Auditing

7th Edition

A.H. Millichamp

B.A., M.Soc.Sc., F.C.A., F.C.C.A, A.T.I.I.

Alan Millichamp was formerly on the staff of the Business School at the University of Wolverhampton. He is a former examiner and assessor in auditing to the Chartered Association of Certified Accountants, and now teaches accounting to managers at the Open University Business School. He is also the author of Foundation Accounting and Finance for Non-Financial Managers, both published by Letts Educational.

Letts Educational
Aldine Place
142/144 Uxbridge Road
Shepherds Bush Green
London W12 8AW
1996

Acknowledgements

The Author wishes to express his thanks to the following for permission to reproduce past examination questions:

    Institute of Chartered Accountants in England and Wales (ICAEW)
    Chartered Association of Certified Accountants (ACCA)
    Association of Accounting Technicians (AAT)
    London Chamber of Commerce (LCC)
    Institute of Chartered Accountants in Ireland (ICAI)
    Institute of Company Accountants (ICA)
    Institute of Chartered Accountants of Scotland (ICAS)

A CIP Catalogue Record for this book is available from the British Library

First Edition 1978
Reprinted 1979, 1980
Second Edition 1981
Reprinted 1982, 1983
Third Edition 1984
Reprinted 1985
Fourth Edition 1986
Reprinted 1987, 1988, 1989
Fifth Edition 1990
Reprinted 1991
Sixth Edition 1993
Seventh Edition 1996
Reprinted 1997

ISBN 1 85805 163 0

Typeset by Elizabeth Elwin, London

Printed and bound in Great Britain by W M Print, Walsall

Preface

Aims of the manual

1. The primary aim of this manual is to provide a simplified but thorough approach to the understanding of modern auditing theory and practice.

    It is intended for those with little or no knowledge of the subject. However, some knowledge of accounting, company law, and data processing would be an advantage.

    Students who will find this manual essential reading include:

    a. Students studying for the examinations of the Institutes of Chartered Accountants, the Chartered Association of Certified Accountants, the Chartered Institute of Public Finance and Accountancy, the Association of Accounting Technicians, the Institute of Company Accountants and the London Chamber of Commerce.

    b. Students studying auditing as a part of a Foundation Course in a college or University or as part of a BTEC national or higher national course, or as part of the NVQ in Accounting

    c. Other business students, managers, accountants and members of their staff wishing to gain a knowledge of the new techniques used by the modern auditor.

Need

2. The expansion of the basic core of knowledge required to pass the auditing papers of the professional bodies, has led to a need for a comprehensive, systematic manual in one volume, aimed specifically at the requirements of present day auditing examinations.

3. It is hoped that this manual will provide the student with a clear and succinct exposition of the subject and be sufficiently interesting to encourage even the least conscientious student to proceed in easily digestible stages.

Approach

4. The manual has been designed with several uses in mind:

    a. for use with a lecturer and background reading,

    b. for use by those who have previously covered the ground in detail, have failed the examination and now require a revision text with the emphasis on examinations,

    c. for use as a checklist of day to day studies and as an examination primer for those who are using other auditing texts.

    The numerous examination questions are particularly helpful for all types of student.

Ends of chapters

5. At the end of each chapter is found:

    a. Summary of the chapter.

    b. Points to note. These are used for emphasis and clarification of points which students often misunderstand.

    c. Short case studies. The objective of the case studies is to illuminate the material in the chapter. Readers may find it helpful to ponder on the case study while reading the chapter.

d. Questions. These are:

    i.   short questions to test comprehension and learning of the material of the chapter;

    ii. recent examination questions with answers in the appendices; and

    iii. recent examination questions without answers. Use of the questions is explained in Appendix 1. Lecturers can obtain answers to these questions from the publishers, if they recommend the book as a course text.

I have included some exercises at the ends of some of the Chapters.

Appendices

6. The appendices form an integral part of the manual and students should note carefully the purpose of each one:

    a. Appendix 1. This contains notes on using the questions and answers, effective study and examination technique. I have also included a section on the major reasons why students fail auditing examinations and how failure may be avoided;

    b. Appendix 2. Answers to questions at the ends of chapters;

    c. Appendix 3. Some longer case studies have been included for classroom use so that students can become involved in and talk about auditing problems.

Notes to the seventh edition

7. The seventh edition now takes account of:

    a. all the Auditing Standards, Statements of Auditing Standards, Auditing Guidelines and APB Practice Notes issued to date;

    b. all the Accounting Standards issued to date;

    c. the new practice regulations;

    d. the new syllabuses of the professional bodies;

    e. the auditing parts of the Standards of Competence for Accounting NVQ/SVQ levels 2, 3 & 4;

    f. recent papers including the APB's paper on the Audit Agenda and the Cadbury Committee's report on Corporate Governance.

8. In addition opportunity has been taken to:

    a. enlarge and rewrite some chapters and introduce new material;

    b. update the exam questions. However, I have been struck by how relevant older questions still are;

    c. add some more case studies.

Chapter order

9. I have received suggestions that the order of the chapters should be changed, for example to reflect the order in which audit actions are carried out. The order in which study is carried on does not have to follow the order of chapters in the book and lecturers may prefer to take Chapter 44 (planning) before say Chapter 10 and Chapter 24 (evidence) before say Chapter 20. However I think that students would benefit from reading these chapters in the order they appear in the book so as to pull together and make sense of all that has gone before.

Suggestions and criticism

10. The author has received and taken account of many helpful comments on this manual. He would welcome many more so that subsequent editions can be made even more useful to students and teachers alike.

A.H.M.
February 1996

Contents

Review of financial statements

The auditors' report

Particular audits

Planning and control of audits

Holding companies and group accounts

Audits of statements other than the profit and loss account and balance sheet

Auditors and the law

EDP and the auditor

Some auditing problem areas

Contents

Internal auditing

Current issues

Appendices

Index

Introduction to auditing

The first chapter introduces you to the idea of stewardship accounting and the need for an independent and competent auditing profession.

1 Introduction to auditing – the why of auditing

Introduction

1. This chapter attempts to explain why auditing exists as a discipline. The chapter first explains the concepts of stewardship and stewardship accounting. The objectives of auditing are next explained with an introduction to auditors' reports and the organisation of the auditing profession. The different types of audit are introduced in the final part of this chapter.

Stewardship

2. Stewardship is the name given to the practice by which productive resources owned by one person or group are managed by another person or group of persons. This has occurred throughout history. For example, in the middle ages, great landowners would not manage their own land but would appoint persons called *stewards* to *manage* the land. Today most business is operated by limited companies which are owned by their *shareholders* and managed by *directors* appointed by the shareholders. Similarly the public own central government resources including the nationalised industries but they are *managed* by the government and persons appointed by the government.

Stewardship accounting

3. Owners who appoint managers to look after the owner's property will be concerned to know what has happened to their property. A famous example of this is in St. Matthew's Gospel (Chapter 25) when the rich man went on a journey and delivered his goods to his servants to look after while he was away. On his return he asked each of his servants to *account* for the goods with which he had been entrusted. He was not pleased with the servant who had not *profitably* used the goods he had managed in his master's absence. Today the process whereby the managers of a business account or report to the owners of the business is called *stewardship accounting*. This reporting and accounting is usually done by means of *financial statements*.

Financial statements

4. Financial statements can take many forms. The best known are the profit and loss accounts and balance sheets of businesses. In the specific case of limited companies, financial statements are produced annually and take the form of an 'Annual report and accounts' which include a profit and loss account and balance sheet and also other statements including the directors' report and a cash flow statement.

Parties to financial statements

5. Historically, annual reports and accounts of companies are produced by the directors (as managers) to the shareholders (as owners), and other people were not expected to be interested in them. However, today a much wider range of people are interested in the annual report and accounts of companies and other organisations.

   The following people or groups of people are likely to want to see and use financial statements:

   a. Actual or Potential
      i. Owners or shareholders
      ii. Lenders or debenture holders
      iii. Employees
      iv. Customers
      v. Suppliers

   b. People who advise the above – accountants; stockbrokers; credit rating agencies; financial journalists; trade unions; statisticians.

   c. Competitors and people interested in mergers, amalgamations and takeovers.

   d. The government, including the tax authorities, departments concerned with price control, consumer protection, and the control and regulation of business.

   e. The public, including those who are interested in consumer protection, environmental protection, and political and other pressure groups.

   f. Regulatory organisations such as those (eg IMRO, PIA) set up under the Financial Services Act 1986.

   All these people must be sure that the financial statements can be relied upon.

Why is there a need for an audit?

6. The problem which has always existed when managers report to owners is – Can the owners believe the report?

   The report may:

   a. contain errors
   b. not disclose fraud
   c. be inadvertently misleading
   d. be deliberately misleading
   e. fail to disclose relevant information
   f. fail to conform to regulations.

   The solution to this problem of *credibility* in reports and accounts lies in appointing an independent person called an auditor to investigate the report and report on his findings.

   A further point is that modern companies can be very large with multi-national activities. The preparation of the accounts of such *groups* is a very complex operation involving the bringing together and summarising of accounts of subsidiaries with differing conventions, legal systems and accounting and control systems. The examination of such accounts by independent experts trained in the assessment of financial information is of benefit to those who control and operate such organisations as well as to owners and outsiders.

Many financial statements must conform to statutory or other requirements. The most notable is that all company accounts have to conform to the requirements of the Companies Act 1985 but many other bodies (eg Charities, Building Societies, Financial Services businesses etc) have detailed accounting requirements. In addition all accounts should conform to the requirements of Financial Reporting Standards (FRSs) and the still relevant Statements of Standard Accounting Practice (SSAPs). It is essential that an audit should be carried out on financial statements to ensure that they conform to these requirements.

Objectives of auditing

7. The auditor should be an independent person who is appointed to investigate the organisation, its records, and the financial statements prepared from them, and thus form an opinion on the accuracy and correctness of the financial statements. The primary aim of an audit is to enable the auditor to say 'these accounts show a true and fair view' or, of course, to say that they do not. The objects of an audit are:

Primary:

To produce a report by the auditor of his opinion of the truth and fairness of financial statements so that any person reading and using them can have belief in them.

Subsidiary:

a. to detect errors and fraud

b. to prevent errors and fraud by the deterrent and moral effect of the audit

c. to provide spin-off effects. The auditor will be able to assist his clients with accounting, systems, taxation, financial, and other problems.

The auditor's report

8. At the end of his audit, when he has examined the organisation, its records, and its financial statements, the auditor produces a *report* addressed to the owners in which he expresses his opinion of the truth and fairness, and sometimes other aspects, of the financial statements.

The auditor's opinion

9. The auditor, in his report, does not say that the financial statements *do* show a true and fair view. He can only say that *in his opinion* the financial statements show a true and fair view. The reader or user of financial statements will know from his knowledge of the auditor whether or not to rely on the auditor's opinion. If the auditor is known to be independent, honest, and competent, then his opinion will be relied upon.

The vast majority of auditors are well known to be independent. However, a few are perhaps incorrectly thought to be too connected with a client (for example a small firm with a large client) and some may not seem sufficiently competent (again, a small firm with a large client, or an auditor who is not a member of a professional body).

Organisation of the auditing profession

10. A vital part of auditing is that the auditor must be *INDEPENDENT of* the management who are responsible for the accounts and the owners who receive them. In the case of companies, he must not be connected with either the directors or the shareholders. He must also be independent of government agencies or other groups who have contact with the business. For these reasons auditors form themselves into independent firms willing to perform audits for a fee for whoever is able and willing to employ them. Some of these firms are very large with worldwide connections and employing thousands of people. Others are very small with sometimes only one or two principals and a very small staff.

Auditing and other services

11. Auditing firms do not describe themselves as auditors. They describe themselves as *Chartered Accountants* or *Certified Accountants* or in some cases just as accountants. Auditing firms are composed of accountants who perform audits for their clients. They also perform other services. The small firms especially may spend more time on other services than on auditing.

    The other services may include:

    a. Writing up books
    b. Balancing books
    c. Preparing final accounts
    d. Tax negotiations
    e. Government form filling
    f. Financial advice
    g. Management and systems advice
    h. Liquidation and receivership work
    i. Investigations.

Qualities required of an auditor

12. An auditor needs to possess the following qualities:

    a. *Independence*

        An auditor cannot give an unbiased opinion unless he is independent of all the parties involved. Total independence is impossible in that the auditor receives his fees from the client. Nonetheless, independence is very important. Not only must the auditor be independent in fact and in attitude of mind but he must also be seen to be independent.

    b. *Competence*

        An auditor must be thoroughly trained and prove his competence before he can sign an audit report. Parliament has decreed that only members of certain professional bodies can become auditors of limited companies. These professional bodies (the three Institutes of Chartered Accountants and the Chartered Association of Certified Accountants) have developed competence in their members by using difficult examinations, post qualifying education, the publication of auditing standards and guidelines and other material. In addition there are requirements before members can become and continue to be *registered auditors.*

c. *Integrity*

Qualified accountants are renowned for their honesty, discretion and tactfulness. Auditors authorised by their professional bodies to conduct audits are known as *Registered Auditors.* Registered auditor firms are supervised and inspected by their professional bodies acting as supervisory bodies.

Types of audit

13. There are four types of audit:

a. *Statutory audits*

These are audits carried out because the law requires them. Statutes which require audits to be done include the Companies Act 1985, the Building Societies Act 1986, the Friendly Societies Acts 1974 and 1992, and others of no examination importance.

b. *Private audits*

A private audit is conducted into a firm's affairs by independent auditors because the owners desire it, not because the law requires it. Examples are audits of the accounts of sole traders and partnerships.

c. *Internal audits*

An internal audit is one conducted by an employee of a business into any aspect of its affairs.

d. *Management audits*

A management audit is an enquiry into the effectiveness of management. This book is principally about a. and b. but Chapter 46 deals with internal auditing.

Summary

14. a. Stewardship involves the separation of ownership from control.

b. Stewardship accounting is the means by which those who control report to the owners.

c. The reports produced by those who control to the owners are used by many other people.

d. All those who use the reports need to be able to believe in them.

e. The audit is the means by which this belief is obtained.

f. Auditing is concerned also with the detection and prevention of error and fraud.

g. Auditors form independent firms and carry out numerous other services for their clients.

h. There are statutory, private, internal, and management audits.

Points to note

15. a. The auditor must be independent, a man of integrity and competent.

b. The auditor gives an opinion in his report. He does not certify or guarantee.

c. Auditors often prepare the accounts they audit. For examination purposes, students must assume that the auditor does not do this.

d. The Auditing Practices Board (APB) defines an audit as:

"An audit of financial statements is an exercise whose objective is to enable auditors to express an opinion whether the financial statements give a true and fair view (or equivalent) of the entity's affairs at the period end and of its profit or loss (or income and expenditure) for the period then ended and have been properly prepared in accordance with the applicable reporting framework (for example relevant legislation and applicable accounting standards) or, where statutory or other specific requirements prescribe the term 'present fairly'."

Notes:

–   Entity is a general term embracing all types of business, enterprise or under-taking including companies, charities, local authorities, government agencies etc. Some are profit oriented and some are not.

–   The reporting framework is for companies the Companies Act 1985 but other statutory and non-statutory provisions may apply to other types of entity.

–   The accounting standards apply to nearly all entities.

–   'present fairly' instead of 'true and fair' applies mainly to local authorities.

A particular point is made of the fact that responsibility for the preparation of the financial statements and the presentation of the information included therein rests with the management of the enterprise (in the case of a company, the directors). The auditor's responsibility is to report on the financial statements as presented by management.

e. A number of Auditing issues are becoming subjects of anxious debate and contro-versy at the time of writing. These include increased accounting regulation of enter-prises and the effect on auditors, increased regulation of auditors, the extent of auditors' responsibilities for the detection and prevention of fraud, auditors' respon-sibilities for ecological matters, the gap between the public's expectations of auditing and the legal position of auditors and the whole future of auditing as a professional activity. The accounting press has many articles on these and other auditing issues and students should read as much as possible about them.

Case study for Chapter 1

Wren, Gibbs and Angelo are partners in a firm of builders specialising in house alter-ation and improvements. Since commencing in business 15 months ago they have been fairly successful. The books have been kept by Wren who has an HNC in Business Studies as well as in building and Wren has also prepared the first year's Accounts.

The three partners are discussing these Accounts which show a profit in excess of draw-ings. Gibbs and Angelo suggest that they could draw out the excess but Wren counsels caution, talking about working capital needs which confuses the others.

Angelo questions Wren on his interpretation of the partnership agreement which is a fairly complicated document and suggests that they should pay to have the Accounts audited. Wren becomes heated and says that would be a waste of money and he is perfectly capable of doing the Accounts and makes no charge to his partners for this work.

Discussion

–   What benefits would the partners get from employing an independent auditor?

–   Where would they find a suitable auditor?

Student self testing questions *Questions with answers apparent from the text*

1. a. List the people and groups of people who are likely to be interested in financial statements. (5)
    b. What other services do accountants provide in addition to auditing? (11)
    c. State the relationship between the Annual Accounts of a company, the shareholders, the directors, and the auditors. (2, 3, 6)
    d. What may be wrong with an annual report and accounts? (6)
    e. What is the primary objective of an audit? (7)
    f. What other benefits are obtained? (7)
    g. What are the objectives of an audit report? (9)
    h. What qualities are required in an auditor? (12)
    i. Distinguish statutory audits, private audits, internal audits and management audits. (13)
    j. Define an audit. (15)

Exercise

1. Describe the services that a firm of Certified Accountants might supply to the following clients:
    i. Intergalactic Oil plc
    ii. Fred Smith – Butcher
    iii. Go Places Travel Agency Ltd
    iv. Woden Tennis and Squash Club Ltd

    Discuss whether the same firm could carry out all these audits.

Examination question without answer

1. You are approached by one of your friends who says 'You are an auditor! My auditor keeps increasing his fees, he tells me it is because of all the extra work he has to do for me. He doesn't do anything for me – except charge me money'.

    Required:

    Draft a letter to your friend discussing this statement. You should inform him of any benefits you think he derives from the audit.

    (Note: marks will be awarded for style and presentation of the letter).

    (AAT 92)

Auditing and the Companies Act

1. The majority of statutory audits carried out in the UK are of companies formed under the Companies Act 1985. The Companies Act contains detailed regulations on the conduct of an audit, the accounting records on which the auditor will work, the financial statements on which he will report and on the auditor's relations with the company. The next four chapters summarise the Companies Act rules in this areas.

2. The Companies Act 1985 is a codifying Act. Before this Act there were several Acts in force (those of 1948, 1967, 1976, 1980 and 1981). The 1985 Act effectively re-enacted all the part of the previous Acts which were still in force. Some *amendments* were also made.

3. The Companies Act 1989 made a large number of amendments to Company Law primarily in the areas of Auditing and Group Accounts. The objective was to implement into English Law EEC directives on Company Law.

4. The Companies Act 1985 remains the principal Act and the Companies Act 1989 includes a number of sections which are expressed to be Sections of the principal Act in replacement for the original sections. For example S.235. This section is found in S.9 of the Companies Act 1989 but will be known as S.235 Companies Act 1985.

2 The rights and duties of an auditor under the Companies Act

Introduction

1. The law on the rights and duties of an auditor under the Companies Act is principally laid down in Sections 235, 237 and 390. We will consider each section separately.

2. An additional section of importance is Section 389A and this will be considered next.

3. Finally, the duties, rights and powers of the auditor are summarised and reviewed.

Section 235 – the auditor's report

4. Section 235:

   (1) A company's auditors shall make a report to the company's members on all annual accounts of the company of which copies are to be laid before the company in general meeting during their tenure of office.

   (2) The auditors' report shall state whether in the auditors' opinion the annual accounts have been properly prepared in accordance with this Act, and in particular whether a true and fair view is given –

   (a) in the case of an individual balance sheet, of the state of affairs of the company as at the end of the financial year,

   (b) in the case of an individual profit and loss account, of the profit or loss of the company for the financial year,

    (c)   *in the case of group accounts, of the state of affairs as at the end of the financial year, and the profit or loss for the financial year, of the undertakings included in the consolidation as a whole, so far as concerns members of the company.*

  (3) *The auditors shall consider whether the information given in the directors' report for the financial year for which the annual accounts are prepared is consistent with those accounts; and if they are of opinion that it is not they shall state that fact in their report.*

5.   Every company must hold an Annual General Meeting of its members (= shareholders) in each calendar year. At that meeting the Annual Report and Accounts (including the Balance Sheet and Profit and Loss Account and, in the case of holding Companies, Group Accounts) are laid before the meeting.

6.   Included in the Annual Report and Accounts, there must be a report by the Auditor(s) on the Accounts examined by him/her/them.

7.   The auditor is usually appointed at an AGM and holds office from the end of that meeting (say July 19th 19-6) till the end of the following AGM (say July 17th 19-7). That is his tenure of office. He reports on the accounts presented at the AGM of 19-7 which is within his tenure of office.

8.   The auditors' report has very specific content viz:

    a.   The Act contains very detailed requirements (see Chapter 5) on the form and contents of Accounts.The auditor has to say whether in his opinion the Accounts have been prepared in accordance with the Act.

    b.   The Act requires, in Section 226, that the Accounts must give a true and fair view of the state of affairs of the Company (ie by the Balance Sheet) and of its profit or loss (ie by the Profit and Loss Account).

        The Auditor must say in his report whether, in his opinion, the Accounts give a true and fair view.

        The idea of true and fair is a difficult one and we will consider it in a later chapter.

        For the moment consider that true means what it says – factually correct. For example, if the Balance Sheet includes an item 'cash in hand £875.00' then this can be true or false. If it were untrue the auditor could not say that a *true* and fair view was given. If no depreciation had been applied to buildings in the Accounts then a fair view of the state of affairs would not be given by the Accounts and the auditor could not say that a true and *fair* view was given by the Accounts.

        Finally this section requires the auditor to consider whether there is any inconsistency between the information given in the Directors' Report and the Annual Accounts. We will deal with it again later in the manual but for the moment realise that the auditor is not asked to give an opinion on the Directors' Report as such. He is only asked to review the Directors' Report and to consider whether any information in it, is other than consistent with the Accounts. If he forms an opinion that there is an inconsistency he has to say so in his report. For example, suppose the Directors' Report states that production at the Bilston Factory has ceased and that the plant there will be sold for scrap. And the Accounts include the Bilston plant at unamortized cost. There is an inconsistency in that the Directors Report shows the Bilston plant to have no further use and the Accounts assume further use. If the matter was material (= of significant size) then the auditor would have to detail the inconsistency in this report.

Section 237 – duties

9. Section 237 reads:

    (1) *A company's auditors shall, in preparing their report, carry out such investigations as will enable them to form an opinion as to –*

        (a) *whether proper accounting records have been kept by the company and proper returns adequate for their audit have been received from branches not visited by them, and*

        (b) *whether the company's individual accounts are in agreement with the accounting records and returns.*

    (2) *If the auditors are of opinion that proper accounting records have not been kept, or that proper returns adequate for their audit have not been received from branches not visited by them, or if the company's Individual accounts are not in agreement with the accounting records and returns, the auditors shall state that fact in their report.*

    (3) *If the auditors fail to obtain all the information and explanations which, to the best of their knowledge and belief, are necessary for the purposes of their audit, they shall state that fact in their report.*

    (4) *If the requirements of Schedule 6 (disclosure of information: emoluments and other benefits of directors and others) are not complied with in the annual accounts, the auditors shall include in their report, so far as they are reasonably able to do so, a statement giving the required particulars.*

10. Subsection 1 requires the auditor to carry out investigations to determine if proper accounting records have been kept and proper returns from branches (at least branches not visited by the auditor) have been received.

    What are 'proper accounting records' is considered in Chapter 4.

    The subsection also requires the auditor to investigate whether the Accounts are in agreement with the accounting records and with returns from branches.

11. Subsection 2 requires that if the investigations required by subsection 1 lead the auditor to form a negative opinion on proper accounting records or agreement of Accounts and records then the auditor is given a duty. The duty is to state the fact of his negative opinion in his report. If he forms a positive opinion he need say nothing on the matter in his report.

12. Subsection 3 is another duty. If the auditor fails to get all the information and explanations which are necessary for the purposes of the audit he has to say so in his report. For example if the auditor feels he needs to know if the repairs expense account includes any capital expenditure and the invoices have been lost he has to say so in his report. Or if he asks the directors if they have received any benefits in kind from the firm and they refuse to answer he has to say that in his report.

13. Subsection 4 gives the auditor some more duties. The requirements mentioned are concerned with disclosure in the Accounts of dealings with directors (remuneration, loans, etc.), Directors often do not want these matters disclosed. If the Accounts do not disclose them then the auditor is required to give the necessary facts (so far as he can) in his report. This will make him unpopular with the offending directors but duty is duty.

Auditors' rights

14. Section 389A:

    (1) *The auditors of a company have a right of access at all times to the company's books, accounts and vouchers, and are entitled to require from the company's officers such information and explanation as they think necessary for the performance of their duties as auditors.*

    This section gives the auditor some rights. He has a right of access at all times to the company's books, accounts and vouchers. In practice this right is exercised with courtesy and reasonableness. Auditors do not appear at their client's premises at two in the morning demanding to see the petty cash book.

15. There is also the right to require from the company's officer such information and explanations as he (the auditor) thinks necessary for the performance of the auditor's duties. The company's officers can refuse to give information or explanation but that leads to subsection 3 of S.237 (see above). The company's officers can also lie or mislead but that may be a criminal action – see Section 389A(2) later in the chapter.

Publication of the auditor's report

16. The Companies Act has a number of rules for publicising the Auditor's Report:

    a. Firstly Section 238:

        (1) *A copy of the company's annual accounts, together with a copy of the directors' report for that financial year and of the auditors report on those accounts. shall be sent to –*

        (a) *every member of the company,*

        (b) *every holder of the company's debentures, and*

        (c) *every person who is entitled to receive notice of general meetings.*

        not less than 21 days before the date of the meeting at which copies of those documents are to be laid in accordance with Section 241.

    b. Secondly Section 239:

        (1) *Any member of a company and any holder of a company's debentures is entitled to be furnished. on demand and without charge, with a copy of the company's last annual accounts and directors' report and a copy of the auditors' report on those accounts.*

    c. Thirdly Section 240:

        (1) *If a company publishes any of its statutory accounts, they must be accompanied by the relevant auditors' report under Section 235.*

        (4) *For the purposes of this section a company shall be regarded as publishing a document if it publishes, issues or circulates it or otherwise makes it available for public inspection in a manner calculated to invite members of the public generally, or any class of members of the public, to read it.*

    d. Fourthly Section 241:

        (1) *The directors of a company shall in respect of each financial year lay before the company in general meeting copies of the company's annual accounts. the directors' report and the auditors report on those accounts.*

e. Finally Section 242:

(1) The directors of a company shall in respect of each financial year deliver to the registrar a copy of the company's annual accounts together with a copy of the directors' report for that year and a copy of the auditors' report on those accounts.

Thus whenever the Annual Accounts are sent to members and other entitled persons, published, laid before the company in general meeting, or delivered to the Registrar of Companies then the Auditor's Report has to be included.

Every company has a file at Companies House and the Accounts sent to the Registrar are included in the file. The file is open to inspection by members of the public. Thus any interested person has access to the file without the Company being aware of the enquiry.

Auditors' rights to attend meetings

17. Section 390 establishes the right of an auditor to receive notice of and attend at meetings:

(1) A company's auditors are entitled –

(a) to receive all notices of, and other communications relating to, any general meeting which a member of the company is entitled to receive;

(b) to attend any general meeting of the company; and

(c) to be heard at any general meeting which they attend on any part of the business of the meeting which concerns them as auditors.

In practice the auditor usually attends the AGM and speaks if he is asked to do so. The right to attend at meetings if of little use if the directors wilfully refuse to send him notice of the date, time and place of a meeting.

In addition, the auditor has rights to attend any meeting at which it is proposed to remove him from office – we shall deal with this in the next chapter.

False statements to auditors

18. Section 389A:

(2) An officer of a company commits an offence if he knowingly or recklessly makes to the company's auditors a statement (whether written or oral) which –

(a) conveys or purports to convey any information or explanations which the auditors require, or are entitled to require, as auditors of the company, and

(b) is misleading, false or deceptive in a material particular.

A person guilty of an offence under this subsection is liable to imprisonment or a fine, or both.

Auditors might remind the officers of a company of the Section when asking questions. However very few do.

It would seem that fear of commiting a criminal offence should prevent an officer of a company from lying to or misleading the auditor. However there are few prosecutions and the Section cannot be relied on by an auditor.

Sadly, directors and officers of companies and other enterprises do sometimes lie to or mislead their auditors and are sometimes economical with the truth.

A recent suggestion is that this section could be used to nail fraudsters instead of the long, expensive fraud trials currently used.

Powers of an auditor

19. An auditor of a limited company is given burdensome duties by the Companies Act. He is required to make a report on, amongst other things, the truth and fairness of the Annual Accounts. If he is negligent in any way and fails to discover that the Accounts contain an untruth or do not fairly present the position then he may be legally required to compensate from his own pocket any persons who lose money as a result of actions taken as a result of the false Accounts.

20. Because of these onerous duties the Act has given the auditor extensive rights. However he is given no legal powers to assist him in his work. It might be said that the right to report, for example, that the directors have not given him all the information he needs, is a power. But it is not really so as the directors can refuse to publish his report. If they so refuse then there are legal consequences but fundamentally the auditor has no POWER to MAKE anybody do any particular action. There are some powers given in the event of the auditor resigning and these are in the next chapter.

Summary

21. a. The Companies Act has laid down substantial duties for auditors of companies primarily in Sections 235 and 237.

   b. The duties of an auditor include:

   - making a report on all Accounts presented to shareholders
   - including in the report his opinion on whether the Accounts comply with the Act and give a true and fair view
   - investigating whether proper accounting records, proper returns from branches (not visited by the auditor) have been kept and whether the Accounts are in agreement with the accounting records
   - stating in his report IF any of the last three things are not so
   - stating in his report if he has not obtained all the information and explanations that he needs
   - giving certain information about directors if the information is not given in the Accounts
   - some duties re the Directors' Report.

   c. The Act ensures that the Auditors' Report is widely publicised by requiring it to be attached when the Annual Accounts are sent to shareholders and others, laid before the Company at the AGM and filed at Companies House.

   d. Some small assistance is given to an auditor by Section 389A which makes it a criminal offence to give false or misleading information to an auditor.

Points to note

22. a. Note the idea of the tenure of office of an auditor and how it ends at the end of an AGM. The auditor has to report on the Accounts presented at that meeting.

   b. The duties described in this chapter are the principal statutory duties of auditors of companies. There are a number of other duties in special circumstances. For example duties are imposed on the auditor of a private company that is re-registering as a public company.

c. You will have noticed references in the sections to subsidiary companies and to group accounts. These will be dealt with in a later chapter. The Companies Act 1989 has extensively added to the law on these matters.

d. It is essential to grasp the central purposes of an audit of a company:
   - Do the Accounts give a true and fair view?
   - Do the Accounts conform to the requirements of the Companies Act?

   It is easy to get lost in the minutiae of auditing and of auditing techniques. Always remember why an audit test is performed.

e. The subsidiary requirement of the Act re proper accounting records is often overlooked. All audit tests are partially aimed at determining if proper accounting records have been kept.

f. The Act prescribes numerous penalties (fines and imprisonment) for contravention of most of the rules laid out in this chapter.

g. There are some modifications of the rules for small and medium sized companies and these are dealt with in the chapter on small companies.

h. The Companies Act 1985 had an addition by statutory instrument in 1994. This is Sections 249A to 249E and were added by The Companies Act 1985 (Audit Exemption) Regulations 1994. This new addition gives exemption from audit for certain categories of small companies. We will take this up again in Chapter 38.

Case study for Chapter 2

Ananias is the auditor of Shady Deals Ltd. During the audit of the company for the year ending 31st December 19-6 the following matters come to light:

a. £50,000 cheques had been drawn on 31.12.-6 and entered then in the cash book. These cheques were not mailed until 17.1.-7.

b. Plant and Machinery appear in the Fixed Assets section of the Balance Sheet without showing the original cost and accumulated depreciation but just the net carrying value.

c. The turnover in the profit and loss account is reduced from the figures in the accounting records by a large amount of bad debts incurred in the year.

d. The auditor was refused access to the directors' minute book on the grounds that it contained personal information about the company's staff.

e. The Chairman's report states that the company were expected to have lower profits in 19-7 owing to unfavourable settlement of a two year old dispute with a customer. No provision appears in the balance sheet regarding this matter.

f. Ananias asked Elm, a director, if he had been supplied with free timber by the company for an extension to his house. He assured Ananias that this was not so. However Ananias could trace no invoice to Elm but noticed that discarded company packing material was in Elm's garage.

g. The company sell on credit to a number of sub-contractors to the building trade but keep no record of their names or addresses. However all seem to pay satisfactorily despite the invoices stating only Pat or Mick.

Discussion

The company have had the Accounts printed and refuse to alter them. Ignoring questions of materiality what does the Companies Act say about Ananias' duty in respect of these matters?

Student self testing questions *Questions with answers apparent from the text*

1. a. What Act of Parliament codified company law? (1)
   b. What must be contained in the Auditor's report? (4–15)
   c. What is the tenure of office of an auditor? (7)
   d. Which set of Accounts must an auditor report on? (7)
   e. What investigations must an auditor make? (9)
   f. Summarise the duties of an auditor. (4, 9)
   g. What duty has an auditor toward the Directors' Report? (4)
   h. In what ways must an auditor's report be publicised? (16)
   i. Summarise an auditor's rights. (4, 9, 14, 17)
   j. Summarise Section 389(A). (18)
   k. What is the auditor's duty if he discovers that the directors have failed to disclose the remuneration of directors in the Accounts? (9, 13)
   l. What does the Companies Act see as the main purposes of an audit? (4)
   m. Summarise sections 235, and 237 Companies Act 1985. (4, 9)

Exercises

What are the auditor's duties in the following circumstances:

a. The accounts contain an item Land and buildings at cost £340,000 when in fact the land and buildings had cost £360,000 and had been depreciated by £20,000.

b. The accounts contain an item debtors £390,000. In fact this item includes a probable bad debt of £30,000.

c. The accounts show a profit after tax of £200,000. The directors' report states that the profit was £330,000 compared with £240,000 the previous year. It does not say that the £330,000 is the profit before tax or that the £240,000 was the profit after tax.

d. The directors' remuneration is stated at £200,000 without any breakdown.

e. The auditors were not allowed to attend the stocktaking.

f. The company did not have a detailed breakdown of new plant and machinery. The total was obtained from a computer file which was overwritten. The details could with much difficulty be resurrected from the original invoices which are filed with other invoices in supplier name order.

g. A director informed the auditor that the company owned a warehouse in South Africa which had been paid for by the company at £50,000. In fact the director had fraudulently misappropriated the money. The auditor could not go to South Africa and had no other evidence on the warehouse.

h. The auditor had not visited the branch at Glasgow and she found that no returns had been received from that branch and the figures included in the accounts were those of the previous year.

3 The auditor and the Companies Act

Introduction

1. Most statutory audits are conducted for companies and are governed by the rules of the Companies Act 1985, as amended by the Companies Act 1989.

   This chapter sets out the rules on the requirements:
   - of a company to have an auditor
   - on the appointment of an auditor
   - on the remuneration of an auditor
   - on the removal of an auditor
   - on the resignation of an auditor
   - on who can be an auditor of a company

   Finally the current professional body rules on *Registered Auditors* are discussed.

Appointment of auditors

2. Section 384 states that every company shall appoint an auditor. The only exceptions to this rule are that certain small companies and *dormant companies* do not need an auditor. A dormant (= sleeping) company is one where in a period no significant accounting transaction occurred. Such companies need not have an auditor but must still *lay* and *deliver* accounts. For small companies see Chapter 38. The new (1994) rules on audit exemption for some small companies give exemption from appointing an auditor for those companies.

3. Section 385 states how auditors of companies are to be appointed:

   a. The company shall, at each General Meeting at which Accounts are presented (usually at each Annual General Meeting [AGM]), appoint an auditor or auditors. Note that it is the company (ie the shareholders) who appoint the auditor.

   b. The appointment is for the period of time known as the *tenure of office* and that is from the conclusion of the meeting to the conclusion of the following general meeting at which accounts are laid (= presented at the meeting).

   c. On the commencement of a new company the Directors may appoint the auditor at any time before the first AGM.

   d. The only exceptions to this manner of appointment are:

      - private companies which have elected to *dispense* with the laying of accounts at AGMs. Such companies must still hold an AGM and send the Accounts to members. However a company may elect to dispense with the requirement to hold Annual general Meetings. The auditor must, under Section 385A, be appointed at each AGM to hold office from the conclusion of that meeting until the time for appointing auditors for the next financial year. The time for appointing auditors is within 28 days beginning with the day on which copies of the company's annual accounts are sent to members.

- private companies which have elected to dispense with the obligation to appoint an auditor *annually.* In these cases the auditor continues indefinitely as he/she is deemed to be re-appointed at the time for appointment each year.

e. In the event of no auditor being appointed as required, Section 387 states that the company must inform the Secretary of State within one week. The Secretary of State may then make an appointment.

f. Casual vacancies in the office of auditor (perhaps caused by death) may be filled by the Directors.

Remuneration of an auditor

4. Under Section 390A the remuneration of an auditor is fixed by the person/persons appointing. Usually this is the company in General Meeting and many company AGM agendas include something like:

   'To re-appoint the auditors Fussy & Co as the company's auditors until the conclusion of the next AGM of the Company, and to authorise the Board to fix the auditors' remuneration.'

   You will notice that the independence of the auditor is honoured by an appointment by the members in General Meeting but may appear to be compromised by the delegation of the fixing of their remuneration to the Board.

5. Section 390A goes on to require that the remuneration of the auditor shall be stated in a note in the company's accounts. Remuneration disclosable is for auditing services only (ie excluding other services eg taxation) but must include sums paid in respect of expenses and the money value and nature of any benefit in kind.

   Under *The Companies Act 1985 (Disclosure of Remuneration for Non-Audit Work) Regulations 1991,* disclosure in the Accounts must also be made of remuneration (including benefits in kind) paid to the auditor for non-audit work (preparing accounts, tax, consultancy etc). Inclusion must be made of the remuneration from non-audit work paid to associates of the audit firm (eg management consultancy firms which are connected with the auditors) and for work done for subsidiaries of the client. The auditors must supply the necessary information to the company. This requirement does not apply to small and medium-sized companies.

   Thus auditors' remuneration must be disclosed to members and other users of the accounts and cannot be hidden by including it in a global figure such as administration expenses. Look it up every time you see a copy of a company's Annual Report and Accounts.

The removal of an auditor

6. The Companies Act takes a serious view of the removal of an auditor and there are a number of special procedures and rules to go through in order to effect a change of auditor.

   Suppose that the directors prepare the accounts with the inclusion of some unusual accounting policy in order to increase profits in a particular year. The auditors (Fussy & Co), being honourable people, may feel that the unusual policy is not acceptable and inform the Directors that they would qualify their report if the policy is not changed. The directors may decide to abandon the policy for this year and change the auditors to

Flexible & Co in order that in future years the unusual policy may be adopted. Flexible & Co may privately indicate that the unusual policy is acceptable to them.

Company law takes the view that company auditors must be capable of being changed if the MEMBERS wish it but is designed:

- to ensure that the reality of the usual company situation, where the appointment of the auditor which is nominally by the members, cannot be manipulated by the directors to change an auditor who is doing his duty but who does not please the directors.

- to ensure that maximum publicity is given to any proposed change of auditor so that members are aware of the matter and can make informed choices

- to give an auditor who the directors would like to remove every opportunity to state his case.

7. The Companies Act legislation is:

   a. Section 391 states that a company may remove its auditor by ordinary resolution (a simple majority) notwithstanding anything in any agreement between it and him. The Section also requires that the company shall give notice of the resolution to the registrar within 14 days on pain of a fine.

   b. Section 391A requires that

   - Special notice (28 days) must be given to the company of intention to move a resolution to remove an auditor or appoint some person other than the retiring auditor. However most such resolutions are moved by the directors.

   - on receipt of such an intended resolution the company shall forthwith send a copy to the auditor who may be removed and also to the intended new auditor. At least the removal cannot be done behind the auditor's back.

   - the auditor, proposed to be removed, may make with respect to the intended resolution, *representations* in writing to the company and request their notification to members. Thus the auditor who does not wish to be removed can state his case and require it to be sent to the members. Note that representations may not exceed a reasonable length.

   - the company must do two things (unless the representations are received too late): state the fact of representations being received in any notice of the resolution and: send a copy to every member of the company to whom notice of the meeting has been or will be sent.

   - the auditor has a general right to speak at the meeting on the subject of his intended removal and, if the representations have not been sent to the members he/she has the right to have them read out at the meeting.

   Note:

   i.   The object of these rules is not to prevent the auditor being removed, if the members wish to remove him, but to ensure that he has adequate opportunity to put his case to the members before they vote on the resolution.

   ii. Section 391A allows the company to seek an injunction against the auditor to restrain him from using his representations as a vehicle for needless publicity for defamatory matter.

   c. In the case of private companies where an election is in force to dispense with annual appointment of auditors then Section 393 says:

- any member may deposit notice in writing at the registered office proposing that the appointment of the company's auditors be brought to an end.
- the directors must then convene a meeting of the company within 28 days and propose a resolution to decide the matter.
- if the directors do not convene a meeting then the proposer may do so himself

In these cases the rules of Sections 391 and 391A still apply.

Resignation of auditors

8. Auditors can resign. There are two main reasons why they may wish to do so. These are:

   a. The obvious reasons: ill health, the company have grown too large for a small audit firm, the fee is inadequate etc.

   b. Where the auditor concludes that because of fraud or other irregularity the accounts do not show a true and fair view and there is no immediate opportunity to report to members. He would be unable to report to members if the entity refused to issue its financial statements or at another stage in the year the auditor has considerable doubts about management's integrity.

9. Procedures are:

   a. Section 392:

      - an auditor may resign by depositing a notice in writing to that effect at the registered office. This is not effective unless accompanied by a *statement of circumstances.*

      - the company must send a copy of the notice of resignation to the Registrar of Companies within 14 days on pain of a fine. Thus any person searching the file will have notice of the resignation.

   b. Section 394:

      - The statement of circumstances should contain a statement of any circumstances (eg fraudulent trading) which he/she considers should be brought to the attention of members or *creditors* or if he/she considers that there are no such circumstances then a statement that there are none.

      - the auditor can cease to be auditor by simply not seeking re-election. However in that case he must still deposit a statement of circumstances and there are time limits for this.

      - if the statement of circumstances contains matters which the auditor considers should be brought to the attention of members or creditors then the company must within 14 days of receipt of it send a copy to all persons entitled to receive copies of the accounts or apply to the court.

      - the court may order that the statement may not be sent out if it thinks the statement is seeking needless publicity for defamatory matter but otherwise the statement must be sent out.

      - the auditor must send his statement to the Registrar

Section 392A gives further rights and duties to the resigning auditor:

- the auditor may deposit with his notice of resignation and his statement of circumstances, a notice calling on the company to convene an Extraordinary Meeting.
- the directors must call such a meeting within 21 days on pain of a fine and must send out copies of the statement and if they fail to do so the auditor can require that the statement be read at the meeting.

There are the usual caveats re the court and defamatory matters.

Who can be an auditor?

10. The Companies Act 1989 radically changed the law in relation to who can be an auditor. The object of the changes was to incorporate into English Law EC directives and to increase regulation of the auditing profession in line with the general modern tendency to regulate everything that moves.

    The sections involved are of the 1989 Act are sections 24 to 54.

11. Section 24 states the general purpose of the law which is to:

    'secure that only persons who are properly supervised and appropriately qualified are appointed auditors, and that audits by persons so appointed are carried out properly and with integrity and with a proper degree of independence.'

12. Section 25:

    (1) A person is eligible for appointment as a company auditor only if he –

    (a) is a member of a recognised supervisory body, and

    (b) is eligible for the appointment under the rules of that body

    The Section goes on to allow either individuals or firms to be appointed a company auditor.

13. Section 34 concerns auditors who are not members of professional bodies recognised by the Companies 1967. They retain rights to audit individual unquoted companies as a consequence of being in office when the Companies Act 1967 came into force. There are still some of these accountants around and many are now members of The Association of Authorised Public Accountants which is a recognised supervisory body. The Association is responsible for regulating its members but in fact has subcontracted the actual monitoring to the Chartered Association of Certified Accountants.

14. Section 27 repeats earlier legislation but with modifications and states that certain persons with connections to a company are ineligible to act as auditor to that company. These persons are:

    - officers and employees of the company
    - partners or employees of such persons or a partnership of which such a person is a partner.
    - persons who have connection with the company or where the company has a connection with an associate of his of any description specified in regulations made by the Secretary of State.

    Note that:

    a. persons who are ineligible to act as auditor of a particular company are also ineligible to act as auditor of a parent, subsidiary, or fellow subsidiary of that company

b. The whole purpose of this sections is to secure the *independence* of the auditor from the company.

15. Section 28 makes it an offence for a person to act as a company auditor if he is ineligible and requires vacation of office if he becomes ineligible.

16. Section 29 gives the Secretary of State power to require a second audit if the first was carried out by an ineligible auditor. It is likely that this will be a very rare occurrence.

17. Section 30 is on Supervisory bodies.

A supervisory body is a body established in the UK which maintains and enforces rules as to the eligibility of persons seeking appointments as company auditors and the conduct of audit work which are binding on such persons because they are members of such bodies or subject to its control.

Recognition will only be given to a supervisory body if the body has rules on: holding of appropriate qualifications, professional integrity and independence, technical standards, investigation of complaints and meeting of claims arising out of audit work.

There are currently five *supervisory bodies*: the three Institutes of Chartered Accountants, the Chartered Association of Certified Accountants and the Association of Authorised Public Accountants. The last is responsible for regulating its members but in fact has subcontracted the actual monitoring to the Chartered Association of Certified Accountants.

18. Section 31 sets out the persons who hold appropriate qualifications. Essentially the only persons so qualified are members of the three Institutes of Chartered Accountants and the Chartered Association of Certified Accountants plus pre-1967 auditors of certain unquoted companies.

19. Section 32 considers *qualifying bodies*. A qualifying body means a body established in the UK which offers a professional qualification in accountancy. The body must have enforceable rules on: admission to or expulsion from a course of study leading to a qualification, the award or deprivation of a qualification, the approval of a person for the purposes of giving practical training or the withdrawal of such approval, entry requirements, courses of instruction, professional experience, examination and practical training.

The currently recognised qualifying bodies are the three Institutes of Chartered Accountants and the Chartered Association of Certified Accountants.

The Act recognises a distinction between supervisory bodies and qualifying bodies but in practice all bodies except the AAPA are both.

20. Sections 35 and 36 require supervisory bodies to maintain a *register* of persons and firms which are eligible to be company auditors and to make the register available to the public.

Professional body rules

21. The new rules on becoming and retaining eligibility as a registered auditor are somewhat complex and students need not know any more than this paragraph to understand how the qualifying and supervisory bodies are ensuring that only suitable persons act as auditors.

The Chartered Association of Certified Accountants

a. Members who wish to be Registered Auditors must obtain a practising certificate. For ACCA members there is no difference between holding a *practising certificate* and being a registered auditor.

b. Members holding a practising certificate can:
- accept an appointment as an auditor
- sign any report or certificate on accounts concerning any business or company where reliance is likely to be placed on such a report or certificate by any other person (eg a sole trader's accounts are seen by the Inspector of Taxes and probably the bank manager).
- hold themselves out as allowing themselves to be available to carry out such work.

c. Any member who wishes to carry on the activities mentioned in (b) under his/her own name or as a partner or director of a firm that does so must have a practising certificate.

d. Members do not need a practising certificate to do certain kinds of work including VAT, Bookkeeping, Payroll, management accounting or management consultancy. They can also do subcontract work without a practising certificate. There is an Accounting and Consultancy certificate.

e. To obtain a practising certificate a member must:
- have a specified period of continuous membership
- have a specified period of approved accountancy experience under the supervision of an approved principal in the office of a public accountant. For persons who first registered as students after 1 January 1990, experience must be gained in an Approved Training Practice.

To hold or renew a practising certificate a member must:
- be a fit and proper person. There are various criteria for this. But, for example, members must not be bankrupts or patients under the Mental Health Act or subject to disciplinary action under the Association's bye-laws.
- hold appropriate Professional Indemnity Insurance and also Fidelity Guarantee Insurance in respect of all partners, directors and employees.
- make provision for continuity of practice in the event of death or incapacity
- maintain competence by continuing professional development
- notify the association of details so that the Association can maintain its public register of Registered auditors (as required by the Act).
- comply with technical and ethical standards
- co-operate with the Association in its monitoring and enforcement of compliance with bye-laws and regulations

f. Members who have held a practising certificate in the past can re-apply without further experience and interview.

The Institute of Chartered Accountants in England and Wales

a. The Institute allows members to hold a practising certificate without being registered auditors. Such members cannot describe themselves as registered auditors and they cannot audit organisations which require a registered auditor to be the auditor.

b. The Institute registers firms and not members (except sole practitioners) as Registered Auditors.

c. Registered Auditor firms must be controlled by persons qualified to audit. There are special regulations for firms which are not composed wholly of Chartered Accountants and for firms which have corporate status (= are limited or unlimited companies).

d. To be qualified to audit, members must have at least two years unbroken appropriate post qualification experience in an Approved Training Office.

e. Registered Auditor firms must have *Professional Indemnity Insurance* and partners must complete a minimum of *Continuing Professional Education*.

f. Registered Auditor firms are monitored by visits from the *Joint Monitoring Unit*.

g. Firms normally need to be authorised to carry on Investment business by the Institute. This is subject also to regulation.

h. Firms wishing to carry on Insolvency business require separate authorisation.

Summary

22. a. Every company (except dormant companies) must appoint an auditor.

b. Auditors are normally elected by the members (shareholders) at the Annual General Meeting when Accounts are presented.

c. Tenure of office is usually till the end of the next AGM so that they can report on the accounts presented at that AGM.

d. Directors may appoint the first auditor of a company and may fill a casual vacancy.

e. Special rules apply to private companies who have elected to dispense with the laying of accounts at an AGM and /or have elected to dispense with the holding of AGMs.

f. It is possible for private companies to elect to dispense with annual appointment of auditors.

g. In certain circumstances the Secretary of State may appoint an auditor.

h. The remuneration of the auditor is normally fixed by the persons/groups appointing the auditor. Full disclosure of remuneration in the accounts is required.

i. An auditor can be removed from office but the detailed rules must be followed. An auditor, who it is proposed to remove, has rights including the making of representations and the requisitioning of a meeting.

j. An auditor can resign either because he wishes to for his own reasons or to draw attention to some matter (eg illegal conduct) relating to the company. He must then write a statement of circumstances or a statement that there are no notable circumstances and this must be circulated to members and the Registrar of Companies.

k. The statement of circumstances rules apply to any situation where an auditor leaves office.

l. The Companies Act prohibits certain persons who have personal connections with the company from also being its auditor.

m. The Companies Act 1989 radically changed rules as to who can be an auditor in order to ensure that only persons who are properly supervised and appropriately qualified are appointed auditors, and that audits by persons so appointed are carried out properly and with integrity and with a proper degree of independence.

n. The Act established the idea of recognised supervisory bodies and recognised qualifying bodies. Only persons who are members of and authorised by supervisory bodies can be company auditors.

o. The supervisory bodies have set up Registers of eligible company auditors.

p. The supervisory bodies have complex rules for authorising Registered Auditors and have supervisory regimes in force. These include requirements for Professional Indemnity Insurance and Continuing Professional Education and monitoring visits.

Points to note

23. a. The rules require all company auditors to be supervised by a supervisory body. Currently the supervisory bodies are the three Institutes of Chartered Accountants, the Chartered Association of Certified Accountants and the Association of Authorised Public Accountants. All but the last are qualifying bodies. The rules are complex and need not detain students too long until they have qualified and seek to become Registered Auditors.

b. EC auditors can seek membership of, and authorisation by, the ACCA. There are safeguards on the competence of such persons.

c. The ICAEW authorises firms and ACCA individual members.

d. The Companies Act 1989 ended the prohibition on corporate bodies (eg companies) being auditors. This means that professional firms could at least in law incorporate as limited companies.

e. Schedule 11 (on the subject of supervisory bodies) requires that any firm appointed as auditors must be controlled by qualified persons. This means that firms of accountants may have unqualified members or partners but that a majority of the partners/Board of Directors/ shareholdings must be qualified persons. The supervisory bodies have complex rules to cover this point.

f. The objects of all these rules are to:

   – ensure all company auditors are fit and proper persons

   – ensure professional integrity and independence

   – have technical standards

   – have procedures to maintain competence

   – ensure practitioners have insurance

   – investigate complaints

   – maintain a register of eligible auditors

   – monitor and enforce the rules

g. These rules apply to companies registered under the Companies Act 1985. However similar rules apply also to many other bodies. These include bodies registered under other Acts of Parliament eg Building Societies, Financial Service Companies, Clubs and Societies registered under the Friendly Societies Act, Associations registered under the Industrial and Provident Societies Act, Solicitors, members of the Association of British Travel Agents etc.

   Special rules apply to Charities under the Charities Act 1993 and we will deal with these in a later chapter.

Other bodies may have rules in their constitutions which require the audit to be by a Registered Auditor.

h. The rules in this chapter both directly under statute and by the professional bodies as required by statute are very complex. The ACCA publish annual reports to the President of the Board of Trade which report among other matters the shortcomings of firms visited under the monitoring visits. Presumably these shortcomings will be remedied and so the new rules will have raised standards. Whether the rules have improved the independence of auditors is still an open question. The basic structure where auditors are appointed by the shareholders remains but this is manipulated by directors in many cases. They can do this because of the inertia of shareholders. The delegation of auditor's remuneration to the Directors also mitigates against true independence in that it leaves the auditor beholden to the directors for his remuneration and that may affect his attitude in any dispute with the directors. Hopefully auditors maintain an independent attitude in any circumstances.

i. The rules have a large economic cost. Better auditing (eg circularisation of debtors which was not often done in the audit of small companies) has an economic cost but it is less clear if it has any economic benefit. Regulation may seem to be wholly good but in practice bad auditors still manage to survive and not all business people want the burdens of more audit regulation. The impact of extra regulation may be that many businesses do not incorporate and thus lose the benefit of limited liability. The impact of any extra regulation is to change at least some economic behaviour, whether for good or ill is a matter for discussion.

j. The new 1994 rules on the exemption from audit of certain small companies has reduced the audit burden for those companies and it has had an interesting side effect. The number of ICAS and ICAEW registered auditors has dropped as firms with mainly small company audits can now de-register as they have no clients large enough to require registered auditor status.

Student self testing questions *Questions with answers apparent from the text*

1. a. Must every company have an auditor? (2)
   b. Who may appoint a company's auditor? (3)
   c. What period of time is covered by an auditor's tenure of office? (3)
   d. Outline the rules when a private company has:
      – elected to dispense with the requirement to hold AGMs
      – elected to dispense with the requirement to lay accounts at the AGM
      – elected not to appoint its auditor annually? (3)
   e. How is the remuneration of an auditor fixed? (4)
   f. Outline the rules on disclosure of an auditor's remuneration. (5)
   f. How can an auditor be removed from office? (7)
   g. What rights has an auditor whose removal is proposed? (7)
   h. Why may an auditor wish to resign? (8)
   i. What are the rules re the resignation of an auditor? (9)
   j. Who cannot be a company's auditor? (12–14)
   k. What is a supervisory body and which bodies are so recognised? (17)
   l. What rules must such bodies have? (17)

m. What is a qualifying body and which bodies are so recognised? (19)

n. What rules must such bodies have? (19)

o. Outline the rules for becoming, and continuing as, a registered auditor supervised by the ACCA (21)

p. Outline the rules for becoming, and continuing as, a registered auditor supervised by the ICAEW (21)

Case study for Chapter 3

Associated Gargoyles Ltd is a private company with only three shareholders, all of whom are directors. They wish to reduce company formalities to a minimum.

Discuss how this may be done.

They wish to appoint Ted, a director's brother who is a chartered accountant working for British Gas PLC.

Can they do this? They want, in any case, to remove Harry, the present auditor. How can this be done and what rights and duties has Harry?

Examination question *(Answer begins on page 542)*

1. Growfast plc was formed on 1 August 1990 in order to manufacture minicomputers. The directors are unsure as to their responsibilities, and the nature of their relationship with the external auditors. The audit partner has asked you to visit the client and explain to the directors the more fundamental aspects of the accountability of the company and their relationship with the auditor.

Required:

Explain to the directors of Growfast plc

a. Why there is a need for an audit; (5 marks)

b. How the auditor of a public company may be appointed under the Companies Act 1985; (5 marks)

c. What the auditor's rights are under the Companies Act 1985; (6 marks)

d. The responsibilities of the directors in relation to the accounting function of the company. (4 marks)

(ACCA 90) (20 marks)

Examination question without answer

2. The Companies Act includes provisions regarding the appointment, duties and powers of a company's auditor.

Required:

a. State the ways in which an auditor can be appointed; (5 marks)

b. Detail the statutory duties imposed on an auditor; (5 marks)

c. Specify the statutory powers given to the auditor to enable him to carry out his work (5 marks)

(AAT 91) (Total 15 marks)

4 Accounting records

Introduction

1. This chapter details the Companies Act requirements on the keeping of accounting records by companies.

2. An auditor must know these rules because he has to carry out investigations to enable him to form an opinion on whether the company has kept proper accounting records and has proper returns from branches not visited by the auditor. Further, if he forms an opinion that the company have not kept proper accounting records, he has to say so in his report. The word 'proper' here means in accordance with custom or appropriate to the circumstances.

3. Note that the responsibility for keeping proper accounting records lies wholly with the directors.

4. The Companies Act 1989 made some minor amendments to the principal Act (The Companies Act 1985) and it is the amended version that is reproduced here.

5. The chapter also lists the statutory books.

Section 221:

(1) *Every company shall keep accounting records which are sufficient to show and explain the company's transactions and are such as to –*

   (a) *disclose with reasonable accuracy, at any time, the financial position of the company at that time, and*

   (b) *enable the directors to ensure that any balance sheet and profit and loss account prepared under this Part complies with the requirements of this Act.*

(2) *The accounting records shall in particular contain –*

   (a) *entries from day to day of all sums of money received and expended by the company, and the matters in respect of which the receipt and expenditure takes place, and*

   (b) *a record of the assets and liabilities of the company.*

(3) *If the company's business involves dealing in goods, the accounting records shall contain –*

   (a) *statements of stock held by the company at the end of each financial year of the company,*

   (b) *all statements of stocktakings from which any such statement of stock as is mentioned in paragraph (a) has been or is to be prepared, and*

   (c) *except in the case of goods sold by way of ordinary retail trade, statements of all goods sold and purchased, showing the goods and the buyers and sellers in sufficient detail to enable all these to be identified.*

(4) *A parent company which has a subsidiary undertaking in relation to which the above requirements do not apply shall take reasonable steps to secure that the undertaking keeps such accounting records as to enable the directors of the parent company to ensure that any balance sheet and profit and loss account prepared under this Part complies with the requirements of this Act.*

(5) *If a company fails to comply with any provision of this section, every officer of the company who is in default is guilty of an offence unless he shows that he acted honestly and that in the circumstances in which the company's business was carried on the default was excusable.*

(6) *A person guilty of an offence under this section is liable to imprisonment or a fine, or both.*

Subject matter

6. a. Sums of money received and expended and the matters about which the receipts or payments took place – *a cash book.*

   b. A record of assets and liabilities – presumably including sales and bought ledgers.

   c. Where the company deals in goods then:

      i. Statements of stock held at each year end

      ii. Statements of stock takings from which (i) are prepared

      iii. Except for ordinary retail sales (= cash sales over the counter) statements of all goods purchased and sold, showing the buyers and sellers and identifying them – sales and purchase day books.

7. a. The accounting records must be sufficient to disclose with reasonable accuracy, at any time, the financial position of the company at that time.

      It must be pointed out that a Balance Sheet could only be produced if stock was taken and that is only required at year ends.

   b. Enable the directors to ensure that any balance sheet and profit and loss account comply with the Act.

8. Subsection (4) is concerned with subsidiary undertakings abroad.

9. The company's accounting records can be kept wherever the directors think fit.

   Special rules relate to accounting records kept outside Great Britain:

   a. Accounts and *returns* in respect of such business shall be sent to Great Britain.

   b. These accounts and returns sent to Great Britain must be such as to:

      i. Disclose with reasonable accuracy the financial position of the overseas business at intervals not exceeding *six months.*

      ii. Enable the directors to ensure that Accounts comply with the Act as to *form* and *content.*

Statutory books

10. The Companies Act requires a company to keep the following books:

    a. Proper accounting records – Section 407.

    b. A register of directors and secretaries – Sections 288, 289.

    c. A register of charges (fixed and floating) – Section 407.

    d. Minute books of meetings of the company, meetings of its directors and meetings of its managers – Section 382.

    e. An indexed register of members – Sections 352-354.

    f. An indexed register of each director's interest in shares and debentures of the company and those of his spouse, infant children and some other persons, trusts and companies connected with him – Sections 324-328.

    g. Public companies must keep a register of shareholders who have an interest of 3% or more in the nominal value of the voting share capital – Section 211.

The auditor's interest in the statutory books

11. The auditor is interested in the statutory books being properly maintained because:–

    a. They are directly concerned with the Accounts (especially a. and c.).

    b. They are audit evidence to be used in verifying detailed items in the accounts; for example the total share capital shown by the sum of the individual share holdings in the register of members must agree with the share capital recorded in the books of account.

    c. Failure to maintain proper records of any sort casts doubt upon the accuracy and reliability of the records generally.

Summary

12. a. The Companies Act lays down rules for keeping of proper accounting records and for proper returns from branches including those overseas.

    b. The Companies Act also requires a company to keep a range of additional records called the statutory books.

    c. The directors are responsible for the maintenance of accounting records and statutory books.

    d. The auditor has a duty to investigate and form an opinion on whether proper accounting records have been kept.

Points to note

13. a. The Companies Act lays down rules for the keeping of proper accounting records and proper returns from branches overseas.

    b. The directors have the responsibility for seeing that the company obeys the rules.

    c. Failure to obey the rules may mean that:

        i.   Proper books of account have not been kept.

        ii   Proper returns have not been received.

        iii. Sufficient information may not be available for the proper disclosure of matters of which the Companies Acts require detailed disclosure.

        iv. Insufficient evidence may be available for confirmation of items in the accounts.

        All these matters are of direct concern to the auditor who may have to consider a qualified report.

    d. Returns in the context of this chapter are of two types:

        i.   Those from branches in the UK. The auditors must see that proper returns have been received by head office when he has not himself visited the branches. Some companies have numerous branches eg. Woolworths. The auditor cannot be expected to visit them all.

        ii. Those from branches overseas. These are subject to special statutory requirements but the auditor has the same duty to satisfy himself on overseas branch matters as he does for UK branches.

    e. The company law referred to in this chapter may seem very tedious but examiners in auditing frequently require knowledge of these matters.

    f. There are penalties for failing to keep proper accounting records or statutory books.

g. Particular problems that may cause the auditor to reflect on whether proper accounting records have been kept include:

- delays in writing up the records
- frequent alterations in records
- exceptionally large numbers of errors found by the auditor
- audit trail difficulties (audit trail is the ability to follow a transaction through the records and documentation. It may be lost in some computer systems)
- computer problems including failure of software, chaos, hardware breakdowns, changes of computer staff, viruses, loss of data etc.

h. Organisations other than companies may have specific statutory requirements re accounting records (eg financial service companies) and the auditor needs to ensure that these have been complied with.

i. Note the requirement in Section 221(1)(a) 'at any time'.

Case study for Chapter 4

Mr and Mrs Seamus O'Neill jointly own a company, O'Neill Fashion Shirts Ltd operating in London. The company buy from a range of suppliers and sell on credit to retail shops nationwide. Copy sales invoices are retained and when the customer pays, the invoice is so marked. A proper cash book is kept. Output VAT is obtained by adding up the VAT on the invoices using an add-listing machine. All this is done neatly and accurately. Incoming purchases invoices are placed in a box and when paid are marked paid and filed in a proper file. Input VAT is obtained from an analysis column in the cash book. The company have a branch in Dublin run by Mrs O'Neill's sister. The branch operates exactly the same system. At the end of each year a summary of the books is sent to London where accounts are prepared and an audit done by O'Connor, a certified accountant.

Seamus asks O'Connor whether his books of account are adequate. O'Connor also maintains the company's statutory books and makes a separate charge for so doing. To justify the charge O'Connor takes Seamus through the statutory books and explains why they are kept.

Discussion

Are the books adequate?

Does a private company need all the statutory books?

Student self testing questions *Questions with answers apparent from the text*

1. a. What must appear in books of account? (5)
    b. List the statutory books. (10)
    c. Who are responsible for maintaining the books of account and the statutory books? (3)
    d. What is the auditor's interest in these documents? (11)

Exercise

1. List the accounting records that Positron Electrical Wholesalers Ltd. should keep.

5 Accounting requirements of the Companies Act

Introduction

1. This chapter outlines the Companies Act requirements on the accounting reference date, the form and content of company accounts, the procedure on the completion of the accounts, modified accounts and the publication of full and abridged accounts.

2. An auditor must know these rules because:

   a. The majority of audits are company audits.

   b. The principal objective of the audit is to report on the truth and fairness of the financial statements.

   c. Section 235 requires the auditor to state in his report whether, in his opinion, the Accounts have been properly prepared in accordance with the Act.

   d. Examiners in auditing require this knowledge in students.

3. The responsibility for preparing financial statements, laying them before the company (= presenting them to shareholders) and delivering them to Companies House lies wholly with the directors.

Accounting reference date

4. Every company has to have a year end and the profit and loss account is for the year ending on that date and the balance sheet is made up as at that date. A company's year end is known as the *accounting reference date* and the financial statements are made up for the *accounting reference periods* ending on that date.

5. Sections 223 to 225 give the law on this matter in unbelievable length. In short:

   a. the company can give notice to the Registrar of its chosen date.

   b. if this is not done then the date is the last day of the month in which the anniversary of its incorporation falls (or 31 March for companies formed before 1990).

   c. the date can be changed by going through the prescribed procedures.

6. The company must prepare accounts for each and every accounting reference period. The actual date used may be up to seven days either side of the accounting reference date.

Financial statements required

7. The following financial statements must be prepared:

   a. A Profit and Loss account for each accounting reference period – Section 226.

   b. A Balance Sheet as at the accounting reference date – Section 226.

   c. If the company is a holding company then group accounts must also be prepared – Section 227. It is permissible and is the common practice not to publish the company's own profit and loss account but to publish a consolidated profit and loss account which shows how much of the consolidated profit or loss for the financial year is dealt with in the company's individual accounts – Section 230.

d. Notes attached to and forming part of the Accounts:

    i   Giving the detailed information required by Schedule 4 without cluttering the financial statements.

    ii. Giving certain required additional information (eg the emoluments of directors) – Section 232 and Schedule 6.

e. A directors' report – Section 234.

f. The auditor's report – Section 235.

Form of company accounts

8. a. The balance sheet must follow either of the two *formats* included in Schedule 4.

b. The profit and loss account must follow one of the four formats given in Schedule 4.

c. There are complex rules on the interpretation and variation of the format rules in Schedule 4.

d. It is possible to depart from the formats only if special circumstances require departure in order that the overriding requirement of a true and fair view be met. In practice departure from the formats is very rare.

Accounting principles

9. The 4th Schedule paragraphs 9 to 15:

ACCOUNTING PRINCIPLES

Preliminary

9. *Subject to paragraph 15 below, the amounts to be included in respect of all items shown in a company's accounts shall be determined in accordance with the principles set out in paragraphs 10 to 14.*

Accounting principles

10. *The company shall be presumed to be carrying on business as a going concern.*

11. *Accounting policies shall be applied consistently within the same accounts and from one financial year to the next.*

12. *The amount of any item shall be determined on a prudent basis, and in particular –*

    (a) only profits realised at the balance sheet date shall be included in the profit and loss account; and

    (b) all liabilities and losses which have arisen or are likely to arise in respect of the financial year to which the accounts relate or a previous financial year shall be taken into account, including those which only become apparent between the balance sheet date and the date on which it is signed on behalf of the board of directors in pursuance of Section 238 of this Act.

13. *All income and charges relating to the financial year to which the accounts relate shall be taken into account, without regard to the date of receipt or payment.*

14 . *In determining the aggregate amount of any item the amount of each individual asset or liability that falls to be taken into account shall be determined separately.*

Departure from the accounting principles

15. *If it appears to the directors of a company that there are special reasons for departing from any of the principles stated above in preparing the company's accounts in respect of any financial*

year they may do so, but particulars of the departure, the reasons for it and its effect shall be given in a note to the accounts.

The accounting principles required are:

a. going concern

b. consistency

c. prudence/conservatism

d. realisation/accruals.

The principle enunciated in para 14 does not seem to have a name in the accounting literature. It could be applied to stocks – the concept of lower of cost and net realisable value must be applied to individual items of stock and not to stock as a whole.

10. Detailed rules on the application of the accounting principles are also given in Schedule 4 both for *historical* accounts and for *alternative* accounting (current cost, ie adjusting for inflation). For example there are rules or guidance on valuing fixed assets, the value of manufactured work in progress and finished goods and FIFO, LIFO, etc. for fungible items.

Content – detailed disclosure requirements

11. Schedule 4 gives extensive detailed rules on the *minimum* information which must be given in the Accounts or in notes attached to them.

There is no objection made against Accounts giving *more* information than the minimum but in practice most Accounts just disclose the minimum required by the law.

Procedure on completion of the accounts

12. a. The Accounts comprising:
    - the balance sheet
    - the profit and loss account
    - the directors' report
    - the auditor's report
    - the group accounts where required

    must be approved by the board and then the balance sheet must be signed by a director of the company on behalf of the board – Section 233.

  b. A copy of the Accounts must be sent to all persons entitled at least 21 days before AGM – Section 238.

  c. Copies of the Accounts must be *laid before* the company in general meeting (usually the AGM) – Section 241.

  d. A copy of the Accounts must be *delivered* to the registrar of companies –Section 242.

Period allowed for laying and delivering accounts

13. The directors of a company are required by the Act (Section 242) to *lay* and *deliver* the Accounts in accordance with a timescale as:

  a. Private companies – within 10 months after the end of the accounting reference period.

  b. Public companies – within 7 months after the end of the accounting reference period.

These times may be extended by three months in companies with overseas interests.

Abbreviated accounts

14. Sections 246 and 247 and The Companies Act 1985 (Accounts of Small and Medium-Sized Enterprises and Publication of Accounts in ECUs) Regulations 1992 gives a number of *exemptions* to small and medium-sized companies. These are:

    a. exemption for both small and medium-sized companies from the requirement of *disclosure* of whether the accounts have been prepared in accordance with applicable accounting standards.

    b. small companies need only produce a slightly reduced form of Balance Sheet.

    c. small companies are exempt from some filing requirements. Notably they need only file an abbreviated Balance Sheet and need not include many of the notes to the accounts. They do not need to file a Profit and Loss Account or the directors' report.

    d. medium-sized companies can file a slightly abbreviated Profit and Loss Account and there is no need for the note analysing turnover over classes and markets.

15. Small and medium-sized companies are defined as companies which satisfy two or more of the following:

		Small	Medium-sized
i.	Turnover does not exceed	£2.8 million	£11.2 million
ii.	Balance Sheet total does not exceed	£1.4 million	£5.6 million
iv.	Average number of employees does not exceed	50	250

    The exemptions do not apply to a company if in the year it is:

    - a public company
    - a banking or insurance company
    - an authorised person under the Financial Services Act 1986
    - a member of an ineligible group

    An ineligible group is one in which any of its members is:

    - a public company
    - an authorised institution under the Banking Act 1987
    - an Insurance company to which part II of the Insurance Companies Act 1982 applies
    - an authorised person under the Financial Services Act 1986

    In addition, a parent company does not qualify as small or medium-sized unless the group headed by it qualifies as a small or medium-sized group (see chapter on group accounts)

16. There are formalities to be gone through if abbreviated accounts are filed:

    a. The Balance Sheet shall contain:
       - a statement that advantage is taken of the exemptions
       - a statement of the grounds on which, in the directors' opinion, the company is entitled to those exemptions.

    b. Inclusion of a special report by the auditor stating that in this opinion:
       i. the directors are entitled to deliver abbreviated accounts;

ii. the accounts have been properly prepared as abbreviated accounts.

The full text of the auditor's report must be included in the special report.

Publication of accounts

17. Section 240 has some rules on the publication of accounts.

A company may publish its statutory accounts. When it does so, it must also publish its auditors' Report. Statutory accounts means the full accounts or the reduced accounts allowed to small or medium sized companies.

Companies may also publish non-statutory accounts (formerly called abridged accounts) (Section 240). When it does, then it must also publish a statement:

a. that the accounts are not statutory accounts

b. whether statutory accounts have been delivered to the Registrar

c. whether the auditors have made a report

d. whether any such report has been qualified.

Dormant companies

18. Section 250 has some rules on dormant companies:

A company is dormant in a period if during the period no significant accounting transaction occurred. Such companies need not appoint an auditor but must still lay and deliver accounts.

Listed public companies

19. Section 251 has some special rules for limited public companies.

These are new in the Companies Act 1989 and the rules are:

a. Listed companies need not send full accounts to their shareholders but may instead send them a summary financial statement.

b. The company must send full accounts to members who require them..

c. There are regulations as to what must be included in the summary accounts derived from the full accounts.

d. The summary accounts must contain a statement that they are only a summary and also contain a statement from the *auditors* to whether the summary is consistent with the full accounts. The auditors' statement must also state whether their report was qualified or unqualified and if it was qualified give their report in full.

Summary

20. a. The Companies Acts lay down very detailed rules on

    i. What financial statements are required.

    ii. The form of the financial statements.

    iii. The accounting principles to be followed.

    iv. Detailed information to be disclosed.

    v. Accounting period and time limits for laying and delivering accounts.

b. Specified exemptions from these rules are given to small and medium sized companies.

   c.   Listed companies may send out summary financial statements.

Points to note

21. a.   The Companies Act rules are voluminous and complex. They are properly the subject of texts in accounting or publications devoted to them and this chapter gives only a brief summary. Auditors must know the rules because their duties laid down by the Act include a requirement to report on the true and fair view and compliance with statute of the Accounts. Auditors also have specified duties in connection with the abbreviated accounts of small and medium sized companies.

   b.   Auditing examinees are sometimes required to show specific and detailed knowledge of the rules.

   c.   In addition to the Companies Act requirements on Accounts, there are also two other sets of requirements to be fulfilled. These are:

      i.   The Statements of Standard Accounting Practice and the Financial Reporting Standards. The detail of these is dealt with in a later chapter. However note that the SSAPs and FRSs specify detailed principles of preparation, and disclosure requirements of the Profit and Loss Account and Balance Sheet but they also require an additional financial statement (but only for larger companies) – The Cash Flow Statement required by FRS 1.

      ii.   Requirements under the Stock Exchange Listing Agreement for listed companies (and similarly for the Alternative Investment Market).

      Auditing students are expected to know the rules in SSAPs and FRSs in great detail but are not expected to know the Stock Exchange rules.

   d.   Note the distinction between:

      i.   *Laying* Accounts before the company. These must be full but there are some modifications for small and medium sized companies. (See Statutory Instrument 1992/2452)

      ii.   *Delivering* (filing at Companies House). These can be, for small and medium sized companies, abbreviated.

      iii.   *Publication*. These can be *abridged*

   e.   The Companies Act 1989 formally recognised the accounting standards and companies are now required to state, with their statement of accounting policies, whether the accounts have been prepared in accordance with applicable accounting standards and give particulars of any material departure from those standards and the reasons for any such departure.

   f.   Accounts must give a true and fair view. Note Section 226:

      (4) *Where compliance with the provisions of that Schedule, and the other provisions of this Act as to the matters to be included in a company's individual accounts or in notes to those accounts, would not be sufficient to give a true and fair view, the necessary additional information shall be given in the accounts or in a note to them.*

      (5) *If in special circumstances compliance with any of those provisions is inconsistent with the requirement to give a true and fair view, the directors shall depart from that provision to the extent necessary to give a true and fair view.*

Particulars of any such departure, the reasons for it and its effect shall be given in a note to the accounts.

Case study for Chapter 5

Pansy Retail Fashions Ltd was formed and began trading on 6 April 19-5 together with a subsidiary, Fairy Fashions Ltd.

At 31.3.-6 the company and its subsidiary had figures as:

	Pansy	Fairy
Turnover	£1.2 million	£1.4 million
Balance Sheet total	£1.6 million	£0.2 million
Average number of employees	65	20

Discussion

The directors have written to you with a series of questions:

a. What reference date they should use?

b. What financial statements they should prepare?

c. Which formats they should use for the accounts?

d. What is the latest date for the first annual general meeting (the company have a branch in Paris)?

e. Whether full accounts have to be sent to the shareholders and the registrar of companies?

Reply to them in the form of a letter.

Student self testing questions *Questions with answers apparent from the text*

1. a. What financial statements must be prepared? (7)
   b. What are the time limits for laying and delivery of accounts? (13)
   c. Define small and medium sized companies. (15)
   d. What exemptions are available to them? (14)
   e. What are the rules on publishing accounts in abridged form? (17)
   f. What are the rules on sending out accounts in summary form? (19)
   g. What additional reports are required from an auditor? (16, 19)

Exercises

1. Hannah plc have both ordinary and preference shares, some of which have been redeemed out of profits in the year. They have revalued the company's freehold property in the year also and included the new figure in the accounts.

   State the Companies Act requirements on disclosure of these items.

2. Shineton Supplies PLC was formed many years ago by a group of retailers as a supplier of widgets. It is now one of many such suppliers and it is run by Glenk who sees it as his own private property. The shareholding is however very diverse (with 40 shareholders) and Glenk has only a small number of shares. The company is a PLC but is not listed. This year, its turnover was £2.2 million, its Balance Sheet total £1.7 million and it has 20 employees.

Required

a. What exemptions on preparing, filing and laying accounts are available? Glenk is anxious to give as little information as posssible to his shareholders or his competitors.

b. What options are open to the company to secure yet more exemptions?

Professional rules

The next part of the book is concerned with various rules and guidelines on auditing and auditors laid down by the professional accounting bodies. There are chapters on the auditing standards and guidelines, accounting standards, professional conduct, and finally, the letter of engagement.

6 Auditing standards and guidelines

Introduction

1. The professional accounting bodies have among their objectives, the provision of technical papers designed to improve the competence and efficiency of members. In the 1960's and 1970's the ICAEW issued a series of statements on best auditing practice known as the 'U' statements, and on related professional matters (the 'V', 'N' and 'S' statements). Some of these are still in force.

    In 1980, the three Institutes of Chartered and the Chartered Association of Certified Accountants approved the issue of a series of Auditing Standards and Guidelines. These were prepared, after consultation, by the Auditing Practices Committee. After 1980 a stream of these appeared.

    The functions of the APC have now been taken over by the Auditing Practices Board established in 1991 by the Consultative Committee of Accountancy Bodies (CCAB – consisting of ICAEW, ICAI, ICAS, ACCA, IPFA and CIMA). The ABP issues Statements of Auditing Standards which will be mandatory and Practice Notes which will be helpful and indicative of good practice. The status of these two types of statement will also be discussed in this chapter.

Statements of auditing standards

2. Each SAS has two types of material:
    a. Basic principles and essential procedures with which auditors are required to comply. These tend to be general. For example in SAS140, there is a basic procedure – Auditors should ensure that the engagement letter documents and confirms their acceptance of the appointment, and includes a summary of the responsibilities of the directors and of the auditors, the scope of the engagement and the form of any reports. Each basic principle and essential procedure statement within an SAS is given a number For example SAS 440.2 – Auditors should obtain evidence that the directors acknowledge their collective responsibility for the preparation of the financial statements and have approved the financial statements.
    b. Explanatory and other material which, rather than being prescriptive is designed to assist auditors in interpreting and applying auditing standards. For example an essential procedure in SAS 430 is that auditors should, when determining sample sizes, consider sampling risk, the amount of error that would be acceptable and the

extent to which they expect to find errors. These terms (sampling risk etc) are then explained at length and advice given on their interpretation in practice.

Auditors must comply with the numbered Statements of Auditing Standards. Apparent failure to comply may be enquired into by the appropriate committee of the relevant accountancy body and may lead to disciplinary or regulatory action. The professional body may withdraw registration from an auditor, who cannot then conduct company audits and is thus partly deprived of his livelihood. In addition the courts and may take into account the SASs when considering if audit work was adequate in negligence cases. The explanatory and other material has less authority in theory but not much less in practice.

3. Current SASs are:

Responsibility
100. Objectives and general principles governing an audit of financial statements
110. Fraud and error
120. Consideration of law and regulations
130. The going concern basis in financial statements
140. Engagement letters
150. Subsequent events
160. Other information in documents containing audited financial statements

Planning, controlling and recording
200. Planning
210. Knowledge of the business
220. Materiality and the audit
230. Working papers
240. Quality control for audit work

Accounting systems and internal control
300. Accounting and internal control systems and audit risk assessments

Evidence
400. Audit evidence
410. Analytical procedures
420. Audit of accounting estimates
430. Audit sampling
440. Management representations
450. Opening balances and comparatives
460. Related parties
470. Overall review of financial statements

Using the work of others
500. Considering the work of internal audit
510. The relationship between principal auditors and other auditors
520. Using the work of an expert

Reporting
600. Auditors' reports on financial statements

610. Reports to directors or management

620. The auditor's right and duty to report to regulators in the financial sector

There is also a glossary of terms.

An SAS on Computer Auditing and Internal Control was still in course of discussion at the time of writing.

Practice notes

4. The APB also issues Practice Notes which are designed to assist auditors in applying Auditing Standards of general application to particular circumstances and industries. They are persuasive rather than prescriptive and have similar status to the explanatory material in the SASs. Practice Notes may later be developed into or be included in SASs.

   Current ones are:

   PN1. Investment businesses

   PN2. The Lloyds market

   PN3. The auditors' right and duty to report to the Bank of England

   PN4. The auditors' right and duty to report to the building Societies Commission

   PN5. The auditors' right and duty to report to SIB and other regulators of investment businesses

   PN6. The auditors' right and duty to report to the DTI in relation to insurers authorised under the Friendly Societies Commission

   PN7. The auditors' right and duty to report to the DTI in relation to insurers authorised under the Insurance Companies Act 1982

   PN8. Reports by auditors under Companies legislation in the UK

   PN9. Reports by auditors under Companies legislation in the Republic of Ireland

   You will notice that these are specialised and mostly concern the regulated sector. Only PN8 is of general interest.

Bulletins

5. The APB also issues bulletins. These are likely to be developed into, or be included within, SASs or Practice Notes. They are issued to provide auditors with timely advice on new or emerging issues and, like Practice Notes are persuasive rather than prescriptive.

   Current ones are:

   B93/1. Review of interim financial information

   B93/2. Disclosures relating to corporate governance

Other APB documents

6. Other APB documents include The Scope and Authority of APB pronouncements and the SSRA *Audit exemption reports* covered in Chapter 38 of this book. The Scope document outlines the purposes of the APB and scope and authority of APB pronouncements. Most of its points have been dealt with in this chapter but it also says that it will issue Exposure Drafts from time to time and may issue other consultative documents.

The APC and auditing standards and guidelines

7. The APB succeeded the APC and adopted the then extant Auditing Standards and Guidelines. These remain in force until withdrawn or replaced by SASs or Practice Notes. Auditing standards have the same status as SASs and Guidelines as Practice Notes.

    At the time of writing the current ones are:

    Auditing Guidelines – Industries.
    Charities
    Building Societies in the UK
    Trade Unions and Employers' Organisations
    Housing Associations
    The impact of regulations on public sector audits
    Pension schemes in the UK
    Banks in the UK
    Guidance for internal auditors
    General business insurers in the UK
    Life insurers in the UK

    Auditing Guidelines – detailed operational
    Bank reports for audit purposes
    Attendance at stocktaking
    Auditing in a computer environment
    Prospectuses and the reporting accountant

    There is also a Practice Note *Reliance by Banks on Audited Financial Statements*

Summary

8. a. Since the 1960's the professional bodies have published guidance to members on auditing practice.

    b. In 1980 this was formalised by the formation of the Auditing Practices Committee which issued Auditing Standards (all now superseded by SASs) and Auditing Guidelines, many of which are still current.

    c. In 1991 the Auditing Practices Board was formed and issues SASs, Practice Notes, Bulletins and other pronouncements.

    d. The CCAB bodies have undertaken to adopt all SASs promulgated by the APB.

    e. Apparent failures by auditors in the UK to comply with the Auditing Standards contained in the SASs may be investigated and may lead to penalties. The penalties may include withdrawal of registration.

    f. The Auditing Standards are likely to be taken into account in a court of law where the adequacy of an auditor's work is being considered. For example if an auditor is being proceeded against for the recovery of damages caused by his/her alleged negligence. All the APB pronouncements are in practice likely to be taken into account in this way.

    g. The SASs contain numbered Auditing Standards which are mandatory and also explanatory and other material which is persuasive.

Points to note

9. a. The program of replacing the Auditing Standards and Guidelines with SASs is almost complete. However students should check the professional press for the new ones that will undoubtedly appear at intervals.

    b. There have been suggestions that the APB should become an independent body not connected with the six members of the CCAB. Future legislation may bring this about.

    c. There can be no doubt that auditing has improved as a result of the mandatory standards. In particular accountants who both prepared and audited the accounts of small enterprises have to change their thinking and see that preparation of figures is not a substitute for auditing them. The economic cost of this extra auditing has probably been heavy but has been relieved to some extent by the exemption from audit of some small companies.

Case study for Chapter 6

Blameless & Co. have just taken over the audit of Widget Machines Ltd, a company in the machine tool industry. Preliminary indications are that the company has a turnover of £1 million, is owned and run by Jack Martinet who keeps tight control over day to day operations. It seems that the company is in financial trouble. The Accounts of previous years have been subject to a qualification of the auditor's report due to non compliance with SSAP's, inefficiencies in the company's computer system and difficulties in the measurement of work in progress.

Discussion

List the SASs, Practice Notes and Auditing Guidelines that may be relevant to this audit.

Student self testing questions *Questions with answers apparent from the text*

1. a. What documents are issued by the APB? (3–6)
    b. What material is contained in a Statement of Auditing Standards? (3)

7 Accounting standards and the auditor

Introduction

1. In general, published accounts are required to conform to the accounting standards. Part of the auditor's duties is to assess whether or not the accounts he is auditing do comply in general and in detail with the accounting standards. This manual is about auditing and cannot include a detailed description of all the accounting standards. For a detailed understanding my readers will need to consult an accounting textbook or perhaps they are already conversant with the Accounting standards.

2. This chapter summarises the current process whereby accounting standards are set and then lists the current documents which an auditor would need to know. Students are reminded that new *Exposure Drafts* and *Standards* are constantly being issued by the

Accounting Standards Board and it is necessary for students to ensure they have studied the most recent documents that their examiners expect.

3. Finally this chapter reviews the relevance of accounting standards to auditing.

4. In a later chapter the audit relevance of some particular accounting standards is considered.

The standard setting process

5. The body ultimately responsible for standards is *The Financial Reporting Council* together with its subsidiaries *The Accounting Standards Board* and the *Urgent Issues Task Force*.

The financial reporting council

6. The Financial Reporting Council is a company limited by guarantee, so that in theory it is in the private sector, but it was set up by the government who, with the Bank of England, appoint its Chairman and three Deputy Chairmen so that it has statutory backing. Its remit is to give support to its operational bodies and to encourage good financial reporting generally. It has two subsidiaries – the *Accounting Standards Board* (ABS) and the *Financial Reporting Review Panel* (FRRP).

The Accounting Standards Board makes and amends and withdraws Accounting Standards. One of its first acts was to adopt the 22 extant Statements of Standard Accounting Practice which were approved by the professional accounting bodies. The previous system of creation of SSAPs by the Accounting Standards Committee and approval by the professional bodies has now been discontinued. The first new Financial Reporting Standard (FRS 1 – Cash Flow Statements) was issued in 1991 and a programme of new and amended standards is now under way. Before issuing a new Standard the ABS issues its proposals in the form of a Financial Reporting Exposure Draft (FRED) for public comment and sometimes before issuing a FRED it issues a Discussion Paper.

Some industries need accounting standards for their particular purposes and they can produce *Statements of Recommended Practice (SORPS)*. The ABS has a role in the approval of these, by approving bodies who issue them rather than the SORPS themselves.

The Accounting Standards Board has a sub-committee called the Urgent Issues Task Force (UITF). The work of the UITF is to assist the ABS in areas where an accounting standard or Companies Act provision exists but where unsatisfactory or conflicting interpretations have developed or seem likely to develop. A surprising number of matters have been subject to UITF pronouncements, most of them very technical. Pronouncements of the UITF are regarded as accepted practice in the area in question and the intention is they should be considered to be a part of the corpus of practices forming a basis for what determines a true and fair view.

Financial reporting review panel

7. The FRRP is a subsidiary of the FRC. Its role is to examine departures from the accounting requirements of the Companies Act 1985 and if necessary to seek an order from the court to remedy them. As well as having detailed requirements on accounting the Companies Act requires all accounts to show a true and fair view and by implication to comply with the accounting standards. The panel does not seek out departures but acts on matters drawn to its attention directly or indirectly. The panel's concerns are with

the public companies and small and medium sized companies are outside its ambit.

Documents that auditing students should be aware of

Statements of standard accounting practice (SSAPs)

8. 1. Accounting for the results of associated companies
   2. Disclosure of accounting policies
   3. Earnings per share
   4. The accounting treatment of grants
   5. Accounting for value added tax
   6. Extraordinary items and prior year adjustments (superseded by FRS 3)
   7. Accounting for changes in the purchasing power of money (now withdrawn)
   8. The treatment of taxation under the imputation system in the accounts of companies
   9. Stocks and work in progress
   10. Statements of source and application of funds (superseded by FRS 1)
   11. Accounting for deferred taxation (now withdrawn)
   12. Accounting for depreciation
   13. Accounting for research and development
   14. Group accounts (superseded by FRS 2)
   15. Accounting for deferred taxation
   16. Current cost accounting (now withdrawn)
   17. Accounting for post balance sheet events
   18. Accounting for contingencies
   19. Accounting for investment properties
   20. Foreign currency translation
   21. Accounting for leases and hire purchase transactions
   22. Accounting for goodwill
   23. Accounting for acquisitions and mergers
   24. Accounting for pension costs
   25. Segmental reporting

Financial reporting standards

9. The Financial Reporting Standards issued to date are:

   FRS 1 – Cash Flow Statements

   FRS 2 – Accounting for Subsidiary Undertakings

   FRS 3 – Reporting Financial Performance

   FRS 4 – Capital Instruments

   FRS 5 – Reporting the Substance of Transactions

   FRS 5A – Amendment to FRS 5: Insurance broking transactions and financial reinsurance

   FRS 6 – Acquisitions and Mergers

   FRS 7 – Fair Values in Acquisition Accounting

   FRS 8 – Related Party Disclosures

   The current programme of the ASB includes:

   – a Statement of Principles for Financial reporting (issued as an exposure draft in November 1995)

- a review of FRS 1
- Goodwill and intangibles (this topic has produced much controversy and argument)
- Associates and joint ventures
- Accounting for tax
- Pension costs in the employer's financial statements
- Valuation: measurement of tangible fixed assets
- Provisions
- Impairment
- Financial instruments (derivatives)

Urgent issues task force

10. The following abstracts have been issued and should be complied with.
    UITF Abstract 3 – Treatment of Goodwill on Disposal of a Business
    UITF Abstract 4 – Presentation of Long Term Debtors in Current Assets
    UITF Abstract 5 – Transfers from Current Assets to Fixed Assets
    UITF Abstract 6 – Accounting for Post-Retirement Benefits other than Pensions
    UITF Abstract 7 – True and Fair View Override Disclosures
    UITF Abstract 9 – Accounting for operations in hyper-inflationary economies
    UITF Abstract 10 – Disclosure of directors' share options
    UITF Abstract 11 – Capital instruments: issuer call options
    UITF Abstract 12 – Lessee accounting for reverse premiums and similar incentives

Relevance of accounting standards to auditing

11. Auditors must include in their reports, their opinion on whether the financial statements they report on, give a *true and fair view*.

12. The abstract concept of the true and fair view is discussed at length in a later chapter. However it is enough to say at this stage that, in general, in order that Accounts show a true and fair view, Accounts must comply with the accounting standards. There can be situations where a true and fair view will not be given if an accounting standard is followed but these will be extremely rare.

13. The Companies Act 1989 formally recognised the accounting standards and required (Schedule 4 (36A)) that with Disclosure of Accounting Policies there should also be a statement as to whether the accounts have been prepared in accordance with applicable accounting standards and particulars of any material departure from those standards and the reasons for any such departure.

14. Thus an auditor is, in effect, being asked to give an opinion on whether all accounting standards have been complied with in the preparation of the accounts he is auditing. This means that auditors must know and understand the accounting standards in detail.

15. Auditing students are also expected to know the accounting standards in detail. Many auditing questions in examinations require this knowledge and examinees are advised to quote from the accounting standards and state which of the accounting standards are relevant to his answer. For example questions involving depreciation will require mention of SSAP 12 and questions on Groups will require mention of FRS 2. Very many questions also require mention of the fundamental accounting principles discussed in SSAP 2 and the need to disclose accounting policies required by that SSAP.

Small companies and accounting standards

16. The accounting standards and UITF pronouncements are on a continuum from the elements of accounting (eg SSAP 12) through to arcane issues that only affect a few, mostly large, companies (eg FRS 3 or UITF Abstract 11). It is currently a matter of discussion within the ASB and the CCAB (see discussion paper of November 1994) as to whether small companies should be exempt from compliance with all but a small number of essential accounting standards. Watch the professional press for discussion of this issue.

Summary

17. a. The accounting standards are essential knowledge for auditing students.

    b. All financial statements must give a true and fair view. Among the requirements for a true and fair view is compliance with the accounting standards.

    c. The SSAPs have been adopted by the Accounting Standards Board and most (those that have not been superseded by a FRS) remain in force. The first eight FRSs have now appeared.

    d. The UITF abstracts are also relevant to auditing students.

Points to note

18. a. Departures from the accounting standards are now rare as they have achieved full recognition by business. In addition the FRRP may pick up undisclosed departures. Normally when the FRRP finds against a company, the company restates its next set of accounts to adjust the wrong treatment but the FRRP can take a company to court if it declines to do so. A recourse to the court has not yet happened. Under the panel's procedures, the facts of cases requiring changes to the accounts are handed on to the professional body of the auditors and this body may take disciplinary action.

    b. The ASB approves bodies who produce SORPs rather than the SORPs themselves. SORPs are normally issued with regard to the accounts of specialised bodies (eg Universities, pension schemes). SORPs are not mandatory but accounts for a body where a relevant SORP exists are unlikely to show a true and fair view if the SORP is not followed. Examiners do not normally expect students to know the SORPs.

    c. Accounting Standards are mandatory except where a true and fair view would not be given which is very unlikely. FREDs and Discussion documents are not mandatory until they have become FRSs but the discussion in them may indicate what present opinion is on what is a true and fair view. However a present accounting standard must be complied until it is superseded.

    d. In an opinion for the APB in 1993, Mary Arden QC (now Mrs Justice Arden) said that the courts are likely to treat accounting standards as legally binding and that compliance with them is likely to be found necessary if the true and fair view requirement in company accounts is to be met.

Case study for Chapter 7

Shirley is the auditor of Earthy Products Ltd, a small company in Walsall. She is reviewing the accounts for the year ending 31 March 19-6 and notes the following facts:

a. The stock is valued at marginal cost whereas the stock in the previous year was valued at direct cost.

b. Cost of sales includes the costs of closure of the branch at Warley.

c. The company have some shares in a public company supplier and the dividends received are in the accounts as cash received.

d. There is no cash flow statement.

e. The company's freehold factory has not been depreciated.

f. The company have not provided for corporation tax as they have unused capital allowances.

g. The accounts make no mention of the uninsured loss of stock in a fire on 6 April 19-6.

h. Certain development expenditure written off in the 1994/5 accounts has been reinstated in the 1995/6 accounts.

i. A contingent gain has been omitted from the accounts as its effects are almost equal but opposite to an unrelated contingent loss which is also omitted.

j. Some 25% of the sterling amount of Trade debtors includes loans to customers which are recoverable only when the customer ceases trading with Earthy Products.

Discussion

What are the implications of these facts for the audit?

Student self testing questions *Questions with answers apparent from the text*

1. a. What is the Financial Reporting Council? (6)
   b. What is the Accounting Standards Board? (6)
   c. What is the Financial Reporting Review Panel? (6,7)
   d. What has happened to the SSAPs? (6)
   e. What is a SORP? (6)
   f. What is the UITF and what status has its pronouncements? (6)
   g. List the current SSAPs (8)
   h. List the FRSs (9)
   i. Which matters are currently under consideration? (9)
   j. Why are accounting standards relevant to the auditor? (11–15)
   k. What is the relationship between the Companies Act and the accounting standards? (13)

8 Rules of professional conduct

Introduction

1. Auditing is carried out by accountants in public practice. Accountancy is a profession. Professions have certain characteristics including an ethical code and rules of conduct. This chapter is concerned with the rules of conduct prescribed by the professional accounting bodies.

2. I will begin with a general discussion on what a profession is and then describe the rules. This subject is frequently found in examinations in auditing which is considered a suitable paper for ethical matters even when they do not relate to auditing.

3. The rules are found in the handbooks issued to all members. The Association publishes the rules in one cheap volume and all students are advised to obtain a copy.

4. In this chapter we will look at:
   - idea of a profession
   - ethics
   - independence
   - conflicts of interest
   - advertising
   - publicity
   - obtaining professional work
   - remuneration
   - insider dealing.

5. Fraud, changes in professional appointments (professional etiquette) and professional liability are dealt with in separate chapters.

Professions

6. Dictionaries define and describe a profession as a calling or vocation involving some branch of learning. Clearly accountancy does involve a body of knowledge as is well known to students who are endeavouring to acquire it. Whether young people are called or feel a vocation towards accountancy is more doubtful.

7. The idea of a profession rests on the following premises:
   a. a recognisable discrete body of knowledge
   b. an educational process
   c. a system of examinations
   d. a system for licensing practitioners
   e. a professional association
   f. a sense of responsibility to society
   g. a code of ethics
   h. a set of technical standards.

   You will see that all of these premises can be applied to the accountancy profession.

Ethics – general rules

8. Professional accountants are required to observe proper standards of professional conduct whether or not the standards required are written in the rules or are unwritten. They are specifically required to refrain from misconduct which is difficult to define

precisely but which includes any act or default which is likely to bring discredit on himself, his professional body or the profession generally.

Several general points can be made:

a. Professional independence is exceedingly important. This is very much an attitude of mind rather than a set of rules but there are many rules which we will describe later.

b. Integrity is vital. Synonyms for integrity include honesty, uprightness, probity, rectitude, moral soundness.

c. Accountants must not only be people of integrity and independence; they must also be seen to be so. Any interest (eg owning shares in a client company) which might diminish an accountant's objectivity of approach or which might appear to to others, must be avoided.

d. When an accountant has ethical difficulties or is unsure of what course of conduct to follow, he should consult his professional body or take legal advice. If in doubt always seek advice.

Independence

9. An auditor's objectivity must be beyond question when conducting an audit. An auditor must always approach his work with integrity and objectivity. The approach must be in a spirit of independence of mind.

There are number of matters which may threaten or appear to threaten the independence of an auditor. These include:

a. Undue dependence on an audit client. Public perception of independence may be put in jeopardy if the fees from any one client or group of connected clients exceed 15% of gross practice income or 10% in the case of listed or other public interest companies. This general observation needs modifying in the cases of new practices.

b. Family or other personal relationships. It is desirable to avoid professional relationships where personal relationships exist. Examples of personal relationships include mutual business interests with members of the group comprising the client, the audit firm, officers or employees of the client, partners or members of staff of the audit firm.

c. Beneficial interests in shares and other investments. In general, partners, their spouses, and minor children should not hold shares in or have other investments in client companies. An audit staff member should not be employed on an audit if the staff member or some person connected with him has a beneficial interest in the audit client. Some company articles require the auditor to have a qualifying shareholding. In such cases the minimum only should be held and the holding should be disclosed in the accounts.

d. Loans to and from clients. An auditing practice or anyone closely connected with it should not make loans to its clients nor receive loans from clients. The same applies to guarantees. Overdue fees may in some circumstances constitute a loan.

e. Acceptance of goods and services. Goods and services should not be accepted by a practice or by anyone closely connected with it unless the value of any benefit is modest. Acceptance of undue hospitality poses a similar threat. A bottle of Scotch at Christmas is acceptable but a weekend in Paris would probably not be.

f.   Actual or threatened litigation. Litigation or threatened litigation (eg on auditor negligence) between a client company and an audit firm would mean the parties being placed in an adversarial situation which clearly undermines the auditor's objectivity.

g.   Influences outside the practice. There is a risk of loss of objectivity due to pressures from associated practices, bankers, solicitors, government or those introducing business.

h.   Provision of other services. This is acceptable in principle but care must be taken and this is reviewed in the next paragraph.

i.   Auditors should not allow their judgement to be swayed by the receipt of a commission, fee or other reward from a third party as a result of advising a client to pursue one course rather than another. If a commission is to be received the accountant should either give it to the client or, with the client's express or implied consent, retain it. If it is to be retained then the fact of a payment of commission, and the amount or how it is to be calculated, should be disclosed to the client, preferably in the letter of engagement. The client must assent to retention.

Audit firms should review on an annual basis every client to determine if it is proper to accept or continue an audit engagement bearing in mind actual or apparent threats to audit objectivity. The rules of the Financial Services Act must always be followed.

Conflicts of interest

10. Conflicts of interest can arise between an accountant and his client. Conflicts of interest can arise between a client and another client, and an accountant should not act for both parties if the parties are in dispute. For example the accountant may be called upon to advise two clients who are tendering for the same contract. Or he may be advising a company and one of its directors who are in dispute. In all such cases the accountant should not accept assignments where he is put in a position where he must advise both sides. On the other hand he may well be able to put forward proposals to settle the dispute.

Specific examples of conflict of interest include:

a.   Provision of other services to audit clients. It is customary for auditors m many cases to provide other services as well as the audit, for example preparing accounts. This is perfectly acceptable providing the service does not involve performing executive functions or making executive decisions. For example discussing the annual dividend decision with the board would be an executive action and hence unacceptable.

b.   Preparation of accounting records. Care should be taken that the client takes responsibility for the work done and that objectivity in auditing is not impaired. The accounting records of public company clients should not be prepared by the auditor.

c.   A practice should not report on a company if a company associated with the practice is the company secretary to the client. However it is acceptable to provide assistance to the company secretary.

d.   No person in an accounting firm should take part in the reporting function (ie take part in the audit) if he or she has in the accounting period or in the previous two years been an officer or employee of that company.

e.   Receivership, liquidation and audits. In general auditors should not accept receiverships or liquidatorships of client companies without a three year gap between the assignments. Clearly a liquidator of a company would be inhibited from taking a negligence action against the auditor if he had himself been the auditor.

Advertising

11. There are still considerable restrictions on advertising including:

    any advertisement should not:

    a. bring into disrepute himself, any member of his professional body, his firm or the accountancy profession generally;
    b. discredit the services of others by for example claiming superiority;
    c. contain comparisons with other members or firms;
    d. be misleading, either directly or by implication;
    e. fall short of the Advertising Standards Authority as to legality, decency, honesty, and truthfulness.
    f. Adverts *may* refer to the basis on which fees are calculated. However, no hourly or other charging rates are permissible. 'This month's special cheap offer' will not appear in accountants' adverts.

    None of this means that accountants' advertisements need be dull or unimaginative. Many firms have put out exciting adverts but whether they are also 'attractive' is not yet clear.

    Enterprises in all sectors of the economy have sought to reduce costs in recent years. A major cost is the audit fee and other fees paid to the auditor for other work. Many enterprises have asked several firms to tender for the audit and other work. This has led to the practice of "lowballing" or tendering low to get the work. Whether this has had a deleterious effect on the quality of auditing is arguable.

Publicity

12. In the past, accountants were required to be very anonymous in public matters. The rules are now less restrictive but there are still some prohibitions. A general prohibition is on any publicity which would bring the accountant, his professional body or the profession, into disrepute. Presumably, an accountant appearing on a chat show and introduced as John Ticker, certified accountant would be acceptable. But if the conversation revealed him to be a transvestite satanist, it might not.

Obtaining professional work

13. Accountants may now advertise for work and engage in other forms of publicity, for example by posters or hoardings or on motor vehicles, on sportswear or by sports sponsorship. However accountants may not give any commission, fee or reward to a third party for introducing clients. Such commissions may, however, be paid to his employees or other practising accountants.

Remuneration

14. The normal basis for charging for professional work, is on the time spent on the work calculated at appropriate hourly rates for principals, senior and other staff. The hourly rate may vary according to the difficulty or complexity of the work involved. It is up to

the accountant to decide upon his hourly rates depending on his cost structure, greed, market conditions, etc. It is not permissible to charge:

a. On a percentage basis except where statute or custom allows, eg in liquidation and receivership work. Many accountants are jealous of the percentage charging methods of estate agents, architects, solicitors, etc., but these professional people generally do not have recurring work from clients and continually need to seek new clients. In any event other professionals also charge flat rates nowadays.

b. On a contingency basis. This means accountants cannot accept work on a percentage of tax saved basis or anything similar.

It is possible to charge on a contingency basis where the client's capacity to pay is dependent on the success or failure of the venture. Examples could be advising on a management buy-out or the raising of venture capital.

Accountants who receive commissions from stockbrokers, insurance brokers, etc. for transactions effected for clients or for trusts of which the accountant is a trustee should either:

a. Pass on the commissions to the client or trust by deducting the amounts received from his fee invoice and showing the deduction.

b. Keep the commissions if he has been specifically authorised to do so by the client.

Insider dealing

15. Insider dealing is illegal – Company Securities (Insider Dealing) Act 1985. It is also contrary to the ethical rules. People who during the course of their work come across 'unpublished price sensitive information' are prohibited from dealing in securities to which that information relates. Unpublished price sensitive information covers specific matters not generally known to those who normally deal on the stock exchange but which if it were known to them would alter the prices of those securities to which the information relates. The prohibition applies to anyone who has a connection at present or at any time in the previous six months and to any third person who the insider may wish to instruct.

Auditors with their close connection with the accounts of a public company client are often in possession of Insider Information. For example they may know that the profit is £12 million when the market is expecting only £10 million. They must not take advantage of this information by buying shares in the company on the expectation of a rise in the price when the accounts are published.

Other matters

16. In addition to the matters mentioned in this chapter, there are rules on professional conduct in the following areas:

a. Descriptions of members of professional bodies and their designatory letters.

b. Activities through corporate and non-corporate organisations.

c. The obligations of consultants. Alan, an accountant consults Bertha, an accountant with special knowledge of taxation, on behalf of Colin, a client. Bertha should not then obtain further work from Colin unless:

i. Alan consents, or

ii. 3 years has elapsed since the end of the consultancy engagement, or,

iii. exceptionally, if the interests of Colin might be prejudiced.

This is to allay the fears of accountants that if they consult experts, they may lose the client.

d. Membership of trade unions. Accountants may belong to trade unions and go on strike.

e. The incapacity or death of a sole practitioner. Arrangements must be made for continuity of a practice.

f. Client's money. Clients' money should be paid into a separate general client account or into an account opened for the particular client. Such moneys should only be used to cover disbursements on behalf of the client, payments made on the instructions of the client and to pay fees to the accountant. Such fees must have been agreed with the client and an invoice raised. Deposit account interest on clients' accounts belongs to the clients.

g. Estates of deceased persons. This is concerned with the division of work between accountants and solicitors.

Summary

17. a. The professional bodies require their members and students to behave in an ethical manner.

b. In some areas, the codes of ethics and conduct are spelt out in detail.

c. Independence is of particular importance and detailed guidance is issued to members.

Points to note

18. a. The ethical codes are in some areas mandatory. For example a certified accountant cannot describe himself as a 'certified accountant and auditor'.

b. In some areas they give guidance only. For example in the independence ethical guide, the 15% fees rule is for guidance only, a client giving 10% of gross fees may influence an auditor who fears the loss of income if he loses the client.

c. In all these ethical matters, an accountant must not only behave correctly, he must also be seen to be behaving correctly.

d. These matters are occasionally tested in examinations. In recent examinations, independence rules, advertising, remuneration method, and insider dealing have appeared.

e. Ethics are taken very seriously by professional accountants.

f. Professional accountants are not allowed to give investment advice or conduct investment business unless they are authorised to do so by their professional body under the Financial Services Act 1986.

g. Auditors become privy to all sorts of information in the course of their work. I well remember being surprised at the very large investment account of a family friend in the Building Society I was auditing as a trainee. Similarly I was interested to discover the amount paid by a neighbour for his house and his method of financing it when I audited a firm of solicitors (to say nothing of divorce cases). Auditors and their staff must regard all such information as totally privileged and not disclose it to third parties except in circumstances where there is a legal right or duty to disclose it. They may not also use such information for personal gain, eg by insider trading.

h. Partners and staff of audit firms can become so familiar with the management or staff of a client company that they lose their objectivity. This must be avoided perhaps by rotating the partners and staff involved.

i. Independence is a big issue at the time of writing and the practice of audit firms performing other services for their audit clients has come into some criticism. Warnings are made in the ethical guides of the professional bodies of the risks to objectivity in performing these services but these all fall a long way short of prohibition. The real question is whether an audit firm can offer a totally dispassionate opinion if it and/or an associated firm are supplying services like:

- bookkeeping
- preparing the annual accounts
- taxation
- advice on company secretarial matters
- management consultancy
- obtaining staff
- selecting computer systems
- litigation support
- corporate financial advice eg on capital raising or takeovers

In a particular situation an auditor may well feel that he or she is a professional person and is quite capable of giving an independent audit opinion even though:

- the fee for the opinion is fixed by the directors
- the directors can engineer a change of auditor if they wish
- the senior conducting the audit prepared the final accounts
- the firm advised the firm on the choice of a computer firm for the supply of new hardware and software
- the firm investigated a company which the client company purchased
- the firm advised the client on a complex scheme for tax avoidance.

I leave you to think about this.

Case study for Chapter 8

Philip has been in practice for many years. At the present time he is anxious to develop more income to send his sons through University. Amongst the new ventures he has been offered are:

a. the audit of his brother's new company;

b. a 25% share in a new company being formed by a client to market computer software;

c. an agency with a building society who want him to agree to an illuminated sign in his office window;

d. a back duty case client has offered him 20% of the sum saved if he will negotiate a reduction in the estimated assessment.

George, his assistant, has been offered a part time job, by a company client, keeping the client's books.

Discussion

a. How might Philip enlarge his practice?

b. How should he deal with the matters mentioned above?

Student self testing questions *Questions with answers apparent from the text*

1. a. What are the characteristics of a profession? (7)

  b. What general ethical rules are there? (8)

  c. What should an accountant do if faced with an ethical dilemma ? (8)

  d. Enumerate the guidelines to independence. (9)

  e. What should an accountant do about commissions? (9)

  f. Enumerate the areas where conflict of interest may occur? (10)

  g. What restrictions are there on advertising? (11)

  h. How can an accountant obtain publicity in an ethical manner? (12)

  i. May an accountant send a video, showing how he could assist a potential company client, direct to that company? (13)

  j. What are the rules on accountants' remuneration? (14)

  k. What is insider dealing? What does an audit clerk do when he knows his mother has shares in Risky plc and that while on the audit of Risky he discovers that the company's new pharmaceutical product of which the market expects much, has been banned as unsafe? An announcement of the ban will be made next week. (15)

Examination question *(Answer begins on page 542)*

1. Southern Engineering Ltd has undergone a period of substantial growth following its establishment five years ago by two engineers. Because of a lack of accounting expertise within the company it has traditionally looked to its auditors, Smith and Jones, for accounting services in the preparation of annual financial statements as well as for the statutory audit function. Smith and Jones have also provided advice in connection with the company's accounting and internal control systems.

  Smith and Jones is a two partner firm of certified accountants whose clients are mainly sole traders, partnerships and small limited companies. Although Southern Engineering Ltd was originally a typical small company client, its growth over the last 5 years has meant that it now accounts for approximately 20% of Smith and Jones ' gross fee income and the company has indicated that it may wish to issue shares on the unlisted securities market in the near future.

  Required:

  a. Discuss the extent to which it is acceptable and desirable that Smith and Jones have in the past provided the three services of statutory audit, advice in connection with systems, and accountancy services in the preparation of annual financial statements to Southern Engineering Ltd. (7 marks)

  b. Discuss the acceptability and desirability of Smith and Jones continuing to act in the future as auditors to Southern Engineering Ltd while continuing to provide the other services. (5 marks)

c. If, despite having been re-elected as the company's auditors, Smith and Jones decide to resign during the year state the procedures they should go through. (2 marks)

d. What actions should Southern Engineering Ltd take on receipt of the letter of resignation from Smith and Jones? (2 marks)

e. If the directors of Southern Engineering Ltd decided to dismiss Smith and Jones during the year, the auditors having refused to resign, what rights does the Companies Act 1985 give the auditor? (4 marks)

(ACCA)

Examination questions without answers

2. It is important that an auditor's independence is beyond question and that he should behave with integrity and objectivity in all professional and business situations. The following are a series of questions which were asked by auditors at a recent update seminar on professional ethics.

a. Can I audit my brother's company? (4 marks)

b. A B and Co the previous auditors, will not give my firm professional clearance or the usual handover information because they are still owed fees. Should I accept the client's offer of appointment? (5 marks)

c. Can I prepare the financial statements of a public company and still remain as auditor? (4 marks)

d. My client has threatened to sue the firm for negligence. Can I still continue to act as auditor? (5 marks)

e. I am a student of the Chartered Association of Certified Accountants. Am I bound by the ethical guidelines of the Association? (2 marks)

Required:

Discuss the answers you would give to the above questions posed by the auditors.

(20 marks)

(ACCA 93)

3. Your firm has been invited by Mr Thorburn, managing director and majority shareholder of Carling Ltd, to accept appointment as auditor of the company. The present firm of auditors will not be reappointed when its term of office expires as Mr Thorburn is dissatisfied with its services.

In addition Mr Thorburn has requested that:

i. an employee of your firm assumes responsibility for preparing the monthly management accounts to a tight deadline. The continuation of the overdraft facility is dependent on receipt of these accounts within ten days of each month end; and

ii. the audit partner attends the monthly board meetings, mainly to explain the management accounts to the other directors.

Requirement

State the matters that you would consider and the procedures you would perform in deciding whether or not to accept appointment as auditor and provide the additional services requested.

(ICAEW 92) (10 marks)

4. The Guide to Professional Ethics agreed by the professional accountancy bodies lays down rules governing auditors' independence.

You are required to state, with reasons, whether an accountant would be entitled, having regard to these rules, to accept a new appointment as auditor in the following circumstances:

a. he is already providing an accountancy service to the company by writing up the accounting records;   (4 marks)

b. he was an employee of the company until he left to set up in practice as a public accountant three years ago;   (3 marks)

c. his wife is a director of the company;   (3 marks)

d. his current total recurring fees amount to £80,000 per annum and the expected annual fee for the new appointment would be about £10,000;   (3 marks)

e. his 23 year old son owns a substantial shareholding in the company;   (4 marks)

f. he is a trustee of the company's pension fund, which owns 15 per cent of the issued share capital of the company.   (3 marks)

(ICA 91) (Total 20 marks)

9 Letters of engagement

Introduction

1. Before commencing any professional work, an accountant should agree, in writing, the precise scope and nature of the work to be undertaken. This is done through the medium of an engagement letter.

2. There is a Statement of Auditing Standards SAS 140 *Engagement letters*.

Purposes

3. a. To define clearly the extent of the auditor's responsibilities.

   b. To minimise misunderstandings between auditor firm and client.

   c. To confirm in writing verbal arrangements.

   d. To confirm acceptance by the auditor of his engagement.

   e. To inform and educate the client.

   f. Unless the terms of engagement are agreed in writing there may be an implied contract arising out of the Articles of Association or previous conduct of the auditor. The terms of such an implied contract may not be to the auditor's liking.

When to send a letter

4. a. To all NEW clients before any professional work has been started.

   b. To all existing clients who have not previously had such a letter.

   c. Whenever there is a change of circumstances (eg extra duties, a significant new auditing guideline, or a major change in ownership or management). The engagement letter should be reviewed every year to see if there is a need for a revised letter.

d. In the case of groups an engagement letter should be sent to each member company of the group that is to be audited by the firm. Or if a standard letter is satisfactory then a letter to the group board requesting that the letter be sent to all group members and that acknowledgement be received from all of them.

Procedure

5. a. On or before acceptance of a new client, discuss the precise terms with the management (the board in the case of a company).

b. Draft and sign the letter before commencing any part of the assignment.

c. Receive the client's written acceptance.

d. Every year review the letter and consider if revision is necessary.

Principal contents

6. The letter should outline the clients' statutory duties (eg on accounting records) and the auditors' statutory (eg to report) and professional (eg to follow the auditing standards) responsibilities. The sections may include:

a. The board's responsibilities re proper accounting records and financial statements which show a true and fair view and comply with the Act. Also the board's responsibility to make available to the auditors all the accounting records, other relevant records and related information and minutes of meetings.

b. The auditor's responsibility to report on the financial statements and on the consistency of view of the directors' report. Also a list of Companies Act responsibilities (S.235 and S.237).

c. The scope of the auditor's work:
   - auditing standards
   - accounting systems review
   - collection of audit evidence
   - tests and reliance on internal controls.

d. The sending of a letter of weakness to the management.

e. Any special factors:
   - relations with internal audit
   - audit of divisions or branches
   - any overseas location problems
   - other auditors if any
   - significant reliance on supervision of the directors in small proprietory companies.

f. The need for a letter of representation from the management.

g. Irregularities and fraud
   - the directors' primary responsibility
   - the auditors' planning of his audit to have a reasonable expectation of discovering MATERIAL misstatements in the ACCOUNTS
   - non-reliance on the auditor to uncover irregularities and frauds.

h. Any agreement for the auditors to carry out work of a bookkeeping or accounting nature – this could be covered in a separate letter.

i. Any agreement for the auditor to provide taxation services – this could also be a separate letter.

j. Where accounting or tax services are carried out the staff may be different from those engaged on audit work and so information given to tax or accounting staff is not thereby given to audit staff. This is known as the CHINESE WALL idea.

k. The fees and the basis on which they are charged.

l. A request for written acknowledgement of the letter and that it creates contractual obligations. In the case of a company the letter of acknowledgement should be signed on behalf of the board.

Example

7. Here is an example:

QUIBBLE, QUERY & CO
CHARTERED ACCOUNTANTS   28 Feb 19-6
to THE DIRECTORS
HEDONITE LTD

GENTLEMEN

The purpose of this letter is to set out the basis on which we are to act as auditors of your company and the respective areas of responsibility of ourselves and yourselves.

AUDIT

a. You are responsible for maintaining proper accounting records, preparing financial statements which give a true and fair view and which comply with the Companies Act, supplying us with the records and with such explanations and information as we may require.

b. We are responsible for giving an opinion on the truth and fairness and compliance with statute of those financial statements in a report.

c. We are required to consider and if necessary report on:

– whether proper accounting records have been kept

– whether the Accounts are in agreement with the records

– whether we have received all the information and explanations we think necessary

– whether the information in the directors' report is consistent with the financial statements.

d. We have a professional duty to report if the financial statements do not conform to the Accounting Standards.

---

e. Our audit will be conducted in accordance with the auditing standards. We shall gather such relevant and reliable evidence as is sufficient to draw reasonable conclusions therefrom. We shall assess your systems of accounting and internal control and our tests will vary according to that assessment. We may wish to place reliance on the system of internal control. We shall report any significant weaknesses in the systems to you.

f. We may request you to provide written confirmation of oral representations given to us.

g. We shall require sight of all documents to be issued with the Accounts and we will wish to receive notice of and attend all general meetings.

h. The responsibility for prevention and detection of fraud and irregularities rests with yourselves. We shall endeavour to plan our audit to detect material misstatements in the Accounts but we cannot be relied upon to disclose frauds or other irregularities which may exist.

ACCOUNTING

We shall prepare the Accounts based on the accounting records maintained by you.

TAXATION

a. We shall agree the corporation tax liabilities of the company with the Inspector of Taxes.

b. You will be responsible for all other tax matters including returns, payment of advance corporation tax and forms P11D.

FEES

Our fees are based on the time necessarily spent by our partners and staff at a level commensurate with the skill and responsibility involved. The audit work will be billed separately from other work.

AGREEMENT OF TERMS

We will be grateful if you would confirm in writing your acceptance of the terms of this letter.

Yours faithfully

Note: This letter has been slightly abbreviated from the usual length of real letters.

It may be desirable to have separate letters for the audit, other services and the giving of investment advice.

Some accountants may also include clauses on any complaints the client may have about the service offered and a note of the country by whose laws the engagement is governed.

Summary

8. a. All assignments given to accountants should be subject to an engagement letter agreeing the terms of the assignment with the client.

b. SAS 140 governs this subject.

Case study for Chapter 9

Juliet, a certified accountant, receives a telephone call from Chateaubriand who is starting up in business as a restaurateur specialising in the business trade. He wishes to appoint Juliet as his accountant. Juliet requests him to call.

Discussion

a. What matters should be discussed at the meeting?

b. In the light of a. draft an engagement letter.

c. What might be the consequences of omissions from the letter?

Student self testing questions *Questions with answers apparent from the text*

1. a. List the purposes of an engagement letter. (3)

   b. What are the procedures connected with engagement letters? (5)

   c. List the principal contents. (6)

   d. Write out an engagement letter for a public company client. (7)

Examination question *(Answer begins on page 543)*

1. It is common practice for auditors to send a letter of engagement to new clients and increasingly to existing clients. Set forth below are matters usually included in such letters.

   i.   Definition and Scope of Audit   (8 marks)

   ii. Fraud and Irregularities   (4 marks)

   iii. Accounting, Taxation and Other Services   (3 marks)

   iv. Fees   (2 marks)

   Required:

   a. Explain why a letter of engagement is desirable for the auditor.   (3 marks)

   b. In the case of each matter referred to above show what points will be included.

   (You may assume that the client is a Limited Company.)

   (ACCA)

Examination question without answers

1. You are the external auditor to Fleeting & Flotsam, a large firm of international architects with branches worldwide. The basis of your audit is an engagement letter.

   Give reasons suggesting the desirability of frequent renewal of your engagement letter.
   (LCC 88) (10 marks)

2. Effective audit planning is essential to ensure both quality of service to the client and the minimising of risk to the practitioner.

   Required

   a. What general points should an auditor consider before accepting a new audit client?
   (3 marks)

   b. What is the purpose of the letter of engagement; what major matters should it refer to?   (12 marks)
   (AAT J 89) (Total 15 Marks)

The modern audit

The next part of the manual explains in outline how an audit is conducted, the timing of audit work and the Auditing Standard– the auditor's operational standard.

10 The modern audit – stages

Introduction

1. An audit can be carried out on enterprises both large and small, and both new and well established. The audit of smaller enterprises has special features that are dealt with in Chapter 38 and the first audit of a new business and first audit by a newly appointed auditor of an established business presents special features which are dealt with in Chapter 37.

2. This chapter describes the stages in the audit of an established client enterprise which is big enough to have a comprehensive system of accounting and record keeping and a system of controls over those records.

Outline stages in the audit

3. The stages in the modern audit can be summarised as:
   - Background research
   - Preparation of the audit plan
   - Accounting system review
   - Internal control system review
   - Substantive testing
   - Analytical review techniques
   - Analytical review of financial statements
   - Preparation and signing of report

The stages explained

4. **Background research**

   Before commencing the audit proper the auditor must discover as much as possible about:

   a. The present condition and future prospects of the *industry* of which his client is a part.

   b. The past history and the present condition and future prospects of his *client*.

   c. The management and key *personnel* of his client and any recent changes.

   d. The *products* and manufacturing and trading *processes* of the client and any recent changes.

   e. The *locations* of all his client's operations.

f. Any *difficulties* encountered by the client in manufacturing, trading, expanding, contracting, labour relations or financing.

g. Any problems in *accounting* or in *internal control systems*.

h. Any problems in *accounting measurement* eg in stock valuation or income recognition.

i. Any problems likely to lead to *audit risk* eg the difficulty of assessing the value of long term contracts in a civil engineering business.

j. Any problems likely to be met in *carrying out* the audit eg distant locations, tight timing problems, or large staff requirements on stocktaking attendance.

k. Any *changes* in *law* or *accounting practice* which may affect the client.

This background research will be done by reading or interviewing:

i. Previous years audit files.

ii. Audit staff who have been previously engaged on the audit.

iii. Published material concerning the client company and the industry.

iv. The company's interim, internal and management accounts.

v. The management of the enterprise.

In order to carry out a comprehensive and effective audit which is nevertheless efficient in terms of time spent, the modern auditor must focus his audit particularly on areas of particular difficulty and risk. In addition the evaluation of many areas in the financial statements, must entail a consideration of the whole circumstances of a client. As simple examples, the evaluation of the life of fixed assets liable to obsolescence or the value of the investment in a subsidiary company can only be effected by a knowledge of all factors having a bearing on the matter and many of these factors are external to the company. For these reasons, the modern audit requires a more detailed knowledge of the client company and its problems that was required in earlier years. This does make auditing more interesting and rewarding to the auditor and potentially also to the client.

5. There is a comprehensive Statement of Auditing Standards SAS 210 *Knowledge of the business*. Among the points it makes are:

a. Auditors should obtain a knowledge of the business which is sufficient to enable them to *identify* and *understand the events, transactions and practices that may have a significant effect on the* financial statements and the audit thereof.

b. This knowledge may be used in assessing *risks of error,* planning the *nature, timing and extent* of audit procedures, and considering the *consistency and reliability* of financial statements.

c. There are a seemingly infinite number of sources for such knowledge. Examples include the previous experience of persons engaged on the audit, visits to the entity, trade journals, promotional literature and even job advertisements by the company.

d. Specific instances of use of knowledge of the business include recognising conflicting information, recognising the reasonableness of answers given to questions, assessing the effectiveness of internal controls by considering management's whole attitude to the control environment.

e. Matters to consider in relation to knowledge of the business. There is an appendix which sets out over 50 matters to consider. A questionnaire derived from this and other matters would enable a very comprehensive picture of an audit client to be gained.

An example

6. Jane is about to start to plan the audit of Metalbash Pressings Ltd, a company which manufactures parts for two UK lorry manufacturers. She will need to research the background as:

    - the industry. She finds that UK lorry output is 75% of normal and she considers the problems for higher unit costs and greater competition resulting in lower prices for component suppliers.

    - the company. The company may be suffering from price and cost squeezes, plant closures and redundancies. She finds that a factory has closed and 50 workers have been made redundant. However the company have purchased for cash (with a bank loan) the business of a company in receivership which is in a related industry. This business has a factory in a neighbouring town and Jane has to plan visits there.

    - Management and personnel. Any changes may weaken controls, change policies or worsen accounting records. Jane finds that there is now a new chief accountant.

    - products and processes. These may have changed with possible consequences in stock values or the value of redundant equipment.

    - locations. Closures may involve closure costs with disclosure problems from FRS 3.

    - difficulties experienced by the client (eg on labour relations or cost and quality control) may impact on internal controls. Jane finds that the new accountant has streamlined several accounting processes and controls may be weaker.

    - accounting systems change frequently nowadays as a consequence of new information technology. The accounting records of the new business have been incorporated into existing systems and some teething problems have occurred.

    - accounting measurement problems may arise in product costs, redundant stocks, closure costs, redundancy costs, lives of fixed assets etc

    - audit risk. Some lorry makers have gone into receivership and there is a risk of Metalbash losing its business or incurring fatal bad debts. Jane will need to concentrate consequently upon the value of debtors and the going concern applicability. There may be risks of wrong values of stocks and fixed assets. Cuts in staffing may give a risk of weakening in systems or controls.

    - in planning the audit, Jane will need to consider locations, timing problems, staff requirements, and the quality of audit staff needed for some of the risky areas including a possible need to look into and assess new systems.

    She will do all this by reading the previous years' files, talking to the staff member responsible for last year's audit, talking to the management, reading minutes, management accounts, newspaper and magazine articles and previous annual report and accounts.

7. **The audit plan**

    The auditor must plan his audit in some detail and the plan will involve preparation of a overall audit plan showing:

a. an outline of the audit work to be done on each area of the client's systems and financial statements.

b. the staff who will do the work.

c. the location of the audit.

d. the timing of the work to be done.

e. a budget of time and costs.

The plan must be made to fit in with the client's timing requirement and with the client's ability to produce necessary analyses and summaries.

8. **The Example of Metalbash**

In preparing the audit plan, Jane will need to complete the following:

- ensure there is an up-to-date engagement letter and ensure the plan encompasses all the work required by the letter of engagement.

- update the permanent file (all the details about the client which are of permanent significance) with details of changes in nature of trade, areas of activity, organisation, accounting systems, internal controls and personalities.

- identify the areas of high risk, that is, areas where material errors may occur and plan accordingly. We have already seen some of these.

- consider materiality limits. Essentially this means that some things are too small or trivial to be worth any audit effort. In practice this is difficult and we will come back to it.

At the planning stage a number of actual audit actions need to be planned (eg attendance at stock take) but we will look at these as we discuss the later stages of the audit.

9. **Accounting system review**

The auditor must:

a. ascertain by asking questions.

b. record on paper.

c. corroborate his record (confirm that the record is correct).

d. review for adequacy and for planning of tests.

e. test to determine that it always works as it is supposed to.

f. evaluate.

g. form a conclusion on the adequacy of the client's system for documenting and recording the transactions, assets and liabilities of the client in the books of account and other records. This is because

i. the Companies Act requires the auditor to investigate and report on the company keeping of 'proper' accounting records.

ii. the books of account and other records form the basis for the preparation of the financial statements.

10. **The Example of Metalbash**

Jane will need to be sure that the company has maintained adequate accounting records throughout the year both as a specific Companies Act requirement and also to ensure that the records form a reliable basis for the preparation of the annual accounts.

She will need to review the integration of the new business records with the old and ensure that all the records adequately enable the directors to produce true and fair accounts. Especial care will be needed with stock records which are also a Companies Act requirement.

11. **Internal control system review**. The auditor should:

   a. ascertain

   b. record

   c. corroborate the record

   d. review

   e. test

   f. evaluate

   g. form a conclusion on the adequacy of the client's system of internal control.

   Internal control is exhaustively explored in Chapter 14 but, in short, internal controls are *procedures* which ensure that *all* transactions, assets and liabilities are recorded *correctly*.

12. The objectives of the accounting systems and internal control systems investigations are to enable the auditor to have *evidence* that:

   a. The client maintains adequate books and records.

   b. The client has a system of internal controls over the processing and recording of transactions such that *all* transactions are recorded *correctly* both numerically and in principle.

   c. The books of account can be relied on to form a reliable basis for the preparation of the Accounts.

   Thus it is not necessary for the auditor to *vouch* every transaction recorded in the books. He will rely upon the system. If the system is satisfactory then he can substitute an investigation and test of the system for a detailed examination of every entry. This is both more economical and is more effective because only by examining the system can he have evidence that *all* the transactions are recorded.

13. In practice in some areas of the firm Internal controls may not exist or may be weak. In such cases the auditor cannot rely on the controls and other evidence needs to be sought for the completeness and accuracy of the record. The basic audit process today is for the auditor to consider the internal controls and if she wishes to place reliance on any of them, she must then ascertain and evaluate them and perform compliance tests on them. Compliance tests will be considered again but are those tests which seek to provide evidence that internal control procedures are being applied as prescribed.

14. **The example of Metalbash**

   Jane finds that there have been many areas in the client where her predecessors have place reliance on internal controls. She finds now that she needs to investigate, document, and evaluate the controls operating currently especially with regard to the records of the new business. The controls on which she considers that reliance may be placed need to be compliance tested.

   As an example a series of controls are applied to ensure invoices are passed for payment are all for goods or services which have been authorised, delivered, inspected and approved. Jane will compliance test these controls.

15. **Substantive testing**

Substantive testing is defined in the auditing standards as:

'Those tests of transactions and balances, and other procedures such as analytical review, which seek to provide audit evidence as to the completeness, accuracy and validity of the information contained in the accounting records or in the financial statements.'

We have seen that the reliability of the records is established by the auditor by him investigating the system. However not all data can be verified in this *indirect* way and some transactions, balances and items in the financial statements must be verified with *direct* evidence.

In particular substantive tests are applied to:

a. Transaction records where internal controls are weak or non-existent and where the *system cannot be relied on.*

b. Unusual, extraordinary or one-off transactions and transactions which are not covered by a system. For example if the client sold a part of its premises, this transaction is clearly rare and the client will not have a system for dealing with it and thus the auditor must seek evidence that the transaction was fully and accurately recorded and was carried out with proper authority.

c. All assets and liabilities at the balance sheet date. For some assets (eg debtors and creditors) the *system* will provide good audit evidence, but additional audit evidence is always sought.

In practice an auditor has to consider on grounds of effectiveness and cost whether to rely on systems controls or whether to carry out substantive tests in each area of the audit. In some areas sufficient evidence can be obtained by analytical review. In many areas a combination of internal control reliance, substantive testing and analytical review provides the necessary audit evidence.

16. **The example of Metalbash**

Much of the audit consists of substantive testing and examples could be culled from any of the assets or liabilities or elsewhere. We will consider one important area. The valuation of finished goods stocks. She must seek evidence that prices used are in accordance with the requirements of SSAP 9. This will be a practical problem as the build up of costs will be very detailed. And this will also be a conceptual problem as fixed overheads may need to be added in accordance with normal level of activity and the idea of normal may be difficult to assess.

17. **Analytical review techniques**

This is defined as:

The study of relationships between elements of financial information expected to conform to a predictable pattern based on the organisation's experience and between financial and non-financial information. Information is compared with compatible information for a prior period or periods, with anticipated results and with information relating to similar organisations.

In general audit evidence is gained from internal control, from substantive tests and increasingly from analytical review.

For example, the wages item in the accounts of a company may be investigated firstly by analytical review. Supposing that:

– no problems had been encountered in the past in this area
– the total payments were within 2% of budgets adjusted for output variation and global wage awards
– the notes to the accounts and the accounts agreed
– inter-firm comparison indicated that gross wage payments were within 3% of mean wage costs of firms of this turnover.

The auditor now has valid evidence that wages are correctly stated within materiality limits. He/she may well feel that some substantive testing to supplement the analytical review may be desirable but that internal control investigation is unnecessary.

18. **The example of Metalbash**

Analytical review is an economical and powerful way of obtaining audit evidence. However in times where upheavals have occurred with disposals and acquisitions and plant closures and redundancies, patterns are harder to find. Nonetheless, industrial wages may be an area where analytical review may be helpful.

19. **Analytical review of financial statements**

At the conclusion of the detailed work of the audit, when all the systems testing and substantive testing has been done, the auditor will have audit evidence that:

a. proper books of account have been kept which form a reliable basis for the preparation of the Accounts.

b. the Accounts have been properly drawn up from those books.

c. all assets, liabilities and transactions, balances and items in the account have been confirmed indirectly by systems investigation and/or directly by substantive testing.

Nonetheless, the auditor will then subject the Financial Statements to an overall *final analytical review* to determine whether:

a. Acceptable, consistent and appropriate *accounting policies* have been applied. For example, the Accounts would not show a true and *fair* view if the depreciation policy had been changed from straight line to reducing balance without this being disclosed or the stock had been valued at marginal cost contrary to the requirements of SSAP 9.

b. All the information in the Financial Statements is *compatible* with all other information. For example, an industrial firm using straight line depreciation may have items of plant which have been fully depreciated. However in determining product cost for valuing work in progress and finished goods, notional depreciation on fully depreciated plant may have been taken.

c. All items in the Accounts are compatible with the auditor's knowledge of the enterprise and its circumstances. For example, the auditor may have read in the press that new processes have been invented in a client's industry which makes some of the client's plant obsolete.

d. There is adequate disclosure of all items requiring disclosure. Numerous disclosure requirements are in the Companies Act and also some items may require special disclosure for proper understanding of the accounts. For example, if farm product sales have been changed from free market credit sales to a purchasing cooperative giving regular monthly cheques, then the change in the debtors/sales ratio may mislead readers unless the change is disclosed.

e. The Accounting requirements of the Companies Act and other regulations have been complied with.

f. Overall, whether the auditor has sufficient evidence to enable him to give an opinion on the truth and fairness of the Accounts.

20. **The example of Metalbash**

Jane will need to ensure a wide range of things including:

- adequate audit evidence for all account items
- proper accounting records
- appropriate accounting policies
- Companies Act compliance
- SSAP and FRS compliance
- adequate disclosure of all items

and many others.

She might find that her firm have a series of audit working papers including checklists which enable her to be sure she has covered everything. She might also consider using the ACCA Audit Guide and Accounts Disclosure Checklist for small businesses.

21. Preparation and signing of the report

The ultimate aim of an audit is the report by the auditor to his client. This is a formal statement giving:

a. a title identifying the persons to whom the report is addressed (eg Auditors' report to the members of XYZ plc)

b. an introductory paragraph identifying the financial statements audited (eg Profit and Loss Account, Balance Sheet etc)

c. separate sections, appropriately headed, dealing with:

i. respective responsibilities of directors and auditors

ii. the basis of the auditors' opinion (we conducted our audit in accordance with Auditing standards ...)

iii. the auditors' opinion (eg the financial statements give a true and fair view ...)

d. the manuscript or printed signature of the auditors

e. the date of the report

22. **The example of Metalbash**

Jane will use a checklist to confirm that she has thought of everything in preparing the report of the auditor. She may have to consider a qualified report if there are areas of the accounts for which she has insufficient evidence or if she disagrees with any material aspect of the accounts. However before qualifying an audit report much agonising would occur with her and the partners in the firm.

Summary

23. The modern audit can be seen as having the following stages:

    a. Background research into the client's place in the economy generally and its industry in particular, the client's constitution, history, operations and personnel.

    b. Preparation of an audit plan.

    c. Accounting system review.

    d. Internal control system review.

    e. Substantive testing including analytical review techniques.

    f. Analytical review of financial statements.

    g. Preparation and signing of the auditor's report.

Points to note

24. a. The audit as outlined in this chapter is sometimes called the systems audit approach or the Balance Sheet audit approach. This idea of a systems based audit is still current. However a newer idea the risk based audit – is now prevalent because if its inclusion in the new Statement of Auditing Standards. Risk based audits still involve investigation of systems and usually some reliance on internal control.

    b. The idea to grasp is that in the past, auditors had the time and resources to vouch or verify every transaction. The modern view is that this approach was both inefficient (expensive on time and resources) and ineffective (no certainty that all transactions had been entered).

    c. The modern auditor is not concerned with individual routine transactions but with the system for documenting and recording them. He is still concerned with material non-routine transactions.

    d. The modern audit is characterized by the search for audit evidence. Some evidence is obtained directly. For example, evidence that a building exists is best obtained by direct inspection of the building. Some evidence is obtained by indirect means. For example, evidence that all deliveries of goods to customers in a period have been followed by the sending of an invoice is best obtained by verifying that a system exists which is good in principle, works in practice and has worked throughout the period. The system will include such ideas as raising pre-numbered advice notes, prohibition of goods leaving the factory without an advice note, and regular comparisons of advice notes issued with invoices issued.

    e. In the modern literature on auditing, the system of accounting is seen as separate from the system of internal controls over the books and records. For example, in setting up a system for continuous inventory (stock records) the elements of the system would include use of goods inwards notes, stores requisitions, stock cards etc. To ensure that the records were complete and accurate, internal controls such as pre-numbering documents with sequence checks to ensure all items were accounted for and regular independent comparisons of actual stock items with the corresponding record to ensure accuracy of recording would be superimposed.

    The auditor would obviously examine the whole system together, viz both the accounting and the controls over the accounting. However it is essential to appreciate that there is a difference.

f. In this chapter I have described the stages in a modern systems based audit. However, the audit is not done all at one time but is spread out over a period of time. The timing of audit work is discussed in the next chapter.

g. The modern audit is concerned largely with a search for evidence. Evidence can be of several kinds including:

   – internal control reliance

   – substantive testing

   – analytical review

   The costs of modern audits and the pressure on fees has meant that audit firms have sought greater effectiveness in their audit procedures together with greater efficiency. This has led to:

   i. Greater use of combinations of evidence from all three sources

   ii. Greater reliance on analytical review

   iii. Greater reliance on substantive tests where internal control review and testing have been considered too expensive for the degree of reliance gained.

h. The definition of substantive testing includes analytical review but analytical review can also be viewed as a separate evidence collecting technique.

i. The concept of audit risk is also now very important. I cover it in a later chapter but for the moment note that auditors now try to identify areas of high risk (eg bad debts, wrong valuations of stock, inappropriate presentation of continuing and discontinuing business under FRS 3, going concern etc in the case of Metalbash). The auditor can concentrate resources on the areas of high risk but of course all areas have to be covered.

j. As a by-product of the investigation of records and systems, the auditor usually sends a letter to the company pointing out weaknesses in the system. Such Letters of weakness have their own chapter in this manual.

Case study 1 for Chapter 10

CARNAC COMPUTERS PLC are a company making, importing, and retailing computers and computer software. They have branches in several European countries. They have recently suffered from falling sales and excess stocking of outdated hard and soft ware and have survived by cutbacks and reducing staff, both management and workers.

The auditors, Earnest and Worried, are planning the audit of the Accounts for the ensuing year.

Discussion

Outline the stages required in the audit of the Accounts of Carnac noting, in particular, difficulties or requirements which this audit will entail.

Case study 2 for Chapter 10

Dream Boatbuilders plc are builders of large luxury yachts. Many of their boats are built to order mainly for the export market when the boats' prices are quoted in US dollars. Some boats are built without orders in the hope of obtaining buyers. The company is experiencing trading difficulties and is heavily indebted to the bank. To improve trading a new managing director was appointed on 1.4.-8. You have been asked to conduct the audit by your firm. The company's year end is 31.12.-8. The date is now 2.6.-8. On reading the previous audit file you find that the company has always had weak internal controls.

Discussion

Outline the stages in the audit of the company noting any particular difficulties or requirements that this audit will entail.

Student self testing questions *Questions with answers apparent from the text*

1. a. List the stages in the modern audit. (3)
   b. What background facts must an auditor discover? (4)
   c. How will the background facts be determined? (4)
   d. What will be included in an audit planning memorandum? (7)
   e. What are the steps in an accounting system review? (9)
   f. What are the steps in an internal control systems review? (11)
   g. Define substantive testing. (15)
   h. What are the objectives of analytical review? (17)
   i. What are the objectives of analytical review of financial statements? (19)
   j. What are the contents of the auditor's report? (21)
   k. What forms of evidence are available to an auditor? (24)
   l. Why and in what ways has the search for audit evidence changed over the years? (24)
   m. Distinguish between direct and indirect evidence. (24)
   n. When are substantive tests used? (24)
   o. In what circumstances can an auditor not place reliance on internal controls? (24,15)

11 The timing of audit work

Introduction

1. Audit work on the records and financial statements relating to a financial year are carried out at various times during, at the end and after the end of the financial year. This chapter discusses the timing of audit work usually found in practice.

Audit visits

2. In all but the very smallest of audits, the audit work will be carried on at the client's premises. Where the client has branches, this can create problems of travelling for the auditor but in such cases some branches are visited as samples or all the branches are visited by rotation.

3. In the majority of cases, three extended visits are made by the auditor to the client's premises to carry out audit work:

a. During the year – the *interim* audit.

b. At the year end.

c. After the year end – the *final* audit.

Interim audit

4. The interim audit will be carried out during the financial year. Very often the interim audit will be about two-thirds of the way through the year eg September or October for a December year end.

5. The work done will be:

a. Ascertain the system of accounting and internal control.

b. Record the system by flow chart or other method.

c. Evaluate the systems for adequacy and presence of apparent weaknesses.

d. Design and carry out compliance tests to determine if the system is operated at all times in accordance with the description of the system evaluated by the auditor.

e. Design and carry out tests to determine if, in areas where controls are weak or non existent, the records can be relied upon.

f. Draw conclusions on the adequacy of the systems and hence of the reliability of the books of account and other records.

g. Seek evidence, by substantive tests, that unusual or one-off transactions have been fully and correctly recorded.

h. Where possible carry out tests on assets and liabilities. Tests on assets and liabilities should be carried out *after* the year end but with clients with strong systems, some verification can be done at the interim stage. Examples are physical verification of stock records and debtors circularisation.

On modern audits a decision has to be taken on whether to place reliance on internal controls. If there is to be a decision to rely on analytical review and/or substantive tests instead then a detailed review of the internal control system will be wasted. Consequently the auditor at some stage in his examination of the accounting records has to decide on whether to complete his examination and review and do compliance tests or to go no further than becoming sure that proper accounting records are being kept.

Year end work

6. On the last day of the client's year end it will be possible to verify some year-end assets and liabilities in a way impossible at any other time. Thus attendance will be required for:

a. Observation and testing of the stock count.

b. Observation and testing of cut off procedures.

c. Counting of cash balances.

d. Inspection of Investments, for example, share and loan certificates.

Final audit

7. The final audit will take place after the year end and is designed to seek evidence that Financial Statements give a true and fair view and comply with statutory and other requirements.

8. The timing of the final audit varies from client to client. Some final audits are commenced within days of the year end and the financial statements are published within as short a period as two months after the year end. Others are commenced many months after the year end. The advantage of an early audit and early publication of the Accounts is that the information given to members and others is up to date. From the audit point of view, transactions in progress at the year end are often not resolved and estimates of outcome have to be made and evaluated. The advantage of a late audit is that transactions in progress at the year end are often resolved and fewer estimates need to be made. For example, after a few months it will have become clear whether or not a doubtful debt is in fact bad. The disadvantage of a late audit is that information reaching members and others is out of date. The Accounts will have become truly historical.

9. The work carried out after the year end will be:
    a. Updating of the auditor's review of the systems of accounting and internal control. This will involve:
        i.   Determining if the systems changed between the interim audit and the year end by interviewing officials and a few 'Walk through' checks.
        ii.   Thoroughly testing new systems.
        iii. Compliance tests of the unchanged systems from the interim audit to the year end.
    b. Drawing conclusions on:
        i.   Adequacy of the accounting system and the system of internal controls thereon.
        ii.   Whether proper books of account have been kept.
        iii. Whether the book of account and other records form a reliable base for the preparation of the Accounts.
    c. Comparing the Financial Statements with the underlying records and books of account to see that they correspond.
    d. Performing substantive tests on all assets and liabilities.
    e. Performing the final analytical review.
    f. Preparing and signing the auditor's report.

Summary

10. a. Audit work is usually accomplished on several visits to the client's premises.
    b. The work is usually distributed between
        i.   An interim audit during the financial year.
        ii.   A year end attendance.
        iii. A final audit after the year end.
    c. The interim audit is principally for the investigation and testing of the systems of recording and internal control.
    d. The year end work is mainly for the observation and testing of the stock count but also the examination of cash balances and investment certificates.
    e. The final audit is all the rest of the work and includes:
        i.   testing systems for the period from the interim audit to the year end

    ii. substantive testing of transactions and balances

    iii. the analytical review

    iv. preparation and signing of the report.

Points to note

11. The timing of audit work depends upon many factors including:

a. Deadlines fixed by the client. For example the client may arrange an AGM for three months after the year end.

b. The organisation of the accountant's office. For example bunching of client year ends around certain dates (eg 31st December) can create severe problems.

c. The extent to which the client can provide schedules and analyses. If these are not available more time is required on the final audit.

d. The extent to which the client has very strong systems in routine areas such as debtors, creditors, stock control, fixed asset registers. Where the systems are very reliable substantive tests can often be performed at the interim instead of the final audit. For example debtors and creditors circularisation and comparison of physical stock or fixed assets with records can be performed mainly at the interim with only small samples being tested at the final.

e. When an audit is carried out for the first time on a new client, an additional visit may be necessary, in order that the auditor may obtain knowledge of the client, its background, personnel, accounting problems, audit risk areas, etc. Following this visit the audit plan, which will be carried out on the other visits, can be prepared.

f. In some very large audits, the audit work is so great that audit staff are on the client's premises the whole year round. This is called a *continuous* audit.

g. In some large audits with very highly computerised records, audit evidence is sometimes available on a temporary basis only. For example where internal control (say over the credit worthiness of customers) is operated by a computer program which is changed at intervals. Then the auditor needs to be present at fairly frequent intervals to test the functioning of the controls on which he wishes to rely.

Case study 1 for Chapter 11

AUTOMATED MANUFACTURING PLC are a very large manufacturer of electrical appliances with factories in the Midlands and the North. The company prides itself on the excellence of its systems and its very tight financial control run by its large staff of qualified accountants. The year end is 31st December and stock is taken during the Christmas holidays while the factories are closed. The Annual General Meeting is held before the end of February.

Discussion

Give an outline audit plan for use by Pooter Brothers, the auditors, noting specially the timing of the audit work.

What special problems may arise in this audit?

Case study 2 for Chapter 11

O. Nix Ltd is a family owned chain of some 12 jewellers shops in Birmingham and the West and East Midlands. Their year end is 31st January. The company buy some stock centrally but delivery is always direct to the branches. Each branch has the power to buy on its own account but all bills are settled centrally. Some stock is transferred between branches depending on demand. The books are reasonably well kept by a member of the family who is a part qualified accountant. She prepares draft annual accounts which are ready by the end of April each year.

Discussion

Give an outline audit plan for use by Hex and Co of Darlaston, the auditors, noting particularly the timing.

Student self testing questions *Questions with answers apparent from the text*

1. a. What work will be done on an interim audit? (5)
    b. What work will be done at the year end? (6)
    c. What work will be done at the final audit? (9)
    d. What factors determine the timing of particular audit work? (11)

Examination questions without answers

1. You are a manager in a medium sized auditing firm and you have just been informed by one of the partners that you are to be responsible for the audit of SOLSTICE Ltd., a newly acquired client. SOLSTICE Ltd. has just incorporated as a limited company after trading for many years as an unincorporated business.

    It is expected that SOLSTICE Ltd. will have a turnover of about £10 million in its first year as a limited company and, as such, will be one of your largest clients. The Managing Director has written to you asking about the current year audit and, in particular, about the audit process.

    Requirement

    Prepare a draft letter to the Managing Director of SOLSTICE Ltd. explaining each of the following:

    a. The reasons why an audit is necessary.   (2 marks)
    b. The effects that the audit requirement will have on his company.   (4 marks)
    c. The different stages of the audit process.   (18 marks)

    (ICAI 92) (Total 24 marks)

2. You are the auditor of RIGNEY Ltd., a company involved in the manufacture and distribution of bathroom fittings. Currently, the company is experiencing trading difficulties resulting in cash flow problems. The bank requires the signed year-end accounts by 31st January in order to be able to review the present overdraft facility.

    As the company's year-end is 31st December, you have agreed with the Finance Director that a roll forward type of audit approach would be the most appropriate. You have decided to start the audit in early December, carry out the necessary audit procedures based upon the 30th November management accounts, and then finish the audit in the last two weeks in January.

Requirement

a. Set out the audit procedures that you would carry out at both stages of the audit, assuming that you plan to rely on internal controls. (16 marks)

b. With regard to the approach considered appropriate in relation to (a) above, outline the amendments that would be necessary, if you did not plan to rely on internal controls. (4 marks)

(ICAI 92) (Total 20 marks)

*N.B. You are **not** required to detail the specific procedures to be carried out in the individual balance sheet or profit and loss account areas.*

3. You have been approached by Mr Martin, the Managing Director of *Domestic Appliances Limited*, a company of which you are the auditor. He states: 'There is no need for you to carry out an interim audit of the accounts for the year ended 30 June 1994. Interim audits are only a way for you to increase your fee income; they are of no use to me and you have to do all the work again at the final audit.'

Required:

a. State why an interim audit is desirable and how it can be of benefit to the client. (10 marks)

b. What work that would normally be carried out at the final audit could be carried out at the interim stage? (5 marks)

(AAT 94) (Total 15 marks)

12 Objectives and general principles

Introduction

1. There is a Statement of Auditing Standards SAS 100 *Objectives and general principles governing an audit of financial statements*. This chapter is derived from that SAS and offers some commentary on its requirements.

Objectives

2. SAS 100 begins with a statement of the objective of an audit. The objective of an audit of financial statements is to enable auditors to give an opinion on those financial statements taken as a whole and thereby to provide reasonable assurance that the financial statements give a true and fair view (where relevant) and have been prepared in accordance with relevant accounting or other requirements. Let us look at this.

a. **Opinion** – not a guarantee or a certificate just an opinion – see paragraph 9 of Chapter 1.

b. **Taken as a whole.** This is a difficult point. Essentially there is a degree of imprecision in all but the very simplest of financial statements because they contain accounting estimates about uncertainties and unresolved transactions. There may even be some non-material misstatements in some of the individual items. However we hope that the auditor's activities provide an opinion that the overall view given by the financial statements is a true and fair one (or that it is not).

c. **Reasonable assurance.** This is also difficult! An audit enhances the *credibility* of financial statements. However the user cannot assume that the auditor's opinion is a guarantee as to the *future viability* of the enterprise nor an assurance as to the *efficiency or effectiveness* with which management has conducted the affairs of the enterprise. Reasonable, as a word, contrasts with absolute.

d. **True and fair view.** This is a difficult concept too – see Chapter 29. Note that some financial statements (eg those of local authorities) have different requirements from true and fair view.

e. **Relevant accounting and other requirements.** These usually include Statutes (eg the Companies Act) and the Accounting Standards but may also include various industry specific SORPs (eg those of colleges) and Codes of Practice (eg those of local authorities).

Required procedures

3. SAS 100 *requires* that, in undertaking an audit of financial statements, auditors should:

   a. Carry out procedures designed to obtain sufficient appropriate audit evidence, in accordance with Auditing Standards to determine with reasonable confidence whether the financial statements are free of *material misstatement*.

   b. Evaluate the overall presentation of the financial statements, in order to ascertain whether they have been prepared in accordance with relevant legislation and accounting standards

   c. Issue a report containing a clear expression of their opinion on the financial statements.

There is a lot in these short requirements. Note that some of the wording is new in SAS 100 which is dated March 1995 and came into effect for audits of periods ending on or after 23 December 1995.

Some comments:

i. **Sufficient appropriate audit evidence.** This is a phrase to be committed to memory. It looks right in most auditing answers! Audit evidence is the whole thrust of this book but it is the special subject of chapter 24. The gathering of evidence is a matter of judgement in deciding on the *nature, timing and extent* of audit procedures. Even when evidence has been gathered it is a matter of judgement what conclusions are drawn from the evidence. For example an auditor may gather much evidence on the future useful life of some plant and machinery – its natural life, the possibility of obsolescence, the cost of repairs as against replacement etc but still has to determine whether he thinks the life selected by the directors is reasonable in the circumstances.

ii. **The Auditing Standards.** These are discussed and listed in Chapter 6 and are to be found throughout the book.

iii. **Reasonable confidence.** A problem with this idea is that not all auditors will see an audit problem in the same way. In any event the view given by financial statements is a mixture of fact (true) and judgement (fair). As a result financial statements cannot be correct. There are no absolute right treatments, judgements or accounting policies

iv. **Free of material misstatement.** Materiality is discussed in Chapter 32. Misstatement is usually in terms of fact. For example the creditors item does not include an actual creditor or the development expenditure carried forward does not comply with SSAP 13 or the requirements of the Companies Act re fixed assets have not been fully complied with.

v. **Report.** The auditors' report is discussed in Chapters 31 to 36.

Influences on an audit

4. There are many influences on how an actual audit is conducted. These include:

a. The Statements of Auditing Standards. These have to be complied with – see Chapter 6.

b. Professional body rules – see Chapter 8. These are now very extensive.

c. Legislation – for companies this is The Companies Act 1985 but most enterprises seem to be affected by some legislation or other. We live in a very regulated age.

d. The terms of the engagement – see Chapter 9.

e. Codes of practice. Some audits are influenced by codes of practice – local authorities are an example.

f. Audit risk – see Chapter 25. Risk (the possibility that an auditor may give an inappropriate audit opinion eg say the accounts give a true and fair view when they do not) permeates all auditing. Risk arises due to:

  i. Inherent risk in some areas. For example the risk of obsolescence in hi-tec industries, or the viability of construction companies in an industry in depression with excessive competition.

  ii. Control risk. The risk that internal controls fail to prevent or detect some misstatement. No system is perfect and human failings amongst other reasons may lead to some inability to detect or prevent some error or fraud.

  iii. The impracticality of examining all items within an *account balance* or *class of transactions*. Auditors test check or sample most populations of items. This raises the possibility of detection risk which is the possibility that the auditors' procedures may fail to detect some misstatement.

  iv. The possibility of some fraud or misrepresentation which is committed with *collusion* by staff or management.

  v. Audit evidence is usually persuasive rather than conclusive. Auditors do not expect a standard of evidence like that in a criminal trial where the decision as to a person's guilt has to be beyond all reasonable doubt. As a result an auditor may give an inappropriate opinion.

g. Fear of litigation. Actions under the law of tort to recover losses alleged to be caused by the negligence of auditors are common and very expensive for auditors in terms of cost, time and loss of clients and reputation. – see Chapter 49.

h. Ethics. SAS 100 requires that in the conduct of any audit of financial statements auditors should comply with the ethical guidance issued by their relevant professional bodies. These guides are now fairly extensive – see Chapter 8. Relevant matters include integrity, objectivity, independence, professional competence, due care, professional behaviour and confidentiality.

i. The individual auditing manual of the firm of auditors. These may be influenced by quality control standards.

Summary

5. a. SAS 100 *Objectives and general principles governing an audit of financial statements* is a general statement which governs all audits.

    b. SAS 100 has a statement of the objective of an audit. This should be learned by heart.

    c. SAS 100 requires certain procedures. These can be summarised as obtain evidence, evaluate the financial statements for truth and fairness, compliance with statutes and for compliance with accounting standards and finally make a report.

    d. There are numerous influences on the actual conduct of an audit including the risk of giving an inappropriate audit opinion

Points to note

6. a. This is a very important (if rather general) Statement of Auditing Standards. Many of the phrases should be memorised and reproduced in auditing answers.

    b. SAS 100 appears to be prescriptive in requiring auditors to do certain things (like gather evidence) and the requirements are expanded in detail in all the other SASs. However the reality is that the role of judgement is still paramount in auditing. Note words like sufficient, reasonable, risk, judgement, imprecision, uncertainties, opinion, material, conclusions.

    c. Note that financial statements are drawn up by the directors (or other managing bodies) who take full responsibility for them.

Case study 1 for Chapter 12

DRACULA STONEWARE LTD are a small company retailing gravestones in a small town. Their auditors are Simple & Co. Bram Simple, a partner, performs the audit like this:

–   After the year end John Goole, a senior audit clerk. is sent to the company's premises.

–   He finds that the books are in excellent shape but that no postings have been made to the nominal ledger which in fact is kept at the accountants.

–   He reconciles the cash book to the bank statements, prepares and balances total accounts for the sales and purchase ledgers, reconciles the VAT, PAYE and NI payments, posts the nominal ledger, extracts a trial balance, prepares a list of prepayments, accruals and other adjustments, prepares the Annual Accounts, directors report etc.

–   He then shows drafts to the directors, settles any queries and returns to Simple & Co. where Mr. Simple glances through the drafts comparing the figures with previous years.

–   The Accounts are then typed and copies sent to the Client and to the Inland Revenue.

Discussion

Relate this approach to the Standard.

Can the standard be applied to audits such as that of Dracula?

How could Simple & Co's office organisation be adapted to the requirements of the Standard?

Does this have any bearing on costs and welfare economics?

Case study 2 for Chapter 12

Boffin is the junior technical partner of Wood, Tree & Co., Certified Accountants. His partners have asked him to draw up a statement contrasting and comparing the audit work required by the Companies Act and by SAS 100.

Discussion

Draw up the Statement.

Case study 3 for Chapter 12

Delbert is about to commence the audit of Sandcastle PLC. This a company in the construction and speculative housing industry which has expanded greatly in recent years. It is run by Gogetter who is known as very autocratic but charismatic entrepreneur. He has expanded the company rapidly by both acquisition and internal growth. The company is heavily geared and the share price has fallen from an absurd high to a very low figure in the past two years.

Discussion

a. In what ways is there a risk of misstatement in the auditor's opinion on the financial statements?

b. What influences would act on Delbert in conducting the audit?

Student self testing questions *Questions with answers apparent from the text*

1. a. Define the objective of an audit. (2)
   b. What is meant by opinion, taken as a whole, reasonable assurance, true and fair view? (2)
   c. State the procedures required by SAS 100. (3)
   d. List possible influences on the conduct of an audit. (4)
   e. What risks are relevant to an auditor? (3)
   f. Why is an audit not just a set of mechanical procedures? (5)

Examination question *(Answer begins on page 543)*

1. You are the partner in charge of the audit of Q Limited for the year ending 30 September 1984. Q Limited is a small company which has expanded rapidly during the last year.

   Turnover has increased by 80% from £1M to £1. 8M, trading profit by 65% from £120,000 to £198,000 and net assets by 90% from £1. 7M to £3.23M. The share capital is entirely owned by the Smith family with Mr. James Smith and his two sons managing the business on a day to day basis.

   As a result of the increased activity during the last year the accounting staff has increased from 2 clerks under the control of Mr. James Smith to 4 staff comprising a qualified chief accountant under the supervision of Mr. James Smith and 3 clerks. As a result of the increased accounting work load and staff numbers, sales and wages systems have been introduced. Purchases are still dealt with on a purely manual cash book basis.

   You have indicated to Mr. James Smith that you have to request an increase in the audit fee. Mr. Smith has always considered the audit of his family company unnecessary and considers this request for an increased fee as being a complete waste of money.

Required:

a.   i.   Explain to Mr. Smith why an audit is required.   (2 marks)

     ii. Outline the basis for determining the fee which your firm would charge.

                                                                                    (2 marks)

b.   Describe in outline the stages of the audit of Mr. Smith's company indicating in what order the audit work would be carried out.   (8 marks)

c.   Describe the benefits of the audit and give FOUR specific uses of audited accounts.

                                                                                    (8 marks)

                                                                                    (ACCA)

The conduct of the audit

1. The next section of the book describes the auditor's interest in his client's system of accounting and internal control (Chapters 13 and 14). Chapters 15 and 16 explain audit testing of the books and records of an enterprise and Chapter 17 describes the manner in which an auditor records and documents his work.

2. At the conclusion of a session of audit testing, an auditor will usually discover a number of weaknesses in the way his client is recording, documenting and controlling his transactions. The penultimate chapter in this section shows how an auditor informs his client of these weaknesses.

3. The final chapter deals with an old subject which has recently received renewed attention – the auditor's duty toward error and fraud.

13 Accounting systems

Introduction

1. This chapter considers:
   a. The auditor's interest in a client's accounting system.
   b. The management's interest in the accounting system.
   c. The need for controls over the system.
   d. The auditor's procedures concerning the accounting system.

   The relevant Statement of Auditing Standards is SAS 300 *Accounting and internal control systems and audit risk assessments*

The auditor's interest in a client's accounting system

2. The auditor's interest in a client's accounting system comes from two sources:
   a. SAS 300 requires that auditors should obtain an understanding of the accounting and internal control systems sufficient to plan the audit and develop an effective audit approach. Further SAS 300 requires that auditors should, in planning the audit obtain and document an understanding of the accounting system and control environment sufficient to determine their audit approach.
   b. The Companies Act 1985 Section 237 states:
      (1) A company's auditors shall, in preparing their report, to carry out such investigations as will enable them to form an opinion as to:
         (a) whether proper accounting records have been kept by the company and proper returns adequate for their audit have been received from branches not visited by them,
         (b) whether the company's balance sheet and (if not consolidated) its profit and loss account are in agreement with the accounting records and returns.
      If the auditors form a contrary opinion, they must state the fact in their report.

The management's interest in an accounting system

3. The management of an enterprise need *complete* and accurate accounting and other records because:

   a. the business cannot otherwise be controlled.

   b. day to day records of debtors and creditors are indispensable.

   c. assets can only be safeguarded if a proper record of them is made.

   d. financial statements which are required for numerous purposes can only be prepared if adequate primary records exist.

   e. statutes (eg the Companies Act) often have specific requirements on record keeping for specific types of business.

   f. record keeping for PAYE NHI VAT and statutory sick pay and statutory maternity pay is also a statutory requirement.

4. What constitutes an adequate system of accounting depends on the circumstances. A small shopkeeper may find that a 'Simplex' book and a spike for unpaid invoices may suffice but an international company clearly needs rather more sophisticated records. The basic needs of a system is that it provides for the orderly assembly of accounting information to enable the financial statements to be prepared but all the other requirements of paragraph 3 must be borne in mind.

The need for controls over the system

5. A system of accounting and record keeping will not succeed in completely and accurately processing all transactions unless controls, known as internal controls, are built into the system. The purposes of such internal controls are:

   a. to ensure transactions are executed in accordance with proper general or specific *authorisation*

   b. to ensure all transactions are *promptly recorded* at the *correct amount*, in the *appropriate accounts* and in the proper *accounting period* so as to permit preparation of *financial statements* in accordance with relevant legislation and accounting standards

   c. to ensure *access to assets* is permitted only in accordance with proper authorisation

   d. to ensure recorded assets are compared with the existing assets at reasonable intervals and appropriate action is taken with regard to any differences

   e. to ensure errors and irregularities are avoided or made apparent.

Auditor's procedures

6. The auditor's procedures will depend on the circumstances but may include:

   a. Obtaining an understanding of the enterprise as a whole in order to see the accounting system in context and thus being able to assess the system's effectiveness and appropriateness.

   b. Ascertaining the complete system by enquiry, use of an internal control questionnaire or requesting the client to supply full details.

   c. Recording the system in the form of flowcharts, narrative notes, check lists or in the answers to the ICQ.

d. If the auditor intends to rely on the internal controls, he should record the system of controls in especial detail.

e. If the system specification was supplied by the client, then perform walk through checks to confirm the correctness of the description.

f. Perform a preliminary evaluation of the system.

g. If the system of controls seems adequate and the auditor is able to and wishes to rely upon the controls, then design and perform compliance tests.

h. If the auditor does not feel able to rely on the controls then perform substantive tests on the records. In any case, some substantive tests must be planned and performed on all material items.

i. Evaluate his evidence and form an opinion on whether proper books of account have been kept and whether the records form a reliable basis for the preparation of financial statements.

SAS 300 requires that auditors should obtain and *document* an understanding of the accounting system and control environment sufficient to determine their approach. This does not mean that a detailed knowledge of the accounting system or internal controls is required. However SAS 300 suggests that what is required is an understanding of the system sufficient to enable them to identify and understand:

a. major classes of transactions in the entity's operations

b. how such transactions are initiated

c. significant accounting records, supporting documents and accounts in the financial statements

d. the accounting and financial process, from the initiation of significant transactions and other events to their conclusion in the financial statements.

This seems to be very comprehensive! However note the words major and significant.

More detailed knowledge of internal controls may be required if the auditor, after evaluating risk matters, decides that her approach is to rely on some internal controls as audit evidence. In practice an understanding of accounting records often goes hand in hand with an understanding of internal controls. In any event the auditor needs to have evidence on The Companies Act 1985 S 237 requirements.

Summary

7. a. The auditor needs to evaluate the accounting system in order to form a conclusion on whether the records form a reliable basis for the preparation of the Accounts and whether proper books of account have been kept.

b. Authority for this view comes from The Companies Act 1985 S.237 and from SAS 300.

c. No enterprise can be managed and controlled successfully without adequate records.

d. Adequate accounting systems must incorporate internal controls to ensure authority, completeness and accuracy and to prevent or uncover error and fraud.

e. Auditors need to investigate, record, test and form an opinion on the accounting system.

Points to note

8. a. The expression 'accounting systems' must be seen as wider than books of account. It encompasses all the procedures necessary to record transactions in the form of documents (eg goods inward notes, clock cards etc.) as well as the actual books of account.

   b. In recent auditing literature, internal controls have been seen as a separate system superimposed upon the accounting system. In practice the accounting system and the system of internal controls are really one system and investigation and testing of both systems is carried out simultaneously.

   c. It is essential to realise that auditors are interested in accounting systems not only as a step along the way of forming an opinion on the truth and fairness and compliance with statute but also as an audit aim in itself.

   d. Commit to memory the phrase 'whether or not the accounting records form a reliable basis for the preparation of the accounts'.

Case study for Chapter 13

Sunbeam Ltd own a garage in Hightown. They sell imported Yaki cars, have a spares service for Yaki, and offer servicing, petrol and motor accessories to the public.

The records are:

All cash sales are recorded daily for each section in a giant cash book. Credit sales are evidenced by copy invoices. Each invoice is marked 'paid' on the date when it is paid. No sales ledger is kept.

Incoming invoices are placed on a spike. When they are paid, they are marked as such and filed away.

Cheques are entered consecutively in the cash book.

There is a wages book and a rudimentary petty cash book.

A private ledger is written up annually by Manuel Day & Co, Certified Accountants the auditors.

Discussion

Relate this system to the requirements of Section 237 Companies Act 1985.

Student self testing questions *Questions with answers apparent from the text*

1. a. Detail the auditor's interest in a client's accounting records. (2)
   b. Why should management maintain good accounting records? (3)
   c. Why are internal controls necessary? (5)
   d. Summarise the auditor's procedures in connection with a client's accounting systems. (6)

Examination question without answer

1. The external auditor has duties in connection with the client's accounting system.
   a. What are these duties?
   b. What procedures does an auditor adopt to discharge these duties?

(LCCI 91)

14 Internal controls

Introduction

1. This chapter considers the auditors approach to internal control systems as outlined in SAS 300 and then considers what internal control is and then gives a detailed review of internal control in specific areas. At the end we take a look at the ideas on control environment and control procedures and consider the limitations of internal control.

The auditor and internal control

2. SAS 300 requires auditors:

   a. to obtain an understanding of the accounting and internal control systems sufficient to plan the audit and develop an effective audit approach

   b. in planning the audit, to obtain and document an understanding of the accounting system and control environment sufficient to determine their audit approach

   c. if after obtaining an understanding of the accounting systems and control environment, they expect to be able to rely on their assessment of control risk to reduce the extent of their substantive procedures, they should make a preliminary assessment of control risk for material financial statement assertions, and should plan and perform tests of control to support that assessment.

   Control risk is defined as the risk that a misstatement that could occur in an account balance or class of transactions and that could be material, either individually or when aggregated with misstatements in other balances or classes, would not be prevented, or detected and corrected on a timely basis, by the accounting and internal control systems.

   Tests of control are tests to obtain audit evidence about the effective operation of the accounting and internal control systems – that is, that properly designed controls identified in the preliminary assessment of control risk exist in fact and have operated effectively throughout the relevant period. Such tests are also called *compliance tests*.

3. Suppose the auditor, Rosemary, of Sheinton Widgets Ltd is starting her audit. She explores and obtains an understanding of the accounting and internal control system of the whole company but we will consider sales. She is concerned that the figure for sales is complete and that no sales have been omitted. In effect we can say that the directors in putting sales at £x in the Profit and Loss Account are asserting things about sales including that all are included. Our auditor needs to have evidence of this.

   She considers the internal controls applied to sales and assesses that they seem well designed and effective in theory. However there is a control risk that a misstatement (a material amount of sales are omitted) may occur and that the internal control system will not prevent it or detect it and correct it. Rosemary decides that part of her audit evidence on the completeness of sales will be reliance on the internal controls applied to sales. Rosemary now has to design, perform, document and draw conclusions from tests of control.

   A notable point from SAS 300 is that "regardless of the assessed levels of inherent and control risks, auditors should perform some substantive procedures for financial statement assertions of material account balances and transactions classes." In this case possible omission of sales is a material matter and Rosemary will need to perform some substantive tests as well as testing the controls.

Definition

4. Internal control is defined as:

'Internal control system – the whole system of controls, financial and otherwise, established by the management in order to carry on the business of the enterprise in an orderly and efficient manner, ensure adherence to management policies, safeguard the assets and secure as far as possible the completeness and accuracy of the records. The individual components of an internal control system are known as 'controls' or 'internal controls'.'

5. In this paragraph, we will consider the definition in detail:

a. **The whole system**. Internal controls can be seen as single procedures (eg Clerk A checks the calculations performed by Clerk B) or as a whole system. The whole system should be more than the sum of the parts.

b. **Financial and otherwise**. The distinction is not important. Perhaps *financial* would include the use of control accounts and *otherwise* may include physical access restrictions to computer terminals.

c. **Established by the management**. Internal control systems are established by the management, either directly or by means of external consultants, internal audit, or accounting personnel. External auditors may be asked to advise on the setting up of systems.

d. **'Carry on ... efficient manner'**. Clearly the converse is unacceptable in any business.

e. **Ensure adherence to management policies**. Not all management have *expressed* policies. But as an example a budget is an expression of management policy and adherence to the budget can be achieved by procedures such as variance analysis. Another example might be the selling prices of the enterprise's products being laid down by management and controls existing to ensure that these prices are adhered to.

f. **Safeguard the assets**. Obviously allowing assets to be broken, lost or stolen, is unacceptable and procedures are always devised to safeguard them. Examples are locks and keys, the keeping of a plant register, regular reviews of debtor balances etc. An aspect of this which is often overlooked is that payment where no benefits have been received, as payment for piece work not done, or the setting up of liabilities where no benefit has been received as in fraudulent purchase and subsequent embezzlement of goods by employees are both examples of failure to safeguard assets.

g. **Secure ... completeness**. It is especially important that *all* transactions are recorded and processed. Procedures which do this include checks that no goods leave the factory without a delivery note followed by regular comparison of invoices with delivery notes to see that no goods sold (always evidenced by a delivery note) have failed to result in an invoice.

h. **And accuracy of the records**. Again, the converse is unacceptable. Examples of procedures to achieve this include checking of the work of one clerk by another or, the use of control accounts, independent comparison of two sets of records eg stock records and stock, or piecework payments and good work put into store.

Types of internal control

6. The types of internal control can be categorised as:

   a. **Organisation**. An enterprise should:

      i. have a plan of organisation which should –

      ii. define and allocate responsibilities – every function should be in the charge of a specified person who might be called the *responsible official*. Thus the keeping of petty cash should be entrusted to a particular person who is then responsible (and hence answerable) for that function

      iii. identify lines of reporting.

   In all cases, the *delegation of authority* and responsibility should be clearly specified.

   An employee should always know the precise powers delegated to him, the extent of his authority and to whom he should report. Two examples:

      1. Responsibility for approving the purchase of items of plant may be retained by the Board of Directors for items over £X and within the competence of the works manager for a budgeted amount agreed by the board.

      2. Responsibility for the correct operation of internal controls may be delegated by the board to specific management personnel and to the internal audit department.

   b. **Segregation of duties**.

      i. No one person should be responsible for the recording and processing of a complete transaction.

      ii. The involvement of several people reduces the risk of intentional manipulation or accidental error and increases the element of checking of work.

      iii. Functions which for a given transaction should be separated include initiation (eg the works foreman decides the firm needs more lubricating oil) authorisation (the works manager approves the purchase), execution (the buying department order the oil), custody (on arrival the oil is taken in by the goods-in section and passed with appropriate goods-in documentation to the stores department) and recording (the arrival is documented by the goods inward section and the invoice is compared with the original order and goods-in note by the accounts department, and recorded by them in the books).

   Another example is the area of sales where initiation is by a representative, authorisation by credit control and the sales manager, execution is by the finished goods warehouse staff who physically send the goods, custody is transferred from the warehouse staff to the transport department, and the transaction is recorded by the goods outward section, the invoicing section and the accounts department.

   c. **Physical**.

      i. This concerns physical custody of assets and involves procedures designed to limit access to authorised personnel only.

      ii. Access can be direct, eg being able to enter the warehouse or indirect, that is by documentation eg personnel knowing the correct procedures, may be able to extract goods by doing the right paper work.

iii. These controls are especially important in the case of valuable, portable, exchangeable or desirable assets. Examples are the locking of securities (share certificates etc.) in a safe *with procedures for the custody of use of the keys*, use of passes to restrict access to the warehouse, use of password to restrict access to particular computer files.

d. **Authorisation and approval**. This is a special case of type a. above. All transactions should require authorisation or approval by an appropriate person. The limits to these authorisations should be specified. Examples:

   i. All credit sales must be approved by the credit control department.

   ii. All overtime must be approved by the works manager.

   iii. All individual office stationery purchases may be approved by the office manager up to a limit of £n. Higher purchases must be approved by the chief accountant.

e. **Arithmetical and Accounting**.

   i. These are the controls in the recording function which *check* that the transactions have been *authorised*, that they are *all* included and that they are *correctly* recorded and *accurately* processed.

   ii. Procedures include checking the arithmetical accuracy of the records, the maintenance and checking of totals, reconciliations, control accounts, trial balances, accounting for documents (sometimes known as sequence checks or continuity checks), *preview* that is before an important action involving the company's property is taken, the person concerned should review the documentation available to see that all that should have been done, has been done. Examples of all these:

   1. Clerk A checking the extensions of a sales invoice, the extensions having been made by Clerk B.

   2. The purchases invoices checked by the purchase invoice section of the accounting department being prelisted by that section before sending them to the computer department for processing.

   3. An official in the accounting department independent of the cash book officials, making a *bank reconciliation*.

   4. An accountant independent of the sales ledger function making a sales ledger control account.

   5. A clerk in the buying department examining purchase requisitions to ensure that they are correct, complete and authorised before making out an order.

   6. A clerk in the accounting department comparing the incoming purchase invoices with copy order forms and goods inwards notes.

   7. An accounting official going through the goods outward records to verify that all have been followed by an invoice.

   8. Checking that the copy cash sales invoices are in numerical sequence. (If one is missing a clerk may have made a sale and misappropriated the cash received.)

f. **Personnel**.

   i.   Procedures should be designed to ensure that personnel operating a system are competent and motivated to carry out the tasks assigned to them, as the proper functioning of a system depends upon the competence and integrity of the operating personnel.

   ii.   Measures include appropriate remuneration and promotion and career development prospects, selection of people with appropriate personal characteristics and training, and, assignment to tasks of the right level.

g. **Supervision**. All actions by all levels of staff should be supervised. The responsibility for supervision should be clearly laid down and communicated to the person being supervised.

h. **Management**.

   i.   These are controls, exercised by management which are outside and over and above the day to day routine of the system.

   ii.   They include overall supervisory controls, review of management accounts, comparisons with budgets, internal audit and any other special review procedures.

     Examples:

     1.   Senior management must be aware of day to day activities and be seen by staff to be so. Glaring failures of control (stock thefts, excess stocking, unnecessary overtime) will become apparent and staff will be motivated to perform well.

     2.   Management accounts should be designed to summarise performance in fine detail. Any anomalies (cost overruns, travelling expense fiddles) should become apparent.

     3.   Budgeting and variance analysis is a management tool which should prevent or at least detect departure from management's intended plans.

7. In addition to the above, two other categories are

a. **Acknowledgement of Performance**. Persons performing data processing operations should acknowledge their activities by means of signatures, initials, rubber stamps, etc. For example, if invoice calculations have to be checked, the checker should initial each invoice. Acknowledgement of performance not only allows blame to be ascribed but also has a powerful psychological effect. Audit clerks usually initial the audit programme when they have completed a part of the work. Even audit clerks are reluctant to confirm in writing that they have examined a thousand credit notes when they have looked at only one hundred!

b. **Budgeting**. A common technique used in business is the use of budgets, which can be defined as quantitative plans of action. Budgets having been agreed, can be compared with actual turn out and differences investigated.

Design of systems of accounting and internal control

8. The design of accounting and control systems is a specialised activity and an auditing manual is not the place for a detailed description of the processes involved. However we will look at one example. Luso books Ltd run a small mail order operation selling

specialist books. The firm advertise and the customers send in their requirements through the post with cheques. Clearly there is a risk of employees misappropriating the cheques and other problems and to avoid these a system like this may be installed:

1. all post to be opened by one member of an authorised group of staff in the presence of another.

2. all orders are transcribed onto a pre-printed form (the blank forms are numbered consecutively)

3. cheques are entered into a 'post cash book' which is totalled daily and initialled by all staff members present

4. cheques are sent to the cashier for banking and accounting in the computer system

5. orders are sent to dispatch for processing

6. other mail is sent to the appropriate manager

7. totals banked shown on a print out are compared weekly with the sales invoices prepared by dispatch and with the bank paying in slip and the post cash book by a senior manager

8. the completed forms are checked for consecutivity by a senior manager.

9. In practice this system will have complications – what happens to orders without cheques or cheques for the wrong amount etc etc? Clearly there are other parts to the whole system of the company. However you may be able to discern some features of the system:

   – organisation – specified responsibilities, specified procedures

   – segregation of duties – several people are involved and no one person has complete charge of all aspects of the transactions

   – arithmetic – reconciliations of post cash book, sales invoices and bankings. Also numerical sequence checks.

Internal control in specific areas of a business

10. This section is divided up into the areas of activity usually found in a business. At the beginning of each area are stated the objectives of internal control in the area and some measures then follow which will achieve the objectives.

    a. **Internal control generally**

       Objectives

       To carry on the business in an orderly and efficient manner, to ensure adherence to management policies, safeguard its assets, and secure the accuracy and reliability of the records.

       Measures

       1) An appropriate and integrated system of accounts and records.

       2) Internal controls over those accounts and records.

       3) Financial supervision and control by management, including budgetary control, management accounting reports, and interim accounts.

       4) Safeguarding and if necessary duplicating records.

5) Engaging, training, allocating to specific duties staff who are capable of fulfilling their responsibilities. *Rotation* of duties and cover for absences.

b. **Cash and cheques received by post**

Objectives

To ensure that *all* cash and cheques received by post are accounted for and accurately recorded in the books.

To ensure all such receipts are *promptly* and *intactly* deposited in the bank.

Measures

1) Measures to prevent interception of mail between receipt and opening.

2) Appointment of an official to be responsible for the opening of the post.

3) Two persons to be present at the opening of the post.

4) All cheques and other negotiable instruments to be immediately given a restrictive crossing eg account payee only, not negotiable.

5) Immediate entry of the details of the receipts (date, payer, amount, cash, cheque, or other) in a 'rough cash book' or post-list of money received. The list should be signed by both parties present.

6) Regular independent comparison of the post list with banking records. The tests should be of total, detail and dating to detect teeming and lading at a later stage in the processing.

c. **Cash sales and collections**

Objectives

To ensure that all cash, to which the enterprise is entitled, is received.

To ensure that all such cash is properly accounted for and entered in the records.

To ensure that all such cash is promptly and intactly deposited.

Measures

1) Prescribing and limiting the number of persons who are authorised to receive cash eg sales assistants, cashiers, roundsmen, travellers, etc.

2) Establishing a means of evidencing cash receipts eg pre-numbered duplicate receipt forms, cash registers with sealed till rolls. The duplicate receipt form books should be securely held and issue controlled.

3) Ensuring that customers are aware that they must receive a receipt form or ensuring that the amount rung up on the cash register is clearly visible to the customer.

4) Appointment of officers with responsibility for emptying cash registers at prescribed intervals, and agreeing the amount present with till roll totals or internal registers. Such collections should be evidenced in writing and be initialled by the assistant and the supervisor.

5) Immediate and intact banking. Payments out should be from funds drawn from the bank on an imprest system.

6) Investigation of shorts and overs.

7) Independent comparison of agreed till roll totals with subsequent banking records.

8) Persons handling cash should not have access to other cash funds or to bought or sales ledger records.

9) Rotation of duties and cover for holidays (which should be compulsory) and sickness.

10) Collections by roundsmen and travellers should be banked intact daily. There should be independent comparison of the amounts banked with records (eg duplicate receipt books) of the roundsmen and salesmen.

11) Wherever possible roundsmen should have a controlled issue of merchandise with a check, on their return, that they have cash or goods to the value of the controlled issue on the lines of an imprest system.

d. **Payments into bank**

Objectives

To ensure that all cash and cheques received are banked intact.

To ensure that all cash and cheques received are banked without delay at prescribed intervals, preferably daily.

To ensure that all cash and cheques received are accounted for and recorded accurately.

Measures

1) Cash and cheques should be banked intact.

2) Cash and cheques should be banked without delay preferably daily.

3) The bank paying-in slip should be prepared by an official with no access to cash collection points, bought or sales ledgers.

4) Bankings should be made with security in mind eg for large cash sums, security guards should be used.

5) There should be independent comparison of paying-in slips with collection records, post lists and sales ledger records.

e. **Cash balances**

Objectives

To prevent misappropriation of cash balances.

To prevent unauthorised cash payments.

Measures

1) Establishment of cash floats of specified amounts and locations.

2) Appointment of officials responsible for each cash balance.

3) Arrangement of security measures including use of safes and restriction of access.

4) Use of imprest system with rules on reimbursement only against authorised vouchers.

5) Strict rules on the authorising of cash payments.

6) Independent cash counts on a regular and a surprise basis.

7) Insurance arrangements eg for cash balances and fidelity guarantee.

8) Special rules for IOUs. Preferably these should not be permitted.

f. **Bank balances**

Objectives

To prevent misappropriation of bank balances.

To prevent teeming and lading.

Measures

1) Reconciliations should be prepared at prescribed frequency.

2) They should be performed by independent personnel.

3) Arrangements should be made for bank statements to be sent direct to the person responsible for the reconciliations.

4) Work on reconciliations should include:

A comparison of each debit and credit in the cash book with the corresponding entries in the bank statements.

A comparison of returned cheques with the cash book entries noting dates, payees and amounts.

A test of the detailed paying-in slips with the cash book.

The dates of credits in the bank statements should be carefully compared with the cash book to detect any delays.

All outstanding cheques and lodgements should be traced through to the next period and their validity verified.

Any unusual items eg contras or dishonoured cheques should be investigated.

5) The balances at the bank should be independently verified with the bank at intervals.

6) Special arrangements should be instituted on the controls and recording of trust monies eg employees' sick pay or holiday funds, attachment of earnings.

g. **Cheque payments**

Objectives

To prevent unauthorised payments being made from bank accounts.

Measures

1) Control over custody and issue of unused cheque books. A register should be kept if necessary.

2) Appointment of an official to be responsible for the preparation of cheques or traders credits.

3) Rules should be established for the presentation of supporting documents before cheques can be made out. Such supporting documents may include GRNs, orders, invoices, etc.

4) All such documents should be stamped 'paid by cheque no. …' with date.

5) Establishment of who can sign cheques. All cheques should be signed by at least two persons, with no person being permitted to sign if he is a payee.

6) No cheques should be made out to bearer except for the collection of wages or reimbursement of cash funds.

7) All cheques should be restrictively crossed.

8) The signing of blank cheques must be prohibited.

9) Special safeguards where cheques are signed mechanically or have pre-printed signatures. Such signings are often made for dividend payments, salary cheques and other reasons.

10) Rules to ensure prompt despatch and to prevent interception or misappropriation.

11) Measures to ensure cash discounts are obtained.

12) Special rules for authorising and checking direct debits and standing orders.

13) Separation of duties: custody, recording and initiation of cheque payments: cash records and other areas eg debtors and creditors.

h. **Wages and salaries**

Objectives

To ensure that wages and salaries are paid only to actual employees at authorised rates of pay.

To ensure that all wages and salaries are computed in accordance with records of work performed whether in respect of time, output, sales made or other criteria.

To ensure that payrolls are correctly calculated.

To ensure that payments are made only to the correct employees.

To ensure that payroll deductions are correctly accounted for and paid over to the appropriate third parties.

To ensure that all transactions are correctly recorded in the books of account.

Measures

1) There should be separate records kept for each employee. The records should contain such matters as date of engagement, age, next of kin, agreed deductions, skills, department, and specimen signature. Ideally these records should be maintained by a separate personnel department.

2) Procedures for, and specified officials responsible for, engagements, retirements, dismissals, fixing and changing rates of pay. Procedures should be laid down for notification of these matters to the personnel and wage roll preparation departments.

3) Time records should be kept, preferably by means of supervised clock card recording. These should be approved and approval acknowledged. All overtime should be authorised.

4) Output or piecework records should be properly controlled and authorised. Procedures should exist for reconciling output or piecework records with production records.

5) The payroll should be prepared by personnel unconnected with other wage duties. Special procedures should exist for dealing with advances, holiday pay, lay off pay, luncheon vouchers, new employees, employees leaving, sickness and other absences and bonuses.

6) The payroll should be checked by separate personnel. All work on the preparation and checking of the payroll should be initialled. All such work should be supervised and the payroll scrutinised and approved by a senior official.

7) The net amount due to be paid out in cash should be drawn after a coin analysis. Tight security should be imposed on the security of cash, both on collection from the bank and at all times up to the receipt of pay envelopes by the workforce. Ideally collection of cash from the bank should be by a Security organisation.

8) Wage envelopes should be made up by personnel independent of the wage roll preparation team.

9) Specified times should be laid down for distribution of wage packets. These should either be acknowledged by the recipients or distribution should be made in the presence of (but not by) foremen or others capable of identifying employees.

10) Surprise attendance at payouts should be made at intervals by internal audit or by a senior official.

11) Unclaimed wages should be subject to special procedures. These should include a record to be maintained of unclaimed wages, safe custody of such pay packets, a requirement for investigation, subsequent payout only after proof of entitlement, breaking down and rebanking after a specified period of time.

12) Payments by cheque and credit transfer should be subject to special procedures. These could include maintenance of a separate bank account with regular reconciliation.

13) Deductions such as PAYE, national insurance, pension contributions, save as you earn, and union dues should be subject to prompt payment over to the institutions concerned. Control totals subject to frequent review should be kept. Independent comparisons of such totals with records such as tax deduction cards should be performed regularly.

14) Regular independent comparisons should be made between personnel records and wages records.

15) Regular independent comparisons of payrolls at different dates.

16) Regular independent comparisons of wages paid with budgets and investigation of variances.

17) Surprise investigation of wage records and procedures by internal audit or senior officials.

18) An independent official should be appointed to be responsible for settling queries.

19) Wage records should conform to the requirements of Statutory Sick Pay.

Note that most firms now credit employees bank accounts through the banking system.

i. **Purchases and trade creditors**

Objectives

To ensure that goods and services are only ordered in the quantity, of the quality, and at the best terms available after appropriate requisition and approval.

To ensure that goods and services received are inspected and only acceptable items are accepted.

To ensure that all invoices are checked against authorised orders and receipt of the subject matter in good condition.

To ensure that all goods and services invoiced are properly recorded in the books.

Measures

1) There should be procedures for the requisitioning of goods and services only by specified personnel on specified forms with space for acknowledgement of performance.

2) Order forms should be pre-numbered and kept in safe custody. Issue of blank order form books should be controlled and recorded.

3) Order procedures should include requirements for obtaining tenders, estimates or competitive bids.

4) Sequence checks of order forms should be performed regularly by a senior official and missing items investigated.

5) All goods received should be recorded on goods received notes (preferably pre-numbered) or in a special book.

6) All goods should be inspected for condition and agreement with order and counted on receipt. The inspection should be acknowledged. Procedures for dealing with rejected goods or services should include the creation of debit notes (pre-numbered) with subsequent sequence checks and follow up of receipt of suppliers' credit notes.

7) At intervals, a listing of unfulfilled orders should be made and investigated.

8) Invoices should be checked for arithmetical accuracy, pricing, correct treatment of VAT and trade discount, and agreement with order and goods-in records. These checks should be acknowledged by the performer preferably on spaces marked by a rubber stamp on the invoices.

9) Invoices should have consecutive numbers put on them and batches should be pre-listed.

10) Totals of entries in the invoice register or day book should be regularly checked with the pre-lists.

11) Responsibility for purchase ledger entries should be vested in personnel separate from personnel responsible for ordering, receipt of goods and the invoice register.

12) The purchase ledger should be subject to frequent reconciliations in total by or be checked by an independent senior official.

13) Ledger account balances should be regularly compared with suppliers' statements of account.

14) All goods and service procurement should be controlled by budgetary techniques. Orders should only be placed that are within budget limits. There should be frequent comparisons of actual purchases with budgets and investigation into variances.

15) Cut off procedures at the year end are essential.

16) A proper coding system is required for purchase of goods and services so that the correct nominal accounts are debited.

j. **Sales and debtors**

Objectives

To ensure that all customers orders are promptly executed.

To ensure that sales on credit are made only to bona fide good credit risks.

To ensure that all sales on credit are invoiced, that authorised prices are charged and that before issue all invoices are completed and checked as regards price, trade discounts and VAT.

To ensure that all invoices raised are entered in the books.

To ensure that all customers claims are fully investigated before credit notes are issued.

To ensure that every effort is made to collect all debts.

To ensure that no unauthorised credits are made to debtors accounts.

Measures

1) Incoming orders should be recorded, and if necessary, acknowledged, on pre-numbered forms. Orders should be matched with invoices and lists prepared at intervals of outstanding orders for management action. Sequence checks should be made regularly by a senior official.

2) Credit control. There should be procedures laid down for verifying the credit worthiness of all persons or institutions requesting goods on credit. For existing customers, credit worthiness data should be kept up-to-date and checks made that outstanding balances plus a new sale does not cause the pre-set credit limit to be exceeded. For new customers, investigative techniques should be applied including enquiry of trade protection organisations, credit rating agencies, referees, the company's file with the Registrar of Companies, etc. A credit limit should be established. This may be fixed at two levels, a higher one such that further sales are not made and a lower one such that management are informed and a judgement made on granting credit.

3) Selling prices should be prescribed. Policies should be laid down on credit terms, trade and cash discounts, and special prices.

4) Despatch of goods should only be on properly evidenced authority. Goods out should be recorded either in a register or using pre-numbered despatch notes. Unissued blocks of despatch notes should be safeguarded and issue recorded. Sequence checks of despatch notes should be made regularly by a senior official. Where appropriate acknowledgement of receipt of goods should be made by customers on copy despatch notes.

5) Invoicing should be carried out by a separate department or by sales staff. Invoices should be pre-numbered and the custody and issue of unused invoice blocks controlled and recorded. Sequence checks should be regularly made by a senior official and missing or spoiled invoices investigated.

6) All invoices should be independently checked for agreement with customer order, with goods despatched record, for pricing, discounts, VAT and other details. All actions should be acknowledged by signature or initials.

7) Accounting for sales and debtors should be segregated by employing separate staff for cash, invoice register, sales ledger entries and statement preparation.

8) Sales invoices should be pre-listed before entry into the invoice register or day book and the pre-list total independently compared with the total of the register.

9) Customer claims should be recorded and investigated. Similar controls (eg pre-numbering) should be applied to credit notes. At the year end, uncleared claims should be carefully investigated and assessed. All credit notes should be subject to acknowledged approval by a senior official.

10) A control account should be regularly and independently prepared.

11) Debtors statements should be prepared by personnel separate from the sales ledger personnel. Posting should be subject to safeguards so that no statements are misappropriated before posting.

12) Procedures must exist for identifying and chasing slow payers. Very overdue balances should be brought to the attention of senior management for legal or other action to be taken.

13) All balances must be reviewed regularly by an independent official to identify and investigate overdue accounts, debtors paying by instalments or round sums, and accounts where payments do not match invoices.

14) Bad debts should only be written off after due investigation and acknowledged authorisation by senior management.

15) At the year end, an aged analysis of debtors should be prepared to evaluate the need for a doubtful debt provision.

16) Also at the year end, cut off procedure will be required. Particular attention will be paid to orders despatched but not invoiced.

k. **Stock and work in progress**

Objectives

To ensure that stock is adequately protected against loss or misuse.

Measures

1) Separate arrangements for each type of stock eg raw materials, components, work in progress, finished goods, consumable stores.

2) Control over the receipt of goods (see under purchases).

3) Stock should be stored under conditions which deter deterioration due to physical causes eg heat, cold, damp, microbial action. Special arrangement for stock which is dangerous or classified secret.

4) Stock should be safeguarded against loss by theft by appropriate physical controls including restriction of access.

5) Where appropriate, stock records should be maintained. Entries should be made by personnel independent of staff responsible for purchasing and custody of goods.

6) Documentation should be controlled by the use of controlled pre-numbered forms with regular sequence checks.

7) Work in progress and finished goods stocks may be subject to recording by value including the charging of material, labour and overhead costs. Control over the latter items can be exercised by the use of control accounts and reconciliation with payroll or records of machine hours.

8) Stock records should be continuously compared with actual stocks held by independent officials. All differences should be corrected and causes investigated.

9) Ideally all stock items should be subject to established maximum and minimum stock levels with re-order levels.

10) Special arrangements should be applied to returnable containers, other's stock on our premises, our stock on other's premises, scrap and waste.

11) Whether or not a continuous inventory is maintained, there should at least be an annual stock take. Procedures should be prescribed for this with emphasis on identifying damaged, slow moving, and obsolete stock and on cut off procedures.

l. **Fixed assets**

Objectives

To ensure that fixed assets are only acquired with proper authority.

To ensure that fixed assets are properly maintained and used only in the business.

To ensure that fixed assets are properly accounted for and recorded.

To ensure that disposals are properly authorised and that proceeds of disposals are accounted for and recorded.

Measures

1) Capital expenditure should be subject to authorisation procedures which in all cases should be evidenced. In appropriate cases (eg new products or production methods), capital investment appraisal techniques should be applied to acquisitions. It may be desirable in such cases for proposed expenditure to be reviewed by a special committee and for board authority to be required. Other capital expenditures (eg replacement of equipment) may be subject to requests on specified forms with board approval. In yet other cases (eg motor vehicles) the Board may lay down overall policy and detailed approval may be given by a designated senior official (eg transport manager) subject to review by or reports to the Board. In other cases (eg routine replacement or update of equipment) the expenditure may be subject to budget limits with actual expenditure approved by a senior official after review that the proposed expenditure is within the budget.

2) All capital expenditure should be monitored by a senior official (eg chief accountant) with approvals; and any excess expenditure investigated and approval sought.

3) Allocation of expenditure between capital and revenue should be approved.

4) Adequate recording of fixed assets should be made with detailed breakdowns as necessary. In many cases (eg for plant, vehicles or buildings) detailed registers should be maintained.

5) Where registers are maintained, frequent and regular review of the record with actual assets should be made by senior independent officials. Where necessary (eg land and buildings) this should include a check of documents of title. In all cases, condition and use should be checked.

6) Disposals whether by scrapping, sale, or trade in should be subject to authorisation procedures. Receipt of and assessment of reasonableness of proceeds should be monitored by a senior official (eg chief accountant).

7) Arrangements to see that fixed assets are properly maintained by regular inspection and reporting of location, operation and condition. This can be combined with the physical verification of the asset registers.

8) Depreciation policy should be laid down by the Board (subject to a minute). Policy should accord with the requirement of SSAP 12. Officials should be appointed to calculate and check the actual calculations.

Control environment and control procedures

11. In this chapter I have continued the definition and understanding of internal controls used in previous editions of this book. SAS 300 has introduced a new analysis and we will consider it now. This new analysis is useful but perhaps not as clear cut as older analyses.

The control environment means the overall attitude, awareness and actions of directors and management regarding internal controls and their importance in the entity. The control environment encompasses the management style, and corporate culture and values shared by all employees. Factors reflected in this idea include:

– the philosophy and operating style of the directors and management

– the entity's organisational structure and methods of assigning authority and responsibility (including segregation of duties and supervisory controls): and

– the directors' methods of imposing control, including the internal audit function, the functions of the board of directors and personnel policies and procedures.

Control procedures are those policies and procedures in addition to the control environment which are established to achieve the entity's specific objectives. They include in particular procedures designed to prevent or detect and correct errors. Specific control procedures include:

– approval and control of documents (eg custody and use of purchase orders)

– controls over computerised applications and the information technology environment (see Chapter 53)

– checking the arithmetical accuracy of the records (eg checking sales invoice calculations)

– maintaining and reviewing control accounts and trial balances

– reconciliations

– comparing the results of cash, security and stock counts with accounting records

– comparing internal data with external sources of information (eg bank statements, customers remittance advices, suppliers statements of account)

– limiting direct physical access to assets and records (eg passwords and locks and keys)

Auditors are expected to make an assessment of the control environment in a client. A good control environment may well mean that internal control is strong but nonetheless internal control may be weak at the level of control procedures. It is generally felt that a poor control environment will mean unreliable control procedures but not necessarily so.

Limitations of internal control

12. Internal controls are essential features of any organisation that is run efficiently. However it is important to realise (especially for an auditor) that internal controls have inherent limitations which include:

   - a requirement that the cost of an internal control is not disproportionate to the potential loss which may result from its absence.

   - internal controls tend to be directed at routine transactions. The one-off or unusual transaction tends not to be the subject of internal control

   - potential human error caused by stress of workload, alcohol, carelessness, distraction, mistakes of judgement, cussedness, and the misunderstanding of instructions

   - the possibility of circumvention of controls either alone or through *collusion* with parties outside or inside the entity

   - abuse of responsibility

   - management override of controls

   - fraud

   - changes in environment making controls inadequate

   - human cleverness – however secure the computer code designed to prevent access, there is always some hacker who gets in !

   SAS 300 requires that auditors must always perform some substantive tests of material items as well as relying on internal controls. The inherent limitations of internal controls are the reason.

Summary

13. a. Internal control is defined as the whole system of controls, financial and otherwise, established by the management in order to carry on the business of the enterprise in an orderly and efficient manner, ensure adherence to management policies, safeguard the assets and secure as far as possible the completeness and accuracy of the records.

   b. The types of internal control include:
       i.   Organisation
       ii.   Segregation of duties
       iii. Physical controls
       iv.   Authorisation and Approval
       v.   Arithmetic and Accounting
       vi.   Personnel
       vii. Supervision
       viii. Management controls
       ix.   Acknowledgement of performance
       x.   Budgeting.

   c. The control environment is a new concept in auditing.

   d. internal controls have limitations.

Points to note

14. a.   The definition of internal control should be memorised.

b.   All entities have some sort of accounting system with some internal controls over the transactions. Indeed listed companies are required to have systems and report on them in accordance with the Cadbury Code. Auditors may rely on these controls as evidence of prevention or detection and correction of errors and irregularities but whether or not they do so depends on their assessment of the risks attached. In any event some substantive tests must be performed on all material balances and classes of transaction.

Case study for Chapter 14

Jason, Ian and Caroline Ltd operate a large shop in the centre of North Bromwich. They sell expensive reproduction antique furniture. Normally customers see the furniture in the shop and place an order for delivery in the company van within 4 weeks. The delay occurs because each sale results in a purchase order for one of the suppliers. On placing the order the customer pays by cash, cheque, credit card or signs a hire purchase agreement. There are 4 sales assistants and a van driver and a cashier in the shop. Accounting and purchasing is done by the manager and a part-time bookkeeper.

The three directors all have other businesses and review the company operations once a month at an all-day board meeting.

Discussion

Devise an internal control system for the shop.

Relate your system to the definition of internal control.

Identify the types of internal controls in your system.

Identify some costs of control that the auditor could perform.

Consider the auditor's attitude to the system.

Student self testing questions *Questions with answers apparent from the text*

1. a.   Define internal control (4) and control risk and tests of control. (2)
b.   List the types of internal controls. (6)
c.   What categories of internal controls are comprised in the term 'organisation'? (6)
d.   What functions should be segregated so that no two are under the control of one person? (6)
e.   What kinds of access to assets and records are there? (6)
f.   What types of arithmetical and accounting controls are possible? (6)
g.   What are the internal control objectives of personnel policies? (6)
h.   What personnel policies achieve these ends? (6)
i.   List some management controls. (6)
j.   What are the effects of acknowledgement of performance? (7)
k.   What budgeting benefits have internal control implications? (7)
l.   When are physical controls especially important? (6)
m.   List some physical controls. (6)
n.   How can theft of cheques in the post be prevented/detected? (10)

o. How can theft of cash sales be prevented/detected? (10)

p. How can teeming and lading be prevented? (10)

q. List suitable controls over a petty cash system. (10)

r. How can the issue of Fraudulent cheques be prevented? (10)

s. List some possible wages frauds. (10)

t. A plc pays B, a cousin of C who is an employee of A plc, for goods not supplied. How could this be engineered and how can it be prevented? (10)

u. E Ltd supplies F with goods but these are not charged to him. What measures could prevent this? (10)

v. List the benefits of a stock control system and how the benefits are achieved. (10)

w. How can the accuracy of a fixed asset register be assured? (10)

x. What is a control environment ? (11)

y. List some limitations of internal control. (12)

Exercises

1. Devise detailed internal control systems for the following:

   a. **Cheques through the post and over the counter**

   Joe's garage Ltd repair and service cars and vans. About half the customers are given credit and pay by cheque through the post. The garage also deal with new and used cars and sell petrol. Customers for these items pay by cash or credit card. There are some five clerical staff in the firm.

   b. **Cash tills in a public house**

   The Bull and Bear has a single bar/lounge and usually there are some 4 bar staff on duty sometimes including the manager. Bar meals are also sold.

   c. **Cheque payments**

   Scarecrow Fashions Mfg. Ltd have some 100 suppliers and a healthy balance at the bank. Many suppliers offer settlement discount. The four directors are often away on business and the office staff is run, in the absence of the financial director, by Mrs Tan who is a part qualified accountant. She has 6 staff.

   d. **Wages**

   Dolerite Builders Ltd carry out repairs and extensions to domestic and business premises. They have 50 workmen all of whom are paid weekly in cash and some 30 firms of subcontractors who are paid weekly by cheque. The company have some 6 office staff. Turnover of workmen and sub-contractors is fairly rapid as the company do not pay well.

   e. **Sales and debtors**

   Caxgut Publishers Ltd publish books (some 150 titles). Books are kept in a large warehouse. Orders are received by post and telephone from bookshops and from individuals.

   f. **Plant and machinery**

   OBSO Manufacturing manufacture electrical apparatus using a mix of sophisticated and traditional machinery (lathes, presses etc). The company regularly change the sophisticated machinery as items become obsolete and also have a need for constant servicing and maintenance of the plant. The company have some 10 clerical staff.

2. a. In Smoothe Tyres Ltd, a company that supplies and fits new tyres to customers' cars, a year end purchase/sales./stock reconciliation revealed that over 200 tyres valued at £11,000 were missing. There are no continuous stock records and the 7 tyre fitters select the tyres from stock, fit them and make out the invoices at the computer terminal.

   b. Jezebel is the cashier of Gungho Ltd, a company which supplies security services. She is in sole charge of payments of expense claims by security personnel. On examining the draft annual accounts, Saif, the chief executive is appalled to find that the total of expenses claims is double that of the previous year when turnover was only 5% lower.

   c. The gross profit of Sundree Ltd, a firm of wholesalers was lower than expected. An investigation revealed that Margaret who produced the sales invoices (using a computerised system) had priced many invoices in the East Anglian region at below the correct prices. Her husband, Michael is the sales rep for that region and his commission had increased by 50% in the year.

   d. The treasurer of St Mary's Church confessed to the newly appointed honorary auditor (a certified accountant) that she had misappropriated the weekly offering envelopes of several parishioners over a period of years. The Church Wardens always counted and banked the notes and coins in the collections but handed the envelopes to the treasurer.

   e. The newly appointed auditor of Tinpot PLC, a small manufacturing company attempted to reconcile the individual items of plant with purchases and disposals since the last such reconciliation five years previously. This revealed some forty machines were unaccounted for.

   What might have happened in each of these cases?

   Design internal control procedures to prevent recurrence.

Examination question (Answer begins on page 543)

1. Southern Engineering Ltd has undergone a period of substantial growth following its establishment five years ago by two engineers. Because of a lack of accounting expertise within the company it has traditionally looked to its auditors, Smith and Jones, for accounting services in the preparation of annual financial statements as well as for the statutory audit function. Smith and Jones have also provided advice in connection with the company's accounting and internal control systems.

   Smith and Jones is a two partner firm of certified accountants whose clients are mainly sole traders, partnerships and small limited companies. Although Southern Engineering Ltd was originally a typical small company client, its growth over the last 5 years has meant that it now accounts for approximately 20% of Smith and Jones' gross fee income and the company has indicated that it may wish to issue shares on the unlisted securities market in the near future.

   During the course of their five year period as auditors of Southern Engineering Ltd., Smith and Jones have been particularly concerned that the company, as it grew, should develop internal control systems appropriate to its size and complexity.

   Required:

   a. State what you understand by internal control. (3 marks)

b. State and explain any four types of internal control giving an illustration of each type of control as it might be found in Southern Engineering Ltd's system for the purchasing of materials and the control of stocks. Your answer should suggest possible consequences if your illustrated control was not in operation.   (12 marks)

c. Discuss the difficulties which Southern Engineering Ltd might have faced in establishing efficient and effective internal control as it grew over its first five years of existence.   (5 marks)

(ACCA)

Note that the unlisted securities market has been replaced by the Alternative Investment Market.

Examination questions without answers

2. Give four examples of internal controls, with a description of each.

(LCC 89) (12 marks)

3. Internal control is defined in the Auditing Guideline, L204, *Internal Controls,* as 'the whole system of controls, financial and otherwise, established by the management in order to carry on the business of the enterprise in an orderly and efficient manner, ensure adherence to management policies, safeguard the assets and secure, as far as possible, the completeness and accuracy of the accountancy records'. The individual components of an internal control system are known as 'controls' or 'internal controls'.

In most businesses it is possible to identify an 'internal control structure' which comprises the following three 'tiers' or elements:

− The control environment
− The accounting systems
− The internal accounting controls

Requirement

a. Explain briefly your understanding of each of these three elements of internal control and how they interrelate.

b. Set out the key elements of the control environment which should be assessed by the auditor.

c. Set out the main objectives of an effective accounting system.

(ICAI 95)

4. In the accounts department of your client, Merchants plc, there is a section devoted to the calculation and authorisation of discounts, and allowances for returned goods, to customers.

i. What internal control would you recommend for this section?   (12 marks)

ii. How far is the external auditor concerned with this section?   (3 marks)

(LCC88) (Total 15 marks)

5. a. A company's system of internal control governing wages should ensure that fraud and error cannot occur.

Four possible frauds which might exist in a poorly controlled wages department are:

i. inclusion of dummy (non-existent) names on the payroll;

ii. overcasting of wages sheets, thus inflating the cash drawn for wages and allowing the surplus to be removed;

iii. inclusion of unauthorised overtime;

iv. misappropriation of unclaimed wages.

You are required to state and briefly explain, for *each* type of fraud listed above, *two* controls which would contribute towards preventing the fraud. (12 marks)

b. To what extent is the external auditor currently required, as part of the audit, to concern himself with the detection of fraud? (3 marks)

c. What action should the external auditor take if the audit reveals that the system of internal control over wages is unsatisfactory? (5 marks)

(ICA 92) (Total 20 marks)

6. You are the auditor of SELLIT Ltd., a large furniture manufacturing company with a well established sales department.

Prior to the commencement of the current year audit, you are considering changing the audit approach in the sales and cash receipts cycle from a fully substantive approach to an approach where reliance would be placed on internal controls ie a reliance approach. You have decided to commit your thoughts to paper and to prepare some guidance notes for your audit team.

Requirement

a. Describe briefly the reasons why a reliance approach *may* be preferable and detail the issues that should be considered before deciding to change to a reliance approach. (2 marks)

b. Prepare a list of internal control objectives that you would expect to find in a reliable system of internal controls over the sales and cash receipts cycle. (4 marks)

c. Set out the more common features of internal control over sales and cash receipts that should exist to meet the control objectives outlined at (b) above. (16 marks)

(ICAI 92) (Total 22 marks)

7. As a senior partner in the auditors to Fat & Thin plc, you are concerned about the efficiency of your client's internal control covering the acquisition of small tools.

Prepare an Internal Control Questionnaire, covering the acquisition of small tools. (13 marks)

(LCCI 90)

15 Audit testing

Introduction

1. This chapter discusses the vocabulary of audit testing and describes the purposes and uses of the different types of testing.

Walk through checks

2. The modern audit requires the auditor to have in his working papers a record of the accounting system and its associated internal controls. This record may be in the form of simple written descriptions, the answers to an Internal Control Questionnaire or as flow charts, checklists or a combination of these.

3. Auditors need to have an understanding of a client's accounting system and control environment. From this initial understanding it is possible to plan the audit and deter-

mine the audit approach. The audit approach may be to rely on substantive tests alone or, in some areas, to rely partly on internal control evidence as well as substantive tests. The problem is how to gain an initial understanding of the accounting system and associated control environment. One way is to use walk-through tests.

Walk-through tests are defined as tracing one or more transactions through the accounting system and observing the application of relevant aspects of the internal control system. For example the auditor might look at the sales system in a wholesaler and trace a sale from its initiation through to the sales figure in the Profit and Loss Account. This will involve looking at customers orders, how the orders are documented and recorded, credit control approval, how the goods are selected and packed, raising of an advice note and /or delivery note, invoicing procedures, recording the invoice in the books of account and so on. At each stage the controls applied (for example applying consecutive numbers to customer order documents and subsequent sequence checks to ensure all orders are invoiced) are examined.

4. When the auditor has done the audit for several years then the audit files will contain a record of the systems but each year the auditor needs to confirm her understanding by:

   – enquiries of supervisory and other staff at all levels of the enterprise

   – inspection of client documentation such as procedure manuals, job descriptions and systems descriptions. You will appreciate that a lack of these may imply a weak control environment. Note that the existence of procedure manuals etc does not necessarily imply that the prescriptions in them are actually carried out in practice!

   – inspection of relevant documents and records produced by the system

   – observation of the entity's activities and operations including watching personnel actually performing procedures.

5. If the preliminary understanding of the systems and control environment leads the auditor to plan the audit to include some internal control reliance then the system needs to be investigated in more depth than the knowledge provided by walk-through tests. See Chapter 17 for ICQs and flowcharts etc.

6. Walk through checks will also be applied:

   a. In any situation where the auditor has not obtained his description of the system from a personal investigation of the system by questioning operating staff and examining documents and records.

   b. At the final audit when he needs to review the system from the date of the interim completion to the year end. He must first determine if the system has changed and walk through checks will achieve this.

Tests of control

7. Test of control are tests to obtain audit evidence about the effective operation of the accounting and control systems – that is, that properly designed controls identified in the preliminary assessment of control risk exist in fact and have operated throughout the relevant period.

   Test of control are sometimes called *compliance tests*.

8. The first stage in the auditor's assessment of the reliability of a system is a preliminary review of the effectiveness of the system by using an internal control evaluation ques-

tionnaire which contains key questions. For example, to test the effectiveness of the wages system, he would ask questions including:

Can wages be paid to piecework personnel for work not done?

The system would then be inspected to see if it included procedures to ensure that this could not happen.

9. If the system appears to be defective or weak then the auditor may need to abandon the systems approach and apply substantive tests. If the system is effective, then the next stage is for the auditor to obtain evidence that the system is applied as in his description *at all times*. This evidence is obtained by examining a sample of the transactions to determine if each has been treated as required by the system, ie to see if the system has been complied with.

10. Two points must be made about compliance tests:

    a. It is the application of the system that is being tested not the transaction although the testing is through the medium of the transactions.

    b. If discovery is made that the system was not complied with in any particular, then:

        i.   he may need to revise his system description and re-appraise its effectiveness

        ii. he will need to determine if the failure of compliance was an isolated instance or was symptomatic.

    It may be that a larger sample may need to be taken.

11. As an example of a test of control, suppose that a system provided that all credit notes issued by the client had to be approved by the sales manager and that a space was provided on each credit note for his initials. Then the auditor would inspect a sample of the credit notes to determine if all of them had been initialled. In practice other internal controls (eg checking of calculations or coding) would be tested on the same credit notes.

Substantive tests

12. Substantive procedures are tests to obtain audit evidence to detect material misstatement in the financial statements. They are generally of two types:

    a. analytical procedures – see Chapter 16.

    b. other substantive procedures, such as tests of details of transactions and balances, reviews of minutes of directors' meetings and enquiry.

13. From this definition, you may deduce that all audit work comes within the compass of substantive testing. However it is usually used to mean all tests other than tests of control. A substantive test is any test which seeks *direct evidence* of the correct treatment of a transaction, a balance, an asset, a liability, or any item in the books or the Accounts. Analytical review is also seen as a separate type of test.

14. Some examples:

    a. Of a transaction – the sale of a piece of plant will require the auditor to examine the copy invoice, the authorisation, the entry in the plant register and other books, the accounting treatment and some evidence that the price obtained was reasonable.

    b. Of a balance – direct confirmation of the balance in a deposit account obtained from the bank.

    c. Analytical review – evidence of the correctness of cut off by examining the gross profit ratio.

d. Completeness of information – obtaining confirmation from a client's legal adviser that all potential payments from current litigation had been considered.

e. Accuracy of information – obtaining from each director a confirmation that an accurate statement of remuneration and expenses had been obtained.

f. Validity of information – validity means based on evidence that can be supported. For example, a provision for future warranty claims may be extremely difficult to estimate in precise monetary terms. If such a provision is made in the Accounts, the auditor would need to apply substantive tests to determine its validity, ie that it was supported by adequate evidence.

Techniques of audit testing

15. There are several categories of auditing test technique:

a. **Inspection** – reviewing or examining records, documents or tangible assets. Examples are:

    i. examining a sample of piecework records for evidence of inspection by inspection staff and approval by the works manager, gives evidence of compliance with the system presented.

    ii. examining copy sales invoices for initials of the member of staff charged with checking invoice calculations, gives evidence of compliance with a system which prevents calculation errors.

    iii. inspecting buildings provides evidence of the existence (but not ownership or value) of the building.

b. **Observation** – looking at an operation or procedure being performed by others with a view to determining the manner of its performance. Examples:

    i. observing the giving out of wage packets to see that internal control procedures are adhered to.

    ii. observing the counting of stock at the year end with the same end in view.

Observation gives evidence of how the procedures are performed at the time of observation but perhaps not at any other time. It is a general truth that actions are rarely performed in the presence of the observer without the observer affecting the operation in some way.

c. **Enquiry** – seeking relevant information from knowledgeable persons inside or outside the enterprise, whether formally or informally, orally or in writing. Examples are:

    i. Routine queries to client staff such as 'Why is invoice copy 643 missing?'

    ii. Seeking formal representations from management on the value of a large subsidiary company in a volatile country.

    iii. Circularising debtors.

d. **Computation** – checking the arithmetical accuracy of accounting records or performing independent calculations. Examples:

    i. Checking (by sampling!) the accuracy of stock extensions (quantity x cost price).

    ii. Verifying the accuracy of detailed interest calculations by a global calculation.

Rotational tests

16. Rotational tests are of two kinds:

    a. Rotation of audit emphasis – the auditor performs a systems audit on all areas of the client's business every year but each year he selects one area (wages, sales, stock control, purchasing, etc) for special in–depth testing.

    b. Visit rotation – where the client has numerous branches, factories, locations, etc., it may be impractical to visit them all each year. In such cases the auditor visits them in rotation so that while each will not be visited every year, all will be visited over a period of years.

17. There is an opinion that each yearly audit is independent of all others and adequate evidence must be found in all areas each year. However, auditors normally serve for many years and rotational testing makes sense in terms of effectiveness and efficiency.

18. It is vital that rotational tests are carried out randomly so that client staff do not know which areas or locations will be selected in any one year.

Summary

19. a. The language of audit testing includes the following definitions:

    i. Walk-through tests are defined as tracing one or more transactions through the accounting system and observing the application of relevant aspects of the internal control system.

    ii. Test of control are tests to obtain audit evidence about the effective operation of the accounting and control systems – that is, that properly designed controls identified in the preliminary assessment of control risk exist in fact and have operated throughout the relevant period.

    iii. Substantive procedures are tests to obtain audit evidence to detect material misstatement in the financial statements

    iv. Rotational tests are tests carried out on the assumption that the auditor will be in office for several years and can in any individual year bring to bear special emphasis on a particular area of the affairs of his client or visit particular branches.

    b. Techniques of audit testing include:

    i. Inspection – looking at records, documents and tangible assets.

    ii. Observation – looking at procedures actually taking place.

    iii. Enquiry – seeking relevant information by asking questions, orally or in writing, to persons or institutions inside or outside the clients.

    iv. Computation – checking or performing calculations.

Points to note

20. a. The language of audit testing varies from firm to firm but in this manual I have followed the words used in the auditing standards.

    b. The language used is less important that understanding the *purpose* of a test. One common audit test is the checking of codings put on purchase and expense invoices.

Such codings are extremely important because an error may lead to mis-analysis between capital and revenue expenditure. The auditor may check a large random sample. By so doing he may be:

i.   testing that the *system* works. Various controls may be applied to the coding. Do the controls work? A good way of seeking evidence that the controls are applied (compliance testing) may be to verify a sample of the results.

ii. seeking direct evidence that the accounting records correctly reflect the nature of expenditure incurred. This will be a substantive test. The difference is a little subtle but it is important in practice that the auditor knows precisely what evidence he is getting from a test.

c.   The distinction between *inspection* and *observation* should be noted. Use observation to mean only the looking at the actual performance of an operation or procedure.

Inspection has a much wider meaning including that of inspecting written records to obtain evidence that an operation or procedure did take place. Another word for observation is witnessing.

d.   Two old words, still much used are depth tests and block tests. These words describe what auditors do but do not explain why they are doing the tests. As many audit staff follow audit programmes without really knowing what they are doing, these words are best avoided.

e.   The definition of the various types of tests should be commited to memory.

f.   The extent of use of each type of test can be summarised as:

  – Walk-through test are used in making the preliminary assessment of the accounting system and control environment.

  – all items should be subject to substantive tests but the extent of such tests depends on the materiality of the item and the inherent risk of misstatement attached to the item. As an example of materiality consider petty cash which, even if grossly wrong, may be unlikely to be affect the view given by the financial statements. As an example of inherent risk, consider the evaluation of the value of work in progress in a civil engineering company. The valuation may be critical to the financial statements yet it may be very difficult to establish precisely.

  – the auditors may expect to be able to rely upon their preliminary assessment of control risk to reduce the extent of their substantive procedures. In such cases they should make a preliminary assessment of control risk for material financial statement assertions and should then plan and perform tests of control to support that assessment. For example the preliminary walk-through tests might indicate good controls over fees in a college. The auditors may then assess the control risk attached to the assertion that all fees, that should have been invoiced, have been invoiced. Tests of control should then be planned and performed to support that assessment. If such tests do support the assessment, then the extent of substantive tests can be reduced.

  – in particular cases (especially small enterprises) the auditors may conclude that accounting and internal control systems are not effective or they may conclude that it is likely to be inefficient to adopt an audit approach which relies on tests of control.

g. Tests of control may include:

- corroborative enquiries about, and observation of, internal control functions. For example being present at the post opening of a mail order firm

- inspection of documents supporting controls or events to gain audit evidence that internal controls have operated properly. For example inspecting works manager approval for capital expenditure and reports of completed installation of new plant before payment was made.

- examination of management reviews. For example examination of minutes of management where salary rates were decided upon.

- testing of the internal controls operating on specific computerised applications – see Chapter 53.

- reperformance of control procedures. For example, making sequence tests or re-reconciling bank statements to the cash book.

Case study for Chapter 15

Foley Widgets Ltd are a wholly owned subsidiary of a German group. Foley trade as stockists of the German parent's products and sell to engineering companies all over the UK and the Republic of Ireland. All sales are on credit. Tiswas & Co. are the newly appointed auditors and are planning their audit of the sales area. The system is as laid down in a manual (in English) which has been given to Tiswas. The system in essence is:

a. Orders are received by telephone, telex or through the company's 4 representatives.

b. Orders are first cleared to a list of acceptable customers provided weekly by credit control.

c. Accepted orders are transcribed onto pre-numbered order forms. These are in triplicate – 1 retained, 2 to accounts, 3 to warehouse.

d. Warehouse pack the goods and send them with the order and pre-numbered despatch note to despatch section. The despatch note is in quadruplicate (1 to retain in packing, 2 to customer, 3 to accounts, 4 to retain in despatch).

e. Despatch send goods by carrier.

f. Accounts invoice the goods – pricing and VAT are added at this point. Invoice is in triplicate – 1 retained, 2 customer, 3 sales. You may invent or assume controls added to this outline.

Discussion

What audit tests would be done on this system?

What audit evidence would be obtained from these tests?

Relate these tests to the overall audit objectives.

Student self testing questions *Questions with answers apparent from the text*

1. a. Define walk through checks. (3)
    b. What is the purpose of a walk through check? (3)
    c. Define test of control. (7)
    d. What is the purpose of a test of control? (9)
    e. Define substantive test. (12)

f. List the techniques of audit testing. (15)

g. When are Walk-Through tests used? (4, 6)

h. What is tested by a test of control? (10)

j. What might an auditor do if tests of control show that a control, on which he wishes to rely, is not always complied with? (10)

k. Give examples of a substantive test:
   - of a transaction
   - of a balance
   - in analytical review
   - for completeness of information
   - for accuracy of information
   - for validity of information (14)

l. Distinguish inspection and observation. (15, 20)

m. List the sub-categories of enquiry (15)

n. When are rotational tests used? (16)

o. What two views of auditing are involved in the decision to or to not test rotationally? (17)

Exercises

1. Devise audit tests in the following situations:

   a. *Industrial wages.* Gong Manufacturing plc are makers of motor car parts in a factory in North Bromwich. They employ 500 factory workers paying on a mixture of time, piecework and bonus systems. They have a sophisticated system of budgetary control and standard costing. They have a very good personnel department with full records and excellent systems of internal control over wages.

   b. *Industrial wages.* Backward Ltd are an engineering company, also in North Bromwich. They have 100 workers and pay by a mixture of time and piecework. They have no system of budgetary control or standard costing. Pricing is by an ad hoc system of rather rudimentary costing and market based pricing. They are none the less profitable. They have no personnel department but the wages department have a wages system which holds some information about each employee. Basically the wage calculation/payment is:

   The wage department has 4 staff (who do have other duties not connected with accounting). Each Monday morning they take the previous weeks clock cards from the gate (which is well supervised). The piece work cards are taken from the works manager who signs them as approved. They are completed by the various foremen who also sign them.

   The cards and piecework sheets are summarised by Angela and Jill and then exchanged and checked. Brian then enters the data on duplicate wage sheets and calculates the wages due and the deductions. Philip checks a sample of the calculations and does the totalling. New employees/leavers are subject to a system of weekly reports from the works manager (pre-numbered).

   Georgia, the chief accountant checks the totalling and prepares the cheque for signature by two directors, both of whom inspect the wages sheets. The cheque is cashed by Simon the security guard using a different car and route each week.

The wages envelopes are made up by Walter and Ellen the sales ledger clerks in a locked room and the copy wage slips inserted in the envelopes.

Payment to the workers is made by Henry, a director in the presence of the foreman. A signature is obtained from each worker in a special book.

c. *Sales and debtors.* Ficab Ltd sell office furniture on credit from a large warehouse in Dudley to industrial and commercial customers.

Orders are obtained through representatives, agents and directly from customers. Deliveries are by the company's own pantechnicons. The system is:

– orders are received by various means and transcribed onto quadruplicate pre-numbered order forms with details for customer name etc, codes and description of furniture and also source of order (important for commission).

– firstly a credit check is made. New customers are credit enquired and the SOF is held until completed or the customer is rejected. Existing customers are enquired into as to outstanding amounts.

– the goods are always in stock as all catalogue items are held.

– copy one of the order is sent to accounts for invoicing using a micro computer which produces a disc (daily) with details of each invoice including a consecutive number.

– print outs are made of each invoice in duplicate with top copy going to the customer. The computer also produces a daybook listing. The disc is used to update the sales ledger disc and also to calculate commissions. Copy invoices are filed with the SOF.

– the second and third copies of the SOF are sent to the warehouse where the goods are assembled for despatch. Goods are labelled with the SOF number. The second copy is retained in the warehouse on a file. The third and fourth copies go with the goods to the customer. The third copy is signed by the customer and is brought back for attachment to the second copy. The gatekeeper ensures that no goods leave the factory without a label and a SOF.

– cheques are received through the post and paid into bank. Bankings are put on disc. The disc is used to update the sales ledger file. Matched invoices and cheques and discounts are eliminated after customers statements of account are printed out in duplicate. Copy one to customer, copy two retained.

– the chief accountant add lists the totals of the statements and prepared a monthly control account using the invoice listing and the cash book listing. He also reviews and actions any overdue accounts.

(This exercise can also be used as a flowchart exercise).

2. *Purchases.* Steel is in charge (with two assistants: Thicke, who is his cousin and Thynne, who is his next door neighbour) of the components warehouse of Pieces Manufacturing Ltd. Dodd is the chief buyer (he also has two assistants) and Peck is the works manager. Tulp is in charge of the bought ledger. The system for purchases of components is:

a. Peck's secretary makes out requisitions on a word processor for new components and Steel does the same for stocks of components where the bins are nearly empty. Dodd or his assistants make out purchases orders on duplicate forms which are pre-printed. They order from the firms that normally supply the components but obtain tenders for new components after discussion with Peck. Most of the components are standard things that many firms can supply. Dodd puts consecutive numbers on the order forms and the top copy goes to the supplier and the bottom copy is sent to Steel. Peck or Dodd usually chase overdue orders when they have difficulties because of shortages.

When the goods arrive, they are signed for by Lewis, the gatekeeper, who sends them through to Steel. Steel checks them against the order and sends the delivery note to Tulp. Tulp checks the invoice, when it arrives, against the delivery note and enters the details in the computer. The computer gives each invoice a consecutive number. At the end of the month the computer adds invoices due for payment to each supplier and prints out a cheque and a remittance advice. The remittance advices and the cheques are sent to Britten who is the very busy chief executive. She signs them and Tulp sends them off.

Short deliveries etc are taken up with the suppliers by Steel. Tulp ignores creditors' statements.

Required

a. Enumerate the weaknesses in this system and the possible consequences.

b. Suggest some improvements.

c. What are the audit objectives in connection with the purchase of components?

d. What controls might be relied upon by Mills, the auditor?

e. How might these be tested by Mills?

f. What other audit tests might Mills apply to detect any misstatement in the Profit and Loss Account figure for purchases of components?

Note: After Chapter 17, you should also be able to flowchart this system.

Examination questions without answers

1. The senior audit clerk in charge of the audit of a small company observes from the previous year's flow chart that Mr. Lennonserp was the only staff member authorised to make changes in rates of pay for the company's salaried and weekly staff. Half way through the current year, Mr. Lennonserp retired and this particular function was not allocated to anyone else.

   What action should the senior audit clerk take?

   (LCC 89) (15 marks)

2. Draft out an Audit Programme to cover that part of the wages audit of a large manufacturing company that relates to the *actual payment of wages*.

   Note: You are not required to deal with the collection of information for wages, preparation of wage sheets, or calculation of wages.

   (LCC 88) (12 marks)

3. You are a senior working on the audit of a large chemical engineering company. One of your assistants on the audit has heard you mentioning the term 'audit objectives' and is confused as to exactly what the different audit objectives are in relation to various account balances.

   Requirement

   a. Identify the 7 audit objectives which are applicable to all account balances and classes of transactions. Define and illustrate each objective by reference to:

i.   trade debtors and sales; and

ii. trade creditors and purchases.

b.   Select *any 5* of the audit objectives identified at (a) (i) above. *For each one* of the 5 audit objectives selected, describe briefly *any* 2 audit tests that would provide the auditor with sufficient evidence to achieve the specific audit objective selected.

(ICAI 94)

16 Analytical review techniques

Introduction

1. Auditors are required to carry out procedures designed to obtain sufficient appropriate audit evidence to determine with reasonable confidence whether the financial statements are free of material misstatement. They are also required to evaluate the overall presentation of the financial statements, in order to ascertain whether they have been prepared in accordance with relevant legislation and accounting standards. The auditors have to give an opinion on whether the accounts give a true and fair view and comply with regulations.

2. Amongst the methods of obtaining audit evidence are internal control reliance, substantive tests and analytical review. This chapter is about analytical review.

3. There is a Statement of Auditing Standards SAS 410 *analytical procedures*. This SAS requires that auditors should apply analytical procedures at the planning and overall review stages of the audit. It also suggests that analytical procedures can be applied as *substantive procedures designed to obtain audit evidence directly.*

Definition

4. Analytical review can be defined as:

   The study of relationships between elements of financial information expected to conform to a predictable pattern based on the organisation's experience and between financial information and non-financial information. Information is compared with comparable information for a prior period or periods, with anticipated results and with information relating to similar organisations.

   In addition, analytical review involves:

   a.   Investigating unexpected variations identified by analytical review.

   b.   Obtaining and *substantiating* explanations for such variations.

   c.   Evaluating the results of analytical review with other audit evidence obtained eg by systems and substantive tests.

5. In an actual case this definition might be applied by examining:

   – increases in magnitude corresponding to inflation

   – changes in amounts consequent on changes in output levels

   – comparisons with previous periods

   – trends and ratios

- comparisons with budgets and forecasts
- comparisons with other, similar organisations eg by inter-firm comparison.

6. Similar techniques are also applied by management, investment analysts and internal auditors to provide information on the performance of an entity, the efficiency of its operations or the quality of its management. Note that in performing these techniques an auditor has a quite different purpose.

7. Analytical review can be simple tests comparing absolute magnitudes of different years, comparing ratios with earlier years, budgets and industry averages but also:

   a. using computer audit software

   b. using advanced statistical techniques eg multiple regression analysis.

Timing

8. Analytical review techniques will be applied throughout the audit but specific occasions include:

   a. At the planning stage. The auditor will hope to identify areas of potential risk or new developments so that he can plan his other audit procedures in these areas. As a simple example, the auditor might discover that the gross profit ratio in a retail organisation had changed from the 28 –30% of previous years to 24%. Or he might discover that a sales analysis revealed that exports had increased from 3% to 26% of turnover.

   b. Obtaining evidence. Modern audits with their emphasis on efficiency and economy depend heavily on analytical review as a valid audit technique used alone or in conjunction with internal control reliance and substantive testing.

      It can be reasonable to obtain assurance of the completeness, accuracy and validity of the transactions and balances by analytical review as by other types of audit evidence. For example, if the relative amounts under different expense headings repeat the pattern of previous years the auditor has evidence of the accuracy of expense invoice coding.

   c. At the final review stage of the audit. Analytical review techniques can provide support for the conclusions arrived at as a result of other work. For example, indications from external sources that profit margins have declined by 10% may support the declined Profit figure in a segment of the company whose figures have been audited by other means and found to be correct. The techniques are also used to assess the overall reasonableness of the financial statements as a whole.

Extent of use

9. Factors which might influence the extent of use of analytical review include:

   a. The *nature* of the entity and its operations. A long-established chain of similar shops which have changed little in the period under review will offer many opportunities for analytical review to be used as the primary source of audit evidence. Conversely a newly established manufacturer of high tech products will not.

   b. Knowledge gained in *previous audits* of the enterprise. The auditor will have experience of those areas where errors and difficulties arose and of those areas of greatest audit risk.

c. *Management's* own use of analytical review procedures. If management has a reliable system of budgetary control then the auditor will have a ready made source of explanation for variance. Also the reliability of information prepared for management will be a factor. Information subject to internal audit will be an example of reliable information.

d. Availability of *non-financial information* to back up financial information. Many companies record non-financial statistics (eg on production, input mixes etc). Some companies have to make returns of output (eg newspapers on circulation, dairies on gallonage etc). All this data can be used as evidence by an auditor.

e. The reliability, relevance and *comparability* of the information available. Clients that take part in inter-firm comparison exercises will be especially appropriate for analytical review evidence.

f. The *cost effectiveness* of the use of analytical review in relation to other forms of evidence. In general, analytical review is cheap but requires high quality (and therefore expensive) staff. Some analytical review techniques can be expensive if for example they involve complex statistical techniques (eg multiple regression) and computer audit software.

g. The availability of staff. Analytical review requires high quality staff with much intelligence, experience and training.

h. SAS 410 has a mandatory requirement that auditors should apply analytical procedures at the *planning* stage to assist in *understanding the entity's business,* in identifying areas of *potential audit risk* and in planning the *nature, timing and extent* of other audit procedures.

Procedures

10. The following remarks can be made:

a. Analytical review procedure can best be carried out on particular segments of the organisation eg the branch at Walsall or the paint division or the subsidiary in France. They can also be used on individual account areas such as creditors or fixed asset depreciation.

b. Analytical review is a *breaking down* of data into sub divisions for analysis over time, by product, by location, by management responsibility etc.

c. Analytical review techniques are not effective in reviewing an entity as a whole unless it is very small. The greater the *disaggregation* the better.

d. One approach is to identify the *factors* likely to have an effect on items in the accounts; to ascertain or assess the probable *relationship* with these factors and items; and then to *predict* the value of the items in the light of the factors. Then the predicted value of the items can be *compared* with the *actual* recorded amounts. As an example gas consumption is a function of temperature. A knowledge of temperature daily will permit an auditor to estimate gas consumption. If actual consumption is similar to that expected the auditor has evidence of the correctness of sales value of gas.

e. The auditor should consider the implications of significant *fluctuations,* unusual items or relationships that are unexpected or inconsistent with evidence from other sources. Similarly he should consider the implications of predicted fluctuations that fail to occur.

The expense of heating oil consumed at the Bridgnorth factory increased by 6% over the previous year. The auditor knows that in the Period heating oil prices were 23% on average lower than in the previous period.

f. Any significant variations should be discussed with management who usually have an explanation for them. Independent evidence must then be sought.

g. The auditor's reactions to significant fluctuations or unexpected values will vary according to the stage of the audit:

- at the planning stage, the auditor will plan suitable substantive tests

- at the testing stage of the audit, further tests and other techniques will be indicated

- at the final stage the unexpected should not happen!

h. All fluctuations and unexpected values must be fully investigated and sufficient audit evidence obtained.

i. As with all audit work, analytical procedures should be fully documented in the working papers. The files should include:

- the information examined, the sources of that information and the factors considered in establishing the reliability of the information

- the extent and nature of material variations found

- the *sources* and *level* of management from which explanations were sought and obtained

- the *verification* of those explanations

- any further action taken eg further audit testing

- the *conclusions drawn by the auditor*.

Example of use of analytical techniques

11. Zilpha Fashion Shops plc own a chain of high fashion shops in major towns. Each shop is operated by a separate subsidiary company. All subsidiaries buy from the Parent. The auditor of the Covhampton shop is reviewing the accounts for the year ending 31.1.-6 before starting the audit.

These reveal (in extract):

(all in £'000)	19-5	19-6	budget 19-6
turnover	600	638	640
cost of sales	400	459	425
gross profit	200	179	215
wages	78	71	70
overheads	70	75	74
net profit	52	33	71
stock	58	53	62
creditors	71	79	74

External data known to Fiona the auditor includes:

- rate of inflation – 5%

- a University survey of the traders in the Precinct in which the shop is situated indicates a 5% growth in real terms

- the rate of gross profit achieved by other shops in the group was 34% and average stock was 45 days worth
- creditors in three other shops averaged 13% of turnover
- wages in the other shops averaged 13% of turnover.

12. From all this data, Fiona could:

   a. Compute estimated turnover as $600*1.05*1.05 = 661$. The actual turnover is significantly less. The difference must be investigated.

   b. Gross Profit from the turnover should be $638*.34 = 217$. Actual rate of gross profit is only 28%.

   c. Stock should be about 45 days worth – $459*45/365 = 56$. Actual is lower but not materially so.

   d. Creditors should be $459*65/365 = 82$. This confirms the figure. In any case this figure can be confirmed by head office.

   e. Wages perhaps ought to be $638*.13 = 83$. If the direction of causation was reversed turnover should be $71*100/13 = 546$. Wages do agree with budget and should be confirmable by considering the numbers on the staff.

   f. Other expenses should perhaps have risen by 5% but they should be reviewed after disaggregation.

Conclusions:

   a. Stock and creditors are in line with expectations.

   b. Globally other overheads are out of line and disaggregation is required.

   c. Sales are lower than expected. Causes may be misappropriation of stock or cash. Close investigation is required.

   d. Gross profit is way out of line. This does not appear to be cut off errors as stock and creditors seem to be about right. Debtors are negligible in this type of retail business. (Customers pay by cash, cheque or credit card). It seems that misappropriation of stock or cash has occurred. Full investigation is required. It may be of course that the management have other explanations – burglary losses, excessive shoplifting, price competition, sales of old stock at low prices etc.

Summary

13. a. Amongst the Procedures for obtaining audit evidence available to an auditor are analytical review techniques.

   b. Analytical review can be and should be carried out at all stages of the audit from Planning to final review.

   c. The extent of use of analytical review depends on:
      - nature and operations of the client
      - knowledge from previous audit
      - management's use of similar techniques
      - availability of non-financial information
      - reliability, relevance and comparability of available information

       – cost effectiveness of analytical review techniques in comparison with other audit techniques

       – quality of audit staff.

   d. Procedures include:

       – disaggregation

       – concentration on segments or single areas

       – identifying influences, assessing mathematical relationships, predicting values, comparing predictions with actual

       – examining unexpected values and seeking explanations which must be fully verified.

Points to note

14. a. Any relationship perceived between variables must be plausible. Thus debtors and sales have a plausible relationship. The relationship found should be reasonable. The relationship in this example is clearly relevant to audit objectives. However no plausible relationship can be established between say selling expenses and work in progress in a manufacturing company.

   b. Reliable substantive evidence of the correctness of the magnitude of an item might be established by comparing it with another magnitude eg salaries from staffing numbers. However both magnitudes may be wrong.

   c. The nature of analytical review includes a comparison over time and the use of past experience on the audit. Therefore it is desirable to build up a picture of the organisation and the relationship between magnitudes in the permanent files.

   d. There is a relationship between the use of analytical review and the reliability of the information being reviewed. Information which is subject to good control procedures is clearly more susceptible to analytical review techniques than other information.

   e. Materiality is very important here. The auditor will often rely largely or wholly on analytical review techniques in areas judged to be not material. He would normally rely on a combination of analytical review, substantive testing and internal controls for material items.

   f. Finding that the gross profit ratio is unchanged from one year to the next is not of itself good audit evidence of the correctness of that ratio. All years may have the same built in errors.

   g. Analytical review is especially useful in obtaining evidence of *completeness* of accounting magnitudes.

   h. If anomalies are found and inadequate explanations are received then further audit work will be necessary. If doubts remain and cannot be resolved then the auditor may consider qualifying his report for uncertainty.

Case study 1 for Chapter 16

Odo Einstein MBA, FCA is about to embark on the audit of HOSIAH WHOLESALE HEALTH FOODS LTD. The company have been established for 5 years and have been modestly successful. Einstein has not encountered many problems in the past except for debt collection problems and bad debts. A feature of the accounts each year has been the large amount of stock. The management is good and monthly accounts are prepared by Hortensia Goodbody FCCA who was head hunted from the auditors. The accounts are disaggregated for management purposes into dried goods, tinned goods and specialty imports.

Discussion

a. To what extent can Odo engage in analytical techniques?

b. Devise analytical techniques using financial and non financial data for verifying the expense 'motor van running expenses'. The company have 20 vans.

c. Devise analytical techniques for verifying sales figures. Odo is particularly worried that he has no systems assurance that all sales have been invoiced.

Case study 2 for Chapter 16

The Annual Accounts of Dorb Paints plc are being audited by Ann Tick of Sooper Brothers, Certified Accountants. She is investigating the item salaries and national insurance. There is also an item Wages and national insurance. The company is large (turnover £40 million) and salaries is material. The company have separate personnel and wages departments with extensive records.

Discussion

Devise a selection of analytical review procedures to enable Ann to avoid detailed investigation of the salaries area.

Student self testing questions

Questions with answers apparent from the text

1. a. What methods of obtaining audit evidence are there? (2)
    b. Define analytical review. (4)
    c. When can analytical review be used? (8)
    d. What factors influence the extent of use of analytical review? (9)
    e. List the procedures that can be used. (10)
    f. List some analytical review procedures. (5)
    g. What actions can an auditor take if he finds fluctuations or unexpected magnitudes? (10)

Exercises *(on Chapters 15 and 16)*

1. Aleph Ltd import and then wholesale widget fittings. Turnover is £3 million and the company is fully computerised and has an excellent system of budgetary control. They also subscribe to the inter firm comparison scheme of the national association of widget importers and traders.

    Devise analytical review tests for the following items:

    a. Total Sales
    b. Wages
    c. Stocks

    d. Debtors

    e. Bad debts (this item is material)

    f. Motor expenses

    g. Petty cash expenditure

2. Cheepo Animal Feeds Ltd wholesale animal feed in sacks to farmers and wholesalers. Sales are obtained largely through agents and some 20,000 invoices a year are put through with commission being due on about 15,000. There are some 80 agents.

   Most orders are telephoned to the company but a few come by post or fax. Many of the orders are phoned through by the agent concerned but much repeat business (on which commission is due) is phoned in by the customer. The sales department clerks make out a sales order form and perform the following work:

   a. Check customer is approved or perform credit control checks for new customers.

   b. Check goods are in stock (form is held until stock is in).

   c. Mark SOF with name and code number of agent if commission is due. This is obtained from a list of customers with agent (if any) stated. The credit control procedure includes adding customer and agent to this list.

   All SOFs are checked and countersigned by the sales manager or his assistant. They include a check on the agent coding.

   The SOFs go to despatch and a good system exists to ensure all goods are invoiced. The invoices are made out by computer from details input from the SOF. All such inputs must have an agent code and invoices where no commission is payable must have code 00 input to be accepted.

   The invoice disc is used to make out commission statements for the agents monthly.

   Required:

   a. The commission is 10% of sales price and is material to the company. What aspects of the item 'sales commission' appearing in the accounts would the auditor seek evidence on?

   b. What audit tests could be devised to acquire such evidence?

3. Nixon Ltd is a second hand car dealer. He acquires cars from auctions, from other dealers, from the public, and from trade-ins. He always pays by cheque and maintains a cash book and a file of vouchers appertaining to these purchases.

   Sales are made to the general public and occasionally to other dealers. The money from these sales comes in the form of cash, cheques or from hire purchase companies. All sales are on invoices which are consecutively numbered. He obtains a commission from the hire purchase companies which comes by cheques monthly with commission statements.

   All purchases are entered in a stock book with details of the car, the supplier and the price. Any repairs etc required are done and invoiced by another company and paid by cheque monthly against a monthly statement. Such repairs are noted in the stock book also.

   Sales are entered in the stock book with details of price, customer etc.

   Some 500 cars are sold annually.

   Required:

   a. What aspects of the items 'sales', 'purchases' and 'stocks' would require audit evidence?

   b. What audit tests would tend to provide such audit evidence?

Examination question *(Answer begins on page 000)*

1. In the course of your audit review of the accounts of Ramos plc, you have tabulated the following statistics:

Year	Gross Profit Ratio	Stock Turnover
49	19.8%	12.0 times
50	18.5%	11.3 times
51	18.6%	11.3 times
52	25.7%	9.4 times
53	30.6%	8.6 times

Required

a. What conclusions may be drawn from the above statistics? (6 marks)

b. As a consequence, what auditing procedures would you consider undertaking?
(9 marks)
(LCCI 92) (Total 15 marks)

Examination questions without answers

2. You are the audit senior in charge of the audit of Tetterby Tools plc, a large manufacturing company. The following information has been provided to you in advance of the finalisation of the audit for the year to 30 April 1990:

PROFIT AND LOSS	1990	1989
	£'000s	£'000s
Turnover	48,000	38,250
Cost of sales	(36,000)	(27,050)
	12,000	11,200
Distribution costs (see note)*	4,950	4,800
Administration expenses (see note)*	3,300	3,150
	8,250	7,950
Trading profit	3,750	3,250
Interest paid	1,200	620
Profit before taxation	2,550	2,630
*Note – Depreciation included as part of these figures	3,200	2,950

BALANCE SHEET	1990	1989
	£'000s	£'000s
Fixed assets	33,525	33,260
Current assets		
Stock	8,373	6,428
Debtors	8,166	4,922
	16,541	11,350
Current liabilities		
Trade creditors	4,500	4,200
Other creditors	1,000	500
Bank overdraft	2,850	1,400
	8,350	6,100
Net current assets	8,191	5,250
Total assets less current liabilities	41,716	38,510
Long term loan (repayable 1999)	(10,000)	(8,000)
	31,716	30,510
Shareholders' funds		
Share capital	3,000	3,000
Reserves	28,716	27,510
	31,716	30,510

Required

a. Identify SIX matters which you consider require special attention when auditing the accounts of Tetterby Tools plc; (6 marks)
b. For each of these state why you consider them to be of importance; (12 marks)
c. Briefly explain the purpose of analytical review and the stages at which such a review should be carried out. (2 marks)

(AAT 90) (Total 20 marks)

3. a. Explain how analytical review procedures can contribute to an audit,
   b. explain how the results of analytical review can influence the nature and extent of other audit work, and
   c. give THREE specific examples of analytical review procedures that might be carried out as part of the audit of a company that operations a chain of departmental stores.

(ICAEW I 88) (12 marks)

4. An important aspect of any audit is an analytical review of the financial statements.

   a. Explain how you think the analytical review can potentially assist each stage of the audit.
   b. Explain how ratios or other steps in the analytical review could draw the auditor's attention to the following possible problems:
      i. an overstatement of the stock in trade;
      ii. misclassification of repairs expenditure as fixed assets;
      iii. substantial misappropriation of sales takings or amounts received from debtors.

(IComA 93)

17 Working papers

Introduction

1. An audit has been defined as a process by which the auditor amasses paper. The more paper he has collected the better the audit he has done. This view is by no means a totally frivolous one for modern audits do involve the collection of papers in such large numbers that an index is invariably required. Note that working papers may in part be held in computer form.

2. There is a Statement of Auditing Standards SAS 230 *Working Papers*. The SAS requires that:

   - auditors should document in their working papers matters which are important in supporting their report
   - working papers should record the auditors' *planning, the nature, timing and extent* of the audit procedures performed, and the *conclusions* drawn from the audit evidence obtained.
   - auditors should record in their working papers their *reasoning* on all significant matters which require the exercise of judgement and their *conclusions* thereon.

3. This chapter will consider working papers under the following headings:

   - Purposes
   - Nature and content
   - Form
   - Permanent and current files
   - Internal control questionnaires
   - Internal control questionnaires
   - Internal control evaluation questionnaires
   - Flowcharting
   - Audit programmes
   - Standardisation
   - Ownership of audit working papers
   - Accountants' Lien
   - Retention of working papers

Purposes

4. Audit working papers are produced and collected for several reasons. These include:

   a. To control the current year's work. A record of work done is essential for:

      i. The audit clerk to see that he has done all that he should.

      ii. His supervisor, manager, the partner to whom he is responsible, and other persons who will review the work he had done.

iii. Enabling evidence to be available in the *final overall review* stage of an audit so that it can be considered whether the Accounts show a true and fair view and comply with statutory requirements.

iv. Working papers collected in the investigation of one part of an enterprise may be used in the verification process for another part.

v. The audit of one part of an enterprise is not conducted in isolation. The whole is not just the sum of the parts. Audit verification includes a review of each part in the context of the whole. This is considered further in Chapter 28.

b. To form a basis for the plan of the audit of the following year. Clearly a starting point for a year's audit is a review of the previous year's work. However, a slavish following of the previous year's work must be avoided and new initiatives taken. Rigidly following the same audit procedures year after year can lead to:

i. Client staff getting to know the procedures.

ii. Client staff designing frauds which the procedures will not uncover.

c. **Evidence of work carried out**

i. Audit clerks need to provide evidence to their superiors that they have carried out work.

ii. More importantly in recent years, evidence that work was carried out may need to be provided in a court of law. *For example*, if a company becomes insolvent and is put into liquidation, the liquidator ought to consider if the company has a justification for action against any person to recover some of the losses. Company A has severe trading losses but shows a profit in its accounts by the inclusion in stock of non-existent stock. Out of this false profit it pays a dividend. The following year the company becomes insolvent and the assets are found to be negligible in relation to the liabilities. Clearly the dividend should not have been paid and if it had not been paid then more money would be available to the creditors. Somebody was to blame for the wrong payment of the dividend and the liquidator can sue the guilty parties and make them compensate the company for the loss. Who is to blame? Presumably the directors, who are responsible for the stock take and the preparation of the Accounts, are primarily to blame. But what about the auditors? They would have to prove in court they did all that they should have done which would include their attendance at the stock take. The evidence they would need to produce would be from their working papers showing the work they did on attendance at the stock take. It would seem obvious in the case mentioned (based on an actual case) that they failed to carry out their duties conscientiously, but all auditors should remember that working papers are evidence of the work they have done and may need to be presented in court.

Nature and content

5. Audit working papers should be sufficiently complete and detailed to enable an experienced auditor with no previous connection with the audit subsequently to ascertain from them what work was performed and to support the conclusions reached.

6. In the case of *significant* matters that may require the exercise of judgement, the working papers should contain:

    a. Details of the matter and all information available.

    b. The management's conclusions on the matter.

    c. The auditor's conclusions on the matter.

    This is because:

        i. the auditor's judgement may be questioned later;

        ii. by someone with the benefit of hindsight;

        iii. it will be important to be able to tell what facts were known at the time when the auditor reached his opinion;

        iv. it may be necessary to demonstrate that, based on the then known facts, the conclusions were reasonable.

    For example, the matter in doubt may be the amount expected to be paid under a guarantee given by the client company to a bank which has lent money to a related company which is in financial difficulty. The working papers should contain:

        i. All the facts with copies or extracts from relevant documents (the related company's financial statements, the document containing the guarantee).

        ii. The management's conclusions. Perhaps that the related company will survive and meet its commitments so that no payment will be required of the client company. The reasons for this conclusion will be summarised.

        iii. The auditor's conclusions. Perhaps that a payment of £x will be required. Again reasoning will be spelt out in detail.

7. The auditors working papers will consist of:

    a. Information and documents which are of continuing importance to each annual audit.

    b. Audit planning and control information.

    c. Details of the client's systems and records with the auditor's evaluation of them.

    d. Schedules in support of the accounts additional to, or summarising the detail in the client's Books.

    e. Details of the audit work carried out, notes of queries raised with action taken thereon and the conclusion drawn by the audit staff concerned.

    f. Evidence that the work of the audit staff has been properly reviewed by more senior people.

    g. A summary of significant points affecting the financial statements and the audit report (eg the guarantee above), showing how these points were dealt with.

    h. Evidence of the inherent and control risk assessments and any changes thereto (see Chapter 25).

    i. evidence of the auditors' consideration of the work of internal audit and their conclusions thereon.

8. Working papers can be in any form desired by the auditor but a usual division is between the *permanent* file and the current file.

The permanent file

9. The permanent file usually contains documents and matters of continuing importance which will be required for more than one audit. It will usually be *indexed*.

   a. **Statutory material** governing the conduct, accounts, and audit of the enterprise. For example, if auditing a Building Society, one would need a copy of the Building Societies Act 1986 and subsequent regulations. In the case of companies this would not be necessary as all auditors know the Companies Act by heart! However, a copy of the Stock Exchange regulations may be required.

   b. **The Rules and Regulations** of the enterprise. For companies, this means the Memorandum and Articles of Association. For partnerships, it means the partnership agreement; for sports clubs, the club rules, and so on.

   c. **Copies of Documents** of continuing importance and relevance to the auditor. Examples are:

      i.   Letter of engagement and minutes of appointment of the auditor. This is particularly important in non-statutory audits as it embodies the auditor's instructions.

      ii. Trade, licence, and royalty agreements entered into by the client.

      iii. Debenture deeds.

      iv. Leases.

      v.   Guarantees and Indemnities entered into.

   d. **Addresses** of the registered office and all other premises, with a short description of the work carried on at each.

   e. An organisation chart showing:

      i. The principal departments and sub-divisions thereof, with a note of the numbers of people involved.

      ii. The names of responsible officials showing lines of responsibility. Extra details should be given for accounting departments.

   f. **List of books and other records** and where they are kept. Names, positions, specimens of signatures and initials of persons responsible for books and documents should also be included. Account codes and classifications should also be held.

   g. **An outline history** of the organisation. Special mention must be made of the history of Reserves, Provisions, Share Capital, Prospectuses, and acquisition of subsidiaries and businesses. There should also be a record of important accounting ratios.

   h. **List of Accounting matters** of importance. Accounting policies used for material areas such as stock, work in progress, depreciation, research and development.

   i. Notes of interviews and correspondence re *Internal Control* matters and all past letters of weakness.

   j. A note of the position of the company in *the Group* and of all subsidiaries and associated companies with holdings therein.

   k. Clients' *Internal Audit* and Accounting Instructions.

   l. A list of the *directors*, their shareholdings, and service contracts.

   m. A list of the company's *properties and investments* with notes on verification.

n. A list of the company's *advisors* – bankers, merchant bankers, stockbrokers, solicitors, valuers, insurance brokers, etc.

o. A list of the company's *insurances*.

This is rather a longer list than some authorities suggest but it does have the merit of reasonable completeness. It will be seen that a reading of the permanent file will be an excellent introduction for staff coming new to an audit. It is very important that on the occasion of each audit, the permanent file is updated.

The current file

10. The current file will contain matters pertinent to the current year's audit. It will contain:

a. A *copy of the Accounts* being audited, authenticated by director's signatures.

b. An *index* to the file.

c. A description of the *Internal Control* system in the form of an ICQ, flowcharts, or written description together with specimen documents.

d. An *Audit Programme*. This will contain:

   i. A list of work to be carried out by audit staff.

   ii. A list with details of the tests actually carried out.

   iii. The results of the tests and the conclusions drawn from them.

   iv. Cross reference to the Internal Control records and letter of weakness.

   v. Where rotational testing over a period of years is used, reference to the appropriate part of the Permanent File.

e. A *schedule* for each item in the *Balance Sheet*. Each schedule should show:

   i. The item at the beginning of the year, changes during the year, and the balance at the end.

   ii. Details of how its existence, ownership, value and appropriate disclosure have been verified.

   iii. Documents of external verification eg a bank letter.

f. A *schedule* for each item in the *Profit and Loss Account* showing its make up.

g. Checklists for compliance with statutory disclosure requirements. Accounting Standards, Auditing Standards etc.

h. A records showing *queries* raised during the audit and coming forward from previous years. This record will show how the queries have been dealt with, by whom (ie audit clerks, supervisor, manager or partner) and, if not satisfactorily answered, the treatment adopted, which may be a qualification of the auditor's report.

i. A *schedule* of important *statistics*. These will include quantitative matters such as output, sales composition, employment, and also accounting ratios such as return on capital employed, gross and net profit ratios, and liquidity ratios. Comparison of these statistics with those of previous years (noted in the Permanent File) must be made to determine significant variations. These variations need to be investigated and explanations sought.

j. A *record* or *abstract* from the *Minutes* of:

   i.   The Company

   ii. The Directors

   iii. Any internal committee of the company whose deliberations are important to the auditor. Examples might be an Internal Audit Committee, a Budget Committee, a Capital Expenditure Committee, the Audit Committee, the Remuneration Committee etc.

k. Copies of *letters to the Client* setting out Internal Control weaknesses.

l. *Letters of Representation*. These are letters written by the *Directors* (or equivalent in organisations other than companies) to the Auditors, being written confirmation of information given or opinions expressed by the Directors on such matters as the value of stock, value of properties, uncertain obligations, and contingent liabilities.

It will be seen that both Permanent and Current Files contain material on Internal Control. It is a matter of opinion where this data is filed; some audit firms adopt a filing system whereby Internal Control matters are stored in a third file, the *Internal Control File*.

Throughout the current file, reference should be made as to how each item is used as audit evidence. Conversely, for each type of transaction and balance, the nature of the audit evidence supporting it should be demonstrated. This evidence may be from internal control reliance, substantive testing or from analytical review or from a combination of these sources.

Internal control questionnaires

11. These documents can have several functions:

   a. A method of *ascertainment* of the system.

   b. Enabling the auditor to *review* and *assess* the adequacy of the system.

   c. Enabling the auditor to identify areas of *weakness*.

   d. Enabling the auditor to *design a series of tests*. In effect this means enabling the auditor to draw up his audit programme.

   e. Enabling audit staff to *familiarise* themselves with the system quickly and comprehensively.

The advantage of using an ICQ are implicit in the functions just stated but in addition they include:

   i.   The use of *standardised* ICQ ensures that *all* the important questions are asked and the important characteristics of a system are brought out.

   ii. The ICQ is a comprehensive, all in, inclusive method of ascertaining, recording, and evaluating a system of internal control.

Next follows an example of a part of an ICQ. Note the separate columns for:

   i.   Questions.

   ii. Answers – if possible Yes/No.

   iii. Assessment of Internal Control strength.

iv. Disposal of weaknesses.

v. Cross reference to Audit Programme.

Internal control questionnaire (extracts)

Client name: **HEDONITE MANUFACTURING LTD**
Subject area: **BANK RECONCILIATIONS**

Symbols: Satisfactory ✔
Weakness ✗

Q No.	Questions	Answers	Assessment	Weakness dealt with	Audit programme
1	How often is a bank reconciliation prepared.	4 weekly	✔		5(a)
2 (a)	Is the person responsible for function independent of the receipts and payment function.	Yes	✔		5(a)
(b)	Alternatively is the reconciliation independently checked.	n/a	✔		
3	Where the reconciliation is prepared as in 2(a) above does he obtain statements direct from the bank and retain them until the reconciliation is effected.	Yes	✔		5(a)
4	Does the independent reconciliation include:				5(a)
(a)	A comparison of the debits and credits shown on the bank statements with the cash book.	Yes	✔		
(b)	A comparison of paid cheques with the cash book as to names, dates and amounts.	Yes	✔		
(c)	A test of the detailed paying-in slips with the cash book.	No	✗	Letter of weakness 12.1.x2.	
(d)	An enquiry into any contra items	Yes	✔		
(e)	Are items more than one month old investigated to establish that they are genuine.	Yes	✔		5(a)

Subject area: UNCLAIMED WAGES				
Q No. Questions	Answers	Assessment	Weakness dealt with	Audit programme
1 What records are maintained of unclaimed wages?	Entered in unclaimed wages book by Mr Smith	✔		14(c)
2 When are unclaimed wages recorded.	After pay out, on return to wages department	✔		14(c)
3 To whom are unclaimed wages packets handed for safe keeping?	Wages dept. manager	✔		14(c)
4 (a) Is he responsible for any other cash funds?	Yes	✔		14(c)
(b) If so, which?	Wages	✔		14(c)
5 Is the authenticity of each unclaimed wage envelope or container investigated by a person independent of the payroll preparation?	Yes	✔		14(c)
6 How long after the pay-out are unclaimed wages broken down and rebanked?	At intervals	X	Letter of weakness 12.1.x2	14(c)
7 Who authorises payment of unclaimed wages?	Wages dept. manager	✔		14(c)
8 (a) Are receipts obtained?	Yes	✔		14(c)
(b) If not, how are employees identified?	n/a			
9 Is an authority required before an employee can collect unclaimed wages on behalf of another?	Yes	✔		14(c)
10 Is the unclaimed wages record signed by:				
(a) The employee receiving the payment?	Yes	✔		14(c)
(b) The person making the payment.	Yes	✔		

Internal control evaluation questionnaires

12. Some audit firms use ICQ's exclusively, others prefer to ascertain the system by questioning staff and recording the system by means of Flowcharts or by written notes. With all methods, specimen documents and other exhibits are also collected. If the Flowchart and written notes method of recording the system is adopted, it is necessary to evaluate the system's strengths and weaknesses. An ideal method of doing this is by means of an *Internal Control Evaluation Questionnaire*. This is a standardised set of questions which has

the advantage, like the ICQ, of ensuring all the right questions are asked and the strengths and weaknesses of a system are brought out.

The basic questions in an ICEQ are called control questions. An example from the sales area is 'can sales be invoiced but not recorded in the books?' Each control question requires an answer yes or no. To determine the answer, a series of detailed questions are then asked. To answer the control question referred to, the back-up questions would be:

a.   Are invoices pre-numbered?

b.   Is there an independent sequence check of the ledger posting copy of the invoice with acknowledgement of performance?

c.   Are there procedures for spoilt and cancelled invoices?

d.   Is there control over 'sale or return' goods?

e.   Is there control over 'pro forma' invoices?

Here is an example of an ICEQ and a list of control questions.

Internal control evaluation questionnaire (extract)

Subject area: **PURCHASES**

Control Question	Criteria	Answer	Might weakness be material?
CAN ORDERS BE PLACED FOR GOODS (OR SERVICES) WHICH ARE NOT AUTHORISED	1. Control over custody of unused requisitions.		
	2. Specified authority for requisitions.		
	3. Limits to authority for issue of requisitions.		
	4. Custody of unused purchase orders.		
	5. Measures for issue of purchase orders.		
	6. Purchase orders pre-numbered.	No	Yes
	7. Purchase orders complete with specification and prices.		
	8. Purchase orders valued and compared with budgets.		
	9. Segregation of duties between officials responsible for, requisition, orders and other sections.		
	10. Requisitions matched with orders and subsequent documents.		

List of control questions to be used in an ICEQ (extracts)

General

1. Is the business conducted in an orderly manner?
2. Are the records accurate and reliable?
3. Are the assets safeguarded?

Cash and bank

1. Can monies be received but not accounted for?
2. Can cash balances, bank accounts or negotiable instruments be misappropriated?
3. Can unauthorised payments be made?
4. Can wage payments be made for work not done?
5. Can the payroll be inflated?

Purchases and creditors

1. Can orders be placed for goods or services which are not authorised?
2. Can goods or services be accepted without being ordered?
3. Can goods or services be accepted without inspection?
4. Can goods or services be paid for without being received?

Sales

1. Can goods be despatched to a bad credit risk?
2. Can goods be despatched but not invoiced?
3. Can goods be invoiced but not recorded in the books?
4. Can debtors' accounts be improperly credited?
5. Can debtors' accounts remain uncollected?

Stocks

1. Are stocks protected against loss or misuse?
2. Are period end stocks properly evaluated as to quantity, condition, and value?

Fixed assets

1. Can fixed assets be acquired or disposed of without proper authority or record?

Investments

1. Can investments be acquired, disposed of or pledged without proper authority or record?
2. Can documents of title be lost or misappropriated?
3. Can income fail to be collected or be misappropriated?

Flowcharts

13. Flowcharts are a method of recording internal control systems from the auditor's standpoint.

14. The *advantages* of Flowcharts are as follows:

    a. Flowcharts enable the system to be recorded in such a way that it can be *understood* by:

       i. New staff coming to the audit.
       ii. Supervisors, managers and partners.
       iii. Client staff, who can have weaknesses pointed out more easily.

b. The *overall* picture of a firm can be seen, and in particular the auditor can be assured he has the whole picture as flowlines going nowhere can be easily spotted.

c. Flowcharting is a *consistent* system of recording.

d. Flowcharting is a *disciplined* method of recording. Full understanding must be gained to draw them.

e. Flowcharting highlights the *relationships* between different parts of a system.

f. *Weaknesses* are easier to spot.

g. *Superfluous* forms and bottlenecks are easily spotted. This is really of use to Organisation and Method Study practitioners but auditors often help their clients in this area.

h. Flowcharts are a permanent record but are easily *updated*.

i. In complex cases, flowcharting is the only way to gain an understanding of a system.

15. The *disadvantages* of Flowcharting are:

a. Their creation can be very *time consuming*.

b. They can become a *fetish* ie ends in themselves.

c. They are of little use in systems (eg small concerns) where internal control is ineffective or very simple.

d. Numerous symbol systems abound which can cause confusion.

16. When preparing Flowcharts the following points should be borne in mind:

a. An *organisation chart* is an essential concomitant.

b. *Simplicity and clarity* are fundamental.

c. Flowcharts must not be congested. Use separate charts for sub-procedures, exceptional procedures etc. *Small congested charts lose examination marks*.

d. Use only *horizontal and vertical lines*.

e. Chart the flow of *goods and documents* on separate charts.

f. *Serial number* operations.

g. *Cross reference* to ICQ, ICEQ, Audit Programme, letter of weakness, etc.

h. Charts must *show*:

   i. Initiation of each document and operation.

   ii. Sequence of all operations on documents and all copies of documents, especially operations of control, inspecting, checking, comparing and approving.

   iii. The sections or individuals who perform operations.

   iv. The ultimate destination, ie where is it filed?

   v. Explanatory notes where required.

i. Use flowchart symbols only, if possible. There is not usually a need for verbal description *and* symbols.

j. Specimens of documents should be attached and cross referenced.

The objective of a flowchart is that it is complete in itself and can be read and understood quickly and comprehensibly. However this takes practice. A verbal description of the system on page 141 might be:

a. The company has a number of separate departments (eg sales, credit control). This is important for separation of duties.

b. Orders are received from customers in various forms.

c. All orders are transcribed onto prenumbered official 'sales order forms'. Prenumbering ensures all orders will be fulfilled or discovered as unfulfilled.

d. The blank order forms are kept locked in the manager's safe. Order forms are important as they key the release of goods.

e. The sales order forms are in duplicate. One copy is attached to the original customer order and filed in a temporary file.

f. The second copy is sent to credit control. Credit control check that the customer is credit worthy by reference to their records and the customer's ledger account print out (to see the customer is not overdue or has not exceeded his credit limit).

g. If credit is not approved then the sub-routine (Flow Chart 54, not given here) is operated.

h. The order is then sent to the warehouse. There, the goods on the order are checked for availability. If the goods are not available then a routine is operated (presumably to order more from the supplier).

i. A despatch note in triplicate is made out from the details in the sales order form. This despatch note is prenumbered.

j. One copy of the despatch note is put with the goods (which are presumably picked off the shelves and packed) and signed by the goods-out foreman who compares the goods with the despatch note.

k. This copy is attached to the sales order form and filed in despatch note number order in the warehouse.

l. The second copy of the despatch note is checked against the goods and sent with the goods to the customer.

m. The third copy is used to make out the invoice. It is subsequently attached to a copy of the invoice and filed in invoice number order in the invoice section. But before being so attached it is checked for sequence (to see none are missing, meaning goods were despatched but not invoiced) by the invoice section manager.

n. The invoice has four copies. The top copy is sent to the customer.

o. The third copy has been dealt with (see m.).

p. This copy is checked for accuracy and initialled by the checker. The second copy is batched daily. From the batch a prelist is made out in duplicate. The top copy is filed in numerical sequence in the invoice department.

q. The second copy of the prelist is sent with the batch of copy invoices daily to computer input(this is on Flow Chart C2 not shown).

r. The fourth copy of the sales invoice is sent to the sales department.

s. From the order forms and the invoice copies, a schedule of outstanding orders is made out weekly in duplicate.

t. The matched order forms and invoices are attached to each other and filed monthly in alphabetical order of customer.

u.   The top copy of the schedule is filed. The second copy is sent to the managing director.

Note:

i.   The symbols used are explained below and the internal control features listed.

ii.   You may well feel that the flow chart explains the system in a much more digestible manner than the narrative above.

Flowchart for audit purposes

Gremlin Wholesale Co. Ltd. – Flowchart of Sales Orders and Invoicing Procedures

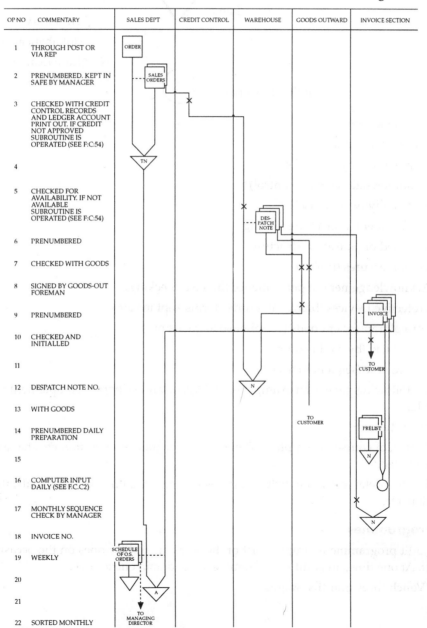

OP NO	COMMENTARY	SALES DEPT	CREDIT CONTROL	WAREHOUSE	GOODS OUTWARD	INVOICE SECTION
1	THROUGH POST OR VIA REP					
2	PRENUMBERED. KEPT IN SAFE BY MANAGER					
3	CHECKED WITH CREDIT CONTROL RECORDS AND LEDGER ACCOUNT PRINT OUT. IF CREDIT NOT APPROVED SUBROUTINE IS OPERATED (SEE F:C:54)					
4						
5	CHECKED FOR AVAILABILITY. IF NOT AVAILABLE SUBROUTINE IS OPERATED (SEE F:C:54)					
6	PRENUMBERED					
7	CHECKED WITH GOODS					
8	SIGNED BY GOODS-OUT FOREMAN					
9	PRENUMBERED					
10	CHECKED AND INITIALLED					
11						
12	DESPATCH NOTE NO.					
13	WITH GOODS					
14	PRENUMBERED DAILY PREPARATION					
15						
16	COMPUTER INPUT DAILY (SEE F.C.C2)					
17	MONTHLY SEQUENCE CHECK BY MANAGER					
18	INVOICE NO.					
19	WEEKLY					
20						
21						
22	SORTED MONTHLY					

Notes to flowchart

1. Symbols used are:

    Document

    Prepared using details in   - - - - -

    Action or Check   ✕

    File   ▽

T	Temporary
A	Alphabetical order
N	Numerical order
D	Date order

    To another flowchart   ◯

2. Note incidence of:
    a. Separation of duties:
        –   initiation (by customer)
        –   authorisation (credit control)
        –   custody (warehouse)
        –   documentation and recording
    b. Specified organisation structure
    c. Proof measures (prelist)
    d. Acknowledgement of performance (invoice checking)
    e. Protective Devices (blank sales order forms kept in safe)
    f. Formal transfer of goods (warehouse to goods out)
    g. Pre-review (by credit control)
    h. Post review (sequence checks)

    On the following page is an example of an Organisation Chart to complement a systems flowchart.

    Notes to student:

    1. This is, of course, incomplete. The warehouse, goods-out section etc., have not been included.
    2. Further detail could be included if desired, eg actual names of officials, their location, etc.

Audit programmes

17. An audit programme is simply a list of the work an auditor does on the occasion of his audit. At one time, an audit programme would contain entries like:

    'Vouch three months' wages'

There would be columns for the periods selected and for the initials of the audit clerk and the date of the test. In the modern audit programme these columns would still be found but the tests would be different, being designed to test the Internal Control system or to substantiate balances or transactions rather than the authenticity of individual entries. The results of tests, particularly if based on statistical sampling, would need some evaluation and the audit programme would provide space for this.

18. The advantage of using audit programmes are:

   a. They provide a clear set of *instructions* on the work to be carried out.

   b. They provide a clear *record* of the work carried out and by whom.

   c. Work can be *reviewed* by supervisors, managers etc.

   d. Work will not be *duplicated*.

   e. No important work will be *overlooked*.

   f. *Evidence* of work done is available for use in defending actions for negligence, etc.

19. The disadvantages of audit programmes are:

   a. Work may become *mechanical*.

   b. Parts may be executed without regard to the *whole* scheme.

   c. Programmes are *rigidly* adhered to although client personnel and systems may have changed.

   d. *Initiative* may be stifled.

   e. There is an audit theory that when an auditor's suspicions are aroused (the usual term is *put upon enquiry*) he should *probe the matter to the bottom*. A fixed audit programme and limited time tend to inhibit such probings.

   f. If work is performed to a pre-determined plan, client staff may become aware of the fact and fraud is facilitated.

Here are examples of Audit Programmes.

Extract from a procedural audit programme

Client: Hedonite Manufacturing Ltd.
Year end: 31st January 19-2
Area: Purchases

Tests	**Signature**	**Date**

1. Select randomly 25 invoices and 10 credit notes for detailed checking in the manner described in the following paragraphs. The items selected for test should include the following types of transaction:

   production purchases
   production services
   capital expenditure
   non-production goods and services
   imports

2. Obtain up-to-date specimen signatures and initials of all officials operating in this area. This should be obtainable from the permanent file.

3. Prepare a schedule of the items selected together with the tests to be applied. On conclusion of each test, the results should be entered on the schedule.

4. For each item selected (where applicable):

   a. Verify that each invoice is supported by a properly signed requisition.

   b. Verify that each invoice is supported by a properly signed copy order.

   c. Verify that each invoice for goods is supported by a Goods Received Note (GRN) bearing evidence that the goods have been inspected and approved as being in good condition and order and in agreement with the purchase order.

   d. Verify that invoices for services have been approved by the person requisitioning the service.

   e. Verify that capital expenditure requisitions have been made within authorised limits.

   f. Verify that prices are as authorised by examining priced copy, orders, estimates, tenders or other evidence.

   g. Verify calculations and additions have been checked.

   h. Check calculations, extensions, and additions.

   i. Check that invoices have been correctly expense and cost record coded and that entries in the invoice register and cost records correctly reflect the coding.

   j. Verify that credit notes are supported by a goods returned note or by other authority if they are for services or adjustments.

   k. Verify that appropriate acknowledgements in the form of initials or signatures appear on each document.

   l. Verify that each invoice has been passed for payment and that invoices on which cash discounts can be claimed have been correctly treated.

   m. Check postings from the invoice register to the purchase ledger accounts.

   n. Verify correct treatment of VAT.

5. Verify sequence of:

   Orders
   Goods received notes
   Copy orders
   Invoice numbers applied internally.

6. Enquire into missing numbers.

7. Enquire into outstanding orders.

8. Enquire into unmatched GRNs.

9. Enquire into unprocessed invoices.

10. Examine pre-lists for control accounts.

11. Test additions and crosscasts of invoice register.

12. Test postings to nominal ledger.

13. Scrutinise the invoice register and the file of invoices for unusual and extraordinary items.

After test review

Did the tests reveal:

a. Any changes in the system of internal control?

b. Any weaknesses in the system of internal control?

c. Any instances of the system being short-circuited or not being followed?

d. Any delays in processing which may affect:
   i. efficiency of the system?
   ii. year end cut off?

e. Any evidence of fraud?

f. Any matter that should put the auditor on enquiry?

After review action

Does the review require any of the following actions?

a. Updating the ICQ and Flowcharts.

b. Revision of the audit programme.

c. Further tests.

d. Queries to raise with the management which could not be answered at the time.

e. Matters to be cleared with supervisor, manager, or partner.

Extract from a vouching audit programme

Client: Smallfry Manufacturing Ltd.
Year end: 31st July 19-1
Area: Industrial wages

	Number Examined	Signature	Date

1. Select one week's wages sheets from each month and:
   a. Check additions of each column.
   b. Trace totals to summaries.
   c. Check additions and cross casts of summaries.
   d. Trace summary totals to nominal ledger.
   e. Vouch totals with actual payments recorded in the cash book.

2. Vouch data recorded on wage sheets for calculation of gross pay with:
   a. Time clock cards.
   b. Piecework records.
   c. Overtime authorisation.

3. Vouch gross pay with tax records.

4. Vouch employees' names with personnel records and contracts of employment.

5. Select 20 employees in one week of each quarter (all departments should be covered) and vouch:

   a. Hours worked with time records.

   b. Piecework with records.

   c. Overtime with authorities.

   d. Other gross Pay (eg lay off pay) with authority.

   e. Rates of pay with union or other agreements or with authority.

   f. Check calculations of gross pay and all deductions.

   g. Trace deductions through to separate records of each deduction (eg income tax, national insurance, pension contributions, union dues, savings schemes).

   h. Inspect receipts where these were given.

   i. Inspect authority for non-statutory deductions.

   j. Investigate any advances of pay ('subs').

6. Select five employees at random and vouch holiday pay paid to them.

7. Investigate five payments of sick pay.

8. Investigate statutory sick pay records.

9. Verify that the procedure for dealing with unclaimed wages has been applied correctly by vouching the unclaimed wages book.

10. At intervals averaging three years witness wages pay out procedure by:

    a. Attending at the pay out of wages.

    b. Inspecting the application of physical controls over wage packets.

    c. Verifying that wage packets are handed over to identified workmen.

    d. Counting the cash in some selected wage packets and verifying with net wages recorded.

    e. Verifying treatment of unclaimed wages.

Overall tests

1. Select two dates some three months apart and compare wages sheets to identify new employees and leavers:

   a. Verify correct employment of new employees by examining tax records, personnel records, and other documentation.

   b. Verify procedures have been correctly carried out when employees have left including a test of redundancy pay, correct notice, etc.

2. Compare wage payments in total and by department with budgets and costing records and obtain explanations for differences.

Internal control

1. Do the procedures as investigated by the above audit programme:

    a. Prevent employees being paid for work not done?   Yes/No

    b. Allow the payroll to be inflated in any way?   Yes/No

    c. Prevent errors occurring in the wage calculation?   Yes/No

2. a. Is there adequate evidence of time worked and piecework performed?   Yes/No

    b. Is there adequate evidence for rates of pay?   Yes/No

    c. Are there independent checks on the arithmetical accuracy of the payroll? Yes/No

    d. Is that payroll presented to check signatories as support for the cheque? Yes/No

    e. Can 'dummy' men be paid?   Yes/No

Conclusions

1. Have proper accounting records been kept in this area?   Yes/No

2. Does the figure for industrial wages give a true and fair view?   Yes/No

Other working papers

20. Other audit working papers may be mentioned:

    a. *Manuals*. Most audit firms of any size have printed audit manuals which complement internal instruction given to staff. They contain general instructions on the firm's method of auditing in each area and on the audit firm's procedures generally.

    b. *Audit note books*. These were common at one time but now most notes made by audit staff are incorporated in the current or permanent files.

    c. *Time sheets*. These are not strictly a part of the audit working papers but are of great importance in controlling the work of audit staff and making a proper charge to the client.

    d. *Audit control and review sheets*. These, again, are usually incorporated in the working files.

They are papers which are concerned with a review of the work done by audit staff and acceptance of the work by supervisors, managers, partners, and reviewing committees. This is further discussed in Chapter 45.

Standardisation of working papers

21. Most firms adopt a system of standard working papers which can be used on all audits. This has many advantages including:

    a. Efficiency

    b. Staff become familiar with them

    c. Matters are not overlooked

    d. They help to instruct staff

    e. Work can be delegated to lower level staff

    f. Work can more easily be controlled and reviewed.

22. The disadvantages are:
    a. Work becomes mechanical
    b. Work also becomes standard
    c. Client staff may become familiar with the method
    d. Initiative may be stifled
    e. The exercise of necessary professional judgement is reduced.

Ownership of books and papers

23. The ownership of the working papers of an accountant hinges on whether the accountant is acting as an agent for the client. The leading case is Chantrey Martin & Co. v Martin 1953.

    The general rules are:
    a. Where the relationship is that of client and professional man, then all documents are the property of the accountant. The only exceptions are original documents, eg bank statements, invoices etc., which remain the property of the client.
    b. Where the relationship is that of principal or agent. This relationship will exist in situations like dealing with the inland revenue, negotiating loans, and arranging the sale or purchase of a business or other property. In these cases all the papers are likely to be the property of the client.

    The ownership of working papers may not seem important, but it may be relevant in situations such as changes in professional appointments, legal proceedings for the recovery of documents, negligence actions etc.

Accountant's lien

24. Accountant's are considered to have a particular lien over any books of account, files and papers which their clients have delivered to them and also over any documents which have come into their possession in the course of their ordinary professional work.

    A particular lien gives the possessor the right to retain goods until a debt arising in connection with those goods is paid.

    The leading case is Woodworth v Conroy 1976.

Retention of working papers

25. It is a general principle that working papers should be retained for as long a period as possible. The precise period is dependent on a number of factors including:
    a. Prospectus requirements are for accounts for the preceding six years.
    b. Tax assessments can be made up to six years after the end of the chargeable period but in fraud cases, can be made at any time.
    c. Actions based on contract or tort (eg professional negligence) must be brought within six years.

Summary

26. a. Working paper collection is an essential part of an audit.

b. The reasons for collecting working papers include:

i.   The reporting partner needs to satisfy himself that all audit work has been properly performed. He does this by reviewing the working papers.

ii. Working papers provide for future reference, details of work preformed, problems encountered, and conclusions drawn. Future reference needs may include a court hearing.

iii. The preparation of working papers encourages the audit staff to adopt a methodical approach.

c. Audit working papers will typically contain:

i.   Information and documents of continuing importance to the audit.

ii. Audit planning information.

iii. The auditor's assessment of the client's accounting system *and* if appropriate, a review and assessment of internal controls.

iv. Details of all audit work undertaken, problems and errors met and of all conclusions drawn.

v.   Evidence that all audit work by the staff has been reviewed by more senior staff and/or a partner.

vi. Records of relevant balances and other financial information including summaries and analyses of all items in the Accounts.

vii. A summary of significant points affecting the Accounts and the auditor's report, and how they were dealt with.

viii.The working papers detail what evidence has been obtained for each class of transaction and balance.

d. Working papers are often divided into Permanent and Current files.

e. Working papers will include:

Internal control questionnaires.

Internal control evaluation forms.

Flowcharts.

Audit programmes.

Points to note

27. a. The actual conduct of any audit where internal control is relied on is fundamentally the same but the detailed methods vary from firm to firm. The collecting of working papers is universal but the precise labels to these vary as do the detailed audit methods. Here is a summary of the standard audit method showing how some of the working papers might fit in:

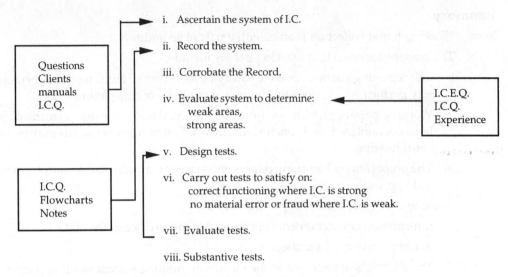

i.   Ascertain the system of I.C.

ii. Record the system.

iii. Corrobate the Record.

iv. Evaluate system to determine:
    weak areas,
    strong areas.

v.   Design tests.

vi. Carry out tests to satisfy on:
    correct functioning where I.C. is strong
    no material error or fraud where I.C. is weak.

vii. Evaluate tests.

viii. Substantive tests.

ix. Analytical review of financial statements.

b. Modern Accounts are subject to much regulation (by Companies or other Acts and by accounting standards). Modern audits are regulated by the professional bodies acting as supervisory bodies. It is essential that auditors perform all the tests and reviews that are necessary to ensure that Accounts comply with the regulations and that the audit is comprehensive and that nothing has been overlooked. All actions must be fully recorded. One way of ensuring that all is done is to have checklists which must be completed, signed and reviewed by managers and partners.

c. Working papers can be stored in a choice of media – paper, film, electronic or other.

d. Auditors use many schedules, analyses and other documentation prepared by the client. It is essential that there is adequate audit evidence that such information is properly prepared. This is especially true of computer print-outs.

e. SAS 230 requires that auditors should adopt appropriate procedures for maintaining the *confidentiality* and *safe custody* of their working papers.

f. Auditors should retain their working papers for some years at least. They may be needed for a prospectus or for regulatory requirements or even in inland revenue investigations.

Case study 1 for Chapter 17

Charlatan Furniture Ltd are a large company engaged in the manufacture and import of self-assembly furniture kits. Their system for the placing of purchase orders is:

a. Requisitions are drawn up by production control, by marketing and by stores accounting who keep stores records on a micro computer. Requisitions are not pre-numbered.

b. All requisitions must be cost allocation coded and be signed as approved by a departmental manager. Certain codes (eg capital expenditure) are excluded from this process.

c. Requisitions are passed to the purchasing department. They approve requisitions and complete purchase orders. Orders are placed with approved suppliers. There is an ongoing programme to find the optimal suppliers.

d. The orders are in triplicate – 1. retained 2. to requisitioner and 3. to the supplier. Orders are pre-numbered and are valued. Cost codes and total purchases for that cost code are entered on the order together with budgeted allowance for that code.

e. The orders are checked and signed by the purchasing manager.

Discussion

a. Flowchart this system.

b. Evaluate its strengths and weaknesses (you may use the ICEQ in this chapter).

c. What audit tests could be applied?

d. Relate this system to the overall audit objectives.

Case study 2 for Chapter 17

During the final audit of the Accounts of Zap pesticides plc it appeared that large quantities of Anophocide had been sent to customers in certain African countries on sale or return terms. Only a small proportion has been sold and cash received. Payment is due in US dollars. The banks have reported that several of the countries concerned have difficulties with foreign currencies. There is a strong rumour that the chemical causes environmental damage and that its use may be banned in the US and other countries.

Discussion

What problems are identifiable in determining the choices open to the company's directors in accounting for this item on the Annual Accounts?

How would the Auditor deal with the matter with special reference to his working papers?

Student self testing questions *Questions with answers apparent from the text*

1. a What are the objectives of working papers? (4)
   b. List the contents of working papers. (5, 6, 7)
   c. List the contents of a permanent file. (9)
   d. List the content of a current file. (10)
   e. What are the functions of an ICQ? (11)
   f. What are the functions of Internal Control Evaluation questionnaires or forms? (12)
   g. Enumerate the advantages and disadvantages of Flowcharting. (14, 15)
   h. Who owns an accountant's working papers? (23)
   i. What is a lien and why might it be important to an accountant? (24)
   j. How long should an auditor retain his working papers? (25)
   k. In the case of significant matters that require the exercise of judgement, what should working papers do? (6)
   l. List the advantages and disadvantages of standardising working papers. (21, 22)
   m. What should an auditor do if his suspicions are aroused? (19)
   n. Distinguish an ICQ from an ICEQ. (11, 12)

Exercises

1. Rapidrise Ltd are a firm of plumbers' and electricians' merchants which have expanded very rapidly to a turnover of some £3 million in five years. There are three founder director/shareholders and some 20 staff + six clerical staff including Ted who is a part qualified accountant. The system for ordering and paying for incoming goods is:

   Each morning Ted visits the warehouse and the foreman and his deputy tell him precisely what to order in order to replace existing stocks and to obtain new lines. New lines are usually suggested by the directors. Ted telephones through the orders to the regular suppliers. Some suppliers require a written order and for them he writes out an order from a duplicate pad which is not sequentially numbered.

   On arrival of the goods, the goods are checked by the foreman or his deputy and the delivery note marked 'OK' and passed to Ted. Ted places the delivery notes in a file. When the invoices arrive they are placed in a box. Approximately once a week, Jean, a clerk, compares the invoices with the delivery notes, settles queries and staples the invoices to the matching delivery notes. She then enters the details of the invoices (supplier, Net, Gross, Vat) into a micro computer floppy disc used only for this purpose. At the end of each month the file is printed out and a listing obtained of the outstanding invoices in supplier name order. When the monthly statements are received, Jean compares them with the print-out and settle any queries over the phone with the supplier or with the foreman.

   She then passes the statements to Ted who decides which items are to be paid (the company has cash flow difficulties caused by its rapid expansion). He marks the items to be paid and gives the lot back to Jean. Jean makes out cheques for these items and sends them to Ted. He signs the cheques (only his is required) and Jean hands them to Mary who sends out the post.

   Jean enters the cheques in the invoice disc. The computer system also:
   - prints out lists of invoices (and credit notes)
   - prints out lists of cheques drawn
   - updates the cash book disc which is used by Ted to control the bank overdraft
   - matches cheques with items and eliminates them where possible.

   Jean journalises entries to match and eliminate invoices where several are settled with one cheque.

   Jean has no other duties apart from some typing and the keeping of the petty cash.

   There are no stock control systems and the warehouse is open during the day to all staff and to customers. Good security operates at night and at weekends.

   Required:
   a. Flowchart this system.
   b. Identify and list the weaknesses in this system.
   c. List the possible consequences of these weaknesses. These should include possible frauds as well as errors.
   d. Suggest a better system.

2. Alset Ltd have 12 electrical appliance shops in the Midlands. The company maintain a warehouse in Bilston and supply goods to the branches using 2 lorries. There is a central accounts department at the warehouse with 5 staff under the chief accountant Louise.

Supplies are ordered for the central warehouse from specific suppliers (these are changed as necessary and a director Toby is in charge of an effective system for selecting suppliers) using an effective system. A stock control system is used in the central warehouse which works well.

The twelve shops are in the charge of individual managers who have autonomy over most aspects of the shop including hiring staff. They are expected to indent for supplies from the central warehouse but are permitted to buy some supplies elsewhere if the central warehouse does not stock items and there is customer demand. Prices for items supplied from head office are fixed by head office as there is central advertising with prices (low) given.

The accounting system is:

– shop managers send in a weekly form of requisition for supplies to the central warehouse. The supplies are invoiced to the shops at cost and the invoices form input for the warehouse stock control system.

– supplies bought for individual shops are paid for by head office when the invoices and delivery notes are sent to head office with a covering letter from each manager stating why they were purchased.

– sales are made in the shops for cash or cheque (no credit cards). These are recorded in till rolls and the managers count the takings daily each morning and bank the proceeds. They agree the till rolls and retain the bank paying in counterfoils and the till rolls. Petty cash and wages are taken out of takings before banking. Each manager maintains his own wages records but payments to the inland revenue are made centrally. A weekly return is sent to head office showing takings and payments made from takings.

– Overheads of the branches such as rent, rates and electricity are paid for centrally.

– stock is counted half yearly by the managers and accounts prepared for each shop based on the data at head office. Action is taken if the profit margins are less than expected.

– some sales are made on hire purchase. The managers fill in the HP forms and keep the recording in the branches. They collect the instalments which are normally paid in cash. Full details are sent to head office on the weekly return. Some HP customers pay direct to head office bank account by standing order.

– each shop manager is remunerated up to 50% by a commission on the net profit of the shop he/she manages.

Required:

a. List the weaknesses in this system indicating the possible frauds and errors that could occur.

b. Prepare a flowchart/flowcharts of a system which would prevent/detect errors and frauds.

c. Devise auditing tests for the existing system indicating whether these are compliance tests, substantive tests or analytical review.

d. Devise auditing tests on the system you have designed for b.

Examination question *(Answer begins on page 544)*

1. You have recently received the following letter from a client company, Andrew Engineering plc.

'Dear Sirs,

Purchase system – raw materials and components

Following our recent expansion we have been reviewing our systems in connection with the above. You may be aware that difficulties have arisen because some items in excess of requirements have been ordered whilst on other occasions vital materials and components have been out of stock.

The following system is therefore proposed for the future.

1. The system will involve the storekeeper, works manager, purchasing department and the production control department.

2. Minimum stock levels will be established by the works manager and production control departments.

3. The storekeeper will maintain a bin card for each type of stock showing the quantity held and production control will maintain a similar record but including value.

4. When stock is required the production control department will issue a sequentially numbered requisition note.

5. The requisition note will be signed as authorised by the works manager who will pass it to the purchasing department.

6. Purchasing department will raise a three part sequential purchase order. One part will be filed with the requisition note, one part passed to the storekeeper and one part passed to production control. The order will quote prices.

7. On receipt of goods the storekeeper will check the quantity and quality of goods received from his copy of the purchase order and raise a three part sequential goods inwards note. He will retain one copy on file and use it to enter his bin card. One copy will be attached to the purchase order and passed to the works manager who will sign the goods inwards note and pass the two documents to the accounts department as their authority to pay the invoice when it arrives. The final copy of the goods inwards note will be passed to the production control department.

8. The production control department will use the goods inwards note to update their physical stock records and will contact the accounts department to ascertain the actual cost of the goods. It will then be filed together with the copy purchase order.

We would be pleased to have your comments on our proposed system.

Yours faithfully,
Andrew Engineering plc.'

Required:

a. Flowchart the company's proposed system. (10 marks)

b. State FOUR proposed internal controls which strengthen the new system. (4 marks)

c. State with reasons TWO areas in which you consider that the internal control is still inadequate and give the possible consequences in each case. (6 marks)

(ACCA)

Examination questions without answers

2. Your firm has recently been appointed auditor of Falmouth Manufacturing Limited, a small manufacturing company that employs 100 staff in the production department (divided into four sections of 25 staff in each) and administration staff of 35 (including 10 office staff). The personnel department consists of a manager and secretary. The wages

department prepares manual wages records, employing two wage clerks who are responsible for making up pay-packets and the payment of wages. The production staff work a single eight-hour daytime shift with overtime. All employees clock in and out each day. The section foremen authorise overtime and calculate the weekly bonus payable to employees based on the weekly production of the department; the bonus is calculated at a standard rate and is sent to the wages department on a standard form. In addition to PAYE and National Insurance (Social Security) deductions, certain employees also have trade union dues, holiday fund and staff saving schemes contributions deducted from their wages. Wages are paid each week on a Thursday based on the time worked in the week to the previous Friday.

Required:

a. Design an Internal Control Evaluation Questionnaire to apply to the above system.

(5 marks)

b. Draft an audit programme to audit the existing production wages system.

(10 marks)

(AAT D 88) (Total 15 marks)

3. a. Why is it important to ascertain and review a client company's system of internal control?

b. Give *five* types of internal control and explain their importance to the client's business.

c. A number of techniques are available to an external auditor to ascertain the client's internal control procedures. Give *five* examples of these techniques and briefly explain them. At least two of your examples should be suitable for use for a smaller client company (indicate which).

d. What action may an external auditor take if the ascertainment procedures reveal weaknesses in the control systems?

(IComA 93)

4. In connection with a new audit of a medium-sized merchanting company, you are required to draw up an Internal Control Questionnaire relating to the method of making payments to trade creditors.

Prepared the questionnaire in good style and layout.

(LCC 89) (12 marks)

5. a. For what purposes do auditors prepare and retain working papers? (12 marks)

b. What are the rights of an auditor to exercise a lien over a company's books for unpaid fees? (8 marks)

(ICA 90) (Total 20 marks)

6. You are the audit partner in charge of the audit of Watson Manufacturing plc. The audit senior who conducted the audit presents you with the files on completion of the audit for the year ended 31 March 1992.

Required

a. List FOUR reasons why audit working papers are prepared. (4 marks)

b. List the categories of items that will be included in a complete set of audit working papers. (3 marks)

c. Briefly state the advantages and disadvantages of following pre-prepared audit programmes. (8 marks)

(AAT 92) (Total 15 marks)

18 Reports to directors or management

Introduction

1. Auditors *may* consider that they should report some matters which come to their attention during the audit to the directors (or other governing body) including any audit committee or to management. The object of the report is to assist the directors and managers. It is in no way a substitute for a qualified audit report. The practice of issuing such a report now seems to be universal.

2. This chapter outlines the purposes, the timing, the procedures, the addressees, the contents and the format and presentation of such letters.

3. There is a Statement of Auditing Standards SAS 610 on the subject.

4. The title of letter to management varies from firm to firm. Such titles include: letter of weakness, management letter, post audit letter, letter of comment, letter of recommendation, internal control letter, follow-up letter.

Purposes

5. These include:

   a. To enable the auditor to give his comments on the accounting records, systems and controls.

   b. To enable the auditor to bring to the attention of management areas of weakness that might lead to material errors.

   c. In some audit engagements there is a requirement to make a report. These include local authorities, stock exchange firms, housing associations and the financial services sector.

   d. To enable the auditor to communicate matters that may have an impact on future audits.

   e. To enable the management to put right matters that may otherwise have led to audit report qualification.

   f. To enable the auditor to point out areas where management could be more efficient or more effective or where economies could be made or resources used more effectively. For example unnecessarily large balances may occur occasionally in the bank. The auditor could point out that facilities exist in the banking sector for short term investment of surplus funds. This is clearly outside the audit assignment but can be very helpful to management and may well make the audit fee more palatable.

Timing

6. a. As the report is a natural by-product of the audit the production of the report to management should be incorporated in the audit plan.

   b. The report should be sent as soon as possible after the end of the audit procedures out of which the report arises.

   c. Where the audit is spread over several visits then it may be appropriate to send a report after each visit. Frequently two reports are sent – one after the interim and one after the final.

d. Where procedures need to be improved before the year end (eg on stock control or identification of doubtful debts or undisclosed liabilities) then the report must be sent as soon as the weaknesses are identified by the auditor.

Procedures

7. a. As weaknesses or breakdowns are identified they should be discussed in detail with the operating staff involved and/or with more senior management. It is vital that the auditor has his facts right.

b. The report should then be written, and then discussed with the addressee.

c. The report should then be sent.

d. An acknowledgement should be obtained from management stating what they propose to do about the weaknesses.

e. The weaknesses should be followed up on the next visit.

Addresses

8. It is usual to address the report to the Board or the audit committee who may then choose to send it down the line for action. Alternatively with the agreement of the Board the report may be sent to the management of the appropriate section, branch, division, region, etc. In some cases separate reports are prepared for the Board and for line management.

Contents

9. The report will include:

a. A list of weaknesses in the structure of accounting systems and internal controls. This means where the client has records or controls which are ill-designed or inadequate. For example there may be no serial numbering of sales invoices so that it is possible for sales invoices to be lost and not be entered in the records.

·b. A list of deficiencies in operation of the records or controls. In principle good records and controls have been designed but they may be by-passed or not always carried out. For example the system in a department store may require all credit notes to be approved by a departmental manager. But in practice the auditor may find that not all credit notes are so approved so that fraudulent credit notes may be issued.

c. Unsuitable accounting policies and practices.

d. Non-compliance with accounting standards or legislation.

e. Explanations of the risks arising from each weakness. For example the possibility of non-collection of the sum due on an invoice or the issue of a fraudulent credit note.

f. Comments on inefficiencies as well as weaknesses.

g. Recommendations for improvement. In some cases the required changes may be complex and the auditor should not delay his report if suggestions cannot be made quickly. Also improvements may require much research and in such cases the auditor would not be able to recommend specific action.

Note that items a, c and d may require the auditor to qualify his report to the MEMBERS as required by statutes (eg the Companies Act on proper accounting records, accounting requirements and true and fair view and a professional duty re compliance with

Accounting Standards). The report to management is not a substitute for the auditor's report.

Format

10. The report should be clear, constructive and concise. It should contain:
    - an opening paragraph explaining the purpose of the report;
    - a note that it contains only those matters which came to the auditor's attention and cannot be a comprehensive list of all weaknesses;
    - if required the report may be tiered by having major weaknesses separated from minor weaknesses;
    - a request that the management should reply to each point made.

Response

11. It is essential that the auditor should obtain a response from his client on each point in the report. The auditor should expect an acknowledgement of receipt, a note of the actions to be taken and in some important cases the directors' discussions should be recorded in their minutes.

The report and third parties

12. At the present time auditors are much frightened of legal actions for negligence and are also much concerned with confidentiality. The auditor should not himself disclose the report to any third party without permission from the client.

It may be that the client may disclose the report to others (eg the bank, regulatory bodies). The report may be relied upon by the third party and the auditor may then have a potential claim for damages arising out of his negligence. The auditor may include paragraphs stating that the report has been produced for the private use of his client only and/or requesting that it not be shown to third parties without permission from the auditor.

As the report may be critical of individuals care should be taken that all its contents are factually accurate and that there are no gratuitously derogatory remarks.

Examples

13.   **Internal control letter following interim audit**

Albert Hall, Esq., FCA,
Financial Director
Hedonite Manufacturing Ltd
Cloghampton   17th October 19-4

Dear Sir

Internal Control

During our interim audit we examined the accounting records of your company and the system of internal control over those records established in your company. This system was designed to ensure accurate and reliable records and to safeguard the company's assets.

As discussed in our meeting on 14th October 19-4 we set out below the principal weaknesses in the system which we found together with our recommendation for improvement. We also attach a schedule of minor weaknesses.

We must point out that our examination was necessarily limited by considerations of cost and time and that the matters dealt with in this letter are not necessarily all the shortcomings in your company's system.

Sales

The system incorporates measures to ensure that all goods leaving the factory are subject to goods outward notes and are invoiced. On checking the GONs. with the copy invoices, we discovered six instances of goods leaving the factory without corresponding invoices. It appeared on closer investigation that all these items were sales of scrap with a corresponding receipt of notes and coin recorded in the cash book. It was not possible to confirm that the receipt corresponded to the amounts charged. Scrap sales are material in amount and we recommend that:

a.   Scrap sales be subject to the invoicing procedure.

b.   A responsible official should have the task of comparing goods outward notes with invoices at specified intervals.

Credit Control

The system requires that among other procedures the sales ledger account is consulted before credit is granted to category 2 customers (not regular customers but customers who have dealt with the company previously). In our investigations we came across two material instances where credit was granted to a customer from whom sums had been due for more than the allowed credit period. We recommend that the clerk checking the creditworthiness of each customer should initial the sales order to confirm that all procedures have been gone through with satisfactory results.

Wages

We detected some errors in keying in the number of hours worked by hourly paid operatives. As a result some workers were overpaid and these errors were not corrected. Some workers were underpaid and these errors were detected as the workers concerned complained. There is some propensity for fraud in these circumstances and we recommend that the keying in be checked or verified in some way such as the use of hash totals or prelisting.

Cheque payments

We would also like to point out that the company's system for dealing with cheque payments is slow and cumbersome although effective. Several cash discounts taken for early payment were disallowed by the suppliers for being out of time. We suggest that the system of payments be examined in detail to consider if it could be speeded up and made more efficient in terms of administrative time.

Raw materials

In previous years raw material stock has been priced on the Highest Price of the year basis. The difference globally between this basis and acceptable bases such as FIFO has been not material. However prices have fluctuated to a greater extent this year and the difference may be material. We recommend that the computer programme extracting this data be amended to value stock on a FIFO basis.

We should be glad if you would tell us in due course what measures you decide to adopt about these matters. We should also like to be informed about any changes you make to the system.

Yours faithfully

Quibble, Query & Co.

Schedule of minor weaknesses.

1. We recommend that the functions of (a) ordering, (b) recording and (c) passing invoices for payment, of catering supplies in the directors' dining room should be performed by separate persons.

2. It is not clear who is responsible for hiring coaches for the works football team and controlling this cost. We recommend that specific responsibility should be ascribed to specified personnel.

3. Purchase invoices are checked as to casts and extensions by Miss Robinson and Miss Smith. No acknowledgement of this check appears on the invoice and we recommend that the rubber stamp should be extended to provide for such an acknowledgement.

4. Small tools such as electric drills are frequently lent by one department to another with no documentation recording these transfers. We recommend that a simple pre-numbered transfer form with spaces for signatures of both parties be used.

5. The petty cash drawer containing up to £200 is kept in Mr William's desk with the key left in the lock during his temporary absences. We recommend that more rigorous control be kept over the key to the petty cash holding.

6. Cash sales of small items at the company's branch at Great Bromwich are evidenced by a book kept at the branch. No review is made as to how these sales correspond with the cash banked and we recommend that such a review is instituted.

14. **Internal control letter following the final audit**

Albert Hall, Esq., FCA,
Financial Director
Hedonite Manufacturing Ltd
Cloghampton   30th April 19-5

Dear Sir

Internal Control

At the conclusion of our interim audit we wrote to you pointing out certain weaknesses in your company's system of internal control. We have now completed the final audit and wish to confirm in writing our discussions on March 14th concerning three more matters.

1. Stocktaking

    Stock sheets were issued by the Chief Accountant and were returned to him. The stock-taking instructions require that these should be numbered to ensure all had been accounted for. This was not done and there is therefore no assurance that all completed stock sheets were returned to the Chief Accountant.

2. Plant

    Our investigation of the physical items of plant with the records revealed two machines which had been scrapped and some parts used to repair other machines. No record of the scrappings had been made in the accounting records.

3. Loans to employees

    It is the company's practice to make loans to employees for car purchase etc., and approval for each loan must be granted by the board. Four loans included in the debtors at the year end had been made to employees who left the company between the making of the loans and the year end. Each of these debtors had ceased to make payments on leaving the company.

We recommend:

1. Stock sheets be pre-numbered.
2. a. Scrapping of machinery be approved by the board.
    b. A plant register should be instituted with regular comparison with actual and record.
3. a. Loans outstanding by employees leaving should where possible be deducted from out-standing remuneration.
    b. A senior official should supervise the collection of all employees' loans.
    c. Consideration should be given to employees giving security for loans made to them.

Please tell us in due course, what action you have taken on these matters.

Yours faithfully,
Quibble, Query & Co.

Note that both these reports (paras 13 and 14) should contain disclaimers of liability.

Summary

15. a. A report to directors or management has several purposes:

    i. Constructive advice to client on economies or more efficient use of resources.

    ii.   Formal request to client to rectify weaknesses which, if not rectified, may require the auditor to qualify his report.

    iii. To enable the auditor to comment on accounting, records, systems and controls with weaknesses and recommendations for improvement.

    iv. To communicate matters that have come to the auditor's attention that might have an impact on future audits.

    v.   Formal information to directors to make clear that they know their legal responsibilities for the consequences of weakness in internal control.

  b. The usual procedure is:

    i.   Verbal discussion.

    ii. Formal letter.

    iii. Follow up.

  c. Letters of weakness can be after interim or final audit or both.

  d. The contents should be:

    i.   Note of purpose of letter.

    ii. Note of purpose of internal control investigation.

    iii. Disclaimer.

    iv. Weaknesses – primary and secondary.

    v.   Recommendations for improvement.

    vi. Request for information on remedial action.

Points to note

16. a. Clearly distinguish the auditors' report required by Section 235 Companies Act 1985 and the subject of this chapter which is on a report to MANAGEMENT.

  b. The audit plan should include the preparation of the report to management and a review of actions taken (if any) on previous reports.

  c. In some cases the weaknesses are not material enough to merit a full scale report or the auditor chooses not to send a report. In these cases the auditor should reduce the discussions to writing, agree them with the management, supply a copy to management and file a copy with the audit working papers.

  d. Make sure that the weakness really is a weakness. The auditor must be sure that he really understands the system not only in detail but as a whole. A well known example is the multiple retail store which abandoned detailed stock control on the grounds of cost. The weakness of the system (or lack of it) is in the possibility of stock losses. Statistical analysis showed that the cost of losses were less than the cost of a control system. It is also a fact that sampling procedures can be as effective as a fully controlled system.

  e. A notable misapprehension is that the letter of weakness can absolve the auditor from blame and hence a legal responsibility to pay for any losses which flow from weakness in internal control. If a weakness is discovered by an auditor and he is unable to satisfy himself that to a material extent:

    i.   Losses have not occurred,

    ii. The records can be relied upon,

he must qualify his report.

An example will illustrate the point:

In re the London and General Bank 1895. (Cases that are headed in re ... means that the company was in liquidation).

The auditor discovered that the assets of the bank included material loans which were inadequately secured.

The auditor wrote to the *directors* pointing out that a larger provision against bad debts was required. The Accounts were not amended and as a profit was thereby shown a dividend was paid.

The directors *and* the auditor were jointly and severally made to pay to the company the amount of the dividend wrongly paid.

Had the auditor reported the facts on the value of the loans in the Auditor's Report, he would have been in the clear but it was held by the Court that reporting to the directors was *not* sufficient.

The auditor reports on the truth and fairness of the Accounts in his Report; any facts he discovered whether on weaknesses of internal control or otherwise, which cast doubt on the truth and fairness of the Accounts must be mentioned in his Report. The letter of weakness none the less has a utility as we have seen.

Case study for Chapter 18

FOLLY MANUFACTURING PLC are a multi-product manufacturing company with 4 factories around the country. The auditors Careful & Co. have completed the interim audit for the year ending 31.12.-6 in September 19-6 and are considering their report to MANAGEMENT.

The matters they have discovered include:

a.   Each factory has a separate bank account. Sometimes the individual accounts are overdrawn but the bank have agreed to set-off for interest calculation. At times there is a net credit balance.

b.   The factory at Tipton shares the policy of straight line depreciation for its plant but unlike the others does not keep a plant register.

c.   The factory in Oldham buys large quantities of scrap copper from scrap merchants paying by cash. Each purchase is approved in writing by the plant works manager but there is no regular check of the cash balance kept to make these purchases.

d.   The stock of finished goods at Oldham is valued at total absorption cost using budgeted global direct wages for overheads purposes. The other factories use a more sophisticated system of departmental overhead recovery based on machine hours.

e.   In all the factories about half the manual workers are paid in cash. Their wages packets are simply given to the foremen to hand out with no formalities.

f.   The factories each use a computerised sales ledger system with complex analytical facilities. One facility, to analyse sales on a month to month and year by year basis for each customer is not used.

Discussion

How should these matters be treated in a report/reports to management? Draft such a report/reports.

Student self testing questions *Questions with answers apparent from the text*

1. a. What reports should be made to management? (5)
   b. When should these reports be made? (6)
   c. What names are given to these reports? (4)
   d. List the contents of such reports. (9)
   e. What is the lesson for auditors of the London and General Bank case? (16)

Examination question *(Answer begins on page 546)*

1. Your firm has acted for many years as auditors to Dodds Ltd which operates a hardware store in Sheffield. The following matters have been noted during the audit of the accounts for the year to 31st March 1985:

   1. It has been agreed that, as in previous years, the audit report will be qualified because the company's system of internal control is largely dependent upon the close involvement of the directors who are also the major shareholders. This internal control matter was last drawn to the attention of the directors in the letter of weakness which arose out of the audit for the year to 31st March 1980. At that time, the directors replied stating that such control is adequate, having regard to the resources, size and nature of the company.

   2. In the letter of weakness following the audit for the year to 31st March 1984 it was reported that a weakness existed in the petty cash system. The managing director acknowledged that letter and advised that the matter would receive due consideration. However, no further action has been taken and the weakness still exists.

   3. The company's bookkeeper has not attempted to reconcile creditors' statements since June 1984.

   4. The company banks its takings once a week, usually on a Friday afternoon. Unbanked cash is held in a petty cash box which is kept in the drawer of a desk in the general office for which only the directors have keys.

   Required:

   Write a letter of weakness to the directors dealing with each of the above matters. Write as from a firm, using fictitious names and addresses. (Marks will be awarded specifically for style as well as for content).

   (ICAEW)

Examination questions without answers

2. At the end of the audit of a company the auditor presents the statutory audit report to the members. He or she will also make a report to the management of the company covering points which have arisen during the audit and which should be brought to the attention of management.

   You are required to:

   a. explain the purposes of a management letter;
   b. explain the types of matter which are likely to be raised in a management letter, and

c. give *two* examples, with brief details, of specific matters which might be raised in relation to the purchasing department of a manufacturing company.

(IComA 94)

3. The management letter should be clear, concise and constructive. Careful presentation will help the recipient to understand the significance of the comments and devise corrective action. The letter may contain matters of varying levels of significance and may well be read by a person who does not have an accounting background. The following paragraphs are extracts from draft management letters prepared by inexperienced members of audit teams.

   i. *Extract from a management letter to the managing director of a large privately owned company.*

   At present there is no control over amendments to the master file data in either the creditors or wages system. Because of this, unauthorised amendments to the data could be made, thus affecting all related transactions processed. Somebody should check amendment data before it is input through the master file suite of programs.

   ii. *Extract from a management letter to the managing director of a medium sized public limited company.*

   Calculations of the net monthly and weekly payroll figures should be independently checked on a random sample basis. At present there is no evidence that checks of this nature are carried out. Independent checks are an essential element of internal control and will help eliminate the possibility of computational errors remaining undetected.

   Required:

   a. Discuss the weaknesses in the above extracts from management letters and redraft the extracts in a more suitable form. (14 marks)

   b. Describe the principal purposes of a management letter. (6 marks)

(ACCA 92) (20 marks)

4. You have recently been designated as the audit senior in charge of the audit of Lightwood & Wegg plc, a manufacturing company. After spending some time at the company's premises, you have ascertained the system controlling the purchase of goods and have drafted the chart shown on the following page.

   Required

   Draft a letter to the managing director of Lightwood & Wegg plc highlighting five potential weaknesses in the purchase system and describe for each of them the effect of the weakness and what action you would recommend.

   (NOTE – Marks will be awarded specifically for the style of the letter as well as the content.)

(AAT 91) (20 marks)

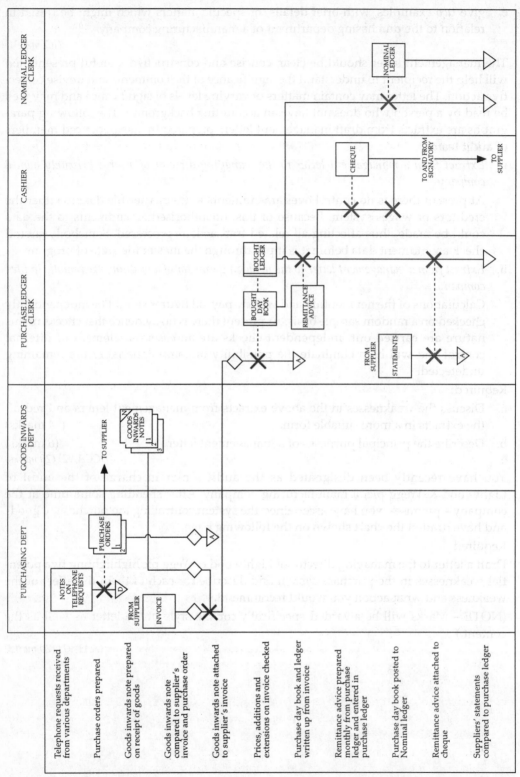

Chart for examination question 4

19 The auditor and errors and frauds

Introduction

1. There is a difference of perception between the public and the auditing profession in relation to an auditor's duty regarding errors and fraud.

2. The auditor sees his duty as:

    'the independent examination of, and expression of opinion on, the financial statements of an enterprise by an appointed auditor in pursuance of that appointment and in compliance with any relevant statutory obligation'.

    The emphasis is on the financial statements. However, the public including much of the business community, tend to see an auditor's duties in terms of the detection and possibly prevention of fraud and error. This chapter explores the relationship which an auditor has with the prevention, discovery and reporting of fraud and also error.

3. There is a lengthy Statement of Auditing Standards SAS 110 *Fraud and Error*.

Error

4. Errors can be described as *unintentional mistakes*. Errors can occur at any stage in business transaction processing-transaction occurrence, documentation, record of prime entry, double entry record, summarising process and financial statement production. Errors can be of any of a multitude of kinds – mathematical or clerical, or in the application of accounting principles. There can be mistakes of commission or mistakes of omission, or errors in the interpretation of facts.

5. Auditors are primarily interested in the prevention, detection and disclosure of errors for the following reasons:

    a. The existence of errors may indicate to an auditor that the accounting records of his client are unreliable and thus are not satisfactory as a basis from which to prepare financial statements. The existence of a material number of errors may lead the auditor to conclude that proper accounting records, as required by Section 221 CA 1985, have not been kept. This is a ground for qualification of the auditor's report under Section 237(2).

    b. If the auditor wishes to place reliance on any internal control, he should ascertain and evaluate those controls and perform compliance tests on their operations. If compliance tests indicate a material number of errors then the auditor may be unable to place reliance on internal control. For example, a client invoices goods of both zero rated and standard rated VAT supplies, the VAT is calculated by Clerk A on a calculator and checked by Clerk B. The auditor tests the control by reperforming a sample of the calculations and a significant number of errors are found. The auditor cannot rely upon the control.

    c. If errors are of sufficient magnitude they may be sufficient to affect the *truth* and *fairness* of the view given by the financial statements. If errors in VAT calculation are made then the liability to HM Customs and Excise will be incorrect. The affect of the total number of errors may not be *material* enough to affect the true and fair view. In that case, the auditor is not concerned with the error, except that he will inform his client in the management letter. However, the auditor has to have good *evidence* that the effect of the errors is not *material*.

Fraud and other irregularities

6. The term 'Fraud and other irregularities is used for several sins including:

   a. Fraud, which involves the use of deception to obtain an unjust or illegal financial advantage. An example of fraud might be the action of J. the principal shareholder and director of J Ltd in intentionally stating stock to be larger than it actually was. This may be criminal deception in that he is intending to obtain an illegal advantage for J Ltd by continuing to receive trade credit from K Ltd who have reviewed J Ltd's accounts. There is a possibility that J Ltd may not be able to fulfil its obligations under the continued credit line.

   b. Intentional misstatements in, or omissions of amounts or disclosures from, an entity's accounting records or financial statements.

   c. Theft. whether or not accompanied by misstatements of accounting records or financial statements.

   Illegal acts is another term. This is any act which is contrary to law. It may be committed intentionally or inadvertently. In our over-regulated society acts contravening laws relating to planning, health and safety, pollution, employment etc are easy to commit either intentionally or in ignorance of the law.

   The auditor may be concerned with a known or proven fraud or other irregularity but the problems arise mainly with suspected frauds and situations where the auditor suspects wrongdoing but has no hard data.

7. The auditor's responsibility towards fraud and other irregularities is not dissimilar to that in relation to errors:

   a. Irregularities may mean that proper accounting records have not been kept. For example, the financial position of the company may be unable to be disclosed with reasonable accuracy S.221(1)(a) or *all* sums of money received are not entered in the accounting records, S.221(2)(a).

   b. The existence of irregularities may indicate that some internal controls are not effective and that the auditor cannot place reliance on those internal controls.

   c. Irregularities may exist which prevents the financial statements from showing a true and fair view and complying with Companies Act requirements. Examples:

      i. Theft of stock by employees and the public from a supermarket chain is commonplace and readers of financial statements presume that some thefts will have occurred. Providing the thefts are within normal tolerances, the accounts do not need to show the fact of or the amount (always unknown) of such thefts.

         However, a *material* theft of cash concealed by suppression of copy invoices, in one particular year, by the company accountant would need to be *disclosed* in the accounts. Otherwise, readers would have a wrong view of the annual profits in relation to trends in annual profits.

      ii. Intentional inclusion in the accounts of debts which are known by the directors to be bad would lead to a wrong view being given to readers of the accounts, of profits and capital.

Materiality

8. A true and fair view may be given by financial statements of Huge plc with or without disclosure of a minor petty cash defalcation. On the other hand, a theft by an employee of £50,000 from Small Ltd., would have to be disclosed if the profits were reported as £45,000. The latter is material to the accounts and the former is not.

9. Materiality is discussed elsewhere and should be fully understood by my readers. However, if an auditor, knows or suspects that an error or irregularity has occurred or exists, then he cannot apply materiality consideration until he had sufficient evidence of the *extent* of the error or irregularity. Consequently, investigations may need to be made (by the auditor or by the client) into all errors and irregularities so that the auditor can have evidence of the materiality of the matter concerned.

Responsibility for prevention and detection of errors and irregularities

10. Primary responsibility for the prevention and detection of errors and irregularities rests with management. This responsibility arises out of a contractual duty of care by directors and managers and also because directors and other managers act in a stewardship capacity with regard to the property entrusted to them by the shareholders or other owners. How they exercise this duty of care is a matter for them, but in most cases their duty may be discharged by instituting and maintaining a strong system of internal control.

There are many ways the Board can discharge their duty toward prevention and detection of fraud and error. These include:

   - complying with the document giving advice to directors following the recommendations of the Cadbury committee.
   - developing a Code of Conduct, monitoring compliance and taking action against breaches
   - establishing systems of internal control, monitoring effectiveness and taking corrective action
   - establishing an internal audit function
   - establishing a compliance function, that is a separate department of the enterprise specifically charges with ensuring compliance with regulations of all sorts
   - having an audit committee.

11. The auditor is not required to assist the directors in this task but the guideline does suggest that an auditor should remind directors of director responsibilities of this kind, (in the engagement letter or other communication) and of the need to have a system of internal control as a *deterrent* to errors and irregularities.

12. The auditor, however, must obtain sufficient relevant reliable audit evidence to support his opinion. In regard to errors and irregularities he should have sufficient evidence that no material errors and irregularities have occurred or if they have occurred, then they have been either corrected and/or been properly disclosed in the financial statements.

The auditor's responsibility is to properly plan, perform, and evaluate his audit work so as to have a reasonable expectation of detecting material misstatements in the financial statements, whether they are caused by fraud, other irregularities or errors.

Audit planning

13. Before preparing the audit plan, the auditor should appraise the risk of material errors and irregularities having taken place. Factors to take into account would include the situation facing the client (eg financial difficulties) or known problems with internal controls. The whole approach to the audit may be coloured by the risks involved.

14. In detail, the matters to be considered might involve:
    - The nature of the business, its services and its products (which may be susceptible to misappropriation). Organisations which involve cash takings (eg retailers) and easily portable and valuable assets (eg jewellers) are particularly at risk. As also are organisations where assets are held in a fiduciary capacity (eg solicitors who hold clients monies before handling them on to the appropriate persons).
    - Circumstances which may induce management to understate profits, eg the impact of taxation on profits.
    - Circumstances which may induce management to overstate profits (or understate losses) eg to retain the confidence of investors, bankers or creditors, to meet profit forecasts, to increase profit related remuneration or to stave off the threat of insolvency proceedings, or where management have shares or share options.
    - The known strength, quality and effectiveness of management.
    - The internal control environment including the degree of management involvement and supervision and the degree of segregation of duties, and where there is excessive authority vested in a senior officer.
    - The ability of the management to override otherwise effective controls.
    - The existence and effectiveness of internal audit.
    - The accounting record type. Changeovers to computers are notorious for giving opportunity for error and fraud.

15. In particular account areas matters to consider include:
    - The susceptibility of an area to irregularity, eg cash sales, portable and valuable stock, exclusion of liabilities.
    - Unusual transactions.
    - Related party transactions.
    - Materiality.

16. The information on the matters outlined above will come from prior experience and the annual review of the business and environment. Weight given will depend upon:
    - The type of error or irregularity that may occur or is known to have occurred.
    - The relative risk of occurrence.
    - Materiality.
    - The relative effectiveness of the different audit tests available.

Internal control

17. Internal controls are designed, in part, to prevent and deter errors and irregularities. The auditor has a duty to ascertain the enterprise's system of recording and processing transactions and assess its adequacy as a basis for the preparation of financial statements. In so doing, he will inevitably examine also the internal controls since they are inextricably

linked with the system of recording and processing. The auditor may wish to place reliance on some internal controls and must then ascertain and evaluate those controls and perform compliance tests on their operation. Thus the auditor is most likely to acquire some knowledge of the existence and effectiveness of internal controls and this knowledge may be very extensive.

18. This review of internal control may indicate potential or actual instances of fraud and error which may lead to the auditor determining by audit tests if fraud or error has taken place and to what extent. In any event, the auditor should inform his client of any potential fraud or error in the management letter.

19. The auditor does not have a specific responsibility by statute to consider internal controls except as outlined in Para 17 above.

Indications of irregularities

20. Possible indications of the existence of irregularities include:

   a. Missing vouchers or documents. An employee may destroy an invoice copy and pocket the cash paid in connection with the invoice.

   b. Evidence of falsified documents. Note the Thomas Gerrard case where invoice dates were altered to place the documents in a different year to bolster profits.

   c. Unsatisfactory explanations. Auditors should always say 'show me' and insist on hard evidence when asking for explanations.

   d. Evidence of disputes. Late or partial payments by debtors may indicate disputed invoices.

   e. Unexplained items on reconciliation or suspense accounts. Differences on bought and sales ledger control accounts may indicate trivial non-material errors but may indicate real fraud or major errors.

   f. Evidence that internal control is not operating as it is intended to. Explanations that short cuts have been made to achieve greater efficiency may in fact have been made to facilitate fraudulent conversion.

   g. Evidence of unduly lavish life styles by officers and employees. Suspicion may be in order but other explanations (eg inheritances) may be possible.

   h. Failure of figures to agree with expectations produced by analytical review. An unexpectedly low gross profit ratio or a surprisingly high breakage rate in a glass factory may hide defalcations.

   i. Investigation by government department or the police, or a regulatory authority.

   j. Substantial fees, commissions or other payments which are larger or smaller than is usual or are to consultants or advisers for unspecified services.

   k. Transactions with overseas 'shell' or tax haven companies or numbered bank accounts.

   l. Payments made to officials of home or overseas governments.

Companies may be involved in frauds on investors, creditors, or governments or may be involved in 'laundering' monies from criminal, drug dealing or mafia activities.

Audit tests and irregularities

21. Audit tests may unearth irregularities although their primary purpose is to simply obtain audit evidence. Compliance tests are designed to seek evidence that the controls, which the auditor may desire to place reliance upon, are effective. Compliance tests may also reveal actual or possible irregularities. Substantive tests are designed to obtain audit evidence of the completeness, accuracy and validity of information. Again irregularities may be revealed as a by-product of the tests.

22. Some audit tests are designed to detect irregularities in addition to obtaining audit evidence. For example, tests may be designed to reveal understatements of liabilities or overstatement of assets such as stock and debtors.

23. In general, an auditor is a watchdog not a bloodhound and tests designed specifically and uniquely to detect irregularities will be performed only when the auditor's suspicions are aroused.

Action to be taken on discovery by an auditor of potential errors or irregularities

24. The following sequence of actions may be appropriate:

   a. Consider materiality. If the matter could not be material in the context of the accounts then take no further action apart from informing management. Consider again paragraph 9 above.

   b. If the matter may be material, perform appropriate additional tests.

   c. If it appears that irregularities or errors have occurred, and may be material, then consider the effects on the financial statements and ensure that these have been prepared with such adjustments and amendments (and disclosures) as may be required.

   d. If further investigations are required and the accounts cannot be delayed, then the auditor's report may have to be qualified for uncertainty.

   e. In events where errors or irregularities have occurred ensure top management are aware of such events.

   f. Any weakness in the system of accounting and internal control which may give or have given rise to error or irregularity should be fully discussed with, and reported to, management.

Reporting

25. a. *To members.* Errors and irregularities need not be reported to members as such. But if financial statements or any part of them do not or may not give a true and fair view or conform to statute or if proper accounting records have not been kept, then the auditor has his statutory duties under sections 236 and 237.

   b. *To top management.* In the event of the auditor suspecting that management may be involved in or condoning irregularities, then a report to the main board or the audit committee may be necessary.

   c. *To management.* All actual or potential irregularities discovered should be in the management letter, with recommendations for changes.

   d. *To third parties.* This is a very difficult area and has been covered in the chapter on unlawful acts of clients and their staffs.

The auditor should:

i. Take legal advice or advice from his professional body.

ii. Ensure the accounts give a true and fair view.

iii. Disclosure to third parties (eg the police) only matters where he has a clear public duty to disclose (eg if a serious crime is contemplated).

iv. Consider resignation and its effects under Section 392. SAS 110 considers resignation as the step of last resort.

Requirements of SAS 110

26. SAS 100 has a number of specific requirements:

a. auditors should plan and perform their audit procedures and evaluate and report the results thereof *recognising* that fraud or error may materially affect the financial statements

b. When planning the audit the auditors should assess the *risk* that fraud or error may cause the financial statements to contain material *misstatements*

c. Based on their *risk* assessment, the auditors should design audit procedures so as to have a reasonable expectation of detecting *misstatements* arising from fraud or error which are *material* to the *financial statements*.

d. When auditors become *aware* of information which indicates that fraud or error may exist, they should obtain an *understanding* of the nature of the event and the circumstances in which it has occurred, and sufficient other information to evaluate the possible effect on the *financial statements*. If the auditors believe that the indicated fraud or error could have a *material* effect on the financial statements, they should perform appropriate modified or additional procedures

e. When the auditors become aware of, or suspect that there may be, instances of error or fraudulent conduct, they should *document* their findings and, subject to any *requirement to report them direct to a third party*, discuss them with the *appropriate level* of management.

f. The auditor should consider the *implications* of suspected or actual error or fraudulent conduct in relation to *other aspects* of the audit, particularly the reliability of management representations.

g. The auditors should as soon as practicable *communicate* their findings to the appropriate level of management, the Board or the Audit Committee if:

– they suspect or discover fraud, even if the potential effect on the financial statements is *immaterial*

– material fraud is actually found to exist

h. Where the auditors conclude that the view given by the financial statements could be affected by a level of *uncertainty* concerning the consequences of a suspected or actual fraud which, in their opinion, is *fundamental*, they should include an *explanatory paragraph* in their report.

i. Where the auditors conclude that that a suspected or actual instance of fraud or error has a material effect on the financial statements and they *disagree* with the accounting treatment or with the extent, or the *lack of disclosure* in the financial statements they should issue an *adverse or qualified* opinion.

j. If the auditors are unable to determine whether fraud or error has occurred because of *limitation of scope* of their work, they should issue a *disclaimer or a qualified* opinion.

k. Where the auditors become aware of a suspected or actual fraud they should:

  – *consider* whether the matter may be one that ought to be reported to a *proper authority* in the public interest; and where this is the case

  – except where there is possible director involvement, *discuss* the matter with the Board including any audit committee.

l. Where, having *considered* any views expressed on behalf of the entity and in the light of any *legal advice* obtained, the auditors conclude that the matter ought to be reported to the proper authority in the public interest, they should notify the directors in writing of their view and, if the entity does not do so voluntarily itself or is unable to provide evidence that the matter has been reported, they should *report* it themselves.

m. When a suspected or actual instance of fraud casts doubt on the *integrity* of the directors auditors should make a report direct to a proper authority in the public interest without delay and without informing the directors in advance.

Notes:

  – a proper authority may be the Serious Fraud Office, the Police, the Securities and Investments Board, the Bank of England or many others

  – qualified auditors' reports are covered by Chapter 32

  – fraud is a delicate matter and before doing anything precipitate an auditor should take legal advice and discuss the matter with her professional body.

Summary

27. a. There is a difference in perception of auditor's duties on errors and fraud between auditors and the public.

  b. An auditor's duty is to give his opinion on the truth and fairness etc., of financial statements.

  c. Discovery of some errors and frauds may be a by-product of the audit.

  d. Discovery of the existence of and disclosure of errors and fraud may be essential to the true and fair view.

  e. Errors are unintentional misstatements in, or omissions of amounts or disclosures from, an entity's accounting records or financial statements. Frauds and other irregularities include frauds (which involves the use of deception to obtain an unjust or illegal financial advantage), intentional misstatements in or omissions of amounts or disclosures from, an entity's accounting records or financial statements and theft as defined in the Theft Act 1968.

  f. Materiality is an important concept in this area and the auditor must have evidence that a matter is not material.

  g. Audit planning must take into account the risk of material misstatement due to errors or irregularities.

  h. Auditors should disclose irregularities to their clients, should ensure their responsibilities under Statute have been observed but should not, in general, disclose irregularities to third parties.

Points to note

28. a.   Some audits under statutes or regulations other than the Companies Act give auditors more extensive duties towards internal control and irregularities. For example, the Building Societies Act 1986 requires the auditor to review and report on a society's establishment and maintenance of a system of control, supervision and inspection. The Local Government Finance Act 1982 requires the auditor of a local authority to actively seek out irregularities and to certify losses due from persons responsible and to recover the sum from them.

   b.   The engagement letter should educate the client in the true nature of an audit and outline the auditor's duties towards irregularity and fraud. The letter should say that the auditor will endeavour to plan his audit so that he has a reasonable expectation of detecting material mis-statements in the financial statements resulting from irregularities or fraud, but that the examination should not be relied upon to disclose all irregularities and frauds which may exist. Some clients may desire a special examination for irregularities and fraud outside the audit.

   c.   In some audits, the possibility of fraud is especially high (eg banks and other financial service businesses). In these types of businesses reliance on the work of the internal auditor may be very important.

   d.   Irregularities in the form of falsifying financial statements are a special risk in companies with going concern problems. The auditor must always be aware of temptations of management to dress or falsify their financial statements to present an untrue but desirable view of the results and position.

   e.   An auditor has the right to require from management any information and explanations he may need. It is reasonable for an auditor to ask management if any irregularities have occurred and, if any are discovered, for the full facts. Section 389A may be helpful here.

   If the auditor feels that he has not been given all the information and explanations that he needs then *the scope of his audit has been restricted* and he should consider qualifying his report.

   In extreme cases he should resign and invoke the Companies Act rules outlined in Chapter 3.

   f.   A number of Acts of Parliament (Financial Services Act 1986, Building Societies Act 1986 and the Banking Act 1987) have changed the rules on the regulation of many financial services businesses. One change has been the imposition of a duty on auditors in certain circumstances to report improprieties directly to a regulatory body. This is a very interesting and controversial new idea which remains to be worked out in practice.

   Guidance on this matter is now given to auditors in the Statement of Auditing Standards SAS 620 *The auditors' right and duty to report to regulators in the financial sector.* This is a very sensitive matter but it does allow the auditor to report serious misconduct or incompetence to the regulatory body in order to protect the investing public.

Case study 1 for Chapter 19

Kwizeene Products Ltd., are wholesalers of household improvement goods with a network of twenty depots in England and Wales. The auditors, Watchhound & Co., are conducting the final audit of the financial statements for the year ending 31st December 19-6 in March 19-7.

The accounts include the following figures (in £'000).

	19-6	19-5
Turnover	10,500	10,100
Gross Profit	2,415	2,223
Net Profit	256	388
Stock	1,245	1,031
Debtors	1,472	1,211
Creditors	861	998

The auditor discovers the following:

a. The company is owned by the Gull family and controlled by Hugo Buzzard, a very dominating character who married the younger daughter of the company founder.

b. Hugo is negotiating for a renewal of overdraft facilities and for a loan to expand turnover.

c. In the interim audit, the wages area (with 95 employees) was found to have very weak controls. Limited tests at that time showed no major errors.

d. A routine test on the 21 representatives' expenses has just revealed that 13 of the 34 items were not supported by vouchers and appeared to be of expenses not actually incurred. The accountant responsible for payment of them referred Watchhound & Co. to Hugo who told them to mind their own business but that all such expenses were properly paid.

e. The auditors have discovered that certain stock lines were sold but were not purchased. They suspect that the items were stolen goods. The amount of the sales of these goods is not determinable without an analysis of the thousands of sales invoices.

Discussion

Discuss the implications of the figures in the accounts and all the other data for the auditors and for the audit of the 19-6 accounts of the company.

Case study 2 for Chapter 19

Offa Builders Merchants plc have many branches in the Midlands and a total turnover of £20 million a year. Profits are £2 million and net assets £8 million. In the financial year ending 31.12.-8 the audit clerk on a routine visit to the large branch at Darlafield accidently overhead the accountant at the branch being given cash by a customer for some goods. Her suspicions were aroused and further investigations and questioning revealed that the accountant and the general manager had systematically defrauded the company of some £300,000 over the previous 3 years by selling goods for cash at a discount or by misappropriating cheques. In both cases no invoices were raised or if they were then they were suppressed.

The main Board were informed and the two miscreants dismissed but not prosecuted. Some £30,000 of the missing money was eventually recovered.

Discussion

Consider this case from the point of view of:

a. Materiality.
b. Internal control and the audit.
c. Previous years.
d. The Annual Accounts.
e. Accounting Records.
f. The auditor's report.
g. Reports to outsiders (eg the police)
h. Reports to Management.

Student self testing questions *Questions with answers apparent from the text*

1. a. Define errors, irregularities, frauds, illegal acts. (4, 6)
   b. What are the auditors duties towards errors? (5)
   c. What are the auditors duties towards the detection of irregularities? (7)
   d. What is the relevance of materiality to these matters? (8)
   e. Who is responsible for internal control in a company? (10)
   f. What factors may indicate a risk of irregularities? (14)
   g. Explain the dictum 'an auditor is a watchdog not a bloodhound'. (23)
   h. What should an auditor do if he discovers an irregularity? (24)
   i. To whom should an auditor report irregularities? (25)
   j. Explain the relevance of the Companies Act 1985, Section 237 (1–4) to all this. (25)
   k. Summarise the requirements of SAS 110. (26)

Examination question *(Answer begins on page 546)*

1. a. 'If the auditor wishes to place reliances on any internal controls, he should ascertain and evaluate those controls and perform compliance tests on their operation.'
      Required:
      Critically evaluate the methods which an auditor may employ to ascertain a business's internal controls. (6 marks)
   b. Two employees of the Western Printing Co. Ltd have for a number of years been committing frauds which have remained undetected.
      i. George Smith, the head storeman, is responsible for checking deliveries of raw materials for quantity and quality against copy purchase orders prepared by the purchasing department. In collusion with a supplier's delivery driver he has consistently accepted short deliveries but signed a receipt for the quantity of goods ordered. The delivery driver has subsequently sold the goods delivered short and shared the proceeds with George Smith.
      ii. John Brown, the chief purchasing officer, has had an arrangement with a stationery supplier that they will pay directly to him a commission on all orders placed by the company. He has sole responsibility for choosing suppliers and has ensured that all stationery orders have been given to this supplier.

Required:

a. List internal controls which could have been employed to minimise the possibility of each of these frauds taking place. You should give the reason for the control in each case. (5 marks)

b. Draft a substantive or vouching audit programme covering the procedures from the requisitioning of raw materials through to the approval of the invoice for payment. (6 marks)

c. Discuss the auditor's general responsibility with regard to the prevention and detection of fraud. (3 marks)

(ACCA)

Examination questions without answers

2. During your interim audit tests of the wages and salaries payrolls of Burnden Ltd., you discover the following exceptions and note them for subsequent discussion with the company's management.

a. The production manager had dismissed an employee but had not informed the wages department. He had submitted clock cards to the wages department and misappropriated the employee's wages. The employee had been dismissed two months prior to the matter being discovered by you. (5 marks)

b. Payments for casual labour are made by the company out of petty cash and recipients are asked to sign a petty cash voucher on receipt of their wages. The total amount paid for casual labour in the seven months to the date of the interim audit was £15,000. No record other than the petty cash voucher is maintained by the company and no deductions for income tax and national insurance are made by the company. The factory manager notifies the petty cashier verbally of the wages due to the casual labour force. (5 marks)

c. An amount of £1,000 per month was being deducted from the gross pay of the managing director of the company. On enquiring why this deduction was being made, you were told by the managing director that the company had purchased a small house for him and he was repaying the capital cost of that house back to the company on an interest free basis. The capital cost was being repaid in twenty-four monthly instalments and he had repaid £3,000 of the amount to date. On reviewing the directors' minutes, no reference to the transaction could be found. (5 marks)

You are required to discuss the significance of the above audit findings.

(ACCA 2 88) (Total 15 marks)

3. Princeton and Yale are in partnership. Previously accounts have been prepared by their bookkeeper but as their business is growing they are considering asking your firm to act as auditors to the partnership.

Required:

a. State how a non-statutory audit could assist the partnership. (6 marks)

b. Mr Yale has stressed that, from his point of view the main purpose of the audit would be to detect fraud. Briefly state your opinion of this viewpoint. (6 marks)

c. Identify the major difficulty you could potentially face in a non-statutory audit, and state how you would try to overcome it. (3 marks)

(AAT J'87) (Total 15 marks)

Asset and liability verification

1. A large part of the Final Audit stage will be taken up with the verification of the assets and liabilities appearing in the balance sheet. There are well established techniques for verifying specific assets and liabilities. All auditing examinations contain one or more questions on this subject.

2. Chapter 20 sets out the methods of verification which are applicable to assets generally and also considers the detailed methods of verifying specific fixed assets and investments. Chapter 21 describes the verification of current assets other than stock. Chapter 22 is concerned itself with liability verification and contains some of the matters which are currently worrying the profession.

20 Asset verification

Introduction

1. The auditor has a duty to verify all the assets appearing on the balance sheet and also a duty to verify that there are *no other* assets which ought to appear on the balance sheet.

Aspects to be verified

2. The following aspects of each asset must be verified:
   a. Cost.
   b. Authorisation.
   c. Value.
   d. Existence.
   e. Beneficial Ownership
   f. Presentation in the Accounts.

   These aspects can be remembered by the mnemonic CAVEBOP.

   Most examination questions in this area can be answered adequately by running through each of these and devising means of verifying each aspect.

   You will also appreciate that the amount of evidence required will depend partly on the risk of misstatement.

3. Older text books tended to stress *existence, ownership* and *value* only. The addition of presentation reflects the relatively greater importance attached now to the *fair* as well as the *true* view given by accounts and the importance of an appropriate selection and disclosure of *accounting policies.*.

4. When verifying assets at a balance sheet data it is possible to divide the assets into two classes:
   a. Those *acquired* during the year under review.
   b. Those *held* at the date of the *previous* balance sheet.

For a. type assets it will be necessary to *vouch* their acquisition. This is why the terms *cost* and *authorisation* have been included in paragraph 2.

For b. type assets, the acquisition will have been dealt with in a previous year. The presentation will, of course, need to be *consistent* with the presentation adopted in previous years. Most examination questions state whether or not the assets concerned were purchased in the year under review. You will appreciate that the distinction does not arise with current assets.

Verification methods

5. a. Make or request from client's staff a *schedule* of each asset. This schedule will show the following and suggest the associated verification procedures:

   i. **Opening balance**
       - Verify by reference to *previous year's* balance sheet and audit files.

   ii. **Acquisitions**
       - Vouch the *cost* with documentary evidence eg invoices.
       - Vouch the *authority* for the acquisition with minutes or with authorised delegated authority.

   iii. **Disposals**
       - Vouch the *authority* – minutes or company procedures.
       - Examine *documentation*.
       - Verify *reasonableness* of the proceeds.
       - Pay special attention to *scrappings*.
       - Note *accounting* treatment.

   iv. **Depreciation, amortisation** and other *write downs*
       - Vouch *authorisation* of policy with minutes.
       - Examine adequacy and appropriateness of policy.
       - Investigate *revaluations*.
       - Check *calculations*.

   v. The above should *reconcile* both as to physical quantity and sterling value of the closing balance.

   vi. The use of plant or other asset *registers* can be of great use to the auditor.

   vii. **Internal control** procedures for the purchase, disposal, accounting and maintenance of assets are very relevant.

   b. **Existence and Ownership.** These are treated together but note that existence does not imply ownership. For example, my television set *exists* and is in my house, but is in fact owned by the Co-op from whom I rent it!

   Verification procedures include:

   i. **Physical inspection**. Auditors should not sit in offices but should get about seeing things. Of course, sitting in a client's office goes to confirm the existence of that office!

   ii. Inspection *of title deeds and certificates of ownership* eg, share certificates. This is a technique that confirms together existence and ownership. Problems arise if the deeds are held by third parties (a certificate from the third party is needed) possibly as security for a loan.

iii. External verification. This applies primarily to 'choses in action' eg, bank accounts debtors, loans etc. A letter of acknowledgement is sought from the bank, debtor etc.

iv. Ancillary evidence. Examples are:

The confirmation of the existence of property by examination of rate demands, repair bills and other outgoings. Ownership is not necessarily implied.

Investment ownership and existence tend to be confirmed by the receipt of dividends and interest.

c. Presentation and Value

i. **Appropriate accounting policies** must be adopted, consistently applied, and adequately disclosed.

ii. **Accounting Standards** must be followed.

iii. **Materiality** must be considered. For example, in a balance sheet of a large company it would be misleading to show an asset such as patents in a class by itself it its total value was negligible in relation to other assets.

iv. The *classification* of assets can be difficult. Certain industrial structures can be considered as buildings or as plant with consequent major differences in depreciation, profit, and asset and equity values. A number of interesting examples have cropped up in tax cases. A dry dock including the cost of excavation has been held to be plant (Barclay Curle 1969), as has a swimming pool for use on a caravan site (Beach Station Caravans 1974). The auditor may take a contrary view to the tax courts and of course to the Board of the Company he is auditing.

v. The choice of *disclosure* of an asset as a separate item or as part of a single figure representing a class of asset is important for a true and fair view. Also important is the choice of words used in the description. In some cases, assets could be classed as fixed or as current eg, investments.

vi. The distinction between *revenue* and *capital* is important. Sometimes this is a matter of accounting policy eg research and development. Sometimes it is a matter of opinion; for example repair expenditure is revenue but may include an element of improvement which is capital.

d. **Other matters relevant to verification**

i. The *letter of representation*. This is dealt with in Chapter 30.

ii. **Reasonableness** and being *'put upon enquiry'* In all audit assignments, the auditor investigates thoroughly and seeks adequate assurances on the truth and fairness of all the items in the Accounts. However, he does not do so with a suspicious mind. He should not assume that there is something wrong, but if he comes across something which seems to him unlikely, unreasonable, suspicious he is said to be *'put upon enquiry'*. In such circumstances he is required to *probe the matter to the bottom* to adequately assure himself there exists nothing untoward or to unearth the whole matter. (Part of the judgement in re the Kingston Cotton Mill Co. Ltd., as long ago as 1896).

iii. Some assets are pledged or mortgaged as securities for loans. This may involve deposit of title deeds etc., with a lender, or in some cases the asset itself. This creates problems for the auditor who must also see that the *liability* is properly described as *secured*.

iv. **Taxation.** Tax and capital allowance computations should be in accordance with asset accounts. Clearly the auditor will be *put upon enquiry* if claims for capital allowances are made for items of plant which do not appear in the plant register.

v. **Insurance.** The auditor would be *put upon enquiry* if there were no correspondence between the assets in the balance sheet and the assets insured, and if there were differences between the balance sheet figures and the insured values.

vi. **Other than balance sheet date verification**. Some assets can be verified at dates other than the balance sheet date. The techniques are discussed later but in sum they are:

Verify at an earlier date and reconcile with acquisitions and disposals to balance sheet date.

Verify at an earlier date and then parcel them up and seal the parcels. At balance sheet date examine acquisitions, vouch proceeds of disposals, and see all other items are still sealed.

vii. Third parties. Auditors must take special care to satisfy themselves that all assets held by third parties are included in the balance sheet and verified. Likewise, no assets owned by third parties may be included in the balance sheet.

Fixed assets

6. It is not possible to discuss in detail the verification of all possible types of fixed asset. We shall discuss in detail only Freehold Land and Buildings. These two assets are obviously inseparable in ordinary circumstances, but accountants are increasingly seeing them as separate assets.

a. *Land*. Consider always for *all* assets if sub-division into separate types is possible. In this case there is:

i. Registered land.

ii. Unregistered land, or

Land bought in the year

Land owned at the end of the previous year.

Existence of all land is best verified by inspection.

Ownership of land is verified by a certificate from the land registry for registered land and by inspection of the deeds for unregistered land. This inspection is carried out by an auditor who is not normally an expert on conveyancing. However, it is enough for him to verify that the deeds are prima facie in order with, for example, the last conveyance being into the name of the client. Land bought in the year will be vouched by reference to the solicitor's completion statement and bill of costs (usual name for a solicitor's fee invoice) and correspondence.

The value of the land will be at

- Cost
- Below cost

– Above cost.

Land at cost will be the norm and creates no problems. Land below cost will be unusual and the auditor will need to:

Examine the reason for the write down.

Examine the director's minute authorising it.

Appraise the adequacy of the write down.

Ensure adequate disclosure of the facts.

Land above cost is dealt with in Chapter 36.

b. Buildings. Buildings can be:

   i. Bought in the year

   ii. Owned at the beginning of the year.

   iii. Under construction at the end of the year.

If under construction or bought in the year they can be:

Manufactured internally by the client.

Constructed by a builder

Bought secondhand.

Buildings can be valued at:

– Cost

– Below cost

– Above cost.

In the past, buildings have usually been valued at cost or above cost when periodic revaluations occur. The question of property revaluations is dealt with in a later chapter. SSAP No. 12 recommends that buildings be depreciated over their useful life. Whatever depreciation policy is adopted the auditor must see that adequate disclosure is made and that the policy is consistently applied.

Investments

7. It is very important to distinguish the categories into which investments can be divided. These include:

a. Variability

   i. Fixed sum deposits.

   ii. Investments of varying value.

b. Quotation

   i. Quoted investments.

   ii. Unquoted investments.

c. Ownership proportion

   i. Investments giving minority interests (ie less than 20%).

   ii. Investments in associated Companies (ie 20-50%).

   iii. Investments in Subsidiary Companies (usually but not necessarily greater than 50%).

    d. Period of Ownership

        i. Short term investments.

        ii. Long term investments.

    e. Treatment in Balance Sheet

        i. Investments which are Current Assets.

        ii. Investments which are not Current Assets.

8. Some special points to note on the verification of investments are:

    a. Internal control is very important. Note particularly the separation of duties of authorisation, custody and recording.

    b. Transaction documents. Students should try to see examples. Look at Extel and Moodie cards and read the Financial Times.

    c. Physical inspection is very desirable; *all* the certificates should be examined *together*.

    d. Sometimes the certificates are examined *before* the year end and parcelled up and sealed. Only unsealed parcels and new certificates need be checked at the year end.

    e. The Companies Act has much to say on the subject.

Summary

9. a Verification of assets always appears in auditing examinations.

    b. The verification is of assertions about each asset. A useful mnemonic is CAVEBOP.

    c. Assets can be:

        i. Acquired in the year

        ii. Held at the end of the previous year.

    d. Verification methods vary according to the asset but many students have found the following list of points useful in examinations:

i.	Schedule of each Asset.	xvi.	Materiality.
ii.	Cost verification.	xvii.	Put upon enquiry.
iii.	Registers of Assets.	xviii.	Insurance.
iv.	Internal Control.	xix.	Lessening in Value – Depreciation.
v.	Physical Inspection.	xx.	Events after BS date.
vi.	Title Deeds	xxi.	Disposal.
vii.	SSAPs.	xxii.	Companies Act.
viii.	Classification.	xxiii.	Held by others.
ix.	Representation Letter.	xxiv.	Ancillary Evidence.
x.	External Verification.	xxv.	Revaluation.
xi.	Authority.	xxvi.	Taxation
xii.	Minutes and *Correspondence*.	xxvii.	Auditing guidelines.
xiii.	Security for obligations.	xxviii.	Proper accounting records.
xiv.	Capital or Revenue.	xxix.	Risk of misstatement.
xv.	Other than BS date.		

The initial letters form useful mnemonics!

Points to note

10. a. All auditing examinations contain questions on asset and/or liability verification.

b. Students fail to answer adequately by making too few points. This chapter will provide enough ideas for students to make enough points in their answers.

c. Questions on asset verification are sometimes on existence, ownership, value and presentation. Some are specifically on one or two aspects only. It is clearly vital to answer the question asked!

d. It is not possible in this manual to give detailed verification procedures for all possible assets. To answer specific questions, remember CAVEBOP and the 29 points and apply them as required.

e. Note that many syllabuses require students to have an appreciation of the accounting requirements of the Companies Act 1985 on disclosure of fixed assets and depreciation.

f. Some companies transfer assets from current assets to fixed assets. Examples are:
   - a vehicle dealer transferring a stock item to fixed assets as the vehicle is to be used as a fixed asset eg as a rep's car or as a delivery van.
   - a speculative builder may transfer unsold houses to fixed assets as the houses will be let as investment properties.

   There may be a tendency in times of trade recession for this to be done to avoid having a stock item valued at below cost ie at net realisable value. UITF Abstract 5 requires that where an asset is so transferred the transfer should be made at the lower of cost and net realisable value at the date of transfer. Thus the difference between carrying value pre transfer and the NRV at transfer date is a loss in the Profit and Loss Account. Depreciation or other fixed asset valuation procedures start at the date of transfer.

g. The extent and manner of verification of an asset depends on the degree of risk of misstatement possible with the asset. Inherent risk depends on many factors including the degree of estimation (eg provision for warranties), the complexity of the assets (eg work in progress), the judgement involved (eg stock at net realisable value) and the susceptibility to loss or misappropriation (eg cash), transactions not subject to ordinary processing (eg the acquisition of subsidiary companies). The extent of reliance on internal control in reducing substantive tests depends on the auditors' perception of control risk.

Case study for Chapter 20

Pinocchio Robots plc are manufacturers of industrial robots. They own a large amount of plant and machinery which is used in the manufacture of their products and is valued at some £14 million. The company maintain good records and internal control systems. There is a plant register based on a micro-computer. Each item of plant is recorded with fields as:

Description	Estimated life
Location	Estimated residual value
Supplier	Insured value
Manufacturer	Depreciation Policy
Serial number/identifying number	Depreciation applied
Cost of purchase	Major repairs

Cost of installation	Capital allowances claimed
Date of purchase	Use in factory
Date of first use	Machine hour rate applicable
Guarantee/Warranty expiry	Responsible officer
Grant Received (if any)	Internal audit inspection dates
Manufacturers invoice number	Statutory inspection/report/Certificate
Internally generated invoice number	

There are some 250 separate items.

Discussion

    a. What facts about the plant need verification by the auditor?

    b. What audit procedures will be applied?

    c. How should plant appear in the annual accounts and notes attached to them?

    d. What Accounting Standards are relevant?

Student self testing questions

Questions with answers apparent from the text

1. a. What are the six aspects to be covered in verifying an asset? (2)

    b. List the points that could be covered in verifying an asset. (9)

    c. How is land and buildings verified? (6)

Exercises

1. Outline an audit programme for the verification of the following assets:

    a. Vehicles in a major haulage contractor.

    b. Farm machinery and equipment in a 10,000 acre mixed farm.

    c. Stock of land of a large speculative builder.

    d. A new factory building on existing land of a major manufacturer.

    e. Aircraft in a small airline.

    f. The investment portfolio of Hopp Breweries plc who make a point of having small holdings in a range of competitor brewers and suppliers.

    g. Holiday homes owned in the UK and overseas by Holiday flats plc.

    h. Plant and machinery of Duv plc a company which has been in the foundry industry but which is rapidly developing into new hi-tec metal bashing while running down its foundry activities.

Assess the inherent and control risks in each one.

Examination question [Answer begins on page 547]

1. As a technician employed on the audit of Thames Engineers plc, a large industrial company you have the task of auditing plant and machinery.

    Required:

    a. Draft an audit programme which you would expect to follow.   (9 marks)

    b. The client has suggested that they wish to change the basis of depreciation from straight line to reducing balance over the same estimated life as the greatest loss in value of the plant occurs in the early years of its life. At the same time it is proposed to revalue certain old items of plant which have been completely written off but which still have a useful life. Draft a memorandum to the partner responsible for the audit suggesting the lines of a letter which he should write to the client indicating the principles involved and the effects of the changes. (8 marks)

c. What information has to be included in accounts with respect to future capital expenditure and how would you verify the figure? (5 marks)

d. What information might have to be included in accounts with respect to land and buildings where they are not regularly independently revalued and what is the auditor's responsibility for this information? (3 marks)

(AAT)

Examination questions without answers

2. It is fundamental to an audit that the auditor should obtain reliable, relevant and sufficient evidence as to the ownership, valuation and existence of the client's assets.

You are required to explain the audit procedures necessary for the auditor to be satisfied on these points for:

a. freehold land and buildings; (8 marks)

b. trade debtors; (8 marks)

c. bank balances. (4 marks)

(ICA 91) (Total 20 marks)

3. a. State what matters contained in the Directors' minute book of a limited Company might be of importance to the auditor of that company. (7 marks)

b. In reviewing the directors' minute book of Tulkinhorn plc you have read the following:

15th March 1986.

RESOLVED: To advance to the sales manager the sum of £2,000 in cash as an advance of the expenses that he is likely to incur on the company's behalf during the next six months.

RESOLVED: That a one year time deposit of £50,000 be made with a finance company.

Required:

State briefly the audit work you would carry out in respect of the two items above.

(8 marks)

(AAT D'86) (Total 15 marks)

4. The draft balance sheet of Chigwell Haulage Limited at 31 July 1990 showed fixed assets as follows:

Cost	At 1/8/89	Additions	At 31/7/90
	£	£	£
Goodwill	20,000	–	20,000
Freehold Land	40,000	–	40,000
Freehold Buildings	120,000	100,000	220,000
Leasehold Buildings	198,000	–	198,000
Plant and Machinery	48,000	30,000	78,000
Motor Vehicles	32,000	24,000	56,000
	458,000	154,000	612,000
Depreciation	At 1/8/89	Charge for year	At 31/7/90

	£	£	£
Goodwill	1,000	1,000	2,000
Freehold Land	–	–	–
Freehold Buildings	2,200	3,800	6,000
Leasehold Buildings	1,800	2,000	3,800
Plant and Machinery	4,600	7,800	12,400
Motor Vehicles	8,000	14,000	22,000
	17,600	28,600	46,200

Net Book Value	At 31/7/89	At 31/7/90
	£	£
Goodwill	19,000	18,000
Freehold Land	40,000	40,000
Freehold Buildings	117,800	214,000
Leasehold Buildings	196,200	194,200
Plant and Machinery	43,400	65,600
Motor Vehicles	24,000	34,000
	440,400	565,800

Required

a. Outline the objectives of the auditor when examining the above items.   (6 marks)

b. Describe the audit work you would carry out in order to satisfy yourself as to the figures shown in the Balance Sheet so that you may express an audit opinion for the year.   (9 marks)

(AAT 90) (Total 15 marks)

21 Current asset verification

Introduction

1. This chapter considers some standard verification techniques for three types of current assets, debtors, cash at bank and loans. The asset verification techniques described in the previous chapter apply to these as to all assets, but as they are common examination subjects and some special techniques are commonly applied it is necessary to describe these particular techniques.

2. There is an auditing guideline – Bank reports for audit purposes.

Debtors

3. Debtors form a large item among the assets of most companies and their verification is essential. The general method of verifying debtors is:

   a. Determine the system of Internal Control over sales and debtors. The system for debtors should ensure that:

      i. Only bona fide sales bring debtors into being.

    ii. All such sales are to approved customers.

    iii. All such sales are recorded.

    iv. Once recorded the debts are only eliminated by receipt of cash or on the authority of a responsible official.

    v. Debts are collected promptly.

    vi. Balances are regularly reviewed and aged, a proper system for follow up exists, and, if necessary, adequate provision for bad and doubtful debts is made.

b. Test the effectiveness of the system.

c. Obtain a schedule of debtors.

d. Test balances on ledger accounts to the schedule and *vice versa*.

e. Test casts of the schedule.

f. Examine make up of balances. They should be composed of specific items.

g. Ensure each account is settled from time to time.

h. Examine and check control accounts.

i. Enquire into credit balances.

j. Consider the valuation of the debtors. This is dealt with in the next paragraph.

Provision for bad and doubtful debts

4. The valuation of debtors is really a consideration of the adequacy of the provision for bad and doubtful debts. The auditor should consider the following matters:

a. The adequacy of the system of internal control relating to the approval of credit and following up of poor payers.

b. The period of credit allowed and taken.

c. Whether balances have been settled by the date of the audit.

d. Whether an account is made up of specific items or not.

e. Whether an account is within the maximum credit approved.

f. Reports on each debtor from collectors, trade associations, etc.

g. Present value and realisability of securities, if any, lodged as collateral.

h. Questions of set-off.

i. The state of legal proceedings and the legal status of the debtor eg in liquidation or bankruptcy.

j. Effect, if any, of the Statute of Limitations.

k. Comparison of debtors to sales with comparison of the ratio with those of previous periods and those achieved by other companies.

l. Evidence of any debt in dispute eg for non delivery, breakages, poor quality etc.

5. Note that:

a. Debts which are considered irrecoverable should be written off to the profit and loss account.

b. Provisions for doubtful debts should be set up against debts which are considered doubtful.

  c. Some companies make round-sum or percentage provisions against doubtful debts. This practice is generally unacceptable to an auditor unless based on good statistical evidence which may come from past experience or may come from data about other similar undertakings which is obtainable from trade associations or which is publicly available.

Debtors circularisation

6. A practice that is becoming very common in the verification of debtors is to circularise the debtors or some of them for *direct confirmation*.

7. The advantages of this technique are:

  a. **Direct external evidence** is available for the existence and ownership of an asset.

  b. It provides confirmation of the effectiveness of the system of *internal control*.

  c. It assists in the auditor's evaluation of *cut-off* procedures.

  d. It provides evidence of items in dispute.

8. There are two methods, which can also be used together:

  a. **Negative** – the customer is asked to communicate only if he does *not* agree the balance. This method is mostly where internal control is very strong.

  b. **Positive** – customer is asked to reply whether he agrees the balance or not or is asked to supply the balance himself. This method is used where there is:

    i. Weak internal control.

    ii. Suspicion of irregularities.

    iii. Numerous bookkeeping errors.

9. The approach is as follows:

  a. Obtain the co-operation of the client – only he can ask third parties to divulge information.

  b. **Select method** – positive, negative, or a combination of the two.

  c. **Select** a sample. All customers can be circularised but this is unusual.

    i. Do not omit – Nil balances

      Credit balances

      Accounts written off in the period.

    ii. Give weight to overdue or disputed balances.

    iii. Use stratified samples, eg all large balances and only some small ones.

  d. The letter should be from the *client*.

  e. It should request a reply *direct to the auditor*.

  f. It *may* contain a stamped,addressed, envelope or a pre-paid reply envelope.

  g. It must be *despatched by the auditor*.

  h. Receive and evaluate replies.

  i. *Follow up* when replies are not received. This is the major problem.

10. Circularisation is sometimes carried out at dates other than the year end. This will occur only when internal control is very strong.

Example of debtors circularisation letter (positive method)

FROM	3 April 19-6

FROM

HEDONITE MANUFACTURING LTD

CLOGHAMPTON

Dear Sir

As part of their normal audit procedures, we have been requested by our auditors Quibble Query & Co to ask you to confirm direct to them your indebtedness to us as shown on the enclosed statement as at 31st December 19-5.

If the statement is in agreement with your records, please sign in the space provided below and return this letter directly to our auditors.

If the statement is not in agreement with your records please notify our auditors directly of the amount shown by your records and if possible send them full particulars of the difference.

It will be of assistance to us if you will give this request your early attention. We enclose a reply-paid envelope for your convenience.

Remittance should not be sent to our auditors.

Yours faithfully,

J. Brown, Company Secretary

....

Please do not detach

Name of Debtor

The balance shown on the statement at 31.12.-5 of £1,432.00 due from us is in agreement with our records at 31.12.-5.

.... Signature

.... Position

.... Company Stamp

To: Ecstatic Mining Ltd.

Newcastle on Tyne

Bank balances

11. Verification of bank balances is effected by:

    a. Appraisal of the Internal Control system.

    b. Examination and Investigation of the Bank Reconciliation, noting particularly:

        i. That all uncleared cheques have been cleared after date.

        ii. Lodgements credited after date, but actually paid in before date.

    c. Title should be verified by the direct confirmation from the bank. The bank must have the permission of the client to do this. The *Bank Letter* is usually on a standard form and opportunity is usually taken to ask the bank a number of questions at the same time.

    d. Value is not usually an issue with bank accounts particularly as banks are now highly regulated. However the Bank of Credit and Commerce International matter has shown that value must not be taken for granted. The auditor must always consider if a bank is in good standing.

The bank letter

12. The guideline – Bank reports for audit purposes makes a number of points. These include:

   a. The bank letter is independent audit evidence of high quality.

   b. It is useful in obtaining evidence of existence, amount, ownership and proper custody of numerous assets and of the existence and amount of liabilities.

   c. A standard letter should be sent. The form has been agreed with the banks.

   d. Before sending the letter, authority to do so has to be obtained from the client and this authority has to be given to the bank.

   e. The letter should be sent at least two weeks before the relevant year end date.

   f. The letter should be sent duplicate, one for the auditor and one for retention by the bank.

   g. If the auditor receives an unsolicited letter from the bank, he should confirm that it is authentic.

13.
Example of standard letter of request for bank report for audit purposes

---

The Manager
Quarry Bank Ltd
Cloghampton   16th December 19-6

Dear Sir

re: Hedonite Manufacturing Ltd

In accordance with your above-named customer's instructions given

1. hereon

2. in the attached authority

3. in the authority dated 14th September 19-3 held by you

please send to us, as auditors of your customer, the following information relating to its affairs at your branch as at the close of business on 31st December 19-6 and in the case of items 2, 4 and 10 during the period since 31st December 19-5.

Please state against each item any factors which may limit the completeness of your reply; if there is nothing to report, state NONE.

We enclose an additional copy of this letter. Please complete the copy in the spaces provided.

It is understood that any replies given are in strict confidence, for the purposes of our audit.

Bank Accounts

1. Full titles of all accounts, together with the account numbers and balances thereon, including nil balances.

2. Full titles and dates of closure of all accounts closed during the period.

3. The separate amounts accrued but not charged or credited at the above date of (a) charges and (b) interest.

4. The amount of any interest charged during the period if not specified separately in the bank statement.

5. Particulars of any written acknowledgement of set-off.

6. Details of loans, overdrafts, and facilities, specifying agreed limits and in the case of term loans, date for repayment or review.

Customer's Assets

7. a. **Security**

    Please give

    i.   Details of any security formally charged to the bank, including the date and type of charge.

    ii. Particulars of any undertaking to assign to the bank any assets.

    b. **Assets held but not charged**

    Please give detail

Contingent Liabilities

8. All contingent liabilities, viz.

    a. Total of bills discounted for your customer, with recourse.

    b. Details of any guarantees, bond or indemnities given to you by the customer in favour of third parties.

    c. Details of any guarantees, bonds or indemnities given by you on your customer's behalf.

    d. Total of acceptances.

    e. Total of forward foreign exchange contracts.

    f. Total of outstanding liabilities under documentary credits.

    g. Others – please give details.

Other Information

9. A list of other banks, or branches of your bank, or associated companies where you are aware that a relationship has been established during the period.

Yours faithfully,

Quibble, Query & Co
Chartered Accountants

Note that this letter is a slightly abridged form of the letter given in the guideline. Each page in the letter should be divided by a vertical line in the middle of the page. Left of the line is the information requested. Right of the line is left blank for the bank's reply.

Loans

14. Loans are not usually material assets of companies other than those whose business it is to make loans. We shall consider two types of loans:

    a. Loans other than to directors.

        Verification will be:

        i.   Examine and evaluate Internal Control. Authority is particularly important.

        ii. Obtain a schedule and test its accuracy.

        iii. Obtain certificates direct from debtors.

        iv. Examine agreements and ensure terms are being adhered to.

        v.   If a loan is secured, examine the security and consider its value and realisability.

        vi. If a loan is guaranteed, examine the status of the guarantor.

vii. Review the adequacy of provisions for bad debts. Bad debts often occur when a loan to an employee is made and the employee leaves before repayment is complete.

b. Loans to directors and connected persons.

This subject is the subject of extensive inclusions in the Companies Act.

The auditor's duties are as follows:

i. Review all loans to directors which were outstanding *at any time* during the year. *Materiality does not apply;* all loans must be reviewed.

ii. Obtain a certificate of confirmation from the directors concerned.

iii. Ensure that all such loans are subject to board minute.

iv. Ensure that the law has been complied with.

v. Ensure that full disclosure is made as required.

vi. If the requisite information is not given in the accounts, the auditor is required to give the *requisite information* in his report. (Section 237 Companies Act 1985).

Summary

15. a. The verification of current assets is a common examination subject.

b. Current assets are verified using the techniques discussed in the previous chapter.

c. Detailed verification techniques for debtors are explained.

d. The valuation of debtors is especially notable.

e. A common technique included in the verification process for debtors is direct circularisation which can be positive or negative or a mixture of both.

f. A part of the verification process for bank balances is the Bank Letter.

g. Loans to directors are subject to company law restrictions which you should know.

Points to note

16. a. The valuation of *all* current assets is the *lower of cost and net realisable value.* It is a common error to assume this method applies only to stock and work progress. Cost is perhaps a peculiar title for sums due to the company and means of course the amount which is due. This amount may differ from the amount collectable and it is the amount which will be collected which is the net realisable value.

b. Note all the detail in the debtors circularisation process.

c. Note in all these verification processes the importance of a proper evaluation and test of the Internal Control procedures.

d. Events after the accounting date (*post balance sheet events*) and before the date of the final audit are very useful in providing evidence to the auditor of existence, ownership and, particularly, value at the balance sheet date.

e. Presentation of assets in the balance sheet is always important and this is particularly so in the case of loans to directors.

f. Students should have an appreciation of the accounting requirements of the Companies Act 1985 on the disclosure of:

– debtors (long and short term) and related interest receivable.

    – cash and bank balances and related interest payable.

g. The make up of figures for debtors and bank balances must be considered to determine if:

    – any items should be separately disclosed

    – bank balances and overdrafts should properly not be set-off

h. UITF Abstract 4 notes that debtors in current assets may include some items which are receivable after more than one year (examples are the trade debtors of lessors or deferred consideration in respect of a sale of an investment). Usually it is acceptable to disclose the long term nature of these items in a note but where the items are so material in the context of total net current assets that readers may misinterpret the Balance Sheet then the amount should be shown on the face of the Balance Sheet.

Case study 1 for Chapter 21

John Dunn Locks Ltd are manufacturers of locks with some 6000 customers in the UK. The auditors Key & Partners, are engaged on the audit of the debtors at 31.7.-6.

Discussion

What factors should the auditors take into account in considering the type and extent of debtors circularisation?

The auditors decide to negatively circularise 300 customers. There were 30 replies. Of these, 26 were timing differences which were easily resolved. The remaining four were:

1. Artichoke Builders Merchants.

    – the goods invoiced in June never arrived.

2. Broccoli Construction.

    – payment was made in April. We have the returned cheque.

3. Cabbage Hardware.

    – the goods invoiced in July were damaged. We are waiting for a credit note.

4. Dill Building.

    – the balance is incorrect. We have been unable to reconcile the balance for some months. We enclose a copy of our purchase ledger account.

What are the implications of these replies for the auditors?

Case study 2 for Chapter 21

Vicarage Eximport plc trade by importing into the UK and also exporting to 60 countries. They have actual branches in 20 countries. They maintain separate bank accounts with 4 UK banks to facilitate foreign trade matters and have bank accounts in the countries where they have branches. They have an overdraft on several accounts and have given security as have the directors.

Discussion

a. Which items on the standard bank letter would be applicable to this company?

b. Which items not included in the standard letter may need to be added?

Student self testing questions *Questions with answers apparent from the text*

1. a. Outline the procedures for verifying debtors. (3)
    b. What matters should be considered in reviewing the provision for bad and doubtful debts? (4)
    c. Outline the procedures for both negative and positive circularisation. (6)
    d. What balances/accounts should not be overlooked? (9)
    e. What audit evidence accrues from the bank letter? (12)
    f. Summarise the contents of the standard bank letter? (13)
    g. When should it be sent? (12)
    h. How should loans be audited? (14)
    i. What are the Companies Act rules on loans to directors and connected persons?
    j. What are the auditor's duties on such loans? (14)

Exercises

1. Outline an audit programme for the following:
    a. Debtors for Spare parts plc who sell to a wide range of commercial and industrial customers in the UK and overseas.
    b. The Hire Purchases Debtors of Scrooge Finance Ltd, a finance company.
    c. A material amount of loans to employees by Libbod plc a baby clothing manufacturer.
    d. The bank balances of Pong plc. The company have large cash surpluses and make a point of switching these between banks both in the UK and overseas to get the best possible interest.
    e. Bills of exchange, both inland and foreign, of Esa Ltd who buy and sell commodities world wide.

Examination question *(Answer begins on page 548)*

1. Sterndale plc is a large company manufacturing a range of tools of various qualities and prices, which it sells to a variety of retail outlets from supermarkets to specialist shops and general stores. Its debtors ledger is maintained on the computer and you have asked for and obtained a computer print-out of individual debtors and certain summarised information (set forth below) relating to the company's debtors at 30 November 1983, three months before the company's year end date. You intend to circularise selected debtors at 30 November 1983.

	Number	%	Value (£)	%
Zero balances	900	15.0	–	–
Credit balances	40	0.7	(234,770)	(4.0)
£1 to £1,000	4,554	75.9	1,468,600	25.0
£1,001 to £10,000	300	5.0	376,500	6.4
£10,001 to £20,000	100	1.7	1,206,900	20.5
Over £20,001	30	0.5	2,719,010	46.2
Sundry debts in the hands of collection agencies	76	1.2	349,856	5.9
	6,000	100.0	5,886,096	100.0

Required:

a. Explain (as if to a non-accountant) your understanding of the objectives to be attained by the circularisation, indicating in your answer which objective is normally met by substantive testing and which by compliance testing. (3 marks)

b. i. State reasons why you would select the following type of balance for circularisation.

   – Zero balances

   – Credit balances

   ii. Show what method of selection for circularisation you would use for the following types of balance:

   – £1 to £1,000

   – Over £20,001

   Give your reasoning in each case.

   iii. Describe the audit steps that you would take in respect of the sundry debts in the hands of collection agencies. (10 marks)

c. Explain what alternative auditing procedures you would adopt if only 30% (in value) of the debtors selected replied to the confirmation requests (including second requests). (4 marks)

d. Indicate the additional audit steps you would take at the year-end to satisfy yourself that the debtors at 28 February 1984 were fairly stated, assuming that following the interim work you had concluded that debtors at 30 November 1983 were, within reason, properly recorded and systems in the area were adequate. (3 marks)

(ACCA)

Examination questions without answers

2. a. In conducting the audit of a mail order company, your internal control question-naires show that the stated system of control on incoming orders with remittances are ineffective. What action will you now take? (10 marks)

   b. Indicate the main points to which you would give attention in arranging a circulari-sation of debtors to obtain confirmation of year end debtors. (10 marks)

   (ICA 90) (Total 20 marks)

3. Audit evidence can be created by processes largely under the control of third parties. This type of evidence can be that which is part of the basic accounting records such as invoices and statements or it can be created by third parties at the request of the auditor. This latter technique is normally referred to as direct confirmation.

   Required:

   a. Discuss the quality of audit evidence generated by direct confirmation techniques, giving three examples other than debtors confirmation of when the technique might be used. (6 marks)

   b. List the sequence of steps involved when directly confirming debtors. (7 marks)

   c. Explain the circumstances when negative confirmation requests may be used. (4 marks)

   d. Explain what evidence may or may not be provided by a positive request for confir-mation from debtors. (3 marks)

   (ACCA 92) (20 marks)

4. You are the auditor of TRENT Ltd., a china manufacturer, which exports 40% of sales to the US. You plan to commence the audit of the accounts for the year ended 30th April, 1990, on 1st July, 1990.

    Trade debtors are included in the balance sheet at the year-end, net of a £150,000 debt provision (5%), at £2,850,000. In previous years there has been an extremely poor response to the debtors circularisation and a decision has been taken not to circularise debtors this year. In an attempt to reduce the exposure to the US dollar, TRENT Ltd. sells 50% of dollar receivables forward.

    Requirement

    You are required to:

    a. explain what substantive audit tests you would carry out in order to verify trade debtors;   (12 marks)
    b. state the audit tests you would carry out in order to form an opinion on the bad debts provision and the action you would take, if you concluded that it was mis-stated; and   (6 marks)
    c. state what adjustment, if any, you would make to US dollar debtors on the basis that they have all been recorded at the actual exchange rate ruling on the date of sale.
                                                                                      (2 marks)
    (ICAI 90) (Total 20 marks)

5. Cricket plc is an expanding company specialising in the developing and marketing of computer software. The net profit for the year ended 31 March 1990 was £763,000 and the net asset value of the company at that date was £6,925,000.

    Required

    State how you would verify the following items appearing in the company's financial statements:

    a. Patents   £500,000   (6 marks)
    b. Bad and doubtful debts   £25,000   (5 marks)
    c. Interest on bank overdraft   £15,000   (4 marks)
    (AAT 90) (Total 15 marks)

6. The petty cashier's department of Dipthong & Stutter plc, a company providing a wide range of specialist delivery and forwarding services, maintains five different cash funds:

    1) General petty cash fund   – For small 'office' expenses
    2) Forwarding department fund   – For sundry expenses at the customs offices etc.
    3) Petrol and oil fund   – To pay for petrol and oil that the van drivers purchase for cash when on the road
    4) Garage sundry expenses fund   – To cover sundry garage expenses paid for in cash
    5) Drivers' subsistence fund   – To reimburse drivers for 'out of town' personal expenses

    i) What problems do you envisage this aspect of the audit will present?
    ii) State how you seek to overcome these problems, in the course of your audit.
    (LCCI 90) (15 marks)

22 Stock and work in progress

Introduction

1. The verification of Stock and Work in Progress has a chapter to itself. It is often the *key* item in accounts.

    As a fairly typical example consider Boots 1995 Accounts. Group profit before tax was £849 million and sales were £4,308 million. Stock was £489 million and the impact of a variation in the stock figure can easily be seen. The problem of stock is that the quantity and value are not derived from the double entry system but:

    a. Quantity is usually ascertained at the year end by counting. Mistakes are extremely easy to make.
    b. Condition is assessed at the same time and is a matter of opinion.
    c. Valuation methods are many and various.

    It will be seen that the figure attributed to stock is very important, is difficult to compute accurately and causes more headaches to auditors than any other problem.

2. It cannot be stressed too much that it is the *directors'* responsibility to ensure that:

    a. Stock and work in progress are correctly identified.
    b. Physical quantities are correctly ascertained and recorded and condition assessed.
    c. Valuation on proper bases is correctly made.

3. There is an auditing guideline: Attendance at Stocktaking issued in November 1983. Students are also reminded of SSAP 9.

4. This chapter considers stock under the following heading:

    a. Categories of stock
    b. Stocktaking procedures
    c. Auditors duties re the physical count
    d. Continuous stock records
    e. Stocktakes other than at year end
    f. Work in progress
    g. Overall tests
    h. Valuation
    i. Cut off
    j. Independent stocktakers
    k. A historical note

Categories of stock

5. In answering any examination question and indeed in considering most problems in life, a first approach is to break the problem down into parts.

    Stock is not different from other matters and a primary division is into:

    a. Goods purchased for resale.
    b. Consumable stores (oils, fuels, spare parts etc.)
    c. Raw materials and components purchased for incorporation into products for sale.
    d. Products and services in intermediate stages of completion.
    e. Finished goods.
    f. Returnable containers.

Cadbury Schweppes have c., e. and f. only. A shop is likely to have only a. and an engineering group all six.

6. A secondary division is:

   a. Stocks assessed by physical count at year end only.

   b. Stocks assessed near the year end and the year end total obtained by adjustment by sales and purchases.

   c. Stocks recorded on a *continuous inventory* system.

Stocktaking procedures

7. Although stocktaking may occur on only one day a year, it is essentially a part of the Internal Control system. A good set of procedures will have the following characteristics:

   a. **Where stock is based on records:**

      i.   Adequate stock records must be kept. They must be kept up to date.

      ii. All categories of stock (ie every item in stock) are checked physically at least once during the year and the amount found compared with the book record.

      iii. This checking is organised and systematic.

      iv. Differences found lead to correction of the records and a *proper investigation of the cause of the difference.*

   b. **When stock is based on a year end count:**

      i.   Good planning so that the work is carried out carefully and systematically – early issue of stocktaking instructions with consideration of feedback from staff.

      ii.   Division of the stocktake into manageable areas for control purposes.

      iii. Proper instructions for counting, weighing, measuring and checking.

      iv.   Proper *cut off* arrangements.

      v.   Identification of defective, damaged, obsolete, and slow moving stock.

      vi.   Identification of stock on the premises owned by third parties and of client's stock held by outside parties.

      vii. Proper control over the issue of blank stock sheets and the return of completed and unused stock sheets.

      viii. Identification of stocks held subject to reservation of title.

      ix.   Identification of stocks and especially of high value items.

      x.   Control of stock movement during the count.

      xi.   Controls to ensure all stock is counted and, at that, once only.

      xii. Nomination of people responsible for each aspect of the count.

      xiii. Appropriate treatment for sealed containers, dangerous goods, and goods with special problems.

      Items iv, v, and viii. are important also for stock based on records.

Stocktaking – the auditor's duties

8. The auditor must satisfy himself as to the validity of the amount attributed to stock and work in progress in the balance sheet. He does this by first considering the client's

system of internal control. This applies to stocktaking as it does to all areas of audit enquiry. It is essential for students to realise that stocktaking procedures are part of the system and the auditor examines the system by finding out what the system is, evaluating its effectiveness, and testing it.

9. The auditor's duties are usually divided into three parts – before, during and after the stocktake.

    a. Before the stocktake:

        i. Review previous year's working papers and discuss with management any significant changes from previous year.

        ii. Discuss stocktaking arrangements with management.

        iii. Familiarise himself with the nature and volume of stocks and especially with high value items.

        iv. Consider the location of stocks (eg at branches) and the problems thus caused for the client and the auditor.

        v. Consider likely points of difficulty eg cut off.

        vi. Consider internal audit involvement and if reliance can be placed upon it.

        vii. Arranging to obtain from third parties confirmation of stock held by them.

        viii. Establishing whether expert help may be needed (eg precious stones, antiques).

        ix. Evaluate the effectiveness of the instructions, especially that they cover all items, meet potential difficulties, are discussed with, and adequately communicated to stocktaking staff. If necessary suggest improvements.

        x. Review surrounding systems of internal control to identify areas of potential difficulty.

        xi. Plan usage of audit staff as to availability to cover all required locations etc.

    b. **During the stocktake:**

    Audit practice now is for the auditor to *attend the stocktake*. The purpose of the attendance is not to take stock or to supervise the stocktake but to *observe* (another word here might *witness*) the client's internal control system in action.

    The actual work to be done is:

        i. Observe the stocktake to ascertain that the client's employees are carrying out their instructions.

        ii. Check the count of a selected number of lines. This must be done by selecting some items found to be present *and* some items recorded on the stock sheets.

        iii. Note for follow up – Details of items selected by the auditors to compare with final stock sheets.

        List of items counted in the auditor's presence.

        Details of defective, damaged, obsolete or slow moving items.

        Instances of stocktaking instructions not being followed.

        Details of items for cut-off purposes.

        iv. Enquiry into, observe and discuss with store keeping staff the procedures for identifying damaged, obsolete and slow moving stock.

        v. Enquire into and test the cut-off procedures.

      vi. Form an impression of the magnitude of stock held for comparison with the Accounts.

     vii. Record fully the work done and his impressions of the stocktake in the working papers.

      ix. If any aspects prove unsatisfactory, inform the management and request a recount.

       x. High value items should be given special attention.

      xi. Photocopies of rough stock sheets should be taken.

     xii. Details of the sequence of stock sheets should be verified.

  c. After the stocktake:

       i. Check the cut-off with details of the last numbers of stock movement forms and goods inward and goods outwards notes during the year and after the year end.

      ii. Test that the final stock sheets have been properly prepared from the count records. In particular the record of stocktake forms issued and returned must be checked.

     iii. Follow up notes made at the attendance.

     iv. Check final stock sheets for pricing, extensions, casting, summarizing, and officials' signatures.

      v. Inform management of any problems encountered in the stocktake for action in subsequent counts.

10. Non-attendance at the stocktake may occur through the auditor having numerous clients all with the same accounting date or the client may have stock at remote or overseas locations. The auditor must still satisfy himself on the stocktake. This can be done by:

  a. Arranging for the stocktake to be at an earlier date.

  b. Appointing agents, eg for overseas locations.

  c. Examining continuous stocktake records more thoroughly.

  d. Intensifying other stocktaking verification methods.

  e. Using *rotational* methods.

None of these solutions is wholly satisfactory and the auditor must make very extensive enquiries before he gives a clean report.

Continuous stock records

11. Some companies which keep continuous stock records may wish to determine the quantity of stock at the year end by extracting the balances from the stock records without physically counting the stock on the year end date. This *may* be acceptable to the auditor if:

  a. The auditor is satisfied that the records are very reliable, accurate, and up to date, and *either*

  b. i. The whole stock is physically compared with the records on at least one day in the year and reasonable correspondence is found, or

      ii. Every item of stock is checked to the records at least once in the year in a systematic and orderly manner. The records of such checking should demonstrate reasonable concurrence between the actual stock and the records.

Stocktakes other than at the year end

12. The auditing guidelines states that stocktaking carried out before or after the year end may be acceptable for audit purposes provided records of stock movements in the intervening period are such that the movements can be examined and substantiated. The greater the interval the more difficult this will be. Acceptability depends also on there being a good system of internal control and satisfactory stock records.

Work in progress

13. All that has been said about stock applies equally to work in progress but this item presents even greater problems of ascertainment and valuation to the *directors* and to the auditors.

14. The auditor's investigations will include:

    a. Inquiry into the costing system from which work in progress is ascertained.

    b. Inquiry into the reliability of the costing system. In particular a costing system integrated with the financial accounting system will prima facie be more reliable because of the discipline of double entry and the inherent checks imposed by external data such as creditors' statements.

    c. Inquiry into the checks made as part of the system on statistical data concerning inputs of materials and outputs of products and expectations.

    d. Inquiry into the system of inspection and reporting thereon to enable due allowance to be made for scrapping and rectification work.

    e. Inquiry into the basis on which overheads are included in costs. This should be based on SSAP 9.

    f. Inquiry into the basis on which any element of profit is dealt with. Profit should be eliminated from work in progress. However it is legitimate to include an element of profit in long term contract work in progress in accordance with SSAP 9.

    g. Where items such as buildings and plant are constructed internally, it is important for the auditor to make sure that if such items are under construction at the year end they are not included twice, ie in fixed assets and work in progress.

Overall tests

15. While detail work on the stocks and work in progress is imperative in an audit, there are a number of overall tests which are very important. These include:

    a. **Reconciliation of changes** in stocks at successive year ends with records of movements, eg purchases and sales.

    b. Comparison of *quantities* of each kind of stock held at year end with those held at previous year ends and with purchases and sales.

    c. Consideration of *Gross Profit* ratio with that of previous years, other companies, and budgeted expectation.

    d. Consideration of *rate of stockturn* with previous years etc.

    e. Comparison of stock figures with budgets for stock, sales, and purchases.

    f. Consideration of standard costing records and the application of variances in the valuation of stock and work in progress.

Valuation of stock in trade and work in progress

16. Two problems in relation to stock which are really very fundamental to reporting profits have existed for many years. They are:

    a. **Valuation** methods are many and various.

    b. **Disclosure** of the methods of valuation used is not made.

    The first problem has been partly solved by SSAP 9. This standard has met with much opposition and is in parts imprecise but it has certainly gone a long way towards solving the problem of variety of method.

    The second problem is still with us and companies have a tendency to be vague on valuation methods. An example from the accounting policies of a major public company:

    'Stocks:

    Stocks are valued at the lower of cost and net realisable value. In respect of work in progress and finished goods cost includes all direct costs of production and the appropriate proportion of production overheads. '

    One can comment that this statement is unnecessary as this is what is required by SSAP 9. What we do not know is how direct costs, production overheads and appropriate proportion are defined.

17. This manual is not going to summarise SSAP 9 but students must be familiar with it.

18. The auditor's duty is to:

    a. Ascertain accounting policies adopted for valuing stock.

    b. Consider the acceptability of the policies selected.

    c. Test the stock sheets or continuous stock records with relevant documents such as invoices and costing records to determine if *'cost'* has been correctly arrived at.

    d. Examine and test the treatment of overheads.

    e. Test the treatment and examine evidence for items valued at net realisable value.

    f. Test the arithmetical accuracy of all calculations.

    g. Test the consistency with which the amounts have been computed.

    h. Consider the adequacy of the description used in the accounts and disclosure of the accounting policies adopted.

19. Note that the Companies Act 1985 codifies in the law many requirements of SSAP 9. Valuation of fungible assets may be FIFO, LIFO, weighted average price or any similar method.

Cut-off

20. This subject has been mentioned already. It is extremely important. Consider a trading account:

Opening Stock	100	Sales	1000
Purchases	750	Closing Stock	150
Gross Profit	300		
	1150		1150

Supposing goods valued at £50 were:

a. Dispatched and invoiced by the supplier before balance sheet date, and

b. Received after balance sheet date owing to delays in transit by rail, then they would be included in purchases as a consequence of a. and they would be excluded from closing stock as a consequence of b. This would mean an incorrect computation of the profit.

Avoiding this possibility is a vital part of the system of internal control as applied to stock and consequently of prime concern to the auditor.

21. A famous case on the subject of cut-off was:

re Thomas Gerrard & Son Ltd., 1967. This was another cotton company. The manager and principal shareholder:

a. Post-dated purchases invoices received before the year end.

b. Ante-dated sales invoice copies in the new year to dates prior to the year end.

He did this quite openly for five half year periods for bigger sums each time thus turning losses into profits and causing the company to pay tax and dividends. The auditors discovered the alterations, asked questions and were put off by answers such as 'these were year end adjustments' or 'it is more convenient'.

The judge awarded damages against the auditors on the grounds that:

i. Once their suspicions were aroused they had a duty to probe the matter to the bottom.

ii. Auditors now have a duty to satisfy themselves as to the validity of stock in trade. This satisfaction cannot arise solely out of the assurances of one official however trustworthy in appearance.

Independent stocktakers

22. In some trades it is found that the stock is counted and valued by an independent firm of stocktakers. Examples include the jewellery, licensed and retail pharmacy trades.

The question arises as to whether this influences the extent of the auditor's examination. The answer is that the auditor has a duty to form an opinion on the amount at which stock is stated. He cannot simply accept an outside stocktaker's valuation but it is usual to do so if:

a. He is satisfied of the stocktaker's independence and standing (ie integrity and competence).

b. He has made enquiries and is satisfied:

i. On the bases of valuation used.

ii. Proper cut-off procedures were employed.

Historical note

23. A study of the history of a subject will often illuminate its present condition. This is true of the audit of stock, and the three cases mentioned below are so well known in the profession as to form part of its folklore or mythology.

a. **re the Kingston Cotton Mill Co. Ltd., 1896.** The auditors failed to detect overstatements of the amounts of stock. They accepted a certificate of the manager on the amount of stock after comparing it with the stock journal which contained accounts for each item or class of items purporting to be in stock and a summary. The summary was determined by the auditors to be in agreement with the detailed accounts. In fact the entries were falsified to show more stock than was actually in existence. The auditors were exonerated on the grounds that it is no part of the auditors duty to take stock and that he is entitled to rely upon other people for the details of stock in trade. The judge's remarks contained the famous phrase *'He is a watchdog, not a bloodhound.'* This means that if he discovers something which is suspicious he should probe it to the bottom but in the absence of suspicious circumstances he is only bound to be reasonably cautious and careful.

Today the judgement in this case would undoubtedly be against the auditor but the comfortable words of the judge have caused auditors for many generations to accept stock sheets without actually attending or enquiring too closely into the stocktake.

b. **McKesson and Robbins Inc., USA 1939.** In this almost unbelievable (except perhaps in America) case, the directors of the company created fictitious records of trading, sales, purchases, bank accounts, debtors, and stock so that the assets were overstated by over 20 million dollars. This extraordinary state of affairs was not detected by the auditors. In particular they did not attend the stocktake. Had they done so they would have rapidly realised that no stock existed!

c. **Allied Crude Vegetable Oil Refining Corporation of New Jersey 1963.** In this scandal, methods were used to fool auditors who were present at the stocktaking. Three methods, at least, were used:

   i.   the quantity of vegetable oil in a tank was checked and before the quantity was checked in the second tank, the contents of the first tank were pumped through to the second tank.

   ii. Using a dip stick to measure the quantity of oil in a tank. In reality the tank was empty and oil was contained only in a thin drainpipe down which the dipstick was dropped.

   iii. Filling the tanks with water instead of oil.

Summary

24. a. Stock on a balance sheet is subject to a correct count, a correct assessment of condition, and appropriate selection of valuation bases.

   b. Stock can be considered under a number of separate categories.

   c. Some firms have stock records (continuous inventory) and some have not. The latter must have a stocktake at the year end.

   d. Stocktaking procedures are a part of the internal control system.

   e. Since Auditing Statement U9 issued in 1968 by the ICAEW, all audit firms must recognize that attendance at stocktaking to observe the incidence of internal control is *normal* audit practice.

   f. Valuation of stock in trade is now governed by SSAP 9. Its contents must be known.

   g. Detailed audit tests must be supplemented by overall tests.

   h. Independent stocktakers can be used by clients and within limitations be relied upon by the auditor.

   i. Cut-off is the most likely source of error and fraud in final accounts.

Points to note

25. a. Internal control assessment is a first consideration in all audit enquiry. Stocktaking methods are part of the internal control system.

 b. This part of the internal control system only applies on one day a year and the auditor needs to witness the procedures being carried out to assess their effectiveness.

 c. The valuation of stock has been done in numerous different ways in the past but SSAP 9 has reduced the number of acceptable methods.

 d. Nonetheless firms still have some latitude in selecting accounting policies and the auditor must see that these are appropriate, consistent with previous periods, apply to all like items in the same period, and are adequately disclosed.

 e. Cut-off procedures are most important.

 f. The auditor's assessment of stock in trade will cover:

 i. existence – stocktaking procedures

 ii. ownership – note goods in transit, goods at other premises, goods owned by others, reservation of title

 iii. value – note problem of net realisable value.

 g. The Companies Act requires companies to keep proper accounting records. Such proper accounting records include statements of stocktakings. Auditors must not only seek audit evidence that a true and fair view is shown by the stock figures in the Accounts but also must investigate to determine that proper accounting records in the form of statements of stocktaking have been kept.

 h. Work in progress can be very difficult to evaluate. Management generally rely on controls to ensure the completeness and accuracy of records of work in progress. Nonetheless inspection of work in progress by the auditor is desirable in that it gives evidence that work in progress exists and helps with determining the state of completion especially of large contracts.

 i. Note that most syllabuses require an appreciation of the accounting requirements of the Companies Act 1985 re disclosure of stocks and work in progress.

 j. Stocks and work in progress are an interesting example of the problem of risk. In most companies stocks are likely to be a material asset and the inherent risk of misstatement is high. Stocktaking is usually accompanied by control procedures designed to minimise misstatements but nonetheless the control risk is often high. Auditors are usually obliged to rely to a large extent on tests of control but if internal controls are weak, alternative substantive tests are often less than persuasive.

Case study 1 for Chapter 22

Aelfric Alchemist Supplies Ltd have a large warehouse in Wapping from which they supply their customers with over 3,000 different chemicals and chemical apparatus purchased from numerous suppliers both in the UK and overseas. They do not maintain a continuous inventory of their stocks. At the year end Thursday 31 July 19-6 they wish to assess the stock physically.

Discussion

 a. Draw up full stocktaking instructions for the stocktake.

b. How should the stock be valued according to:

    i. SSAP 9

    ii. The Companies Act 1985?

c. How should the auditor seek evidence for the physical stock at 31.7.-6?

Case study 2 for Chapter 22

Osocheep Supermarkets Ltd have a main depot and 5 large supermarkets. Their financial year end is Thursday 31 March 19-8 and stock is to be evaluated as at the close of business on that date. The next day is an exceptionally busy one and much business in terms of deliveries from supplier, movements of stock, and sales. The sales margins are narrow and it is very important to obtain an accurate figure for stock. Goods in stock in the warehouse are kept on a continuous inventory system (quantities only) on a micro computer with a printout of the previous day's stock available at noon each day. The stock at branches is not recorded continuously. The bulk of the stock is carried in the back rooms and moved onto the supermarket shelves continuously during the day.

Discussion

What are the problems in this case re:

Cut off

Stock identification and quantity determination

Valuation

Case study 3 for Chapter 22

Bizant Construction plc are civil engineers specializing in large public buildings. At their year end (31.5.-9) the following contracts were in progress:

(All figures in £'000)

	A	B	C	D	E
Value of work done	300	700	800	420	70
Cumulative payments on account	220	730	850	300	65
Total costs incurred	240	600	830	440	95
Transferable to cost of sales	240	580	760	430	67
Provision for foreseeable losses				60	24

Discussion

a. How should these figures be incorporated in the accounts?

b. Outline an audit programme for these items.

Student self testing questions Questions with answers apparent from the text

1. a. What are the directors' responsibilities for stocktaking? (2)

  b. What categories of stock are there? (5, 6)

  c. List the characteristics of good stocktaking procedures. (7)

  d. What are the auditor's duties toward stocktaking:

    i. Before the stocktake?

    ii. During the stocktake?

    iii. After the stocktake? (9)

e. What are the auditor's tasks in connection with work in progress? (14)

f. What overall tests can be applied in respect of stock? (15)

g. Summarise SSAP 9 requirements re the valuation of:
   i. stock
   ii. work in progress
   iii. long term contracts.

h. Summarise the famous cases:
   i. re Kingston Cotton Mill 1896
   ii. McKesson and Robbins Inc. 1939
   iii. re Thomas Gerrard & Son Ltd. 1967. (23)

Exercises

1. Draft an outline audit programme for the following:

   a. The sites under development of Jerry Ltd a speculative builder.

   b. The stock in Cheepy plc a supermarket chain. No perpetual inventory is kept and the count is at the year end.

   c. The work in progress of Robotto plc a manufacturer of complex machine tools partly to order and partly for stock. The company have a standard costing system.

   d. Stock of coal of Birnwell Ltd a private colliery. The stock at the surface was counted at the year end.

   e. The stocks of Drinkie Ltd a chain of public houses and licensed restaurants. All the stocks are counted and valued by independent valuers.

   f. The stock of Nicnac Ltd a wholesaler of components who have 2,000 separate lines. The company maintain a computerised stock control system (using average cost) and do not count at the year end.

   g. The finished goods stocks of Babby Ltd a manufacturer of childrens wear. The stock was counted five days before the year end.

   h. The stocks of Feinwein Ltd wine merchants. The company keep most of the stocks at the premises of customers. Customers are invoiced for wines taken from the stocks kept on their premises.

   i. The stocks of Olde Ltd an antique dealer specialising in small but very valuable items.

Examination question *(Answer begins on page 549)*

1. Fastwheels plc is a wholesaler selling all types of tyres for motor vehicles and motor cycles. The company has a central warehouse from which the tyres are distributed throughout the country. Stock records are maintained by computer and a VDU display or print out is available to authorised users at any time. The information displayed is as follows:

Manufacturer

1			2		3
Stock Level			Stock on Order from Manufacturer		Sales
Tyre Type	Number of Units	Average Cost per Unit £	Number of Units	Cost per Unit £	Number of Units sold during last 12 months

The company's financial accountant has had some doubts as to whether or not input of stock movement to the computer is complete and accurate and ordered a sample physical stocktake at 31 July 1985, three months before the financial year end of 31 October 1985. This was carried out by two storekeepers under the supervision of an accounts clerk. A comparison between the number of units physically counted at 31 July 1985 and the details maintained by computer for three tyre types supplied by one manufacturer are as follows:

Manufacturer: Dunelli Rubber Co.

1			2		3	4
Stock Level			Stock on Order from Manufacturer		Sales	
Tyre Type	Number of Units	Cost per Unit £	Number of Units	Cost per Unit £	Number of Units sold during last 12 months	Physical Stock Take of Units
X27	361	19	100	22	1,343	391
Y91	928	27	–	–	381	1,110
Z32	72	22	150	21	441	46

The discrepancies between physical stocktake numbers and those in the stock records would appear to confirm the financial accountant's fears. As the company's chief internal auditor you have been asked to give assistance in ensuring that: possible input data errors are identified; that adequate stocktakes will be carried out at 31 October 1985; that any discrepancies will be dealt with in an appropriate manner and that stock is properly valued at the year-end.

Required:

a. With reference to Fastwheels plc:

   i. give two possible reasons for recorded stock levels being incorrect as the result of input errors. (2 marks)

   ii. suggest controls which may detect the input errors mentioned by you. (2 marks)

b. List five major matters that should be considered when planning a stocktake indicating the significance of each matter. (10 marks)

c. For the three tyre types, indicate the matters to be considered (assuming that columns 2, 3 and 4 above are correct) when valuing stock as at 31 October 1985.

(6 marks)

(ACCA)

Examination questions without answers

2. Howard plc has a system of continuous stocktaking. Specialist stocktakers verify the stock throughout the year and agree it with the stock records, investigating any differences and reporting as appropriate to the company's management. No 'complete' stocktaking is undertaken at the year end in connection with the company's year end accounts.

   What would the external auditor do in order to verify stocks appearing in the company's balance sheet?

   (LCCI 91) (15 marks)

3. As the auditor to Triptich plc, you are considering attending the company's annual stocktaking.

   What planning of your auditing of the stocktaking would you undertake BEFORE the actual stocktaking begins?

   Note: Do NOT discuss auditing work during or after the actual stocktaking.

   (15 marks)
   (LCC 87)

4. Stocks and work in progress take many different forms, depending on the nature of the business. Many companies undertake contracts for work which last for more than one accounting period. The audit objectives concerning these long-term contracts do not differ greatly from those concerning normal stock and work in progress, except in so far as long-term contracts require the estimation of future revenues and costs in order to identify the profit to be recognised in the profit and loss account.

   Required:

   a. Explain why the audit of stocks and work in progress is often the most complex and time-consuming part of the audit. (6 marks)

   b. Describe the factors which are likely to affect the auditor's assessment of the inherent risk attached to long-term contract work in progress. (6 marks)

   c. Describe the audit work which would be performed in order to verify the value of long-term contract work in progress. (8 marks)

   (ACCA 92) (20 marks)

5. a. Stock and Work in Progress presents one of the major verification difficulties to the auditor. Because of this, the Audit Guidelines require the auditor to observe the stock-take.

   Required:

   State what general procedures would the auditor expect to find a client adopting in order to ensure that the stock-take is carried out correctly. (11 marks)

   b. You are the auditor of Plantagenet Limited, an electrical component manufacturing company. The directors have provided you with the following information concerning some of their company's products:

Product	A	B	C
Unit Selling price	£20	£25	£28
Sales in units	45,000	25,000	7,000
Cost per unit	£15	£21	£26
Selling expenses per unit	£3	£6	£4
Stock in units at year end	5,000	3,000	3,500

Required:

State what values should be attributed to the year end stock value. Give reasons for your answer and state any further considerations required. (9 marks)

(AAT D'87) (Total 20 marks)

6. Rubella Yarns plc manufacturers cotton yarn for sale to the textile industry. The stock of the company is valued on a standard cost basis and you are about to commence the final audit, having attended the physical stock count.

You are required to:

a. State under what circumstances standard cost would be a suitable method of pricing stocks for financial accounting purposes. (6 marks)

b. Describe how you would satisfy yourself as auditor of Rubella Yarns plc that the standard costs had been properly determined. (7 marks)

c. Discuss briefly what action you would take if you discover that there are significant variances between actual and standard prices for stock. (7 marks)

(ACCA 2 88) (Total 20 marks)

7. Plymouth Construction plc is involved in the construction of public buildings in the United Kingdom. The company has a 31 March 1988 year-end. At the year-end there were three major contracts in progress, the details of which are given below:

	PROJECT A	PROJECT B	PROJECT C
Commencement date	1 April 1987	1 June 1987	1 Feb 1988
Estimated completion date	30 June 1988	31 May 1988	31 Dec 1989
Contract value	£5m	£1.5m	£3m
Costs to date	£3.6m	£0.8m	£0.5m
Estimated costs to complete	£0.8m	£0.9m	£1.8m

Required:

a. Outline the basis which Statement of Standard Accounting Practice 9 'Stocks and Work in Progress' states should be used when valuing long-term work in progress. (4 marks)

b. State how the three contracts should be included in the accounts for the year ended 31 March 1988. (6 marks)

c. What special areas of work in progress would need to be considered when auditing the accounts for the year ended 31 March 1988? (5 marks)

(AAT D 88) (Total 15 marks)

8. Gourmet plc operates six food warehouses throughout Great Britain. The company makes bulk purchases from manufacturers and suppliers based within the United Kingdom and abroad. It distributes these goods to supermarkets and cash and carry wholesalers. Each warehouse maintains its own stock records from goods inwards and despatch notes. Head Office maintains a financial control over the stocks based on the daily value of sales and a value of daily purchases (based on selling price).

The company's year end is 30 November, which in 1991 falls on a Saturday. The Financial Director has arranged for a stocktake to be held on the preceding Wednesday and the warehouses will be closed on that day. The stock sheets are to be priced at selling price.

You are required to

a. State the audit procedures you would undertake in respect of the physical stocktake. (10 marks)

b. State the matters to which you would give attention to ensure that the correct quantities and values of stock items are included in the Financial Statements.   (5 marks)

(AAT 91) (Total 15 marks)

23 Liability verification

Introduction

1. A balance sheet will contain many liabilities grouped under various headings. The headings may include:

    a. Share capital

    b. Reserves

    c. Creditors: amounts falling due after more than one year:

        i.   Debenture loans

        ii.   Bank loans and overdrafts

        iii. Payments received on account

        iv.   Trade creditors

        v.   Bills of exchange payable

        vi.   Amounts owed to group companies

        vii. Amounts owed to related companies

        viii. Other creditors including taxation and social security

        ix.   Accruals and deferred income.

    d. Provisions for liabilities and charges

        i.   Pensions and similar obligations

        ii.   Taxation, including deferred taxation

        iii. Other provisions

    e. Creditors: amounts falling due within one year as in c. i. to ix.

    f. Contingent liabilities – incorporated by note only.

2. The auditors' duty is fourfold viz:

    a. To verify the *existence* of liabilities shown in the balance sheet.

    b. To verify the correctness of the *money amount* of such liabilities.

    c. To verify the appropriateness of the *description* given in the accounts and the adequacy of *disclosure*.

    d. To verify that *all* existing liabilities *are actually included* in the accounts.

    The last of these causes the most difficulty.

Verification procedures

3. It is not possible to detail the procedures for verifying all possible liabilities. However, some general principles can be discerned, and these should be applied according to the particular set of circumstances met with in practice or in an examination. These are:

   a. **Schedule.** Request or make a *schedule* for each liability or class of liabilities. This should show the make up of the liability with the opening balance, if any, all changes, and the closing balance.

   b. **Cut-off.** Verify *cut-off*. For example a trade creditor should not be included unless the goods were acquired before the year end.

   c. **Reasonableness.** Consider the *reasonableness* of the liability. Are there circumstances which ought to excite suspicion?

   d. **Internal control.** Determine, evaluate and test *internal control* procedures. This is particularly important for trade creditors.

   e. **Previous date clearance.** Consider the *liabilities at the previous accounting date*. Have they all been cleared?

   f. **Terms and conditions.** this applies principally to loans. The auditor should determine that all terms and conditions agreed when accepting a loan have been complied with. In recent years many loan deeds have contained undertakings by the company borrowing the money that it will keep a minimum proportion of equity (ordinary share capital and reserves) in its total capital (equity and loans). Breach of this agreement which has occurred frequently in property companies can lead to the appointment of a receiver.

   g. **Authority.** The authority for all liabilities should be sought. This will be found in the company minutes or directors' minutes and for some items the authority of the Memorandum and Articles may be needed.

   h. **Description.** The auditor must see that the description in the accounts of each liability is adequate.

   i. **Documents.** The auditor must examine all relevant documents. These will include invoices, correspondence, debenture deeds etc., according to the type of liability.

   j. **Security.** Some liabilities are secured in various ways, usually by fixed or floating charges. The auditor must enquire into these and ensure that they have been registered. The Companies Act requires, for secured liabilities, that an indication of the general nature of the security be given and also the aggregate amount of debts included under the item covered by the security.

   k. **Vouching.** The creation of each liability should be vouched, for example the receipt of a loan.

   l. **Accounting policies.** The auditor must satisfy himself that appropriated accounting policies have been adopted and applied consistently.

   m. **Letter of representation.** This is discussed further in the chapter on letters of representation.

   n. **Interest and other ancillary evidence.** The evidence of loans tends to be evidenced by interest payments and other activities which stem from the existence of the loan.

   o. **Disclosure.** All matters which need to be known to receive a *true and fair view* from the accounts must be disclosed. The Companies Acts provisions must be complied with.

p. **External verification.** With many liabilities it is possible to verify the liability directly with the creditor. This action will be taken with short term loan creditors, bank overdrafts and, by a similar technique to that used with debtors, the trade creditors.

q. **Materiality.** Materiality comes into all accounting and auditing decisions.

r. **Post-Balance sheet events**. These are probably more important in this area than in any other. There is a chapter on this subject later in the manual.

s. **Accounting Standards.** Liabilities must be accounted for in accordance with the accounting standards and UITF abstracts where relevant. Accounting standards that may be relevant to liabilities include FRS 4, FRS 5, SSAPs 15, 17, 18, 21 and 24.

t. **Risk**. Assess the risk of misstatement.

4. Students may well remember these mnemonically. For any given liability all of them will not be required, but mentally going through them should be an excellent guide to what needs to be done.

Inclusion of all liabilities

5. It is not enough for the auditor to be satisfied that all the liabilities recorded in the books are correct and are incorporated in the Final Accounts. He must also be satisfied that no other liabilities exist which are not, for various reasons, in the books and the accounts. Examples of such unrecorded liabilities are:

a. Claims by employees for injury. Note that these should be covered by insurance under the Employers Liability (Compulsory Insurance) Act 1969.

b. Claims by ex employees for unfair dismissal.

c. Contributions to superannuation schemes.

d. Unfunded pension liabilities. A company may have a liability to pay past or present employees a pension in respect of past service and have no funds separated out for this purpose.

e. Liability to 'top-up' pension schemes. When money has been put into separate trusts to pay pensions, inflation has often meant that the amount is insufficient and the company may have to implement Clauses in the scheme whereby they have to put in extra money which could run into millions of pounds.

f. Bonuses under profit sharing arrangements.

g. Returnable packages and containers.

h. Value added and other tax liabilities. The auditor's special knowledge of tax may lead him to suspect a liability of which the directors are blissfully ignorant.

i. Claims under warranties and guarantees.

j. Liabilities on debts which have been factored with recourse. To explain: A owes B £50. B sells (factors) the debt to C for £45. Thus B has no debt any more but £45 in the bank. A fails to pay C. C can claim £50 from B (he has recourse).

k. Bills receivable discounted (a special case of j.).

l. Pending law suits.

m. Losses on forward contracts. A Ltd makes a contract to sell a million tons of hedonite, which it does not have, at £50 a ton in six months' time. No entry will appear in the books or accounts, but when the time comes hedonite has risen on the commodity market to £70 a ton and A Ltd, buys in at that price in order to make the sale for which it has contracted.

6. It is important that the auditor appreciates that such liabilities can exist. He also has a positive obligation to take reasonable steps to unearth them.

The actions he would take would include:

a. Enquiry of the directors and other officers.

b. Obtain a letter of representation – see later in the chapter.

c. Examination of post balance sheet events. This will include an inspection of the purchase invoices and the cash book after date.

d. Examination of minutes where the existence of unrecorded liabilities may be mentioned.

e. A review of the working papers and previous years' working papers.

f. An awareness of the possibilities at all times when conducting the audit. For example, discovery during the audit that the client deals in 'Futures' (5m.) will alert the auditor to the possibility of outstanding commitments.

Provisions

7. Students tend to confuse two words in common use. The correct use of these two words are:

a. **Provision** – any amount retained as reasonably necessary for the purpose of providing for any liability or loss which is either likely to be incurred, or certain to be incurred but uncertain as to amount or as to the date on which it will arise. (CA 1985 4th Sch. 89)

Thus a provision:

i. is a debit to profit and loss account (reducing profit and therefore dividends; hence retained).

ii. for a likely or certain future payment.

iii. where the *amount* or the *date* of payment is uncertain.

b. **Reserve** – that part of shareholders funds not accounted for by the nominal value of issued share capital or by the share premium account.

The need for the creation of provisions is an important consideration for directors who are responsible for Accounts and consequently for the auditors. Post balance sheet events can often cast light on the amount of provision required. The auditor has a duty to see that any provisions set up are used for the purpose for which they were set up and that any provisions which are no longer needed are transferred back to profit and loss account.

8. In late 1995, the ASB issued a new discussion paper *Provisions*. This proposed that items should only be provided for when the company has a firm commitment (not merely an intention) to the expenditure. It also proposes that the only costs to be provided for should be those incremental costs necessary to sort out a past problem. Anything that will bring benefits in the future should be charged in the future period. Supposedly the object of these proposals is to end the practice of profit smoothing using 'big bath' provisions. A company might wish to smooth out its profits over the years by:

- making a large provision in a good year. This might be for some expense like warranties or environmental restoration.
- releasing the provision (ie by not renewing it) in lean years.

The effect of this is to transfer profit in good years to bad years. It is arguable whether this practice now occurs, in view of sharper auditing in recent years. But in any case the proposals should end the practice if they are adopted.

Share capital

9. Share capital is effectively a special sort of liability of a company. When share capital has been issued in a year its verification is as follows:

a. Ensure the issue is within the limits authorised by Memorandum and Articles.

b. Ensure the issue was subject to a directors' minute.

c. Ascertain and evaluate the system for the control of issue.

d. Verify that the system has been properly operated. This will involve examining the prospectus (if there is one), applications, application and allotment sheets, the share register, cash received records, share certificate counterfoils, and repayment to unsuccessful applicants.

e. When the issue was one which was contingent upon permission to deal being received from the Stock Exchange then:

   i. Ensure that permission has been obtained. If it has not been given all the money subscribed is returnable.

   ii. Ensure that all the money was contained in a separate bank account until all conditions were satisfied.

   iii. Ensure that the minimum subscription has been received. If there are not enough subscribers then the whole is returnable.

f. When the issue is not for cash but for other consideration, eg the goodwill and other assets of a business, vouch the agreement and ensure that all entries are properly made.

g. Vouch the payment of underwriting and other fees.

10. When no new issue of shares has been made the audit work will *include:*

a. Determine the total of shares of each class as stated in the balance sheet and obtain a list of shareholdings which in total should agree with the balance sheet total.

b. Test the balances in the share register with the list and *vice versa.*

c. If this is not possible at the balance sheet date, it may be permissible to do it earlier provided that the auditor is satisfied with the system of control over transfers.

d. When the share register is maintained by an independent firm of registrars (which is common with public companies) the auditor should obtain a certificate that the work outlined in a. and b. has been done. The certificate should state that the balances on the share registers agree with the issued capital at the balance sheet date.

Pending legal matters

11. This is a specially difficult area in practice because of the inherent uncertainty involved in estimating the outcome of legal actions. There are some audit actions which will lead

to the verification of the existence but not necessarily the amount of liabilities arising out of legal actions. These include:

a.   Reviewing the client's system for recording claims and disputes and the procedures for bringing these to the attention of the Board.

b.   Reviewing the arrangements for instructing solicitors.

c.   Examining the minutes of the Board or other responsible committee for references to or indications of possible claims.

d.   Examine bills rendered by solicitors. As solicitors are often late in sending in bills they should be requested by the client to send in bills or estimates up to date or to confirm they have no charges unbilled.

e.   Obtain a list of matters referred to solicitors from a director or other responsible official with an estimate of the possible ultimate liabilities.

f.   Obtain a written assurance from the appropriate director or official that he is not aware of any matters referred to solicitors other than those disclosed.

12. If the auditor is at all in doubt he should obtain a direct confirmation of 11 e. from the company's legal adviser. The request must be sent by the client requesting the reply or that a copy of the reply be sent direct to the auditor. The letter to the solicitor should include a request for details of cases referred to the solicitor not mentioned in 11 e.

Letter to a client's legal adviser to confirm contingent liabilities arising out of pending legal matters

Messrs Scrooge & Co
New St.
Oldcastle   26th September 19-6
Dear Sirs,

Joy Manufacturing Ltd.

In connection with the preparation and audit of the accounts for the year ending 31st December 19-5 the directors have made estimates of the amounts of the ultimate liabilities (including costs) which might be incurred, and are regarded as material, in relation to the following matters on which you have been consulted. We should be glad if you would confirm that in your opinion these estimates are reasonable.

Matter	Estimated liability including costs
1. Claim by James Brown for wrongful dismissal	£2,000
2. Claim by Hedonite Manufacturing Ltd for damages in respect of faulty goods	£8,000
3. Action by Sultan of Difur for damages caused by late delivery of equipment	£nil
4. Action by Joyful Mfg plc for breach of copyright in our Catalogue	£4,000

Yours faithfully,

Fussy & Co
Chartered Accountants

Note that solicitor's opinion letters often do not satisfactorily resolve the auditor's uncertainties. Solicitors often say that the outcome of an action is 'unpredictable' or say that the company has 'meritorious defences'.

Debentures

13. Long term loans are often evidenced by a piece of paper called a debenture. For this reason long term loans are often called debentures. Such loans can be unsecured, secured by a fixed charge over a specific asset, or secured by a floating charge on all the assets. Secured liabilities are sometimes called mortgage debentures.

14. The verification procedures are:

   a. Obtain a schedule detailing the sums due at the beginning of the year, additions and redemptions(= repayments) and the sum due at the year end.

   b. Note, or photocopy, for the permanent file the terms and conditions of the loans as evidenced in the debenture deed.

   c. Agree opening balances with last year's papers.

   d. Vouch receipt of new loans with prospectus, board minutes, memorandum and articles, register of debenture holders etc.

   e. Vouch repayments with debenture deeds (terms are correctly interpreted, cash book, register of debenture holders etc.)

   f. Vouch interest payments with debenture deed, cash book and see amount paid is correctly n% of amount outstanding.

   g. Agree total amount outstanding with register of debenture holders.

   h. If loans are secured, verify charge is registered at Companies House.

   i. Verify disclosure is in accordance with Companies Act requirements. Note that long term loans which are repayable within twelve months of the accounting date must be shown as such.

Accounting estimates

15. In this chapter we have considered many liabilities which are uncertain as to existence or amount. Liabilities are sometimes certain (eg most trade creditors) but some need to be estimated. There are many other areas of accounting where estimates need to be made including stock at net realisable value, depreciation and others. Some of these have been dealt with in the appropriate chapter of this book. However it seems a good idea to summarise at this point the auditing processes attached to accounting for estimates in general. There is a Statement of Auditing Standards SAS 420 *Audit of accounting estimates*.

   The following remarks can be made:

   a. Accounting estimates have to be made in all areas where precise means of measurement cannot be applied. We have seen several examples in this chapter already (depreciation, stocks at NRV, lawsuits, warranty claims etc).

   b. The responsibility for these estimates lies with the directors or other governing body and may involve special knowledge and judgement. Some are routine, eg depreciation, and some are one-off eg the outcome of a lawsuit. Many are capable of reasonable estimation but some might not be. In the latter cases and if the matters are material, the auditor might consider that the uncertainty and /or the lack of objective data is so great that there are implications for the audit report – see Chapter 32.

   c. Auditors should obtain sufficient appropriate audit evidence on all material accounting estimates. The evidence should give assurance that the estimates are *reasonable in the circumstances* and, when required, *appropriately disclosed*.

d. Possible audit procedures include:

   i. Review procedures and methods adopted by management to make accounting estimates. These may include internal audit. In some cases a formula will be used (eg in estimating warranty claims or in setting depreciation rates). There should be systems for continually reviewing these formulae. The fact that directors do actually consider the formulae or other methods of calculating estimates on a continuing basis is itself reassuring to the auditor!

   ii. Test these processes in connection with each estimate.

   iii. Evaluate the data and consider the assumptions on which the estimates have been made. For example in looking at depreciation, what assumptions on obsolescence have been made?

   iv. Check any calculations or applications of formulae.

   v. Make an independent estimate on each estimate and compare it with that of the directors. Investigate any difference.

   vi. Compare estimates made in previous years with actual outcomes where known. Do the same for the independent estimates of the auditors.

   vii. Review subsequent events.

e. At the final review stage of the audit, the auditor should make a review of the estimates (as with all the accounting data in the financial statements) and assess them in the light of:

   – her knowledge of the business
   – consistency with other evidence obtained during the audit.

f. If the auditor considers that a material estimate is unreasonable, he should ask the directors to adjust the financial statements and if this is not done then he should consider there is a misstatement and ponder the implications for his auditor's report.

Summary

16. a. The capital and liabilities side of the balance sheet is divided into a number of subheadings.

   b. the auditor must verify the existence, amount, and adequate disclosure of all liabilities. He must also be satisfied that *all* liabilities are included.

   c. Each liability is verified from whatever evidence is available but some general procedures common to most liabilities can be discerned.

   d. Provisions are a difficult area. The auditor must take special care in considering the adequacy of provisions.

   e. Share capital is verified like other liabilities but special procedures apply to new issues.

   f. Pending legal matters can be verified by direct confirmation from the company's legal advisers.

   g. There are some general points which can be made on the audit of all accounting estimates.

Points to note

17. a. The liabilities side of the balance sheet is subject to numerous *Companies Act rules* on disclosure. These must be known.

   b. Be very careful to use the words *provision* and *reserve* correctly. They are *not* synonymous for accruals and prepayments.

   c. Two important matters in connection with liabilities are contingencies and post balance sheet events. They are discussed in Chapter 33.

   d. The letter of representation may be evidence in this area, especially in the problem of inclusion of all liabilities. This is discussed in Chapter 30.

   e. Some companies may have enormous potential liabilities arising out of environmental factors. An example is T & N (formerly Turner and Newall) which was a major supplier of asbestos. Claims for damages amounting to hundreds of millions of pounds have been made against the company and are going through the courts. Similar claims may be made against other companies that supplied products, which at the time of supply were considered acceptable, but which are now seen as damaging. Vulnerable companies include tobacco, pharmaceutical and chemical companies. To some extent claims against such companies may be covered by insurance but that may also be a subject for endless litigation.

Case study for Chapter 23

Horsebox, Postillion & Co. are a city firm of Certified Accountants. The firm's accounts are produced by the administration partner but are subject to audit by Blanket, Mange, another firm of Certified Accountants. In June 19-6, a partner in Horsebox who was suffering from overwork failed to realised that an error had occurred in the preparation and audit of the Accounts of International Maize Ltd. Stocks of maize in transit had been inadvertently included in the company's stocks in both the producing country and the receiving country. The company had been acquired by Universal Porage Inc. who have now discovered the mistake. They have given notice that they intend to bring an action to recover damages from Horsebox on the grounds that they relied on the audited accounts for the year ending 30.4.-6 and that they would not have purchased IM had they known of the error.

The stock of IM was overstated by £2.4 million as a consequence of the error. The profit of IM was reported as £4.3 million and UP paid £21 million cash for IM.

Horsebox carry professional indemnity insurance in the sum of £1 million.

The partners of Horsebox dislike each other and rely heavily on Blanket, Mange. No one at Horsebox has informed Blanket, Mange of the pending legal action.

Discussion

   a. What auditing procedures might allow Blanket, Mange to discover the existence of the action?

   b. How might the amount of the ultimate award and costs be determined by Blanket, Mange?

   c. What other hidden liabilities might Horsebox have at their year end – 31.12.-6?

Student self testing questions *Questions with answers apparent from the text*

1. a. Reproduce the Companies Act Format 1 listing of capital, reserves and liabilities. (1)
   b. List the general procedures for verifying liabilities. (3)
   c. List some liabilities that may be omitted. (5)
   d. How can the auditor determine if all liabilities are included? (6)
   e. Define provision and reserve. (7)
   f. What factors about a liability must be verified by an auditor? (2)
   g. How might audit evidence of the truth and fairness of the item 'Share Capital' be obtained? (9)
   h. How might pending legal matters be dealt with by an auditor? (11, 12)
   i. How can debentures be audited? (14)
   j. List audit procedures in connection with accounting estimates (15)

Exercises

1. Draft an outline audit programme for the following:
   a. The trade creditors of Hurric Ltd a manufacturer of aircraft parts.
   b. The accruals and prepayments of Spit Ltd, a manufacturer of anoraks and similar clothing.
   c. The 16% convertible debentures of Beetroot plc. The redemption date is 2,012 and conversion is possible in any August. 4% of the debentures were converted in the year under review. The debentures are quoted.
   d. The overdraft of Turnip plc which is secured.
   e. Taxation liabilities of Rich plc ,an international property company.
   f. A provision by Mangle Ltd against warranty liabilities in connection with a faulty product.
   g. A note to the accounts re a contingent liability for 'futures' by Pees Ltd a dealer in non-ferrous metals.

Examination question *(Answer begins on page 550)*

1. You are the manager in charge of the audit of Farrington Ltd, a company which manufactures biscuits and confectionery. You wish to employ a junior member of staff to audit the trade creditors, accruals and provisions as shown in the balance sheet at the year-end and are in the process of preparing audit programmes which clearly explain the purpose and extent of the work at each stage of the audit.

   The draft figures for 'creditors – amounts falling due within one year' as at 31 October 1985 (with 1984 comparative figures) are as follows:

	31 October	
	1985	1984
	£	£
Trade creditors	261,521	177,625
Sundry accruals	21,162	18,177
Provisions – Legal action*	40,000	–
– Factory repairs**	72,000	62,000
	394,683	257,802

* This provision relates to a legal action brought by a competitor who claims their manufacturing process has been illegally copied.

** This provision which was first set up in 1984 relates to sums required to be spent on urgent repairs to the factory foundations and structural steelwork. (£58,500 was spent during the year ended 31 October 1985.)

Required:

For Farrington Ltd, set out in tabular form (with an explanation of the purpose of each stage) outline programmes for the audit of:

a. Trade creditors (8 marks)

b. Sundry accruals (4 marks)

c. Provisions. (4 marks)

(ACCA)

Examination questions without answers

2. Your audit supervisor has asked you to audit the liabilities of Glassware ltd ('Glassware'), a small manufacturing company which makes paperweights and other glass ornaments. Included in its draft Balance Sheet are the following liabilities:

	£
Trade creditors	150,343
Obligations under finance leases	50,673
Corporation tax payable	15,404
Accruals	10,023
Bank overdraft	73,920
Other sundry creditors	5,980

Your supervisor has stressed that one of the major audit objectives in the audit of liabilities is that of 'completeness' and that you should ensure your audit work adequately covers this objective.

Required

1. Explain why 'completeness' is a major objective in the audit of liabilities.

2. State the audit tests you would carry out to verify the completeness of Glassware's liabilities.

(ICAS 1994)

3. You are the Senior working on the audit of KINGSTON Ltd., a company engaged in the distribution of specialised health care computer equipment. The equipment is purchased under licence from a large multi-national company and is sold to a small customer base comprising hospitals and health centres.

Due to the fact that stocks are maintained at a minimum level and debtors are easily verified by direct confirmation with customers, you consider the critical audit area to be creditors and accruals. The draft balance sheet of KINGSTON Ltd. includes the following balances within its short-term and long-term creditors.

	£'000
Trade creditors and accruals	4,352
Overhead and wage related accruals	2,356
Finance lease obligations	973
Proposed dividends	5,000
Corporation Tax payable	598
Long-term loan	15,000
	28,279

The net assets as included in the balance sheet amount to £54,345,000. Although the company has sophisticated accounting and internal control systems, you have decided to adopt t a substantive type audit approach, because you have not had sufficient time to test the internal controls. The Manager in charge of the audit has asked you for your comments regarding the audit approach to this critical area of creditors and accruals.

Requirement

Draft a memorandum to the Manager in charge of the audit setting out each of the following:

a. The audit objectives in relation to the validation of creditors.

b. The specific substantive audit procedures that you would carry out in order to verify each of the balances set out above.

c. The general audit procedures that you would adopt in the creditors area.

(ICAI 93)

4. Santa Teresa plc is engaged in importing and exporting goods. As a result, the company has at any one time large balances on its Bills of Exchange Receivable and Bills of Exchange Payable Accounts.

Required

Outline your audit method in connection with Bills of Exchange.

(LCCI 92) (15 marks)

5. In January, 1991 you carried out an interim audit of Bradley Headstone Limited, a medium sized manufacturing company. This audit revealed no significant areas of weakness.

Required

Draft a final audit programme to cover purchases and trade creditors.

(AAT 91) (15 marks)

Audit evidence

1. Auditing is concerned with the verification of accounting data and with determining the *accuracy* and *reliability* of accounting statements and reports.

2. Verification does not mean seeking proof or absolute certainty in connection with the data and reports being audited. It means looking for sufficient *evidence* to satisfy oneself as auditor that the accounts show a true and fair view. What is sufficient evidence depends on what experience and knowledge of contemporary auditing standards tells one is satisfactory.

3. Chapter 24 deals with the theory of audit evidence and Chapter 26 with the value of evidence produced by statistical sampling. Chapter 25 discusses the fashionable subject of audit risk. Finally Chapter 27 deals with reliance on other specialists.

24 Audit evidence

Introduction

1. This chapter may seem somewhat theoretical but in fact the material does make possible an approach to audit problems which can be useful in practice and also in examination.

   There is a Statement of Auditing Standards SAS 400 *Audit evidence.*

Financial statements and assertions

2. Directors produce or cause to be produced financial statements. In doing so they are *asserting* that:

   a. The individual items are:

      i. Correctly described.

      ii. Show figures which are mathematically correct or fairly estimated.

   b. The accounts as a whole show a true and fair view.

3. The idea to grasp is that the *producer* of a set of accounts is making *assertions* about items in the accounts when he puts them in the accounts.

   The sort of assertions he is making are these:

   a. **Existence**: an asset or liability exists at the Balance Sheet date. This is an obvious assertion with such items as land and buildings, stocks and others.

   b. **Rights and obligations**: an asset or liability pertains to the entity at the Balance Sheet date. This means that the enterprise has for example ownership of an asset. Ownership as an idea is not simple and there may be all sorts of rights and obligations connected with a given asset or liability.

   c. **Occurrence**: a transaction or event took place which pertains to the enterprise during the relevant period. It may be possible for false transactions (eg sales or purchases) to be recorded. The assertion is that all recorded transactions actually took place.

   d. **Completeness**: there are no unrecorded assets, liabilities, transactions or events or undisclosed items. This is important for all accounts items but is especially important for liabilities.

   e. **Valuation**: an asset or liability is recorded at an appropriate carrying value. Appropriate may mean in accordance with generally accepted accounting principles, the Companies Act rules, Accounting Standards requirements and consistent with statements of accounting policies consistently applied.

   f. **Measurement**: a transaction or event is recorded at the proper amount and revenue or expense allocated to the proper period.

   g. **Presentation and disclosure**: an item is disclosed, classified and described in accordance with applicable reporting framework. For example fixed assets are subject to the Companies Act rules and to SSAP 12 and other requirements. Exceptional items are subject to FRS 3.

4. As an example, we will look at an item in a balance sheet 'bank overdraft £10,250'. In including this item in the balance sheet, the directors are making these assertions:

   a. That there is a liability to the company's bankers.

   b. That at the balance sheet date this liability was £10,250.

   c. That this amount is agreed by the bank.

   d. That the overdraft was repayable on demand. If this were not so, it would not appear amongst the current liabilities and terms would be stated.

   e. That the overdraft was not secured. If it were secured this fact would need to be stated.

   f. That the company has the Authority to borrow from its Memorandum and Articles.

   g. That a bank reconciliation statement can be prepared.

   h. That the bank is willing to let the overdraft continue.

5. If no item 'bank overdraft' appeared in the balance sheet, it would represent an assertion by the directors that no overdraft liability existed at the balance sheet date.

Audit evidence

6. The auditor's attitude to each item in the accounts will be as follows:

   a. Identify the express and implied *assertions* made by the directors in including (or excluding) the item in the accounts.

   b. Evaluate each assertion for relative importance to assess the quality and quantity of evidence required.

   c. Collect information and evidence.

   d. Assess the evidence for:

      i. appropriateness. Appropriateness subsumes the ideas of quality and reliability of a particular piece of audit evidence and its relevance to a particular assertion.

      ii. sufficiency. More of this in a later paragraph.

   Note that audit evidence tends to be persuasive rather than absolute and that auditors tend to seek evidence from *different sources* or of a *different nature* to support the same assertion. Note also that auditors seek to provide *reasonable* but not *absolute* assurance that the financial statements are *free from misstatement*. Auditors do not normally examine all the information available but reach their conclusions about financial statement assertions using a variety of means including sampling.

7. Having formulated judgement on *each individual item* in (or omitted from) the accounts, the auditor must formulate a judgement on the truth and fairness of accounts *as a whole*. To do this he will need other evidence in addition to the judgements he has made on the individual items. As an extreme example, he may need evidence of the directors' implied assertion that the accounts should be drawn up on the going concern principle.

Limitations

8. The quality and quantity of evidence needs is constrained by the following:

   a. Absolute proof is impossible.

   b. Some assertions are not material.

   c. Time is limited. Accounts must be produced within a time scale and the auditor may have to make do with less than perfection to comply with the time scale.

   d. Money is limited. The ideal evidence may be too expensive to obtain.

   e. Sensitivity. Some items are of greater importance than others (valuation of property in property companies, for example) or capable of greater variations (stock and work in progress).

Varieties of evidence

9. The evidence an auditor collects can be divided into categories like this:

   a. **Observation.**

      i. Examination of physical assets.

      ii. Witnessing the internal control and book keeping procedures.

      iii. Observation of the records to ensure that book keeping and internal control procedures have been carried out.

   b. **Testimony from independent third parties.** eg bank letters, debtors circularisation.

   c. **Authoritative documents** prepared *outside* the firm eg title deeds, share and loan certificates, leases, contracts, franchises, invoices.

   d. **Authoritative documents** prepared *inside* the firm, eg minutes, copy invoices.

   e. **Testimony** from directors and officers *of the company*. This may be formal, for example the letter of representation, or informal, for example in replies to ICQ questions.

   f. **Satisfactory internal control.** For many items this is the most useful evidence.

   g. **Calculations performed by the auditor.** Evidence of the correctness of many figures can be obtained this way.

   h. **Subsequent events.** The audit is usually performed well after the year end and many assertions can be verified by reference to subsequent events.

   i. **Relationship evidence.** Evidence confirming the truth about one item may tend to confirm the truth about another. For example, evidence confirming the correctness of investment income also confirms some aspects of the item 'investments'.

   j. **Agreement with expectations.** Verification can be assisted by the computation and comparison of ratios and absolute magnitudes with those achieved (a) and in the past; (b) by other companies; and (c) budgeted. Conversely, inconsistencies and unusual or unexpected items will alert the auditor.

k. **External events.** The client is not isolated from the world, and the auditor should use his knowledge of current events in assessing a company's accounts. For example, consider revolutions and the value of overseas subsidiaries.

Basic techniques for collecting evidence

10. There are nine:

a. **Physical examination and count.**

b. **Confirmation.** This should be in writing, external sources being preferable to internal sources.

c. **Examination of original documents.** Original documents should be compared with the entries in the books. The usual wording is vouching.

d. **Re-computation.** Additions, calculations, balance extractions, etc.

e. **Retracing book keeping procedures.** Checking postings.

f. **Scanning.** This is somewhat indefinite but is widely used, especially in seeking the unusual or the unlikely.

g. **Inquiry.** Asking questions. This is a necessary and valid technique. However, auditors acquire a habit of always seeking confirmation of oral answers.

h. **Correlation.** Seeking internal consistency in records and accounts.

i. **Observation.** Seeing for oneself is the best possible confirmation especially in connection with internal control systems.

Test checking

11. This subject is explored further in the next chapter but needs some consideration here. It is not always necessary to obtain evidence about each individual transaction. The modern approach is to obtain evidence about each *type of transaction* by examining a representative *sample* of each type. This is called test checking and is applied as much to assets and liabilities as to routine transactions. The size of the sample to be tested depends on:

a. the strength of the internal control system

b. the materiality of the items

c. the number of items involved

d. the nature of the item

e. the audit risk attached.

Legal decisions

12. The amount of evidence an auditor needs to satisfy himself on the truth and fairness on any figure in the accounts is a matter for the auditor to decide basing his decision on his experience and his knowledge of the standards of the profession generally. This knowledge is gained from textbooks, authoritative articles in the professional press, and the pronouncements of the professional bodies.

13. However, the courts have occasionally been called upon to determine what a competent auditor should do. This usual arises when an auditor is sued for the recovery of damages

caused by his negligence. Most of the well known cases are very old and may well be decided differently if heard today when standards are higher. Some of the cases are:

a. London Oil Storage Co Ltd v Seear Hasluck & Co 1904

    The petty cash balance per the petty cash book was £796. The actual balance in hand was only £30, the rest having been misappropriated. The auditor should have been put upon enquiry by the very large amount of the book balance. He should then have counted the cash in the cash box. This he failed to do.

b. The City Equitable Fire Insurance Co Ltd 1924

    i.   The judge decided that the auditor should not have accepted certificate of a third party holder of securities but have actually examined the securities himself. In fact, the securities were held by the company's stockbrokers, one of whose partners was the Chairman of the company. The view now is that it is reasonable for an auditor to accept the certificate of a third party holder of securities if the standing of the third party is un-questionable.

    ii. This fascinating case also raises the question of window dressing. The true facts were that the company's stockbrokers owed the company a large amount. To hide this the stockbrokers bought some securities on the company's behalf immediately before the end and sold them immediately afterwards. The effect of this was to show 'investments' in the balance sheet instead of a 'debt'. In fact the stockbrokers did buy the securities but were unable to take delivery of them, as they had to pledge them as security for the purchase money.

c. **re Thomas Gerrard & Son Ltd 1967**

    Invoice dates were altered to put them onto different years in order to inflate the profit. The auditor noticed the alterations, was put upon enquiry but was satisfied by the managing director's assurances. He should have sought direct confirmation of the amounts outstanding at the year end from the company's suppliers.

Sources

14. Sources of audit evidence include from within: systems, books, documents, assets, management and staff and from without: customers, suppliers, lenders, professional advisers etc.

15. The sources and amount of evidence required will depend on, materiality, relevance, and reliability of the evidence available from a source, and the cost and time involved.

16. Relevance of audit evidence depends upon whether it assists the auditor in forming an opinion on some aspect of the financial statements. For example evidence that indicates that a recorded asset exists is relevant to audit objectives.

Reliability

17. The reliability of audit evidence can be assessed to some extent on the following presumptions:

    a. Documentary evidence is more reliable than oral evidence.

    b. Evidence from outside the enterprise (eg bank letter) is more reliable than that secured solely from within the enterprise.

   c.   Evidence originated by the auditor by such means as analysis and physical inspection is more reliable than evidence obtained from others (auditors always say 'show me' not 'tell me').

   d.   Evidence for a figure in the Accounts is usually obtained from several sources (eg for debtors - a good system with internal controls, debtors circularisation, ratio analysis, payment after date etc.). The cumulative effect of several evidential sources which give a consistent view is greater than that from a single source (ie $2 + 2 = 5$).

   e.   Original docments are more reliable than photocopies or facsimiles.

Sufficiency

18. Sufficiency is the great problem. The auditor's judgement will be influenced by:

   a.   His knowledge of the business and its industry.

   b.   The degree of audit risk. Assessment of this is helped by considering:

      i.   Nature and materiality of items of account (eg stock is material and difficult to measure).

      ii. The auditor's experience of the reliability of the management and staff and the records.

     iii. The financial position of the enterprise (in a failing enterprise, directors may wish to bolster profits by over valuing assets or suppressing liabilities).

     iv. Possible management bias (as iii.) but also the management may wish to 'even out' profits for stock market image or taxation reasons.

   c.   The persuasiveness of the evidence.

   d.   The nature of the accounting and internal control systems and the control environment.

19. The procedures for collecting evidence include:

   a.   Systems and controls testing (with compliance tests).

   b.   Substantive testing.

   c.   Analytical review.

Summary

20. a.   When the directors prepare accounts they are making *assertions* about the items in the accounts, items omitted from the accounts, and the accounts as a whole.

   b.   The auditor conducts an audit by:

      i.   Identifying the assertions made.

      ii. Considering the information and evidence he needs.

     iii. Collecting the evidence and information.

     iv. Evaluating the evidence.

     v.   Formulating a judgement.

   c.   There are some limitations to the ideal approach to the collection of evidence.

   d.   There are many different varieties of evidence. Some varieties are of more value than others.

   e.   There are nine techniques for collecting evidence.

f. An established method of collecting evidence is the sampling.

g. Some legal decisions have appeared to guide the auditor in assessing what evidence he needs.

h. SAS 400 on audit evidence discusses relevance, reliability and sufficiency and gives some criteria for assessing these qualities in audit evidence.

Points to note

21. a. It is a very good idea both in practice and in examinations to identify what express and implied assertions are being made when an item appears in accounts or does not appear. You should get into the habit of doing this as often as possible.

b. A mental review of the varieties of evidence in paragraph 9 and the techniques of evidence collection in paragraph 10 will often suggest a comprehensive answer to practical and examination problems of verification.

c. Note particularly the value of strong internal control as evidence.

d. The legal cases can often be quoted in examinations although knowledge of them is not compulsory.

e. There is a distinction made in the more theoretical books on auditing between evidential matter and audit evidence. The auditor gathers immense quantities of evidential matter from the business records and management and staff and from third parties. This evidential matter is evaluated by the auditor. If it is relevant to the audit objectives (eg ownership of an asset or completeness of a revenue total) and it is reliable to any extent, it becomes audit evidence.

Case study for Chapter 24

Down Market Department Stores plc sell a high proportion of their merchandise on hire purchase. The system for dealing with HP sales is highly organised and well controlled. The HP debtors ledger is kept on a specially designed micro computer system. The HP debtors of the company at 30.9.-6 appear in the accounts at £4.6 million out of gross assets of £19.3 million.

Discussion

a. What assertions are the directors implying in stating the HP debtors at £4.6 million?

b. What possible misstatements could occur?

c. What varieties of evidence may be collected re this current asset?

d. What basic techniques for collecting evidence can be applied to the item?

Student self testing questions *Questions with answers apparent from the text*

1. a. What sort of assertions about items in accounts are directors making? (3)

b. What varieties of audit evidence are there?(9)

c. What basic techniques for obtaining audit evidence are there? (10)

d. What criteria are there for determining the size of a sample to be used in test checking? (11)

e. What criteria are there for assessing reliability? (17)

f. What criteria are there for assessing sufficiency? (18)

g. Summarise three legal decisions relating to audit evidence? (13)

h. Distinguish audit evidence from evidential matter. (21)

i List sources of audit evidence. (14)

j. What presumptions can be made about the reliability of audit evidence? (17)

k. What might influence an auditor's judgement on sufficiency of audit evidence? (18)

Exercises

1. What assertions are being made by the directors including the following items in the accounts of Dahlia plc a manufacturer of building materials and how might they be verified:

   a. A newly completed finished goods warehouse.

   b. Goodwill of a private business purchased in the year. The goodwill is being written off over 5 years.

   c. Debtors less a general provision for doubtful debts.

   d. Purchases.

   e. Directors' remuneration.

   f. Accrued interest on loans to customers.

   g. Stock of spare parts for plant and machinery.

   h. Plant and Machinery.

2. Welth plc is an investment trust company. List and give details of the varieties of evidence available to an auditor (para 9) for the item 'Investments' in the balance sheet. The company have both quoted and unquoted securities.

3. Crisant Ltd are a licensed maker of secured and unsecured loans to members of the public. The principal items in the accounts are interest receivable in the profit and loss account and loans in the balance sheet. Outline how the basic techniques for collecting evidence (para 10) can be applied to the audit of these items.

4. Aster Ltd manufacture and install process plant for customers in the food processing industry.

   a. Consider the evidence to be collected re the item debtors. Rank this in order of reliability (para 17).

   b. The auditors seek assurance that all liabilities have been included in the accounts. Certainty on this matter is not possible. Discuss the matters to be taken into account in considering the sufficiency of evidence that might be collected.

Examination question (Answer begins on page 551)

1. 'The auditor should obtain relevant and reliable evidence to enable him to draw reasonable conclusions therefrom.'

   Required:

   a. List the various kinds of evidence which might be available to an auditor, giving an illustration of each kind. (10 marks)

   b. What general procedures should be gone through to obtain third party evidence? (5 marks)

   c. To what extent do you consider that a certificate from a trade debtor confirming agreement to a year end balance provides relevant, reliable and sufficient evidence of the outstanding debt? What other work might be necessary to verify the debt? (10 marks)

   (AAT)

Examination questions without answers

2. An auditor must ensure that statements made in the accounts for publication bearing the audit report give full information to the readers of those accounts.

   In the accounts for publication of Trimble plc, there is an entry under creditors, amounts falling due within one year:

   'Bank overdraft £1,234,567'

   If the auditor makes no comment upon this entry, what may he expect it to tell the readers of the accounts? (12 marks)

   (LCC 89)

3. One form of audit evidence available to an external auditor is that supplied by the cost accounting section of his client's staff.

   State what audit evidence the auditor might request from this section in relation to plant and machinery and discuss how far the auditor could rely upon it. (13 marks)

   (LCCI 90)

4. a. What is 'third party' evidence? (3 marks)

   b. Why does an auditor obtain such evidence? (3 marks)

   c. Give one example of third party evidence for *each* of the following items and state how reliable you consider that evidence to be:

      i. Land owned by the client, reserved for future factory building.

      ii. Trade creditors.

      iii. Investments held by bank for safekeeping. (9 marks)

      (LCCI 90) (Total 15 marks)

5. Legislation requires all companies to maintain statutory books and registers.

   Required:

   State the matters to which you would direct your attention when reviewing:

   a. The share register.

   b. The register of directors and secretaries and the register of directors' shareholdings.

   c. The minute books.

   d. The register of charges.

   (AAT 94)

25 Audit risk

Introduction

1. In recent years, the phrase audit risk has entered the vocabulary of auditing.

   Audit risk means the chance of damage to the audit firm as a result of giving an audit opinion that is wrong in some particular. Damage to the audit firm may be in the form of monetary damages paid to a client or third party as compensation for loss caused by the conduct (for example negligence) of the audit firm or simply loss of reputation with the client (and perhaps also the audit) or the business community.

A wrong audit opinion means for example saying that the Accounts show a true and fair view when in fact they do not.

2. This chapter considers:
    a. i.   normal audit risk
        ii.   higher than normal risk
        iii. audit work risk.
    b. Audit firm organisation and audit risk.
    c. Particular audits and audit risk.
    d. The Risk based audit approach.

    There is a Statement of Auditing Standards SAS 300 *Accounting and control systems and audit risk assessments*.

Normal audit risk

3. All audits involve risk. However strong the audit evidence and however careful the auditor, there is always a possibility of an error or fraud being undetected.

4. In general , if there are indications that audit risk is normal and there are no indications of higher than normal risk then the auditor who:
    a. Organises his office and staff in a competent manner.
    b. Follows the auditing standards and guidelines.

    is unlikely to be found negligent and to have to pay damages as a consequence of fraud or error not discovered by him.

5. Indications that risk is normal may include:
    a. Past experience indicates risk is normal.
    b. The management and staff of the client are competent and have integrity.
    c. The accounting system is well designed, works and is subject to strong internal controls.
    e. The client is old established and is not subject to rapid change.
    f. The board of directors are actively engaged in the company and control and leadership is of good quality.
    g. The board of directors has competent non-executive directors and better still, an audit committee.

6. Where audit risk is normal, then the auditor may approach his audit by relying on:
    a. Key controls.
    b. Substantive tests.
    c. Analytical review.

Higher than normal risk

7. Some audit assignments involve high audit risk. The majority of audits contain at least one area of high risk.

8. Indications of higher than normal audit risk include:
    a. Previous experience.

b. Future plans of the enterprise include sale or flotation on the Stock Exchange of the company.

c. High gearing.

d. Liquidity problems.

e. Poor management.

f. Lack of controls and/or poor bookkeeping.

g. Recent changes of ownership/control.

h. Dominance by a single person.

i. Rapid staff turnover.

j. In small companies, non involvement of the proprietor or conversely over reliance on management for control.

k. Changes of accounting procedures or policies.

l. Evidence from background research.

m. Over reliance on one or a few products, customers, suppliers.

n. Recent high investment in new ventures or products.

o. Problems inherent in the nature of the business eg stock counting or valuing difficulties, difficulty in determining the extent of liabilities, warranty claims, cut-off.

p. The existence of 'put upon enquiry' situations.

9. The audit approach in high risk situations must be:

a. Sceptical.

b. To use high calibre audit staff.

c. Collection of a wide range of audit evidence in each area.

d. Meticulous preparation of audit working papers.

e. Probing of all high risk areas to the bottom.

f. Extreme care in drafting the audit report.

Audit work risk

10. All audit work involves normal risk and some audit work involves higher than normal risk. This is because there is always a possibility of the Accounts containing a mis-statement due to error or fraud.

In addition to the audit risk arising from client activity there is also a risk that the audit work may be of an inadequate standard.

11. The risk arising from audit work may include:

a. Failure to recognise put upon enquiry situations.

b. Failure to draw the correct inferences from audit evidence and the analytical review.

c. Use of the wrong procedures in a particular situation.

d. Failure to perform necessary audit work because of time or cost considerations.

e. Failure to detect error or fraud because of poor sampling method or inadequate sample sizes.

Audit firm organisation and audit risk

12. It is essential that an audit firm should organise its affairs in such a way as to minimise the risk of paying damages to clients or others arising out of negligent work.

13. Features of organisation which may minimise risk include:

    a. Proper recruitment and training of all personnel.

    b. Allocation of staff with appropriate ability to particular audits.

    c. Planning of the work of the firm in such a way that each audit can be approached in a relaxed but disciplined way and timing problems can be accommodated.

    d. Two way communication with staff on matters of general concern and in connection with specific audits.

    e. Use of audit manuals which conform to the audit standards and guidelines.

    f. Use of audit documentation which is comprehensive and yet which allows for special situations.

    g. Use of budgeting and other techniques to ensure that audits are remunerative and yet risk-minimising.

    h. Use of precise and frequently updated letters of engagement.

    i. Use of review techniques for all audits.

    j. Existence of a technical section so that all new developments (accounting, law, audit procedures) are rapidly incorporated into the firm's actions.

Particular audits and audit risk

14. Risks arising from a particular audit can be minimised by:

    a. Techniques for recognising the existence of audit risk.

    b. Segregating normal risk areas from high risk areas.

    c. Allocating staff who are competent to do the work especially in high risk areas.

    d. Extensive background research into the client and its industry.

    e. Careful planning with emphasis on high risk areas.

    f. Comprehensive documentation.

    g. Good briefing of audit staff.

    h. Emphasis to staff on the need for recognition of high risk situations and good communication when high risk or put upon enquiry situations are discovered.

    i. Particular attention to the conclusions reached from audit evidence.

    j. Special emphasis on the analytical review.

    k. Review of the audit work by a senior auditor unconnected with the particular audit.

    l. Emphasis on materiality considerations and sample sizes.

The risk based audit methodology

15. Audit costs have been rising steadily in the last few years due to higher salaries (accountants are among the highest paid people), high office costs (accountants like to be in plush city centre offices) and higher professional indemnity premiums (accountants, it seems, make lots of mistakes).

At the same time audit fee resistance has risen due to competition, low growth in the market (except for the public sector) and the growth of competitive tendering for audits.

Consequently, audit firms are continually trying to reduce audit costs while at the same time reducing audit risk. This has led to the idea of risk based auditing being in some sense a distinct approach to auditing. Historically, auditing has progressed from being a largely *substantive testing* process, through a largely *systems* based process into a risk based method which uses a range of audit techniques including: substantive testing, internal control compliance, analytical review and the use of *inherent factors*.

Inherent factors include background knowledge of the client and past audit record indicating no special difficulties. According to Mautz and Sharaf, it is a valid auditing postulate that 'in the absence of evidence to the contrary what has held true for the client in the past will hold true in the future'.

Essentially auditing is the gathering of evidence about each part of the accounts but as absolute assurance is impossible, there is always some element of residual risk which has to be accepted. The extent of that acceptable risk is a matter of judgement. It can be seen as the product of the separate risks accepted in each type of evidence gathering. Thus:

Overall risk = Inherent risk × Control Risk × Analytical review risk × substantive risk.

Thus if, for example an audit situation was examined, found to be material and the risk factors assessed, the following set of figures might be assembled:

(the area may be debtors)

Overall acceptable risk 5% (= 5 chances in 100 of giving a wrong opinion).

Inherent risk (client is old established, well managed and no problems have been encountered in the area previously) 50%.

Control risk (internal control is strong, unchanged from last year, little possibility of management override) 20%.

Analytical control risk (figures tie up with credit sales, with previous years and with budgets subject to small changes stemming from different external conditions) 50%.

Thus substantive risk $= \text{OR}/\text{IR} \times \text{CR} \times \text{AR} = 0.05/0.5*0.2*0.5$

$$= 1$$

This means the audit assurance required from substantive testing is 100% – 100% ie no assurance is required. Assurance from the other sources of evidence are sufficient to support an audit opinion with 5% risk. Most auditors would find this a bit strong but if you change the risk factor from control to 30% then the substantive risk becomes 67% and the level of assurance required from the evidence source substantive testing is only 100% – 67% = 33%. In effect, in designing statistical sampling tests for substantive testing the level of confidence required is only 33%. The sample sizes corresponding to this are likely to be very small.

Using the risk based audit strategy

16. a. The risk based equation outlined above is one of several possible. Others include:

$$\text{AR} = \text{IR} \times \text{CR} \times \text{DR}$$
$$\text{AR} = \text{IR} \times \text{DR} \times \text{SR}$$

where: AR is overall audit risk – the risk that the auditor will draw an invalid conclusion and wrongly qualify or not qualify his/her report.

IR is inherent risk – risk which derives from the nature of the entity and of its environment prior to the establishment of internal controls. Some enterprises are inherently more risky than others eg new v old established, high tech (computer manufacture) v low tech (hand- made up-market furniture).

DR = detection risk – the risk that the auditor's substantive procedures and his review of the financial statements will not detect material errors.

SR = sampling risk – detection risk arising out of sample based substantive tests.

Some of these are sub-sets of others (eg sampling risk of detection risk).

b. Care must be taken to weigh the risk from each source of evidence as it is gathered and then to avoid over auditing in the remaining evidence gathering. For example, if adequate weight is given to inherent factors and analytical review it may be that minimal internal control evaluation and/or substantive testing will be required.

c. It may be undesirable to carry out detailed ICQ and compliance testing techniques if:

   i.   a high level of assurance can be gained from inherent factors and analytical review

   ii. a preliminary review indicates that controls appear to be very strong

   iii. a high level of assurance was obtained in the previous year and the system has not changed

   iv. the area is not material

   v.   a preliminary review indicates that controls are not strong and a high level of assurance will have to come from substantive testing.

d. Use computer aided auditing techniques wherever possible.

e. Use the same sample as far as possible for several tests both compliance and substantive. This takes us back to the old idea of block and depth tests. However care must be taken to think through each sample and clearly record what evidence is being obtained whether it be compliance (if so on what controls) or substantive. In any event random samples never include blocks of transactions.

f. In using sampling, always look for rational sampling methods including stratification.

g. Increase the role of internal audit. Smaller and smaller firms are turning to internal audit and audit firms should make maximum use of this resource.

h. Increase the use of accounting technicians for the actual sampling and employ high level staff for the thought behind the audit work. As a matter of comment, the use of clever recent graduates for audit work seems to be expensive (high salaries, low output as learners and with time off for study) and a turn off from auditing.

Summary

17. a. Audit risk is a term which has grown in importance in recent years.

   b. Audit risk may be defined in two stages:

    i.   The possibility that the financial statements contain material mis-statements which have escaped detection by both, any internal controls on which the auditor has relied and on the auditor's own substantive tests and other work.

    ii. The possibility that the auditor may be required to pay damages to the client or other persons as a consequence of:

       1. the financial statements containing a mis-statement, and

       2. the complaining party suffering loss as a direct consequence of relying on the financial statements, and

       3. negligence by the auditor in not detecting and reporting on the mis-statement can be demonstrated.

c.   Audit risk can be seen as normal or higher than normal.

d.   Normal audit risk exists in all auditing situations.

e.   Higher than normal audit risk can be associated with particular clients or with particular areas of a client's affairs.

f.   Audit risk can arise from a client which is high risk as a whole, for particular areas of a client's affairs, or, from inadequacies in audit work.

g.   Audit risk can be minimised by appropriate audit firm organisation and appropriate audit work on a particular client.

h.   Many modern writers consider the use of risk based auditing as a new direction in auditing, contrasting with the older substantive testing and systems based auditing. Risk based auditing takes account of substantive test risk, internal control risk, detection risk, analytical control risk, sampling risk and inherent risk.

Points to note

18. a. Risk is a useful concept in planning all audit work. It is also a useful buzz word in examination answers.

    b. Modern audit firms are increasingly adopting a *risk based* audit approach. This means that audits are divided into normal and high risk audits and individual audits are divided into normal risk areas and high risk areas. The normal risk areas are covered with emphasis on key controls and analytical review and the larger part of the audit effort is placed on the high risk areas.

    c. This approach of focussing the audit on the high risk areas both minimises the auditor's risk and also makes economic sense from the auditor's, the client's and the public's points of view.

    d. Spotting high risk areas is the important skill. Ideas which assist in this, include:

      Identifying large or high value (material) items.

      Recognising error prone conditions, eg capital/revenue coding, stock and work in progress.

      Briefing staff on the importance of put upon enquiry situations, the investigation of related parties, and the interpretation of new legislation and accounting standards.

    e. One way to reduce audit risk is to acquire the quality standard ISO 9000 either on its own or as part of Total Quality Management. This subject is reviewed in more detail in Chapter 45 on quality control.

Case study 1 for Chapter 25

Stoke, Poges & Co., certified accountants are planning their workload for the three months ending 31 March 19-7: their busy time. They have two partners, one highly skilled senior clerk and several trainees and semi-seniors in the firm. Audits to be done include:

Burke & Hare Ltd., an old established firm of funeral directors.

Growbig Construction Ltd., a newly established firm of speculative builders.

Safe and Sound Supermarket Ltd.

The Heartbreak Hotel Chain Ltd., whose aged proprietor lives in Jamaica.

Smart, Alick & Partners, estate agents.

Halley Electronics Ltd., who are looking for a listing on the Stock Exchange. They manufacture computer peripherals.

Giles Farm Products Ltd., whose major problem is excessive cash resources.

AHM Construction Ltd., a fast expanding firm of civil engineering contractors.

Cultural Video Shops Ltd.

Farcical Funnies Ltd., who run a series of scandal magazines and who recently changed management.

Discussion

a. Distinguish the normal risk companies from the higher than normal risk companies.

b. Who would you put in charge of these audits?

c. Does this case say anything about 'work risk'?

d. Identify possible high risk areas in each of these clients.

Case study 2 for Chapter 25

In the audit of Wodenfield Windows Ltd., a three year old replacement window company, the following data has to be considered:

The company's first two years have been successful but internal controls have been minimal and the control is in the hands of the founders Bill and Ben who are strong characters.

The director/shareholders seem determined to take all profits out of the company as directors' remuneration, leaving a minimum of capital for everyday use and expansion. The company are heavily financed by the bank.

In the year under review turnover and profit are up 50% while stock and debtors are up 65%, creditors are up 50% also.

Discussion

Assess this company from the risk point of view, considering likely risks from the perspectives of inherent risk, control risk, analytical review risk, detection risk, sampling risk, substantive risk.

Student self testing questions *Questions with answers apparent from the text*

1. a. What is audit risk? (1)
    b. What factors might indicate that risk is normal? (5)
    c. What factors might indicate higher than normal audit risk? (8)

d. What is the audit approach in areas of high risk? (9)

e. What is audit work risk? (10)

f. How might audit work risk arise? (11)

g. What audit firm organisation features might minimize audit risk? (13)

h. How can risk in particular areas be minimised? (14)

i. What is a risk based audit? (16)

j. How can high risk areas be spotted? (16)

k. Define overall audit risk, inherent risk, control risk, analytical review risk, detection risk, sampling risk, substantive risk. Put these risks into sets or categories.

Examination questions without answers

1. Some areas of an audit have a higher risk element than others.

    a. How may an external auditor identify such areas?

    b. What action should the auditor take upon discovery of such areas? (15 marks)

    (LCCI 91)

2. It is important for an auditor to consider risk when planning, carrying out and coming to an opinion on the financial statements of a company. Audit risk has been categorised into:

    a. inherent risk

    b. control risk, and

    c. detection risk.

    The following equation is often used in determining audit risk:

    $$AR = IR \times CR \times DR$$

    where:

    AR = audit risk

    IR = inherent risk

    CR = control risk

    DR = detection risk.

    You are required:

    a. To define the following terms:

        i. audit risk

        ii. inherent risk

        iii. control risk

        iv. detection risk. (4 marks)

    b. To explain the factors which affect inherent risk in an audit. (7 marks)

    c. To describe the work you will carry out to quantify the control risk in a purchases system. (7 marks)

    d. In relation to detection risk:

        i. to consider the effect on the detection risk of the inherent risk and control risk, if the auditor requires a particular value of audit risk.

        ii. to briefly describe the audit checks you will perform in verifying trade creditors and accruals, and how these tests are affected by the value of the detection risk.

        (7 marks)

        (ACCA 93)

26 Statistical and other sampling methods

Introduction

1. A complete check of all the transactions and balances of a business is no longer required of an auditor. The reasons for this are:

   a. Economic – the cost in terms of expensive audit resources would be prohibitive.

   b. Time – the complete check would take so long that accounts would be ancient history before users saw them.

   c. Practical – users of accounts do not expect or require 100% accuracy. Materiality is very important in accounting as well as auditing.

   d. Psychological – a complete check would so bore the audit staff that their work would become ineffective and errors would be missed.

   e. Fruitfulness – a complete check would not add much to the worth of figures if, as would be normal, few errors were discovered. The emphasis in auditing should be on the *completeness* of record and the true and *fair* view.

2. In some cases a 100% check is still necessary. Some of these are:

   a. Categories which are few in number but of great importance eg land and buildings.

   b. Categories with special importance where materiality does not apply eg directors' emoluments and loans.

   c. Unusual, one-off, or exceptional items.

   d. Any area where the auditor is put upon enquiry.

   e. High risk areas.

3. In most areas a 100% check is not necessary and a test check is made, or, to put in audit terminology – evidence about a whole class of transactions or balances is obtained by examination of a sample of items taken from that class.

4. There are two approaches to sampling in auditing:

   a. judgement sampling

   b. statistical sampling.

   We will deal with each in turn and then review statistical sampling in more detail.

5. Note that the objective in all sampling is to *draw conclusions* about a large group of data, eg all the credit sales made in a period, or all the PAYE calculations or all the debtors, from an examination of a sample taken from the group.

6. There is a Statement of Auditing Standards SAS 430 *Statistical Sampling*

Objectives of audit sampling

7. SAS 100 requires that auditors should carry out procedu..s designed to obtain sufficient appropriate audit evidence to determine with reasonable confidence whether the financial statements are free of material misstatement.

Two words in the last sentence are relevant here – reasonable and material. It is not necessary that auditors should financial statements are absolutely 100% accurate. Sampling does not provide absolute proof of 100% accuracy but it can provide reasonable assurance that some elements of the financial statements are free from material misstatement.

Audit sampling means drawing conclusions about an entire set of data by testing a *representative* sample of items. The set of data which may be a set of account balances (eg debtors, creditors, fixed assets) or transactions (eg all wage payments, all advice notes) is called the *population*. The individual items making up the population are called *sampling units*.

Materiality and risk

8. a. An auditor is not required to have evidence that all items in a set of Accounts are one hundred per cent correct. His duty is to give an opinion on the truth and fairness of the Accounts. Errors can exist in the Accounts and yet the Accounts can still give a true and fair view. The maximum error that any particular magnitude can contain without marring the true and fair view is the *tolerable* error. Tolerable error is auditing materiality.

In his audit planning, the auditor needs to determine the amount of tolerable error in any given population and to carry out tests to provide evidence that the actual errors in the population are less than the tolerable error. For example, stock can be a large amount in a set of accounts. Stock is computed by counting and weighing, by multiplying quantity by price and by summing individual values. Errors can occur at any of these stages. Applied prices may be incorrect. The effect of incorrect prices may be to compute a stock figures that is above or below the correct stock figure by an amount that is above the tolerable error.

b. *Audit risk*. This term applies to the risk that the auditor will draw an invalid conclusion from his audit procedures. Audit risk has several components:

i. *Inherent risk* is the risk attached to any particular population because of factors like:

The type of industry – a new manufacturing hi-tech industry is more prone to errors of all sorts than a stable business like a brewery.

Previous experience indicates that significant errors have occurred.

Some populations are always prone to error, eg stock calculations, work in progress.

ii. *Control risk*. This is the risk that internal controls will not detect and prevent material errors. If this risk is large the auditor may eschew compliance tests altogether and apply only substantive tests.

iii. *Detection risk*. This is the risk that the auditor's substantive procedures and analytical review will not detect material errors.

The assurance that an auditor seeks from sampling procedures is related to the audit risk that he perceives. The sample sizes required will be related to the audit risk that he perceives. The sample sizes required will be related to materiality and to audit risk.

To sample or not?

9. The auditor, in considering a particular population, has to consider how to obtain assurance about it. Sampling may be the solution. Factors which may be taken into account in considering whether or not to sample include:

    a. Materiality. Petty cash expenditure may be so small that no conceivable error may affect the true and fair view of the accounts as a whole.

    b. The number of items in the population. If these are few (eg land and buildings), a hundred per cent check may be economic.

    c. Reliability of other forms of evidence – analytical review (eg wages relate closely to number of employees, budgets, previous years, etc.) – proof in total (VAT calculations). If other evidence is very strong, then a detailed check of a population (100% or a sample) may be unnecessary.

    d. Cost and time considerations can be relevant in choosing between evidence seeking methods.

    e. A combination of evidence seeking methods is often the optimal solution.

Stages of audit sampling

10. The stages of audit sampling are:

    a. Planning the sample.

        –   *Audit objectives*. Why is this test being carried out? What contribution does it make to the overall assessment of true and fair view?

        –   *The population*. The population has to be defined precisely. This may be all sales rather than all sales invoices. (Can you see the difference?)

        –   *The sampling unit*. Note that in compliance testing it is the operation of the control on a transaction not the transaction which is the sampling unit.

        –   *The definition of error in substantive tests*. In stock calculations, an error of greater than £1 only may constitute an error for this purpose.

        –   *The definition of deviation in compliance tests*. The deviation may be any failure to carry out a control procedure or it may be a partial failure.

        –   *The assurance required*. This is a function of the other sources of evidence available.

        –   *The tolerable error or deviation rate*. This is related to materiality.

        –   *The expected error/deviation rate*. This is a factor which is not intuitively expected by students. In fact, errors increase the impreciseness of conclusions drawn from sampling and larger sample sizes are required if there are many errors.

        –   *Stratification*. It may be desirable to stratify the population into sub-populations and sample them separately or in some cases, such as high value items, do a hundred per cent check.

    b. Selection of the items to be tested. This is dealt with in detail later in the chapter.

    c. Testing the items.

    d. Evaluating the results. This should also be done in stages:

        –   Analyse the errors/deviations detected in relation to the planning definitions.

 – Use the errors/deviations detected to estimate the total error in the population. This is called *projection* of the errors from the sample to the population.

 – Assess the risk of an incorrect solution. This will be related to the amount of *projection* of error compared with the tolerable error and the availability of alternative evidence.

Judgement sampling

11. This means selecting a sample of appropriate size on the basis of the auditor's judgement of what is desirable. You could call it the 'seat of pants' approach.

    This approach has some advantages:

    a. The approach has been used for many years. It is well understood and refined by experience.

    b. The auditor can bring his judgement and expertise into play. Some auditors seem to have a sixth sense.

    c. No special knowledge of statistics is required.

    d. No time is spent on playing with mathematics. All the audit time is spent on auditing.

12. There are some disadvantages:

    a. It is unscientific.

    b. It is wasteful – usually sample sizes are too large.

    c. No quantitative results are obtained.

    d. Personal bias in the selection of samples is unavoidable.

    e. There is no real logic to the selection of the sample or its size.

    f. The sample selection can be slanted to the auditors needs eg selection of items near the year end to help with cut-off evaluation.

    g. The conclusions reached on the evidence from samples is usually vague – a feeling of 'it seems OK' or of vague disquiet.

13. Overall, judgement sampling is still the preferred method by a majority of auditors. Partly this can be defended on the grounds that the auditor is weighing several strands of evidence (internal control, business background, conversations with employees, subjective feelings, past experience, etc.) and is usually investigating several things at once (eg more than one control evidenced on an invoice, proper books, internal control compliance and substantive testing of totals) so that the whole process is too complex to reduce to the simple formulations of the statistician. On the other hand, the statistician can reply that judgement sampling in the past worked well because very large samples were always taken. Today, the small samples required by economic logic require careful measuring of the risks attached and this can only be done by the use of statistical techniques.

Statistical sampling

14. Drawing *inferences* about a large volume of data by an examination of a sample is a highly developed part of the discipline of *statistics*. It seems only common sense for the auditor to draw upon this body of knowledge in his own work. In practice, a high level of mathematical competence is required if valid conclusions are to be drawn from

sample evidence. However most firms that use statistical sampling have drawn up complex plans which can be operated by staff without statistical training. These involve the use of tables, graphs or computer methods.

15. The advantages of using statistical sampling are:
    a. It is scientific.
    b. It is defensible.
    c. It provides precise mathematical statements about probabilities of being correct.
    d. It is efficient – overlarge sample sizes are not taken.
    e. It tends to cause uniform standards among different audit firms.
    f. It can be used by lower grade staff who would be unable to apply the judgement needed by judgement sampling.

    There are some disadvantages:
    a. As a technique it is not always fully understood so that false conclusions may be drawn from the results.
    b. Time is spent playing with mathematics which might better be spent on auditing.
    c. Audit judgement takes second place to precise mathematics.
    d. It is inflexible.
    e. Often several attributes of transactions or documents are tested at the same time. Statistics does not easily incorporate this.

    The rest of this chapter describes some of the facts and considerations that auditing students should digest.

Sample selection – characteristics

16. In auditing, a sample should be:
    a. Random – a random sample is one where each item of the population has an equal (or specified) chance of being selected. Statistical inferences may not be valid unless the sample is random.
    b. Representative – the sample should be representative of the differing items in the whole population. For example, it should contain a similar proportion of high and low value items to the population (eg all the debtors).
    c. Protective – protective, that is, of the auditor. More intensive auditing should occur on high value items known to be high risk.
    d. Unpredictable – client should not be able to know or guess which items will be examined.

17. There are several methods available to an auditor for selecting items. These include:
    a. **Haphazard** simply choosing items subjectively but avoiding bias. Bias might come in by tendency to favour items in a particular location or in an accessible file or conversely in picking items because they appear unusual. This method is acceptable for non-statistical sampling but is insufficiently rigorous for statistical sampling.
    b. **Simple random** all items in the population have (or are given) a number. Numbers are selected by a means which gives every number an equal chance of being selected.

This is done using random number tables or computer or calculator generated random numbers.

c. **Stratified** this means dividing the population into sub populations (strata = layers) and is useful when parts of the population have higher than normal risk (eg high value items, overseas debtors). Frequently high value items form a small part of the population and are 100% checked and the remainder are sampled.

d. **Cluster sampling** this is useful when data is maintained in clusters (= groups or bunches) as wage records are kept in weeks or sales invoices in months. The idea is to select a cluster randomly and then to examine all the items in the cluster chosen. The problem with this method is that this sample may not be representative.

e. **Random systematic** this method involves making a random start and then taking every nth item thereafter. This is a commonly use method which saves the work of computing random numbers. However the sample may not be representative as the population may have some serial properties.

f. **Multi stage sampling** this method is appropriate when data is stored in two or more levels. For example stock in a retail chain of shops. The first stage is to randomly select a sample of shops and the second stage is to randomly select stock items from the chosen shops.

g. **Block sampling** simply choosing at random one block of items eg all June invoices. This common sampling method has none of the desired characteristics and is not recommended.

h. **Value weighted selection** this method uses the currency unit value rather than the items as the sampling population. It is now very popular and is described more fully later in the chapter, under *Monetary Unit Sampling*.

Sample sizes

18. There are several factors which must be considered when deciding upon the sample size. These include:

a. **Population size** – Surprisingly, in most instances this is not important and is only relevant in very small populations.

b. **Level of confidence** – Even a 100% sample (for human concentration reasons) will not give complete assurance. Auditors work to levels of confidence which can be expressed precisely. For example, a 5% confidence level means that there is 19 chances out of 20 that the sample is representative of the population as a whole. Of course, the converse view is that there is one chance in twenty that the sample, on which the auditor draws conclusions, is non-representative of the population as a whole.

c. **Precision** – from a sample, it is not possible to say that I am 95% certain that, for example, the error rate in a population of stock calculations is $x\%$ but only that the error rate is $x\% \pm y\%$ where $\pm y$ is the precision interval. Clearly the level of confidence and the precision interval are related, in that for a given sample size higher confidence can be expressed in a wider precision interval and vice versa.

d. **Risk** – risk is a highly important concept in modern auditing and in high risk areas (eg coding of expense invoices into capital and revenue) a large sample will be desirable, because high confidence levels and narrow precision intervals are required.

In statistical sampling, risk can be quantified and a particular level chosen.

There are two types of risk:

i. α risk – the risk of rejecting a population (eg all the stock calculations) when it is in fact right.

ii. β risk – the risk of accepting a population (eg debtors) when it in fact contains an unacceptable proportion of errors.

The alpha and beta risks are related, in that reducing the alpha risk involves an increase in the beta risk and vice versa. If an auditor rejects a population (eg stock calculations) he must put his client to more work and also give himself more work. Thus the consequences of alpha risk are only more work and thus economic loss to the auditor. The consequences of beta risk are greater in that Accounts may be approved by the auditor but contain serious error. The costs to the client, the business community and others may be serious. If the errors are subsequently discovered the auditor may lose reputation and may suffer an action for negligence.

Fortunately, the scientific nature of the auditor's use of statistical theory may well indicate that despite the actual erroneous opinion given by the auditor, his work was satisfactory and he was not negligent.

e.   **Materiality** – this is really a subset of risk. Materiality is fundamental to modern auditing and with all populations being sampled, materiality should be considered in fixing the sample size because:

i.   Populations that are material to the overall audit opinion (eg stock in most clients) must be sampled with smaller precision intervals and higher confidence levels.

ii. Within a population, a materiality factor can be subjectively estimated (eg 5% either way on debtors) and precision intervals fixed accordingly.

f.   **Subjective factors** – this is a most important and yet difficult area of consideration. The auditor expects to gain audit evidence about a population from a sample. However other audit evidence is available in addition to the evidence from the sample:

The existence of internal controls.

The auditors knowledge of the company, its staff and its environment.

Correlation evidence from other areas subject to audit.

Previous years' experience.

Analytical review.

Gut feeling.

Thus if the only evidence about a population is from the sample then a large sample is required. If the sampling evidence is merely topping up other evidence, then the sample need not be so large.

Most sampling plans used in practice explicitly build in these subjective factors.

g.   **Expected error/deviation rate** – the theory requires that the sample size required is a function of the error/deviation rate. This is only known after the results have been evaluated. However, an estimate based on previous experience and knowledge of other factors may give a good indication. If the results indicate that the level of error/deviation was higher than expected, a larger sample may have to be taken.

The level of confidence and precision interval are statistical terms. The level of confidence is a function of the risk that the auditor is willing to accept. It is related to the subjective factors considered. The precision interval is equivalent to the materiality factor or tolerable error.

Tolerable error

19. Tolerable error is the maximum error in the population that auditors are willing to accept and still conclude that audit objectives have been achieved. The tolerable error in a population is usually determined in the planning stage. It is related to and affected by:

   – materiality considerations

   – assessment of control risk

   – results of other audit procedures.

   The essential procedure is to set a tolerable error rate and then to *project* the error rate in the population implied by the sampling results and then to compare the two. If the projected error is larger than the tolerable error then further auditing procedures will be necessary in the area.

Statistical sampling audit uses

20. Statistical sampling plans can be used in all auditing situations when evidence about a population is obtained by sampling.

21. Some popular uses include:

   Compliance testing – the issue of sales credit notes is controlled by the requirement that all such should be approved by a departmental manager and this approval evidenced by a signature. The auditor would wish to confirm that this control was complied with by sampling the sales credit notes.

   Substantive testing – in a client with very unreliable internal controls, the auditor may wish to verify that all despatches in a year have resulted in invoices in that year. The correspondence between despatch note and invoice can be sampled.

   – stock calculations can be sampled.

   – a sample of debtors only need be circularised.

Sampling methods

22. These include:

   a. Estimation sampling for variables – this method seeks to estimate (with a chosen level of confidence and precision interval) the total value of some population. For example the total value of debtors, stock or loose tools. The procedure is to extrapolate from a sample to an estimate of the total value. This estimate can be compared with the book value and if any difference is within the materiality limits pre-established, the auditor has evidence for the book value of the item.

   b. Estimation sampling for attributes – this method seeks to estimate the proportion of a population having a particular characteristic (= attribute), for example overdue debts or damaged stock or errors in coding invoices.

Attribute sampling has the disadvantage that it only measures deviations from some norm but does not measure the monetary affect of that deviation. It is generally used in compliance testing where the extent of application of a control is to be determined.

c. Acceptance sampling – this method seeks to discover the error rate in a population to determine whether the population is acceptable. It involves pre-determining a maximum error rate. Its uses are legion, including:

i. Whether a control can be relied upon – if non compliance is greater than an acceptable rate, the control will not be relied upon and other audit tests will have to be applied.

ii. Whether stock calculations can be relied on.

If the error rate is greater than some acceptable proportion then the auditor will have to request the client to do the calculations again.

d. Discovery sampling – this method extends acceptance sampling to an acceptance level of nil. For example, a system, with controls, exists in an Investment Trust Company to ensure that all bonus issues are accepted and recorded. If even one bonus issue has not been recorded, the auditor will be unable to accept the controls and will have to seek other evidence. This method has been compared with seeking a needle in a haystack. It requires large samples.

Monetary unit sampling

23. This is a relatively new variant of discovery sampling which is thought to have wide application in auditing. This is because:

a. Its application is appropriate with large variance populations. Large variance populations are those like debtors or stocks where the members of the population are of widely different sizes.

b. The method is suited to populations where errors are not expected.

c. It implicitly takes into account the auditor's concept of materiality.

24. Procedures are:

a. determine sample size. This will take into account:

i. the size of the population

ii. the minimum unacceptable error rate (related to materiality)

iii. the Beta risk desired.

b. List the items in the population (we will use debtors) eg

Debtor name	Amount of balance £	Cumulative £
Jones	620	620
Brown & Co.	4	624
XY Co. Ltd.	1,320	1,944
JB plc.	220	2,164
RS Acne	4,197	6,361
. . .	. . .	. . .
. . .	. . .	. . .
	384,200	384,200

c. If the sample size were 100 items then take a random start say 1,402 and every 3,842th item thereafter; that is using systematic sampling with a random start.

The idea is that:

   i. the population of debtors is not the 1,250 debtors but 384,200 single £'s.

   ii. if the particular pound is chosen then the whole balance of which that £1 is a part will be investigated and any error quantified.

In our example, XY Co. Ltd., would be selected since 1,402 lies in their balance and RS Acne would also be chosen as 1,402 and 3,842 lies in their balance.

Note that the larger balances have a greater chance of being selected. This is protective for the auditor but it has been pointed out that balances that contain errors of understatement will have reduced chance of detection.

d. At the end of the process, evaluate the result which might be a conclusion that the auditor is 95% confident that the debtors are not overstated by more than £x. £x is the materiality factor chosen. If the conclusion is that the auditor finds that the debtors appear to be overstated by more than £x then he may take a larger sample and/or investigate the debtors more fully.

25. MUS has some disadvantages:

a. It does not cope easily with errors of understatement. A debtor balance which is underestimated will have a smaller chance of being selected than if it was correctly valued. Hence there is a reduced chance of selecting that balance and discovering the error.

b. It can be difficult to select samples if a computer cannot be used as manual selection will involve adding cumulatively through the population.

c. It is not possible to extend a sample if the error rate turns out to be higher than expected. In such cases an entirely new sample must be selected and evaluated.

26. MUS is especially useful in testing for overstatement where significant understatements are not expected. Examples of applications include debtors, fixed assets and stock. It is clearly not suitable for testing creditors where understatement is the primary characteristic to be tested.

Working papers

27. As in all audit work, the work done in audit sampling situations should be fully documented in the working papers. In particular the documentation in the working papers should show:

Planning the sample

a. Stating the audit objectives.

b. Definition of error or deviation.

c. The means of determining the sample size.

d. The tolerable error rate.

Selecting the items to be tested

e. The selection method used.

f. details of the items selected.

Testing the items

g. The tests carried out.

h. The errors or deviations noted.

Evaluating the results of the tests

i. Explanations of the causes of the errors or deviations.

j. The projection of errors or deviations.

k. The auditor's assessment of the assurance obtained as to the possible size of actual error or deviation rate.

l. The nature and details of the conclusions drawn from the sample results.

m. Details of further action taken where required (eg a larger sample or other forms of evidence gathering).

Summary

28. a. Traditionally, auditors have relied upon test checks or samples in forming conclusions about populations of data.

b. The size and composition of samples can be determined by the judgement of the auditor.

c. Alternatively statistical methods can be used. These have the advantage of enabling the auditor to draw conclusions like 'I am 95% certain that the error rate in the wage calculations is 1.4% ± .3%.'

d. Samples should be random, representative, protective and unpredictable.

e. Sample selection methods include haphazard, random, stratified, cluster, random systematic, multistage, block, and value weighted.

f. Sample sizes are a function of:

population size, confidence levels and precision limits.

g. Confidence levels and precision limits are a function of risk assessment, materiality and other subjective factors relating to other forms of audit evidence (internal control, analytical review, knowledge of the business, correlative factors).

h. Statistical sampling can be used in all areas of an audit and with both compliance and substantive tests.

i. Sampling methods include estimation sampling for variables, estimation sampling for attributes, acceptance and discovery sampling.

j. A newly developed method of interest is monetary unit sampling (MUS).

Points to note

29. a. The design of the sampling plans used by firms of accountants is a technical matter best done by the statistically trained.

b. A manual of this kind is not the right place to teach the mechanics of sampling. There are several excellent works available on statistical sampling for accountants and auditors.

c. Professional auditing examiners do not require a knowledge of the technical aspects of sampling beyond that given in this chapter.

d. Materiality is very important in auditing. In sampling, materiality manifests itself in the term 'tolerable error' which is related to the statistical term precision interval.

e. Risk is also a very important concept in auditing. The degree of risk determines the degree of assurance an auditor requires in an audit area. In statistical sampling this is related to the level of confidence required.

f. Statistical sampling as an audit tool, like risk analysis, promises much but in practice delivers little. The problem presents itself to an auditor as 'What is an acceptable risk?' or 'What is the probability that these accounts or that figure contain an inaccuracy?'. These problems are incapable of quantification although most auditors could make a subjective assessment as to the risk being low, medium or high.

All auditors take a risk when they express a clean opinion on a set of accounts. However the risk may seem less acceptable in some circumstances. For examples:

– when external users are sure to use the accounts (eg the bank in renewing a loan or a potential buyer of the company)

– when the company is in facing financial problems if say it is possible that the company may go into receivership

Case study for Chapter 26

Hoopoe plc are an old established large food processing company mainly buying poultry from local farmers, freezing them and selling them to retailers on credit terms. Assets employed total £6 million, turnover £15 million, profits are £1.8 million and debtors are £3 million. The company have excellent internal controls which the auditor has evaluated at the interim audit. The auditor is examining the debtors schedule. He finds that there are 3,900 items upon it. Four balances are over £100,000, being to large supermarket chains. 162 balances totalling £114,000 are for customers overseas.

Discussion

a. Discuss the tolerable error that might be acceptable in the case of debtors.

b. What audit risk factors are relevant? What substantive tests and analytical review techniques will enable the audit to reduce the detection risk?

c. What stratification will be required?

d. Outline the stages of a suitable audit sampling approach to the debtors in this case, determining the audit objectives, the population, the sampling unit, the definition of error, the sample selection method, and the sampling method. In each area, discuss the difficulties which might be encountered.

Student self testing questions *Questions with answers apparent from the text*

1. a. Why is a 100% check no longer usual in auditing? (1)
   b. Where is 100% check still applied? (2)
   c. What is meant by: representative, population; sampling units? (7)
   d. What is 'tolerable error' and how is it related to materiality? (8, 19)
   e. What is inherent risk, control risk, detection risk? (8)
      Give examples of each.
   f. What factors are relevant in considering whether to sample? (9)
   g. List the stages in sampling. (10)

h. An auditor is looking at purchases. Should he see the population to be sampled as all goods entered in the goods received book or all purchase invoices? (10)

i. An auditor is sampling (statistically) purchase invoices to ensure that all are checked against goods inwards notes. Such checks are evidenced by the signature of a clerk in a grid. Given the population size (25,000), the sample size (500) and that 24 items carried no signature, what should the auditor do? What conclusions can be drawn? Do this mathematically if you can or give the type of statement that can be made. Relate this statement to the audit objectives. (10)

j. When is stratification desirable? (10)

k. List the sampling methods available. (22)

l. List the advantages and disadvantages of judgement sampling and of statistical sampling. (11,12,15)

m. List some sample selection methods. (17)

n. Distinguish level of confidence from precision interval. (18)

o. Distinguish α (alpha) risk from β (beta) risk. (18)

p. List some statistical sampling techniques. (22)

q. Explain monetary unit sampling. (23)

r. Why is MUS not good for testing understatement? (25)

s. What is tolerable error? (19)

Examination question (Answer begins on page 551)

1. As a recently qualified accountant you joined the staff of a small professional firm a short time ago. Your first responsibility was to conduct the audit of the firm's major client, Western Chemicals plc. You followed the traditionally audit programme which has been used by your employer for many years and relies extensively on traditional judgement sampling.

During the audit a number of ideas occurred to you which you feel would be of benefit to your employer for future audits of his client.

Required:

Draft a memorandum to the partner responsible for the audit in which you:

a. briefly state the advantages and disadvantages of following audit programmes which rely on traditional judgement sampling; (10 marks)

b. describe the statistical sampling techniques of random sampling and stratified sampling; (3 marks)

c. outline the advantages and disadvantages of statistical sampling techniques as opposed to traditional judgement sampling. (7 marks)
(ACCA)

Examination questions without answers

2. It is important to recognise that audit sampling may be constructed on a non-statistical basis. If the auditor uses statistical sampling, probability theory will be used to determine sample size and random selection methods to ensure each item or £1 in value of the population has the same chance of selection. Non-statistical sampling, is more subjective than statistical sampling, typically using haphazard selection methods and placing no reliance upon probability theory. However, in certain circumstances statistical sampling

techniques may be difficult to use. The auditor will review the circumstances of each audit before deciding whether to use statistical or non-statistical sampling.

Required:

a. List three situations where the auditor would be unlikely to use audit sampling techniques. (3 marks)

b. Explain what you understand by the following terms:
   i.   attribute sampling
   ii. monetary unit sampling. (6 marks)

c. Describe the factors which the auditor should consider when determining the size of a sample. (6 marks)

d. Describe to what extent statistical sampling enhances the quality of the audit evidence. (5 marks)

(ACCA 93)

3. Healthy Milk Ltd buys milk from dairy farmers, processes the milk and delivers it to retail outlets. You are currently auditing the debtors system and determine the following information:

i.   The company employs 75 drivers who are each responsible for delivering milk to customers. Each driver delivers milk to between 20 and 30 shops on a daily basis. Debtors normally amount to approximately £450,000. Payments by customers are not normally made to the drivers but are sent directly to the head office of the company.

ii. The sales ledger is regularly reviewed by the office manager who prepares a list for each driver of accounts with 90 day balances or older. This list is used for the purpose of intensive collection by the drivers. Each driver has a delivery book which is used for recording deliveries of milk and those debtors with 90 day balances.

iii. The audit program used in previous audits for the selection of debtor balances for direct confirmation stated: 'Select two accounts from each driver's customers, one to be chosen by opening each driver's delivery book at random and the other as the fourth item on the list of 90 day or older accounts.' Each page of the driver's delivery book deals with a single customer.

Having reviewed the debtors system, you conclude that statistical sampling techniques should be used to assist your audit work. On the completion of your review and testing of the 2,000 debtor balances, your statistical sample of 100 accounts disclosed 10 errors. You therefore conclude that there must be 200 accounts in the entire population which are in error as you are sure that the errors detected in the sample will be in exact proportion to the errors in the population.

Required

a. Explain the reasons why the audit procedure used in the previous audit for the selection of debtors for audit confirmation would not produce a valid statistical sample. (4 marks)

b. Explain briefly the audit objectives in selecting a sample of 90 day accounts for direct confirmation. (3 marks)

c. Discuss whether the application of statistical sampling techniques would help in the attainment of the audit objectives set out in b) above. (5 marks)

d. Discuss whether it is reasonable to assume that the errors detected in the sample of debtor balances tested are in exact proportion to the errors in the total population of debtors. (4 marks)

e. Discuss the view that since statistical sampling techniques do not relieve the auditor of his responsibilities in the exercise of his professional judgement, then they are of no benefit to the auditor. (4 marks)

(ACCA 90) (Total 20 marks)

27 Reliance on other specialists

Introduction

1. SAS 100 requires that an auditor should carry out procedures designed to obtain *sufficient appropriate audit evidence* to determine with reasonable confidence whether the financial statements are free of material misstatement.

2. In general the auditor's programme of work will provide him with sufficient reliable relevant evidence to enable him to give an unqualified opinion. However there can be circumstances where the auditor's knowledge is insufficient and he may then need to rely on the opinions of experts or specialists to help him form an opinion. This chapter is about reliance on other specialists.

3. There is a Statement of Auditing Standards SAS 520 *using the work of an expert.*

Examples

4. Examples of specialists whose work may be relied upon by auditors include:

    a. Valuers – on the value of fixed assets such as freehold and leasehold property or more rarely plant and machinery and on the value of specialist stock in trade such as works of art, antiques, precious stones etc.

    b. Quantity surveyors – on the value of work done on long term contracts.

    c. Actuaries – on the liability to be included for pension scheme liabilities.

    d. Geologists – on the quantity and quality of mineral reserves.

    e. Stockbrokers – on the value of stock exchanges securities.

    f. Lawyers – on the legal interpretation of contracts and agreements, or the outcome of disputes and litigation.

When will specialist opinions be relied on?

5. In certain kinds of businesses specialist opinions are a primary source of evidence. For example civil engineering businesses often employ independent quantity surveyors to value work in progress. Often an auditor has little other evidence on which to base his opinion on such values. Property companies incorporate values of properties in their accounts. The source of such valuations being specialist valuers. The auditor may have no other evidence except the specialist valuer's opinion.

6. Except in cases such as those in paragraphs 4 and 5 the auditor does not need to seek specialist opinions because he has sufficient internal evidence or because the matter is not material. However there can be situations where an expert opinion may be essential evidence. For example the client, an entertainment management agency, has a contract which may or may not involve the payment of royalties to a former manager of an entertainer under contract. The matter has not yet gone to litigation and may well be settled amicably. If the amount payable is either nil or £50,000 depending on the interpretation of the contract then if the client's profit is £2 million then the matter is not material and the auditor will be content to accept either interpretation. If however the client is a small one and £50,000 is very important to the view given by the Accounts, then the auditor may wish the client to seek specialist legal advice.

7. In general in deciding whether the auditor needs to have specialist opinions he will consider:

   a. The materiality of the item.

   b. The risk of significant error in an item. For example the amount of the value of some antiques valued at net realisable value may be material but any error in valuation may have only a small chance of being materially wrong. On the other hand, the risk of significant error in an assessment of the extractability of mineral from a mine may be very high.

   c. The complexity of the information and his own understanding of it and any specialism relating to it. The obligations of a client under a complex lease agreement involving a development property in Spain may require the opinion of a lawyer skilled in both English and Spanish Law.

   d. Other sources of audit evidence available on the matter.

The reliability of the specialist

8. Factors which may influence the auditor to rely upon or not to rely upon the work of a specialist include:

   a. **The competence of the specialist**. This may be indicated by technical qualifications, certification and licensing, membership of professional bodies, experience and reputation.

   b. **The independence of the specialist**. The degree of relationship with the client may be the key factor. Any specialist who is related to the directors or employees of the client or who has financial interest (other than his fee) with the client is clearly less than wholly independent. Apparent dependence may be mitigated by professional body disciplinary and ethical codes.

Agreement

9. If it is the intention of the auditor to place reliance on the work of a specialist, it is important to hold a consultation between auditor, client and specialist, at the time the specialist is appointed, to reach agreement on the work to be performed. The agreement should cover:

   a. Objectives, scope and subject matter of the specialist's work.

   b. Assumptions upon which the specialist's report depends and their compatibility with the accounts. For example, are going concern or market values to be taken.

   c.   A statement of the bases used in previous years and any change to be made.

   d.   The use to be made of the specialist's findings. (He may need this for professional indemnity insurance purposes).

   e.   The form and content of the specialist' report or opinion.

   f.   The sources of information to be provided to the specialist.

   g.   The identification of any relationship which may affect the specialist's objectivity. An example of this may be the case of an architect who though in private practice obtains most of his commissions from the client who is subject to audit.

It is possible to use a specialist's opinion without this process but it is desirable to go through this procedure.

Evaluation of the specialist evidence

10. The sufficiency and reliability of such evidence will depend upon the nature of the evidence, the circumstances necessitating its preparation, the materiality of the matter and the auditor's assessment of the competence of the specialist and his independence from the client. In particular, the auditor should consider:

   a.   Whether the opinion is given in accordance with an agreement such as that specified in paragraph 9 above.

   b.   Whether the data is compatible with the data used in preparing the financial statements.

   c.   Whether the consistency convention has been followed.

   d.   Whether the evidence appears to be reasonable. The auditor can often have an opinion on property values but the assessment of geological data may not be possible.

   e.   Whether the specialist's findings have been incorporated correctly in the accounts.

   f.   The effective date of the specialist's findings is acceptable. This relates to the importance of the date of the auditor's own report.

   g.   Whether the specialist has qualified his/her opinion, or expressed any reservations.

   h.   When the specialist has reported in previous years, whether the findings are compatible with those of earlier years.

In any event, the auditor must apply his intellect to understanding at least the assumptions made and bases of valuation used.

If the auditor is unable to reply upon the findings (eg if the specialist did not use data specified to him and also used in the accounts), then he may request the client to obtain an opinion from another specialist. This may seem extreme but in some cases it might avoid an audit report qualification.

The audit report

11. The auditor should not refer in his own report to any specialist opinion he has relied on because the auditor is solely responsible for his opinion and cannot share this responsibility.

12. The auditor may have to qualify his report when:

   a.   The matter is material.

b. There is no specialist evidence available and no satisfactory alternative evidence is available or when the auditor cannot rely on the specialist's evidence.

13. Qualification is only likely to be necessary:

   a. Where management are unable or unwilling to obtain necessary specialist evidence.

   b. Where the relevance or reliability of the specialist's evidence is uncertain.

   c. Where management refuses to accept or incorporate the evidence in the accounts.

   d. Where the management refuse to obtain a second opinion when the auditor deems it necessary.

Summary

14. a. In some cases, the opinion of a specialist would be essential evidence to an auditor.

   b. The specialist should have his terms of agreement drawn up after consultation with the auditor.

Points to note

15. a. An expert may be engaged by or employed by the entity or the auditor. When the expert is employed by the auditor then SAS 240 *Quality control for audit work* will apply to the work.

   b. Auditors should never uncritically accept the opinion of a specialist.

   c. Corroborative evidence should always be sought.

   d. In all cases, the auditor has to consider whether he has relevant and reliable audit evidence which is sufficient to enable him to draw reasonable conclusions.

Case study 1 for Chapter 27

The Lonzim Co. Ltd., has invested 30% of its funds in a tract of land in Mambabwe. The company have spent the money on the land, mineral licences, prospecting and sundry works preparatory to extraction of the mineral Hedonite from which the rare metal Millenium can be obtained. The viability of the scheme is totally dependent on the quantity of ore in the mine and the quantity of Millenium in the ore. The company have taken a gamble on the matter following the findings of Clem Entyne, an employee of long standing, who has measured the size of the lode to his satisfaction with 'on site' borings and has sent to London samples which have been analysed and show a high proportion of Millenium. The auditor of the company John Orr is planning the audit of the year ending 31st December 19-7 in August 19-7.

Discussion

   a. How, in detail, might Orr obtain sufficient evidence for the appropriateness of the going concern basis for the assets in Mambabwe?

   b. How might the actual value of the assets there be verified?

Case study 2 for Chapter 27

HERMIT GALLERIES PLC are international art dealers with a turnover of £30 million a year. They specialise in impressionist paintings and have a stock valued at £10 million. Recently it has been rumoured that some £4 million worth of their stock may be the work of a particularly brilliant forger.

Towards the end of the financial year the company have agreed with the auditor to commission a report on the authenticity of the stock from a well known academic expert.

Discussion

Draw up the terms of reference for the expert.

Draft a check list to examine the expert's report as audit evidence.

The actual expert's opinion was certainty on the authenticity of 1.1 million pounds worth, certainty on the forged nature of 1.6 million pounds worth and doubt about the remainder.

What should the auditor do?

Student self testing questions *Questions with answers apparent from the text*

1. a. Give examples of reliance by auditors on the evidence supplied by specialists. (4)
   b. In what conditions may such reliance be required? (5)
   c. What factors indicate the reliability of the specialist? (8)
   d. What terms should appear in the agreement? (9)
   e. How should the auditor evaluate the evidence? (10)
   f. What might appear in the auditor's report on these matters? (11,12)
   g. What should not appear in the report? (11)

Examination questions without answers

1. When verifying assets, the auditor will often have to rely on external confirmation of assets by third parties.

   Required:
   a. Indicate the major items which may need to be verified in this way. Who would be responsible for making the confirmation? (6 marks)
   b. What points should the auditor consider when seeking to rely on third party verification? (3 marks)
   c. What are the main items that should be included in the letter sent to a bank for audit purposes? (6 marks)
   (AAT J'87) (Total 15 marks)

2. Paragraph 4 of the Auditing Standard L101, *The Auditor's Operational Standard*, states that the auditor should obtain relevant and reliable audit evidence sufficient to enable him to draw reasonable conclusions therefrom.

   During the course of the audit, the auditor may need to consider audit evidence in the form of statistical data, reports, opinions, valuations or statements from specialists.

   Requirement
   a. List 5 examples of situations where an auditor may wish to rely upon the report of a specialist. (5 marks)
   b. Describe the principles that the auditor should follow when he wishes to place reliance on audit evidence provided by specialists. (11 marks)
   (ICAI 92) (Total 16 marks)

Review of financial statements

1. The final stage of an audit is the analytical review by a senior member of the audit team of the financial statements. The objectives of this review are:

   a. to provide audit evidence by determining if the financial statements provide information which is both internally consistent and consistent with other information in the possession of the auditor (knowledge of the environment, the enterprise and of his detailed audit tests).

   b. to determine if the financial statements have been prepared using acceptable accounting policies, comply with Accounting Standards and other requirements and that there is adequate disclosure of relevant matters.

2. To conclude this section there are chapters on the true and fair view and on representations by management.

28 The final review stage of the audit

Introduction

1. At the end of the detailed work of the audit, auditors make an *overall review* of the financial statements before preparing their report. The review should be sufficiently detailed to enable the auditors, in conjunction with the conclusions drawn from the other audit evidence obtained, to give them a reasonable basis for their opinion on the financial statements.

2. There is a short Statement of Auditing Standards SAS 470 *Overall Review of financial statements*

The stages of an audit

3. The auditor next gathers audit *evidence* about *individual* items and *groups* of items which together make up the accounts.

4. The auditor is then in a position of knowing that he has sufficient evidence to substantiate the details of the accounts. He then needs to determine if the *accounts as a whole* have certain qualities. The final review assists in this determination.

The qualities required of final accounts

5. The final review is designed to elucidate the following qualities which hopefully are possessed by the final accounts.

   a. That they use acceptable accounting policies, which have been consistently applied and are appropriate to the business. Note that an acceptable policy (eg reducing balance depreciation) may be inappropriate for some assets (eg leaseholds or quarries).

   b. The results of operations (profit and loss account), state of affairs (balance sheet) and all other information included in the financial statements are *compatible* with each other and with the auditor's knowledge of the enterprise.

c. There is adequate *disclosure* of all appropriate matters and the information contained in the financial statements is suitably *classified* and *presented* (for example, a loan to a subsidiary should not be described as cash at bank).

d. There is compliance with statutory requirements (for example, the Companies Act).

e. There is compliance with other relevant regulations (for example stock exchange regulations).

f. There is compliance with accounting standards.

Auditor qualities

6. The auditor who performs a review needs certain qualities. These are:

a. An ability to distinguish between non-material, *material* and *fundamental* items.

b. An ability to assess the information gathered in the audit, for *accuracy* and *completeness*.

c. Skill, imagination and judgement.

d. An ability to recognise apparent *inconsistencies* which might indicate areas where errors, omissions, frauds or irregularities have occurred which might not have been revealed by the routine auditing procedures.

e. An ability to assess whether or not an audit opinion is possible at all.

Procedures

7. The following set of procedures should be adopted for the final review:

a. Accounting policies

Consider if they:

i. are acceptable

ii. are acceptable to the particular circumstances

iii. are commonly adopted in the particular industry

iv. are consistently applied over the years

v. are consistently applied throughout the enterprise

vi. comply with all relevant accounting standards

vii. are adequately disclosed in accordance with SSAP 2.

b. The circumstances of the enterprise

i. Consider if the accounts are consistent with the auditor's knowledge of the underlying circumstances of the business and the information, explanations and conlcusions reached on the audit.

ii. Review the information in the accounts to determine if there are any abnormalities or inconsistencies. Background knowledge of the company is clearly essential for this.

c. Presentation and disclosure

i. Consider if any conclusion that a reader might draw from his reading of the accounts would be justified and is consistent with the circumstances of the enterprise.

    ii.   Consider if the substance of any transactions or activities is disclosed and not merely their form.

    iii. Consider if the presentation might have been unduly influenced by management's desire to present facts in a favourable light.

    iv. Consider if the review has indicated that there are new factors which might alter the policies used or the presentation of the accounts, and, special attention needs to be paid to going concern difficulties.

  d. Consider if the accounting policies chosen comply with *generally accepted accounting principles*. GAAPs should accord with the fundamental accounting concepts:

    – going concern (of especial importance in times of recession)

    – accruals

    – consistency

    – prudence

In addition accounts should accord with the *'substance over form'* convention which is receiving increased attention currently.

Example

8. A final review by the auditor of Elspeth Carpet Manufacturing Ltd., using checklists revealed:

  a. Stocks of raw wool had been valued at replacement price. This was not equal to net realisable value.

  b. Interest was shown in the profit and loss account as one sum notwithstanding that the company has both short and long term loans.

  c. Debtors included a loan to a director of £7,500.

  d. The relationship between disclosed wages costs and disclosed social security costs had changed from the previous year.

  e. Trade creditors had changed from 38 days last year to 23 days this year.

  f. No depreciation had been charged on the company's new warehouse.

  g. The gain on the sale of an unwanted piece of land had been credited to administrative costs.

I will leave to the reader to work out the implications of these.

Summary

9. The final stages of an audit include a review of the financial statements, carried out by a suitably experienced senior or partner. The matter is covered by SAS 470.

Points to note

10. The final review is particularly important as current auditing opinion is moving more towards a consideration of the view given to users by financial statements. Of course, the detail is still important but emphasis must be on the view given by the accounts which must be true in detail and fair in totality.

11. The final review may reveal:

  a. That all is well.

b. That further audit evidence may be required in some areas.

c. That amendment to the accounts may be desirable. The client should be requested to make any such amendment.

d. That a qualified audit report may be required.

12. An historical progression can be discerned in audit evidence gathering:

a. Vouching of all transactions.

b. Vouching of a sample of transactions – test checking.

c. Reliance on systems with compliance testing.

d. Analytical review techniques.

The emphasis in earlier times was on a. There is much more emphasis today on analytical review techniques. The final review stage of an audit is really a subset of the analytical review techniques spelt out in Chapter 16.

13. The Overall Review of Financial Statements is concerned with:

a. Accounting Policies.

b. The results etc. are compatible with each other and with the auditor's knowledge of the enterprise.

c. Disclosure.

d. Statutory and other regulations.

e. What type of opinion, if any, can be given.

Case study for Chapter 28

Angela is engaged on the 19-6 audit of Feloni Ltd who are printers and publishers of sheet music. She has noted the accounting policy disclosure statement which shows:

a. Stock is valued at the lower of cost and net realisable value. Cost includes production overheads based on a global labour hour rate based on output in 19-6. Unsold stocks of sheet music printed before 31.12.19-5 are written down to £1.

b. Advances to composers are written off as they are paid.

c. Plant is written off on the straight line basis over ten years.

d. The freehold property is amortised over 30 years.

She has also noted that:

a. The directors' report is optimistic about the current year and future year's success in selling old titles due to a revival of 70's music.

b. Stocks appear simply as stocks £120,000.

c. The company rents out a leasehold property it owns but has no use for. The notes to the accounts say Gross Rental Income £4,900.

d. No mention is made of the entry into liquidation on 13.3.-7 of a wholesale music warehouse who owed Feloni £142,000 on 13.3.-7 and £71,000 on 31.12.-6. Angela knows of the liquidation as her boss is the liquidator.

e. No mention is made of an action against a pop group for breach of copyright. The action was commenced on 31.3.-6 and already uncharged legal fees of about £10,000 have been incurred.

f. The list of directors shows 14 names and the remuneration breakdown only 13.

g. The directors report shows that Joe Gigli a director has 1,000 shares in the company. She happened to note that the dividend paid to him indicated a shareholding substantially greater than that.

Discussion

What should Angela do about these matters?

Student self testing questions *Questions with answers apparent from the text*

1. a. What qualities are required of final accounts? (5)
   b. What qualities are required of auditors? (6)
   c. List the procedures required. (7)
   d. What actions may be required as a result of a final review? (11)
   e. Distinguish analytical review from overall review of financial statements. (12)

Exercises

1. The Harbridge Group plc include in their annual report and accounts a statement of accounting policies. This statement includes the following:

   a. Government grants received in respect of capital expenditure on plant are being amortised to revenue over a period of five years.
   b. Stock has been valued at the lower of cost and net realisable value. Cost in the case of manufactured finished goods is standard total absorption cost.
   c. All plant and machinery is depreciated on a straight line basis over its estimated life which varies from seven to twelve years.
   d. Development expenditure on new products is included in stock in trade.
   e. Land and Buildings including the Investment properties in central London are depreciated on the straight line method over 50 years.
   f. Profits on sales to certain South American countries are taken to Profit and Loss Account on receipt of the relevant cash which may be before or after the despatch of the goods.

   Required:
   Discuss these policies from the point of view of the true and fair view.

2. In conducting her final analytical review of the Accounts of San Serif Ltd a printing company, Geraldine the auditor discovers:
   - All plant is written off over 5 years but much of the plant is much older and works very well.
   - The company print a line of analysis paper which is sold by mail order to the accounting profession. Stocks of this paper are valued at paper cost only.
   - There is a 10% general provision for doubtful debts. Actual bad debts are few.

   The Managing Director is asked about these items and points out:
   - these policies have been used for many years;
   - surely it is OK to understate profits;
   - we do not want to pay lots of corporation tax or dividends.

   Required:
   Discuss this matter from the point of view of the true and fair view. (Hint – you may find it useful to consider expectation).

Examination question (Answer begins on page 551)

1. You are the auditor of M Ltd, a company which manufactures three basic products, all of which are components for the electronics industry. The company sells to three major customers who account for 90% of the company's turnover, the remaining 10% of sales being to overseas customers. The company's year-end is 31 December and for stock valuation purposes all completed components in stock at that date are valued using their standard costs.

    (Note: There is no work in progress and no production takes place on the last day of the year.)

    The standard costs are revised quarterly and those set at 1 October are used for year-end stock valuation purposes. Details of stock for the year ended 31 December 1984 are as follows:

	Component			Total Value of Stock at 31 Dec 1984
	A	B	C	
Number in stock at 31 December 1984	25,200	8,150	17,700	
Standard cost at 1 October 1984	£0.73	£2.16	£1.85	
Value at 31 December 1984 (using 1 Oct standard costs)	£18,396	£17,604	£32,745	£68,745
Number of components sold in year	55,420	48,900	92,400	
Standard cost of components sold in year	£39,600	£100,245	£166,320	
Actual cost of components sold in year	£40,350	£140,345	£150,850	
Revised standards for the quarter commencing 1 Jan 85 are as follows	£0.74	£2.20	£1.55	

    Required:
    a. Explain under what conditions standard costs may be used for year-end stock valuation purposes. (2 marks)
    b. Using the figures given above carry out a review to determine the areas that do not appear to make sense and thus the areas on which the auditor would concentrate when substantiating the stock valued at £68,745 in the financial statement as at 31 December 1984. (12 marks)
    c. State the TWO critical matters to be considered when auditing the standard labour cost and describe TWO audit tests that you would perform in substantiating such cost. (6 marks)
    (ACCA) (20 marks)

Examination questions without answers

2. You have gathered sufficient audit evidence to allow your review of the final accounts for publication of Frog plc.
    What matters would you look for in the final accounts for publication? (15 marks)
    (LCC 89)

3. You are the senior in charge of the audit of Heath Products Limited for the year ended 30 September 1991. The company which is a wholesaler of plumbing products, operates

from rented accommodation: its fixed assets comprise motor vehicles, a micro-computer, fixtures, fittings and office equipment. The accounting records (consisting of a sales ledger, purchase ledger, nominal ledger and payroll) are kept on the microcomputer by the company book-keeper. A part time accountant prepares quarterly management accounts and the annual accounts.

The draft accounts for the year ended 30 September 1991 and the previous year's audited accounts are summarised below:

Profit and Loss Account

	1991	1990
	£	£
Sales	2,087,800	1,013,400
Cost of Sales	1,361,200	710,400
Gross Profit	726,600	303,000
Overheads	544,200	294,800
Profit Before Tax	182,400	8,200
Taxation	63,840	2,200
Retained Profit	118,560	6,000

Balance Sheet at 30 September

	1991	1990
	£	£
Fixed Assets	40,800	17,800
Current Assets:		
Stock	346,000	105,200
Trade Debts	478,400	191,000
Prepayments	11,000	3,000
	835,400	299,200
Current Liabilities:		
Trade Creditors	357,600	142,600
Accruals	75,600	42,400
Taxation	63,840	2,200
Bank Overdraft	172,200	41,400
	669,240	228,600
Net Current Assets	166,160	70,600
Net Assets	206,960	88,400
Directors' Loan Account	(30,800)	(30,800)
	176,160	57,600
Called up Share Capital	2,000	2,000
Profit and Loss Account	174,160	55,600
	176,160	57,600

The company sells substantial quantities of low value items to a large number of customers. Only 5% of the sales are for cash, the rest are on credit. The sales ledger has over 700 'live' accounts, of which 70% are new customers beginning in the past year. You have conducted compliance tests on the systems during your interim audit and have concluded that the systems are generally reliable. There is however, no formal system for recording the receipt of goods (apart from the supplier's delivery note). From this you conclude that there is a greater risk of purchase cut-off errors.

As part of your final audit planning process you have decided to conduct an analytical review.

Required

a. Calculate FIVE appropriate ratios for both years.   (5 marks)

b. Comment on the financial performance of Heath Products Limited for the year ended 30 September 1991, both in comparison with the previous year and in absolute terms.   (5 marks)

c. From you review of the financial statements and the other information given, detail the audit work you would carry out on the following:

    i.   Stock and the Gross Profit Margin;   (4 marks)

    ii. Trade Debtors;   (3 marks)

    iii. Trade Creditors.   (3 marks)

(AAT 91) (Total 20 marks)

29 The true and fair view

Introduction

1. The expression 'true and fair view' is central to auditing and yet it is an abstraction whose meaning is far from clear.

2. a. The Companies Act states that every company balance sheet and profit and loss account must give a true and fair view of the state of affairs and of the profit or loss respectively (CA 1985 S.226). This requirement overrides the requirement to use a format.

    b. The auditor must report to the members on whether the financial statements show a true and fair view (CA 1985 S.235).

    c. SAS 600 *Auditors' reports on financial statements* applies mainly to those financial statements intended to give a true and fair view.

    d. This chapter reviews the concept under a number of headings:

    historical, legal requirements, truth and fair view.

Accounting Standards

3. Schedule 4 requires that:

    a. Accounting policies shall be stated (original para 36 of 4th Schedule).

    b. 'It shall be stated whether the Accounts have been prepared in accordance with applicable accounting standards and particulars of any material departure from those standards and the reasons for it shall be given'.

In effect this gives statutory recognition to the idea that to give a true and fair view, Accounts must comply with accounting standards.

Legal requirements

4. The true and fair view is a Companies Act concept and is therefore a legal notion. However neither the Acts nor the courts have ever attempted to define it. The legal considerations have been discussed in a counsel's opinion published in Accountancy in November 1983.

5. The idea of 'true and fair view' is at a high level of *abstraction*. Similarly abstract words and phrases include 'reasonable care'. The idea must be applied to an infinite variety of different concrete facts. Clearly there will always be a *penumbral* area (neither completely in the sun nor completely in shadow) where opinions can differ as to whether a financial statement gives a true and fair view, or not, of a particular set of facts. For example valuing stock, sold after date at a profit, at cost gives a true and fair view, valuing damaged stock, which can only be sold at a loss, at cost would not give a true and fair view. But what precise value of net realisable value would give a true and fair view is subject to several opinions.

6. The *meaning* of true and fair view is constant in law and has not changed since 1947. However the *content* of the concept is subject to change and development. As a analogy consider the phrase 'poverty line'. The meaning of the word may be commonly understood in the same way but the content will be differently perceived in India and England, in 1884 and 1984 and between individuals at any one time or in any particular country.

7. The courts have rarely given a view in any particular set of circumstances as to the content of a true and fair view. However the law appears to require that Accounts follow the *correct principles of commercial accountancy*. What are correct principles of commercial accountancy can be established by determining what accountants actually do. The courts will consider the evidence of expert witnesses. Today what accountants actually do is to conform to the statements of Standard Accounting Practice and to this extent the requirements of the Accounting Standards and the true and fair view coincide.

8. The idea to grasp is that of *expectation*. Users (investors etc.) of financial statements expect that Accounts will conform to the Accounting Standards and to other generally accepted accounting principles. For example, a true and fair view will be given by a set of Accounts in which freehold properties are valued at cost because anyone familiar with accounting, would *not expect* valuation at market value.

9. The Companies Act now gives substantial detailed disclosure requirements but spells out also the principles underlying the preparation of Accounts (CA 1985 4th schedule).

Truth

10. Investigation and discovery of anything is assisted by breaking down or classifying the thing into parts. We therefore will breakdown true and fair view into parts, beginning with true.

11. In practice the work 'true' is difficult to pin down as it also incorporates a high level of abstraction. However in accounting terms we can consider synonyms like – in accordance with fact or reality; not false or erroneous; representing the thing as it is.

12. Numerous Accounts items can be seen in this light. For example 'Freehold Land ... at cost £2,000,000.'

It is either true or false that:

a. Freehold Land exists.

b. The Freehold Land is the property of the company who hold a good title.

c. The Freehold Land did cost the company £2,000,000.

d. All the Freehold Land belonging to the company is included.

On the other hand, the matter may not be as simple as it seems. For example:

i. good title may be a matter of opinion.

ii. Historical cost may be a matter of opinion – are legal costs included? Subsequent costs (drainage, fencing) may be considered capital or revenue.

13. A dictionary definition of true also includes 'in accordance with reason or correct principles or received standard' which brings us back to generally accepted accounting principles and the Accounting Standards.

Fair view

14. The word 'view' is important in that Accounts cannot give a view in an abstract way. The view given cannot be divorced from the perceptions of a reader/user of the Accounts.

15. The idea of fairness involves a number of thoughts including:

a. **Expectation**. Any user has certain expectations from a set of Accounts. He/she presumes that the Accounts will conform to generally accepted accounting principles and the Accounting Standards. This had already been discussed under the legal considerations above.

b. **Relevance**. The fair view from the point of view of a user must mean that the view given by the Accounts will be relevant to the informational *needs* of the user. This needs some qualifying. It is assumed that Accounts show:

   – the resources (assets) employed in the enterprise

   – the claims (capital and liabilities) against the resources

   – the changes in resources and claims over a period (profit and loss account, cash flow statement).

   That is: The Accounts *report* on historical events. They are not intended for decision making even though they may be used for this purpose.

c. **Objectivity** – consisting of externally verifiable facts, rather than subjectively considered opinions. In practice, as we have seen under 'truth', most accounting figures are subjective or contain a substantial subjective element. As SSAP 2 puts it '... many business transactions have financial effects spreading over a number of years. Decisions have to be made on the extent to which expenditure incurred in one year can reasonably be expected to produce benefits in the form of revenue in other years ...'

d. **Freedom from bias** – the producer of Accounts (directors, managers) should not allow personal preferences to enter into their Accounts preparation work. For example, a desire to show a favourable profit should not influence a manager's assessment of the expected life of fixed assets, or the saleability of stock. In practice, all human activities are influenced by personal experience and prejudice. The important thing is to be aware of this and for an auditor to be aware of the tendency to bias in all financial reporting.

e. **Beyond simple conformity** – users of Accounts expect Accounts to conform to generally accepted accounting principles and the Accounting Standards. However simple rigid conformity can lead to a misleading view. For examples inclusion of profits from overseas branches may mislead shareholders when those profits are not available to shareholders because of exchange control restrictions.

f. **Least as good** – at one time, the prudence convention was so highly esteemed, that shareholders and auditors' expectations went no further than making sure that the true position was at least as good as that shown by the balance sheet. This extremely cautious and conservative view would be of little comfort to an investor who sold his shares for £1 each when if all the facts had been known, the shares would have fetched £5 each. Despite modern insistence on fairness up *and* down, the least-as-good syndrome lurks in every accountant's subconscious.

g. **Accounting principles** – the accounting *principles* and *policies* used should be:
   - in conformity with Accounting Standards (mostly!)
   - generally accepted
   - widely recognised and supported
   - appropriate and applicable in the particular circumstances.

In most areas, more than one policy will satisfy these criteria. For example, there are several different acceptable methods for depreciation and therefore several different measures of profit, all of which may give a true and fair view.

h. **Disclosure** – accounting is an aggregating and summarising process. A million transactions in a year can be summarised in a relatively few lines in a set of Accounts. The overall results and final position can only be appreciated by aggregating transactions and balances into suitable classes or categories. For an investor, a list of 10,000 sales ledger balances has little informational value but debtors £3.6 million is useful as it can be compared with previous years, sales, other figures on the Accounts etc. Too much disaggregation causes confusion between the wood and the trees and a general indigestibility. On the other hand too much aggregation can hide individual figures or sub-classes that ought properly to be disclosed. As an example, in 19-4 The Lemon Drop Trading Co. Ltd. suffered a major bad debt of £300,000 and this was included in 'administrative expenses £720,000' in the profit and loss account. The net profit was £240,000 against £510,000 in 1983. Would not failure to disclose that administrative expenses included bad debts £300,000 (19-3 £6,500) mislead shareholders as to the *trend* of profits?

i. **Materiality** – the elusive accounting principle of materiality is intimately bound up with the true and fair view. An item is material if its disclosure or non disclosure would make any difference to the view received by the user of the Accounts. Fairness is therefore a function of materiality. For example, a clerk in a company embezzled £50,000 and this sum proved irrecoverable. The company did not wish to disclose this loss separately as it was not material as the profit was over £2 million. The auditor might argue that disclosure would change the view given by the Accounts as shareholders might then have doubts about the directors' ability to control the company's affairs and shareholders might also wish to know company policy on prosecuting offenders of this sort.

Summary

16. a. The expression 'true and fair view' is an *abstract* idea of immense importance and difficulty.

   b. The idea has a long history in company law but first came into its modern form in the Companies Act 1947.

   c. The *meaning* of the phrase in company law is fairly clear but its content is both unclear and capable of development.

   d. The meaning is closely bound up with the *expectations* of Accounts users. In particular they expect generally accepted accounting principles and policies and the Accounting Standards to be followed.

   e. The phrase can be broken down into parts viz *true* and *fair view*. True can mean in accordance with the facts.

   f. Fair view has many elements – accordance with expectations, relevance, informational needs, concordance with accounting purposes (reporting not decision making), objectivity, freedom from bias, disclosure and materiality.

   g. Least-as-good ideas have to be avoided.

Points to note

17. a. Most people expect Accounts today to be accurate and comprehensive and to give a reasonable man a right understanding of the underlying results and position of the enterprise. This sounds reasonable but a closer inspection will reveal that most of these words are abstractions which are very difficult to interpret into the precise words and figures of financial statements.

   b. Accounts are apparently very precise. The profit was £141.3 million for example. This is very misleading. Accounting is not deterministic but probabilistic. There are many estimates and guesses in Accounts (eg depreciation) and different policies (eg FIFO or weighted average cost for stock valuation) that it has been suggested that a statement that the profit was in the range of £50–£300 million might be more realistic.

   c. Note the precise requirements of the Companies Act on format, accounting principles and disclosure are submerged in an overriding requirement that Accounts give a true and fair view.

Case study for Chapter 29

Trumpton Foundries plc manufacturing cast iron plaques for all purposes. They have just published their accounts for the year ending 31.12.-6. Chigley, a shareholder, is thinking of selling his shares and is reading through the accounts to help him in his decision on selling or retaining his holding.

Some of the items in the accounts are:

	all in £'000	
	19-5	19-6
Turnover	2,369	2,576
Cost of sales	1,500	1,620
Net Profit	215	220
Fixed Assets	1,456	1,367
Stocks	245	289
Overdraft	167	260

Unrevealed by the accounts are the following items:

a. The company has substantial amounts of plant which have been fully depreciated.

b. In 19-6, the company accepted, at marginal cost + 10%, an order from America. The invoiced amount was £370,000. This was the company's first export order.

c. Cost of sales includes £213,000 being the cost of a research and development project carried on jointly with the local University. The project has led to significantly better and cheaper products.

d. In December 19-6 the company bought a very large consignment of fuel oil for £35,000 to take advantage of low prices.

Discussion

a. From the point of view of Chigley can these accounts be said to give a true and fair view?

b. Do the accounts conform to a legal view of truth and fairness?

c. Do accountants prepare accounts with a view of reporting wholly past activities to shareholders?

d. Consider the bank overdraft. To what extent can this be seen as being composed of matters which can be regarded as objectively 'true'? Are there also matters which are matters of opinion?

e. Should accounts offer 'point' figures of profits? Should they perhaps offer a range of profit figures or probabilistic estimates? Should a commentary be offered on matters with significance to understanding or the future of the enterprise? Where does this idea leave the auditor?

Student self testing questions *Questions with answers apparent from the text*

1. a. Relate true and fair to the Accounting Standards. (3)
   b. Summarise the legal view of true and fair. (4–8)
   c. What does true mean in the context of accounts? (10–13)
   d. What ideas are involved in the idea of fair? (14)
   e. Do accounts need to be relevant to the needs of users to show a true and fair view? (15)
   f. Can accounts be both objective and true? (15)
   g. Why should an auditor be aware of the problem of bias in accounts? (15)
   h. Contrast 'least as good' with 'true and fair'. (15)
   i. What qualities will accounting principles and policies used in accounts conform to? (15)
   j. Contrast disclosure with materiality. (15)

Examination question without answer

1. The standard unqualified audit report for a company requires the auditor to express an opinion as to whether the financial statements show a true and fair view.
   You are required to
   a. explain what you understand by the phrase 'a true and fair view';   (8 marks)

b. give three examples from each of:
   i. company accounting legislation, and
   ii. pronouncements from the Accounting Standards Committee or Accounting Standards Board, requirements contributing to the true and fair view of financial statements prepared in accordance with them. (12 marks)

(ICA 92) (Total 20 marks)

30 Representations by management

Introduction

1. It is now normal audit practice for the auditor to obtain a letter *from the management* addressed *to the auditor* confirming any representations given by the management to the auditor. This letter is known as the management letter or the letter of representation.

   Representations in this context can be defined as 'a statement made to convey an opinion.'

2. This chapter outlines the reasons why auditors obtain this letter, the procedures for so doing and finally the contents. We also consider audit action if management decline to sign such a lettter.

3. There is a Statement of Auditing Standards SAS 440 *Management representations*.

Reasons why the letter of representation is obtained

4. *The Companies Act 1985 Section 389A* entitles the auditor to require from the officers of the company such information and explanation as he thinks necessary for the performance of the duties of the auditors. Further Section 237 (3) gives a duty to the auditor to include in his report, any failure to obtain all the information and explanations which he deems necessary for the purposes of the audit.

5. *The Companies Act 1985 Section 389A (2)* strengthened CA85.S 389A (1) by making it a criminal offence, punishable by fine and/or imprisonment to make any statement (orally or in writing) which conveys, or purports to convey, any false or misleading information or explanation to the auditors.

6. Auditors are required to carry out procedures designed to obtain sufficient appropriate audit evidence to determine with reasonable confidence whether the financial statements are free of material misstatement. Representations from management are a source of evidence.

Management representations as audit evidence

7. In the course of an audit, numerous questions are asked of the client's management and staff. Replies are usually verbal. Most of the queries are:
   a. *Not material* to the financial statements. Examples are queries re missing documents or errors in bookkeeping, or

b. Capable of being *corroborated* by other evidence. For example, provisions in respect of litigation can be confirmed by the client's solicitors or the life of plant can be confirmed by examining technical literature.

8. However, in some cases:

a. Where knowledge of the facts is *confined to management*, for example, the management's intentions to close or keep open a material loss-making branch. This would have an affect on the value of the assets at the branch.

b. Where the matter is principally one of *judgement* and *opinion*, for example, the realisability of old stock. Then:

i. the auditor should ensure that there is no *conflicting* evidence;

ii. the auditor may be unable to obtain *corroborating* evidence;

iii. the auditor should obtain *written confirmation* of any representations made;

9. The auditor must decide for himself whether the total of other evidence and management's written representations are sufficient for him to form an unqualified opinion.

Procedures

10. The following procedures should be adopted:

a. The auditor should summarise in his *working papers* all matters that are material and also subject to uncorroborated oral representations by management.

b. In addition these matters should be *either*:

i. formally minuted as approved by the Board of Directors at a meeting ideally attended by the auditor;

ii. included in the signed letter of representation.

c. Standard letters should not be used as:

i. each audit is different;

ii. the letter is important and should receive very careful attention;

iii. the management should participate in its production. There should be much drafting, review and discussion.

d. The letter should be:

i. signed at a high level – eg chief executive, financial director. SAS 440 suggests the chairman and secretary;

ii. approved and minuted at a board meeting at which, ideally, the auditor would be present.

e. The preparation of the letter should begin at an early stage, eg at the beginning of the final audit in order to avoid the possibility of the auditor being faced with a refusal to sign by the management. If there is a refusal by management to cooperate then the auditor should:

i. do all he can to persuade management to cooperate;

ii. prepare a statement setting out his understanding of the principal representations made, with a request that management confirm it;

iii. if management disagree with this statement, discuss and negotiate until a correct understanding has been reached;

    iv. if management refuse altogether to cooperate, either on principle or because they are themselves uncertain about a particular matter, consider if he has obtained all the information and explanations he requires and consequently may need to qualify his report on grounds of limitation of scope.

   f. The representation letter or board resolution making representations should be approved as late as possible in the audit, after the analytical review, but, as it is audit evidence, before the audit report is prepared. If there is a long delay between the approval of the representation and the audit report, the auditor may need to do other audit work/or obtain a supplementary letter of representation. SAS 440 suggests dating the letter on the day the financial statements are approved.

Contents

11. The contents of the letter of representation should *not* include *routine* matters, for example, that all fixed assets exist and are the property of the company or that stock is valued at the lower of cost and net realisable value.

12. The letter should include *only* matters which:

   a. are material to the financial statements, and

   b. the auditors cannot obtain independent corroborative evidence.

13. SAS 410 *requires* that the auditors should obtain evidence that the directors acknowledge their collective responsibility for the presentation of the financial statements and have approved the financial statements. The place for this is the letter of representation. It also *requires* that auditors obtain written confirmation of representations from management on matters material to the financial statements when those representations are critical to obtaining sufficient appropriate audit evidence. This will include matters on which directors intentions are vital or where knowledge of the facts are confined to management. Examples might be intentions on capital investment so that deferred tax does not become payable or the continuation of a project which might have little value if abandoned.

14.   **Example of a letter of representation**

To Puce, Watermelon & Co.
Chartered Accountants.

Gentlemen,

We confirm that to the best of our knowledge and belief, and, having made appropriate enquiries of other directors and officials of the company, the following representations given to you in connection with your audit of the company's financial statements for the year ending 31st December 19-3:

1. We acknowledge as directors our responsibility for the financial statements, which you have prepared for the company. All the accounting records have been made available to you for the purpose of your audit and all the transactions undertaken by the company have been properly reflected and recorded in the accounting records. All other records and related information, including minutes of all management and shareholders' meetings, have been made available to you.

2. The provision for warranty claims has been estimated at 2% of annual turnover as in previous years. This amount is in accordance with our opinion of the probable extent of

warranty claims. We know of no events which would materially effect the amount of these claims.

3. As stated in Note 12 to the Accounts there exists a contingent liability in respect of the company's guarantee of the bank overdraft of NBG Ltd, an associated company now in receivership. In our opinion the assets of NBG Ltd will realise sufficient to satisfy the bank and no actual liability will arise.

4. It is the intention of the Board of Directors to continue production at our Trumpton plant for at least the next three years so that valuation of the assets and liabilities of that plant should appropriately be on the going concern basis.

Yours faithfully,

NJ Brown, Company Secretary

Signed on behalf of the Board of JBS Ltd.

14 April 19-4

Summary

15. a. A letter of representation is a letter from the management to the auditor confirming in writing opinions conveyed to the auditor orally.

   b. It is obtained on the occasion of each audit.

   c. The Companies Act 1985 Section 389A entitles the auditor to such information and explanation as he may require. In giving such information and explanation management should remember that the same section makes it a criminal offence to give false or misleading information to an auditor.

   d. SAS 440 governs this subject.

   e. The letter should contain only matters which are material and for which the auditor cannot obtain corroborating evidence.

   f. The principal items will be matters of which management alone have knowledge and matters of judgement and opinion.

   g. The letter should also contain the directors' acknowledgement for their responsibilities under CA 1985 for preparing financial statements which give a true and fair view and a statement that all accounting records have been made available to the auditor and that all the transactions undertaken by the company have been properly reflected and recorded in the accounting records. It should also say that all other records and related information including minutes of all management and shareholders' meetings have been made available to the auditors.

   h. Ideally the representation letter should be dated the same day as the directors formally approve the accounts.

Points to note

16. a. The letter of representation is a form of audit evidence but not of course the only form. Thus the auditor cannot rely on the letter of representation to save doing the audit.

b. The letter is used only on the restricted number of matters discussed in this chapter. This is a departure from previous practice when a wide range of routine matters were included.

c. The inclusion of only a limited range of matters tends to sharpen the focus on those matters included.

d. Special problems exist in this area for auditors of Groups.

e. It is advisable for the auditors to ascertain that the persons responsible for the letter should understand what it is that they are being asked to confirm!

Case study for Chapter 30

Bouncy, Gamine & Co are auditors of the Zombrit Group. The accounts for the year ending 31.12.-6 are being subjected to the final review. The following matters have been noted by Maureen, the manager in charge:

a. The company has engaged in a number of long term contracts in Africa. During the last few years a minority of these have sustained losses. Work in progress at 31.12.-6 includes a substantial amount of African contracts. Some are valued at cost and some include attributable profit in accordance with SSAP 9. One contract has been valued with a provision for ultimate loss.

b. The group has set up a subsidiary in Zombaland to manufacture motor parts for sale in Central Africa. The group have lent this subsidiary material amounts but so far production difficulties, political problems and difficulties in finding adequate markets have plagued the project. All assets acquired by the subsidiary have been valued at cost.

c. The group have a property in Milton Keynes which they used as the regional head-quarters. This office has been closed and the staff transferred, with considerable opposition, to London. The property has been let to another company on a two year lease and has been treated in the accounts as an investment property in accordance with SSAP 19.

d. The company have a project to manufacture and sell a range of televideo kits so that executives can see each other whilst talking on the telephone. Production should commence in 19-7. All expenditure so far has been deferred in accordance with SSAP 13.

Discussion

a. Identify the matters connected with these items which the auditor may include in a letter of representation.

b. Draft such a letter.

Student self testing questions *Questions with answers apparent from the text*

1. a. Why should a letter of representation be obtained? (4–6)
   b. What kind of matter should be included in a letter of representation? (8)
   c. What procedures should be used? (10)

Examination questions without answers

1. i. What are 'representations made by managements to the auditor'? (3 marks)
   ii. How far is the auditor justified in accepting management representations as audit evidence? (6 marks)
   ii. If the auditor is not satisfied with such representations, what action should be taken? (6 marks)

   (LCC 89) (Total 15 marks)

2. You are the audit senior in charge of the audit of Dorlcote Mill Limited for the year ended 31 July 1992. The Managing Director, Dr Turnbull, has given you a draft of the letter of representation he proposes to issue, and has asked for your comments. The text of the letter is as follows:

   'Dear Sirs,

   I confirm the following representations given to you to assist you in preparing your accounts and conducting your audit:

   a. You have been given all the information and explanations you need to form your opinions.
   b. You have been given access to all the books and records of the company.
   c. No material instances of fraud or irregularity have occurred.
   d. The stock has been valued at £50,000, by the Directors.
   e. The Freehold Premises are valued at £300,000, by the Directors.
   f. No material event has taken place since the Balance Sheet date of which you are unaware.

   Yours faithfully

   J. Turnbull'

   Required

   a. Comment on the content of the draft letter. (5 marks)
   b. Redraft the letter making appropriate assumptions where necessary. (10 marks)

   (AAT 92) (Total 15 marks)

The auditors' report

1. The auditors' report is the end product of the audit. It has been traditionally very short but has been expanded considerably in Statement of Auditing Standards 600 – Auditors' reports on financial statements, issued in May 1993.

2. Most auditors' reports are positive and end with a statement expressing the auditors' opinion that the financial statements show a true and fair view and comply with statutory requirements. Some, however, express this opinion with reservations or express a contrary opinion. These are *qualified* reports.

3. The chapters in this part of the manual are:

    31. On the clear or unqualified opinion
    32. On qualified opinions
    33. On events after the Balance Sheet date which may have a bearing on the opinion
    34. On the vital subject of going concern
    35. On the special problems of amounts derived from preceding financial statements
    36. On the impact on audit opinions of accounting standards.

4. The principal authority on auditors' reports is the Statement of Auditing Standards 600 – Auditors' reports on financial statements issued in May 1993. SAS 600 is expanded by Practice Note PN 8 *Reports by auditors under company legislation in the UK* and by PN 9 *Reports by auditors under company legislation in the Republic of Ireland.*

31 The auditors' reports

Introduction

1. The content of the auditor's report is governed by:

    a. statute – for companies this means the Companies Act 1985 (as amended by the Companies Act 1989) Sections 235–237.

    b. The Statement of Auditing Standards 600 – Auditors' reports on financial statements

The Companies Act 1985

2. The Companies Act 1985 Section 235 requires that the auditor's report shall state whether, in the auditor's opinion, the financial statements:

    a. have been properly prepared in accordance with the Act

    b. give a true and fair view

    The auditor *must* state these matters in his report.

    Section 235 also requires that the auditor's report shall state the names of the auditors and be signed by them.

3. In certain circumstances Sections 235 and 237 require the auditor to make further statements in the report. the circumstances are:

a. if, in the auditor's opinion, proper *accounting records* have not been kept

b. if, in the auditor's opinion, proper *returns* adequate for their audit have not been received from *branches* not visited by them

c. if, in the auditor's opinion, the company individual accounts are not in *agreement* with the accounting records and returns

d. if, in the auditor's opinion, they have failed to obtain all the *information and explanations* which to the best of their knowledge and belief, are necessary for the purpose of their audit

e. if, in the auditor's opinion, the information given in the *directors' report* is not consistent with the annual accounts.

These matters are expanded upon in the next chapter.

4. The Companies Act Section 237(4) gives the auditor a specific duty to include in his report certain information if that information is not given in the accounts. The information relates to Schedule 6 and concerns disclosure of information on emoluments and other benefits of directors and others.

Statement of Auditing Standards 600

5. We will begin by reproducing an unqualified auditors' report in full:

Auditors' report to the shareholders of ABC PLC

We have audited the financial statements on pages 34– 46 which have been prepared under the historical cost convention (as modified by the revaluation of certain fixed assets) and the accounting policies set out on page 38.

Respective responsibilities of directors and auditors

As described on page 33 the company's directors are responsible for the preparation of financial statements. It is our responsibility to form an independent opinion, based on our audit, on those statements and to report our opinion to you.

Basis of opinion

We conducted our audit in accordance with Auditing Standards issued by the Auditing Practices Board. An audit includes examination, on a test basis, of evidence relevant to the amounts and disclosures in the financial statements. It also includes an assessment of the significant estimates and judgments made by the directors in the preparation of the financial statements, and of whether the accounting policies are appropriate to the company's circumstances, consistently applied and adequately disclosed.

We planned and performed our audit so as to obtain all the information and explanations which we considered necessary in order to provide us with sufficient evidence to give reasonable assurance that the financial statements are free from material misstatement, whether caused by fraud or other irregularity or error. In forming our opinion we also evaluated the overall adequacy of the presentation of information in the financial statements.

Opinion

In our opinion the financial statements give a true and fair view of the state of the company's affairs as at 31 May 1996 and of its profit for the year then ended and have been properly prepared in accordance with the Companies Act 1985.

Laurel and Hardy   22 High Street
Certified Accountants and Registered Auditors   Boghampton
22 September 1996

---

6. To comment on this report:

   a. The title must clearly distinguish the report from other documents in the annual report and accounts

   b. The addressees must be clearly identified. For companies the report is addressed to the shareholders but other types of entity may have other addressees.

   c. The financial statements concerned must be clearly identified. The auditor is not expressing an opinion on the photograph of the Chairman on page 18!

   d. There may be a reference to the accounting convention (eg cost) and accounting policies but this is not a requirement. Many auditors omit it.

   e. Note the sub-headings (Respective responsibilities, Basis of opinion etc). Sub-headings are a new idea in the Standard.

   f. It is important to distinguish the responsibilities of the directors from those of the auditor. The Standard requires a statement that the financial statements are the responsibility of the reporting entity's directors and this can be done as in our example (on page...) or could be in the auditor's report. The matters to be included are detailed later in this chapter. The Standard requires a statement that the auditor's responsibility is to express an opinion on the financial statements.

   g. The Standard requires that the auditors explain the basis of their opinion by including:

   – a statement as to their compliance or otherwise with Auditing Standards and any reasons for departures therefrom

   – a statement that the audit process includes: examining, on test basis, evidence: assessment of the significant estimates and judgments made by the directors: a consideration of the accounting policies, and their consistency and their disclosure.

   – a statement that they planned and performed the audit so as to obtain reasonable assurance that the financial statements are free from material misstatement, whether caused by fraud or other irregularity or error, and that they have evaluated the overall presentation of the financial statements.

   h. an auditor's report should contain a clear expression of opinion on the financial statements and on any further matters required by statute or other requirements applicable to the particular engagement

   i. the report should contain the manuscript or printed signature of the auditors

   j. the report should be dated. See separate paragraph below.

Dating the report

7. The Standard states that auditors should not express an opinion on financial statements until those statements and all other financial information contained in a a report of which the audited financial statements form a part (eg the Annual Report and Accounts) have been approved by the directors, and the auditors have considered all necessary available evidence.

8. Thus the auditors will sign only after:

   a. Receipt of the financial statements and accompanying documents in the form approved by the directors for release

   b. Review of all documents which they should consider in addition to the financial statements (eg the directors' report, the Chairman's statement etc)

c. completion of all procedures necessary to form an opinion including a review of post Balance Sheet events.

Summary financial statements

9. The Companies Act 1985 S 251 allows listed companies to send shareholders a *summary financial statement* instead of the full annual report. This is governed by the Companies (Summary Financial Statement) Regulations 1992 and the auditors response is covered by an *auditing guideline* – the *Auditor's Statement on the Summary Financial Statement* and by PN8.

10. The summary financial statement must be derived from the annual financial statements and directors' report and must explicitly follow the detailed requirements concerning the form and content, set out in the 1992 regulations. It is required to contain a statement by the company's auditors expressing their opinion as to whether these requirements have been met.

    The summary statement must also state whether the auditors' report on the full financial statements included a qualified opinion and if so must give the auditors' report in full.

11. A suitable report would be:

Auditors' statement to the shareholders of ABC PLC

We have examined the summary financial statement set out on page...

Respective responsibilities of directors and auditors

The summary financial statement is the responsibility of the directors. Our responsibility is to report to you our opinion on its preparation and consistency with the full financial statements and directors' report.

Basis of opinion

We conducted our work in accordance with the Auditing Guideline 'The auditor's statement on the summary financial statement' adopted by the Auditing Practices Board.

Opinion

In our opinion the summary financial statement is consistent with the full financial statements and directors' report of ABC PLC for the year ended.... and complies with the requirements of the Companies Act 1985, and regulations made thereunder, applicable to summary financial statements.

Laurel and Hardy	1 High Street
Registered auditors	Sheinton
23 March 19....	

The auditors' duties in respect of the summary financial statements may include:

a. Refer to the Statement in the Engagement Letter

b. Include the matter in the Audit Plan – it is desirable that work on the summary should be done at the same as the main audit.

c. Verify that the summary Financial Statement is consistent with the annual accounts and the directors' report. Inconsistencies may include:

   – simple mistakes

- matters of opinion. An example of this may be in the summary of the directors report where the summary may include all the optimistic matters and exclude all the more gloomy prognostications for the future.

- exclusion of matters which although not required by the Regulations may be required (in the auditor's opinion) for a proper understanding of the accounts. An example may be the exclusion of a very large exceptional item or a non-adjusting post balance sheet event.

d. Verify that the statement complies with the requirements of S. 251 and the Regulations.

e. While the auditors do not have to say that the summary statement gives a true and fair view (it cannot!) they should ensure that a statement is included in a prominent position like:

'This summary financial statement is only a summary of information in the group's financial statements and the directors' report. It does not contain sufficient information to allow for a full understanding of the results of the group or the state of affairs of the company or the group. For further information the full annual financial statements should be consulted. These can be obtained from the company's secretary.'

f. As the summary statement may be sent out as part of a newsletter or some other form of communication, the auditor should examine the whole communication and ensure that the summary financial statement forms an identifiable section and that the whole communication does not mislead.

g. If the auditor cannot give an unqualified report she should request the directors to make changes and if they do not she should issue a qualified report.

Statement of directors' responsibilities

12. Matters to be included in a description of the directors' responsibilities for the financial statements are:

a. Company law requires the directors to prepare financial statements for each year which give a true and fair view

b. The directors are required to:

- select suitable *accounting policies* and apply them *consistently*

- make *judgments* and *estimates* that are reasonable and prudent

- state whether applicable *accounting standards* have been followed (large companies only)

- prepare the financial statements on a *going concern* basis unless it is inappropriate to presume that the company will continue in business

c. The directors are responsible for keeping proper *accounting records*, for saf*eguarding the assets* and for taking reasonable steps for the prevention and detection of *fraud* and other irregularities.

Financial statements

13. The Standard takes the view that the auditors' report does not need to specify the individual *financial statements* subject to their opinion. FRS 3 specifies several *primary* statements in addition to the Balance Sheet and Profit and Loss Account.

Summary

14. a. The Companies Act 1985 requires inclusion in the auditors' report of an opinion on:
    - true and fair view
    - proper preparation in accordance with the Act

   b. The Statement of Auditing Standards 600 – Auditors' reports on financial statements – has many requirements and suggestions including:
    - basic elements (title, addressees, financial statements identification, responsibilities of directors and auditors, basis of opinion, the opinion, signature of auditor, date)
    - a sample unqualified report

   c. Summary financial statements can be sent by listed companies and there are requirements for content , audit and auditor's report. Note that there are rules as to when a summary financial statement can be sent to a shareholder instead of a the full report and accounts.

   d. The Companies Act 1985 requires in certain circumstances that the auditor report:
    - on proper accounting records not being kept
    - on proper returns from branches not visited by the auditor not being received
    - on the accounts not being in agreement with the accounting records
    - not receiving all the information and explanations he requires
    - certain items connected with directors if they are not included in the accounts as required by the Act
    - information in the directors' report is not consistent with that in the financial statements.

   e. The date of the auditor's report is important

   f. The Standard requires a statement of directors' responsibilities in the accounts or in the auditors' report.

Points to note

15. a. The standard unqualified report should be learned by heart.

   b. The purpose of the new requirements of Statement of Auditing Standards 600 is to aid communication between the auditors and the readers of the financial statements by tackling the *expectation gap*. The expectation gap exists because the public, including the investment community, generally are unclear about the role of the auditor. Many people think the auditor prepares the accounts and /or deals with tax and /or keeps the books but few realise precisely the restricted role the auditor actually plays. Essentially people expect more from an auditor than his actual role can supply, hence the expectation gap. The new and expanded report may help people to have a clearer view of what the auditor does and is responsible for.

c. In Statement of Auditing Standards 600, material is defined so that a matter is *material* if its omission or mis-statement would reasonably influence the decisions of a user of the financial statements. Materiality may be considered in the context of the financial statements as a whole, any individual primary statement within the financial statements or individual items included in them.

d. The material in this chapter relates to companies but may be adapted to other kinds of entity. For examples a Committee of Management may be the responsible body instead of directors, The Code of Audit Practice for Local Authorities and the NHS in England and Wales may be the appropriate standards instead of the Auditing Standards, the Building Societies Act instead of the Companies Act etc.

e. The auditor must not sign the report until the Board have approved the accounts, the auditor has reviewed all documents that he/she is required to consider in addition to the financial statements, and, he/she has completed all procedures necessary to form an opinion including a review of post Balance Sheet events.

The dating of the auditor's report indicates that the auditor has completed these things. If the date is later than the directors' formal approval then the auditor must:

– obtain assurance that the directors still approve the accounts

– review subsequent events up to the date of signing the auditor's report.

Case study 1 for Chapter 31

Hall, Purpose and Co. Chartered Accountants are the auditors of General Trading PLC a company whose accounts are wholly based on the cost convention. The letter of engagement requires that the accounts and directors reports are in fact prepared as well as audited by Hall, Purpose. In the year ended 31 March 19-5, the company made a small loss and the Board approved the accounts on 28 July 19-5. Due to holidays, the partner in charge at Hall, Purpose did not sign the accounts until August 29.

Discussion

a. Draft a full auditor's report assuming that there is no need for a qualified report.

b. What must Hall, Purpose do before signing their report on August 29?

c. The audit senior discovered that on August 19 the company announced that a contract it fully expected to get had in fact gone to another company and as a consequence the company would need to close its factory in Hartlepool which formed 10% of its fixed assets. What effect would this have on the auditor's report?

Case study 2 for Chapter 31

Stubby Lane Hockey and Social Club is an unincorporated club with a set of rules and a committee of management. They have 400 members and own their own ground and clubhouse. The freehold is registered in the names of trustees who are also members of the committee.

Discussion

Draft an unqualified auditor's report by the auditors (who are paid) Bully & Co.

Student self testing questions *Questions with answers apparent from the text*

1. a. State the principal authorities for a company auditor's report. (1)
    b. List the items the Companies Act requires in an auditor's report. (2 and 3)
    c. What does CA 1985 S 237(4) say? (4)
    d. Write out a full unqualified auditors' report. (5)
    e. When can an auditors' report be dated? (7)
    f. Write out a full auditors' report on a summary financial statement. (11)
    g. List the auditors' duties in respect of a summary financial statement. (11)
    h. List the matters to be included in the description of directors' responsibilities. (12)
    i. What is the expectation gap? (15)
    j. Define material. (15)

Examination questions without answers

1. You are the senior in charge of the audit of Denham Limited. On referencing the file, an audit junior realised that the audit report for the company had not been drafted and in the absence of any reference books he drafted an audit report which reads as follows:

    REPORT OF THE AUDITORS TO THE DIRECTORS

    The attached accounts have been audited by us.

    We certify that the accounts give a fair and reasonable view of the Directors' Report, Profit and Loss Account and Balance Sheet for the year ended 31 March 1990.

    In our opinion, the Company has maintained proper books during the year and we believe that all the relevant sections of the Companies Act have been complied with.

    ABC & ASSOCIATES

    Accountants

    Required

    Draft a memorandum to the audit junior pointing out the errors that have been made in drafting the report. Explain why the errors are significant and how they should be corrected. (15 marks)

    Note: You are not required to redraft the audit report.

    (AAT 90)

32 Qualified audit reports

Introduction

1. When auditors give a report like those in Chapter 31 they are said to give a clean, clear or unqualified opinion. In some cases, the auditor is unable to give such an opinion for one or more of a large variety of reasons. In these cases an auditor is said to give a *qualified opinion*.

    The Companies Act 1995 Section 262 describes a qualified auditors' report as one where the auditor does not state the auditors' unqualified opinion that the accounts have been properly prepared in accordance with the Act.

A qualified auditors' report is a disadvantage to a company for several reasons:

   a. it has legal consequences, notably in possibly restricting dividend payments – S.271.

   b. it may lead to the Accounts being seen as less reliable by contact groups such as banks and other lenders and potential buyers of the business.

   c. it reflects badly on the directors.

2. The principal source materials on qualified auditors' reports are:

   a. The Companies Act 1985

   b. The Statement of Auditing Standards 600 – Auditors' reports on financial statements.

3. This chapter deals with the subject as:

   a. Qualifications in practice

   b. Companies Act requirements

   c. Types of qualification

   d. Inherent uncertainty

   e. Accounting Standards

   f. Examples of qualified reports

   g. Example of an unqualified report with inherent uncertainty

   h. Materiality

Qualifications in practice

4. For many years, qualified reports were very rare. With the introduction of SSAPs, many of which were controversial, in the 1970s and 1980s qualified reports became commoner. However only a minority of reports were or are now qualified.

5. Private companies usually lack internal controls and many have cash dealings. for this reason it is very difficult for auditors to have adequate evidence of completeness of recording of transactions. As a result many auditors used what was called the type 6 qualified reports and a great number of auditors' reports were qualified in this very general way. SAS 600 requires that any qualification must be specific.

Companies Act requirements

6. The Companies Act 1985 Sections 235 and 237 requires a qualified report:

   a. if the financial statements have not been properly prepared in accordance with the Act

   b. if the financial statements do not give a true and fair view

   c. if proper accounting records have not been kept

   d. if proper returns adequate for their audit have not been received from branches not visited by the auditors

   e. if the company individual accounts are not in agreement with the accounting records and returns

   f. if the auditors have failed to obtain all the information and explanations which to the best of their knowledge and belief, are necessary for the purpose of their audit

g. if the information given in the directors' report is not consistent with the annual accounts.

The Act does not state that non-compliance with an accounting standard is grounds for a qualified report but this may be so. We will discuss this later in the chapter.

These things may be matters of fact but may also be matters of opinion. Examples of matters that may lead to qualification under the above heads are:

a. Detailed disclosure as required by the Act is omitted in some area eg fixed assets.

b. True and Fair view is a difficult subject and is discussed in another chapter. However adoption of an inappropriate accounting policy, perhaps on depreciation, may be an example.

c. See Chapter 4 on what is required by the Act. Any shortfall may lead to a qualification

d. See Chapter 4 again.

e. This seems unlikely but directors may deliberately produce financial statements which are not in agreement with the books

f. Insufficient audit evidence is a common form of qualification.

g. The Directors report may say that the prospects for the company are poor and that steps will be taken to improve things by closing the company's factory in Tipton. However the Balance Sheet included the factory and its associated assets on a going concern basis.

Types of qualification

7. There are several types of qualification. These can be summarised as:

Nature of Circumstances	Very material and Pervasive	Less Material
Limitation of scope	Disclaimer	Possible adjustments
Disagreement	Adverse	Except for

To explain these terms:

Limitation of scope means a limitation of scope of the auditors' work that prevents them from obtaining sufficient evidence to express an unqualified opinion. Examples might be

a. a limitation imposed on the auditor as, for example, if he were not permitted to carry out an audit procedure considered necessary. Perhaps the directors may not permit a debtors' circularisation or may not allow the auditor to attend a stocktake.

b. a limitation outside the control of both auditors and directors. Perhaps necessary records existed but have been destroyed by fire or the auditor was prevented from attending a stocktake by a car breakdown.

Disagreement means that the auditors do not agree with the accounting treatment or disclosure of some item in the accounts. The financial statements may have an accounting policy (eg inclusion of overheads in finished goods stock on a global percentage of overheads to prime cost) when the auditor considers that a more complex apportionment is essential to the true and fair view.

Very material and pervasive. This term applies when the possible effect of the limitation of scope is so material or pervasive that the auditors are unable to express an opinion on the financial statements. Similarly when the matter giving rise to the disagreement is so material and pervasive that the financial statements are seriously misleading.

Less material means when the effect of the limitation is not so material or pervasive as to require a disclaimer. Similarly when the disagreement is not so material or pervasive as to require an adverse opinion.

Adverse opinion. An adverse opinion is one where the auditors state that the financial statements do not give a true and fair view.

A *disclaimer of opinion* occurs when the auditors conclude that they have not been able to obtain sufficient evidence to support, and accordingly are unable to express, an opinion on the financial statements.

Possible adjustments. The wording of the opinion should indicate that it is qualified as to the possible adjustments to the financial statements that might have been determined to be necessary had the limitation not existed.

Except for. The opinion is qualified by stating that the financial statements give a true and fair view except for the effects of any adjustments that might have been found necessary had the limitation not affected the evidence available to the auditors.

Inherent uncertainty

8. Inherent uncertainties are inevitable in accounting. Suppose that the company is engaged in litigation and the case will not be heard for many months and the verdict cannot be predicted. The only way to determine the uncertainty is to wait on the outcome of the trial but the financial statements must be produced to accord with Companies Act time limits and because shareholders need the accounts.

The directors should analyse the situation, obtain advice, make estimates, include them in the financial statements and disclose the situation in the notes to the financial statements in as clear a manner as possible.

The auditor should then form an opinion on the adequacy of the accounting treatment of this inherent uncertainty. This will involve consideration of:

– the appropriateness of any *accounting policies* dealing with the matter
– the *reasonableness* of the estimates included in the financial statements
– the adequacy of *disclosure*.

Some inherent uncertainties are *fundamental*. These are uncertainties where the degree of uncertainty and its potential impact on the view given by the financial statements may be very great. In determining whether an inherent uncertainty is fundamental, the auditors consider:

– the risk that the estimate included in the financial statements may be subject to change
– the range of possible outcomes
– the consequences of those outcomes on the view given by the financial statements

Inherent uncertainties are regarded as fundamental when they involve a significant level of concern about the validity of the *going concern* basis or other matters whose potential effect on the financial statements is *unusually great*.

9. What to do about the auditors' report:

	Not Fundamental	Fundamental
Uncertainty is adequately accounted for and disclosed	Do nothing	Explanatory Paragraph
Uncertainty is misstated or inadequately disclosed	'Except for' qualified opinion	Adverse qualified opinion

An *explanatory paragraph* is one which is included in the section of the auditors' report which sets out the basis of the opinion. It is not a qualification.

10. Students should appreciate that an inherent uncertainty is different from a limitation of scope. In this respect SAS 600 is different from the previous standard. An inherent uncertainty should be resolved by the passage of time when, say, the verdict of the court is given or when a vital loan is given (which was in doubt) or a business is sold at a satisfactory price (which was also in doubt). A limitation of scope occurs when evidence does or did exist (or reasonably could be expected to exist) but that evidence is not available to the auditors. In such cases a qualification or disclaimer of opinion is appropriate.

Accounting standards

11. The Companies Act 1985 requires financial statements to give a true and fair view. Financial statements that do not accord with applicable accounting standards will not in general give a true and fair view. Thus company financial statements should comply with applicable accounting standards. Further, large companies are required to state in their financial statements whether the financial statements have been prepared in accordance with accounting standards and to give particulars of any material departures from them and the reasons for the departures.

12. When an auditor concludes that there has been a departure that auditor should:

– assess whether there are sound reasons for the departure

– assess whether adequate disclosure has been made re the departure

– assess whether the departure is such that the financial statements do not give a true and fair view of the state of affairs or profit or loss.

Normally a departure from an accounting standard will result in the issue of a qualified or adverse opinion.

Examples of qualified reports

13. Here is an example of an *'except for'* opinion caused by *disagreement*:

Qualified opinion arising from disagreement about accounting treatment

Included in the stock shown on the Balance Sheet is an amount of £x valued at cost price. In our opinion as this stock is unsafe for consumption it is unlikely to be sold in the normal course of trade and it should be valued at scrap value of £y. This would reduce the profit after tax and net assets by £z.

Except for the incorrect valuation of stock, in our opinion the financial statements give a true and fair view of the state of the company's affairs as at 31 May 1996 and of its profit for the year then ended and have been properly prepared in accordance with the Companies Act 1985.

I have omitted the addressee etc, the names of the auditor and the standard parts.

You will note that most of this report is as usual apart from the *explanation* and the *qualified opinion*. It is important that the report contains a description of the *reasons* for the qualification and *quantified* effects on the financial statements. It is not sufficient to refer to notes attached to and forming part of the financial statements. The report itself must make the matter clear.

14. Here is an example of qualified opinion – *limitation on the work of an auditor*:

Basis of opinion

We conducted our audit in accordance with Auditing Standards issued by the Auditing Practices Board, except that the scope of our work was limited as explained below.

An audit includes examination, on a test basis, of evidence relevant to the amounts and disclosures in the financial statements. It also includes an assessment of the significant estimates and judgments made by the directors in the preparation of the financial statements, and of whether the accounting policies are appropriate to the company's circumstances, consistently applied and adequately disclosed.

We planned and performed our audit so as to obtain all the information and explanations which we considered necessary in order to provide us with sufficient evidence to give reasonable assurance that the financial statements are free from material misstatement, whether caused by fraud or other irregularity or error. However the evidence available to us was limited because £x of the company's purchases of metal scrap residues were paid for in cash from itinerant dealers. There was no system of control over these payments on which we could rely for the purpose of our audit. There were no other satisfactory audit procedures that we could adopt to confirm that these cash purchases were properly recorded.

In forming our opinion we also evaluated the overall adequacy of the presentation of information in the financial statements.

Qualified opinion arising from limitation of audit scope.

Except for any adjustments that might have been found to be necessary had we been able to obtain sufficient evidence concerning cash purchases, in our opinion the financial statements give a true and fair view of the state of the company's affairs as at 31 May 1996 and of its profit for the year then ended and have been properly prepared in accordance with the Companies Act 1985.

In respect alone of the limitation on our work relating to cash purchases:

– we have not obtained all the information and explanations that we considered necessary for the purpose of our audit; and

– we were unable to determine whether proper accounting records had been maintained.

I have omitted the standard parts of the report. Note the reference at the end to *Companies Act requirements*.

15. Here is an example of a *disclaimer*:

> We planned and performed our audit so as to obtain all the information and explanations which we considered necessary in order to provide us with sufficient evidence to give reasonable assurance that the financial statements are free from material misstatement, whether caused by fraud or other irregularity or error. However, the evidence available to us was limited because we were prevented from travelling to Gomboland because of the state of war between that country and Ruritania. We were thus unable to obtain adequate evidence for the existence, ownership and value of the company's assets situated in Gomboland appearing in the Balance Sheet at £x.. Any adjustment to this figure would have a consequential significant effect on the profit for the year.
>
> In forming our opinion we also evaluated the overall adequacy of the presentation of information in the financial statements.
>
> **Opinion: disclaimer on view given by the financial statements**
>
> Because of the possible effect of the limitation of evidence available to us, we were unable to form an opinion as to whether the financial statements give a true and fair view of the state of the company's affairs as at 31 March 19-9 or of its profit for the year then ended. In all other respects, in our opinion the financial statements have been properly prepared in accordance with the Companies Act 1985.
>
> In respect alone of the limitation on our work relating to the assets in Gomboland:
>
> – we have not obtained all the information and explanations that we considered necessary for the purpose of our audit; and
>
> – we were unable to determine whether proper accounting records had been maintained.

I have omitted the standard parts of the report. Note again the reference at the end to Companies Act requirements.

16. Here is an example of an *adverse* opinion:

> **Adverse opinion**
>
> As more fully explained in the note... development expenditure on the Mark iv widget in the sum of £y has been deferred to future periods on the grounds that the Mark iv widget is technically feasible and is ultimately commercially viable. In our opinion the case for technical feasibility and commercial viability had not been made out at the date of our report and we consider that the expenditure should be written off in the current year.
>
> In view of the effect of the treatment of the development expenditure , in our opinion the financial statements do not give a true and fair view of the state of the company's affairs as at 31 May 19-8 and of its profit then ended. In all other respects, in our opinion the financial statements have been properly prepared in accordance with the Companies Act 1985.

Once again I have omitted the standard parts of the report.

Example of an unqualified opinion with an explanation of a fundamental uncertainty

17. Here is an example. Note that is unqualified!

> ... we also evaluated the overall adequacy of the presentation of information in the financial statements.
>
> **Fundamental uncertainty**
>
> In forming our opinion, we have considered the adequacy of the disclosures made in the financial statements concerning the possible outcomes of the litigation against the company in respect of alleged breach of a patent. The future settlement of this litigation could result in additional liabilities of unknown amount. Details of the circumstances relating to this fundamental uncertainty are described in note... Our opinion is not qualified in this respect.
>
> **Opinion**
>
> In our opinion the financial statements give a true and fair view of the state of the company's affairs as at 31 May 1996 and of its profit for the year then ended and have been properly prepared in accordance with the Companies Act 1985.

Materiality

18. Auditors are reluctant to qualify their reports and usually will not do so on trivial matters. It is important therefore to consider in all cases when a qualification is contemplated whether or not the matter is *material*.

Materiality is a particularly difficult matter in practice but, is of great importance . It is always tempting to avoid the need to qualify a report by convincing oneself that the matter is not material. Great care should be taken before coming to a conclusion on matters of materiality.

The following considerations may be helpful in deciding matters of materiality:

a. **The Companies Acts** are full of of references to materiality. For example, there must be shown separately in the profit and loss account the amount, if material, charged to revenue in respect of sums payable for the hire of plant and machinery.

b. **Materiality is fundamental to accounting** which consists of aggregating, classifying, and presenting financial information. It is an area of professional judgement. It has been said that a good accountant is one who can competently judge matters of materiality.

c. **When materiality arises**. Suppose a company incurs a large bad debt. The question will rise as to whether the debt is material (= large) enough to require disclosure. If it is, should it be presented:

   i. as part of an omnibus figure (administrative expenses)

   ii. as a separate item (eg the note to the accounts might show a bad debt of £x caused by the collapse of Gone Broke Ltd.)

   iii. as a matter of special emphasis (eg show the profit before and after the bad debt)?

d. Supposing the bad debt was discovered after the accounts have gone to the printers, should the accounts be altered?

e. A further instance of materiality is whether a formula or accounting basis properly allows for special factors. For example, a company servicing cold stores may have a formula for evaluating future liabilities in respect of service contracts signed. Consistency requires that the accounts are always prepared on the same basis. However a special factor (eg inflation) may require a change of formula.

f. **How to assess an item's materiality**.

    i. Compare the magnitude of the item with the overall view presented by the accounts.

    ii. Compare the magnitude of the item with the magnitude of the same item in previous years.

    iii. Compare the magnitude of the item with the total of which it forms a part. (Eg 'debtors' may include employee loans but if employee loans become large ie material, then ,the description 'debtors' may be inadequate).

    iv. Consider the presentation and context of the item. Does it effect the true and fair view?

    v. Are there any statutory considerations?

    vi. Some items are *always* material eg Directors' Remuneration.

g. **Some overall considerations**.

    i. Whether or not an item is material may depend on the degree of approximation of the item of which it is a part. Depreciation errors are often not material because depreciation is itself subject to a great deal of approximation.

    ii. Small errors may seem large in years when profits are very small.In such cases materiality should be judged in the light of the normal dimensions of the business.

    iii. There can be critical points when materiality can be important, for example in turning a small profit into a small loss, or just making a company's assets exceed its liabilities, or in reversing a trend.

    iv. Some items have a significance disproportionate to their size, eg income from investments.

19. There is a Statement of Auditing Standards SAS 220 *Materiality and the auditor.* The SAS requires that auditors consider materiality and its relationship with *audit risk*. It points out a number of issues:

    i. Materiality is a matter of professional judgement and it has both quantity (amount) and quality (nature) dimensions. Auditors should take it into account when considering the nature, timing and extent of audit procedures.

    ii. Materiality should be taken into account at the planning stage and re-considered if the outcome of tests, enquiries or examinations differs from expectation.

    iii. In evaluating whether the financial statements give a true and fair view, auditors should assess the materiality of the *aggregate of uncorrected statements*. These may be those identified during the audit and their best estimate of others which they have not quantified specifically. Examples might be numerous small errors in the sales ledger or in coding expense invoices. If the directors adjust the financial statements for these, all may be well but if not the *aggregate* misstatement may be material when each individual misstatement is not.

Summary

20. a. Some auditors' reports are qualified for one or more of several reasons.

   b. The principal sources of material on qualified reports are the Companies Act 1985 and SAS 600 *Auditors' report on financial statements*.

   c. Qualified reports are relatively rare. Small companies with little control especially over cash transactions will often have qualified reports.

   d. The Companies Act 1985 ss 235 and 237 specify several reasons for qualifications.

   e. The main reasons given for qualified reports in SAS 600 are limitation in the scope of the work of the auditor and disagreement.

   f. The effects of some limitations of scope are so material and pervasive that a disclaimer of opinion is required.

   g. The effects of some disagreements can be so material and pervasive that the financial statements are seriously misleading. An adverse opinion is then required.

   h. With other less material limitations of scope a qualified opinion should be given with the wording that the opinion is qualified as to the possible adjustments that might have been determined if the limitation had not existed.

   i. With less material and pervasive disagreements an except for qualification is required.

   j. Inherent uncertainty is endemic in accounting and inherent uncertainties do not lead to qualifications unless the matters are inadequately dealt with or disclosed.

   k. Fundamental uncertainties will not lead to a qualification but to an explanatory paragraph.

   l. In general departures from accounting standards lead to qualified reports.

   m. SAS 600 gives some examples of qualified and other auditors' reports. This chapter includes some reports which conform to the wording in these examples.

   n. Materiality is vital to accounting measurement and disclosure. Auditors' reports are only qualified for material matters.

Points to note

21. a. Auditors who feel a qualification is necessary for disagreement will normally request the directors to change the accounts. The directors will usually do this, so that no qualified report is necessary.

   b. Because of the serious nature of a qualified report, auditors are always reluctant to qualify their report. However after XYZ PLC has called in the receivers three months after the publication of financial statements showing a profit, everybody says 'surely something was wrong and the auditors should surely have qualified their report'.

   c. Conversely, the auditors would be much criticised if they qualified their report, perhaps for going concern reasons, and this caused the company's collapse. The new unqualified report with a fundamental uncertainty explanation helps here because the auditors can comment on the uncertainty without actually qualifying their report.

d. Qualifications are only used for material matters. What is material is a matter of judgment but SAS 600 suggests that a matter is material if its omission or mis-statement would reasonably influence the decisions of a user of the financial statements.

e. Note that many qualifications also imply that the auditors cannot say that proper accounting records have been kept in some area and also that all necessary information and explanations have not been received.

f. Qualifications should be well written:

- they should give information. They should not arouse suspicion or induce the reader to ask for more. They should not be like a newsvendors placard: 'world leader dead'. This statement is intended to induce the passer-by to ask for more

- they should be concise as is consistent with clarity. They should be long enough to be clear but not so long as to bore the reader

- they should be specific as to items and facts and as far as possible as to amounts

- the effect on the financial statements as a whole should be made clear

- the auditors' opinion should not be capable of being misinterpreted.

g. If a qualified audit report has been given on any company's accounts and the company wishes to pay a dividend then the auditor has certain additional duties.

Case study 1 for Chapter 32

Althea Printing Machinery plc have just had their accounts audited by Such, Loss Certified Accountants. The manager and the partner in charge of the audit are considering the following matters which arose in the final review:

a. The accounting records did not adequately identify and separately record development expenditure on the project to create a new type of machine. £408,000 has been capitalised and is being amortised over three years including this year. The project is likely to be very successful and the capitalised expenditure was incurred.

b. The notes to the accounts state that:

'The company's assets in Southern Utopia have been nationalised and the amount to be paid as compensation is being negotiated. £100,000 has already been paid but the balance is totally uncertain.

Provision has been made (as an exceptional item) of half the remaining book values of £27,000'

c. The directors estimate the total net realisable value of four obsolete machines at one-half of cost ie £50,000. The manager knows of such a machine recently purchased by a client from another manufacturer at £5,000.

d. The directors refused permission for the auditors to circularise the creditors. The auditors wished to do this as some doubts ocurred over cut-off. Alternative tests have not proved totally convincing.

e. The new office block in the city which is partly used by the company and partly let out has not been depreciated. The directors expressed a view in the statement of accounting policies that the building is high quality and has suffered no diminution of value.

f. The company sold scrap metal from its operations for cash in the sum of £50,000. There is little audit evidence on the correctness of this sum.

g. The accounts show in the balance sheet:

'Preliminary expenses and discount on debentures £120,000.'

The manager has already discussed these items with the board who are determined to make no alteration to the accounts as they stand at present.

Student self testing questions *Questions with answers apparent from the text*

1. a. Why is a qualified report difficult for a company? (1)
    b. What are the main sources for information on qualified reports? (2)
    c. List the circumstances in which Sections 235 and 237 require qualification. (6)
    d. Reproduce the table in para 7. (7)
    e. Define limitation of scope. (7)
    f. When is an adverse opinion required? (7)
    g. When is a disclaimer of opinion required? (7)
    h. Define inherent uncertainty. (8)
    i. What should an auditor do about inherent uncertainties? (9)
    j. Define materiality. (18, 21)
    k. What qualities are required of qualifications? (21)

Exercises

1. Write out in full audit reports in the following circumstances:
    a. The sales ledger of A Ltd is in a mess such that the debtors of £2,400,000 can be substantiated with a 95% probability only to within 10%.
    b. B plc includes in its assets some properties valued at £3 million in a central American country which is undergoing civil war. The directors are happy to give a letter of representation that the properties exist, are owned by the company and are fairly valued. However the auditor is unable to visit the country or to verify the continued existence, ownership or value of the properties.
    c. C Ltd is engaged in litigation over some alleged copyright infringed by C Ltd. The alleged infringement took place over the previous year and the claim is for £4 million. The action is not expected to be heard for over a year and the outcome is anybody's guess. No provision has been made.
    d. D Ltd have included the goodwill arising on the acquisition of Joe's business (£500,000) in the balance sheet and are writing it off over 10 years. The auditor considers the life of the *purchased* goodwill as only 2 years.
    e. E Ltd failed to take stock at Branch 12 and included the stock at an estimated amount £400,000.
    f. F Ltd refused to disclose in the accounts:
       i. The loss of £300,000 caused by the defalcation of a director (now removed from office)
       ii. Payments of an unfunded pension of £50,000 to a former director.
    g. G Ltd had income from gaming machines of an unknown amount and all this money was properly spent on legitimate cost of sales items. The balance sheet is fully acceptable to the auditor.

h. The directors report states that the profit for the year of H plc was £13 million. The profit and loss account shows a profit of £11 million + £2 million extraordinary item. Answer if:

a. the auditor considers the item to be exceptional and not extraordinary

b. the auditor thinks the item is extraordinary.

All these items are material but not fundamental.

Examination question *(Answer begins on page 552)*

1. During the course of your audit of the fixed assets of Eastern Engineering plc at 31 March 1986 two problems have arisen.

i. The calculations of the cost of direct labour incurred on assets in course of construction by the company's employees have been accidentally destroyed for the early part of the year. The direct labour cost involved is £10,000.

ii. The company has received a government grant of £25,000 towards the cost of plant and equipment acquired during the year and expected to last for ten years. The grant has been credited in full to the profit and loss account as exceptional income.

Required:

a. List the general forms of qualification available to auditors in drafting their report and state the circumstances in which each is appropriate. (4 marks)

b. State whether you feel that a qualified audit report would be necessary for each of the two circumstances outlined above, giving reasons in each case. (8 marks)

c. On the assumption that you decide that a qualified audit report would be necessary with respect to the treatment of the government grant, draft the section of the report describing the matter (the whole report is not required). (4 marks)

d. Outline the auditor's general responsibility with regard to the statement in the directors' report concerning the valuation of land and buildings. (2 marks)

(ACCA) (Total 18 marks)

Examination questions without answers

1. You have been asked by the partner in charge of your firm to provide guidance to audit staff about materiality. He believes that if this guidance is provided to staff it will allow them to carry out audits more effectively.

You are required to:

a. Provide a definition of the term 'material' and explain why the concept of materiality is important to auditors. (4 marks)

b. Provide guidance on materiality. Your answer should consider:

i. errors in compliance tests on accounting systems

ii. errors in the profit and loss account

iii. errors in balance sheet items

iv. compliance with the Companies Acts and Accounting Standards

v. aggregation of errors and uncertainties. (21 marks)

(ACCA 91) (25 marks)

2. Statement of Auditing Standards 600 – *Auditors' Reports on Financial Statements* – has modified the previous reporting standards in two important respects:

i. it requires the inclusion in the auditors' report of an extended number of basic elements, and

ii. it changes the types of qualified report available to the auditor.

You are required to:

a. list the basic elements of the auditors' report on the financial statements of a company as required by SAS 600, briefly explaining what you consider to be the reasons for including each of them, and

b. explain the types of qualified audit report now available, with an example of the application of each of them.

(IComA 95)

3. TOP BAKERS Ltd. owns a chain of bakeries and one tea shop. Management bought this chain from the previous owners three years ago and financed the acquisition from personal borrowing. They are repaying these borrowings from the dividends which they are paid by the company.

TOP BAKERS Ltd. was a client of the Senior Partner of your firm in previous years. Following his untimely death, you assumed responsibility for this engagement at the commencement of this year's audit. The following details have been taken from the 1990 audited accounts and the 1991 draft accounts on which you will be expressing your opinion shortly. These figures include the results of the tea shop and bakeries.

	Year ended 30th June	
	1991	1990
	£'000	£'000
Stocks	560	500
Net current liabilities	(275)	(250)
Net assets	275	200
Profit for the year (after tax @ 40%)	820	750
Dividends paid	745	500
Turnover	5,450	5,400

You are aware that, from the time of the management buy-out, the company adopted a policy of not including labour or overhead in stock valuation because operating management considered that these costs were really related to the period in which they were incurred. If labour and overhead were included in stock valuation, their inclusion would increase the amount at which stocks are stated by approximately 60% in each year.

TEA SHOP

The accounting records show the tea shop sales at £420,000 in the year ended 30th June, 1991, and £400,000 in the year ended 30th June, 1990, with profit margins of 67% and 72% respectively. Margins generally accepted for the tea shop type of business indicate that they should be between 65% and 75%. The tea shop turnover is comprised of cash sales only and there are no controls over the completeness of the recording of these sales other than monitoring of the achieved profits. Transactions between the tea shop and the bakeries are on an arm's length basis.

Requirement

You are required, on the assumption that the Directors refuse to make any changes to the draft 1991 accounts and that your audit, which has now been completed, has revealed no problems or errors other than the matters discussed above, to set out the audit report which you would give on the 1991 accounts, giving reasons for your treatment in the report of the matters set out above.

NB You should ignore any matters which relate only to amounts included as comparative figures in the profit and loss account for the year ended 30th June, 1991, – ie those relating to the profit and loss account for the year ended 30th June, 1990.

(ICAI 91) (20 marks)

4. a. What must an audit report state in order to ensure that it is fully understood?

    b. State what you understand by the terms 'adverse opinion' and 'disclaimer of opinion' and give an example of each.

(LCCI 91) (15 marks)

33 **Events after the balance sheet date**

Introduction

1. This chapter deals with the auditor's consideration of events that occur after the balance sheet date by considering:

    a. the reason for the auditor's interest in such events

    b. SSAPs 17 and 18

    c. the dating of the audit report

    d. some unusual but possible circumstances

    e. the auditor's procedures in this area.

2. There is a Statement of Auditing Standards SAS 150 *Subsequent events.*

The auditor's interest in post balance sheet events

3. The preparation of a profit and loss account and balance sheet always involves the consideration of events which have or will occur after the date of the balance because at the year end there are numerous transactions in progress where the outcome is uncertain and post balance sheet events which have occurred or are expected to occur, must be examined to determine the appropriate values of assets and liabilities.

    For example, the collectibility of debts, the net realisable value of old stock, the outcome of legal action are a function of future uncertain events. Almost all assets and liabilities are carried in the balance sheet at values which imply some judgement of future events. Even the value of fixed assets is a function of their expected future useful life.

4. Since the preparer of a set of final accounts must use post balance sheet events in preparing Accounts, the auditor must seek evidence that:

    a. all post balance events have been considered and where appropriate used;

    b. balance sheet values correctly incorporate post balance sheet events.

SSAPs 17 and 18

5. In his review of post balance sheet events the auditor should seek evidence that SSAP 17 Accounting for Post Balance Sheet events and SSAP 18 Accounting for contingencies have been complied with.

6. SSAP 17 broadly requires that:

   a. Financial statements should be prepared on the basis of conditions existing at the balance sheet date, that is, for example, the subsequent destruction of an asset existing at the balance sheet date can be ignored.

   b. Material post balance sheet events require changes in balance sheet values if they are:

      i. adjusting events

      ii. indications of going concern non-applicability.

   c. Non adjusting events should be disclosed if:

      i. non disclosure would affect the view given to users by the Accounts

      ii. the outcome of transactions entered into before the balance sheet date would seriously alter the appearance of the company's balance sheet (eg window dressing).

   Adjusting events are those which provide additional evidence of conditions existing at the balance sheet date. There are two types:

   – events such as sale of old stock, collection of debts, settlement of a court action, agreement of disputes etc,

   – incorporation of statutory or conventional requirements eg declaration of a final dividend.

7. SSAP 18 broadly requires:

   a. Material contingent losses should be accrued (incorporated) in the Accounts where it is probable future events will confirm (or have confirmed) a loss which can be estimated with reasonable accuracy.

   b. Material contingent losses not accrued (because they cannot be reasonably quantified or are not probable) should be disclosed unless the possibility of loss is remote.

   c. Contingent gains should *not* be accrued and need be disclosed only if it is probable that the gain will be realised.

Dating of audit reports

8. The auditor should always date his audit report. The date should be as close as possible to the date of approval of the financial statements by the directors but must be *after* that date. Note that SSAP 17 requires disclosure of the date of approval of the Accounts by the directors.

Period end to date of auditor's report

9. SAS 150 requires that auditors should perform procedures designed to obtain sufficient appropriate audit evidence that:

   a. All material subsequent events up to the date of their report *which require adjustment of the financial statements* have been identified and incorporated in the accounts

b. All material subsequent events up to the date of their report *which require disclosure* (but not accounts alteration) have been identified and disclosed.

There are a number of possible procedures including:

i. *Focusing* on matters, encountered in the audit, which are susceptible to change. These include cut-off, collection of debts, sales of stock at below cost etc.

ii. Enquiring into management's procedures (if any) for dealing with subsequent events

iii. Reviewing accounting records

iv. Reviewing interim financial statements, budget reports, cash flow forecasts and other management information

v. Reading minutes and agendas of meetings of shareholders, directors and management committees

v. Enquiring of management as to any events which may be relevant

vi. Reading external documents such as stock exchange pronouncements and press reports which may affect the client's business. For example press discussion of the housing market may trigger enquiries as to the valuation of a house building company's stock of land.

Some specific enquiries may be made. The ones below are general but specific enquiries may occur to an auditor of a specific company. Some specific enquiries:

– current status of items involving subjective judgement eg litigation, sale of fixed assets or negotiation of new or renewable loans.

– any new borrowings or similar commitments

– any sales of assets, actual or planned

– any disasters eg loss of assets or incurring of liabilities eg initiation of litigation against the client

– any intentions to merge, sell or to liquidate the undertaking (or part of it)

– any intention to make issues of shares or loans

– any intentions to take over another company

– any change in the risk profile of the company eg a major change in product or market extension

– any events which may change the going concern status of the company or any part of it.

Date of auditors' report to issue of financial statements

10. This may be a very short period but, in any event, SAS 150 advises that auditors have no obligation to perform procedures or make enquiries regarding the financial statements after the date of their report.

11. However auditors may become aware of subsequent events which may materially affect the financial statements. SAS 150 gives no examples but the settlement of major litigation may be a good example. In these cases the auditors should consider if the financial statements need amendment, discuss the matter with the directors and if necessary conduct further audit procedures and finally consider the implications for their report.

Issue of financial statements to annual general meeting

12. Similar remarks can be made as in paras 10 and 11 above. However there are differences between events which occurred before the date of the audit report but of which the auditors only became aware after that date (this seems unlikely) and events which occurred after the date of the report. In the former case there are statutory provisions for amending the financial statements (Section 245). There are no such provisions in the latter case.

Summary

13. a. Post balance sheet events have an effect on the Accounts.

b. Auditors must review these events.

c. Authority for the treatment of post balance sheet events in Accounts is found in SSAPs 17 and 18.

d. Audit reports should be dated as soon as possible after the date of formal approval of the Accounts by the directors.

e. Subsequent events are dealt with in SAS 150.

f. Auditors should apply procedures to discover the existence of relevant subsequent events which occur from the date of the financial statements to the date of signing the auditors' report.

g. There is no obligation on auditors to apply procedures to discover relevant subsequent events form the date of signing their report to the date of laying the financial statements before the company.

h. However, if the auditors become aware of such events they should discuss the matter with the directors, consider the implications for their report and take such actions as may seem necessary.

Points to note

14. a. Note that SSAP 18 perpetuates the accountants 'least-as-good' syndrome in that:

   - A material contingent loss not accrued should be disclosed except when the possibility of loss is remote.
   - Contingent gains should not be accrued. Disclosure should only be made if it is probable that the gain will be realised.

b. The auditor should be aware of window dressing. For example:

   Subsidiary A has some unsaleable widgets it has manufactured. On 31.12.-6 (the year end) it invoices these to Associate Company B. After date the sale is reversed by a credit note. The objective of the 'sale' was to value the widgets at cost or above to remove the real loss in value in the widgets from the accounts. It is unlikely that the auditors of Subsidiary A or Associated Company B would realise the significance of the supposed transaction.

Case study for Chapter 33

Claribel is conducting the final audit of Westwood plc who are importers and dealers in timber and manufacturers of packing materials. The accounts show results which are comparable to those of the previous year. Claribel is puzzled by this as she knows that the company are having difficulties and that creditors are pressing and the bank is making difficulties over the overdraft. She is suspicious of the accounts and resolves to be especially vigilant in the audit of post balance sheet events. The company's year end is 31.3.-6 and she is doing the audit in mid June. Two specific items have come to her attention:

a. In the sales office she came across some promotional literature offering special very low prices for obsolete stock in July.

b. In conversation with the purchasing manager she discovers that the company has signed a barter deal with an exporter in Zombaland for the exchange of hard woods from Africa for some woodworking machinery of Westwood that is surplus to requirements. The contract was signed in February for completion in the winter of 19-6/7.

Discussion

List the procedures that Claribel should adopt re post balance sheet events.

What particular further facts should she elicit re a. and b.?

What might be the significance of these items for the accounts?

Student self testing questions *Questions with answers apparent from the text*

1. a. Summarise SSAP 17 and its significance for the auditor. (6)
   b. Summarise SSAP 18 and its significance for the auditor. (7)
   c. Comment on the dating of audit reports. (8)
   d. List general and specific procedures to be adopted to identify relevant subsequent events. (9)
   e. Summarise an auditor's duties in respect of events occurring between the date of the auditors' report and the laying of the financial statements before the company. (10–12)

Examination question *(Answer begins on page 552)*

1. An unqualified audit report normally states that the financial statements to which the report refers give a true and fair view of the state of the company's affairs at the balance sheet date and of its profits for the year ended on that date.

   Bearing in mind the above statement the directors of Midland Builders Ltd have drawn up accounts for the year ended 30 April 1987 which do not reflect certain events which have occurred since the year end. They justify their action on the grounds that the books and records correctly reflect what was known at the year end. The following are the events which are not reflected in the draft financial statements (in all cases the figures are material).

   i. At a meeting in May 1987 the local planning authority rejected the company's plans to develop one of its freehold sites. The site was included in the company's assets at its cost of £50,000 but it is likely that the site will have to be sold and will realise no more than £35,000 because of its reduced development potential.

   ii. Following the completion of a long-term contract in June 1987 it has been possible to calculate the final profit on the contract. It appears that the profit accrued at 30 April 1987 was underestimated by £20,000. This arose from a material error at 30 April 1987 in estimating the amount of work still to be completed.

iii. A public company in which Midland Builders Ltd held shares as a long-term trade investment announced in June 1987 that it was going into liquidation. The investment is shown in the balance sheet at its historical cost of £40,000 and a note of its stock market value at 30 April 1987 of £46,000 is included in the notes to the accounts. It now appears likely that the investment will prove worthless.

Required:

a. Discuss generally the effect which facts and events relating to a period but becoming known or occurring after the the end of an accounting period can have on the financial statements for the period in question. Comment on the directors' view that the books and records reflect what was known at the year end and that no further adjustments are required. (4 marks)

b. List FOUR detailed procedures which an auditor should adopt in order to detect post balance sheet events. (4 marks)

c. In respect of each of the three events described above, list the detailed work which the auditor should undertake and comment on the acceptability of the company's decision not to adjust its financial statements.

   i.   Refusal of planning permission. (4 marks)

   ii. Completion of long-term contract. (5 marks)

   iii. Liquidation of trade investment. (3 marks)

   (ACCA)

Examination questions without answers

2. A contingency is a condition which exists at the Balance Sheet date, where the outcome will be confirmed only on the occurrence or non-occurrence of one or more uncertain future events.

Required

a. Give details of 6 possible contingent gains or losses. (6 marks)

b. Describe briefly the treatment of material contingent gains or losses. (4 marks)

c. What type of circumstances can give rise to uncertainty? How should the auditor attempt to deal with this in his report to the members of a company? (5 marks)

   (AAT) (Total 15 marks)

3. An auditing Guideline has been issued on events after the balance sheet date. Your firm is the auditor of Bestwood Electronics plc which assembles microcomputers and wholesales them and associated equipment to retailers. Many of the parts for the computers and the associated equipment are bought from the Far East. These computers are used by businesses for accounting, word processing and other computer tasks.

You have been asked by the partner in charge of the audit to consider your firm's audit responsibilities in relation to post balance sheet events, and the audit work you will carry out on these matters.

You are required to:

a. Briefly describe the responsibilities of the auditor for detecting errors in the accounts during the following periods:

   i.   from the balance sheet date to the completion of the detailed audit work

   ii. from the completion of the detailed audit work to the date the directors sign the financial statements

iii. from the date the directors sign the financial statements to the annual general meeting which approves the accounts. (6 marks)

b. List and describe the audit work you will carry out in period (a) (i) above which involves consideration of post balance sheet events. (14 marks)

c. Briefly describe the work you will carry out in period (a)(ii) above to ensure no adjustments are required to the accounts. (5 marks)

(ACCA 91) (25 Marks)

34 Going concern

Introduction

1. In recent years, many companies and other enterprises have failed. That is: they have gone bust, into bankruptcy, into receivership or liquidation. The reasons for failure are many and varied but high gearing and high interest rates are often blamed. A fundamental accounting concept in SSAP 2 is going concern. This is defined as: an assumption that the enterprise will continue in operational existence for the foreseeable future. It means in particular that the Profit and Loss Account and Balance Sheet assume no intention or necessity to liquidate or curtail significantly the scale of operations. *Foreseeable future* is not defined further and we will consider it again later. the Companies Act 1985 Sch 4 (10) says that the company shall be presumed to be carrying on business as a going concern.

2. There have been many instances when a company have issued financial statements prepared on the going concern basis, have an unqualified auditors' report and then go bust shortly afterwards. The auditors are then much criticised. Surely, people say, they must have known the company was likely to fail! Hindsight is a valuable property as is an ability to see into the future! The modern view is that:

   a. the directors should consider the appropriateness of the going concern very carefully before preparing the financial statements

   b. the auditors should form an opinion likewise

3. There is a lengthy Statement of Auditing Standards SAS 130 *The going concern basis in financial statements.*

Consequences of going concern

4. The adoption of the going concern basis in financial statements means among other things:

   a. assets are recognised and measured on the basis that the enterprise expects to recover through use or realisation the recorded amounts in the normal course of business. For example the plant and machinery is expected to be used for many years into the future and its net book value recovered through use. An abandonment of going concern basis would mean that the enterprise would immediately sell the plant and machinery when it may fetch only a small fraction of its book value.

b. liabilities are recognised and measured on the basis that they will be discharged in the normal course of business. The Balance Sheet shows creditors due after 12 months and creditors due in less than 12 months. Abandonment of going concern basis would make them all payable immediately.

5. If financial statements are drawn up without the going concern basis then:

a. all assets would be valued at net realisable values. Most would have much lower values than going concern values.

b. all liabilities would be shown at the amount due. One notable change would be the inclusion of redundancy pay which is presumed not to be payable if the enterprise is continuing for ever or at least not until a long time into the future.

Directors duties

6. The directors should consider carefully whether the going concern basis is appropriate. They do this by considering all available information. This does mean that they have to make a judgement about future events which are inherently uncertain. The question that arises is 'how far into the future do they need to look?'. The answer to that depends on a number of factors:

– the nature of the business. The future of a civil engineering contractor is inherently more uncertain than that of a firm of funeral directors.

– the riskiness of the company or its industry. A one customer firm is more at risk than a firm with many customers. A highly geared company is more at risk than an all equity one.

– external influences. A sudden increase in interest rates or a change in exchange rates can make some businesses unviable. Even a change in the weather from wet to dry can ruin an umbrella company.

7. So, how do directors review the going concern basis? Here are some procedures:

a. reflect on how long into the future to look by considering the matters in paragraph 6 above.

b. consider all the factors which are relevant: risk, known or expected changes in the economy and the circumstances of the company, ongoing transactions the outcome of which is uncertain.

c. forecast financial statements

d. budgets and strategic plans

e. cash flow forecasts

The auditors' procedures

8. SAS 130 requires that the auditor, when forming an opinion as to whether financial statements give a true and fair view, should consider the entity's ability to continue as a going concern, and any relevant disclosures in the financial statements.

The latter idea is relatively new. It suggests that when a reader of the financial statements might be expected to have doubts about the viability of the company and hence the appropriateness of the going concern basis, then some note or other disclosure should be made in the financial statements justifying the adoption of the going concern basis. More of this later.

Some possible procedures are:

a. assess the adequacy of the means by which the directors have satisfied themselves that the adoption of the going concern basis is appropriate

b. examine all appropriate evidence

c. assess the adequacy of the length of time into the future that the directors have looked

d. assess the systems or other means by which the directors have identified warnings of future risks and uncertainties.

e. examine budgets and other future plans and assess the reliability of such budgets by reference to past performance

f. examine management accounts and other reports of recent activities

g. consider the sensitivity of budgets and cash flow forecasts to variable factors both within the control of the directors (eg capital expenditure) and outside their control (eg interest rates or debt collection)

h. review any obligations, undertakings or guarantees arranged with other entities for the giving or receiving of support. Other entities may mean lenders, suppliers, customers or other companies in the same group. A UK company may be viable in itself but may have given guarantees to other members of the group and when, say the holding company in Australia fails, the company goes down with it.

i. survey the existence, adequacy and terms of borrowing facilities and supplier credit

j. appraise the key assumptions underlying the budgets, forecasts and other information used by the directors

k. assess the directors' plans for resolving any matters giving rise to concern (if any) about the appropriateness of the going concern basis. Such plans should be realistic, capable of resolving the doubts, and the directors should have firm intentions to put them into effect.

Finally the auditors should review all the information they have and all the audit evidence available and consider whether they can accept the going concern basis. They should always have all their evidence documented and their reasoning explained fully in the working papers.

Borrowing facilities

9. For many entities, survival is a matter of continuing to borrow, especially from the bank. Bank refusal to renew facilities is perhaps the most common precipitation of receivership and liquidation. Consequently the auditor, in cases where borrowing facilities are critical, needs to examine and review these facilities in detail. Procedures will include obtaining written confirmations of the existence and terms of borrowing facilities and assessing the intentions of the bank or other lenders.

Situations where these matters are of special importance include when the entity:

a. has had difficulty in negotiating or renewing finance

b. finds such facilities essential for survival

c. is expected to experience cash flow difficulties

d. finds that assets granted as security are declining in value

e. has breached the terms of borrowing or covenants made

Auditors reports

10. Several possibilities exists and the auditor needs to vary his action according to the situation. We discuss each in turn.

    a. **The entity is clearly a going concern.** This will mainly arise when the *headroom* (as SAS 130 puts it) is large between the financial resources required in the foreseeable future and the financial resources available. The directors should still undertake an exercise to determine that this is so and the auditors should seek evidence that the directors have done so and that the going concern basis is appropriate.

    b. **The entity is not, in the opinion of the auditors, a going concern.** There are two possibilities here. One is that the directors have prepared accounts on the going concern basis and the auditors disagree with that basis. In such cases the auditors should issue an *adverse* audit opinion. The second possibility is that the directors have prepared the accounts on a basis other than going concern. This will be rare. It can however arise if a company was formed with a specific purpose in mind (eg developing an estate or running a specific exhibition) and is to be wound up when the purpose has been achieved. In these cases the auditors need not qualify their report providing the financial statements contain the necessary disclosures so that readers of the accounts can understand the position. Annual financial statements are unlikely to be prepared at all if a company is about to go into insolvency and then the auditor's opinion does not really arise.

    c. **The auditors may have concern about the appropriateness of the going concern basis.** In such cases they may be able to allay their concern by obtaining audit evidence that the directors have satisfied themselves that the going concern basis is appropriate by a thorough appraisal and taking specialist advice. Where the concern persists the auditor may feel that his fears will be allayed by some relevant disclosure in the financial statements. In this case the auditor should consider whether the disclosures are sufficient to give a true and fair view. If, in the auditor's opinion, they do not, then a qualification on grounds of disagreement is required. For example:

> **Qualified opinion arising from disagreements as to the adequacy of a disclosure in the financial statements.**
>
> In our opinion, the financial statements should disclose the following matters. The company are required to repay a term loan on ...... 19... They have been unable to obtain further long term finance but their projections of trading and cash flow indicate that it will be possible to meet the repayment on the due date. The directors have informed us that their views are based upon their plans and their intentions to sell their American distribution company. Such a sale has not yet been agreed and, inherently, there can be no certainty that the company will be able to meet its obligation to repay its term loan.
>
> Except for the absence of the disclosure referred to above. in our opinion...

If the auditors consider that there is a considerable measure of concern but that it is adequately met by disclosures in the financial statements then they should not qualify their report but should include an explanatory paragraph in their report. For example:

Extract from the 'basis of opinion' section of the auditor's report

---

Going concern

In forming our opinion, we have considered the adequacy of the disclosure made in note 4 of the financial statements concerning the uncertainty over the possible outcome of the litigation on the alleged infringement of a patent by the company. In view of this uncertainty we consider that it should be drawn to your attention, but our opinion is not qualified in this respect.

(Note 4 will have adequately explained that the company are alleged to have infringed a patent and if the allegation is proved the company will be unable to continue to make its main product. However the company vigorously deny the allegation and expect to win the action but there is still much doubt.)

The real world of small companies

11. In the past, very little attention was paid to going concern. It tended to be assumed except in circumstances where obvious worries existed. Now, it receives a great deal of attention and directors are expected to consider their position very carefully. For example the following considerations might be appropriate in a small retail company:

    – the company have prepared cash flow forecasts for the next six months including the five months after approval of the financial statements. These show adequate cash resources.

    – the directors do not consider that forecasts for a longer period are necessary as they would be too uncertain to be useful and the current forecast shows a reasonable surplus.

    – the directors have reviewed in detail the assumptions underlying the forecast including the level of turnover, the trend of expenses and capital expenditure and input pricing and found them acceptable.

    – the company have recently renewed their overdraft facilities for the ensuing twelve months.

    – the lease of the premises has three more years to run at the present rent

    – further retail development in their precinct is likely to attract more customers without adding to competition, at least in the next year.

    If the directors have undertaken this review, are prepared to represent this fact in writing to the auditor, the auditor has reviewed the directors' work and found evidence that the conclusions are reasonable, then the auditor can accept the going concern basis.

    The new thing is that this work has to be done in all cases.

Cadbury code reporting

12. The Cadbury Code requires directors to report on a number of aspects of corporate governance (see Chapter 63). You will usually find in modern reports and accounts a statement like:

    'After making due enquiries, the directors have a reasonable expectation that the group has adequate resources to continue in operational existence for the foreseeable future. For this reason, they continue to adopt the going concern basis in preparing the accounts.'

The auditors should review and seek evidence to confirm this view. They do this by reviewing the directors' minute book, supporting documentary evidence on going concern basis, enquiring of the directors and obtaining written confirmations of the directors' oral representations on the subject.

They should not report directly to the directors on going concern basis but their report on compliance generally with the code includes going concern basis by implication. They should report specifically however if they feel that it is misleading, i.e. it is not consistent with other information they become aware of in the course of the audit of financial statements on the appropriateness of the going concern basis or the adequacy of related disclosures in the financial statements.

You will appreciated that the auditors need to investigate and assess evidence on going concern basis for the audit of the financial statements. This makes an assessment of the directors statement on compliance with the Code in respect of going concern basis relatively easy. However they do not specifically mention it but will do so if it is misleading. As an example the financial statements may have a note that the going concern basis is appropriate on the basis that a maturing loan will be renegotiated favourably and that the negotiations are at an advanced stage. The compliance statement is as in our example above. The auditors might think that is misleading without specific mention again of the loan negotiations.

Summary

13. a. Going concern is now a major issue.

b. SAS 130 is relevant to this subject

c. The definition of going concern should be learned

d. Abandonment of the going concern basis means that assets will be valued at net realisable values and some liabilities will become payable including redundancy pay.

e. The directors have a duty to consider the going concern basis very carefully and make suitable enquiries.

f. The auditors have a duty also to consider the going concern basis and review and seek audit evidence on the directors own considerations and opinions.

g. A major issue in many going concern basis doubts is borrowing facilities. If in doubt the auditors need to confirm these directly with the bank and form an opinion on the bank's attitude toward supporting the company.

h. There are numerous situations where going concern basis is an issue. Some of these are financial, some operational, and some external to the entity.

i. The auditor will make no mention of going concern basis in his report if the company is clearly a going concern.

j. If it clearly is not then an adverse opinion is called for if the financial statements are prepared on a going concern basis

k. If the financial statements are not prepared on a going concern basis, there are adequate explanations of the circumstances and the auditor concurs then an unqualified opinion is appropriate.

l. The grey area is when there are doubts about going concern but the auditor considers that the going concern basis gives a true and fair view. In such cases the notes to the accounts should give adequate explanations of the situation and the directors' assumptions. If they do then the auditor should include an explanatory paragraph in the opinion but not qualify his report. If the notes are inadequate then the auditor should qualify for disagreement.

m. The going concern basis is one of the issues requiring mention in the directors' report on compliance with the Cadbury Code.

Points to note

14. a. The going concern principle can be considered in relation to the enterprise as a whole or a part only. For example, if a branch were not a going concern, realisable value of assets would need to be substituted for book values and new liabilities may appear in respect of the branch.

b. The probability that a going concern qualification of an auditor's report may bring about a receivership or liquidation is a very real problem to auditors who have doubts about a client's future. The auditor should give his opinion without fear of the consequences to his client.

c. The recession of the early nineties has produced many company failures and in many surviving companies substantial retrenchment has occurred, including closures and asset sales. Many apparently strong companies have suffered declines in sales which have led to redundancies and rationalisations. As a result the going concern principle has come into prominence and can no longer be taken for granted. In addition the business community has come to expect more information from the annual report and accounts and in particular feels it needs more information on the future and the risks and uncertainties besetting each company.

d. Note the definition of going concern and the paradox that efforts to continue a company (eg by closing factories) may lead to the going concern basis being inappropriate for part of a company.

e. SAS 130 has much on the period to review for going concern basis. The length of the period clearly relates to the circumstances of the entity and the consequent risks. Directors should pay attention to a period of at least one year from the date of approval of the financial statements. If not they should disclose this fact. If they do not so disclose, then the auditor should do so in the basis of opinion sections but need not qualify the report.

f. If the auditors consider that representations from the directors are critical to obtaining sufficient audit evidence on going concern basis and the directors decline to provide them, then they may feel a need to qualify their report on grounds of limitation of scope. This could be *except for* or a *disclaimer*.

Case study 1 for Chapter 34

CONGLOM PLC is a quoted company primarily in the home computer industry but with a wide range of divisions, many in other industries. It has expanded fast by heavy borrowing from banks and the issue of loan stock.

Discussion

What indications might the auditor find that may cast doubts on the appropriateness of the going concern concept for the company?

What alternative strategies may Conglom adopt to survive and hence to allow the auditors to give an unqualified report?

Suppose that the survival of the company was wholly conditional on very large sales of the company's new home computer over the next six months in the so far untried market in continental Europe.

Draft a suitable set of alternative audit reports.

Case study 2 for Chapter 34

Widget Manufacturing Co Ltd have traded successfully for many years and in the boom years of the late eighties planned an extension to the factory to enable a doubling of turnover. The factory was completed in 19-2 with the aid of a very large bank loan. The company have always been short of working capital and also have a substantial overdraft which frequently exceeds the facility. The expected increase in turnover never occurred because of the recession. The auditor is John Jumpy FCCA.

Discussion

What evidence might the directors produce to justify their opinion that the company is a going concern and how might Jumpy validate the evidence?

Suppose the directors based their opinion on an assumption of an end to the recession and a large increase in turnover both in the UK and overseas. How would this affect Jumpy?

Student self testing questions *Questions with answers apparent from the text*

1. a. Define the going concern basis (1)
    b. List the consequences of the going concern basis (4,5)
    c. List the directors' duties in respect of going concern basis (6,7)
    d. List the auditors' procedures (8)
    e. List the possible auditors' reports (12)
    f. State the Cadbury Code requirements on going concern basis (14)

Examination questions without answers

1. a. Explain the going concern concept.   (3 marks)
    b. According to Auditing Guideline L410, The Auditor's Consideration in Respect of Going Concern, –

        '...a company rarely ceases to carry on business without any prior indications, either of inability to meet debts as they fall due, or of problems that raise questions about the continuation of the business.'

        Requirement

        You are required to identify any 7 examples of such 'prior indications' and write a short explanatory note on each of the examples you have selected.   (14 marks)
        (ICAI 91) (Total 17 marks)

    N. B. You are not required to comment on the relative significance of each example.

2. You are a senior with a firm of Chartered Accountants. You are about to commence working on the audit of CRUSADER Ltd., a family owned and managed limited company. You have been informed by a business contact that the company has not been trading very successfully and is having difficulties with its bankers. However, you are not aware of any of the specific details.

The manager in charge of the audit is also aware of this information and is concerned about the ability of CRUSADER Ltd. to continue trading. He has asked you to visit the company in order to ascertain the current state of affairs.

Requirement

a. Draw up a list of questions that you would wish to ask, and details of any information that you would wish to obtain from, the Finance Director of CRUSADER Ltd. during your visit so as to enable you to assess the future viability of the company.

b. Explain briefly the audit opinion that you would give assuming you concluded, after carrying out appropriate audit procedures, that there was a fundamental uncertainty regarding the ability of the company to continue trading. The audit opinion should be in accordance with SAS 600, *Auditors' Reports on Financial Statements*.

You are *not* required to draft the audit report.

(ICAI 94)

35 Opening balances and comparatives

Introduction

1. This chapter is concerned with the Accounts of the business for the year *before* the Accounts being audited. The first part considers the Companies Act requirements, the second explains the auditor's interest, the third the auditor's procedures and the final part reviews some problems which may arise in practice.

2. There is a Statement of Auditing Standards SAS 450 *Opening balances and comparatives*.

Companies Act requirements

3. The Companies Act (Schedule 4(4)) states that corresponding amounts are required to be disclosed in respect of every item in a company's balance sheet and profit and loss account for the financial year immediately preceding that to which the balance sheet and profit and loss account relates.

4. Corresponding amounts for the previous year are commonly known as the comparative figures and current practice is to print one narrative and two sets of figures as:

	19-6	19-5
	£'000	£'000
Fixed Assets	£6,420	£6,180

Where the corresponding amount is not comparable (= able to be compared) with the amount shown in the previous years' Accounts then:

a. the previous year's figure should be adjusted, and

b. particulars of the adjustment and the reasons for it shown in the notes.

5. Note also the requirements of FRS 3 on acquisitions, discontinued operations, prior period adjustments and comparatives. In particular see paragraphs 7, 29, 30 and 60–64.

The auditor's interest

6. The auditor is interested in the preceding year's figures because:

    a. These figures form the opening position from which the present year's figures are derived. For example, the opening stock is a component of the cost of sales figure. Thus the auditor must be assured that the opening figures have been properly brought forward.

    b. Accounting policies must be applied consistently from year to year.

    c. Corresponding amounts must be shown (see paragraph 3. above) and the auditor must seek evidence that they are properly shown.

7. The auditor is *not* required to express any opinion on the corresponding figures as such but he is responsible for seeing that they:

    a. are the amounts which appeared in the preceding period's Accounts, or

    b. have been restated to achieve consistency or comparability, or

    c. have been restated due to a change in accounting policy or a correction of a fundamental error as required by FRS 3.

Audit procedures

8. If the auditor was the auditor of the preceding Accounts (a *continuing auditor*) *and* issued an unqualified report then he should:

    a. Consider whether his audit of the current period has revealed any matters casting doubt on the previous year's figures.

    b. Satisfy himself that the balances have been properly brought forward and incorporated in the books.

    c. Satisfy himself that the preceding period's figures have been properly and consistently classified and disclosed as comparative figures.

    d. Satisfy himself that consistent accounting policies have been applied.

Problem situations

9. When the preceding period's Accounts were *audited by another firm* (known as *predecessor auditors*). In order to be satisfied on the items in paragraph 8. above, the auditor will have to perform additional work as:

    a. Consultations with the *client's* management.

    b. Review of the *client's* records, working papers and accounting and control procedures for the preceding period particularly as they affect the opening position.

    c. Consider whether work on the present year's Accounts provides also evidence regarding opening balances.

    d. *If* the above are insufficient then the auditor may have to perform some substantive tests on the opening balances.

e. It may be that the auditor may wish to *consult with the previous auditor*. This is often done but is usually limited to seeking information on the previous auditor's audit of particular areas (usually high risk areas such as stock), or on matters not adequately dealt with in the client's records.

10. Normally, the actions outlined will enable the auditor to give an unqualified report at least in respect of use of the previous year's figures but it may be that some material matter cannot be adequately evidenced and then a report like the following may be required:

AUDITORS' REPORT TO THE MEMBERS OF XYZ LIMITED

As usual down to '… or other irregularity or error.'

However, the evidence available to us was limited because we were not appointed auditors of the company until… and in consequence did not report on the financial statements for the year ended …. There were no satisfactory audit procedures that we could adopt to confirm the amount of stock and work in progress included in the preceding period's financial statements at a value of £x.

In forming our opinion we also evaluated the overall adequacy of the presentation of information in the financial statements.

Qualified Opinion arising from limitation in audit scope

Except for any adjustments that might have been found to be necessary had we been able to obtain sufficient evidence concerning opening stock and work in progress, in our opinion the financial statements give a true and fair view of the state of the company's affairs as at … and of its profit for the year then ended and have been properly prepared in accordance with the Companies Act 1985.

In respect alone of the limitation on our work relating to opening stock and work and progress:

– we have not obtained all the information and explanations that we considered necessary for the purpose of our audit and

– we were unable to determine whether proper accounting records had been maintained

Laurel and Hardy   22 High Street
Certified Accountants and Registered Auditors   Boghampton
Dated…

---

11. When the preceding period's audit report was qualified:

a. If the matter has been resolved and no qualification is required in respect of the current Accounts then no qualification will be required.

b. If the matter is still unresolved then the auditor should qualify his report as:

AUDITORS' REPORT TO THE MEMBERS OF ......

as usual down to the complete Basis of Opinion paragraph then:

Qualified opinion arising from disagreement about accounting treatment

As indicated in note… to the financial statements debtors include an amount of £.. which is the subject of litigation but against which no provision has been made. We have not been able to satisfy ourselves that this amount will be recoverable in full. We qualified our audit report on the financial statements at … (date of preceding financial statements) with regard to the same matter.

Except for the absence of this provision, in our opinion the financial statements give a true and fair view of the state of the company's affairs as at 31 May 1996 and of its profit for the year then ended and have been properly prepared in accordance with the Companies Act 1985.

Stringent & Co etc

---

c. If the previous period's accounts contained:
   i. actual or possible mis-statement in the profit and loss account (not therefore affecting the opening figures).
   ii. misclassification of the preceding period's financial statements.
   iii. a restatement of the previous figures with which the auditor disagrees or does not have a restatement that the auditor does want, then a qualified report is required.
12. When the previous period's accounts were not subject to audit. This may be because the exemption provisions of the Companies Act Section 249 applied to the previous year and the accounts were not audited. Points that may be made include:
   - the opening balances must be substantiated. This may be done by work on current year matters, special substantive tests on opening balances, consultations with management and review of records, working papers and accounting control procedures for the preceding period.
   - much depends on the accounting policies followed (a complex one eg on the learning curve or deferment of development expenditure may need confirmation of calculations), the materiality of the opening balances and the nature and risk of misstatement of them.
   - if sufficient evidence cannot be obtained then a report like that in para 10 may be required.

Summary

13. a. Preceding financial statements have a bearing on current year's statements because:
   i. they are the opening figures to the current year's Accounts;
   ii. consistency of accounting policy is required;
   iii. they are comparative figures.
   b. The Companies Acts have requirements for comparative figures to be shown.
   c. The auditor has a duty towards these figures.

d. Problems arise if the previous year's audit was performed by another firm or if the previous year's audit report was qualified.

Points to note

14. a. If an uncertainty exists in the opening stock then the auditor cannot say the profit gives a true and fair view since the opening stock is part of the profit computation. However he can say the balance sheet gives a true and fair view since the opening stock is not part of the balance sheet.

b. FRS 3 (as the successor to SSAP 6) has also pronounced on prior year adjustments.

c. FRS 3 also pronounces on comparative figures:

'Comparative figures should be given for all primary statements and such notes as are required by FRS 3. The comparative figures in respect of the Profit and Loss Account should include in the continuing category only the results of those operations included in the current period's continuing operations.' The auditor should verify that correct comparatives of continuing, discontinued and acquisition operations are shown.

d. To some extent SAS 450 is not specific but uses terms like 'the auditors should consider the implications for their report'. In essence the auditor will normally check only that the comparatives agree with previous year's accounts and consistent policies have been applied. The auditors must also bear in mind FRS 3 and acquisitions, prior year adjustments etc. Problems arise when there are report qualifications in the current or previous year's audit reports, when the previous year's accounts were audited by predecessor auditors or were not audited, when the auditor comes across material misstatements in the previous year 's accounts or if the opening balances cannot be substantiated.

Case study for Chapter 35

Lettice & Co. have been appointed auditors of Limp Ltd. manufacturers of handkerchiefs in succession to Celery who retired due to ill health. Suresh is currently reviewing the final accounts and discovers the following:

(The audit is on the year ending 31.12.-6)

a. An examination of the stock sheets at 31.12.-5 reveals that stock has been valued at prime cost £85,000 instead of £120,000 the full cost. Celery had not picked this up.

b. A freehold property had been purchased on 23.2.-5 for £800,000 (inc. land £200,000). No depreciation had been charged in 19-5. The building is old and Suresh estimated its useful economic life at 25 years.

c. The auditors' report on the 19-5 accounts was qualified. Celery had discovered that there was a cut-off uncertainty on creditors in the amount of £30,500. This will never now be resolved.

d. In view of the errors found in the 19-5 accounts Suresh is unhappy about all the figures in the 19-5 balance sheet.

Discussion

a. What work should Suresh do on the figures in the 19-5 balance sheet?

b. How should the items a, b, c, be treated in the accounts for 19-6 with their corresponding figures?

c. Draft the auditor's report on the 19-6 accounts. Assume no problems arose other than those stated.

Student self testing questions *Questions with answers apparent from the text*

1. a. What is the auditor's interest in corresponding figures? (3)

   b. What aspects of the corresponding figures is the auditor responsible for? (6)

   c. What should the auditor do re previous accounts if he audited them and gave a clean report? (8)

   d. What additional work should be performed if the previous accounts were audited by another firm? (9)

   e. What paragraphs would appear in an auditor's report if there was an uncertainty in the opening stock? (10)

Examination question without answers

1. You are the senior assigned to the audit of PARADOX Ltd., a new audit client of the chartered accountancy firm for which you work.

   At the pre audit meeting attended by Mr. Grant, the company's Financial Director, you learn that the company has a significant debt collection problem arising mainly from the complete lack of internal controls over the sales and debtors transaction flows.

   You have been advised that the lack of controls has given rise to incorrect invoicing, loss of customers and little or no formal debt follow-up procedures. From discussions with Mr. Simms, the company's Financial Controller, you have also learned that the previous auditors were never successful in their attempts to secure replies to their debtor circularisation letters.

   You have noted that the previous year's audit report was qualified with regard to the auditor's inability to substantiate the closing trade debtors balance as a result of inadequacies in the sales and debtors records.

   The manager in charge of the audit has advised you that the standard client acceptance procedures have been completed, including professional clearance from the previous auditors and that the partner has accepted the company as a client of the firm.

   Requirement

   a. Prepare a very brief plan for the audit of sales and debtors and outline the difficulties which you might encounter in the circumstances outlined above.

   b. Set out the basic internal controls that you consider should be established in the areas of sales and debtors.

   c. Draft a brief letter to Mr. Grant, the company's Financial Director, advising him as to the type of audit report he may expect in the current year:

      i. assuming that the current year's trade debtor balance *can* be substantiated and that there are no other unresolved audit issues; and

      ii. assuming that the current year's trade debtor balance *cannot* be substantiated and that there are no other unresolved audit issues.

   In both circumstances, you are to assume that you will be unable to substantiate the prior year trade debtor balance from work carried out in the current year.

You should set out clearly the opinion that would be given in each of the circumstances in (c) (i) and (c) (ii). You are *not* required to draft the audit report.

(ICAI 95)

36 Auditing and accounting standards

Introduction

1. Accounting standards are authoritative statements of how particular types of transaction and other events should be reflected in financial statements and accordingly compliance with Accounting standards will normally be necessary for financial statements to give a true and fair view.

2. The professional bodies expect their members (including auditors) who assume responsibilities in respect of financial accounts to *observe* accounting standards.

3. *Significant departures* from standards should occur rarely and only to preserve the true and fair view. The effect of such departures should be disclosed and explained. Auditors should ensure that significant departures are disclosed and to the extent that their concurrence is stated or implied, justify them.

   The Companies Act requires that such departures are disclosed, explained and the reasons for the departure given. If the auditor, after much thought, agrees with the departure he must ensure that the matter is properly disclosed and explained in the accounts but need not mention the matter in his report. If he does not approve the departure then he must qualify his report.

4. The SSAPs and FRSs have some legal backing. The Companies Act has included some specific items included in SSAPs notably on accounting principles and stock. In *Lloyd Cheyham* v *Littlejohn* 1985, the judge stated that SSAP 2 was very strong evidence as to what is the proper standard and unjustified departure from it would be a breach of duty.

   The Companies Act 1989 requires a statement concerning conformity with Accounting Standards in the statement of accounting policies.

5. This chapter summarises the auditors duties in respect of each current Accounting Standard. Each Accounting Standard is very detailed and the best practice is to have a detailed check list for each Accounting Standard and apply it on all audits. I have given the main points only

SSAP 1 – Acounting for associated companies

6. The auditor should:

   a. Consider if the companies consolidated as associated companies come within the Definition in the Standard.

   b. Consider if any other companies in which the group has share holdings should properly be treated as associated companies.

   c. Determine that income from each associated company is properly brought into the consolidated financial statement.

d. Determine that the investing company's share of the net assets of the associated companies are properly brought into the consolidated balance sheet.

Note that there are very detailed descriptions of how c and d are to be done and how to deal with special situations such as extraordinary items and non co-terminous accounts.

The Companies Act 1989 introduced the concept of subsidiary *undertakings*. In some circumstances an associated company in SSAP 1 terms could be regarded as a subsidiary undertaking and would need to be consolidated. This matter is considered further in the chapter on groups.

SSAP 2 – Disclosure of accounting policies

7. The auditor should:
   a. Determine that the accounts have been prepared on the basis of the fundamental accounting concepts: going concern, accruals, consistency and prudence.
   b. Ensure that if there are any departures from the fundamental concepts these are justified and have been fully explained.
   c. Identify those accounting policies (eg depreciation method, stock and work in progress, consolidation policies etc) which have been followed for dealing with items which are material or critical in determining profit or loss for the year and in stating the financial position.
   d. Ensure that all these policies have been clearly and fairly explained in the notes to the accounts.

SSAP 3 – Earnings per share

8. The definition of Earnings per share has changed in FRS 3 paragraph 25 and the auditor should ensure that EPS is properly calculated in accordance with FRS 3 as 'the profit in pence attributable to each equity share, based on the profit (or consolidated profit in the case of a group) of the period after tax, minority interests and extraordinary items and after deducting preference dividends and other appropriations in respect of preference shares, divided by the number of equity shares in issue and ranking for dividend in respect of the period'. This is a different definition from that in SSAP 3 and has caused some consternation in investment circles. This area is controversial and students should examine articles in the magazines and press on the subject.

9. The auditor should:
   - ensure that earnings per share has been correctly calculated.
   - ensure that the prescribed calculations and disclosures re dilutions of capital have been followed
   - ensure that EPS has been properly shown on the Profit and Loss Account.
   - if another version of EPS has been used ensure that para 25 of FRS 3 has been followed and both that and the orthodox version are given.
   - ensure that the basis of calculation has been properly shown on the Profit and Loss Account or in the notes.

SSAP 4 – The accounting treatment of government grants

10. The auditor should:

    a. Identify any government grants related to fixed assets received or receivable in the period under review.

    b. Ensure that all such grants have been properly treated in accordance with the standard. This means that grants related to fixed assets should be credited to revenue over the expected useful life of the asset. This may be achieved by reducing the net cost of the fixed asset by the amount of the grant or by treating the amount of the grant as a deferred credit, a portion of which is transferred to revenue annually.

SSAP 5 – Accounting for value added tax

11. The auditor should ensure that:

    a. Turnover shown in the profit and loss account excludes VAT on taxable outputs.

    b. *Irrecoverable* VAT allocable to fixed assets and to other items disclosed separately in published accounts should be included in their cost where practicable and material.

    Clearly the auditor will also see that the VAT is properly treated throughout and that the legal requirements have been properly dealt with.

SSAP 8 – The treatment of taxation under the imputation system in the accounts of companies

12. The auditor should:

    a. Ensure all taxation items relevant to the standard have been properly identified and quantified. Provisions may be required for many items.

    b. Ensure that the taxation charge in the profit and loss account shows separately:

    i. the amount of UK Corporation tax specifying the separate items of tax on the income of the year, tax attributable to franked investment income, irrecoverable ACT and relief for overseas taxation;

    ii. total overseas taxation relieved and unrelieved.

    c. Ensure outgoing dividends are shown net, ie without ACT or attributable tax credit.

    d. Ensure incoming dividends from UK resident companies (F.1.1) are included gross, ie as cash received plus tax credit.

    e. Ensure that dividends proposed should be included in current liabilities (net) and that the associated ACT should be included as a current tax liability.

    f. Ensure that ACT on proposed dividends if recoverable should be treated by deduction from deferred tax account or if there is no deferred tax account, as a deferred asset.

    g. Determine if any ACT is irrecoverable. This can be a source of disagreement.

SSAP 9 – Stock and work in progress

13. This very important standard is discussed further in the chapter on the audit of stock and work in progress. Although the standard specifies precisely the methods of stock valuation to be followed, the methods still leave room for differences of opinion. For example, overheads should be included in production costs based upon the *normal* level of activity. Auditors and management may well differ on the meaning of normal in any

given situation. Stock and work in progress are usually key figures in accounts and the auditor needs to be especially vigilant in this area.

SSAP 12 – Accounting for depreciation

14. The standard is fairly straight forward but leaves scope for disagreement between auditor and management on such matters as useful life and the recoverability of unamortised cost.

15. The auditor should ensure:

   a. Provision for depreciation of fixed assets having a finite useful economic life should be made by allocating the cost (or revalued amount), less estimated residual values of the assets as fairly as possible to the periods expected to benefit from their use.

   b. Where there is a revision of the estimated useful life of an asset following regular reviews the unamortised cost should be charged over the revised remaining useful economic life.

   c. Where assets are revalued in the financial statements the provision for depreciation should be based on the revalued amount and current estimate of remaining useful life, with disclosure in the year of change, of the effect of the revaluation, if material.

   d. That for each major class of depreciable asset, there are disclosed the depreciation methods used, the useful economic lives or depreciation rates used, total depreciation for the period and the gross amount of depreciable assets and the related accumulated depreciation.

SSAP 13 – Accounting for research and development

16. The auditor should ensure that:

   a. The cost of fixed assets acquired or constructed in order to provide facilities for research and development over a number of accounting periods should be capitalised and written off over their useful life.

   b. Other expenditure on pure and applied research (as defined in the Standard) should be written off in the year of expenditure.

   c. Development expenditure (as defined) should be written off except in the circumstances specified in the standard. If development costs are deferred they should be amortized on the basis of sales or use of the product or process. Deferred expenditure should be reviewed each year and if in doubt written off immediately. It should not then be reinstated.

   d. Movements and balances of deferred development should be fully disclosed. Deferred development expenditure should be separately disclosed and should not be included in current assets. The accounting policy adopted should be fully explained.

   e. The total amount of research and development expenditure charged in the profit and loss account should be disclosed, analysed between the current year's expenditure and amounts amortised from deferred expenditure. This applies only to public companies who are 10 times as large as medium sized companies as defined in the Act.

   Clearly any expenditure regarded as development expenditure and deferred should have the closest attention of the auditor.

SSAP 15 – Accounting for deferred tax

17. This standard requires that the auditor:

   a. Ensures that any deferred tax is computed under the liability method (ie calculated at the rate of tax that it is estimated will be applicable when the timing differences reverse).

   b. Should ensure that tax deferred or accelerated by the effect of *timing* differences should be accounted for to the extent that it is probable that a liability or asset will crystallise. It should not be accounted for if it is probable (because of the continuing nature of the enterprise) that a liability or asset will not crystallise.

   c. Should ensure that whether deferred tax liabilities or assets will or will not crystallise is based on reasonable assumptions. This is clearly a challenge to the auditor.

   d. Should ensure that all relevant information is taken into account up to the date of approval of the accounts by the board.

   e. Ensure full disclosure of deferred tax matters is made in the accounts and notes as detailed in the standard.

The after-tax profit is important as it is used in the calculation of earnings per share and the price earnings ratio. It is vital that the auditor is satisfied with the treatment of deferred tax.

SSAP 17 – Accounting for post balance sheet events

18. This SSAP is a fruitful source for questions in auditing papers. There is some scope for disagreement between auditor and management. There is a special difficulty for an auditor in that he has to be sure that all post balance sheet events have been reviewed by him and their impact on the accounts (if they are adjusting events) considered. See Chapter 33.

SSAP 18 – Accounting for contingencies

19. Contingencies can be a problem for an auditor in that:

   a. He has to be sure that *all* contingencies have been considered.

   b. Proper treatment according to the standard has been made (to accrue, to disclose or to ignore?)

   c. Contingencies involve estimates.

   d. Auditor and management may disagree.

   See also Chapter 33.

SSAP 19 – Accounting for investment properties

20. This SSAP concerns investment properties which are defined in the standard as interests in land and buildings which:

   a. are complete;

   b. are held for their investment potential with rental income being negotiated at arm's length.

It excludes properties occupied by the company itself or another company in the group.

Note that SSAP 19 was amended by SSAP 19A in July 1994.

21. The auditor should ensure that:

   a. Investment properties are *not* depreciated in accordance with SSAP 12 except lease-holds which should be depreciated especially if the lease period if 20 years or less.

   b. Investment properties should be included in the balance sheet at their open market value.

   c. The names of persons making the valuation, their qualifications and the basis of valuation should be disclosed.

   d. Changes in value should be taken to investment revaluation reserve and not to profit and loss. If the reserve becomes negative, it should then be written off to profit and loss.

SSAP 20 – Foreign currency translation

22. The auditor should ensure that:

   For individual companies:

   a. Each asset, liability, revenue and cost arising from a transaction in a foreign currency is translated into the local currency at the exchange rate in operation at the date on which the transaction occurred. If the rates do not fluctuate significantly, average rates may be used.

   b. At each balance sheet date, monetary assets and liabilities should be translated using the closing (year end) rate or rates fixed under the terms of the relevant transactions.

   c. All exchange gains and losses should be reported as part of the profit or loss from ordinary activities unless they arise out of extraordinary transactions.

SSAP 21 – Accounting for leases and hire purchase contracts

23. The auditor should ensure that:

   a. A finance lease (as defined) is recorded in the balance of a lessee as an asset and as an obligation to pay future rentals.

   b. Rental payments under finance leases are allocated between the finance charge and a reduction of the obligation. Finance charges in successive periods should recognise that the obligation is reducing.

   c. The asset is depreciated over the shorter of the lease term and its useful life.

   d. Hire purchase contracts are treated similarly but the asset should be depreciated over its useful life.

   e. Rentals under operating leases (as defined) are charged on a straight line basis over the lease term unless some more rational basis is appropriate.

   f. In the books of the lessor, a finance lease is recorded as a debtor.

   g. The total gross earnings under the finance lease (or HP contract) are allocated to successive periods to give a constant periodic return on the net cash investment in each period.

   h. Assets held for use in operating leases by a lessor are recorded as fixed assets and depreciated over their useful lives.

   i. Rental income from operating leases is recognised on a straight line basis or more rational basis.

j. A manufacturer or dealer lessor does not recognise any selling profit under an operating lease.

k. The detailed disclosure requirements of the standard are fully complied with.

Normally the leases can be categorised into finance or operating leases by the terms of the agreement.

SSAP 22 – Accounting for goodwill

24. The auditor should ensure that:

a. No amount is attributed to non-purchased goodwill in the balance sheets of companies or groups.

b. Any amount attributed to purchased goodwill is the difference between the fair value of the consideration and the aggregate of the fair values of the separable net assets.

c. Purchased goodwill is not carried in the balance sheet as a permanent item. It should be written off immediately to reserves.

d. Negative goodwill should be credited directly to reserves. Purchased goodwill may instead be amortised over its useful economic life. Note that goodwill purchased will decline and be replaced by non-purchased goodwill (eg old customers leave and are replaced by new ones).

e. Full disclosure is made.

This standard is unlikely to cause disagreements between auditor and management.

UITF Abstract 3 deals with the treatment of goodwill on disposal of a business. Situations occur when A PLC acquires B Ltd and writes off the goodwill on acquisition against reserves. When the B Ltd is sold again for a consideration which includes goodwill, Abstract 3 requires that accounting for the profit or loss on sale should include the purchased goodwill. Thus the effect of the two transactions of a purchase and sale goes through the Profit and Loss Account.

SSAP 24 – Accounting for pension costs

25. This SSAP was issued early in 1989. Its provisions are highly technical and very detailed. An auditing manual is not the place to summarise the provisions.

Where a client company provides pensions for its current or former employees, whether the scheme is contractural or ex-gratia and whether the scheme is funded or not, the company needs to account in accordance with the standard. The auditor should have a check list to see that compliance with the standard has occurred.

26. UITF Abstract 6 deals with post-retirement benefits other than pensions.

SSAP 25 – Segmental reporting

27. The Companies Act 1985 Schedule 4 para 55 requires all companies to show in the notes:

a. if the company had (in the directors' opinion) two or more substantially different classes of business then

  – turnover attributable to each class

  – profit or loss attributable to each class

b. if the company had supplied two or more substantially different markets
   - turnover from each market.

SSAP 25 goes further and requires analyses of geographical segments (turnover, profit and net assets). Segments can be defined in relation to turnover by origin (supplied from) and destination (supplied to).

These requirements apply only to public companies and companies which are ten times the size of medium sized companies.

This standard and the Act are somewhat vague and the auditor's task is not clear cut. Obviously the auditor has to have audit evidence that the Standard and the Act have been complied with or report the contrary. However, if the directors do decide that the two areas of activity are significantly different and require segmental reporting then the auditor must be satisfied that the sums are correctly done.

FRS 1 – Cash flow statements

28. This standard was issued in September 1991. It does not apply to small companies (as defined) or wholly owned subsidiaries.

    The auditor's duty is to see that a cash flow statement is included where one is required, that the standard is followed in the preparation of the statement and that the figures are all correctly taken from the other financial statements and the records.

FRS 2 – Accounting for subsidiary undertakings

29. This FRS is dealt with in the chapter on group accounts.

FRS 3 – Reporting financial performance

30. This accounting standard has had a major impact on all annual reports and accounts. Auditors need to have evidence that all its provisions have been properly applied.

31. Specific problem areas for auditors may be:
    - ensuring all gains and losses are included in the financial statements for the period either in the Profit and Loss Account or the Statement of Total Recognised Gains and Losses.
    - ensuring appropriate division of results between continuing operations, acquisitions (as a component of continuing operations) and discontinued operations. The minimum disclosure level is of turnover and operating profit. Where an analysis between these activities includes interest and /or tax the method of allocation and the underlying assumptions must be disclosed.
    - ensuring only income and costs related to discontinued operations are included under the heading of discontinued operations. Any reorganisation or restructuring of continuing operations as a result of a sale or terminations should be treated as a part of continuing operations.
    - ensuring that discontinued operations should not include any operation unless there is a binding sale agreement or a detailed formal plan for termination from which the reporting entity cannot realistically withdraw.
    - ensuring all exceptional items are identified, divided into those related to discontinuing operations and continuing operations, disclosed and described. FRS 3 Sections 20 items (profits or losses on sales, terminations, fundamental reorganisations etc)

should be shown on the face of the Profit and Loss Account after operating profit and before interest.

- ensuring profits or losses on disposals of assets are shown as the differences between proceeds and net carrying amount.

- ensuring that the primary statement: Statement of Total Recognised Gains and Losses is included.

- ensuring a note is present reconciling the opening and closing totals of shareholders funds of the period.

FRS 4 – Capital instruments

32. This FRS is very technical and beyond the scope of a general work on auditing.

FRS 5 – Reporting the substance of transactions

33. This FRS requires transactions to be recorded, accounted for and disclosed in accordance with their substance rather than their legal form. In fact this is an old accounting convention and has been dealt with in a number of SSAPs including SSAP 21 *Accounting for leases and hire purchase contracts.* However FRS 5 deals with a number of very technical situations like quasi-subsidiaries which are also beyond the scope of a general work on auditing.

FRS 6 – Acquisitions and mergers

34. This FRS is concerned with determining if new business combinations are mergers or acquisitions and the appropriate methods of accounting for them. Clearly these are not everyday issues for auditors but many take-overs/mergers do occur and the auditors must ensure that the provisions of FRS 6 are followed in accounting for the new combination.

FRS 7 – Fair values in acquisition accounting

35. This FRS is dealt with in Chapter 47.

FRS 8 – Related party disclosures

36. This FRS is dealt with in Chapter 55.

Summary

37. a. Auditors are expected to ensure Accounting Standards are observed.

   b. Departures from Accounting Standards may occur to preserve the true and fair view. Auditors must consider all departures and ensure they are disclosed and explained. If they disagree with the departure then they must qualify their report. If they agree they must justify but need make no mention in their report.

   c. Details of auditor duties re Accounting Standards are summarised.

Points to note

38. Students are expected to know the SSAPs and FRSs when sitting auditing examinations.

Case study for Chapter 36

Trying plc are desperately trying to fight off a hostile takeover by Goth plc. In the attempt to fight the takeover the company have turned to creative accounting to raise profits in the current year.

They have engaged in substantial research and development on a new product Hedonite which they hope to sell in the USA. They have several investment properties in the London area, one of these was acquired in the year and is held on a lease of 60 years. They have received a large investment grant for an investment made in Scotland two years before. They have contracted to buy a substantial amount of a commodity in twelve months time. Prices of this commodity have collapsed on world markets.

They own a ship which has fallen into disrepair but which will shortly need its Lloyds certificate. They have just agreed to settle a substantial product liability claim in the USA but have as yet paid no money. They have been forced to write down the value of a large stock of oil products in a division which is to be reduced to skeleton trading only.

They do not depreciate the permanent way or rolling stock on their private railway in Venezuela. The company do not this year pay corporation tax due to timing differences on capital investment but have paid ACT on dividends.

They intend to close down the hotel division which has been and is still loss making.

Discussion

Consider:

a. How the group may raise profits by adopting accounting policies which give the highest possible short term profits.

b. How the group may raise profits in the short term by adopting accounting policies or dealing with items in contravention off the Accounting Standards.

c. What auditing activities may detect the contraventions in b.

Student self testing questions *Questions with answers apparent from the text*

1. a. What do Accounting Standards try to do? (1)
    b. What responsibilities have qualified accountants towards the Accounting Standards. (2)
    c. What rules apply to departures and auditors? (3)

Exercises

1. Discuss the auditors responsibilities in the following situations:
    a. Client A plc, has not included the group's share of an associated company's extraordinary item in its consolidated profit and loss account.
    b. B Ltd, a department store has not included stock in its statement of accounting policies.
    c. C PLC has calculated EPS as net profit after tax on continuing operations excluding extraordinary items.
    d. D plc has accounted for government grants by means of a deferred credit and has included the deferred credit in shareholders funds.
    e. E Ltd has included VAT on customers' accounts in debtors.

f. F plc has included the profit on sale of its factory in extraordinary items. It has built and is occupying a new factory. The move involved some redundancy costs which it has not disclosed.

g. G Ltd has ACT recoverable and a deferred tax account. The ACT recoverable has been shown as a deferred asset.

h. H plc has some redundant stocks. These have been valued at realisable value without taking account of sales commission.

i. I plc, a civil engineering contractor has included in turnover the estimated value of work done on a very large overseas contract. The contract was very keenly priced and some 8% of the contract has been completed.

j. J PLC has omitted a Statement of Total Recognised Gains and Losses from its accounts on the grounds that all gains and losses except the immediate write off goodwill arising on its acquisition of JJ PLC have gone through the Profit and Loss Account.

k. K plc is an engineering company with numerous items of plant. In the past plant at the Willenhall factory has been depreciated by the reducing balance method although the other factories have used the sum of digits method. The Willenhall items have been brought into line with the rest of the factories this year but no disclosure of this fact has been made.

l. L plc, a consumer electronics company, have five major development projects on hand. All of these have been treated under the deferral method. The company is going through a thin time with regard to sales and has liquidity problems.

m. M plc has a large transfer to deferred tax this year.

n. N plc has sold a piece of surplus land adjacent to its factory after date for 30% more than its book value.

o. O Ltd has guaranteed the overdraft of Oo Ltd, a customer, to ensure continuity of sales to that customer. No note to this effect appears in the accounts as the directors say that the possibility of payment is unlikely but not remote and disclosure would tell PP Ltd, another customer, about the relationship and cause PP Ltd to withdraw their custom.

p. P plc is a tour operator and also owns a block of flats at Bournemouth which it lets to holiday makers. The block is depreciated on the straightline basis per SSAP 12.

Examination question *(Answer begins on page 553)*

1. Burghley Industries plc is a company with divisions in several parts of the United Kingdom. For several years, it has received regional development grants in respect of some of its capital expenditure.

    Required:

    a. State how these grants should be treated in the financial statements.　　(5 marks)

    b. Tabulate the steps you would take in order to verify the receipt of these grants.

    (6 marks)

    c. If the directors of Burghley Industries plc decided to credit the whole of the grants to the profit and loss account in the current period, what action (if any), would you take?　　(4 marks)

    (AAT) (Total 15 marks)

Examination questions without answers

2. You are the audit senior in charge of the audit of Rosanna Spearman (Industrial) Limited. You have been informed of the following occurrences in the year ended 31 December 1988.

    Required:

    State how each item should be treated in the financial statements, the authority for your advice, and any additional audit considerations that are applicable.

    a. Contributions made by the company to the company self-administered pension scheme totalling £175,000. (4 marks)

    b. During the year a business was acquired and goodwill of £500,000 was purchased. (4 marks)

    c. Shortly after the year-end the company started to incur costs totalling £1,397,000 on the closure of one of its two factories. (4 marks)

    d. The company guaranteed the sum of £35,000 borrowed by one of the directors from a local bank to enable him to purchase a boat. (3 marks)

    (AAT J 89) (Total 15 marks)

3. During the year under audit, Millhouse plc decided to change its method of calculating depreciation on machinery from a reducing balance method to a revaluation method. This is fully reported by the company in the accounts for publication presented to you for audit.

    As auditor, what would you do in connection with this change in the accounting method? *(LCC 87) (14 marks)*

4. You are the audit manager of Gowest Youngman plc ('Gowest'), a company registered in Scotland, which trades mainly outwith the UK both on its own account and through its wholly-owned Madalian subsidiary, Goeast Oldgal Ltd.

    The investment in the subsidiary, which was acquired at the beginning of Gowest's current financial year, is included in Gowest's Balance Sheet at £1,500,000. The Madalian currency has over the last two years devalued by approximately 15% per annum against sterling.

    Required:

    1. Explain, in rfespect of foreign currency balances and transactions, the audit considerations relating to the following audit objectives:

        a. Completeness   b. Accuracy   c. Valuation   d. Disclosure

    2. Specify, in relation to the audit of the company and group accounts of Gowest:

        a. the foreign exchange concerns to be addressed in the audit of the investment in, and consolidation of, its Madalian subsidiary; and

        b. the audit work you would carry out to deal with these concerns.

    (ICAS 1995)

5. In its annual accounts, a company states its 'Accounting policies'.

    Required

    a. What should an auditor look for in reviewing the client's accounting policies. (9 Marks)

    b. How far might the results of the review of the client's accounting policies affect the audit and audit report? (6 Marks)

    (LCCI 92) (Total 15 marks)

6. You are in charge of the audit of The Varden Lock Company Limited for the year ended 30 September 1990. Recently you have been informed of the following occurrences by the Managing Director:

a. On 25 October 1990 a debtor who owed the company £50,000 at the year end was declared bankrupt. It is not expected that the receiver will pay a dividend to the unsecured creditors. The balance is part of the total debtor balance of £650,000;

b. A lease has been entered into during the year. It is a five year lease of equipment at £75,000 per year. The total lease payments (less a finance charge) have been capitalised, the costs being written off on a straight line basis over 6 years:

c. An actuarial review of the Company's occupational pension scheme has revealed that the scheme is overfunded. The directors have therefore decided to take a 'Pension Holiday', with no payments being made for the next three years and no charges being made to the profit and loss account for the same period.

Required:

Discuss each of these points and advise as to how they should be treated, referring where appropriate to the relevant legislation or Statement of Standard Accounting Practice. In addition state any other information that you might require before giving a definitive answer.

(15 Marks)

(AAT 90)

Particular audits

1. This section considers the audit problems of particular audit clients. Chapter 37 describes the preliminaries required on all audits and concludes with a note on the effect of client size on the relative audit emphasis to be placed on vouching, systems reliance and analytical review.

2. Small companies present special problems which are discussed in Chapter 38 and the relative emphasis to be placed on vouching in small (and other) companies is discussed in Chapter 39.

3. Specialised audits are discussed in Chapters 40 and 41, the audit of Local Authorities in Chapter 42 and Accountant's Reports in Chapter 43.

37 The first audit

Introduction

1. Usually when audit firms are appointed as auditors to an enterprise, they remain auditors for many years. In the first year after appointment they have to set up the permanent file and make themselves familiar with the client and its history. Subsequently, the audit will be easier as much of the information necessary as background to the audit will already be on file subject to review and updating.

   Hence, the first audit will be of particular importance and will take rather longer and use more experienced staff than later audits.

Stages in the first audit

2. These are as follows:

   a. Before accepting an audit engagement an accountant should first consider whether or not he can take on the work from an ethical, legal and practical point of view. The ethical considerations have been dealt with in Chapter 8. As an example, an accountancy firm whose senior partner has been a director of the proposed client for some years, could not accept the audit, even if the partner resigned as a director.

   The legal considerations have been dealt with in Chapter 3. As an example an unqualified accountant who was not recognised by the Department of Trade could not become auditor of a company.

   The practical considerations concern whether or not the auditor has the physical resources to carry out the audit satisfactorily. The problems that might arise here include the size of the client in relation to the audit firm. Ford Motors may be too much for a small firm in downtown Walsall. Other problems include geographical location and the need for special knowledge for example, of computers or the special nature of the client's trade, and bunching of client year ends.

b. **Professional etiquette**. If the organisation has an auditor who is ceasing to act, ie one is replacing another accountant, then the professional bodies require the new auditor to communicate with the previous auditor. The detail of this procedure is dealt with in paragraph 3.

c. **Confirmation of Appointment**. The new auditor must confirm that he has been properly and legally appointed. He does this by examining the minute books of meetings at which he was appointed and placing a copy of the appropriate minute on his new permanent file. In companies the minutes will be of the company in general meeting or in some cases of the directors.

d. **Letter of Engagement**. In companies, the auditor's work is laid down by the Companies Acts but even in these cases the auditor may be asked to perform additional work, perhaps in the areas of taxation, accountancy, systems, etc. In partnerships, the work to be performed by the auditor must be a matter of agreement between the partners and the auditor. The letter of engagement sets out the agreement between the auditor and his client. This matter has been dealt with in Chapter 9.

When and if the first four matters have been dealt with the auditor can commence work.

e. The *permanent file* should then be set up. This should contain the items detailed in Chapter 17 on working papers.

In addition, the following work should be done to complete the file:

i. Review the business, its industry, markets, customers, processes, personnel, etc.

ii. If the company is a member of a group, determine the group structure and the trading and financial arrangements between the client and other group members.

iii. If the company has related company relationships or is in common ownership with other companies, research the trading and financial arrangements.

iv. Obtain a copy of the company's file at Companies House. A complete copy can now be obtained on microfiche.

v. Determine the business interests, both past and present, of the client management. This information can be obtained by interview and by file searches of companies who have directors in common.

vi. Determine if there are any unusual clauses in the Memorandum and Articles, past qualified audit reports, unusual accounting policies, dependence on single suppliers or customers, important franchising or royalty agreements.

f. Tour the company's premises, noting the nature of the business and any special difficulties which might arise in Accounting or Valuation. The sort of difficulties which might occur which would be noted in the first visit would be assessing quantity and value of stock and work in progress in manufacturing or chemical process industries. On this tour opportunity can be taken of meeting the organisation's officers and senior staff.

g. Make a note of important dates, eg dates of directors, partners, and company meetings, date of interim accounts, final accounts, dividend payments, etc.

h. *Risk assessment.* SAS 300 requires the auditor to:

- obtain an understanding of the accounting and internal control systems sufficient to plan the audit and develop an effective audit approach
- use professional judgement to assess the components of audit risk and to design audit procedures to ensure it is reduced to an acceptably low level.

On the first audit, these requirements are particularly important.

i. Prepare an *audit* plan.

j. Prepare a *time budget* and *allocate staff*.

The first audit can now be commenced.

Professional etiquette

3. All professional bodies have codes of conduct governing the relationship between members of the profession and their brother and sister members and the relationship with their clients. Some of the ethical code is explicit and some is implicit but usually understood by members as a consequence of their professional training and experience.

One of the more well known aspects of the ethical code concerns changes in auditor. Organisations can change their auditors at will providing they follow the statutory rules and the particular rules governing the organisation. In the case of a company, this means the Companies Acts and the Company's Articles of Association. However, the professional bodies, eg the Institutes of Chartered Accountants and the Chartered Association of Certified Accountants have special rules which their members follow. These are:

a. A member (of an accounting body) on being asked to act as auditor should request the *client's permission* to communicate with the previous auditor (if there is one).

b. If this permission is refused, refuse the appointment as auditor.

c. If permission is given *request in writing*:

all the information which ought to be made available to him /her to enable him/her to decide whether or not he/she is prepared to accept the appointment.

d. A member receiving such a request should, in turn, request the *client's permission* to discuss the client's affairs with the proposed new auditor.

e. If this permission is *refused*, the old auditor will inform the new auditor who will then refuse the appointment.

f. If permission is given then the old auditor:

   i. Discloses to the proposed auditor all information which he will need to decide whether or not to accept the appointment.

   ii. Discuss freely with the new auditor all matters relevant to the appointment which the new auditor will need to know.

The reason for this rigmarole is:

i. It is a matter of courtesy between professional men.

ii. It enables the proposed auditor to know if it is proper for him to accept the appointment.

iii. It safeguards the position of the retiring auditor.

iv. It protects the shareholders and others interested in the Final Accounts.

Here is an example of a professional etiquette letter:

Letter to be sent to existing auditors on proposed change of professional appointment (professional etiquette)

> Messrs. Little, Small & Co.   24 June 19-9
>
> Dear Sirs,
>
> **Going Places Limited**
>
> We have been invited to accept nomination as auditors to the above company and have been informed that your firm currently acts in that capacity.
>
> We should be grateful if you would let us know whether there is any information of which we should be aware when deciding whether or not to accept this nomination.
>
> Yours faithfully,
>
> Bigg, Large & Co.

Preceding financial statements

4. The new auditor will obtain copies of at least the previous five years' financial statements. This will be important because:

    a. Analytical review includes absolute and ratio comparisons with previous Accounts.

    b. Previous year's figures form the opening position for a current year's Accounts.

    c. Comparative figures must be shown.

    d. Previous years' Accounts may have qualified auditor's reports.

    This matter is dealt with in Chapter 35 in that part of the manual dealing with auditors' reports.

Summary

5. a. The first audit of a new client is a specially important one as there is much work to be done which will not need to be repeated, but will require review and updating in later audits.

    b. The main work before commencing the detailed work of the audit is:

        i.   Communicate with retiring auditor *if any*.

        ii. Confirm *appointment* is valid.

        iii. Send and obtain acknowledgement of the *letter of engagement*.

        iv. Set up the *permanent file* – in an examination give the headings of the contents.

        v.   Tour the enterprise and meet directors and staff.

        vi. Note important dates.

        viii. Examine accounting and control systems and make risk assessments.

        vii. Prepare the audit programme.

        ix. Prepare time budget and allocate staff.

    c. The rules of professional conduct require proposed new auditors to communicate in writing with the previous or existing auditors.

Points to note

6. a. Much of the work set out in paragraph 2(e) is directed towards:

      i. determining if there are any related parties;

      ii. identifying areas of audit risk.

  b. Professional Etiquette. The communication process between existing and proposed auditors is rigidly adhered to in practice. Note that it is a rule of the professional bodies, not of statute.

  c. Before commencing any audit, it is necessary to decide upon the audit approach. In particular, this means determining the relative emphasis to be placed on vouching, reliance on systems and analytical review. Where the emphasis is to be placed depends on the size of the enterprise (small companies have simpler systems and fewer controls) and its nature (in the audit of a trust fund, all transactions would be vouched).

Case study for Chapter 37

Honest & Co. (gross fees £60,000) have been introduced to George Brash, Director and principal shareholder in George Brash Ltd., manufacturers of kitchen units. The introduction has been arranged by the bank manager who wishes the company to appoint a qualified accountant and registered auditors instead of Cyril who is not qualified. George agrees to this and meets Honest. At the interview Brash talks the whole time as if the sole task of the auditor is to minimise his tax liabilities. He mentions casually that he had just received a letter from the Inspector of Taxes asking him if his tax return is complete in all particulars. George also states that the company have 30 employees, a turnover of £600,000 and an audit fee of £3,000 which he considers high but Cyril did save him a lot of tax.

It turns out that both George and Honest are members of the Stuffs Golf Club but have never met. George is also an uncle of Gladys, Honest's newly appointed junior typist.

The company's last accounts were for the year ending 31.3.-6 and the interview was on 28.5.-6.

It appears that the company keep excellent records using a commercial micro computer package.

Discussion

  a. Go through Honest's routines for considering acceptance of new clients. Should George Brash be taken on?

  b. Draft the letter to Cyril.

  c. Assuming Honest & Co. accept the audit, outline the procedures to be gone through before starting the audit proper.

  d. Prepare an outline audit plan emphasising the timing aspects.

Student self testing questions *Questions with answers apparent from the text*

1. a. What work should be done before commencing the detail work on a new audit? (2)

  b. List the stages of a professional etiquette exchange of letters. (3)

  c. What work should be carried out on previous accounts? Explain the purposes of the work in each case. (4)

Examination question *(Answer begins on page 553)*

1. The firm of Lee & Co. was re-appointed as auditor of Eastern Engineering PLC at the last annual general meeting. Subsequently, however, Eastern Engineering PLC has grown considerably as a result of acquiring other companies and Lee & Co., has decided that it does not have the resources to audit the enlarged group.

   Required:

   a. How can Lee & Co. resign its appointment before the next annual general meeting? What statement must accompany the resignation. (3 marks)

   b. What actions must the company take on receipt of the notice of resignation? (2 marks)

   c. How may the casual vacancy arising be filled and what procedures are necessary before the company's next annual general meeting at which the appointment will be confirmed? (3 marks)

   d. The new auditor will undoubtedly contact Lee & Co. to ascertain certain matters. Draft the letter which the new auditor should send to Lee & Co. (4 marks)

   e. What actions should Lee & Co. take on receipt of the letter from the proposed new auditor and what information should be given? What are the reasons for the various procedures involved? (6 marks)

   f. What do you understand by 'the auditor's lien'? Lee & Co's files relating to Eastern Engineering PLC contain many working papers including:

      i. schedules prepared for audit purposes;

      ii. a fixed assets register maintained at the client's request; and

      iii. computations and correspondence relating to corporation tax.

      Discuss the extent to which in normal circumstances they are required to make these documents available to their former client and the new auditor. (7 marks)

      (AAT) (Total 25 marks)

Examination question without answers

2. You have just been appointed as auditor of Bolivar plc. You have discussed the audit within the company's previous auditors who have given you much information about the audit and client as possible.

   Required

   Outline carefully what work you would undertake before your staff begin the first audit.

   (LCCI 92) (12 Marks)

38 Small companies

Introduction

1. Most companies are small. The law allows small businesses to trade with the protection of limited liability. The price of limited liability is compliance with the Companies Act requirements including those for laying and delivering Accounts and for audit.

2.   This chapter considers small companies and includes a historical note, audit requirements, filing requirements and small company qualifications.

Historical notes

3.   Until 1967 most small companies came into the category of exempt private companies. They were exempted from filing their Accounts at Companies House. The Companies Act 1967 abolished this exemption.

4.   The Companies Act 1981 introduced new categories of small and medium-sized companies with *reduced* filing requirements.

5.   The companies Act 1989 changed the rules on small and medium sized companies. See Chapter 5 for details.

6.   New sections of The Companies Act 1985 were inserted by the Companies Act 1985 (Audit Exemption) Regulations 1994. As a result some small companies are exempt form audit. This subject is dealt with in Chapter 43.

Financial statements of small companies

7.   The Companies Act 1985 S.246 and Schedule 8 parts I and II give exemptions to small companies in the *preparation* of the financial statements and the directors' report. These are listed in the schedule and include exemption for giving details of staff and staff remuneration and employee involvement. Financial statements which are prepared using these exemptions can still give a true and fair view.

If a small company takes advantage of these exemptions it must include a statement by the directors above their signatures:

–   that special exemption provisions have been applied

–   and a statement of the grounds on which, in the directors' opinion, the company is entitled to those exemptions

A similar statement is required on the directors' report.

If a small company takes advantage of the exemption then the auditors' report *opinion* section should be:

'In our opinion the financial statements give a true and fair view of the state of the company's affairs as at 31 May 19… and of its profit for the year then ended and have been properly prepared in accordance with the provisions of The Companies Act 1985 applicable to small companies.'

Filing requirements

8.   The Companies Act 1985 S.246 and Schedule 8 part III gives small and medium sized companies the right to file *abbreviated* accounts.

Chapter 5 sets out the definitions of small and medium sized companies and summaries the filing requirements for them.

The procedures are:

a.   Full Accounts must be produced and audited. The auditor must produce the usual audit report.

b.   Where a company takes advantage of the need only to file abbreviated accounts then the balance sheet must contain:

A statement that advantage is taken of the exemptions conferred by schedule I or II.

A statement of the grounds on which in the directors' opinion the company is entitled to those exemptions.

Note that 'grounds' means being small or medium sized.

c. The auditors must then consider whether in their opinion the requirements for exemption are satisfied. If they are not, they must report this to the directors and the company does not proceed further in producing abbreviated Accounts.

d. The auditors should prepare a report to the directors stating whether in the auditor's opinion:

- the company is entitled to the exemptions
- the abbreviated accounts have been properly prepared in accordance with part III of schedule 8.

e. The auditors should also prepare a report to accompany the accounts being filed at Companies House as:

Auditors' report to NBG Limited pursuant to paragraph 24 of Schedule 8 to The Companies Act 1985

We have examined the abbreviated accounts on pages ... to ... together with the financial statements of NBG Limited prepared under S 226 of The Companies Act 1985 for the year ended 31 August 19...

Respective responsibilities of directors and auditors

The directors are responsible for preparing the abbreviated accounts in accordance with Schedule 8 to The Companies Act 1985. It is our responsibility to form an independent opinion as to the company's entitlement to the exemptions claimed on page... and whether the abbreviated accounts have been properly prepared in accordance with the schedule.

Basis of opinion

We have carried out the procedures we considered necessary to confirm, by reference to the audited financial statements, that the company is entitled to the exemptions and that the abbreviated accounts have been properly prepared from those financial statements. The scope of our work for the purpose of this report does not include examining or dealing with events after the date of our report on the full financial statements.

Opinion

In our opinion the company is entitled under sections 246 and 247 of The Companies Act 1985 to the exemptions conferred by Section A (or Section B) of part III of Schedule 8 to that Act, in respect of the year ended..., and the abbreviated accounts on pages ... to... have been properly prepared in accordance with that schedule.

Other information

On ... we reported, as auditors of NBG Limited, to the members on the financial statements prepared under S 226 of The Companies Act 1985 for the year ended... and our audit report was as follows:

(here include the full auditors' report)

Bunkum & Co.	1 Low Street
Registered auditors	Mediumville
23 November 19...	

If the full audit report was qualified (it often is with small companies) then the auditor must include any further material required to understand the qualification. This may not be necessary as qualifications must be fully understandable. However the qualification may refer to a note to the accounts and in that case the note also must be reproduced.

A problem may arise if the company has a turnover of say £2.7 million and the qualification is that evidence is not available that all sales have been included. Clearly the sales could have been over £2.8 million putting the company from the small to the medium sized category. In this case the auditor can only reasonably give a report that the company is a medium-sized one.

Small company audit qualifications

9. a. The auditor needs to obtain the same degree of assurance in order to give an unqualified opinion in both small and large enterprises.

   b. The problem with owner dominated companies and companies where the management can override internal controls is that there may not be evidence of the *completeness* and *accuracy* of the recording transactions.

   In such cases the auditor will usually obtain management assurances as to the completeness and accuracy of recording. These assurances will be in the form of a paragraph in the *letter of representation*. If the auditor has obtained evidence in the form of substantive testing of transactions and analytical review and in particular a review of costs and margins he may well decide that he can accept management's assurances. He will then make *no* reference to either the representations received or the less formal nature of internal control. To do so would imply a qualification and in these cases he is giving an *unqualified* report.

   On the other hand the auditor may conclude that in particular areas the representations and other evidence are insufficient to support an unqualified opinion. For example this might occur where transactions are mostly in cash and there is no regular pattern of costs and margins. Some retailers are like this. If the auditor knows of no reason why an adverse opinion should be given, he may give a 'subject to' opinion specifying in his report his reasons for qualification and the areas and amounts affected by the uncertainty.

   Where it is not possible to identify specific areas of uncertainty or where uncertainty is *pervasive* in the enterprise then a disclaimer is required. In exceptional cases of this type where there is some other evidence available then a 'subject to' qualification mentioning the reservation as the 'completeness and accuracy of recording of transactions.'

Summary

10. a. All companies have the same audit requirements, but some small companies are now exempt.

    b. Small and medium-sized companies need only *file* abbreviated accounts.

    c. Due to the limited internal control in small companies and the possibility of management override auditors may seek management assurances on the completeness and accuracy of accounting records in a letter of representation. This may lead to an unqualified audit report.

Points to note

11. a. Note the changes in the law in the Companies Act 1989 which reduces the burdens of small companies with regard to holding AGMs, laying accounts and annual appointment of auditors.

    b. Note also the change in the rules in the new auditing standard.

    c. However all companies (unless dormant, unlimited and some small companies) need full annual accounts and full audit.

    d. In March 1991, the Auditing Practices committee issued an exposure draft for a proposed guideline on The Audit of Small Businesses. This says nothing really new but is a good summary of the problems of auditing small businesses. Some good points are made and these include:

       i. The close involvement of the proprietor in day to day activities may either increase or decrease the risk of material misstatements being present in the accounts. The active participation of the proprietor will reduce the possibility of staff committing fraud or error but on the other hand the proprietor may himself arrange for misstatements eg by omitting whole transactions such as cash sales.

       ii. An auditor should neither assume that the proprietor is honest nor dishonest but should evaluate all audit evidence with professional detachment.

       iii. There can be internal controls on which the auditor can rely. For example the director may insist on reviewing all documentation before signing cheques prepared by his bookkeeper.

       iv. The major problem is on completeness of record and approaches to this may include:

          – there may be some internal control as for example sequential numbering of invoices

          – correspondence between physical records of 'outs' and sales records

          – correspondence of documents such as time records and job sheets and sales

          – reconciliations of total quantities of goods bought, sold and in stock. This could be done, for example, with a steel stockholder

          – predictive analytical review procedures including gross profit ratios

          – if sufficient time has elapsed since the year end a review of post balance sheet events can be very useful

          – representations by the proprietor could provide at least corroborative evidence.

       v. The Exposure Draft does suggest that qualifying the audit report for completeness will only be required if sufficient assurance does not come from a combination of all the sources of evidence stated above.

    e. The Companies Act 1985 (Accounts of Small and Medium-Sized Enterprises and Publication of Accounts in ECUs) Regulations 1992 allows a slightly abbreviated Profit and Loss Account for small companies. It also allowed companies to set out the amounts in the annual accounts in ECUs as well as sterling. There may instead be an additional copy of the accounts in ECUs. In both cases the exchange rate must be as at the Balance Sheet date and the rate disclosed.

f. Note that small companies can claim some exemptions from the accounting require-
    ments in preparing their accounts – schedule 8: Part I (financial statements) and part
    II (directors' report). Small and medium sized companies can file abbreviated
    accounts – schedule 8 Part III.

Case study for Chapter 38

Winfred Metal Reclamation Ltd. buy scrap metal residues from local companies and
treat the residues to recover the metal which is then sold to other local companies. Some
purchases are made from itinerant scrap merchants. No evidence is available for the
purchase of this scrap which totalled £60,000 in the year ending 30 November 19-6.
However there is no evidence that it is incorrect and a director is willing to give a letter
of representation containing the usual assurances re completeness and validity. The
auditors find all other matter to be satisfactory and records are good.

Figures in the year ending 30.11.-6 are:

	£
Purchases	376,000
Net Profit	24,000
Balance sheet total	121,000
Employees	5

Discussion

a. What addendum should appear on the balance sheet if abbreviated accounts are to
    be filed?
b. Draft the letter from the auditor to the directors.
c. Draft the auditors report on the alternatives of:
    i.   Unqualified report.
    ii. A report qualified only on the purchases.
    iii. A report qualified only on accounting records
    iv. A disclaimer.

Student self testing questions *Questions with answers apparent from the text*

1. a. Define small and medium sized companies. (Chapter 5)
    b. What exemptions are available to such companies? (Chapter 5)
    c. What procedures are required? (8)
    d. Reproduce the special report. (8)
    e. What alternatives are proposed for small companies? (9)

Examination questions without answers

1. The audit of the accounts of small companies creates additional problems for the auditor,
    when compared with auditing the accounts of large companies. Also it has been
    suggested that the statutory audit requirement for small companies should be abolished.
    You are required to:
    a. Briefly discuss the problems of auditing the accounts of small companies. Your
        answer should describe the circumstances where it is possible to give an unqualified
        audit opinion on:

    i.   the balance sheet,

    ii. the profit and loss account.   (7 marks)

b. Briefly consider the extent to which the statutory accounts of small companies and the statutory audit thereof satisfy the needs of the following users of accounts:

    i.   directors of the company,

    ii. shareholders, who are not directors of the company,

    iii. creditors including banks,

    iv the Inland Revenue and Customs & Excise (for VAT).   (6 marks)

c. Discuss the arguments for and against the audit of the accounts of small companies, and give your view on whether the statutory audit of small companies should be abolished.   (12 marks)

(ACCA) (Total 25 marks)

2. It is widely recognised that the way in which audits of small, owner-managed businesses are conducted will, of necessity, be different to those of larger businesses with formal and well developed systems of internal control on which the auditor can place reliance. It is also generally accepted that the most effective practical form of internal control for a small, owner-managed business is the close involvement of the owner-manager.

Requirement

a. Describe and explain, with the use of appropriate examples, the ways in which an owner-manager can exercise control in such a business.

b. Discuss briefly the issues that an auditor would need to consider before planning to place reliance on the 'control' provided by the close involvement of the owner-manager in the running of the business.

c. Discuss the substantive evidence that an auditor may seek to rely upon in order to assure himself as to the completeness of income in a small, owner-managed business. You are to assume that there is no effective internal control upon which the auditor can rely.

(ICAI 95)

39 The vouching audit

Introduction

1. In large company audits, modern economics dictate that the approach will be:

a. Review previous year's experience and background information to identify areas of audit risk so that the audit can be focussed thereon.

b. Review the accounting systems and internal controls.

c. Where audit risk is low and internal control good, minimal testing is required.

d. Where audit risk is high, concentrate resources to gain maximum audit evidence.

e. Conduct an analytical review to obtain audit evidence that the financial statements are both internally consistent and consistent with the auditor's background and environmental knowledge and comply with generally accepted accounting principles.

2. This approach is inappropriate in most small enterprises because:

    a. Sales, margins, assets and liabilities can fluctuate so much that audit risk assessment and analytical review procedures are less effective.

    b. Internal controls are few or ineffective or easily overridden.

    c. The most important determinant of accuracy and completeness of recording of transactions is managerial and proprietorial involvement and supervision.

    d. The small size and small number of transactions allows greater contact with detail by the auditor.

    e. In the majority of very small cases, the auditor also balances subsidiary books (eg bank reconciliation, sales and bought ledger total accounts), enters the nominal ledger, extracts a trial balance and prepares the final accounts.

3. The very small end of a continuum of audit clients from the very small to the very large requires a vouching audit approach. As a client becomes larger the emphasis will change until the approach in paragraph 1 becomes appropriate.

Vouching audit

4. a. **Usage**. Vouching audits are used:

    i. In very small audits when the number of transactions are not too large.

    ii. In audits where internal control is weak or non-existent.

    iii. In certain types of specialised audit such as that of trusts or estates.

    b. Method. The vouching audit involves a consideration of each entry in the books and *vouching* the available evidence to support each entry. The evidence usually consists of documents and papers and should satisfy the auditor that:

    i. The transaction was authorised by management.

    ii. The transaction came within the aims and objects of the organisation.

    iii. The transaction was correctly and adequately described by the entry in the books.

    iv. The entry is correctly incorporated in the Final Accounts.

A comparison of the vouching system approaches

5. As an example we will consider purchases.

    a. **Vouching audit**. The auditor should examine the books in which the purchase invoices are recorded and the file of purchase invoices. Each invoice will be examined and the following details looked for:

    i. The invoice should be addressed to the firm.

    ii. It should at least appear to be an authentic invoice from the supplier.

    iii. The goods should be of a nature relating to the business carried on.

    iv. The invoice should bear the signature or initials of the clerk deputed to check them.

v. The invoice should have attached to it a docket signed by the gate-keeper acknowledging receipt of the goods or bear reference to a goods inwards book or some other evidence that the goods have actually been received.

vi. The entry should be extended into the correct column in the purchase day book or be otherwise correctly coded so that it ends up in the right place in the final accounts. Particular attention should be paid to goods of a capital nature.

vii. The detail relating to VAT and discounts should also be checked.

viii. Calculations and extensions should be checked.

ix. The date should fall in the accounting period.

x. If the invoice date and the date of supply of the goods or services fall in different periods, the auditor must see that the correct treatment has been given to the item in the final accounts.

b. **The risk based audit.**

i. obtain an understanding of the accounting and control systems sufficient to plan the audit and develop an effective audit approach.

ii. use professional judgement to assess the components of audit risk and to design audit procedures to ensure it is reduced to an acceptably low level.

iii. if reliance on an assessment of control risk can be used to reduce the extent of substantive procedures, make a preliminary assessment of control risk for material financial statements assertions (eg that all purchases are included or that no material non-'purchase' items are included), and plan and perform tests of control to support that assessment.

iv. plan and perform appropriate substantive tests (eg examine invoices after date to ensure none relate to the financial year under examination) including analytical reviews (eg assessing gross profit ratio).

v. review the work done to see if there is sufficient audit evidence to determine with reasonable confidence whether the financial statements are free of material misstatement.

Examination papers

6. You should now appreciate that the procedural and vouching audit approaches to an audit are different. However, the precise approach adopted for any given audit will be a matter of judgement depending, as we have seen, on such matters as client size, the degree of internal control applied, and statutory requirements. The necessary information is not always given in examination questions.

Consider the following questions:

'How would you verify the item rents received appearing in the cash book of a limited company?'

The vouching audit approach would give the following answer:

i. Inspect the agreements and lease counterparts noting terms.

ii. Check all rents have been received.

iii. Vouch rent books.

iv. Vouch collectors' accounts with cash banked.

v. Investigate arrears.

vi. Enquire into unlet property.

vii. Verify correct accounting treatment and disclosure.

The risk based audit approach would be like that of paragraph 5b.

In practice the approach would be:

i. obtain an understanding of the accounting and control systems sufficient to plan the audit and develop an effective audit approach

ii. use professional judgement to assess the components of audit risk (inherent risks may be omission of rents, misappropriation of rents, bad debts, etc) and to design audit procedures to ensure it is reduced to an acceptably low level

iii. if reliance on an assessment of control risk can be used to reduce the extent of substantive procedures, make a preliminary assessment of control risk for material financial statements assertions and plan and perform tests of control to support that assessment

iv. plan and perform appropriate substantive tests (eg investigate arrears) including analytical reviews (eg comparing with previous years and known changes to let property and rent reviews)

v. review the work done to see if there is sufficient audit evidence to determine with reasonable confidence whether the financial statements are free of material misstatement.

Reliance on controls or substantive testing?

7. In practice, auditors prefer to rely on systems with compliance testing and with reduced substantive testing. But in areas where controls are weak or not always complied with then substantive testing is applied entirely.

8. Let us consider what we mean by this, by considering an example. In the accounts of Kinver Key Co. Ltd., there is a material item – scrap sales £6,000. The company manufacture steel keys by stamping out the keys from sheets of metal. The scrap is what is left of the steel sheets after the keys have been stamped out from them. The system for dealing with the scrap is found to be as follows:

Scrap Steel is placed by the operatives in a large bin placed in the yard outside the workshop. At intervals, the bin is collected by a local scrap merchant who removes the bin and scrap and leaves an empty bin. The weight is found on the company weighbridge by the gatekeeper who notes the weight in a book kept for that purpose. During the week following each collection the scrap merchant sends a cheque with a statement showing the weight collected, the price and the amount of the cheque. The cashier who also opens the post inspects the statement to see if it is more or less the same amount as usual and pays it in.

9. Now this is not a very strong system because:

a. The weight of scrap taken could be falsified by the collusion of the gatekeeper with the scrap merchants or their driver.

b. There is no check by the cashier that:
   i.   All scrap collections are paid for;
   ii. The scrap weight is correct.
   iii. The scrap price is the current market price.
c. The cashier could misappropriate the cheques.

The reader will readily be able to suggest improvements to the system as it stands, but the system is very weak.

10. For that reason the auditor must seek direct evidence of:
   a. the completeness – all the scrap has been paid for and the receipts properly banked and recorded;
   b. the accuracy – all cheques have been correctly computed from the product of correct weight price;
   c. the validity – the scrap price was the current market one;
   of the figure in the accounts – scrap sales £6,000.

11. He could do this by substantive tests which would include:
   a. Comparing the gatekeeper's record with scrap merchant's statements and vice-versa.
   b. Checking a sample of the calculations.
   c. Verifying that all the statements were complemented by an entry in the cash book of the same amount.
   d. Obtaining a technical estimate of the proportion of scrap which would be obtained from a steel sheet and verifying that the total scrap bore the appropriate relationship to total steel sheets purchased.
   e. Verifying a sample of the prices paid with prices determined from discussion with management, trade sources, the audit assistant's experience with other clients, etc.

   From all these tests it should be possible to substantiate the item in accounts.

Summary

12. a. In planning his audit, an auditor must decide on the relative emphasis to be placed on substantive testing, systems and compliance testing and an analytical review.
    b. In small audits, the substantive testing or vouching audit is more commonly applied.

Case study for Chapter 39

The Bumpkin Group plc is a manufacturer of agricultural equipment. The group have recently sold off a company in a different industry for cash and have invested the proceeds in stock exchange securities. The year-end and final audit are being planned and members of staff briefed for the different sections of the audit.

The item 'investments – quoted £4.2 million' consists of some thirty securities. Investment policy is delegated to the financial director who takes advice from the firm's stockbrokers and makes changes as he sees fit.

The item 'trade creditors £3.9 million' consists of some 250 accounts kept on a micro-computer using a commercial software package.

Discussion

   a. Assess the audit risk in these two items.

   b. Detail the audit work to be done on these two items. When should each item of work be carried out? Discuss approaches and the weight to be given to internal control, substantive testing and analytical review.

   c. What quality of audit staff should be used on each item?

Student self testing questions *Questions with answers apparent from the text*

1. a. Distinguish the methods usable on small and large audits. (1, 2)

   b. When are vouching audits appropriate? (4)

   c. How should a supplier's credit note be vouched? (5)

   d. How should the internal control be assessed in the wages area of a large company? What alternative audit approaches may be possible? (5)

Exercises

1. You are the auditor of the Richville Community Centre. The centre has a large hall and several other lettable rooms. It has, as full time staff, a manager, an assistant manager, a secretary and a bartender who also caters. There are several part-time staff.

   Draft an audit program. The accounts are produced by the manager who also keeps the books.

Examination question *(Answer begins on page 554)*

1. During the course of an audit an auditor examines many documents.

   Required:

   In respect of each of the following documents state:

   i.   its value to the auditor

   ii. the information the auditor would specially look for; and

   iii. the tests he would perform on it.

   a. Vehicle registration document for delivery lorry.   (4 marks)

   b. Suppliers statement.   (5 marks)

   c. Certificate from a building society in respect of an investment by the client.

        (5 marks)

   d. Hire purchase agreement signed by the client for the purchase of office equipment.

        (6 marks)

   e. Property fire insurance policy and renewal date.   (5 marks)

        (AAT)

Examination question without answers

2. You are the auditor of Laura Lyons Fashions Limited. As part of your audit for the year ended 30 June 1992 you examined entries in the payments section of the cash book. Extracts from the cash book read:

Dates	Details	Cheque No.	Gross	VAT	Net
2.4.92	Corporation Tax	107901	25,973.85		25,973.85
5.4.92	Telephone 753-3561	107935	276.85	41.23	235.62
7.4.92	Road Tax H973DBC	107954	100.00		100.00
10.4.92	Local Business Tax	107977	2,935.50		2,935.50
15.4.92	Income Tax and National Insurance contributions for employees	107993	2,635.45		2,635.45
17.4.92	C & E 1/1 to 31/3/92 – VAT	108035	6,392.75		6,392.75
19.4.92	Directors' Expenses	108062	450.00		450.00
21.4.92	Petty Cash	108083	150.00		150.00
24.4.92	Mrs. B. Mann – purchase of 200 shares in Laura Lyons Fashions Limited	108133	560.00		560.00
28.4.92	Wages	108199	7,482.99		7,482.99

Required

For each of the items referred to above, detail the audit work you would carry out to verify the items of expenditure. (Total 20 marks)

(AAT 92)

40 Audits of different types of business

Introduction

1. There are innumerable types of business and all of them have Accounts prepared and most of them have these accounts audited. Ideally students would meet every kind of business in their training but in practice only a few are encountered.

2. Every type of business has its audit problems but the sheer number of different types makes it impossible to discuss these problems in this manual in any other than a general way.

3. Some enterprises, for example Local Authorities or Building Societies are subject to specific *statutory* requirements on conduct of affairs, Accounts preparation and audit.

4. Some enterprises should have their audits conducted in accordance with specific auditing guidelines. These include Charities, Building Societies, Trade Unions and Employers' organisations, Housing Associations, Pension Schemes and Banks. These guidelines are very detailed and giving a detailed account of how to do an audit for all of them would require a manual of unacceptable length. It is unreasonable to expect students to have detailed knowledge of the audit of every type of enterprise and this is not really necessary. For exam purposes it is usually possible to apply a general approach to an audit which will conform to the specialised guidelines giving a general knowledge about enterprises and some imagination.

However the next chapter does give some indications on the audit of specific types of enterprise. This chapter is of a more general nature.

Common approaches

5. The approach to any particular audit will clearly require some modification to any general approach.However there are many ways in which a general pattern can be used in planning any audit.

    These ideas include setting up a permanent file with:

    a. A copy of any statutory material relating to the conduct of the enterprise, its accounts or its audit. For companies this is unnecessary as all auditors know the Companies Act by heart.

    b. A copy of the rules and regulations, constitution or other document governing the specific enterprise. In the case of companies this means the Memorandum and Articles and in a partnership, the agreement.

    c. An engagement letter.

    d. A copy of the minute relating to the appointment of the auditor.

    e. Notes on the background to the enterprise, the industry it is part of, and its history and prospects.

    f. Notes on the internal structure of the enterprise, products, locations, production systems, personnel, management etc.

    g. Copies of all past accounts with notes on accounting policies and significant ratios. Include also any prospectus.

6. The audit will need to be planned with audit risk in mind. The balance of audit approach between reliance on internal control, substantive testing and analytical review will need to be determined and documented.

Specific enterprises

7. The specific approach to a particular audit is a function of the type of business involved. A good approach might be:

    a. **Revenues and Expense.** Consider the kinds of revenue and expense you would expect and the particular problems which might arise in controlling them and recording them.

    b. **Assets and Liabilities.** Consider the kinds of assets and liabilities which are likely to be found and any particular problems which might arise in verifying their existence, ownership, valuation and presentation in the accounts.

    c. **Internal Control.** Consider any special problems which might arise. A likely area is cash receipts.

    d. **Accounting Polices.** Consider any problems of accounting measurement which may affect the accounts.

    e. **Audit risk.** Consider any matters which might give rise to greater than normal audit risk. In some enterprises these might be cash receipts, in others the valuation of stock and work in progress.

    f. Consider any accounting or auditing rules required by statute. For example the audit of Building Societies are governed by the Building Societies Act 1986.

    g. Consider the requirement of any regulatory body. For example the Building Societies Commission or PIA.

h. Consider the form of report which should have the following sections:

- Addressee.
- Financial Statements.
- Auditing standards followed.
- The Audit opinion (which is usually in true and fair terms).
- Any other opinions prescribed by statutory or other requirements (eg Companies Act, Building Societies Act etc).
- Identity of the Auditor.
- Date of the report.

Summary

8. a. Audits can be conducted on the Accounts of any enterprise. All are different and present different auditing problems.

b. All audits should be conducted in accordance with the Auditing Standards and with any relevant statute.

c. A general approach to all audits can be determined.

d. Each audit can present special features in revenues, expenses, assets, liabilities, internal control, accounting polices and audit risks.

Points to note

9. Examiners do not expect detailed knowledge of special sorts of enterprises but do expect imagination from the examinee. The tendency is to a case study approach so that the student can apply general auditing principles to specific cases.

As an example the auditing of a Housing Association may present special features but primarily it is just an audit.The rental income should be verified as in any rent receivable situation. Outgoings can be verified with vouchers and other evidence as in any business. Students with imagination will realise that outgoings should be authorised by the management committee and the authorisation evidenced by a minute. Outgoings must also be within the constitutional powers of the Association.

Case study 1 for Chapter 40

Suburbelec Ltd is a private company owned and directed by Wyre. The company have a shop in the suburbs of Wentown and repair and sell televisions, videos and other electrical and electronic appliances and apparatus.They also sell records and tapes and run a video library. They also offer television and video rentals. The company is heavily indebted to the bank but is reasonably profitable. The company rent the premises on a seven year lease with three years to run.

Discussion

a. Draw up a memorandum detailing:
- types of revenue
- types of expense
- types of asset
- types of liability

- internal control problems
- audit risk areas.

b. List the contents of a permanent audit file for this company.

Case study 2 for Chapter 40

Alan, Bruce, Cheryl and Donna are in a partnership as dental surgeons. Their accounts are prepared for years ending 31st March by Evan a certified accountant. The Partners have requested that this year (year to 31st March 19-7) the accounts should be done as early as possible and should be subject to a full audit.The practice does both national health service and private work. A legally drawn Partnership agreement exists. The Partnership own the freehold of the building in which they carry on their practice. The building is subject to a mortgage. The partners employ four dental nurses, three receptionists, one whom keeps the excellent accounting records.

Discussion

a. Draw up an engagement letter. Evan has not previously agreed one with the partners.

b. Draw up the audit plan in detail.

c. Identify any accounting problems that may occur.

d. Draft an auditor's report assuming all is well and no qualification is necessary.

e. What problems may arise if the audit is to be completed by 30th April 19-7?

Student self testing questions *Questions with answers apparent from the text*

1. a. List the contents of a permanent file. (5)

   b. List the areas which the auditor of a new business might initially direct his attention in planning his audit. (7)

Examination questions without answers

1. You have been appointed auditor of Coombe Tracy Squash Club. The club has 1,000 members and a clubhouse containing 10 squash courts with a bar and catering facilities. Members pay an initial joining fee of £25 and thereafter an annual subscription of £50. In addition they pay £2 per hour to use the squash courts (which must be booked in advance). The bar steward retains 50% of the profits from catering facilities, but all bar profits belong to the club. The club professional is paid a retainer of £10,000 per year and retains all fees for lessons together with the profits from the sale of sports equipment. There is one other full time employee who maintains the courts etc, he is paid an annual salary of £8,000 and is paid overtime when necessary (eg during tournaments). There is a committee of 6 members which makes all other decisions affecting the club.

   Required

   a. Describe the steps you would take to ensure that all annual subscriptions were properly received. (4 marks)

   b. Describe the steps you would take to ensure that all initial joining fees were properly received. (4 marks)

   c. What internal control procedures should there be to ensure that the bar steward properly accounts for all bar takings? (4 marks)

d. What internal control procedures should exist to control overtime worked by the full time employee? (3 marks)

(AAT 92) (Total 15 marks)

2. Your firm has recently been appointed auditors of Beeston Investment Trust plc. You have been asked to describe the work you will carry out in certain areas of the audit of the company's accounts for the year ended 30 September 1990.

    The main items in Beeston Investment Trust's draft balance sheet at 30 September 1990 are:

    a. Investments quoted on the UK Stock Exchange – £29.6 million.

    b. Investments in unquoted UK companies – £3.9 million.

    c. Investment properties – £11.1 million.

    Annual income from investments is approximately £1.4 million, and rents from investment properties are about £730,000.

    In the balance sheet the following valuation bases are used:

    a. Quoted investments at the mid-market value at the balance sheet date.

    b. Unquoted investments at the directors' valuation.

    c. Investment properties at an external professional valuation every five years and at directors' valuation in intermediate years. The last professional valuation was two years ago.

    You are required to:

    a. List and describe the work you will carry out to verify that all income has been received for:

        i.   dividends from quoted and unquoted investments, (7 marks)

        ii. rents from investment properties. (5 marks)

    b. List and describe the work you will carry out to verify that the value placed on the company's investments at 30 September 1990 is correctly stated for:

        i.   quoted investments, (4 marks)

        ii. unquoted investments, (4 marks)

        iii. investment properties. (5 marks)

(ACCA 90) (Total 25 marks)

41 Specialised audits

Introduction

1. The auditing guidelines and APB Practice Notes include many on specific industries. They are:

    Charities
    Building Societies
    Trade Unions and Employers' Organisations
    Housing Associations
    Pensions Schemes in the UK

Banks in the UK
General Business Insurers in the UK
Life Insurers in the UK
Investment Businesses
The Lloyds Market

Also several Practice Notes on the auditors' right and duty to report to regulators.

2. These guidelines tend to be very long and complex and examiners cannot really expect a detailed knowledge of them in a general professional exam. However occasionally they are examined but usually in a way that can be answered without *special* knowledge. Students can say how to verify rents received in a Housing Association or expenditure in a Trade Union from first principles. With a little imagination they can also say how to verify mortgage advances in a Building Society or employers' contributions to a pension scheme.

3. In this chapter I have summarised the main points in the audits of:

Charities
Financial Services firms.

Charities

4. There are thousands of charities, some very large like the NSPCC or Oxfam and some very small. Many are professionally managed and have sophisticated accounting systems, but many rely on volunteers who may be unversed in accounting. All should produce accounts and be subject to audit. To assist the auditor there is an auditing guideline: charities.

Charities may be companies limited by guarantee. They are then governed by The Companies Act 1985 and all its regulations apply. Others are registered under various other Acts. The main Act, covering all charities is the Charities Act 1993. However many of its provisions, notably those relating to accounting, have not yet come into force.

5. Auditing regulations depend on the constitution of the charity – if the charity is a company, then The Companies Act applies. The guideline of 1981 should be followed and the auditing standards should also be applied, especially SAS 600 and, where relevant SAS 620. Accounting regulations will eventually come into force (probably early in 1996) but in the meantime there is a SORP, issued by the Charity Commission and charities should follow its prescriptions.

6. The SORP requires:

   a. Accounts should comply with the four fundamental accounting concepts (SSAP 2) and follow all the relevant accounting standards.

   b. All accounting policies should be disclosed. There will be a diversity of policies in practice – think of life member subscriptions.

   c. Separate funds must be itemised. It is a feature of charities that funds are collected for different purposes. Sometimes funds collected are for restricted use and such restricted funds must be shown.

   d. Financial statements should include:
      – a Statement of Financial Activities bringing together the various funds and gains and losses on revaluations and disposals of investments

       – a Summary Income and Expenditure Account

       – a Balance Sheet

       – a Cash Flow Statement

e. Fixed assets should be at cost/valuation less depreciation. Fixed assets held as investments should be shown at market value. Current assets should be at the lower of cost and net realisable value.

f. There are many detailed requirements which should be complied with.

7. Some general points about the audit of charities include:

a. The auditor must understand the constitution of the charity. Many are companies limited by guarantee, some are constituted under the law of trusts, some are just unincorporated bodies.Whatever the constitution the auditor must understand it in detail with particular reference to any accounting or auditing regulations.

b. A letter of engagement is essential. In particular the letter should make clear who the auditor should report to.

c. Funding must be investigated and evidence found for the inclusion of *all* funds received. Some of these may be grants and a notable point is that grants may be repayable in certain circumstances. A provision may be required for this or at least a note to the accounts.

d. Legacies form another form of income and it is difficult for an auditor to be sure all have been received especially if these are reversions. The auditor should see that the charity has procedures to ensure all legacies are received. This may require legal assistance to search all notified wills.

e. Direct donations can often be verified by a proper system for opening the post or by the publication of a list of donors.

f. Cash collections are impossible to verify for completeness but some work can be done. The charity should have a system for issuing collecting tins and for recording their return. Counting should be done by several people and cash counts acknowledged in writing. A good system is required not only for the benefit of the charity but also for the protection of the volunteers.

g. Expenditure can be verified by reference to written evidence, eg invoices and receipts but also by reference to *authority*. Expenditure should be authorised by committee minute or by delegated authority. Year end liabilities should be particularly examined to ensure all are included.

h. Fixed assets can be verified in the usual way. However a particular problem arises with gifts of fixed or other assets in kind. These should be valued in some appropriate way to recognize and account for the asset.

i. A point arises on liquidity and going concern. Some charities are government, local authority or other grant dependent. In the wake of lowered expenditure by these bodies, some charities may have liquidity problems and may not even be going concerns.

j. The auditor should always make a report. Here is an example which covers many charities and voluntary organisations:

> REPORT OF THE AUDITORS TO THE MEMBERS/TRUSTEES OF ......
>
> We have audited the accounts on pages ...to...
>
> *Responsibilities of the committee/trustees and auditors*
>
> As described on page... the Committee/Trustees are responsible for the preparation of the accounts. It is our responsibility to form an independent opinion, based on our audit, on those accounts and to report our opinion to you.
>
> *Basis of opinion*
>
> We conducted our audit in accordance with Auditing Standards issued by the Auditing Practices Board. An audit includes examination, on a test basis, of evidence relevant to the amounts and disclosures in the accounts. It also includes an assessment of the significant estimates and judgements made by the Committee/Trustees in the preparation of the accounts, and of whether the accounting policies are appropriate to the charity's circumstances, consistently applied and adequately disclosed.
>
> We planned and performed our audit so as to obtain all the information and explanations which we considered necessary in order to provide us with sufficient evidence to give reasonable assurance that the accounts are free from material misstatement, whether caused by fraud or other irregularity or error. In forming our opinion we also evaluated the overall adequacy of the presentation of information in the accounts.
>
> *Opinion*
>
> In our opinion the accounts give a true and fair view of the state of the charity's affairs as at .... and of its surplus for the year then ended.
>
> Wind, Bagg & Co.
>
> Certified Accountants and Registered Auditors, Oxford
>
> 7 December 19...

The audit of charities

8. Most charities produce accounts although these are often just cash receipts and payments accounts. Most of these receive some form of audit although the auditor is often not a qualified accountant and is often not paid for his pains. Contact groups of a charity usually do require assurance that the financial affairs of a charity are competently and honestly dealt with and reported upon. Contact groups include members, subscribers, beneficiaries, donors, management committees, professional managers and employees, the treasurer, grant givers and others.

   It is essential that the auditor takes his duties seriously and applies his skills with proper care.

Financial services companies

9. The financial services sector covers all types of investment including shares, debentures, government securities, options, warrants, unit trusts, futures contracts and some long term life insurance contracts. It involves dealing in, arranging deals in and managing and advising on investments as well as setting up and operating collective investment schemes. In the past investing members of the public often lost their savings due to the activities of fraudulent, reckless or just plain incompetent financial service businesses. However, since the Financial Services Act 1986, all such businesses have been *regulated*. As a result investors should be protected from the depredations of the dishonest, the

incompetent and the insolvent. However it is important to note that the investor protection legislation does not take the *risk* out of risk capital. If I pay money to a unit trust management company I should find that it is actually invested as I expect (and not stolen from me) but I am not protected against falls in value of the shares the Unit trust is invested in. As the SIB put it, the FSA 1986 no more removes the need for investors to pay attention to where they place their money than the existence of the Highway Code removes the need to look before crossing the road.

10. Actual regulation is delegated to an agency called the *Securities and Investments Board (SIB)*. The SIB is assisted by several Self-Regulating Organisations (SROs) and Recognised Professional Bodies (RPBs). The three SROs are:

   – Investment Management Regulatory Organisation (IMRO). Primarily for businesses that engage in managing investments, manage occupational pension Schemes, and manage or act as trustee for Unit Trusts.

   – Personal Investment Authority. Primarily for insurance companies, friendly societies and financial advisers who market, advise on and arrange deals in life assurance, unit trust and investment trust savings schemes, shares and warrants and debt instruments for private clients.

   – The Securities and Futures Authority (SFA). Primarily for firms engaged in dealing and arranging deals in and advising on shares, debentures, gilt-edged stocks, futures, options, commodities, derivatives, and for corporate finance customers.

There are nine RPBs including the ACCA and the three Institutes of Chartered Accountants.

Some investment institutions do not come under the FSA 1986. These include Banks, Building Societies and to some extent Insurance Companies. These are regulated by other bodies – the Bank of England, the Building Societies Commission and the DTI respectively.

Regulation is carried out in many ways but includes:

a. Granting authorisation to do investment business only to firms which are 'fit and proper' to carry on the business. Fit and proper firms have adequate financial resources and can show appropriate previous experience and competence. There is a central register of such firms available to the public.

b. Receiving reports and accounts from the firms and from their auditors – see later.

c. Routine compliance visits at appropriate intervals.

Regulated firms and persons must adhere to strict codes of conduct including, for example, requirements that commission must be disclosed before the investor signs the application form and that investment firms must make proper arrangements for the segregation of clients' money. The SIB and SROs have a substantial armoury of regulatory sanctions including fines, suspension and ultimately withdrawal of authorisation.

11. **The auditor and regulated firms.** The auditor of a regulated firm has several duties:

a. To audit the financial statements in the usual way. The requirements here depend on the constitution of the client. Many clients are companies and the Companies Act applies.

b. To make routine reports to the regulators on specific aspects of the client's business. These reports are the subject of a number of APB Practice Notes.

c. To report directly to regulators on matters which come to light while engaging in the above audit activities which the auditors consider should be brought to the attention of regulators sooner than would be achieved by routine reports. This is a very difficult area and is covered by a Statement of Auditing Standards SAS 620 *Right and Duty to report to Regulators.*

12. **Routine reports to regulators on specific aspects**. The report should have several sections including:

a. The addressee

b. The financial statements audited. These will usually be the annual financial statements. In addition further matters will be set out in detail later in the report.

c. The auditing standards followed. These will normally be the Auditing Standards and such procedures as are required for the further matters usually mentioning the relevant Practice Notes.

d. A statement that they have obtained all the information and explanations which they considered necessary.

e. The opinion on the financial statements – true and fair, prepared in accordance with SRO rules, in agreement with the firm's accounting records and returns.

f. The opinion on other matters. These will include:

i. The statement of financial resources is prepared in accordance with SRO rules and shows actual and required financial resources

ii. The firm has financial resources at least to the minimum amount required

iii. The firm has kept proper accounting records in accordance with SRO rules

iv. The firm maintained systems adequate to enable it to comply with Client Money Regulations.

g. The identity of the auditors

h. The date of the report.

The manner in which auditors conducts their investigations to enable them to give an opinion on the other matters is beyond the scope of this book but my readers should be able to think of a number a procedures.

The report may need to be qualified. In such cases it may be necessary to ensure that the regulator is informed immediately an intention to qualify is recognised. The information may be given to the regulator by the client or by the auditor.

13. **Non-routine reports to regulators**. SAS 620 requires that auditors of regulated entities should bring information of which they become aware in the ordinary course of performing work undertaken to fulfil their audit responsibilities to the attention of the appropriate regulator without delay when:

a. They conclude that it is relevant to the regulator's functions having regard to such matters as may be specified in statute or any related regulations; and

b. In their opinion there is reasonable cause to believe it is or may be of material significance to the regulator.

To explain these requirements in more detail:

a. The auditor has contact with the regulated firm in three ways. Firstly as auditor of the financial statements in the usual way, secondly as in order to report on certain other matters as outlined in paragraph 10, and thirdly by doing other work eg taxation, accounts preparation, consultancy etc. SAS 620 has in mind the first two of these. Non-audit work does not come into the scope of this requirement. However the auditor may see non-audit work as part of her audit evidence in the same manner as the work of any expert providing information which is audit evidence.

b.   In due course any qualification of their reports on the financial statements or other matters will come to the attention of the regulators but that may be too late to protect customers of the client firm or other persons from loss. In such cases immediate reporting is required.

c.   If an auditor finds he has come across a matter of importance to the regulator he should firstly obtain such evidence as is available to assess its implications for his reporting responsibilities (financial statements and other matters) and then determine whether, in his opinion, there is reasonable cause to believe that the breach is of material significance to the regulator.

d.   Matters that are likely to be of material significance to the regulator include:
   –   the financial position of the of the regulated entity. If, say, the solvency requirements have been breached.
   –   compliance with requirements for the management of the business. If, say, internal controls are not working effectively.
   –   the status of its directors as fit and proper persons. If, say, the directors have bought expensive houses for their mistresses using clients' monies.
   –   conducting business outside the scope of the entity's authorisation.

e.   Auditors are not required to design or implement procedures beyond the scope of their normal audit work, but they and all their staff should be aware of, and alert to, signs of material matters which ought to be brought to the attention of regulators at all times.

f.   Some of the matters which require immediate reporting to regulators may be of significance to the financial statements. For example a very serious breach (eg of solvency) may lead to the regulator taking away authorisation to trade and that has obvious impact on going concern.

Summary

14. a.   There are several auditing guidelines to specific industries.
    b.   In this chapter I have dealt with charities, and financial services firms.

Points to note

15. a.   Many industries are highly regulated as to the manner of accounting, control, audit and other financial and trading matters. To audit these, the auditor has to be fully aware of all detailed regulations. No general student of auditing and indeed no general practitioner can be expected to carry these details around in his head. However, general principles can be applied (internal control, asset and liability verification etc).
    b.   I have omitted some of the industries dealt with in previous editions as these are now too complex in their legal requirements for easy coverage or seem to be rarely examined.

   c.   Professional accounting bodies do not expect students to have detailed knowledge of the guidelines and legal rules on specialised audits such as banks, building societies and housing associations. The rules and guidelines are immensely complex and detailed and it would be unreasonable to expect detailed learning of them. However, the examiners may use an audit of a building society or other body to examine general auditing principles without expecting detailed special knowledge. For example the audit of rents could be tested in a housing association context, internal controls over lending in a building society context and bad debt provisions in the context of a bank.

Student self testing questions *Questions with answers apparent from the text*

1. a.   Indicate some special problems of the audit of Charities. (7)
     b.   Write out an audit report for a Charity. (7)
     c.   What activities are carried on by Financial Services Companies? (9)
     d.   What is the objective of the Financial Services Act 1986? (9)
     e.   When should an auditor report to a regulatory body? (12, 13)
     f.   On what matters should he report routinely? (12)

Case study for Chapter 41

You are the auditor of the Goodbury Hills Fellowship Ltd, a charity which provides aid and assistance to children who contact Hills Disease and their parents and families. Income comes from:

- an annual street collection which raises £1,500
- social events which raise £2,000
- collecting boxes in pubs, houses and homes which raise £2,000
- deeds of convenant £4,200 gross
- donations £100 this year
- legacies £3,000 this year

Principal expenditures are:

- maintaining a Victorian house, which they own, as a day centre £2,000
- salaries of part time staff at the house £5,000
- grants to the Hills disease research trust £4,000
- administration charges £700
- grants to individuals to provide equipment £2,000.

Discussion

   a.   What controls would you advise over income and expenditure – the charity is run by a board of 10 parents with a chairman, secretary and treasurer none of whom are paid.
   b.   What audit evidence would you seek re. income and expenditure and assets and liabilities.
   c.   Draft a suitable audit report. The charity is a company and is registered with the Charity Commission.

Examination questions without answers

1. You are carrying out the audit of the Mary Davison Charity. It has two branches:
   a. a pensions branch which uses income from investments to pay pensions
   b. a housing branch which provides accommodation for retired people.

A summary of the draft income and expenditure accounts for the year ended 30 September 1992 show:

Pensions branch:		£
Income from investments:		
Dividends from UK quoted companies		3,960
Interest from UK Government securities		9,164
Bank deposit account interest		2,351
Total investment income		15,475
Pensions and grants paid	9,905	
Administration expenses	3,275	
		(13,180)
Net surplus transferred to income account		2,295

Housing branch:	£
Rents received from:	
– flats	8,375
– bungalows	11,310
	19,685
Less: Expenses	(22,124)
Deficit transferred to income account	(2,439)

The charity is supervised by the trustees who meet about four times a year. Rents are collected by a part-time clerk, who also records all cash received and paid by the charity. Cheques are signed by the chairman of the trustees.

For the pensions branch:

a. pensioners are paid £260 a year
b. the trustees authorise payment of new pensions, and periodically they make additional grants to pensioners for urgent repairs to their houses, or equipment to help with disabilities
c. the trustees can authorise payment of pensions to people who have an income of up to £10 a week above the 'poverty level' as defined by government. If an individual's income rises to more than £20 a week above the 'poverty level', the trustees normally discontinue the pension
d. an individual is paid to visit the pensioners to check they are still entitled to receive the pension and to note any deaths
e. at the end of the charity's financial year there were 34 pensioners
f. there are surplus funds in the income account, which are invested in a deposit account with a UK clearing bank
g. income from investments is stated gross in the accounts. However income from dividends and government securities is paid after deduction of basic rate tax, and the

charity reclaims this tax after the year end. The tax due from the government is included in debtors in the accounts.

For the housing branch:

a. there are seven flats and eight bungalows

b. residents in the flats pay £25 a week and those in the bungalows pay £30 a week

c. the trustees advertise the accommodation when it becomes vacant and approve new residents.

You are required to describe the audit work you will carry out to verify:

a. all rents from flats and bungalows have been received   (8 marks)

b. all income has been received from investments, including those bought and sold in the year   (9 marks)

c. pensions and grants have only been paid to pensioners authorised by the trustees.   (8 marks)

(ACCA 92) (25 marks)

2. Your firm has recently been appointed auditor of 'GIVE', a national charity that receives a substantial proportion of its income from voluntary sources. You are the Manager in charge of the audit assignment and have agreed to draft a memorandum to the Senior setting out the matters that should be considered in planning the audit.

Requirement

You are required to draft a memorandum to the Senior detailing the matters peculiar to the audit of 'GIVE' that may warrant consideration at the forthcoming audit planning meeting.   (20 marks)

NB Routine planning steps common to all new audit engagements are not required.

(ICAI 91)

42 Local authorities, the NHS and central government

Introduction

1. The audit of local authorities and Health Authorities in the UK is rather different from the audit of companies and other private sector enterprises. The main reason for this is the emphasis placed on value for money. The detail of local authority audits is complex and requires a manual all to itself. This chapter outlines the statutory arrangements for audit and the role of the audit commission and introduces some of the detail. Students may find that the differences between local authority audits and audits of commercial undertakings illuminate both kinds of audit.

2. This chapter concludes with a brief introduction to the audit of health authorities and with the work of the National Audit Office.

Statutory background

3. The Local Government Finance Act 1982 established the Audit Commission which began its work in 1983. Its responsibilities were extended by the National Health Service and Community Care Act 1990 to include NHS bodies. We will look at the NHS at the end of this chapter. The audit commission employs about 1,000 staff and is self-financing, obtaining its income from fees charged. Its main duties are:

    a. To appoint auditors to all local authorities and health authorities. The auditors can either be its own employees (the District Audit Service) or one of seven approved firms of accountants. In fact 70% of local authorities use the DAS and 30% the private firms.

    b. To promote studies to encourage economy, efficiency and effectiveness in local government and the NHS.

The role of the audit commission

4. The audit commission and its auditors have two major roles:

    a. To ensure that local authorities are spending money and reporting their financial situation in accordance with the law and that there are safeguards against fraud and corruption.

    b. To help local authorities to help themselves by showing how services can be provided as cost-effectively as possible.

5. They carry out their roles by:

    a. Appointing auditors.

    b. Undertaking studies which make recommendations for improving economy, efficiency and effectiveness of services.

    c. Encouraging local authorities to learn from one another and thus to apply good management practice which has proved effective elsewhere.

    d. Carrying out studies to investigate the impact on local authorities of legislation or central government action. For example the commission has carried out studies on homelessness and on the community charge.

6. The Commission have assisted auditors in many ways including:

    – preparing statistical profiles of each authority which contrast cost and other data with national averages. For example costs per child in primary schools might be higher or lower than average.

    – preparing audit guides based on the results of studies into individual services.

    – with advice on good management

7. The Citizen's Charter includes one initiative enacted by the Local Government Act 1992 which obliges the Commission to draw up a list of indicators for measuring the performance of local government services. My reader will, by now, have appreciated that the audit commission has its main purpose in making the provision of local government services more economical, more efficient, more effective, better value for money and better managed.

Auditors' responsibilities

8. Local Authority auditors must carry out their responsibilities in accordance with The Code of Audit Practice for Local Authorities and the NHS in England and Wales which

is approved by Parliament. The code sets out the general duties of auditors and tells auditors how they are to conduct the audit given their special responsibilities in respect of fraud, corruption and value for money and how they should report the results of their audits in the forms of:

- audit opinion
- public interest reports
- management letters

9. At this point it is as well to define some of the terms used:

Economy – the terms under which the authority acquires human and material resources. An economical operation acquires these sources in the appropriate quality and quantity at the lowest cost. As an example a local authority might find it more economical to staff many aspects of its police operations with civilians.

Efficiency – the relationship between goods and services produced and resources used to produce them. An efficient operation produces the maximum output for a given set of resource inputs or it has minimum inputs for a given quantity and quality of service provided. Falling school rolls have meant that many schools have student numbers which are much less than the numbers the schools were intended for or are capable of taking. Consequently the input cost of running schools is much greater than the output merits.

Effectiveness – how well a programme or activity is achieving its established goals or other intended effects. For example in a housing department it might be found that an unresponsive and bureaucratic form of organisation meant that some urgent calls for help were only dealt with after considerable delays.

Fraud and irregularities – intentional distortion of financial statements and accounting records and to misappropriation of assets, whether or not accompanied by distortion of financial statements and accounting records. An example might be the theft of council property perhaps covered up by altering the records of assets.

Corruption – corrupt practices are the offering, giving, soliciting or acceptance of an inducement or reward which may influence the actions taken by the authority, its members or officers. Examples are legion and include tendering and award of contracts, canvassing for appointments, planning permissions etc.

Legality – a local authority has to operate within its legal powers. Some things statute requires it do, some things statute allows it to do at its discretion and some things it is not allowed to do at all.

10. The auditors' duties include:

a. Financial Accounts – the auditor is required to give an opinion as to whether an authority's annual accounts 'present fairly' its financial position. The opinion work will involve a review of accounting systems such as payroll, payments and income, and a detailed examination of the final accounts including cash/bank balances, debtors, stocks and creditors.

b. Fraud and Corruption – the primary responsibility for safeguarding against fraud and corruption rests with the authority but the auditor is required to ascertain whether the authority has taken reasonable steps such as setting up an adequate internal control system to provide segregation of duties, proper authorisation procedures and an effective internal audit function. Where fraud or corruption is suspected auditors will pursue their investigations in collaboration with the authority and where necessary with the police.

c. Value for money – this is now seen as the main thrust of the audit effort. The value for money work at each local authority includes carrying out where relevant the commission's national studies, reviewing the authority's statistical profile and undertaking such local projects as appear relevant to the local situation.

d. Legality – the legality of the authority's spending is still an important part of the audit. However local authorities have wide discretion but there are nonetheless restrictions on their powers.

11. The auditor's objectives will include an assessment of:

 – whether the statement of accounts presents fairly the financial position
 – the general financial standing of the authority
 – the adequacy of the financial systems
 – the adequacy of the arrangements for preventing and detecting fraud and corruption
 – the performance of particular services
 – the effectiveness of management arrangements

The local authority auditor

12. The local authority auditor must be independent and without official, professional or personal relationships which might limit the extent or character of his audit. He may not engage in decision making or in any management operation of his client local authority nor have any substantial financial interest in the transactions or services of the local authority except in an arms-length capacity for example as a council tax payer.

13. He may not undertake any work for the local authority except that of auditor except:

a. Where the cost of the additional work is less than £10,000

b. Where the authority and the appointed auditor are able to satisfy the Commission that the additional work would not risk impairing the auditor's independence and his firm performing the work ensures economy, efficiency and effectiveness in the utilisation of the authority's resources.

14. Local authority auditors have considerable powers. They have the legal power to obtain whatever information they feel is necessary to carry out their function. In addition they have a statutory function in matters involving illegality or losses caused by wilful misconduct. If the auditor feels that the local authority has done something which it has no right to do, they will first discuss the matter with the local authority and then if thought necessary apply to the High Court for a declaration that the item is unlawful.

Conducting the audit

15. In general the local authority auditor must follow the auditing standards of the APB. There is a short auditing guideline: applicability to the public sector of Auditing Standards and Guidelines.

16. In examining the annual accounts, the auditor should ensure that the provisions of the Code of Practice on Local Authority Accounting (issued by CIPFA) have been complied with, figures are not understated or overstated, the description of the figures is neither

misleading or ambiguous, there is compliance with all statutory and other requirements, there is adequate disclosure of all items and that the information contained in the statement of accounts is suitably classified and presented.

17. In reviewing the arrangements made to prevent and detect fraud and irregularities the audit should be planned so that there is a reasonable expectation of detecting material misstatements in the accounts. The auditor should pay special attention to activities which are particularly exposed to the risk of fraud and irregularities. In reviewing internal controls, the auditor should be constantly alert to the possibilities of fraud and irregularities and draw attention of management to any weaknesses. Any indication of fraud and irregularities should be followed up.

Reporting the audit

18. This should be done in the following ways:

   a. An opinion in much the way that the Companies Act requires for companies.

   b. Project Reports made to the authority. These are separate reports on any value for money projects undertaken at the authority. The report will outline the area of activity, the objectives of the work, summarise the findings and conclusions and make recommendations for improved value for money.

   c. Management letter. This is a report to the members of the authority which summarises the main matters which have arisen from the audit and the benefits anticipated from the implementation of agreed action. It also gives a brief account of the regularity (legality) and value for money work undertaken.

Section 18 – Auditor's reports

19. When the auditor has completed his audits of the accounts, he shall enter on the accounts:

   a. A certificate that he has completed the audit in accordance with the Act, and

   b. his opinion on the relevant statement of accounts. He may also enter in his report, any *report* made under Section 15(3) – public interest matters.

   c. The report must be sent to the Audit Commission.

   An unqualified report might be:

> To Smallborough District Council:
>
> I certify that I have completed the audit of the authority's accounts for the year ended 31 March, 19... in accordance with Part III of the Local Government Finance Act 1982 and the Code of Audit Practice.
>
> In my opinion the statement of accounts set out on pages ... to ... presents fairly the financial position of the authority at 31 March 19... and its income and expenditure for the year then ended.
>
> Auditor
>
> (Date)

20. In expressing his formal opinion on whether the statement of accounts presents *fairly* the financial position of the authority, the auditor should satisfy himself in particular on the following matters:

a. The guidance notes of CIPFA on the application of Accounting Standards to local authority accounts.

b. Material accounting policies not subject to guidance from Accounting Standards.

c. Any material understatements or overstatements.

d. That the description of the figures is neither misleading nor ambiguous.

e. Compliance with all statutory and other requirements applicable to the accounts of the authority.

f. Adequate disclosure of all appropriate material items.

g. Suitable presentation and classification of all information.

Qualified reports

21. Qualifications should follow the Auditing Standard – Qualifications in audit reports. An example might be:

> To the City of North Bromwich:
>
> I/we certify that I/we have completed the audit of the authority's accounts for the year ended 31 March, 19… in accordance with Part III of the Local Government Finance Act 1982 and the Code of Audit Practice.
>
> Government grant claims for housing benefit subsidy have not been finalised by the Council since 19… Discussions are currently taking place with the Department of Health and Social Security to clarify difficulties over their completion. The statement of accounts consequently includes an amount of £ … based on the best estimate of grant due to the Council.
>
> Subject to the effects of any adjustment that might be shown to be necessary on the finalisation of the housing benefit subsidy claims, in my/our opinion the statement of accounts on pages … to … presents fairly the financial position of the authority at 31 March 19… and its income and expenditure for the year then ended.
>
> Auditor
>
> Date

22. Unqualified audit opinions can include 'Emphasis of Matter'. For example a paragraph in the middle might say:

I draw attention to note … which refers to a change in accounting policy whereby interest on loans was previously accounted for on a cash payments basis has been accrued up to 31 March 19… The additional charge to revenue resulting from this charge amounted to £ …

23. Two matters are of particular relevance in considering qualification:

a. Capital Accounting. The auditor should ensure that there is full footnote disclosure of the basis on which capital expenditure has been recorded in the accounts. He should also ensure that the current accounting treatment of capital items is acceptable and consistent.

b. Creative accounting. The auditor should ensure that there is full disclosure of instances of creative accounting. Creative accounting occurs on transfers to and from special funds. It is essential that readers of the accounts can distinguish such transfers from actual income and expenditure.

24. The largest number of qualifications so far have been failure to accrue external loan interest followed by inadequate provision for doubtful debts.

Public inspection of accounts and right of challenge

25. Section 17 gives any interested person or any elector the right:

    a. At each audit to inspect the accounts to be audited and all the books and other documents related to them and make copies of them.

    b. to question the auditor about the accounts.

    c. To make objections to the auditor on matters relating to Section 19 (unlawful items), Section 20 (recovery of amounts not accounted for), or Section 15(3) (public interest matters).

    The auditor might find that items requiring his attention are supplied by members of the public.

Right to inspect statements of accounts and auditor's reports

26. Section 24 gives electors rights to inspect and make copies of statements of accounts.

Management letters

27. In addition to routine memoranda for chief officers, at the conclusion of his audit, the auditor should summarize matters that have arisen during the course of his audit which are significant enough to be brought to the attention of the authority (ie the councillors) but which do not merit either a qualification of the accounts or a report in the public interest.

    The letter which must also be sent to the Audit Commission, should summarize those significant matters which the auditor has raised during his audit, officers' responses and the auditor's opinion on the adequacy of the officer's response. Preparation of the letter should follow the pattern suggested in company audits. (See Chapter 18)

Extraordinary audit

28. Section 22 *allows* the Audit Commission to direct an auditor to hold an extra ordinary audit of the accounts if an application on that behalf is made by a local government elector or it appears to the Commission that it is desirable to do so in consequence of a report made by an auditor or for any other reason.

Report in the public interest

29. The Local Government Finance Act 1982 requires that the auditor shall consider whether in the public interest a report should be made on any matter which comes to the auditor's attention in the course of the audit. Examples of matters which, if significant might call for a report include:

    - The fact that the auditor's opinion on the statement of accounts was qualified
    - Delayed preparation of accounts
    - Failure to comply with statutory requirements
    - Excessive or inadequate levels of balances, inappropriate levels of provisions, lack of prudence, prospective budget deficits etc

- Lack of action on matters previously reported including value for money opportunities
- Absence of or weakness in arrangements for securing the three Es.
- Unnecessary expenditure or loss of income due to waste, extravagance, inefficient financial administration, poor value for money, mistake etc
- Weaknesses in management information systems and monitoring arrangements
- High levels of arrears, deficiencies in income collection procedures
- Deficiencies in internal control and internal audit arrangements
- Objections received at the audit of local authorities
- Misconduct, frauds or special investigations.

Note that the report may be made immediately on discovery or within fourteen days of the conclusion of the audit. The Local Government Act 1992 increased the publicity given to these reports by requiring them to be considered at a full meeting of the council. The meeting must be advertised in the local press with a note that the report is to be discussed.

The National Health Service

30. Under the provisions of the National Health Service and Community Care Act 1990 the work of auditing the NHS is now provided by the Audit Commission. The District Audit Service has about 70% of the audits and eight firms of accountants share the remaining 30%. Audits include those of NHS Trust and GP fundholders.

31. The approach to the audit is as for local authorities with emphasis on:
    - value for money: economy, efficiency and effectiveness
    - improving quality and effectiveness of service
    - helping authorities learn from the best authorities

32. The Commission help auditors in their value for money work by:
    - providing a statistical 'profile' of each authority (eg Wednesfield General treated 22,000 patients at an average cost of £x which is £y more than the national average.)
    - providing audit guides based on the results of studies into individual services (eg on day surgery)
    - providing advice on good management

33. As with local authorities the auditor's responsibilities cover:
    - financial reports
    - fraud and corruption
    - legality
    - value for money

34. As with local authorities reporting is by:
    - audit opinions
    - project reports
    - management letters
    - reports in the public interest

An unqualified report might be:

> 'Boghampton Area Health Authority
>
> We certify that we have completed the audit of the authority's accounts for the year ended 31 March 19... in accordance with Part I of the National Health Service and Community Care Act 1990 and Code of Audit Practice.
>
> In our opinion the statement of accounts set out on pages... to... presents fairly the financial position of the authority at 31 March 19... and its income and expenditure for the year then ended.
>
> Boor, Tedius & Co
> Registered Auditor
> 28 February 19...'

35. In the cases of NHS Trusts, the auditors' report may be like this:

> **Auditor's report on the Sheinton Community Health Service Trust**
>
> We certify that we have completed the audit of the financial statements on pages...to... which have been prepared in accordance with the accounting policies relevant to the National Health Service as set out on pages...to...
>
> **Respective responsibilities of directors and auditors**
>
> As described above the directors are responsible for the preparation of the financial statements. It is our responsibility to form an independent opinion, based on our audit, on those statements and to report our opinion to you.
>
> **Basis of opinion**
>
> We carried out our audit in accordance with part 1 of the NHS and CC Act 1990 and the Code of Audit Practice issued by the Audit Commission. which requires compliance with relevant auditing standards.
>
> Our audit included examination, on a test basis, of evidence relevant to the amounts and disclosures in the financial statements. It also included an assessment of the significant estimates and judgements made by the trust in the preparation of the financial statements, and of whether the accounting policies are appropriate to the Trust's circumstances, consistently applied and adequately disclosed.
>
> We planned and performed our audit so as to obtain all the information and explanations which we considered necessary in order to provide us with sufficient evidence to give reasonable assurance that the financial statements are free from material misstatement, whether caused by fraud or other irregularity or error. In forming our opinion we also evaluated the overall adequacy of the presentation of information in the financial statements.
>
> **Opinion**
>
> In our opinion the financial statements give a true and fair view of the state of affairs of Sheinton Community Health Service NHS Trust as at 31 March 19... and of its income and expenditure for the year then ended.
>
> Signature: J Smith
>
> For and behalf of Tickers
> Birmingham
> 24 August 19...

Note:

- the paragraph headings
- the addressees
- the words: estimates and judgements, reasonable assurance, material misstatement, true and fair view (this an NHS Trust).

National Audit Office

36. The audit of central government is handled by the National Audit Office and some 550 public sector accounts, from the Ministry of Defence down to small executive agencies, are audited. The National Audit Office was created by the National Audit Act 1983 and its head is the Comptroller and Auditor General. It has about 850 staff.

   Its objective is to give assurance, information and advice to parliament on the way government departments and other public bodies use and account for taxpayers money (about £500 billion a year). This aim is achieved by high quality financial audit and by in-depth examinations of selected departmental projects, programmes and activities. In carrying out its work it aims to put forward constructive ideas and recommendations and so help departments and agencies achieve better value for money.

   In detail its objectives are:

   a. provide parliament with an assurance that public money has been spent for the purposes parliament intended
   b. improve financial control in government departments and other public bodies
   c. improve value obtained from the resources made available by parliament
   d. improve the techniques and quality of public sector audit

37. The Office is especially concerned with economy, efficiency and effectiveness – words you are now familiar with. Examples of their investigations included how the Department of Energy and HM Customs and Excise determined their requirements for office accommodation in central London. This brought out the need for departments to undertake full and soundly based investment appraisals before making their decisions. Another example was the discovery of the need for the Department of Social Security to set up a Compensation Recovery Unit to recover benefits in cases where the award of damages in tort and social security overlaps. The Parliamentary Public Accounts Committee find the work of the Office invaluable.

Summary

38. a. Local authority auditors are appointed by the Audit Commission.
   b. The main objectives of local authority audits are to ensure fairly presented accounts but, more importantly, to ensure value for money in local authorities.
   c. Value for Money can be seen as economy, efficiency and effectiveness
   d. Comparative studies by auditors are important and local authorities are encouraged to learn from each other
   e. Local authority audits are also concerned with legality, (regularity), fraud and irregularities and corruption.

f.   Local authority audits must be conducted in accordance with the Code of Practice for Local Authorities and the NHS in England and Wales and with the relevant auditing standards and guidelines.

g.   The audit is reported by an audit opinion on the accounts, a management letter and project reports.

h.   The local authority auditor may make public interest reports

i.   The work of the audit commission has now been extended to the NHS with a similar emphasis on value for money

j.   Central government departments and agencies are audited by auditors appointed by the National Audit Office. Such auditors may be the NAO or one of eight approved firms. The emphasis again is on value for money.

Points to note

39. a.   Economy, Efficiency and Effectiveness can be summarised as spend less, spend well and spend wisely. There are overlaps in categorising any particular expenditure. The important thing is value for money.

b.   The findings of the Audit Commission and the NAO are now made very public and my readers are advised to watch out for their reports in the national and local press. You might see 'Boghampton Area Health Authority in expenditure scandal'!

c.   The local authority auditor has some extraordinary powers including the power to serve a notice precluding an action and to apply to the court for a declaration that an item of account is contrary to the law. The court can order repayment or the perpetrator to be disqualified form holding public office. The auditor can, where any person has failed to bring into account any sum which should have been included, certify the sum due and may recover the sum from the person responsible.

d.   The actions of auditors are often perceived as political although strict impartiality is always observed. Clearly obtaining value for money often means redundancy of council or NHS staff.

e.   There are at least three key differences between audit in the public services and audit in the private sector:
   –   greater independence from the organisations they audit
   –   a wider role for auditors (value for money) and an extended scope to the audit
   –   extended reporting to the stake holders

   Perhaps the private sector will tend in the future to come into line with the public sector contrary to the usual happenings where the public sector are encouraged to become more like the private sector!

Case study 1 for Chapter 42

Janet and John are both audit staff members of Mustard & Co Registered Auditor. Janet is handling the audit of Mega PLC and John is handling the audit of Toothroyd City Council.

Discussion

Contrast the two audits in as many ways as you can.

Case study 2 for Chapter 42

Obtain the annual report and accounts of your local authority, a local NHS Authority, and a NHS Trust

Discussion

Contrast and compare the certificate of the reporting authority or its directors, the auditors' report, the type of information given, the accounting policies. How meaningful do you think the information is for the ordinary citizen, qualified accountants, trainee auditors?

Student self testing questions *Questions with answers apparent from the text*

1. a. What are the main duties of the Audit Commission? (3)
    b. What are the main roles of the Audit Commission and its auditors? (4)
    c. How do they carry out their roles? (5)
    d. Define the three Es. (9)
    e. List the LA Auditors' duties. (10)
    f. How should the audit be reported? (18)
    g. Write out an unqualified report (19)
    h. What matters might give rise to a public interest report? (29)
    i. What matters in an audit of an Health Authority need emphasis? (31)
    j. List the objectives of the National Audit Office (36)

Examination question without answer

1. The value for money audit is an important part of a local authority audit. it is a concept which is traditionally analysed into 'Economy', 'Efficiency' and 'Effectiveness'.
    Required:
    1. Explain, providing an example of each, what is meant by the following terms:
        a. Economy   b. Efficiency   c. Effectiveness
    2. Explain the auditor's role in relation to value for money aspects in the statutory audit of a local authority.

        (ICAS 1995)

43 Accountants' reports and audit exemption reports

Introduction

1. Accountants who are appointed as auditors to companies have their duties prescribed by the Companies Acts. They are auditors and they make an Auditor's Report.

    Accountants also do work in connection with the Accounts of sole traders and partnerships. The work may be an audit or it may be the preparation of the Accounts without an audit or including only a partial audit. A partial audit of some aspect only of a client's affairs or into some books only.

Whatever the relationships, it should be agreed precisely in the *letter of engagement*.

2. New sections of The Companies Act 1985 was inserted by the Companies Act 1985 (Audit Exemption) Regulations 1994. These new sections (249A to 249E) conferred exemptions from audit on certain categories of small company. It has been seen as a surprising step back into deregulation in an apparently endless series of new regulations. There is a Statement of Standards for Reporting Accountants SSRA *Audit Exemption reports*.

3. This chapter begins with a consideration of reports on sole traders and partnerships and then reviews the new rules on Audit Exemption Reports.

Accountants' reports

4. Whether the relationship between the accountant and the Accounts is an audit relationship or not, there should be a *report*.

5. The report must make quite clear the relationship which the accountant has with the Accounts and the extent of the responsibility he bears in relation to them.

6. Where Accounts are *audited* then the report should be labelled *Auditor's Report*. In other circumstances the report should be labelled *Accountant's Report*.

7. A typical *Accountant's Report* might be:

Accountant's Report

In accordance with instructions given to us we have prepared, without carrying out an audit, the annexed accounts set out on pages ... to ... from the accounting records of ... and from information and explanations supplied to us.

8. When accountants are instructed to carry out specific checks but not a full audit then the checks will be referred to in the accountant's report but care must be taken to see that there is no suggestions that they have audited the Accounts as a whole.

9. The accounts should conform to accepted accounting principles and if they do not, this fact should be made clear. If any estimates are used, they should be so described.

Client acknowledgement

10. Accounts prepared with or without audit should always be approved by the client before the report is signed. The client should be asked to sign a declaration such as:

'I approve the accounts and confirm that I have made available all relevant records and information for their preparation.'

Audit exemption reports

11. **Turnover not greater than £90,000 and gross Balance Sheet assets less than £1.4 million.**

These very small companies are exempt from audit completely. There are however exceptions:

- public companies
- banking and insurance companies
- insurance brokers and authorised persons and appointed representatives under the Financial Services Act
- Trade Unions and employers' organisations
- parent companies and subsidiary companies

Since there is no need for an audit, there is no need for an auditor. However many such companies will still employ accountants to prepare the accounts and such accountants may include an accountants' report like that in para 7. The company still has to prepare full accounts although the reduced filing requirements (see Chapter 5) may apply. When filing unaudited accounts the directors must include a statement as:

'The exemption conferred by S.249A(1) (or S.249A(2) for companies with turnover over £90,000) not to have these accounts audited applies to the company and the directors confirm that no notice has been deposited under S.249B(2) of The Companies Act 1985.

The directors acknowledge their responsibilities for ensuring that:

i.   The company keeps accounting records which comply with S.221 of The Companies Act 1985 and:

ii.   the accounts give a true and fair view of the state of affairs of the company as at ... and of its profit or loss for the year then ended in accordance with the requirements of S.226, and which otherwise comply with the requirements of The Companies Act 1985 relating to accounts so far as applicable to the company.'

Section 249B (2) confers a right on a member or members holding not less than 10% of the share capital to require the company financial statements to be audited in the usual way.

12. **Turnover greater than £90,000 but not more than £350,000 (£250,000 for charities) and Balance Sheet gross assets not more than £1.4 million.**

These small companies are also exempt from audit but the accounts must be accompanied by a report from a reporting accountant.

The Act says:

a.   The company is exempt from audit if the directors cause a report to be prepared in accordance with S.249C and made to the company's members by a suitably qualified reporting accountant.

b.   The report is required to state, whether in the opinion of the reporting accountants making it:

– the accounts of the company for the financial year in question are *in agreement with the accounting records kept by the company under S.221* and

– having regard *only* to, and on the basis of, the information contained in the those accounting records, those accounts have been drawn up in a manner consistent *with the provisions of the Act* (ie the accounting requirements) specified in S.249C so far as they are applicable to the company.

The report must also state whether in the opinion of the reporting accountant, having regard *only* to the information contained in the accounting records, the company *satisfied the requirements* for exemption and did not fall into the categories of company not entitled to exemption.

You will see that the report is limited in scope and investigations are limited to the books of account. You should also realise that the company still has to comply with The Companies Act requirements as a small company in all other respects.

Compiling the report

13. The SSRA requires that:

a. The reporting accountants should perform such procedures as are necessary to provide a *reasonable* basis on which to express the opinions.

b. The terms of the engagement should be agreed with the directors in a *letter of engagement*.

c. In the conduct of the engagement the reporting accountants should comply with the *ethical* guidance issued by their professional body

d. The reporting accountants should *plan* their work

e. Working papers should adequately *record* the *plan and the procedures* and should provide *evidence* that the work was carried out in accordance with the SSRA and supports the *conclusions* drawn

f. Work delegated to assistants should be *directed, supervised and reviewed* so as to provide confidence that the work was done *competently* and in accordance with the SSRA

g. The reporting accountants should perform procedures as are necessary to provide a reasonable basis for an opinion on whether the accounts are in agreement with the accounting records.

    Appropriate work will include test checking postings to ledger accounts from books of prime entry, checking all balances to the trial balance and checking the trial balance and adjustments to the accounts. **It is not necessary** to determine if proper accounting records have been kept or whether the accounting records are arithmetically correct. It also not necessary to check source documents such as invoices to the books of prime entry. Immaterial differences can be ignored.

h. the reporting accountants should perform such procedures as are necessary to provide a reasonable basis on which to express an opinion on whether, having regard only to, and on the basis of, the information contained in the accounting records, the accounts have been drawn up in a manner consistent with the accounting requirements specified in S.249C(6).

    This means that one of the Formats has been used and that all items are appropriately described For example fixed assets should be shown at cost or valuation less provision for depreciation and current assets should be shown at the lower of cost and net realisable value.

    The reporting accountants are not concerned with existence, ownership or value of assets nor of the completeness of income, liabilities or disclosures nor do they need to make any assessment of any estimates or judgements made by the directors in the preparation of the accounts, nor whether the accounts comply with applicable accounting standards.

i. The reporting accountants should perform such procedures as are necessary to provide a reasonable basis on which to express an opinion on whether, having regard only to, and on the basis of, the information contained in the accounting records, the company is entitled to exemption from an audit.

    The procedures required will be an inspection of the records to see if the report conditions appear to have been met. This will be relatively simple if the accounts are in agreement with the records and the accounts show numbers which are below the limits. In addition the reporting accountants have to determine if the company at any time in the year fell into one of the non-exempt categories. Normally the reporting accountants' knowledge of the business will answer this but they need to be alert to the possibility at all times.

j. If the reporting accountants either

- have doubts about whether the results of their procedures provide a reasonable basis for their opinion

- or become aware of information which indicates to them that the accounts may be misleading

they should discuss the matter with the directors. The directors may be able to explain the matter and dispel the doubts, bearing in mind that the reporting accountants do not seek independent evidence to corroborate any explanations. In any case practising accountants cannot allow their names to be associated with accounts which they believe may be misleading.

k. If the reporting accountants conclude that the conditions for exemption are not satisfied then they should not issue a report and should inform the directors. An audit will then be necessary.

l. If all is well then the reporting accountants should issue a report. An example is:

Accountants report to the shareholders on the unaudited accounts of Tichy Limited

We report on the accounts for the year ended...... set out on pages....

Respective responsibilities of directors and reporting accountants

As described on page ... the company's directors are responsible for the preparation of the accounts, and they consider that the company is exempt from an audit. It is our responsibility to carry out procedures designed to enable us to report our opinion.

Basis of opinion

Our work was conducted in accordance with the Statement of Standards for Reporting Accountants, and so our procedures consisted of comparing the accounts with the accounting records kept by the company, and making such limited enquiries of the officers of the company as we considered necessary for the purposes of this report. These procedures provide only the assurance expressed in our opinion.

Opinion

In our opinion:

a. The accounts are in agreement with the accounting records kept by the company under S.221 of The Companies Act 1985.

b. having regard only to, and on the basis of, the information contained in those accounting records:

   i. the accounts have been drawn up in a manner consistent with the accounting requirements specified in S.249C of the Act; and

   ii. the company satisfied the conditions for exemption from an audit of the accounts for the year specified in S.249A(4) of the Act and did not, at any time, within that year, fall within any of the categories of companies not entitled to the exemption specified in S.249B(1)

Miniscule & Co. (signature)   2 High St
Reporting accountants   Cloghampton
10 November 19...

---

m. If the reporting accountants conclude that in respect of a particular matter either,

- the accounts are not in agreement with he accounting records or
- the accounts have not been drawn up in a manner consistent with the accounting requirements,

they should issue a report including a negative opinion in respect of the relevant part of the opinion section.

An example:

Basis of opinion

As stated in note … the directors have made no provision in the accounts for the depreciation of acquired goodwill shown in the Balance Sheet at £x. Paragraph 21 of schedule 4 of The Companies Act 1985 requires that where goodwill is treated as an asset it should be reduced by provisions for depreciation.

In our opinion:

a. The accounts are in agreement with the accounting records kept by the company under S.221 of The Companies Act 1985.

b. having regard only to, and on the basis of, the information contained in those accounting records:

i. because of the absence of the provision for depreciation referred to above, the accounts have not been drawn up in a manner consistent with the accounting requirements specified in S.249C of the Act; and

ii. the company satisfied the conditions for exemption from an audit of the accounts for the year specified in S.249A(4) of the Act and did not, at any time, within that year, fall within any of the categories of companies not entitled to the exemption specified in S.249B(1)

Note that such disagreement may lead the reporting accountants to have doubts about the company's entitlement to the exemption from audit. For example if a fixed asset has been written off then true and fair presentation may take the gross assets over the limit.

n. There may be a limitation of scope. For example the directors may decline to give some information or explanations or some of the accounting records may have been destroyed. In such cases the reporting accountants issue a qualified opinion. This involves 'except for…'. In some cases a loss of records may be made up by the reporting accountants going back to the original documents. A loss of records of sales may lead to doubts about eligibility to exemption from audit.

o. In circumstances where the reporting accountants become aware that the accounts may be misleading they should add an explanatory paragraph in the basis of opinion section of their report, referring to the matter. It should be made clear that no opinion is expressed on the matter. An example may be apparent failure to provide for a doubtful debt or a contingent liability.

p. In very rare circumstances, the reporting accountants may:

- become aware of information which indicates to them that the accounts may be misleading and they also conclude that the matter cannot be adequately dealt with by modification of the report; or

– have serious doubts about the integrity of the directors.

In such cases the reporting accountants should resign the engagement, notifying the directors of the reason without delay. They may need to take legal advice on the wording of a letter of resignation if the directors' integrity is the problem.

Summary

14. a. Not all work done by accountants in connection with Accounts is auditing.

b. All work, audit or other wise, which is covered by an agreement should be subject to a letter of engagement.

c. The report should be labelled *accountant's report* unless a full audit is carried out.

d. Specific checks do not constitute an audit.

e. The client should sign a declaration.

f. A new Section 249A et seq. added two new privileges for small companies. Those with turnover under £90K are exempt from audit altogether. Those with turnover under £350k (Charities £250K) are exempt from audit but require an audit exemption report. Some companies, including financial service companies, still require an audit.

g. The exemption gives the directors some responsibilities

h. A report must be drawn up by reporting accountants giving an opinion on three. matters: that the accounts agree with the accounting records, the provisions of the Companies Act have been met, the company is entitled to the exemptions claimed.

i. Procedures performed by the reporting accountants are limited and their opinion is given only on the basis of these limited procedures.

j. The reporting accountants cannot give a qualified report on whether exemption is merited. If they are in doubt they cannot give a report and the accounts need an audit.

k. They can give a qualified report on the other matters.

l. They can give an explanatory paragraph if they have doubts about whether the accounts might mislead.

m. They may resign the engagement if they have doubts about the integrity of management.

n. The report must contain a title, the addressees (the shareholders of ... Ltd), an introductory paragraph identifying the accounts reported on, a statement that the directors are responsible for the preparation of the accounts, a description of the basis of the reporting accountant's opinion, the opinion, the name and signature of the reporting accountants and the date of the report.

Points to note

15. a. Failure to agree precisely the work to be done by an accountant (or reduce the agreement to writing) can lead to misunderstanding as to the extent of an accountant's responsibility for the Accounts.

b. Failure to make clear the extent of an accountant's responsibility for a set of Accounts may lead others to rely on the Accounts. This reliance may be misplaced and the accountant be made liable in damages.

c. A reporting accountant need not be a registered auditor but must be a member of one of the three Chartered Institutes or the Chartered Association or the Association of Authorised Public Accountants and must be entitled to engage in public practice and must be independent of the company.

d. Note the words *reasonable, having regard only to and, on the basis of*

e. Note that shareholders can demand an audit and, in practice, the bank and others can request an audit.

Case study 1 for Chapter 43

Dorrit has purchased a small shop with living accommodation at the back. He has opened the shop and is selling home brew and wine making kits and apparatus very successfully. He is largely financed by the bank. He now employs three people part time.

Philip, a Certified Accountant, has been approached to look after his financial affairs. Specifically Philip has been asked to prepare the annual accounts (preparable from an excellent book kept by Mrs. Dorrit; the business has an excellent modern cash register which analyses sales into categories), agree tax liabilities and send a copy of the accounts to the bank. In a few years Dorrit hopes to build the business up sufficiently to sell it.

Discussion

Draw up a letter of engagement.

Draw up a suitable accountant's report.

Case study 2 for Chapter 43

Piddling is a small company wholesaling boating equipment. Its accountants are Wee & Co. Certified Accountants and they summarise the books, extract a trial balance and prepare the accounts. In the past they have been the company's auditors. We are now considering the year ending 31 December 19x8.

The directors desire to take advantage of S.249.

Discussion

a. Outline the laying and delivering exemptions available to the company if the turnover is a. £300,000 or b. £4 million. The Balance Sheet totals are £100,000 and they have 5 employees.

b. Outline the audit exemption requirements and procedures in the same circumstances.

c. How would these be affected by:
    –   for a brief time in June 19x8 the company owned a subsidiary Barely Visible Ltd
    –   the trial balance differs by a material amount. The directors say they cannot find the difference and have ignored the difference in preparing the accounts.
    –   all loans have been lumped together although some are due in four months and some in ten years
    –   the administrative costs on the Profit and Loss Account include a material amount for a bad debt written off in earlier years but unexpectedly recovered. The directors decline to show this separately and Wee & Co. suspect that the better than expected profit is designed to impress the bank.

- the cash book shows some material transactions with a bank in Switzerland. The directors say these are normal trading transactions but decline to expand further on the matter.

d. Write out a clean report on the accounts.

Student self testing questions *Questions with answers apparent from the text*

1. a. What is the importance of a letter of engagement? (1)
   b. Distinguish an auditor's report from an accountant's report. (6)
   c. Draw up an accountant's report. (7)
   d. What is the client's role in connection with the annual accounts? (10)
   e. What companies cannot have exemption from audit? (11)
   f. What are the limits for exemption from audit and an audit exemption report? (11)
   g. What are limits for audit exemption (12)
   h. What three matters must be covered in an audit exemption report? (12)
   i. List the requirements of the SSRA. *Audit exemption reports* (13)
   j. Write out an unqualified report (13)

Planning and control of audits

1. The next section is concerned with effectiveness of organisation in an accountant's office and with the effective planning and control of individual audits.

2. Chapter 44 is on planning and Chapter 45 on quality control in auditing.

44 Planning

Introdution

1. It is of great importance that an audit is planned in advance because:

   a. The intended means of achieving the audit objectives must be established;

   b. The audit can be controlled and directed;

   c. Attention can be focussed on to critical and high risk areas;

   d. The work can then be completed economically and to time scale requirements.

2. There is a Statement of Auditing Standards SAS 200 *Planning*. In addition SAS 210 *Knowledge of the business* is relevant.

3. This chapter looks at matters to be taken into account, and the preparation of an audit plan.

Matters to take into account

4. a. The work to be performed in addition to the audit.

   b. Reviewing last years working papers.

   c. Changes in legislation (eg Financial Services Act 1986) or auditing or accounting practice (a new SAS, a new FRS).

   d. Analytical review of management accounts, consulting with management.

   e. Changes in the business or its management or ownership.

   f. Changes in systems or accounting procedures.

   g. Timing requirements.

   h. Extent of preparation by the client of analyses and summaries.

   i. Use of internal audit.

   j. Degree of reliance on internal controls.

   k. Joint auditors if any.

   l. Rotational testing.

   m. Liaison with the audit committee.

5. As an example of audit planning, we will consider the case of Stubby Widgets Ltd, a manufacturer, importer and wholesaler of widgets and the auditors who are Fastwork and Co. The December 19-6 audit plan is to be prepared by Fiona who is a new member

of staff. She has to consider all the matters mentioned in paragraph 4 and finds the following data requires attention:

a. A special report has to be prepared for the Widget Manufacturers Association on the cost structures in the company.

b. As Fiona is new to the audit she needs to read previous years papers especially carefully as her predecessor has left Fastwork and the audit partner, to whom she reports has also changed as old Mr Tick has retired and gone to live in the Bahamas. The 19-5 audit was completed in May 19-6 and the time is now July 19-6

c. There are several of these as my readers will know. Happily all these are summarised in Fastwork's internal Updating and Fiona is sent on courses regularly.

d. The client produces monthly accounts internally and Fiona finds that turnover increased substantially after March as a new branch was opened in Paris and two major new products began manufacture. These two products are new technology and the company have taken a risk in introducing them at this time. Substantial capital expenditure throughout the first part of the year has already led to liquidity problems and this has been added to by increases in stock and debtors.

e. A structural review of the company consequent on the items mentioned in d. has led to three senior directors and managers being retired early and new appointments made in June. There is a new Financial Manager.

f. A completely new networked computer system was installed in April and is working well.

g. The directors have expressed a wish for the audit to be completed by the end of March and they promise to have the accounts ready by mid February.

h. Every conceivable schedule is available from the computer system. Fiona feels she should think up analyses which will help her prepare her analytical review procedures.

i. The company have no internal audit.

j. The company rely heavily on internal controls. Fiona thinks that much audit reliance on internal controls may well be possible.

k. There are no joint auditors.

l. Fastwork and Co do not generally engage in rotational testing as they see each audit as a single specific task.

m. There is no audit committee.

General strategy

6. SAS 200 suggests that there should be an *Overall Audit Plan* which outlines the *general strategy* and a *detailed approach* specified in an *Audit Programme*. In simpler audits these two documents could be combined.

The general strategy will be directed toward the following matters:

a. **terms of engagement** – work to be done – audit, precise accounting work to be done for client, tax etc, letters to be sent – letter of weakness etc, reports to third parties eg regulatory authorities.

b. **the client and its background** – history, products, locations, especially noting factors like a new managing director, a new computer, a new product.

    c.   **important figures and ratios** – from previous years and if available, from management and draft accounts.

    d.   **audit risk areas** – these might include stock, work in progress, or dealings with a company under common ownership.

    e.   the effect of information technology on the audit.

    f.   **extent of involvement of internal audit.**

    g.   **requirement for involvement of specialists.** These may be from within the audit firm eg computer audit or rarely external specialists.

    h.   **setting of materiality levels.**

    i.   **client assistance.** Assistance from the client may be required in providing documents and analyses, providing computer time, arranging visits to branches.

    j.   **the audit approach.** The extent of reliance on internal control, the use of substantive tests and analytical review procedures.

    k.   **timetable** – dates of interim, year end and final audits and of dead lines to meet eg AGM of company.

    l.   **staffing requirement.**

    m. **budget and fee.**

    n.   the operating style (eg direction from the top or disseminated decision making) and control consciousness of directors and management.

    o.   possibilities of error or fraud.

    p.   involvement with subsidiaries and their auditors, branches, divisions and other components of the audit assignment.

    q.   regulatory requirements (especially important in some types of company eg those in financial services.

    r.   going concern issues.

7.   The overall budget plan which Fiona needs to prepare includes:

    a.   An amendment of the Letter of Engagement to include the report to the Widget Manufacturers Association and the visit to Paris where substantial stocks are held.

    b.   Need for a careful read of SSAP 20 as the Paris branch is the first item in a foreign currency.

    c.   Assessment of the impact of new managers and need for Fiona to meet all the relevant staff and tour the works.

    d.   Extra time needed to audit capital expenditure.

    e.   Identification of risk areas. These include going concern, capital/revenue identification on new plant, the branch in Paris, increased stocks and debtors, identification of all creditors especially as payment is likely to be slower, the new computer system even though this is apparently going well, the viability of the new products.

    g.   Need to plan year end presence at stocktaking including Paris.

    h.   Need to spend time evaluating the new computer system and the internal controls which have been incorporated.

i. Identification of areas which are not material and as far as possible setting materiality levels. Fiona finds that this is essentially very difficult and prefers to wait and see the detailed items as she audits them.

j. The making of a list of all assets and liabilities, revenues and expenses so that detailed schedules of these can be requested from the client. For example she may request a breakdown of sales by product in order to examine the success/failure of the new products.

k. Need to identify and test, at the interim audit, internal controls which she may wish to rely on.

l. Need to audit assets and liabilities as much as possible before the year end in view of the short time available after the year end.

m. Fiona will need staff for the interim (which is flexibly dated), at the year end stock take (including Paris) (an awkward time), and at the final which will be rapid and therefore may need extra staff.

n. Extra work is required this year (capital expenditure, new computer system, faster audit, Paris, liquidity problems) and the fee will need to reflect this. Approach client early on this!

The audit programme

8. The audit programme develops and documents the nature, timing and extent of planned audit procedures required to implement the Overall Audit plan. The audit programme essentially will consist of a very detailed list of things to be done and will show all assets, liabilities, revenues and expenses and such things as sample sizes, bases of selection of samples and when and where the programme is to be carried out. It is a set of instructions to staff.

It needs to take into account:

- risks of error
- amount of audit evidence required in each area
- co-ordination of auditing with accounts preparation (if accounts are prepared by the audit team)
- the co-ordination of any assistance from client staff eg on schedule preparation, availability of records, internal audit
- involvement of other auditors (especially with groups) and experts if required.

Knowledge of the client's industry, business and organisation

9. It is essential that all members of the audit team fully understand the client's industry, business and organisation. This is so because only that way can they judge the risks associated with the engagement. Also an economical and effective audit can only be carried out with a full knowledge of significant environmental, operational and organisational factors. Knowledge of such factors also helps in communication with client's staff, in assessing the reliability of management representations and in judging the appropriateness of accounting policies and disclosures. This knowledge can be gained from:

- the client's annual report and accounts

- analytical review of the clients interim accounts, financial reports, variance analyses etc.
- internal audit reports
- visits to the client's premises and discussions with management and staff
- perusal of minutes of shareholders, directors, audit committee, budget committee etc.
- previous years audit files including the permanent file
- consideration of the state of the economy (audit staff are no doubt avid readers of the Financial Times)
- reports from within the audit firm which may be relevant to the client eg tax department and management consultancy
- perusal of relevant literature from credit rating agencies, stockbrokers, investment analysts
- perusal of relevant trade magazines and journals

Note that there is a Statement of Auditing Standards SAS 210 *Knowledge of the business*.

10. In the case of Stubby Widgets Ltd, background information would be obtained from a variety of sources including the monthly accounts, previous years files and accounts, talking with the clients management and staff, reading minutes etc, review of trade magazines which may have a bearing on the viability of the company and its new products.

Summary

11. a. Planning is very important in auditing if the audit objectives are to be met economically, efficiently and to tight time and cost constraints.

   b. SAS 200 suggests that there should be, for each audit engagement, an Overall Audit Plan and an Audit Programme.

   c. In planning an audit a thorough understanding of the client, its industry and surrounding matters needs to be gained by all audit staff. There are multiple ways of gaining this knowledge from reading the Financial Times to talking to client staff in the staff canteen. SAS 210 covers this topic.

Points to note

12. a. The plan should also emphasize the importance of:

      i. staffing requirements in terms of experience and special skills needed and of availability;

      ii. proper briefing of staff on the client and its industry, high risk areas, related party matters etc.

   b. A modern approach to audit planning is to assess the client for risk. A client which is felt to offer above average audit risk will need the most competent staff and this has to planned for. In addition identification of high risk areas in an audit enables the audit to be focussed and the most resources put into the right areas.

   c. With modern audits resources are limited and costs high. The most effective and efficient audit can only be performed if it is well planned. Planning includes getting the right mix of evidence gathering in terms of analytical review, systems testing and substantive testing.

d. In the case of Stubby Widgets several new factors emerged for the 19-6 audit which necessitated forward planning in detail. These included the new computer system, the change of management, new capital investment, new products, liquidity problems, Paris, and a tight timetable for the final accounts. Without planning for these factors, the audit would be less efficient, less timely and more expensive.

e. However much an audit is planned, it is impossible to take into account every factor which will actually affect the audit. However identifying the probable factors will at least enable the audit firm to take them into account in formulating the plan and the staffing requirements.

f. SAS 200 requires that the audit work planned should be reviewed and, if necessary, revised during the audit. It advises that such changes should be documented.

Case study for Chapter 44

Gnomic Garden Equipment plc manufacture garden tools of all sorts from trowels to motor rotovators. They have three factories and some 800 employees. Turnover in 19-6 is expected to be £13 million about 2% up on 19-5. Exports take about 40% of turnover. Profit in 19-6 is expected to be about £400,000 against £1.2 million in previous years. During the year the company appointed a new dynamic young chief executive to halt the slide in profits. One of his first moves was to replace an old mainframe computer with a system of micros.

Spicy & Co. the auditors have been asked to complete the audit early as the new chief wants the annual general meeting to be in early April instead of early June. The company's year end is 31st December. The chief executive has also stated that the audit fee has always been far too high and he is looking for a much more efficient audit.

Spicy & Co's. partner in charge of the 19-6 audit is considering the audit plan for the year ending 31.12-6 in June 19-6.

Discussion

a. Identify the areas of audit risk that may exist with this audit.

b. List the matters to be taken into account in formulating the audit plan.

c. Discuss ways in which the audit could be made more economical.

d. Draft an Overall Audit Plan for the 19-6 audit.

Student self testing questions *Questions with answers apparent from the text*

1. a. What matters must be taken into account in planning an audit? (4)

b. List matters which are relevant to the preparation of an Overall Audit Plan. (6)

c. What is an audit programme and what must be taken into account in developing it? (8)

d. List ways in which knowledge of the business may be gained. (9)

Examination questions without answers

1. You are the audit manager of Goalatso PLC and at the initial planning meeting with the finance director you are advised that during the year the company acquired a 28 year lease over a piece of land on which it has erected a new office building. The cost of construction was £1.5 million, of which £100,000 related to the capitalisation of the company's own staff costs and overheads. The company had to borrow in order to

finance the project and the final cost includes capitalised interest. the entire property is occupied by Goalatso plc who vacated their existing short term leased premises at the time of the move to the new premises. The old lease has still three years to run.

Required:

Draft paragraphs for inclusion in the audit planning memorandum highlighting:

1. the audit issues arising from the construction of the new premises; and
2. the audit work which you plan to carry out in relation to these matters

(ICAS 1995)

2. Your client, Communico Distributors Ltd., has for several years been a family owned company selling telephones and answering machines through its own dealer network in the South of England. In May 1990, the company was bought by two brothers, Peter and Charles Brown.

Shortly thereafter, the company acquired the exclusive United Kingdom distribution rights to a revolutionary car phone, manufactured in South Korea, which sells for about half the price of competitive products, and is fully compatible with all British mobile telephone networks.

During the year ending 31 August 1991, expansion has been rapid under the new management. Specifically:

1) The new car phone received extensive media acclaim during October and November 1990, which was accompanied by regional television advertising campaigns. Since then, monthly sales have increased from £500,000 to £1,600,000.

   Sales of the new car phone now account for 75% of the company's turnover.

2) The company has purchased dealer networks from three other companies and is negotiating to purchase two more which will then complete its national coverage.

3) Employee numbers have increased rapidly from 40 to 130, of which administration staff at head office have risen from 12 to 28.

4) In June 1991, the central distribution and servicing department moved from head office into larger premises in Milton Keynes.

This was necessary to handle not only the increased stocks and pre-delivery checks necessary, but also the rising level of after sales warranty work caused by manufacturing defects in the new car phone.

Requirement

Prepare an outline planning memorandum for the audit of Communico Distributors Ltd for the year ending 31 August 1991, which identifies the potentially high risk areas of the audit and details how the audit effort will be directed to overcoming these problems.

(14 marks)
(ICAEW 91)

45 Quality control

Introduction

1. It is of primary importance to the business world in general and to the auditing profession in particular that an audit should be a quality product. Audits should be extremely well done and yet be completed expeditiously and economically.

2. There is a Statement of Auditing Standards SAS 240 *Quality control for audit work*

    SAS 240 requires that in all firms, quality control policies and procedures should be implemented both at the level of the **audit firm** and on **individual audits.**

3. This chapter deals with quality control under three heads:

    a. Audit firm organisation.

    b. Planning, controlling and recording individual audits.

    c. Reviews of audit firms procedures in general and of particular audits.

    d. The ISO 9000 series of Quality Management Systems.

Audit firm organisation

4. It is recognised that each firm has its own needs depending on size, geographical spread, special expertise etc, but all firms must organize procedures which ensure audits are performed:

    a. In accordance with approved auditing standards.

    b. In conformity with statutory (eg Companies Act) and contractual (letter of engagement) requirements.

    c. In conformity with personal (ethical) standards.

    d. In conformity with any professional standards set by the firm itself – many firms pride themselves on their professionalism.

    e. Economically and to time schedules.

    f. With minimum risk.

5. The procedures required are:

    a. Each firm should establish a and monitor control policies and procedures and communicate these to all partners and staff. Larger firms employ printed manuals but smaller firms may have to rely on verbal instruction.

    b. *Acceptance and reappointments as auditor.* There should be a procedure for evaluating prospective clients with consideration of the firms ability to meet the client's needs and for making the decision on acceptance which may be made by an individual partner, or by an individual partner, or by a committee.

    c. *Professional ethics.* Procedures to ensure all partners and staff are aware of and adhere to the principles of independence, objectivity, integrity and confidentiality. It is important to instruct staff who are not members of professional bodies and to monitor observance of ethical standards. For example, staff might not be aware on the prohibition on ownership of shares in client companies or may be unwilling to sell them if they are so aware. Consideration should be given to the auditor's independence and ability to serve the client properly and to the integrity of the client's management.

d. *Skills and competence.* The object is to have a fully competent and skilled set of partners and staff. Procedures include:

    i. Recruitment only of suitably qualified and expert staff. Staffing needs should be planned ahead.

    ii. Technical training and updating. All partners and staff should be encouraged to learn, and to keep up-to-date with technical matters. The firm could provide literature, maintain a technical library, send people on courses and hold courses themselves. Some firms produce a special newsletter at intervals to update staff with technical developments.

    iii. On-the-job training and professional development. Planning, Controlling and Recording emphasises the importance of relating staff abilities to client need but opportunities should also be provided for staff to have adequate experience on a range of clients as on-the-job training. Performance of staff should be evaluated and discussed with staff concerned. This kind of assessment and feedback is now common practice in all walks of life.

e. *Consultation.* Individual members of the firm should not take decisions on problem areas without consultation with others. Problem areas might be technical (eg computers where expert members of staff should be consulted) or matter of risk (eg to qualify or not to qualify). Sole practitioners are advised to consult with other firms or with professional advisory services.

f. *Monitoring the firms quality control procedures.* Suitable procedures should be introduced to ensure that all procedures are working adequately. This is dealt with in the review section.

Individual audits

6. The control procedures to be applied to individual audits include:

a. **Allocation of staff** – staff should have appropriate training, experience, proficiency and, if required, special skills (eg in computing)

b. **Proper briefing of staff** – staff should be properly informed on:

    i. objectives of the audit

    ii. timing required

    iii. the overall plan of the audit

    iv. significant accounting and auditing problems

    v. related parties

    vi. the need to bring problems and put upon enquiry situations to superiors.

c. **Audit completion checklist** – with sections for completion by staff and reporting partner. It is a common experience, that in the rush to complete an audit on time, matters of importance can be overlooked.

d. **Contentious matters** – all problems, special difficulties, and potential qualifications must be identified, recorded and discussed by, if necessary, the reporting partner with colleagues or even another practitioner.

e. **Documentation** – all audit work and conclusions reached must be fully recorded in the working papers.

f. **Reviews** – all audit work must be fully reviewed. This is dealt with in the next section.

g. **Acknowledgement** – all audit work and review action should be acknowledged in writing by the performer.

h. **Supervision** – Personnel with supervisory responsibilities should monitor the progress of the audit to consider whether assistants have the necessary skills and competence to carry out their assigned tasks, assistants understand the audit directions and the work is carried out in accordance with the overall audit plan and the audit programme. I well remember carrying out audit work in the distant past without knowing what I was doing or why I was doing it! Times have, I hope, changed.

Review

7. There are several levels of review. Some reviews are concerned with each individual audit. For example before a partner signs an audit report, he should first complete the laid down procedures for reviewing the work of the managers and staff. Before the manager passes on accounts to the partner for signature, he should himself carry out the laid down procedures for reviewing the work of the audit staff.

There should always be a post audit review. This is usually carried out after the completion of the audit but before the partner signs the auditors report. This will involve the partner in completing a check list and acknowledging that he has done so. The check list will include the following:

a. Review of the Accounts. Do they:
   i. Comply with statutory requirements?
   ii. Comply with SSAPs?
   iii. Use and disclose appropriate accounting policies which are consistent with previous periods?

b. Review of Internal Control evaluation. Is all documentation ie flowcharts, ICQs etc, complete? Were all weaknesses investigated and a letter of weakness sent to the client and acknowledged? There should also be a review of the assessments made of inherent and control risks and of any changes made to the overall audit plan or audit programme as a result of tests of control.

c. Review of the audit programme. Has all the work been completed and acknowledged?

d. Review of the files. Were all assets and profit and loss items verified?

e. Are all conclusions expressed consistent with the results of the work performed and do they support the audit opinion? It is very important that conclusions on such matters as going concern basis are fully documented, reasonable, and defensible in court!

8. Some reviews are conducted of particular audits to monitor that the firm's procedures are working in general.

9. Review panels. It is desirable for audit firms to set up internal review panels to consider difficult or contentious points referred to it. All decisions on audit report qualification should be subject to a review panel.

British standard ISO 9000 series

10. One way of adding to quality control in auditing firms is to be certified under the ISO 9000 series. These are the standards that lay down criteria to enable firms to demonstrate to themselves and to the public that they have procedures that, when followed, will provide a consistent, reliable and high quality service. Certification is by an accredited certification body and the audit firm must have written and installed a quality management system. The ISO 9000 series is widely used in manufacturing industry but is also available in service industries. ISO 9001 and ISO 9002 apply to financial service companies.

The benefits of the ISO 9000 series registration include:

– assurance of quality can mean higher client satisfaction

– more efficient use of resources

– higher fees and profitability

– perhaps lower professional indemnity insurance premiums

– some clients may require ISO 9000 series registration from all suppliers. This does not normally apply to service suppliers but may do so in the future.

– higher credibility with third parties such as banks, inland revenue etc

– greater staff satisfaction and confidence

– marketing benefits

There are some drawbacks including:

– loss of client confidentiality as files have to be available to the consultants

– cost

– continuous commitment.

ISO 9000 is clearly a good thing and does ensure a consistent and high quality delivery of service. However it does not address the issue of the correctness of service delivered. To do that an auditing firm must aim for Total Quality Management. I have said that possession of a ISO 9000 certificate implies a high quality delivery of a service but it has been suggested that it actually implies only the delivery of a consistent service of what may be a low standard service.

Summary

11. a. Audit work must be controlled.

   b. This control is implicit in an audit firm's systems and procedures for carrying out audits.

   c. Audit work must be subject to review.

   d. Reviews are carried out in practice by a variety of categories of person from inside and outside the firm.

   e. It is possible for an audit firm to obtain ISO 9000 series certification.

Points to note

12. a. Auditors are under pressure to ensure that audit standards are high because:
    i. Publicly aired failure is bad for business.
    ii. Failure to live up to standards can lead to expensive litigation.
    iii. Inefficiency is unprofitable.
  b. Independent review by persons unconnected with the detail of an audit can lead to the discovery that:
    i. The firm's procedures are not always followed.
    ii. There are gaps in the procedures.
    iii. There are technical matters of general interest which need investigation.
    iv. Staff or partners are overworked.
    v. Deadlines are too tight.
    vi. There are deficiencies in the quality of the staff or in their training.
  c. Quality control can be seen in several stages:
    i. Proper organisation of the firm and its procedures.
    ii. Planning for each audit.
    iii. Control of each audit.
    iv. Working papers.
    v. Review of work done.
    vi. Review of organisation and procedures.
  d. It is important to distinguish between procedures designed to ensure the firm as a whole provide a high standard product in all professional engagements and procedures to ensure that each individual engagement is properly carried out. A review of an audit may be to sample the effectiveness of the overall procedures or may be to ensure that a particular audit was performed effectively.
  e. In order to ensure that all that needed to be done on an audit was done any review should be conducted on the basis of a checklist

Case study for Chapter 45

George Hardprest is a sole practitioner with 12 unqualified staff and gross fees of £200,000.

Discussion

  a. What training facilities should his firm provide?
  b. George has been asked to take on the audit of a small company which has been criticised in the consumer column of the local paper. The proprietor has served a prison sentence for fraud. Should George accept the client?
  c. George is the auditor of a company with cash flow difficulties. He is now inclined to 'include an explanatory paragraph' in his report – but the managing director has said that if he does George will lose the audit and that of another company under the same control. George is desperate to discuss the matter. With whom can he have discussions?

    d.   What ought to be included in George's technical library?

    e.   Would ISO 9000 help George?

Student self testing questions *Questions with answers apparent from the text*

1.   a.   In what ways should audits be performed? (4)

    b.   What procedures might ensure audits are conducted in a quality manner? (5)

    c.   What control procedures should be applied to individual audits? (6)

Examination questions without answers

1.   In your capacity as senior partner in charge of overseas audits in a large London firm of auditors, you are concerned with the effective maintenance of a high standard of work throughout the firm's overseas audits.

    State how you would seek to maintain the highest standard of work in all overseas audits.   (12 marks)

                                                            (LCC)

Holding companies and group accounts

1. Companies frequently have *subsidiary* companies which they own or control. This applies particularly to quoted companies but can apply also to private companies. A *holding* company and its subsidiaries are collectively known as a *group*.

2. Some auditing problems apply to holding companies in their own accounts and these are dealt with in Chapter 46.

3. Groups of companies are required to prepare *group accounts* in the form of *consolidated accounts*. This is a large subject from an accounting point of view and has considerable audit interest as well. This is dealt with in Chapter 47.

4. The Companies Act 1989 amended the Companies Act 1985 substantially in this area. Other sources of information in this section include:

   FRS 2– Accounting for subsidiary undertakings

   SSAP 1 – Accounting for associated companies

   SAS 510 – The relationship between principal auditors and other auditors.

46 Holding companies

Introduction

1. The published Accounts of a holding company will consist of a *Balance Sheet*. Among the assets of the holding company will be *Investments in subsidiary companies*. There will not usually be a published profit and loss account as the Companies Acts allow a holding company to publish only a *consolidated profit and loss Account*.

   However, the notes to the company's individual Balance Sheet must show the company's profit or loss for the financial year.

2. The Companies Act has numerous and detailed requirements on the presentation of a holding company's own balance sheet. If you cannot remember these, you should revise them before continuing.

Audit considerations

3. The audit of the Accounts of a holding company follows the same lines as any company audit. However, special consideration must be given to the dealings with and presentation of the investments in subsidiary companies.

4. The verification of the investments in subsidiary companies will include the following work.

   a. **Audit schedule**

   The current file should contain a schedule with the following data:

i.   All the data which the Companies Act require to be disclosed in the holding company's own accounts.

ii. Companies of the Accounts of each subsidiary with a note of who are the auditors (the holding company auditor may audit all, some or none of the subsidiaries), and of any qualification in any of the auditors' reports.

iii. A summary of all movements in investments in subsidiaries and on current and loan accounts with each subsidiary.

iv. Reconciliation of inter-company balances.

The last item creates much difficulty in practice.

b. **Verification of existence and ownership of investments in subsidiaries**

This is effected:

i.   By examining share certificates. If the certificates are not in the name of the holding company, there should be blank signed transfers and declarations of trust by the persons who own the shares on behalf of the holding company.

ii. If the certificates are held by third parties (eg bankers), by obtaining a certificate from the custodian stating that they are held free of any encumbrance (eg the shares are not held as security for a loan) or, if encumbered, the nature of the encumbrance. The auditor should satisfy himself that the share certificates are held by third parties in the *ordinary course of business* and that no circumstances *putting him upon enquiry* arise.

c. **Verification of current and loan accounts with subsidiaries**

i.   This is normally effected by obtaining a certificate from each subsidiary acknowledging the balances concerned.

ii. If the auditor of the holding company is also auditor of the subsidiary, he can reconcile the entries in both sets of books himself.

iii. The auditor should satisfy himself that dealings between group companies have not been used to cover material fraud.

d. **Verification of value**

i.   If the shares were acquired in the year, vouch the acquisition in the usual way, considering *cost* and *authorisation*. Examine accounting treatment of the premium or discount on acquisition and of any dividends received out of pre-acquisition profits.

ii. The balance sheet date value of each subsidiary must be considered. The auditor should regard such investments as the same as other assets in his duty towards their value.

If ordinary investments are held as *fixed assets* and their value has fallen below book value, then there is *no need* for the book value to be reduced to market value *unless* the fall in value is regarded as permanent.

If ordinary investments are held as *current assets* and their value has fallen below *book value then the book value must be written down to net realisable value.*

Investments in subsidiary companies are *not* current assets but it is necessary for such investments to be written down if their value has fallen *below book value.* Hence the auditor must form an opinion of the value of each investment in a subsidiary company.

There are several points to note in assessing the value.

i. whether the investments were purchased at a premium over net assets.

ii. The present net assets of the subsidiary excluding goodwill.

iii. The profitability of the subsidiary.

iv. Whether the subsidiary has made losses.

This latter point can cause confusion. If the subsidiary makes a loss then it is reasonable to suppose its value has fallen *but it does not follow that its value will fall below book value.* If, however, since acquisition, losses have exceeded profits then it is reasonable to suppose that the value has fallen *below* cost.

Special consideration must be given to the value of overseas subsidiaries which are located in politically unstable countries.

Summary

5. a. Holding companies often have as their principal asset, investments in and loan and current accounts with subsidiary companies.

   b. The Companies Act says a great deal about disclosure and presentation of data about subsidiaries.

   c. The auditor has a duty to verify the asset 'investment in group undertakings'.

   d. Special considerations are

   i. Compliance with Companies Act requirements.

   ii. Verification of existence and ownership.

   iii. Investigation of current and loan accounts with subsidiaries.

   iv. Verification of value.

Points to note

6. a. Students must be careful to distinguish examination questions on *holding companies* from those on *group accounts.*

   b. The Companies Acts disclosure and presentation requirements *must be known.*

   c. The valuation of investments in subsidiaries is a difficult area. It is important to realise that such an investment need not be written down unless its value has fallen below book value (usually original cost).

Case study for Chapter 46

Foss Chemicals Ltd make chemicals for the defence industry. They had no subsidiary companies but in mid 19-6, they acquired 60% of the share capital of an American company for £600,000 paid partly in cash and partly in shares in Foss. The net assets of the American company, Forrus Inc, were about £800,000 at the time of purchase. Since then the company has made a loss of £200,000, but is expected to break even next year and make a large profit after that.

Discussion

a. Draw up a list of audit procedures that Paul, the auditor of Foss, should carry out in connection with Forrus. The audit of Forrus is carried out by an American firm. Paul is engaged on the audit of Foss's 19-6 accounts.

b. How should the matters connected with Forrus appear in Foss's own accounts? Foss advanced £120,000 as a loan to Forrus and has a trading balance of Dr £60,000 at 31.12. -6.

Student self testing questions *Questions with answers apparent from the text*

1. a. What should appear in the work papers of an auditor in connection with the subsidiary companies of the client and the client's own balance sheet? (4)

b. What audit procedures should be applied to subsidiary companies as an asset in the books of a client? (4)

c. How should subsidiary companies be valued? (4)

47 Groups of companies

Introduction

1. Group accounts consist of three statements.

a. The Consolidated Balance Sheet.

b. The Consolidated Profit and Loss Account and the Statement of Total Recognised gains and losses.

c. The Balance Sheet of the Holding Company.

In addition there are other statements which are discussed in Chapters 48 and 49.

The balance sheet of the holding Company was discussed in the previous chapter. This chapter discusses the two consolidated statements and the auditor's duties towards them.

There is a Statement of Auditing Standards SAS 510 *The Relationship between principal auditors and other auditors*.

Group accounts

2. Group accounts cause much difficulty to students but it is assumed that readers of this manual are totally familiar with both the Companies Act material in this area and with the methods commonly employed to prepare consolidated accounts. If you are uncertain of this subject please revise before continuing.

Note particularly when consolidated accounts are not required and the alternatives to consolidated accounts.

Students should also be familiar with the requirements of FRS 2, FRS 6 and FRS 7.

Small and medium size groups

3. Small and medium-sized groups are exempt from the requirement to prepare group accounts providing no member of the group is a public company, an authorised institution under the Banking Act 1987, an Insurance Company or an authorised person under the Financial Services Act 1986.

    The group must satisfy TWO of the following conditions:

	Small		Medium-Sized	
	Net	Gross	Net	Gross
Turnover	£2.8M	£3.36M	£11.2M	£13.44M
Balance Sheet Total	£1.4M	£1.68M	£5.6M	£6.72M
Number of employees	50		250	

    Note: – M = Million

    – Net means with the set-offs and other adjustments required by Sch 4A (eg reducing assets to values excluding intra-group profit margins)
    – Gross means before such adjustments
    – Either net or gross figures can be used.

    Clearly, a small company also qualifies as a medium-sized one and the difference between the two is as to whether the parent company qualifies to file abbreviated individual accounts.

    To take advantage of this exemption, the directors need a report from the auditor stating whether, in the opinion of the auditor, the company is entitled to the exemption. The report has to be attached to the individual accounts of the company.

Auditors duties

4. The auditors duties are somewhat onerous. He is required to express an opinion on the truth and fairness and compliance with the Companies Act of the consolidated accounts. This involves two stages:

    a. Forming an opinion on the truth, fairness, and compliance with statute of Accounts of each material company in the group.

    b. Forming an opinion on the truth, fairness, and compliance with statute of the consolidated accounts as a whole which are, of course, prepared from the Accounts of the individual companies.

    This task is difficult in all cases but is especially so in cases where a material amount of the net assets and profits of the group arise in subsidiaries which are audited by *other auditors*. This subject is dealt with later.

5. The work required in considering consolidated accounts is as follows:

    a. **Current audit file data**

        1. A complete list of subsidiaries showing the share holdings of the holding company or of other group members where there are sub-subsidiaries (sometimes known as vertical groupings).

        2. Copies of the Accounts of each subsidiary noting.

            i.   Qualified audit reports.

            ii. Agreement of inter-company balances.

       iii. The division between pre- and post-acquisition profits.

       iv. Accounting policies adopted.

       v. That each set of accounts is properly signed by directors and auditors.

    3. Questionnaires used to determine the work undertaken by subsidiary company auditors (discussed later).

    4. Letters of weakness sent by each subsidiary company auditor.

    5. A check list showing Companies Act requirements.

    6. A check list showing FRS 2, FRS 6 and FRS 7 requirements.

    7. A note of whether or not the group is entitled to small or medium-sized group filing exemptions.

b. **Accounting policies.** These should preferably be uniform throughout the group and proper disclosure of material policies should be made. If they are not uniform, the auditor should request that they should become so and if it is not possible (for overseas legislation reasons for example) then a full disclosure must be made.

c. **Consolidated adjustments** and the preparation of the consolidated accounts. The auditor must verify that the adjustments have been correctly carried out both conceptually and mathematically.

d. **Companies Act requirements.** The auditor must verify that all required disclosures have been made in the form prescribed. Alternative presentation to consolidated accounts must be considered. Consolidation may give a misleading view, but this would be very rare.

e. **See that all material subsidiaries have been audited.** Otherwise an opinion cannot be formed.

f. **Investigate non co-terminous accounts.** This should apply only to overseas subsidiaries, who may have year ends different from the holding company for legal or for other reasons.

g. **Investigate for 'window dressing'.** H Ltd, a holding company has a subsidiary S Ltd. H has a cash at the bank and S has an overdraft. The group directors would prefer that the overdraft was not shown in the consolidated Balance Sheet. They arrange that H draws a cheque in favour of S to repay the overdraft immediately before year end. Immediately after year end a cheque for the same amount is sent by S to H. Neither cheque is cleared. This is a sample of window dressing or artificial creation of a situation which though true does not fairly represent the underlying reality.

h. **Consider foreign subsidiaries.** There are special problems such as blocked currencies and political issues which may make the consolidation misleading. Accounting policies on currency conversion should conform to SSAP 20.

i. As with all auditing assignments the inherent risks must be evaluated. The extent of auditing procedures in each area will depend on this assessment and also on the materiality of each area.

Subsidiaries with different auditor

6. The auditor of the Holding Company (the *principal auditor*) has to give an opinion on the consolidated accounts which may incorporate the Accounts of material subsidiaries audited by other firms (the *other auditors*).

7. The directors of the Holding Company have a duty to produce Consolidated Accounts which show a true and fair view and comply with statute. The principal auditor has a duty to express an opinion on the consolidated accounts as a whole *even though* he has not carried out an audit on some of the figures that are included in them.

8. The principal auditor, then, is responsible for Accounts which he did not audit. He must make sufficient enquiries to satisfy himself that all the figures are reliable.

9. The work that the principal auditor must do to satisfy himself of the reliability of the Accounts audited by a secondary auditor is:

   a. **Accounting policies.** The primary directors should have arranged for uniform accounting policies to be applied to all group company accounts. Where this is not so (perhaps for overseas legislative reasons) the principal auditors should ensure that full information is available for altering the Accounts, or if this is not possible that the differing policies are fully explained.

   b. **Availability of information.** The primary directors should have sufficient control over the subsidiaries to enable them to secure all the information that is needed about:

      i. Accounting policies

      ii. Items needing disclosure

      iii. Consolidated adjustments

      If the primary directors lack sufficient information, then the principal auditor should seek *from the primary directors*, permission to approach the subsidiaries or the secondary auditors direct.

      The Companies Act 1985 Section 389A gives:

      1. A subsidiary company and its auditor a duty to give a principal auditor any information or explanation that he needs.

      2. A holding company a duty to obtain data from a subsidiary if the principal auditor requires it.

   c. **Scope of the work of the other auditors.** The principal auditors will need to be satisfied that:

      1. All material aspects of the subsidiaries' Accounts have been audited.

      2. That the work of the secondary auditors can be relied on. The answer to the latter problem is clearly difficult in that it boils down to a professional man asking himself if he can rely on the work of a fellow professional man.

      Whether or not he can depends on:

      i. What does the principal auditor know of the other auditor? After some years this will be resolved.

      ii. What auditing 'standards' govern the work of the other auditor? Standards are higher for example in the United States than they are in Gombovia.

    iii. What are the legal auditing requirements in the country where the other auditor works?

    iv. Who appointed the other auditor and to whom does he report? There may not be an arms length relationship between the primary board and the other auditors.

    v. Has any limitation been placed on the work of the other auditor?

    vi. Are the other auditors independent in all respects?

    vii. Is the other auditors' examination adequate and reasonable *in the principal auditor's opinion?*

Having considered the above, the principal auditor will have to consider whether any of the answers to the point above will cause him to qualify his report. He will also have to consider if any *qualifications* in the other auditors' reports need to be carried through to the principal auditors' report.

d. **Materiality.** Some subsidiaries will be so small in relation to the whole group that the problem of reliability of their Accounts can be ignored.

Note that a subsidiary can be not material in the context of the group but that several subsidiaries taken together can be material. In such cases each subsidiary has to be seen as material.

Consultations with secondary auditors

10. In all material cases it will be necessary for the primary auditor to consult with the other auditors.

The steps required are:

a. Obtain authority to do so through the respective boards of directors.

b. Request *written explanations* of the other auditors' *procedures* and *findings* with oral back up if necessary.

c. Examine the other auditors' *files* and *working papers.*

11. In practice, the principal auditor will compile a questionnaire to be completed by the other auditors. It is important to discuss the questionnaire with the other auditors *before* they undertake their audit.

Audit reports and other auditors

12. In the past it was common to find audit reports with statements that certain subsidiaries were audited by other auditors. SAS 510 advises against this idea as readers should not be misled into thinking that the principal auditor was other than fully responsible for his opinion on the group accounts.

It is suggested that the notes to the accounts could give an indication of material subsidiaries not audited by the principal auditor.

Post balance sheet events

13. The auditors of a group must carry out a review to identify events after the balance sheet date which are of significance to the group. This review must identify events which are significant to the group as a whole and which may occur in subsidiary companies. Where subsidiaries are audited by other auditors, an additional burden is put upon the principal auditor to ensure that an adequate review is carried out by other auditors.

Representations by management

14. The directors of a holding company have responsibility for producing group accounts. It may be that the group auditor may require representations from the directors of the holding company in respect of group matters. It may also be that the group auditor may require representations on group matters from subsidiary company boards. The source of representations depends on the management structure of the group.

Associated companies

15. The rules relating to the incorporation of the results of Associated companies in group accounts are not found in the Companies Acts but in SSAP 1. If you cannot remember these rules, you should revise them before continuing.

16. All that has been said in this chapter about subsidiary companies applies equally to associated companies. The principal auditor is likely to have even more difficulty in forming an opinion on consolidated accounts when the results of associated companies are included. This is because:

   a. An associated company is less likely to have the principal auditor as its auditor.

   b. The holding company is likely to have less influence on an associated company than on a subsidiary.

   c. The Companies Act 1985 assigns no duties to directors and auditors of associated companies to disclose information to principal auditors. However, some associated companies may be required to be consolidated as they are 'subsidiary undertakings' and their boards must give information to the principal auditors.

   d. An associated company is likely to have a different year end from the Holding Company.

   e. An associated company may well have different accounting policies.

Summary

17 a. Group accounts are subject to audit opinion in the same way as individual company accounts.

   b. Some of the figures in the consolidated accounts may relate to material subsidiaries audited by secondary auditors.

   c. There are established methods of assessing the reliability of such accounts.

Points to note

18. a. Before taking an examination in auditing in which the audit of group accounts may be included, students must be familiar with legal and accountancy aspects of group accounts. Especially note the occasions when group accounts are not necessary and the alternatives to the usual consolidated accounts.

   b. Note that the principal auditor is responsible for his opinion on the consolidated accounts even if he did not audit all companies in the group.

   c. Because of this he has to make such enquires as he thinks necessary to assess the reliability of the subsidiary company accounts and the subsidiary company's auditors.

   d. He can only do this after obtaining the authority of the Holding Company directors.

e. In auditing a group, the principal auditor seeks *evidence*. The work of the other auditor provides evidence as to the amounts included in the subsidiary accounts. Whether it is sufficient evidence is the nub of the matter.

f. Note that a other auditor is responsible for forming an opinion on the accounts of his clients, and he can do this *without considering the need to incorporate the accounts in consolidated accounts*. He will for example not be looking for stocks valued at above cost to the group or for accounting policies which are different from those adopted by the rest of the group.

g. SAS 510 recommends that the group audit report should not make reference to the fact of subsidiaries being audited by other firms.

h. Factors which may influence a principal auditor's approach to the work of a secondary auditor include the degree of *risk* which the principal auditor considers acceptable and the existence of specific audit problems (eg on stocks).

i. If the principal auditor is not happy that the secondary audit was carried out in accordance with approved auditing standards then, after consulting the Board, he may:

    i. Request additional audit tests by the other auditor.

    ii. Request additional audit tests to be conducted by him and the other auditor jointly.

    iii. Exceptionally, conduct his own additional tests.

j. In general a company which is itself a subsidiary is not required to produce group accounts unless it is itself quoted.

k. Subsidiaries should nearly always be accounted for under the acquisition method. Occasionally the merger method may be acceptable if the very stringent conditions of Sch 4 A are met.

l. Before accepting appointment as group auditor, a firm should consider whether their own participation is sufficient to enable them to act as principal auditors. They should consider:

    – the materiality of the portion of the financial statements they audit

    – what they know of the components of the business

    – the nature of their relationship with the other auditors

    – their ability to perform additional procedures

    – the risk of material misstatements in the subsidiaries' accounts.

m. A modern view of the acceptability of other auditors' work is that acceptability might depend on the quality control procedures in the other auditors' firm.

n. Other auditors are required by SAS 510 to co-operate with and assist the principal auditor.

Case study for Chapter 47

Take up again the case study in Chapter 46. Foss Chemicals have gross assets of £14 million and profits of £700,000.

Discussion

    a. Review FRS 2 in the light of the Foss – Forrus case.

    b. What matters should Paul consider when reviewing the group accounts?

    c. What actions should Paul take with regard to the audit by the American firm of the accounts of Forrus?

    d. Identify the risks and the risk areas that Paul should worry about.

Student self testing questions *Questions with answers apparent from the text*

1. a. State the rules re. small and medium sized groups. (3)

    b. List the procedures required in auditing a group. (5)

    c. List the principal auditor's rights to information about subsidiaries. (9)

    d. List the factors to be taken into account in evaluating the evidence, ' the work of a secondary auditor'. (9)

    e. State a selection of group matters that might not be of concern to a secondary auditor. (18f)

Examination questions without answers

1. You are employed in a practising firm of chartered accountants which has recently acquired a new client, URBINO Ltd., in which the principal shareholders are also directors. The directors are currently preparing the consolidated financial statements for the year ended 31st December, 1994, and, as the final audit is due to begin quite shortly, you recently held a planning meeting with the audit partner.

At that meeting, the partner noted that an audit approach had yet to be determined in respect of directors' remuneration and interests and their proper disclosure in the financial statements of URBINO Ltd. He is aware that these areas can be complex and is anxious that, in accordance with L203, *Audit Evidence,*, the audit approach chosen should balance the relevance and reliability of evidence available from each source with the time and cost involved in obtaining it.

You have assembled the following background information:

(1) URBINO Ltd. is a large privately owned holding company with a number of subsidiary and associated undertakings.

(2) The board of directors of URBINO comprises both non-executive and executive directors. The boards of all subsidiary undertakings are made up from these same persons. Certain directors also sit on the boards of associated undertakings.

(3) Non-executive directors receive fees for their services. Executive directors receive remuneration packages related solely to their executive appointments. These packages include salaries, bonuses, pension contributions and other benefits.

(4) Each director holds shares in URBINO Ltd. and in some of its subsidiary undertakings.

You have completed your interim audit visit during which your compliance testing confirmed that the system of accounting and internal control within URBINO Ltd. and its subsidiary undertakings had operated effectively during 1994.

Requirement

Prepare a short memorandum to the audit partner in which you should:

a. identify the principal audit procedures which might be adopted in order to verify that the disclosures included in the draft consolidated financial statements in relation to:

   i.   directors' remuneration;

   ii. directors' interests

   are complete and accurate in all material respects; and

b. conclude as to the most appropriate audit approach to adopt in the light of the audit partner's wish to balance the relevance and reliability of available evidence with the time and cost involved in obtaining it.

NB: Your answer should *not* deal with directors' loans or transactions.

(ICAI 95)

2. Ipanema plc has one subsidiary company called Copacabana Ltd. In your capacity as auditor of Ipanema plc and as group auditor, you have been investigating the inter-company current accounts and discover that they fail to agree.

Required

a. What possible reasons might there be for the lack of agreement?   (3 marks)

b. What is the group auditor's responsibility in connection with the difference?

(3 marks)

c. What audit method should you adopt?   (6 marks)

(LCCI 92) (Total 12 marks)

3. You are the group auditor to Erewash plc. During the year under audit review, the group acquired a majority shareholding in Trent Valley Ltd. You are not the auditor of Trent Valley Ltd, whose present auditors will continue in office.

State what specific audit methods you might undertake in connection with the acquisition of Trent Valley Ltd.   (15 marks)

(LCCI 90)

48 Other statements and interim accounts

Introduction

1. The other statements we are concerned with are:

a. The Chairman's report.

b. The Director's report.

c. Group accounts.

d. Cash flow statements.

e. Notes to Accounts.

f. Comparative figures.

g. Statistical summaries.

h. Lists of subsidiary and associated companies.

i. Accounting policies.

j. Any other information or statements in the Annual Report.

There is a Statement of Auditing Standards SAS 160 *Other information in documents containing audited financial statements.*

2. We will use this chapter to cover a new topic – the auditors' review of and report on interim financial statements. There is an APB bulletin B93/1 *Review of interim financial information.*

Directors' report

3. The Companies Act requires that a directors' report shall be prepared each financial year.

4. The auditor is not responsible for the directors' report and does not audit it or give an opinion on it. However S.235(3) The Companies Act 1985 requires:

'The auditors shall consider whether the information given in the directors' report for the financial year for which the annual accounts are prepared is consistent with those accounts; and if they are of the opinion that it is not they shall state that fact in their report.'

SAS 160 requires that the auditors should read the directors' report and if as a result they find any material inconsistencies with the audited financial statements, they should seek to resolve them. An example of an inconsistency is if the plant and machinery at the Birmingham plant was in the Balance Sheet at cost less depreciation but the directors' report said that this plant and machinery was to be scrapped and replaced with modern plant in the coming year.

If any inconsistencies come to light then the auditors should ask the directors to resolve the differences and make any necessary alterations to the accounts and/or to the directors' report. The directors will normally accede to this and the matter ends there.

If the directors decline to make any alteration then the position could be either or both of:

a. the financial statements are incorrect. In this case the auditors will possibly need to qualify their report – see Chapter 32.

b. the directors' report is incorrect. In this case the precepts of S.253(3) apply and the auditor should include a reference in his report. As an example:

'Inconsistency between the financial statements and the directors' report

In our opinion, the information given in paragraph 8 of the directors' report is not consistent with these financial statements. That paragraph states without amplification that the company achieved a 10% growth in profitability in the year. The Profit and Loss Account shows that the operating profit declined by 5% and the growth in net profit after tax was experienced only because of the inclusion of an exceptional item of £3.1 million on gains on the disposal of a subsidiary company.'

Note: This form of report is not a qualified report as the opinion on the financial statements is unaffected.

If the auditors consider that there is a *material misstatement* in the directors' report but it does not require that the financial statements be amended and the directors decline to change the alleged misstatement then the auditors should take legal advice as to what to do or possibly resign the engagement. SAS 160 gives no example but an example might be if there were major misstatements on the identity of the directors' or their shareholdings. You will appreciate that such is a misstatement but is not an inconsistency.

Schedules and statements

5. Company auditors are required to express an opinion on the financial statements. These are not simply the Profit and Loss Account and Balance Sheet but may include a number of separate schedules and statements:
    - The company accounts
    - the Group accounts
    - notes, attached to and forming part of, the accounts
    - comparative figures
    - schedule of accounting policies
    - lists of subsidiary and associated companies
    - cash flow statement

    The auditor's responsibility for these is as for the Profit and Loss Account and Balance Sheet. However see Chapter 35 for the comparative figures

Other documents

6. The annual report of a company may include other documents and material. For example, the Chairman's statement, statistical summaries, a photograph of the Board of directors and yet others.

    SAS 160 requires that all other statements, documents and information issued with audited financial statements should be reviewed by the auditors for inconsistencies with the financial statements and for misstatements within the other material. This is a new requirement. As with the directors' report any misstatement or inconsistency should be discussed with the directors and normally they make the necessary alterations and that is the end of the matter. However if the director fail to make the required alterations then:

    a. if the financial statements are incorrect, qualify their report
    b. if the matter does not affect the financial statements then take legal advice and, possibly, resign.

    A reference in the auditor's report to an inconsistency is only required where the inconsistency is between the financial statements and the directors' report.

    Clearly, the step of taking legal advice or resigning would only apply if the directors refuse to make necessary changes to the other information and the matter was very serious. Legal advice is necessary as the auditor may not be protected by qualified privilege against actions for defamation in all cases. Resignation, you will recall, gives the auditor a duty to make a statement of circumstances and gives him various other rights including the right to be heard at the AGM.

Interim accounts

7. In the past the Stock Exchange rules have required listed companies to issue interim accounts half way through the year as well as the annual report and accounts. This was usually just an abbreviated Profit and Loss Account. However rules have advanced and the Cadbury committee has reported. Consequently most listed companies now include a Balance Sheet and a Cash Flow Statement. It is not thought that these financial statements should be audited. However they should be *reviewed* by the auditors and a report issued.

8. The objective of a review is to provide the auditors with a basis for reporting:

   a. whether in their opinion the interim financial information has been prepared using accounting policies consistent with those used in the company's preceding financial statements; and

   b. whether they are aware of any material modifications that should be made to the interim financial information as presented. These objectives imply procedures which are substantially less than an audit.

9. **Procedures.** The procedures that should be adopted for a review are suggested at length in the bulletin and consist in essence of:

   - plan the work including undertaking an update of the auditors' knowledge of the business and assessing the potential risk of material misstatement.
   - obtain evidence by a process of enquiry and analytical procedures
   - review prior year matters including any points raised in management letters
   - consider the subsequent events review carried out on the previous audit
   - enquiry about any changes, planned or actual, to systems, operations, controls, risks etc
   - checking significant balances from the accounting records to the trial balance and to the accounts
   - reviewing minutes etc
   - reviewing accounting policies used
   - enquiry about subsequent events up to the date of approval of the interim accounts
   - reviewing the going concern basis
   - obtaining written representations from the directors
   - read any other information sent out with the interim accounts (see earlier part of this chapter)
   - discuss findings with the directors and the audit committee
   - report.

10. **The report** An example might be:

> *Report of the Auditors – Report to Interim PLC*
>
> We have reviewed the interim financial information set out on pages ... to... in respect of the six months ended 30 June 19x2., which is the responsibility of, and has been approved by, the directors. Our responsibility is to report on the results of our review.
>
> Our review was carried out having regard to the bulletin, 'Review of Interim Financial Information', issued by the Auditing Practices Board. This review consisted principally of obtaining an understanding of the process for the preparation of the financial information, applying analytical procedures to the underlying financial data, assessing whether accounting policies have been consistently applied, and making enquiries of the Group's management responsible for financial and accounting matters. The review excluded audit procedures such as tests of controls and verification of assets and liabilities and was therefore substantially less in scope than an audit performed in accordance with auditing standards. Accordingly we do not express an audit opinion on the interim financial information.
>
> On the basis of our review:
>
> – we are not aware of any material modifications that should be made to the interim financial information as presented; and
>
> – in our opinion the interim financial information has been prepared using accounting policies consistent with those adopted by Interim PLC in its financial statements for the year ended 31 December 19x1
>
> Tickers
> Certified Accountants, Sheinton   27 August 19x2

You might ask yourself:
- what did Tickers do and what did they not do?
- who is responsible for what?
- is this an audit?
- what do Tickers say positively?
- what procedural rules did Tickers follow and not follow?
- who are Tickers reporting to?

11. **Qualified reports.** It is possible to give a qualified report. These are much like those for fully audited financial statements discussed in Chapter 32.

Summary

12 a. A directors' report is a requirement of The Companies Act.

   b. The auditor is not responsible for the directors' report and does not give an opinion on it. However he is required to consider if any information in it is inconsistent with the financial statements.

   c. The auditor needs to clarify any inconsistency. Normally any inconsistency will be resolved and documents amended.

   d. If amendments are not made the auditor may need to qualify his report on the financial statements or include a statement on the matter in his report.

   e. SAS 160 has similar requirements for all other documents and information which accompany audited financial statements. However the requirement for a statement in his report where the other documents are inconsistent with the financial statements (but the financial statements are correct) applies only to the directors' report.

f. SAS 600 also covers misstatements in the other documents and information. Serious misstatements may require the auditor to seek legal advice on what to do and possibly to resign.

g. Interim accounts issued by listed companies now usually contain a Balance Sheet and Cash Flow statement as well as a Profit and Loss Account. The auditor should review these and give a report on his findings.

h. The report covers a small range of requirements including accounting policies used and whether any material modifications may be required to the financial statements.

Points to note

13. a. The auditor's report usually contains a statement like:

    'We have audited the financial statements on pages ... to ...'

    Auditors must take great care to see that the pages concerned cover all the statements subject to audit examination and opinion and only those statements. Cases have been known of the auditor's report apparently covering a colour photograph of Miss Bilston Boilerhouse 19-7.

   b. The annual report and accounts of a public company consists of a number of separate statements and schedules, some of which are, and some of which are not, subject to audit opinion. However it can also be viewed as a unitary whole. When viewed as a whole a view may be given of the results of the period or the state of affairs at the end of the year, which is different from the view given by the accounts which form a part of the whole.

    It is therefore desirable for, and SAS 160 requires that, the auditor to examine all other statements and if individually or collectively they give a different view from the accounts, he has a duty to feel put upon enquiry and to investigate the differences.

Case study for Chapter 48

Alice is engaged on the audit of Miss Lead plc a manufacturer of fashion dresses. She has read the proposed Directors' report and Chairman's Statement. She finds that:

1. The Directors' report, in discussing developments, states that the company intend to close down the factory at Liverpool and shift production to a newly built extension at the Bolton factory. The accounts include £48,000 as the unamortised cost of the plant at Liverpool. The factory there is leasehold with only one year of the lease to run.

2. The dividend per share is stated in the Directors' report to be 4.5p against 4.0p in the previous year and the Directors' report makes much play on the increase. In fact the final dividend has gone from 4.0p to 4.5p but the total dividend has gone from 6.3p to 6.2p.

3. The Chairman's statement states that the company is poised for a large increase in turnover and profit. Alice has seen the budgeted accounts and forecasts for the next year and further projections in a long range forecast and plan. These show a short term decline in business and profit and a very slow recovery in the long term.

The company turnover is £6 million, profits are about £450,000 and net assets £4 million.

The directors have lost the confidence of institutional shareholders and fear a take-over bid.

Alice has discussed these items with the Board and they adamantly refuse to make any changes.

Discussion

a. What should Alice do about these items?

b. Draft the audit report assuming nothing else was wrong.

Student self testing questions *Questions with answers apparent from the text*

1. a. What statements appear in an annual report and accounts? (1)

   b. What is the auditors duty towards:
      - The Chairman's statement, (6)
      - The Directors' report, (4)
      - cash flow statements, (5)
      - interim accounts. (7)

Exercise

Julia, the manager in charge of the audit of Chaotic PLC is reviewing the draft annual report of the group. Among other matters she notes:

a. The general tenor of the directors' and chairman's reports are optimistic but the accounts show a downward trend in profits and this is confirmed by the medium term forecasts prepared for the Board by consultants.

b. The financial statements include a stock of Thingies valued at £640,000 at cost. The Chairman's statement states that production of Thingies has ceased as they were loss making. Further enquiries by Julia, indicates that the stock will be sold as a job lot to Opp plc at a substantial loss.

c. The directors' report states that Subsida Ltd was sold for £3 million to Poke plc, giving a profit of £0.5 million. However the accounts include a provision for £1.3 million for a series of payments to Poke to compensate them for lower than expected profits earned by Subsida, as agreed in the sale contract.

d. The directors' report states without amplification that "Successful conclusion of the development of the Whatsit, a new product, will bring substantial profits to the group". Julia knows that prototypes have been plagued with faults and that a competitor will certainly beat Chaotic to the market.

e. For three months during the year, George Goon was a director of the main group board, having been a director of a subsidiary for several years. He resigned shortly before the year end before pleading guilty to drug smuggling offences. His name does not appear in the list of directors nor is his remuneration included in the directors' remuneration.

The board adamantly refuse to change any of these matters in the report and accounts. What should Julia's firm do, given that the profit of the group is shown as £6.1 million before tax.

Auditors and the law

1. You will already have appreciated that the law has relevance for auditors. The Companies Acts and their effect on auditors have taken up a large part of the manual.

2. Other branches of the law have also affected auditors and this part considers some of them. Some of the points made are about controversial issues which have practical and examination importance at the present time.

3. Chapter 49 deals with an auditor's obligations and liabilities under the law. Chapter 50 deals with unlawful acts and Chapter 51 with Dividends.

49 Auditors' liability

Introduction

1. Auditors perform audits and sign audit reports. These reports are the auditors' opinions on the truth and fairness etc. of financial statements. Auditors are known to be competent and honest. So if the auditors say financial statements show a true and fair view, readers of the financial statements will have faith in them because they have faith in the auditors.

2. As his work is relied upon by others the auditor clearly has a responsibility to do his work honestly and carefully. The judge in the London and General Bank case (1895) said:

    'He must be honest – that is, he must not certify what he does not believe to be true, and he must take reasonable care and skill before he believes that what he certifies is true.'

3. What is *reasonable care and skill* depends on the circumstances and is very difficult to assess in any given case. What is clear is that:

    a. An auditor may fail to exercise sufficient skill and care.

    b. As a consequence, some fraud or error may be undiscovered, or he may fail to discover that the accounts fail to show a true and fair view, or may contain a material misstatement.

    c. As a consequence somebody who relies on the work of the auditor may lose money.

    d. This loss of money flows from the failure of the auditor to do his job properly.

    For example, Hank plc., may buy Rabbit plc because inter alia, they believed that the accounts of Rabbit Ltd., showed a true and fair view of the liabilities of that company. It turned out that there were several liabilities excluded from the accounts. Botch & Co., the auditors, had failed to discover this as they had not applied the standard tests. Hank plc would have paid less for Rabbit Ltd., or not bought the company at all had they known about the error in the Accounts.

    e. This point is the vital one, the auditor *may* have to make good from his own resources the loss suffered by another person.

4. The auditor may (this mercifully rare) be dishonest or connive at the dishonesty of others.

5. The problems are:

    a. *What is reasonable care and skill?* We will discuss this later.

    b. *To whom does the auditor have a moral responsibility to do his work properly.* The answer is to his conscience and to any person who relies on his work.

    c. *To whom does the auditor have a legal responsibility?* By legal responsibility we mean an obligation to make good from his own pocket losses suffered by others, or to be more precise 'to pay damages which flow from his negligence'. This is a very difficult question which we shall review in due course.

    d. But first, we shall consider the *criminal law* and the auditor.

6. The criminal law applies to all citizens and auditors could find themselves in the dock if they committed any act which was against the law. Auditors acting as auditors generally do not break the law but it is not impossible to imagine an auditor conspiring with others to defraud the investing public by deliberately publishing a false prospectus. There are some specific crimes or misdemeanours which an auditor may commit. These include:

The Companies Act 1985:

– S.389   Person acting as an company auditor knowing himself to be disqualified

– S.389A   Subsidiary company auditor failing to give information to auditors of parent company

– S.394A   Person ceasing to hold office as auditor, failing to deposit statement as to circumstances

– S.458   Being a party to carrying on company's business with intent to defraud creditors, or for any fraudulent purpose

Insolvency act 1986. Accountants who act as liquidators, receivers or trustees can easily commit technical offences but there are few offences to trap the auditor except perhaps S.208 where, as an officer, he misconducts himself in course of winding up.

Financial services Act 1986. There are a number of offences which an auditor can commit under this Act

Civil liability under the common law

7. What is negligence? One definition is: some act or omission which occurs because the person concerned (eg an auditor) failed to exercise that degree of reasonable skill and care which is reasonably to be expected in the circumstances of the case. What is reasonable is not what a super careful and expert auditor would do but what an ordinary skilled man (or woman) would do in the circumstances. In the circumstances is an interesting idea. Auditors are expected to carry out audits following the requirements and guidance of the Auditing Standards and using their professional judgement. For example an auditor must consider the going concern basis by following the precepts of SAS 130. However auditing is a sampling process and evidence can be gained by such methods as analytical review and internal control evaluation. Not everything is examined in minute detail for cost and timeliness reasons and because the benefits would hardly outweigh the costs. However routine tests may be inadequate if the auditor is:

– put upon enquiry

– encounters increased cause for suspicion

– the bells start ringing

In these circumstances the auditor needs to do more than routine testing and evidence gathering. In the words of the old case, he or she needs to probe the matter to the bottom. For example if the auditor comes across a small number of purchase invoices which seem to have dates altered from pre year-end to post year-end then he is alerted to a possible deliberate attempt to improve the profit as measured. The whole matter is likely to be material and must be probed fully.

A useful equation is that negligence occurs if:

$$\text{Probability of harm or error} \times \text{Gravity of harm or error} > \text{Probability of its discovery by the audit tests conducted}$$

Let us see some examples of this. Suppose in a small company the wages area is controlled by one clerk. In such cases, there is a probability that a fraud could be committed and remain undetected, so the probability of harm is high. On the other hand the gravity of harm done cannot be great as any undetectable fraud could only be a small fraction of the total costs of the enterprise. The auditor might judge that no more tests should be conducted than in cases where internal controls were stronger. In a speculative building company which has built a number of estates on reclaimed land, the probability that damage might occur to the houses is small as all the appropriate tests and certificates were obtained. However the gravity of harm could be very great if a whole estate proved worthless as a result of undiscovered pollution on the reclaimed land. Perhaps in this case the left hand side of the equation would require extra audit procedures. A third example is that of a company which hedged its exposure to losses on its investment portfolio by dealing in derivatives. In such cases the probability of harm is high and the gravity of any harm could be very great (witness Barings Bank). The auditor needs to investigate and find evidence on the matter in very great detail.

8. The famous case of the *London Oil Storage Co. Ltd. 1904* will illuminate the idea of negligence and of loss.

The petty cash was misappropriated over a period of years so that the balance per the petty cash book was £796 in 1902 whereas there was only £30 in the cash box. The auditor did not count the cash and therefore did not discover the embezzlement. It was established that:

a. The auditor was negligent in not counting the cash as he should have been *put upon enquiry* by the surprisingly large amount (in 1902) of the book balance.

b. The company suffered loss.

c. The loss was caused by:

   i. The *directors'* failure to exercise proper control as is their duty.

   ii. The auditors. Not because they failed to discover the loss *already made* (clearly a loss cannot be caused by failing to discover it) but because their failure to discover a loss in previous years led to *further* defalcation.

   The auditors should have appreciated that the unusual size of the petty cash balance indicated a probability of harm or error and the gravity of possible harm was also large (in 1904) and so the audit tests conducted were insufficient.

d. The auditors were ordered to repay the loss caused by their negligence which was assessed at five guineas only.

The Hedley Byrne case

9. The next problem to consider follows from the modern concept that financial statements with auditors reports are relied upon not only by the persons with whom the auditors have contractual relations (the company, for example) but also many other people whom we can call *third parties*.

10. If the auditor is negligent and fails to discover that accounts do not show a true and fair view, then other people who rely on the accounts may suffer loss. Such people may include *lenders* or people who may want to *buy the business* or shareholders.

11. The question is 'Does the auditor have a *legal obligation* to recompense third parties who suffer loss as a consequence of his negligence?' Such an obligation might arise under the *law of tort*, torts being civil wrongs done to people.

12. In the case of *Candler v Crane Christmas & Co. 1959* it was decided that the auditor has no legal obligation in the absence of a *contractual or fiduciary relationship*.

13. However, doubt was cast on this judgement in the case of Hedley, Byrne & Co. Ltd. v Heller & Partners Ltd. in 1963. The House of Lords decided that the Candler case was wrongly decided and that actions for professional negligence can arise if financial loss is suffered by third parties who rely on the professional skill and judgement of persons with whom they have no contractual or fiduciary relationship. The case concerned a bank and not an accountant but the principle could extend to accountants and auditors.

14. The law was substantially clarified in February 1990 by the decision of the House of Lords in the case of Caparo Industries PLC v Dickman and Others. The facts of this case were that Caparo Industries PLC purchased shares in Fidelity PLC from June 1984 and subsequently made a successful takeover bid for Fidelity. Caparo alleged that the purchase of most of the shares were made in reliance on Fidelity's accounts for the year to 31 March 1984 which had been audited by Touche Ross and that those accounts were inaccurate. Caparo alleged that if the true facts had been known they would not have made a bid. The decision was that in these circumstances the auditors owed no duty of care to the shareholders (actual or potential) in respect of investment decisions.

15. Their lordships reviewed the intended purpose of statutory accounts. Primarily the accounts were sent to shareholders in the company in order that they may exercise their proprietary functions that is for the protection of the company and its informed control by the body of shareholders. Clearly accounts can be used for all manner of investment and other decisions but that is not their purpose. If the auditor was negligent and inaccurate accounts were sent to shareholders then they were deprived of their rights to exercise their powers in general meeting. In such cases it is for the company to seek a remedy from the auditors not individual shareholders. To widen the scope of duty of an auditor to include loss caused by reliance on accounts for a purpose for which they were not supplied would be to extend the scope unreasonably.

16. After this decision the profession and insurers breathed a collective sigh of relief. However many commentators were disturbed by the idea that accounts could not be relied upon in making investment decisions. However I take the view that one can rely upon a set of accounts without having the power to sue the auditors if they were negligent. The auditors are not insurers and are not paid to accept a liability to outside parties but only to their clients.

17. However legal opinion is that this decision does not entirely let auditors off the hook. They may still be liable to third parties if at the time of the audit they were aware of the investment in contemplation, knew the investor would receive the accounts and knew the investor was likely to rely on the accounts in considering the investment. Effectively, in auditing a company which is underfunded or vulnerable to takeover the auditor must be careful in his relations with third parties who might be considering an investment so that he is fully aware of his obligations in undertaking the audit.

Minimising liabilities

18. Auditors and accountants can minimise their potential liability for professional negligence in several ways:

   a. by not being negligent

   b. by following the precepts of the auditing standards

   c. by agreeing the duties and responsibilities in an engagement letter. This should specify the specific tasks to be undertaken and exclude specifically those that are not to be undertaken. It should also define the responsibilities to be undertaken by the client and specify any limitations on the work to be undertaken.

   d. by defining in their report the precise work undertaken, the work not undertaken, and any limitations to the work. This is so that any third party will have knowledge of the responsibility accepted by the auditor for the work done.

   e. by stating in the engagement letter the purpose for which the report has been prepared and that the client may not use it for any other purpose.

   f. by stating in any report the purpose of the report and that it may not be relied on for any other purpose

   g. by advising the client in the engagement letter of the need to obtain permission to use the name of the accountant and withholding permission in appropriate cases.

   h. by identifying the authorised recipients of reports in the engagement letter and in the report

   i. by limiting or excluding liability by a term in the engagement letter or, to third parties, by a disclaimer in a report.

   j. by obtaining an indemnity from the client or third party

   k. by defining the scope of professional competence to include only matters within the accountants' competence. Do not take on work you are not proficient at.

You will appreciate that an auditor's report under the Companies Act cannot include disclaimers, etc but it now does include the work done and the responsibilities of the auditors and the directors. However the advice holds good for special investigations and audits for special purposes.

You will also appreciate that auditors and accountants are now required to hold professional indemnity insurance.

The future

19. The problem of liability in tort, and also under contract law, of auditors to companies is currently a very hot potato. Interesting matters that are current include:

a. a campaign for reform in the USA where awards against auditors have been very great

b. statutory capping (limiting) awards in New South Wales

c. proposals for proportionate liability in the UK and elsewhere. Where negligence can be proved against directors and auditors jointly the usual situation is that the directors have not the funds to pay (they are not insured) and the auditors (or their insurers) have to pay the lot.

d. The Companies Act 1989 allowed auditors to be limited liability companies. KMPG partners have voted to turn part of the audit practice into a limited company. KMPG Audit PLC will still be liable for losses occasioned by the company's negligence but the risk of bankruptcy is taken away from the individual partners. Other firms are considering incorporating.

e. potential claims against auditors of astronomical sums exist in a number of very public cases. These include BCCI (a claim of up to $3 billion has been mooted) and Lloyds.

f. As I write, damages have been awarded against a major firm of accountants in the sum of up to £105 million in connection with the audited accounts of a company which was taken over by another company. This sum was not entirely covered by insurance and there may be a substantial personal loss to each of the partners. The matter may go to appeal but the effect of this award will be to speed efforts by the accounting profession to ring fence themselves against such awards.

g. A proposed law in Jersey in the Channel Islands to introduce limited liability partnerships. British firms of auditors should be able to register under this law in Jersey. The effect will be that the firms will have unlimited liability and could go bust. But the individual partners would have limited liability and thus be protected against catastrophic litigation. This is similiar to the situation in the US where firms register under similar legislation in Delaware. This idea is known as the Delaware option.

Should auditors' liabilities be extended?

20. There are some arguments in favour of extending the apparent legal duties of care by auditors to individual shareholders, purchasers of shares and possibly other third parties:

These include:

a. Third parties do rely on the integrity of audited accounts and would seem right that a legal liability should reflect that.

b. Professional men are paid and should therefore be accountable.

c. Where the company suffers loss (eg from fraud or theft) because of the auditors' negligence then the current existing legal remedy by the company against the auditor is appropriate. However if the directors overstate the assets and the auditor fails to discover this then the company does not suffer loss. However the shareholders or potential shareholders may suffer loss and it seems right that they should be able to recover from the auditors.

d. If liability is not extended then the public may perceive that the auditor is liable to no-one, there is no need for the auditor to exercise skill and care and the accounts are not reliable and are of little benefit.

21. There are also many counter arguments including:

   a. It is unreasonable and unrealistic to say auditors have a 'liability in an indeterminate amount for an indeterminate time to an indeterminate class' to use the words of Lord Justice Cardozo in 1931.

   b. Practical difficulties in deciding whether accounts were relied upon or not – a gold-mine for lawyers.

   c. The current legal framework sees the purpose of preparing and auditing accounts as assisting shareholders in assessing the stewardship of the directors not in assisting investors in their investments.

   d. Audit fees would be astronomic if full liability for investment decisions were taken on.

   e. The legal responsibility for producing accounts rests with the directors and it would seem inequitable if the liability arising out of incorrect accounts were transferred to auditors.

   f. The work required on an audit would need to be greatly extended at an enormous cost which, on a welfare economics standpoint, would be a misuse of scarce resources.

   g. The company pays the auditor and consequently expects to recover damages if the company loses as a result of auditor negligence. However investors to not pay the auditor and so should not expect to recover.

   h. Insurance cover for professional indemnity would be even more difficult and expensive to obtain.

Summary

22. a. The criminal law makes possible prosecutions against auditors who act dishonestly or recklessly or connive at dishonesty.

   b. Civil liability can arise under the Companies Act and the Common Law.

   c. In certain circumstances, civil liability can arise under the law of tort. This type of liability is currently a matter of discussion.

Points to note

23. a. Liability can *only* arise if

      i. The auditor can be shown to be negligent.

      ii. Loss has been suffered.

      iii. The negligence is the *direct cause* of the loss.

      iv. The auditor has *legal* liability in the circumstances.,

   b. The section on minimising liabilities is very important. All auditors now have to have insurance cover under professional indemnity policies.

   c. Cases of professional negligence concerning auditors very rarely come before the courts as such cases are settled out of court. That such cases are numerous is evidenced by rocketing professional indemnity premiums. The author takes the view that if more cases were allowed to come to the courts the issues of:

      i. what is negligence;

    ii. to whom does the auditor have a legal responsibility;

would be come clearer.

However in individual cases, a court hearing would involve enormous costs in terms of legal fees, partner time, and adverse publicity.

d. Auditors are required to perform their work with reasonable skill and care. It now seems well established that this means that the auditor must apply the standards of reasonable competent modern auditor. The modern auditor applies all the auditing standards and guidelines. Essentially the defence to a negligence claim is that the auditor followed the auditing standards and guidelines, but see paragraph 7.

e. Auditors are now required to carry professional indemnity insurance. There is a tendency to sue the auditor knowing that he will not have to pay but his insurer will. The effect of this is that the insurer will insist on reasonable skill and care on the part of his insured. In addition the professional bodies are required to act under the Companies Act 1989 as regulators of the conduct of their members. Professional accountants like lawyers, insurance brokers and others are finding themselves highly regulated. Perhaps this will lead to higher standards of care.

f. A recent case which threw some light onto auditors' liability was Berg Sons & Co Ltd and others v Mervyn Hampton Adams and Others 1992. Some of the lessons of the case were:

– auditors are not liable for an indefinite time after publication of the allegedly offending accounts. After a reasonable time it could not be foreseen that accounts would still be relied upon in making decisions (to lend money in this case but presumably any decision).

– audited accounts are only one source of information which a person should take into account in making decisions.

– unsupported representations by management or others, whether oral or written, are insufficient audit evidence.

– auditors are only liable for losses they have actually caused.

Case study 1 for Chapter 49

Wing Prayer & Co a small firm of Certified Accountants are the auditors to AHM Publishing Co Ltd, publishers of text books. During the audit of the December 19-5 accounts the audit senior engaged on the audit fell ill with overwork and was replaced by Guy a third year graduate trainee. Guy finished the audit and the partner signed a report. Shortly after the AGM which was on 23.6.-6 negotiations began for the sale of the company to Amalgamated Publishers plc who acquired the company in November 19-6.

The audit of AHM's 19-6 accounts by Puce, Watermelon in March 19-7 revealed that a printing bill for two of AHM's titles dated 30.11.-5 had been disputed and thus not entered in the books. The matter was resolved in August 19-6 when AHM paid the £8,000 owing. The bill was not accrued in the 19-5 accounts.

Amalgamated paid £60,000 for AHM whose reported profits net of management remuneration were: 19-3 £16,000, 19-4 £13,000, 19-5 £17,000.

Amalgamated sued Wing Prayer & Co. for damages.

Discussion

a. Discuss in detail all the issues raised by this case.

b. How might Wing Prayer & Co. minimise the chances of a repetition of the case?

Case study 2 for Chapter 49

Niggle & Co., the auditors to Daffodil Widgets Ltd, gave an unqualified report on 14 December 19-7 on the accounts for the year ending 30 June 19-7. These accounts were seen by The Wednesfield Bank PLC in September 19-8 and the bank lent £50,000 to Daffodil on short term overdraft in 19th September 19-8. In March 19-9 the company went into liquidation still owing the bank £50,000. The company was hopelessly insolvent and the bank recovered nothing. It turned out that the accounts of June 19-7 were defective in that several substantial creditors were omitted from the accounts. Had these creditors been included it would have been apparent that Daffodil was not a going concern in June 19-7.

Discussion

Can the bank recover from Niggle and Co?

Student self testing questions *Questions with answers apparent from the text*

1. a. How can an auditor be criminally liable under the Companies Act? (6)
   b. How can an auditor be liable for damages under the Common Law? (7)
   c. Summarise the London Oil Storage case and its lessons. (8)
   d. How can an auditor be liable under the Law of Tort? (9–17)
   e. What conditions must be satisfied for an auditor to have to pay damages for a tort? (23)
   f. Summarise the Hedley Byrne case and its lessons. (13)
   g. How can an audit firm minimise its potential for paying damages? (18)
   h. Summarise the Caparo case (14)

Examination question *(Answer begins on page 554)*

1. The accountancy profession is constantly concerned by the problem of auditors' liability. Required:
   a. To which parties might the auditor be liable?   (3 marks)
   b. Under what circumstances might the auditor be liable to third parties?   (5 marks)
   c. Your firm has been the auditor of Bonner Publishing for many years. It has recently been discovered that for the past few years, the managing director has consistently overvalued stock. Prepare a note for your audit partner advising him of the possible defences should a liability claim arise.   (7 marks)

   (AAT) (Total 15 marks)

Examination questions without answers

2. Audit risk is a combination of the risk that the financial statements being audited may contain material errors and that these errors may not be detected by the auditor's testing procedures. A failure to detect such errors may leave the auditor liable for losses suffered by other parties.

Required

a. Briefly describe what you understand by the terms 'inherent risk', 'control risk' and 'detection risk'. (5 marks)

b. Explain, in the light of recent case law, what you understand to be the auditor's liability for losses suffered by other parties. (10 marks)

(AAT 91) (Total 15 marks)

50 Unlawful acts of clients and their staffs

Introduction

1. This subject is a fascinating one for students who may see themselves in the role of Sherlock Holmes. However, the reality of discovering or being involved in crimes committed by a client or members of the client's staff is usually unpleasant or a cause for anguished inner conflict.

2. In practice, an auditor must always act scrupulously and correctly and in accordance with the law.

   He should:

   a. Take legal advice if necessary.

   b. Read the guidance provided by the professional body and by the auditing standards. Current guidance is contained in:

   – *requirements in relations to money laundering (*this a technical release)

   – *professional conduct in relation to defaults or unlawful acts* (this is ICAEW guidance for members in practice)

   – *SAS 110 Fraud and error* (see also Chapter 19)

   – *SAS 120 Consideration of law and regulations*

   – *SAS 620 the auditor's right and duty to report to regulators in the financial sector* – see Chapter 41.

3. An accountant must not himself commit a criminal offence.

   He would do so if he:

   a. Advises a client to commit a criminal offence.

   b. Aids a client in devising or executing a crime.

   c. Agrees with a client to conceal or destroy evidence or mislead the police with untrue statements.

   d. Knows a client has committed an arrestable offence and acts with intent to impede his arrest and prosecution. Impede does not include refusing to answer questions or refusing to produce documents without the client's consent.

   e. Knows the client has committed an offence and agrees to accept consideration (eg an excessive audit fee) for withholding information.

f.   Knows that the client has committed treason or terrorist offences and fails to report the offence to the proper authority.

g.   various activities in connection with money laundering – see later.

Discovery of unlawful acts

4.   If an auditor discovers an unlawful act he will not usually disclose this to the police or other authority unless

a.   The client authorises disclosure.

b.   The disclosure is compelled by process of law, eg a court order.

c.   Disclosure is required in the auditor's own interest eg in defending himself against civil or criminal actions.

d.   The circumstances are such that the auditor has a public duty to disclose. If he discovers an intention to commit a serious crime or tort for example.

e.   disclosure is required in the circumstances envisaged by advice given on money laundering and disclosure to regulators in the financial sector.

5.   The auditor should not disclose unlawful acts (except as outlined in paragraph 4) because a common practice of disclosure would impair the frankness with which client and auditor relationships are characterised. Similar frank relationships are common with professional people including doctors, priests, lawyers and bankers.

6.   The auditor, on discovering an unlawful act, should consider:

a.   That he must do nothing to assist in the offence or to prevent its disclosure.

b.   That he must bring all offences of employees to the notice of his client.

c.   Accounts must have an auditor's report. If the offence is such that its non disclosure means that the accounts do not show a true and fair view, he must insist on disclosure or qualify his report.

d.   Discovery of material defects in previous accounts should be pointed out to the client with a recommendation for disclosure. If the defect requires the treatment required under FRS 3 on prior year items, disclosure must be made or the auditor's report must be qualified.

e.   Should he resign?

Remember that if an auditor resigns, he must make a Statement of Circumstances, detailing the circumstances surrounding his resignation.

Companies

7.   Auditors have a statutory obligation to report on the accounts of their company clients. If a qualification is required, then the auditor's report must be qualified. Auditors appointed under statutes eg the Companies Acts should not avoid *qualifying their reports by resigning*.

8.   If the auditor discovers that previous accounts were materially false then:

a.   FRS 3 prior year items may apply.

b.   If FRS 3 does not apply, nonetheless shareholders and others may need to be informed. This may put the auditor in a tricky position. He should take *legal advice* and possibly *consult his professional body* before doing anything.

   c.   In liquidation the auditor can disclose any matter he wishes to the liquidator who in fact becomes his client. Note that the ethical codes of the professional bodies prohibit an auditor from being appointed liquidator of the same company.

Third parties

9.   Confidentiality is a key part of the professional ethos and is an implied term in an auditor's contract. However there can be circumstances when an auditor is not bound by his duty of confidence but can disclose matters to a proper authority in the public interest or for other specific reasons. The proper authority may be the police, the Stock Exchange, the Investigation division of the Board of Trade, the Serious Fraud Office or the Regulatory Organisations under the Financial Services Act 1986.

As things stand such circumstances include:

   a.   if ordered to do so by a court or a government officer empowered to request such information.

   b.   if obliged to disclose certain information to the liquidator, administrative receiver or administrator of a client.

   c.   in the public sector, where required by statute or the terms of his engagement.

   d.   under the Financial Services Act, to regulators. See Chapter 41.

   e.   when it is in the auditor's own interest to do so, for example to defend himself against criminal charges.

   f.   in the public interest. This is very difficult and an auditor should always take legal advice and consult his professional body before doing so. It is not possible to generalise on when disclosure of a matter such as fraud should be made in the public interest but, as an example, a fraud which is likely to affect a large number of people and which is likely to be repeated with impunity might be such a matter.

10.   The reason why an auditor will not normally disclose matters to a third party is the duty of confidentiality and also because he may fear legal action against him for a breach of confidence or defamation. Before disclosing a matter himself the auditor should:

   a.   Inform senior management and/or the audit committee (if there is one) and request that the proper authorities are informed.

   b.   Obtain evidence to ascertain that the matter has been so reported.

   c.   In the lack of such evidence inform the proper authority direct.

Fraud and the future

11.   The Report of the Cadbury Committee on Corporate Governance did not recommend that the statutory duty to report fraud should be extended beyond the regulated sector (eg financial service companies) to the generality of companies.

However the Report recommended that the Government should consider introducing legislation to allow auditors to report reasonable suspicion of fraud freely to the appropriate investigatory authorities. Such legislation already exists in the regulated sector. Such legislation could strengthen the position of auditors who report fraud against the risk of a suit brought against them for breach of duty to maintain a confidential client relationship or defamation.

Illegal acts and the future

12. Currently all companies are subject to a wide range of regulations in the areas of employ-ment, health and safety, planning, environment etc. Breach of such regulations either intentionally or inadvertently is common. Most of these matters are outside the current remit of the auditor and many are beyond an auditor's competence. However the auditor may come across breaches of regulations in his audit work and normally he will advise his client accordingly. Whether he should inform the proper authorities is a diffi-cult matter although there could be seen to be a public duty to do so in certain very serious circumstances.

The Cadbury committee took the view that it is the responsibility of the Board of Directors to establish what their legal duties are and to ensure that they monitor compli-ance with them. The committee also took the view that this would be enhanced if the auditor's role were to check that Boards had established their legal requirements and that a working system for monitoring compliance was in place. The committee recognise that it would be difficult to ascribe a wider role than this to the auditor as the auditor would be unlikely to have the necessary expertise. The committee recommended that this subject should be further considered by the accountancy and legal professions and representatives of preparers of accounts.

SAS 120 Consideration of law and regulations

13. SAS 120 makes the following points:

   a. Auditors should plan and perform their audit procedures, and evaluate and report on the results thereof, recognising that *non-compliance* by the entity with law or regu-lations may *materially* affect the *financial statements*. Some clients are in heavily regu-lated sectors such as banking or waste disposal and auditors must be particularly aware of the effect of non-compliance with such clients. However all businesses are now regulated generally in such areas as planning, health and safety, racial and sexual discrimination and many others. The effect of non-compliance can be fines or litigation which means that *actual or contingent liabilities* should be included in the financial statements. These may be non-material in amount but the auditor needs to be satisfied that this is so. The effect of non-compliance can be more serious including loss of licences or authorisation to continue in business. This may have implications for the financial statements in many ways including the assumption of *going concern* basis.

   b. It is the responsibility of *directors* to take steps to ensure that their entity complies with laws and regulations, to establish arrangements for preventing and detecting any non-compliance and to prepare financial statements which comply with all laws and regulations.

   c. Directors may fulfil their responsibilities by:

   - maintaining an up-to-date *register* of relevant laws and regulations and moni-toring any changes to these.

   - instituting and operating appropriate systems of *internal control*

   - developing a *code of conduct* to inform employees and to ensure employees are trained and that sanctions exist against breaches

   - engaging legal advisers to assist in this area.

      – maintaining a register of complaints and breaches

      – in large companies, maintaining internal audit and compliance functions as separate departments

d. Auditors plan their work with a reasonable expectation of detecting material misstatements in the financial statements that may arise through non-compliance. As a simple example, an auditor would need evidence that a new building constructed for a client had planning consent and complied with building regulations. Auditors however cannot be expected to find all breaches as many breaches have no material effect on the financial statements, audit procedures include sampling and audit evidence is persuasive rather than conclusive. There is also the points that auditors may rely on internal controls in many areas and these may not always reveal breaches and the auditor cannot be expected to detect non-compliance hidden by collusive behaviour, forgery, override of controls or intentional misrepresentations by management.

e. The auditors should obtain sufficient appropriate audit evidence about compliance with those laws and regulations which relate directly to the preparation of, or the inclusion or disclosure of specific items in, the financial statements. Examples are the Companies Act, other statutes and SORPs.

f. The auditors should perform procedures to help identify possible or actual instances of non-compliance with those laws and regulations which provide a legal framework within which the entity conducts its business and which are central to the entity's ability to conduct its business and hence to its financial statements. Examples of such laws and regulations may be pertinent in entities such as financial service companies, casinos, bus companies. Procedures may include obtaining a general understanding of the rules, inspection of licences and correspondence with authorities, enquiry of the directors on any non-compliance and obtaining written assurance from the directors that they have given the auditors all information on non-compliance.

g. On the audit, staff should be alert for instances of actual or possible breaches which might affect the financial statements.

h. When actual or possible breaches are encountered the auditors should gather all possible information and evidence, evaluate it and fully document their evidence, reasoning, findings and conclusions. The matters should be discussed with management and in rare cases, after due consideration and taking legal advice, reported to third parties.

i. Effects of non-compliance on the auditors' report. There are several possibilities (see Chapter 32):

      – fundamental uncertainty about the consequences – include an explanatory paragraph in the report

      – disagreement with the consequent accounting treatment or disclosure – adverse or qualified opinion

      – inability to determine the existence of or consequences of a non-compliance – a disclaimer or a qualified opinion on grounds of limitation of scope.

Money laundering

14. There is much public disquiet about money laundering by drug traffickers, terrorist organisations and other criminal persons. The government added to the possibilities of preventing and detecting such activities in the Criminal Justice Act 1993 and The Money Laundering Regulations of 1994. The effect of this legislation on accountants and auditors is to add a risk of committing criminal offences. It is now a criminal offence to fail to maintain appropriate procedures for the prevention or reporting of money laundering, while carrying out relevant financial business. Possible professional activities here include banking, insurance and investment business but also advice and administrative services in the ordering of personal affairs, advice on setting up trusts, companies and other bodies, arranging loans and acting as a trustee. In engaging in any such activities accountants need to have procedures to recognise, prevent and report money laundering. Reporting of money laundering suspicions is specifically exempted from *all confidentiality* requirements. It is also notable that it is a criminal offence to disclose (eg to the directors) that a money laundering suspicion has been reported to the authorities. Clearly the guilty parties must not be given the tip off to run or cover up their misdoings.

It is also notable that the Money Laundering Regulations apply to all accounting firms authorised by the ICAEW or other body to carry out investment business. Most firms are so authorised. The consequence of this is that firms must have procedures in place:

- for identification of clients. This means they must know with whom they are dealing with when accepting a new client. Beware the possibility that your new client is a Mafioso in disguise.

- for keeping records of all transactions for five years

- for internal reporting. This means that staff must have the identity of a person to whom they can report.

- as may be necessary for the purposes of forestalling and preventing money laundering.

The ICAEW guidance finishes by saying that members providing services as *auditors*, directors, trustees or professional advisers are obliged to report money laundering suspicions through their own firm's procedures, independently of any procedures that their clients may have for reporting similar suspicions.

Summary

15. a. Auditors may uncover criminal offences committed by a client or an employee of the client.

b. This puts them in a difficult position. The auditor should act carefully and correctly and, if necessary, take legal advice.

c. Auditors must not themselves commit criminal offences and should know the circumstances in which a criminal offence may be committed by not doing something.

d. The auditor should not jeopardize a professional relationship by disclosing offences except in specified circumstances.

e. Auditors have a responsibility to give an opinion on company accounts which they should not avoid by resignation.

f. The Cadbury committee recommend extending the regulations of the regulatory sector which enables auditors to report reasonable suspicion of fraud to the proper authorities to the generality of companies. They do not recommend however that statute establish an obligation to do so.

g. The Cadbury committee recommend some extension of auditor's duties in respect of Directors duties to establish their responsibilities under a wide range of legal requirements and monitor compliance.

h. Auditors must be aware of the possible impact of non-compliance with law and regulations on the financial statements in their audit planning and procedures.

i. Firms of accountants must have procedures in place to recognise and report suspicions of money laundering activities.

Points to note

16. a. The auditor's duty when he discovers an unlawful act or when he is made aware of an unlawful act while conducting his audit is not always clear.

b. In examinations any questions on the subject should be answered by scrupulously following the advice given in this chapter.

c. Many writers have criticised this advice on the grounds that an auditor has a public duty which overrides his inclination to protect himself and his client.

Recent DOT enquiry reports have implied that the auditor should seek disclosure of matters which concern a wider range of people than himself and his client. The matter is currently subject to much debate.

d. An interesting ethical dilemma is when an auditor discovers a material fraud by a member of the client's staff against the client which had been continuing for some years. On looking into the matter the auditor discovers that if he reports the matter to his client, his client could sue him for recovery of the amount lost since the first occasion when the auditor should have discovered the fraud.

e. The general rules to be followed in the circumstances described in this chapter are:

i. Take legal advice

ii. Resign but do not do so if you are the auditor of a company

iii. Advise the client to make full disclosure to the relevant authorities.

iv. Consider whether statutes (eg on money laundering or financial services) or the public interest require disclosure to the proper authorities.

f. Normally disclosure will be preceded by discussion with the directors but in some instances (eg money laundering or where the directors themselves are involved or the auditor has lost confidence in the integrity of the directors) disclosure may be without informing the directors.

g. Essentially the auditor has three duties:

– confidentiality

– to give an unbiased opinion on the financial statements

– to report to the proper authorities in certain circumstances

In the past the first duty tended to overrule the other two but the trend is now the other way.

h. The rules sometimes conflict and are not often clear-cut. Practising auditors need to be very wary.

i. The Financial Services Act requires the auditor to report some matters to the regulating bodies over the heads of his clients.

Case study 1 for Chapter 50

Alien Corn Ltd are dealers in agricultural produce. Data about the company include:

Turnover – £600,000

Profit before proprietoral remuneration – £40,000

Shareholders – 16, all related, of which 4 are directors. 40% of the shares are held by distant relatives.

The auditors are Wright, Pickle & Co.

The audit of the accounts for the year ending 31.10.– 6 is being conducted by Andrew, an unqualified senior. During the audit, he discovers:

a. the company have paid Christmas bonuses to staff amounting to £500 without deducting PAYE. A PAYE inspection is arranged for next week. He advises the company to destroy the petty cash book in which these payments are recorded together with the vouchers. Petty cash books last about 6 months and the payments concerned are in the one before the current one. Andrew has already given it an audit inspection.

b. Andrew discovered by accident that Miss Debra Meenor, who handles purchases invoices had been passing for payment invoices (about £5,000 a year) for goods which had not been purchased. The invoices were from a firm owned by Miss Meenor's father. The practice had been going on for several years.

c. Andrew compared the despatch notes with the sales invoices and discovered that some six despatches of goods had not resulted in invoices. All the despatches were to a firm in the Irish Republic. Quite by chance Andrew had noticed a bank statement in the managing director's in-tray from an Irish Bank and had wondered about it.

Discussion

a. Discuss the implications of these discoveries?

b. What should Andrew and his firm do about them?

Case study 2 for Chapter 50

Gunges Ltd are a chemical company in Wolverhampton making speciality chemicals for export to third world companies. The company is owned by the Gunge family but is run by Bismuth who was recruited because of his sales experience in Africa and South America. The Board consists of four Gunges and Bismuth but rarely meet. The auditor is Raymond and he has made a number of discoveries in the course of his audit:

a. The company are making material payments to a numbered Swiss bank account. Bismuth (who Raymond trusts not at all) tells Raymond that these are commissions to third world government officials who obtain business for the company.

b. Workers appear to be handling what look like dangerous chemicals without proper protective gear. Bismuth tells Raymond that the regulations are known to Gunge and are all followed.

c. A pipe seems to be discharging chemicals into the adjacent canal. Bismuth tells Raymond that he has a licence to do this but declines to show it to Raymond.

Discussion

Discuss the implications of these discoveries for Raymond.

Student self testing questions *Questions with answers apparent from the text*

1. a. When can an auditor disclose unlawful acts to the police? (4)
   b. Why does an accountant have a professional duty of confidence? (5)
   c. Outline the present position on disclosure by an auditor of frauds and other irregularities to the proper authorities and the Cadbury committee's recommendations (13)
   d. Outline the present position on disclosure by an auditor of illegal acts to the proper authorities and the Cadbury committee's recommendations (12)
   e. Summarise the requirements of SAS 120. (13)
   f. What are the rules on money laundering? (14)

Examination question *(Answer begins on page 554)*

1. Several months after the year end, John Collinge (Food Importers) plc is forced into liquidation. It comes to light that the managing director has been defrauding the company by paying amounts received from cash sales into his own private bank account. For several years he had been supplying retailers who paid him in cash which he had not entered into the company records. Further the shareholders of the company, having heard of the inaccurate financial statements and fraudulent activities have decided to sue both yourselves and the previous auditors for negligence.

   You are required to discuss the legal position of:

   a. the managing director, John Collinge   (5 marks)
   b. the current auditors, explaining the general liability of the auditor for negligence if fraud is not detected   (8 marks)
   c. the previous auditors, Navco and Partners.   (2 marks)

   (ACCA 91) (Total 15 marks)

Examination questions without answers

1. During 1993 the Auditing Practices Board issued exposure drafts of Auditing Standards dealing with 'Fraud and error' and 'Consideration of law and regulations'
   Required:
   Explain:
   1. the auditor's responsibilities for the detection and reporting of fraud and error as part of their statutory audit procedures
   2. why there is a need for Auditing Standards in relation to 'Fraud and error' and 'Consideration of law and regulations'

   (ICAS 1994)

   Note: you can now answer this using the actual standards.

2. You are the auditor of BISTRO Ltd., a company that operates five restaurants. During the course of your planning of the audit for the year ended 31st March, 1990, the Managing Director has informed you that he is concerned about the margins achieved in one of the

restaurants and he is particularly worried that cash or stock may have been misappropriated.

You have established that there is one staff member responsible for all of the company's accounting functions, including bank reconciliation's, and that accounting records are maintained for goods inwards, purchases, sales and cash. Stock is counted every three months.

Requirement

You are required to:

a. detail the audit tests you would undertake in respect of cash sales and banking.

(10 Marks)

b. indicate what other steps you might take in addition to those normally undertaken at the year-end, in order to establish whether any misappropriation has taken place; and

(5 Marks)

c. state briefly your responsibilities in respect of the detection of fraud and irregularities.

(5 Marks)

(ICAI 90) (Total Marks 20)

3. You have been the auditor of Dennis Trading Limited for many years. During this period you have never had occasion to qualify your audit report, nor have you had any reason to doubt the honesty of the management or the employees of the company.

The following matters have come to your attention this year:

a. Your audit manager informs you that she has heard from a member of the wages department that the head of the department has recently bought a villa in Barbados, a yacht, a four -seater aeroplane and a new Porsche motor car;

b. A junior carrying out sequence checks on sales invoices from one of the branches has discovered that invoices are missing; it appears that this only happens on one day a week and they always relate to cash sales;

c. During the whole of the period you have been auditor, the managing director has misappropriated substantial (and increasing) sums of money reported as 'Construction Costs'.

Required:

Describe the steps that you might take to attempt to resolve the situations outlined above. Indicate also how they may affect you personally as auditor.

(AAT 90) (15 Marks)

51 Divisible profits and dividends

1. This subject is traditionally a subject for audit manuals and audit papers in examinations. However, it has equal relevance to studies in accountancy and company law.

2. The problem lies in determining what profits are able to be distributed as dividends and what profits cannot be distributed because of the company law doctrine of *capital maintenance*.

Non-distributable funds

3. Some reserves arise out of specific events which make them non-distributable. These are:

    a. Under CA 1985 S.130 Share Premium Accounts.

    b. Under CA 1985 S.170 Capital Redemption Reserve.

4. Most companies have a clause in their articles which allows:

    a. The company to pay a dividend up to the amounts recommended by the directors.

    b. The directors to declare interim dividends.

    The law relating to companies prohibits the payment of dividends except out of profits. This is because the payment of a dividend other than out of profits would be a reduction of capital. A *reduction of capital* is allowed by the Companies Act 1985 (sections 135–141) although it is difficult (a court order may be required) but not by the payment of dividends.

5. The law relating to distributable profits has been in the past, somewhat obscure. The cases on this matter are antique and sometimes conflicting. Fortunately the law had been partially clarified by the Companies Act 1980 and the relevant provisions are summarised below.

The Companies Act 1985. Sections 263 to 281

6. Any company (public or private) that wishes to make a *distribution* must have *profits available for the purpose*.

    Profits available for distribution

    These are:

    >   accumulated *realised* profits
    >
    >   *less* accumulated *realised* losses

    Such profits and losses may be either *revenue* or capital.

7. **Definition of distributions**

    Any distribution of a company's assets to its members, in cash or otherwise, but *not* a distribution that is made by way of:

    a. An issue of either fully or partly paid bonus shares.

    b. The redemption of preference shares with the proceeds of a *fresh* issue of shares and the payment of any premium payable on redemption out of the share premium account.

    c. The *reduction* of share capital by extinguishing or reducing liability in respect of share capital that is not paid up or paying off share capital.

    d. The distribution of assets to members on a *winding up*.

8. **Note:**

    a. The profits available for dividend are the *accumulated* profits. This reversed the decision in Ammonia Soda Co Ltd v Chamberlain in 1918.

    b. The profits must be *realised*. This reversed the decision in Dimbula Valley (Ceylon) Tea Co Ltd v Laurie 1961.

9. **Public companies**

Before public companies can make a distribution the following conditions must be satisfied.

a. As stated above, for all companies.

b. At the time of the proposed distribution, its net assets must exceed the sum of its called up share capital and its *undistributable* reserves.

c. The distribution must not reduce its net assets below the sum of its called up share capital and its undistributable reserves.

10. **Undistributable reserves**

These are:

a. The share premium account.

b. The capital redemption reserve fund.

c. The excess of accumulated *unrealised profits* over accumulated *unrealised losses*.

d. Any reserve that the company, for any other reason, is prohibited from distributing. An example of 'any other reason' is a prohibition contained in the articles of association.

This provision prevents a company paying a dividend out of *realised* profits without making good any realised or *unrealised* capital loss.

This reverses the decision in Lee v Neuchatel Asphalte Co 1889.

11. **Realised and unrealised profits and losses**

The Act does not define these terms. Ordinary accounting practices should be the determinant, noting especially the prudence convention.

However the Act does make one notable point in section 275. Consider the following example:

	Cost	Valuation	Difference
Fixed Assets	100,000	150,000	50,000
Depreciation at 2%	2,000	3,000	1,000

The net profit after tax but before depreciation is £20,000. Section 275 provides that the realised profit should be £20,000 – £2,000 = £18,000. Thus the additional depreciation is disregarded in computing the realised profits.

12. **Relevant accounts**

Before making a distribution, reference must be made to the relevant accounts (Section 271).

The *Relevant* accounts are:

a. The latest audited financial statements.

b. Where the distribution would exceed the amount that is distributable according to the latest audited accounts then interim financial statements should also be referred to.

c. Initial financial statements should be used before the *first* audited accounts are available.

13. **For *public companies* only**

   a. With *initial* financial statements, the auditors must have made a report stating whether in their opinion the accounts have been properly prepared.

   b. *Properly prepared* means being prepared in accordance with the Companies Act 1985 S226 (ie showing a true and fair view) and the 4th schedule (accounting disclosure requirements) with such modifications as are necessary as they are initial accounts.

   c. If the report by the auditors is not an unqualified one, then there must also be a *statement* by the auditors stating whether, in their opinion, the qualification is material for the purpose of determining the distributability of the profits shown. The report and statement (if there is one) must have been delivered to the Registrar.

   d. In order to say that financial statements have been properly prepared, the auditor must carry out a full audit and give a full auditors' report which refers to 'initial accounts' and which has as its opinion paragraph:

   'In our opinion the initial accounts for the period from... to... have been properly prepared within the meaning of S.273 of The Companies Act 1985.'

   e. I should imagine such reports will be exceedingly rare.

Qualified audit reports

14. If a qualified audit report has been given on any company's accounts and the company wishes to pay a dividend then the auditor has certain additional duties.

15. The auditor must state in writing whether, in his opinion, the subject of the qualification is material for the purpose of determining whether the proposed distribution is permitted under the terms of the 1985 Act.

   An appropriate form of report is:

Auditors' statement to the members of XYZ Limited pursuant to Section 271 (4) of The Companies Act 1985

We have audited the financial statements of XYZ Limited for the year ended ..... in accordance with Auditing Standards issued by the Auditing Practices Board and have expressed a qualified opinion thereon in our report dated.....

Basis of opinion

We have carried out such procedures as we considered necessary to evaluate the effect of the qualified opinion for the determination of profits available for distribution.

Opinion

In our opinion the subject matter of that qualification is not material for determining, by reference to those financial statements, whether the distribution (interim dividend for the year ended) of £ proposed by the company is permitted under Section 263 of the Companies Act 1985.

---

16. The work that the auditor has to do depends on the qualification. Suppose York Widgets have available profits of £100,000 and wish to pay a dividend of £50,000. The audit report is qualified for uncertainty because the stock at one location was not counted. If the stock at that location was included at £20,000, then the worst possible position could be that it was in fact nil. In that case the profit would be measured at £80,000 and the dividend could be paid.

Interim dividends

17. Table A and the articles of most companies permit the directors to pay interim dividends.

    The auditors' responsibility lies in seeing that any dividend paid is intra vires the directors and that the accounts show a true and fair view.

    Most established companies have built up revenue reserves, and interim dividends can usually be paid without fear of paying them out of capital.

18. However, in the *first year* of a company's life, there is often a commercial need to pay an interim dividend. If there is a *profit at an interim stage* and an *overall loss* for the year then the dividend will be paid out of capital. If this is so then the directors are *personally* liable to repay the dividend to the company.

19. Sometimes, the auditors are asked to advise the company's directors on the advisability of paying an interim dividend in the first year.

    The following considerations should be brought to the directors' attention:

    a. Do the Articles permit an interim dividend?

    b. Have interim accounts, showing a profit, been prepared?

    c. Do the prospects of the company indicate with a fair degree of certainty that an overall profit exceeding the dividend will be made?

    d. Are there sufficient liquid funds available?

    e. Commercial policy decisions will need to be made concerning:

        i.   The relative sizes of interim and final dividends.

        ii. The establishment of a precedent or expectation from shareholders.

        iii. The relative desirability of dividends and further investment.

20. In the case of public companies any interim Accounts (first year or otherwise) that are needed to support a dividend must be fully audited, filed at Companies House and carry an audit report like that of paragraph 13.

Audit considerations and divisible profits

21. In the London and General Bank case 1895, the judge said:

    'It is no part of the auditor's duty to give advice either to directors or shareholders as to what they ought to do'

    and

    'It is nothing to him whether dividends are properly or improperly declared, provided he discharges his duty to the shareholders'.

22. Is, then, the auditor concerned with the legality or otherwise of dividends? The answer is yes, because:

    a. If the dividend is paid out of capital, this fact must be made plain in the accounts, or the accounts will not show a *true and fair view*.

    b. If the accounts do not show a true and fair view the auditor *must* say so in his report.

    Therefore the auditor cannot form an opinion on the truth and fairness of the accounts without first forming an opinion on the legality of dividend payments.

    c. The Companies Act lays special duties on the auditor as we have discussed in this chapter.

Summary

23. a. The doctrine of capital maintenance in company law restricts the right of a company to pay dividends.

    b. Some reserves cannot be used for the payment of dividend including share premium and capital redemption reserve.

    c. All companies are restricted to paying dividends only out of realised profits less realised losses.

    d. Public companies are in addition restricted to paying dividends only out of realised gains less realised and unrealised losses.

    e. If interim or first accounts are required before there are enough profits available to pay a dividend then the auditor must conduct a full audit and report whether the Accounts have been properly prepared.

    f. If the auditor's report is qualified then the auditor must give a report on whether the qualification is material for the payment of the dividend.

Points to note

24. a. The duty put upon auditors when their report is qualified is a power, in that they can prevent a company from paying a dividend.

    b. It is desirable for students to know (or revise) the company law relating to dividends, their declaration, payment, and disclosure in accounts.

    c. The over-riding consideration in all accounts for the auditor is *'Do the accounts show a true and fair view?'*

    d. Special considerations apply to investment companies and insurance companies.

Case study for Chapter 51

Queer Trades plc has drafted its accounts for the year ending 31st December 19-6 and proposes to pay a dividend of 1.2p per share. Its balance sheet shows (before the proposed dividend):

Ordinary shares (10p each)	1,000,000
Share Premium	500,000
Capital Redemption Reserve	600,000
Profit and Loss Account	100,000
Revaluation Reserve	200,000

The assets section includes land and buildings as revalued at £700,000 less depreciation for 9 years £225,000. The original cost of the land and buildings had been £500,000. The auditor has qualified his report because the company have a debt due from a company in Turkey amounting to £30,000. The company insist that the debt is good but the auditors do not think they have sufficient evidence of this.

Discussion

1. a. Can the company pay the proposed dividend?

    b. What legal formalities are required before payment?

   c.   Draft the auditors' report (by Puce Watermelon and dated 23.4.-7)

   d.   Draft any other report required by the auditors in this case.

Student self testing questions *Questions with answers apparent from the text*

1. a.   What non-distributable funds may a company have? (3)

    b.   When can a company pay a dividend? (4,7)

    c.   What restrictions are there on public companies paying dividends? (9)

    d.   What statement is required from an auditor by Section 271? (15)

    e.   What are duties of an auditor re interim dividends? (19)

    f.   What are the lessons of the London and General Bank case? (21)

EDP and the auditor

1. Electronic data processing has revolutionised the accounting and control methods of many concerns in recent years. The technical innovations have reduced prices to the extent that EDP methods are now available to even the smallest firms.

2. Auditing methods have had to be altered to accommodate the new technology. The application of auditing to EDP situations is still in the process of development. However, some ideas on internal control procedures and auditing methods have become established and are now frequently to be found in examinations.

3. Chapter 52 deals with internal control. Chapter 53 deals with audit considerations and Chapter 54 considers the special problems of smaller companies using micro computers.

4. There is an audit guideline – auditing in a computer environment. An Auditing Standard is in course of preparation.

5. Auditing in a computer environment has in the past been seen as a special sub division of the auditing discipline. Auditing examinations have tended to follow this attitude. This approach still exists but is likely to make way for an approach where auditing will normally be in a computer environment as most companies and organisations will have computerised records.

6. It is important to recognize that the auditing standards and guidelines apply as much in a computer environment as they do in a manual record environment.

52 Internal control in EDP situations

Introduction

1. The approach of an auditor to a computerised system is not fundamentally different from that to a manual, or mechanical or electro-mechanical system. His approach in the majority of audits is to determine, evaluate and test the system to see that it:

   a. Produces records which form a reliable basis for the preparation of accounts.

   b. Safeguards the assets.

2. What is an adequate system is a matter of judgement. The subject has been discussed at length in Chapter 14.

3. However while internal control characteristics as discussed in Chapter 14 apply to EDP and non EDP systems, the special nature of EDP systems has required the development of special internal control characteristics. These are discussed in this chapter.

EDP systems contrasted with non EDP systems

4. The special characteristics of EDP systems of which an auditor must be aware are:

   a. EDP systems take longer and are more difficult to install. Inefficient installation can cause problems including *accounting chaos* that has on numerous recorded occasions led to:

    i.   An auditor being unable to determine the truth and fairness of the accounts.

    ii. Corporate failure.

b. EDP systems are much more complicated. This creates problems of understanding for the auditor.

c. A larger part of the data processing operations becomes centralised with the concentration being in the computer department. The natural division of data processing between the various parts of an enterprise and its accounting department is lost together with the understanding of and interest in data processing which managers have. The concentration of data processing in the computer department may facilitate error and fraud and militate against its discovery.

d. Conversely, the development of the micro computer has allowed firms to install distributed systems whereby accounting records are not kept centrally but are disseminated around the firm and kept on micros. This has caused problems of control. Large systems are usually surrounded by complete systems of control since they would not work if they were not. However, smaller systems kept on micros will often work well without complicated control mechanisms.

e. The steps in computer processing and data storage on magnetic files are not visible unless printed out. Modern systems rely heavily on direct entry of data via keyboards and the storage of data on disc. There is often no regular printing out of output as information can be accessed as required on visual display units.

The name given to the facility to trace individual transactions through a system from source (eg a customer order) to completion (eg turnover in the final accounts) or vice versa is the AUDIT TRAIL. In the more advanced computer systems there are sometimes losses in the traditional audit trail. Causes of this loss include:

    i.   Use of magnetic files. Files stored on magnetic media cannot be directly inspected.

    ii. Deletion of data. A complete file of data (eg a sales ledger account) may be obliterated to save space in magnetic storage. Recent transactions only are retained.

    iii. Sorting. Source documents are often not sorted. The data from them is sorted by the computer. The tracing of source documents from output documents can then be very difficult.

f. Machines do not make mistakes. Generally speaking if correct data is presented to the machine and faultless computer programs are used, the output will be error free. So there is no point in the auditor checking for processing errors which are extremely rare. However there is point in the auditor investigating the accuracy and completeness of data presented to the computer department for processing and, much more difficult, the adequacy of programs. Machines cannot be relied upon to recognize nonsense data as such. A machine will, if programmed to do so (fraudently of course) double the pay of selected employees. In a manual system clerks would notice and query this.

Internal control in EDP systems

5. The possibility of errors and fraud occurring in EDP systems is much larger than in manual systems. The likelihood of discovery is also much less. Therefore there is a need for well designed control systems which are carefully monitored in operation.

6. The control systems in computer systems are considered under two main headings:
   a. General Controls
   b. Applications Controls *or System Controls*

General controls

7. General controls relate to the accounting environment within which computer-based accounting systems are developed, maintained and operated and which <u>therefore apply to all individual applications</u>. The objectives of general controls are to ensure:
   a. proper development and implementation of new applications;
   b. the integrity of program and data files;
   c. the integrity of computer operations.

   <u>General controls can be manual or programmed.</u>

   Paragraphs 8 and 9 cover development and implementation.

   Paragraphs 10 to 14 cover the other general controls.

General controls – development and implementation

8. Any system or program which is put into operation will continue to be used with amendments for a long time possibly many years. If any such system or program can permit or cause error or fraud then its effect will be continuous and not 'one-off'. Consequently inadequate systems can cause large losses or even corporate failure. To prevent inadequate systems being used standards must be prescribed for the design, development, testing and implementing of systems, programs and amendments to them. Controls must be instituted to ensure that these standards are adhered to.

   Methods used to control systems and program creation are:
   a. **Laid down procedures** for working including **consultation** with other interested parties. Note the auditor and the **audit trail** problem.

      Interested parties include management, users and the staff operating the system. It is particularly important to determine the output needs of users. Computers can produce much more information from analysis and users need to be imaginative in expecting much more than they are used to from a manual system.
   b. Full **documentation and recording** of all activity.

      This must be on standard stationery in accordance with prescribed methods.

      <u>Systems documentation will include:</u>
      i. Flow charts of clerical and computer procedures
      ii. Types of input and specimens of input forms
      iii. The form and content of master and other files
      iv. The processing detail and how error conditions will be specified and dealt with whether by rejection or notice on the screen for operator correction.
      v. The output forms specified and who the output is to be distributed to.
      vi. The controls to be operated on the system to ensure completeness and accuracy of processing and how the audit trail is maintained.

      <u>Programming documentation will include:</u>

  i.   Block diagrams as well as program listings

  ii. A statement of control procedures incorporated into the programmes. These will be particularly important to the auditor.

  iii. Detailed instructions to the operators with special reference to error routines.

  iv. how the programmes were tested and the results of testing.

  v.   Details of all amendments to the programmes and how they were tested, authorised, approved and implemented.

c. Fully documented and recorded **testing** including **desk checking, use of test packs, pilot and paralled running.**

    Testing should be with normal volumes of data so that confirmation is available that the system will work in normal operating conditions. Every type of input must be tested. It should be found that in normal operating conditions, time schedules can be met.

d. **File conversion checks** by manual comparison of a print out of each converted file with the original file.

    The use of control accounts to ensure that the file starts balanced is very important. Usually file conversion reveals redundant records, duplicated records and records which have accumulated errors. File conversion is an opportunity to remove these.

e. All new methods, systems, and programs must be **formally accepted and authorised** in writing by senior officials.

    Authorisation must be after approval and acceptance by users operators and management.

f. There must be tight control over systems developers and programmers who are allowed to have access to the computer in order to try out their programs.

    It must be remembered that systems once set up are used operationally without the benefit of human contact with every detail. Thus any errors or frauds incorporated in the systems will be perpetuated. The objective of tight systems of development are to prevent errors and frauds creeping in or if they do then to detect and eliminate them. It is well worthwhile for an auditor to be satisfied that the development stage of systems produces acceptable systems.

    All that has been said of systems development is equally true of amendments and all amendments should go through the same rigorous development, testing and approval mechanism.

9. Where programs and systems are developed by software houses as they usually are for small systems or companies then special problems arise. These include:

a. Inadequate definition of the system objectives so that the system fails to fit the users requirements or fails to supply adequate audit trail.

b. Dependence on overworked software houses can lead to difficulties in implementing the systems to the planned timetables. Consequently systems are often implemented without proper testing.

c. Turn key operations are often implemented without proper adaption or testing.

d. Amendments are poorly done or not done at all due to the collapse of the software house or lack of a proper service agreement.

e. Documentation of files, and programs is not always given to the customer. Copies should be made available.

f. In many cases, failure to control program amendment occurs and staff can gain access to the operational system or program code. This weakness is made worse by an increasing knowledge among ordinary personnel of computer matters and of languages such as BASIC.

Computer systems are now found in the smallest companies. Very often these are systems bought off the peg without all the development of paragraph 8. It is these systems that tend to have error and fraud potential. The auditor can have an advisory role in their implementation to ensure that the information provided from the system will be adequate to produce proper accounting records and accounts which show a true and fair view.

General controls – integrity of data and program files and of computer operations

10. Segregation of duties

a. A basic segregation is between the computer department and the rest of the organisation (the user departments). As an example, purchase invoices could be approved and pre-listed by the buying department and processed by the computer department who produce output totals which the buying department would verify.

b. Within the computer department division is usually:

i.   Development of systems and programs

ii. Operations – actual processing of Data.

iii. Control and management of the EDP functions.

Generally duties should be arranged so that:

i.   Manually maintained records are not accessible to computer personnel.

ii. No person has charge of the complete processing of a transaction.

iii. Development personnel have no access to operational processing.

iv. Input generation is separated from input control and computer operation.

v.   All operations are supervised.

11. Recent problems that have arisen in the area of separation of duties include:

a. *Small installations* tend to lack this segregation as accounts staff (and sometimes other user departments) tend to assume full control over the computer.

b. The use of *remote terminals* in on-line and real time systems makes access available to users, and also to programmers who have been traditionally isolated from the computer.

c. In micro and mini computer systems, development, both initial and continuing, is often undertaken by *software houses* which provides a segregation of duties between the organisation and the software house.

12. **Control over computer operators.** These controls are necessary to prevent errors and frauds or to deter errors and frauds. Common controls include:

a. Segregation of duties, for example data preparation, machine operation and review of logs.

b. The use of a manual prescribing procedures and standards to be followed at all times.

c. Rotation of duties so that no person is responsible alone for any aspect of work.

d. The use of machine generated logs specifying the programs used and processing done. These have to be reviewed by a senior official.

e. Recording of operator intervention in programs. This applies mainly to main frame computers.

f. Physical access. Methods to restrict access to computers include locks and keys, close circuit television surveillance and lockable terminals.

g. Access via terminals. Methods to achieve this include the uses of specific passwords for terminals or particular applications.

h. The scheduling of work to prevent bottlenecks and to promote efficiency and maximum usage of the hardware.

i. Two operators per shift. This is basic internal control and prevents some types of fraud except where there is collusion.

j. Precise and detailed operating instructions for each program.

13. **Accounting Record Controls** The object of these is to ensure that files are maintained correctly and protected from erroneous or deliberate corruption or unauthorised alterations. File integrity is the aim. Common controls include:

a. Software routines to prevent:

i. Other than the most recent file being updated (eg the most recent sales ledger file must be used).

ii. Accidental overwriting of files.

iii. Use of the incorrect file.

b. External labelling (eg tapes, discs and floppy discs) for the same purposes as a. above.

c. File devices (eg tapes, discs and floppy discs) must be kept securely to prevent loss or damage. It must be remembered that staff may corrupt their employer's files on their home computers! In large installations, a librarian may be used.

d. Accessing of files. This has been discussed under control of computer operators.

e. Tight control over the use of utility programs, for example copying and editing programs.

f. Control over programs and their use. These include development and maintenance controls (discussed separately), sequential numbering of programs and revisions with software control over the use of such numbers, and reviews of library contents.

g. Batch processing controls. These involve authorisation of data, its receipt into the computer department, its processing, and the distribution of output. Methods include batch totals (real or hash) and the reconciliation of output with input.

h. On-line software controls. These include document total checks, sequence checks of transactions and automatic reporting of all input transactions for user review.

i. Physical protection, including restriction of access and insurance.

j. Copying of all files, with the dual held elsewhere.

k. Reconstruction facilities. The common techniques are retention of files for a period (grandfather, father, son) and dumping of files onto magnetic media or by printing out.

14. **Fire precautions and standby arrangements.** Fire precautions are obvious but in computer installations flood and dust control are also environmental considerations. Standby arrangements are essential in case of breakdown. Imagine the response if the work force were told there would be no wages this week as the computer had broken down!

Applications controls

15. Applications controls relate to the transactions and data belonging to EACH computer based accounting system and are therefore specific to EACH application. The objectives of applications controls are to ensure:

   a. the completeness of accounting records;

   b. the accuracy of accounting records;

   c. the validity of accounting records. This last means that all entries are properly authorised.

   Applications controls can be manual eg the establishment of a control total on an adding machine of receipts from customers, for subsequent comparison. They may also be computerised. For example the computer might check the completeness of processing by checking the sequence of delivery note numbers.

16. The description of a control as general or application is convenient but not important and sometimes it is not clear. Restricting access by the credit manager to certain programs and files only, by use of passwords is a general control since it applies to several programs and is concerned with the integrity of files – he cannot have access to any programs other than those he needs to have access to.

   A programmed control ensuring that gross wages do not exceed £300 per worker per week is an application control since it relates to the wages calculation application only and is concerned with the validity of entries.

17. **Completeness of accounting records**

   This can be assisted by:

   a. User created control totals.

      For example the purchase and expense invoices for a period can be summed on an adding machine by the purchasing department. Subsequent processing by the computer can ensure the total processed is as the control total established by the adding machine.

   b. Comparison with previously created files, for example sales order entries against sales invoices created.

   c. Sequential numbering.

      All input data such as purchase invoices or sales dockets should have a sequential number put on by the user department (eg purchase invoices) or by the printer (sales dockets).

   d. Batch registers and within batches, record and field numbers.

It is possible for whole batches of data to go missing. A system, whereby the user department prepares all input data in numbered batches with specific numbers of input items in each enables the computer to have checks built in to ensure all items are processed.

e. Listing of sequences against master files for example unpaid commission agents or employees.

The system could produce listings of records not used eg any agent not paid would come to the attention of the sales manager who could confirm no commission was due or that an agent's commission had been omitted in error.

f. The establishment of run to run controls.

Once data has been input (eg sales dockets) then separate programmes may be used to update the various files (eg invoicing, stock, sales ledger, commissions, sales analysis etc). Each programme must use all the data.

g. Listing and review of re-submitted data so that rejected data can be compared with it and data is not rejected and consequently not processed for some non valid reason.

If sales invoice particulars are rejected it may be for some technical reason (eg incomplete data) or because of credit control procedures (eg too much overdue). It is essential this is reviewed to ensure either the amount is invoiced (or we all go bust) or is not (because it will be a bad debt).

18. **Integrity of files**

The integrity of program and data files can be assisted in the following way:

a. Techniques for ensuring the completeness, accuracy and authorisation of amendments to master files and standing data files and for ensuring the completeness and accuracy of the processing of these amendments are similar to the techniques for transaction input discussed in paragraphs 19 to 21.

b. As this is a very important area it may be worth printing out all amendments for one to one checking.

c. At intervals, the whole file should be printed out for detailed manual checking.

d. Master files and standing data files can be controlled by the use of record counts and hash totals which are established and checked each time the file is used.

19. **The validity of input**

Common controls are:

a. On-line or real time access. Restriction of access can be obtained by physical controls (locks and keys), use of passwords and terminal menus (jargon for limited access from particular terminals) for example the credit control departmental terminal may only give access to the program which updates the customer master file for customer description and credit limit.

b. Batch processing. Segregation of user and computer departments. Ideally all input should be authorised by user departments.

c. Responsibility for transaction and master file records should be split between different user personnel.

d. The use of control totals (real or hash) with reconciliation with input prelists.

e. Use of exception reports with checking by user departments, for example sales on special price terms would be printed out for checking by the sales manager.

f. *Small installations.* Inadequate separation of duties makes authorisation of input difficult in small companies. the best approach is the retrospective review of reports and the creation and review of transaction logs by independent officials.

g. Manual authorisation of input documents with evidencing of the authorisation. For example all invoices for payment may have to be approved by the chief accountant who releases for processing only those he has approved and initialled. This is a manual control.

h. Authorisation of cash point withdrawals is an example of a programmed control. Before releasing cash the programme searches files to ensure that a sufficient balance is on the customer's account and that there have been no other cash point withdrawals that week.

i. Program controls can be used to give authorisation – see paragraph 20.

20. **Accuracy of processing**

This verification can be assisted in the following ways:

a. The use of pro forma documents with pre-coding as far as possible.

Coding is a science on its own and I do not intend to use this manual to teach it. However some coding systems can make mistakes possible and so the auditor is concerned that any coding system is found is one that facilitates accurate programming. Important codings such as the coding of incoming expense invoices for expense or capital expenditure accounts, should have checks incorporated to ensure accuracy. Such checks could include redundancy (extra confirming digits) or use of words as well as numerical codes.

b. The independent verification of entry. This basically means doing all input twice.

This technique is now unusual but is clearly very effective!

c. Initial validation, for example, of format, completeness of fields and check digit verification. This can be achieved off line or in the conversion stage.

This is a valid internal control technique in non computer systems also. Pre review and authorisation of data is found in such areas as purchasing where the buying department may review the requisition before inititating ordering procedures.

d. **Program controls**. These include:

i. **Format checks** – names are alphabetic, codes are numeric etc.

ii. **Field presence** – data on a sales might have to include name of customer, code of customer, sequence number of sales order form, code of item being sold, quantity being sold, code number of salesman etc.

iii. **Check digit verification.**

iv. **Master file** compatibility. There may be a master file of say customers of products or employees. Inputs must be of items that correspond to records on the appropriate master file. Thus inputs for an employee not found on the master file would be rejected.

v. **Range checks** – for example electricity usage for domestic premises of 100,000 units a quarter would be rejected as this would be impossibly high. Similarly input of weekly hours worked by an employee could be rejected if it was over say 80 hours.

vi. **Batch totals** – This has already been discussed and ensures not only that all items are input but also that they are accurately input.

vii **Sequence checks** – if all records have externally imposed sequential numbers then the programme can ensure that all items are processed.

viii. **Logical inference** – for example if there is input of net value, VAT and gross value of purchase invoices, the program can check the calculations.

e. Exception reports. These should be used to highlight abnormal exceptional items or missing items (an unpaid employee). Programs can reject data or print a warning.

f. Totalling. Pre-listing of real or hash totals with user verification of agreement with totals processed.

g. Regular user department testing of sample transactions.

21. **Output**. Output can be controlled as:

a. When output is directly related to input eg amendments to standing data files or invoices produced from input but incorporating standing data file information such as prices, then control can be by program controls, clerical verification with input or by agreeing totals.

b. Exception reports cannot be compared with input. For example a list of overdue debts or of stock with lower balances than predetermined reorder levels may not be complete. Controls must be within the programs generating the data.

c. Distribution of output. It is important that all output is received by user departments (eg overdue debts lists to credit control) and to achieve this output should be consecutively numbered.

d. Action taken on output. It is important that output is acted upon. For example the overdue debt list already mentioned or a list of overtime worked. To achieve action, procedures should be laid down for action, written acknowledgement of performance prescribed and reviews of action taken performed.

An example of a system

22. CD Ltd sell domestic appliances on HP to customers in their shop. We can assume that all customers pay instalments by cash or cheque into the shop.

The system might be:

a. All sales on HP are evidenced by an agreement filled in manually by the salesperson. The agreements are sequentially numbered. The interest is computed from tables.

b. The deposit must be at least 25% and is received by cash or cheque and a prenumbered receipt is given.

c. Each hirer is given a card with details and as instalments are paid they are given (a) a prenumbered receipt (b) an entry on the card.

d. The totals of the weeks HP agreements are summed manually by the sales manager to establish a control total.

e. HP agreement details are entered daily in the computer together with the control total and the number of items. The program checks:

i.   All fields are entered and in the right alphanumeric form.

ii.   The prenumbered numbers have a check digit which is checked.

iii.   The total amount of the agreement is more than £20 (the minimum) and £900 (the maximum).

iv.   The net + interest = gross and the gross = deposit + instalments.

v.   The total = the control total and the number of records is correct.

vi.   The numbers are in sequence with no omissions.

vii.   The deposits are at least 25% of the price of the product.

viii.   The interest is checked against data held on file.

ix.   The instalments are calculated at the price + interest − deposit divided by 12, 18 or 24 specified in the input.

x.   On input the name of the hirer is compared with a list of defaulting hirers and if found the record is rejected.

xi.   The input is added to a disc file which records all HP agreements made.

xii.   Hard copy output is made of the input for presentation to the sales manager and the accountant. This output is serially numbered by the computer.

xiii.   The input is added to a file of HP debtors which acts as the sales ledger.

There may be other requirements to accord with current legislation on HP but I am concerned here with computing and internal control principles.

Similar actions are taken manually and by the computer to process deposits and instalments and completed agreements and also settlements before completion. There are also slow payer routines. You may care to design applications complete with controls for these.

Summary

23. a.   Internal control in an EDP system is vital.

    b.   EDP systems have characteristics which have effects on the auditor's approach.

    c.   Some basic ideas about internal control in EDP systems have been developed.

    d.   General controls are concerned with the environment in which the computer is operated and systems and programmes are developed and implemented.

    e.   Applications controls are concerned with the transactions and data specific to each application.

Points to note

24. a.   The use of the word *control* must be understood. The objective of controls is to ensure that:

        i.   The records are accurate, reliable, and free from error.

        ii.   Frauds are not committed, or if they are, that they are promptly uncovered.

        iii.   Assets are safeguarded.

    b.   Examination questions are often set on the concept loss of audit trail. As an example a loss of audit trail could occur in a system for processing hire purchase transactions. The inputs could be new agreement details and cash receipts. The output may be only totals and lists of overdue accounts. There may be no way for the auditor to verify these figures apart from satisfying himself of the satisfactory nature of the programs and systems used.

c. Computer frauds are occasionally uncovered but experts estimate that innumerable frauds occur that are not uncovered. The best known example of a computer fraud is the bank clerk who realised that paying in was documented by a paying in slip with the customer's account number in MICR (magnetic ink character recognition). The computer would automatically update the right account. A customer who forgets his own paying in book, can select one from the counter and fill in his account number. This will then have to be coded manually by the computer operators. However, if the clerk surreptitiously puts his own account paying in slips in the box for customer use, the computer will automatically credit his account.

d. Inadequate computer systems can be disastrous. A firm which wholesales a very large variety of spare parts to thousands of customers may computerise its invoicing and sales accounting. If this is badly done, sales data which is not properly coded may be rejected by the computer and long processing delays may occur. In the end, the delays may cause cash flow problems which may cause the firm to go into liquidation. In addition the preparation of true and fair accounts may prove impossible.

e. I have used the terminology in the guideline – general and applications. Previous documents used the terms administrative controls or organisation controls for general controls. Systems development controls were separately described but are now included in general controls. Application controls have previously been described as procedural controls. No doubt further changes in terminology will occur.

f. There are various sorts of files:

i. transaction files (eg this month's invoices, this week's hours worked);

ii. Master files (eg debtors, creditors, stock balances, cumulative pay and tax) which change each time they are updated, eg daily, weekly or monthly;

iii. standing data files (eg wage rates; sales prices; customer name, address and credit limits) which change only when change is required, eg wage or price changes.

Case study for Chapter 52

Birds Nest Soups plc have the following system for dealing with purchase invoices:

The purchasing department gather and approve all incoming purchase invoices.

After approval the invoices are batched and sent weekly to the computer department.

The computer department process them by updating the purchase ledger and the nominal ledger.

The company do not take settlement discounts.

Discussion

a. What applications controls would you expect to find at each stage of the processing? Controls can be manual or programmed.

b. What general controls would you hope to find to ensure the integrity of program and data files, to prevent or enable recovery from systems, hardware or program malfunction, fraud or sabotage?

Student self testing questions *Questions with answers apparent from the text*

1. a. What special characteristics of computerised systems does an auditor need to take into account? (4)

    b. What two sorts of control exist? (6)

    c. What methods should exist for control over design and implementation of systems? (8)

    d. What problems exist when systems are designed by software houses? (9)

    e. What controls should exist over computer operators? (12)

    f. What controls may be applied to accounting records? (13)

    g. What controls might assist in ensuring the completeness of processing? (17)

    h. What controls may ensure the integrity of files? (18)

    i. What controls assist in ensuring the validity of data and files? (19)

    j. What controls aid the accuracy of processing? (20)

Exercises

1. Whizzo plc have separate departments for purchasing, sales, cheque payments, cheques through the post, accounting, wages and personnel. The company are wholesalers.

    Design computerised systems for sales, purchases and wages.

    You should ensure that the internal control principles as in this chapter are included.

    The controls should also include the principles of internal control in Chapter 14. For example sales controls should ensure all orders are processed, sales are only made to bona fide good credit risks, authorised prices are charged, all invoices are correct as to price, calculations, extensions and VAT, all invoices are entered in the 'books', all invoices are in the sales ledger, every effort is made to collect debts.

2. The 'Save the toad' charity receive donations through the post from covenants given by supporters. Design a computer system to process covenants and the receipts therefrom. The system should ensure that all covenants and receipts are processed and that the income tax recovery is correct. Remember that all covenantors have to sign an R 185 form.

Examination questions without answers

1. You have been asked to recommend the controls which should be exercised over the computerised database system of Thurgaton Plastics plc. The company is a wholesaler of plastic pigments (dyes) and granules which it supplies to manufacturers of plastic products (eg plastic buckets and car fascias). It purchases the plastic pigments and granules from large manufacturers.

    The company has a large computer system in which all accounting data is input from remote terminals. Data from remote branches of the company is sent direct to the main computer using the national telephone system (British Telecom in the UK).

    The company's database system comprises:

    a. an integrated sales, purchases and nominal ledger system;

    b. a payroll system – the wages expense, and credits for deductions (eg PAYE and national insurance) are posted directly to the appropriate accounts in the nominal ledger;

   c. a stock control system which is integrated with the purchases and sales accounting systems;

   d. a sales order processing system, which is integrated with the stock control system. When a customer places an order, it is deducted from the available stock. When the goods are due for delivery and the stock is available the computer produces a dispatch note and sales invoice, and deducts the quantity of stock dispatched from the book stock records – the sales invoice is posted to the sales ledger.

You are required to list and describe the controls you would expect to find in existence:

   a. to prevent unauthorised access to the database system;   (7 marks)

   b. to detect errors in input;   (6 marks)

   c. to guard against hardware and software errors;   (7 marks)

   d. to check the integrity of database.   (5 marks)

(ACCA) (Total 25 marks)

2. Describe the controls you would expect a company with a fully computerised accounting system to adopt in order to reduce the possibility of errors in input.

(16 marks)

(LCC 91)

3. The auditor of Unamuno plc is investigating the client's system of electronic data processing and is particularly concerned with the maintenance of master file integrity.

Required:

   a. What are master files?   (3 marks)

   b. What controls should there be to ensure their integrity?   (12 marks)

(LCCI 92) (Total 15 Marks)

4. The electronic data processing department of Tilpady plc employs a number of computer operators. As auditor of the company, you are required to tabulate the controls to be imposed on the operators in order to avoid errors and fraud.

List and describe five such controls.   (15 marks)

(LCCI 90)

5. If an organisation uses computer facilities it is important that it has procedures in place to ensure that these are available when required and that the integrity and confidentiality of the stored data is maintained.

   a. In what ways might an organisation suffer if it fails to protect its data?   (10 marks)

   b. What are the main risks to data which need to be guarded against and controlled?

(10 marks)

(ICA 92) (Total 20 marks)

6. Microcomputers create many problems for the auditor. The following characteristics are of special concern:

   i. direct access to the computer by users,

   ii. immediate processing of data when it is input,

   iii. frequently, no permanent record of data which has been input into the computer and processed by it.

Required:

   a. Detail the controls which should be exercised to ensure that only authorised persons are allowed access to information on files and to input data to update them.

(5 marks)

b. Describe the procedural controls which should be exercised to ensure that:

   i. only authorised data is input into the computer,   (3 marks)

   ii. a proper record is kept of all data which is input into the computer,   (3 marks)

   iii. any unauthorised amendment of files is highlighted.   (4 marks)

(AAT 92) (Total 15 marks)

7. When considering the feasibility of relying upon EDP controls, the auditor is not trying to gather evidence that a particular computer system is impregnable. Rather the auditor is looking for reasonable assurance that the access to programs and data files is restricted and that sufficient testing has been carried out to ensure the proper operation of the programs in the system. He, needs, however, to be realistic in determining the specific nature and extent of testing of access controls. Access controls can be divided into logical and physical access controls. Logical access controls will identify each user and restrict each identified user to specific programs, functions or data files.

Required:

a. describe two objectives of logical access controls in an EDP system. For each objective describe two controls which would ensure that the objective was fulfilled.

      (8 marks)

b. Explain the considerations which the auditor takes into account when evaluating the effectiveness of the logical access controls.   (7 marks)

c. List the physical access controls which may exist in an EDP system, and in general briefly describe the purpose of physical access controls.   (5 marks)

(ACCA 91) (Total 20 marks)

53 Auditing in a computer environment

Introduction

1. Audits should be executed in accordance with the Auditing Standards and with the guidance of the auditing guidelines. This is true of all audits including those of clients who have computerised accounting records. The basic approach to an audit is the same for all audits. However there are some features of computerised systems which make it necessary to change some of the audit approach.

2. More and more firms are using EDP for their accounting. Methods range from the use of giant mainframe computers to desktop machines, from centralised computer departments to the use of outside bureaux, from real-time systems to electronic invoicing systems.

   The auditor has to adapt himself to this revolution. However, it must be emphasized that the *auditor's duties remain the same* whatever the data processing systems used.

3. The approach adopted by auditors can be:

a. To audit round the computer. This means treating the computer as a 'black box'. The auditor looks at input and output but ignores what goes on in between.

This approach has been much criticised but in fact has many merits. Getting to grips with the system in detail is very time consuming and hence costly. Further, the controls may not be strong enough for the auditor to place reliance on them. Consequently a substantive testing approach with analytical reviews is likely to be the most effective and economical method of auditing.

b. Systems evaluation.

This has been seen as the best modern method for all audits but it does require the auditor to be well trained in EDP. The auditor will need to make detailed contract with the hardware and, with more difficulty, the software.

In fact controls are strong enough to be relied on in very few systems. Therefore the time spent on a detailed review of a system may be unproductive. However some understanding of every system is necessary if the auditor is to have evidence that the company have maintained proper accounting records.

c. **Using the computer**. This means using:

i. Established techniques such as test packs and computer audit programs.

ii. Specially designed tests to be incorporated in the client's own processing. This is perhaps futuristic but may well be necessary as real time systems become more common. They are known as embedded audit facilities.

Difference between manual and computer systems

4. The major differences between computerised and manual systems are:

a. The complexity of computer systems. An auditor can usually fully understand a manual system in a matter of hours at most. A computerised system cannot usually be fully comprehended without expert knowledge and a great deal of time.

b. A separation between computer and user personnel that may be physical but is also likely to be psychological and due to use of jargon in speech communication. The natural checks on fraud and error provided by the interaction of user personnel and accounting and bookkeeping staff no longer apply in a computer environment. For the auditor the lack of controls provided by user/manual – data – processor interaction, which are not always replaced by good controls of the general and applications type, leads to a reluctance to rely on internal control in a computerised environment. Happily computer literacy is growing and the isolation of computer personnel will diminish in the future.

c. Lack of visible evidence. Data is stored in computer systems primarily on magnetic discs. The information contained in the records is not easily examined. This is an obvious problem for the auditor. However the paperless office is by no means a present reality.

Many computer systems produce acres of print-outs and the auditor may well be faced with a surfeit of record rather than a shortage.

d. Much data on computer files is retained for a short period only. Manual records are usually retained for years. It is possible to examine say a sales ledger account going back through years if it is manually written up. But if it is on a disc it is unlikely that more than three or four months records will be maintained. It is likely that copies of the customer's statements of account will be retained but these may be filed in a way which makes access by an auditor difficult and time consuming.

e. Computer systems can have programmed or automatic controls. For example the checking by a computer programme that a stock code is correct by use of check digit verification may be an important control. Its operation is difficult to check by an auditor.

f. As a consequence of computer programs operating automatically without personnel being aware of what the program is doing, any program with an error in it is likely to process erroneously for ever. For example a program for pricing sales invoices may price item xyz at £45 instead of £54 due to an original inputting error. The program will go on making this error unnoticed until prices are changed.

g. Clients may use an outside agency – a computer bureau – to maintain their accounting records. This creates considerable problems for an auditor in examining controls where access is not a legal right.

Changes in audit approach

5. The basic approach to the audit is unchanged but detail changes include:

a. **Systems design** – In conventional audits the auditor finds out about the client's system. In audits of EDP systems, the auditor must be in at the design stage when systems are set-up. This is because:

   i. He is an expert on, and *aware of*, internal control systems. He should make sure that the systems set up will produce reliable records.

   ii. He may need special print outs or special controls to obviate the lack of *audit trail*.

b. **Timing of audit visits** – More frequent visits will be required because:

   i. Systems and programs change frequently.

   ii. Print outs are often pulped and magnetic files over-written.

   iii. Filing order changes are frequently made.

   iv. Audit trails must be followed while they still exist.

c. **Systems review** – This follows the usual pattern but is more difficult because:

   i. EDP systems are much more complex.

   ii. Technical language is used.

   ii. Too much documentation is available.

   iv. Many controls are program controls. Effective evaluation may mean examining the detail of programs which are written in high level languages or in machine code.

   v. Frequent changes are made to systems and programs.

   To overcome these problems, the auditor must distinguish between primary controls which are essential to the reliability of the records and secondary controls which are less important. A basic distinction between systems is that some are clerical control reliant, in these cases the auditor must concern himself particularly with the procedural controls and the organisational controls.

   Others are program control reliant. In these cases the auditor must place special emphasis on the systems development controls.

   An ICQ is essential. Here is an example:

Internal control questionnaire for use in EDP systems

CLIENT NAME: WHIZZO TRADING CO. LTD.
SUBJECT AREA: DEVELOPMENT OF NEW SYSTEMS, APPLICATIONS AND PROGRAMS

Q. no.	Questions	Answers	Assessment	Weaknesses dealt with	Audit programme
	Preliminary				
1	Is a feasibility study always made?	Yes			14
2	Does the study cover:				
	(a) Establishment of need	Yes			
	(b) User co-operation	Yes			
	(c) Costs and benefits	Yes			
	(d) Time scales	Yes			
	(e) Future developments	Yes			
3	Is the auditor consulted at this stage?	Sometimes	X	Discussed with Chief Accountant 25.1.-2.	
	Standard procedures and documentation				
4	Is there a manual detailing procedures to be followed in:				
	(a) Systems specification	Yes			
	(b) Program writing and adaptation	Yes			
	(c) Testing	Yes			
	(d) File conversion	Yes			
	(e) Acceptance and Authorisation?	Yes			
5	Does the standard system specification cover:				
	(a) General descriptions of the new systems with flowcharts	Yes			
	(b) The form of input	Yes			
	(c) Master files	Yes			
	(d) Processing requirements especially on errors and exceptions	Yes			
	(e) Output	Yes			
	(f) Controls required?	Yes			
6	Do the standard program writing instructions include:				
	(a) Instructions on the approach to be adopted	Yes			
	(b) Block diagrams	Yes			
	(c) Description of control procedures	Yes			
	(d) Detailed instructions for operatives	Yes			
	(e) Testing	Yes			
	(f) Documentation retention?	Yes			

Systems and Program testing

7   Are all new systems and programs exhaustively desk checked and tested with test and live data?   *Yes*

8   Are all new systems:
(a) Pilot tested   *Yes*
(b) Run in parallel with existing systems using operational volumes of data?   *Some*

9   Are tests fully documented?   *Yes*

10   Is the documentation retained?   *Yes*

11   Does testing ensure that input can be provided and output distributed within the specified time cycles?   *Yes*

File conversion

12   Are standard procedures laid down for file conversion?   *Yes*

13   Is a complete print out of the converted file made?   *Yes*

14   Is this checked in detail with the original file?   *tested only*   X   *Discussed with computer manager 29.1.-2.*

Acceptance and authorisation procedures

15   Is each major stage in a development reviewed in detail by:
(a) The computer manager or senior official in the Computer Dept.   *Yes*
(b) The manager of the user department concerned?   *Informally*   X   *Discussed with computer manager 29.1.-2. New procedures to be instituted.*

16   Are these reviews acknowledged in writing?   *Yes*

17   Are new systems and programs formally approved in writing before use by:
(a) The computer manager   *Yes*
(b) The manager of the user department concerned   *Yes*
(c) The Board of Directors?   *Only for computerisation of major areas*

	Amendments	
18	Are there written procedures for formal requests to be made for program or system changes?	Yes
19	Are changes subject to the same procedures as for new developments?	Yes
20	Are all amendments subject to:	
	(a) Documentation	Yes
	(b) Testing	Yes
	(c) Pilot running	Yes
	(d) Parallel running	Sometimes
	(e) Approval	Yes
	(f) Is all documentation and test data retained?	Yes

d. **Audit tests**. These will differ from those used in manual systems because:

   i. Manual systems rely upon controls over individual items. EDP systems usually control batches of items.

   ii. Computer processing is almost totally reliable so that emphasis is placed on systems and programs and not on calculations.

   iii. This reliability of computer processing also applies to its use of master files. Thus it is vitally important that what is on master files should be correct, and all changes should be authorised and correctly made.

   iv. Program controls are found only in EDP systems.

   v. In manual systems documents are usually checked before processing. In EDP systems the processing often includes checking documents for validity and other characteristics. Some are then rejected. Control over these rejections and investigations of the causes are very important.

   vi. Audit trail losses are common. This is dealt with in the next paragraph.

e. In computerised systems, internal controls are of two types – general controls and applications controls. The auditor has to consider at an early stage in the audit whether he can place reliance on either or both types of control. In all but the larger systems, general controls tend to be weak which means that the auditor is unlikely to be able to place much reliance on them.

Applications controls are often program based and compliance testing them is difficult.

f. Computer systems are complex and difficult to understand, partly because of the specialist vocabulary used. The larger firms of auditors have tended to set up specialist sections of computer auditors. The relationship between general audit staff and computer audit staff has then to be defined.

In the future it is likely that all staff will be trained to work in a computer environment and specialist staff will only be required for very large and complex systems.

6. Computerised systems present an auditor with problems but also with opportunities. Computer Assisted Audit Techniques (CAATs) have been developed to overcome some

of the problems and to grasp some of the opportunities. The two principal techniques are:

a. Use of 'test data' to test the operation of the client's programs.

b. Use of audit software – computer programs developed for audit purposes to examine the contents and do work on the contents of the client's computer files.

The use of CAATs is dealt with later in the chapter.

Audit trail

7. There is often a lack of audit trail when:

a. The computer generates totals, analyses, and balances without printing out details.

b. Exception reports are produced eg on overdue accounts without any assurance, apart from a knowledge of the correctness of the program, that the list is complete.

8. To overcome the loss of audit trail, the following techniques are available:

a. Special print outs for auditors. Remember the need to be consulted at the design stage.

b. Programmed interrogation facilities. This is a special audit technique described later under 'computer audit programs'.

c. Clerical re-creation. This is very tedious.

d. Total testing and comparison. With other data, budgets, previous periods.

e. Alternative tests eg physical stock counts.

f. The use of test packs to verify program performance. This is described later.

Planning the audit in a computer environment

9. All audits must be planned. In a computer environment the following matters may need to be borne in mind:

a. Auditors need to be involved in computerised systems at the planning, development and implementation stages. Knowledge of the system gained at these stages will enable the auditor to plan his audit with an understanding of the system.

b. Timing is more important in computerised environments than in manual ones. The auditor will need to be present when data and files are available. More frequent visits to the client are usually required.

c. Recording methods may be different. A recent development is the use of portable micro computers to make the audit working 'papers' on floppy discs instead of paper.

d. The allocation of suitably skilled staff to the audit. It may be necessary to use the computer audit department for some parts of the audit and for general audit staff to have had some computer experience.

e. The extent to which CAATs can be used. These techniques often require considerable planning in advance.

Audit firm organisation

10. The difficulties faced by auditors in the presence of EDP methods have led to most large firms setting up special computer audit departments.

11. The duties of *general audit staff* in connection with computer based systems are:

    a. To *inform* the computer audit department when a client installs or amends an EDP system.

    b. To complete the conventional part of systems evaluation and testing, and to draft the audit program.

    c. To carry out tests on the EDP system other than the special techniques.

12. The duties of the *computer audit* staff are:

    a. To develop a working relationship with the client who is installing an EDP system.

    b. To undertake the systems evaluation and write the audit program.

    c. To devise and carry out the special techniques.

    d. To supervise the general audit staff in areas where the special expertise of the computer audit department is needed.

Testing internal controls

13. The auditor tests internal controls when he wishes to place reliance on the controls in determining whether the accounting records are reliable. Testing of controls in computer based systems is for the same purpose as testing controls in manual systems.

14. In manual systems, controls are tested in one of two ways:

    a. By observation. This is principally used when no documentary evidence of the control is retained. Examples are the payout of wages, the physical security of premises or the counting of stock.

    b. Tests of control. These are performed on controls where documentary evidence that the control has functioned is available. Examples are the verification of wage calculations or the approval of purchase invoices. Compliance testing may involve:

        i. Examining evidence that a control has been exercised (in the examples cited, examining acknowledging signatures).

        ii. Reperformance of some or all of the steps that the person exercising the control was supposed to perform.

15. In computer systems, controls are tested in a similar way but differ in the kind of evidence examination possible and the reperformance of steps.

    The examination of evidence will include examination of:

    Exception reports

    Reconciliation reports

    Edit reports

    Missing Document reports.

    However, problems arise in reviewing the evidence gained by such examination. The problems are:

    a. Such reports are not always retained.

    b. The reports may not be complete.

    c. There is still no assurance that the logic of the programmed control was correct.

    d. If there are no exception reports, it may be because there are no exceptions or it may be because the program control does not exist or does not work.

16. Reperformance can therefore be the best approach. Techniques that are used include:

   a. **Manual reprocessing.** This is sometimes possible but difficulties arise because of the sheer volume of input usually found.

   b. **Computer assisted reperformance.** This is more promising and greater assurance is usually gained. The traditional technique is the use of audit test packs which consist of data specially prepared by the auditor. This can be summarised as auditor's data, client's program.

   c. **Parallel simulation.** This technique uses a specially developed program to simulate the operation of the live program. It can be summarised as client's data, auditor's program.

A problem arises in the use of test packs in that there is a choice. The test pack can be used together with 'live' input to test the effect of live programs, carrying out the test during normal processing using live master files. The alternative is to use copy, test or dummy master files. The choice is between live testing and dead testing.

   a. Live testing has the following disadvantages:

      i. If the data is included with normal data, separate test data totals cannot be obtained. This can sometimes be resolved by the use of dummy branches or separate codes to report the program's effects on the test data.

      ii. Side effects can occur. It has been known for an auditor's dummy product to be included in a catalogue!

      iii. Client's files and totals are corrupted although this is unlikely to be material.

      iv. If the auditor is testing procedures such as debt follow up, then the testing has to be over a fairly long period of time. This can be difficult to organise.

   b. Dead testing has the following disadvantages:

      i. Difficulties will be encountered in simulating a whole system or even a part of it.

      ii. A more detailed knowledge of the system is required than with the use of live files.

      iii. There is often uncertainty as to whether operational programs are really used for the test.

      iv. The technique uses a lot of computer time which may upset the client's schedules.

      v. The time span problem is still difficult but more capable of resolution than with live testing.

As an example of the use of test packs consider the example of the HP agreements in the last chapter. The auditor could invent say 20 HP agreements and enter the data into the computer. The simulated agreements could include items with errors:

   – an item with a shortage of one field
   – an incorrect batch total
   – an incorrect number of records
   – total less than £20
   – total greater than £900

- net + interest not equalling gross
- incorrect interest

etc, etc

The auditor would be interested in the response of the program to these items. Hopefully all erroneous items would be rejected. In the case of the incorrect batch total and number of records the program should refuse to send them to file or produce a print out until corrected.

At the end of this piece of audit work the auditor would have evidence that the programmed controls are effective. The file of HP agreements is the starting point for 'interest' and 'HP debtors'. Both of these items are material to the accounts.

Substantive testing

17. Substantive testing of computer records is possible and necessary. Its extent depends on the degree of reliance the auditor has placed on the internal controls. The degree of that reliance will depend on the results of his review and compliance testing of the internal controls over the accounting records.

Substantive testing includes two basic approaches both of which will be used.

a. **Manual techniques.** These include:

   i. **Review of exception reports.** The auditor will attempt to confirm these with other data. An example is the comparison of an outstanding despatch note listing with actual despatch notes.

   ii. **Totalling.** Relevant totals, for example of debtors and creditors can be manually verified.

   iii. **Reperformance.** The auditor may reperform a sample of computer generated calculations for example stock extensions, depreciation or interest.

   iv. **Reconciliations.** These will include reconciliations of computer listing with creditors' statements, bank statements, actual stock, personnel records etc.

b. **Computer Audit programs**

   i. These consist of computer programs used by an auditor to:

      1. Read magnetic files (disks or tapes) and to extract specified information from the files

      2. Carry out audit work on the contents of the file.

   ii. These programs are sometimes known as enquiry or interrogation programs. They are usually written in high level languages such as Cobol. They are usually written by or for an audit firm but clients' own interrogation programs can be used; such programs are available from software houses.

   iii. Staff unskilled in programming can be easily taught to put their search or operating requirements into a simple coded form which the computer audit program can interpret and apply to the files selected.

   iv. **Uses of computer audit programs**

      1. Selection of representative or randomly chosen transactions or items for audit tests, eg item number 36 and every 14th item thereafter.

2. Scrutiny of files and selection of exceptional items for examination eg all wages payments over £120, or all stock lines worth more than £1,000 in total.

3. Comparison of two files and printing out differences eg payrolls at two selected dates.

4. Preparation of exception reports eg overdue debts.

5. Stratification of data eg stock lines or debtors, with a view to examination only of material items.

6. Carrying out detail tests and calculations.

7. Verifying data such as stock or fixed assets at the interim stage and then comparing the examined file with the year end file so that only changed items need be examined at the final audit.

8. Comparison of files at succeeding year ends eg to identify changes in the composition of stock.

v. **Advantages**

1. Examination of data is more rapid.

2. Examination of data is more accurate.

3. The only practical method of examining large amounts of data.

4. Gives the auditor practical acquaintance with live files.

5. Provides new opportunities to the auditor.

6. Overcomes in some cases a loss of audit trail.

7. Relatively cheap to use once set up costs have been incurred.

vi. **Disadvantages**

1. Can be expensive to set up or acquire.

2. Some technical knowledge is required.

3. A variety of programming languages is used in business. Standard computer audit programs may not be compatible.

4. Detailed knowledge of systems and programs is required. Some auditors would dispute the need for this detailed knowledge to be gained.

5. Difficulty in obtaining computer time especially for testing.

vii. There can be no doubt that standard computer audit program packages will be in general use in the near future.

viii. Use of audit software raises the visibility of the auditor in the eyes of the company. It makes the audit more credible.

ix. Interesting 'quirks' in the system are often discovered and can be reported to management. This also makes the audit more credible.

x. Packages are not usually available for small machines.

Computer bureaux

18. Many enterprises use a computer bureau instead of having their own in-house computer. The auditor's duties remain the same whatever the data processing system used by his client but the use of a computer service bureau does present special difficulties to the auditor in evaluating the reliability of the records.

19. Special points to note are:

   a. There must be a clearly defined relationship with the bureau headed by a senior official.

   b. The contact with the bureau must be very precise and comprehensive.

   c. In establishing systems, the manual procedures at the user must be well established.

   d. File conversion must be well done.

   e. Input data should be validated by manual or computer controls at the user before transmission to the bureau.

   f. Records should be kept of all data sent to the bureau.

   g. There should be a high degree of security and control over documents and data in transit. Desirably copies should be kept or originals microfilmed.

   h. Rejection procedures should be carefully planned and action foreseen. All error reports should receive instant attention.

   i. Output should be controlled and all output sequentially numbered to ensure all is received.

   j. The accuracy and completeness of processing should be monitored at the user by means of batch numbering and control accounts.

   k. Master files maintenance is particularly important and checks of print outs of files should be performed regularly by the user.

   l. Security and confidentiality should receive high priority.

   m. Standards at the bureau (both organisational and procedural)must be adequate. It would create difficulty if hordes of auditors descended on a bureau, each one clutching his ICQ. It is possible that in the future the bureau's own auditor or some mutually acceptable neutral auditor will be required to investigate the controls in force in the bureau and issue an opinion to the auditor of each client of the bureau.

On-line systems

20. On-line and real time systems are growing in number particularly in banks, building societies, and other financial institutions.

21. The auditor has the same duties whatever the system but his techniques will need to change to accommodate this type of processing.

22. Special difficulties will arise because:

   a. Information will be stored on magnetic files and will be continuously changed.

   b. There will be a minimum of print outs and a minimum of permanently retained data.

   c. Authority for approval of a transaction, eg cash withdrawal from a bank, will be under program control ie without human intervention.

23. The auditor's problems will however not be insuperable and the following points need to be made.

   a. External evidence will still be available – debtor and creditor circularisation, stock counts, bank letters etc.

   b. The audit trail will still exist as management will need to trace transactions.

   c. The use of computer audit programs will increase and become more sophisticated.

    d.   Internal control evaluation is already very important as audit evidence. In some parts of real time systems the only evidence of record reliability may be adequate internal control.

    e.   the client will himself set up extensive monitoring and testing systems.

    f.   The client will probably set up internal audit support.

    g.   Modern systems feature rapid search facilities on remote terminals.

Data base systems

24. A database system is one where data common to a number of applications is situated on a common database and is accessed by specific computer programs. These systems are as yet rare but it is expected that they will become more common in the future. Clearly data is input from a range of sources including remote terminals and access is by a range of users.

Security and integrity of data is difficult in such systems and the auditor is likely to be worried about the validity of the data since it is from such data that the accounts will be prepared.

Some points in relation to databases and audit are:

    a.   All access to data should be recorded by computer logs which identify the user. These should be regularly reviewed.

    b.   The development of 'hacking' has worried computer users and database systems are more vulnerable to hacking than most.

    c.   All data which ends up in a database must be fully validated both manually and by the computer.

    d.   The auditor should be fully involved in the construction and design of the database. He should be concerned that adequate data dictionaries are produced as well as adequate data maps. Data dictionaries are files which fully describe the information about the data and how it relates to programs and terminals which have access to the data. Data maps describe the interrelationships of the data in databases.

    e.   Auditing databases is very difficult. One approach is to use advanced computer assisted techniques such as having resident audit monitors in the database. These could identify unauthorised situations arising during processing. It is also possible for data to be dumped out onto hard copy or a disc so that the auditor can then apply his tests to it.

Distributed processing systems and networks

25. Distributed processing may have a number of meanings including:

    –   micros and minis at different sites not linked

    –   micros and minis at different sites linked to a central mainframe

    –   a network of micros and minis at different sites linked to each other without a central mainframe.

Essentially these different configurations do not make any difference to an auditors duties but they do create more opportunities for the system to incorporate errors or frauds. The auditor will need to apply some advanced computer audit techniques and much imagination. He will need to have a plan of how the general controls are applied and how the system is linked. He will also need detailed understanding of the controls both manual and computer applied in each application.

Advanced auditing techniques in computer based systems

26. As more advanced computer systems are invented, the auditor needs to match the invention of computer people with his own inventiveness.

Some of the more advanced computer aided audit techniques are:

a. The use of test packs to test program operation and program controls. This has already been discussed.

b. The use of computer audit programs. These have also been discussed.

c. The use of embedded audit facilities. These are additional coding in computer accounting programs designed to perform audit functions. They are designed by and are under the control of the auditor.

Use of this technique may include:

- reperforming particular validation checks on input to ensure that the input checks work

- perform analyses or other analytical reviews on data while the data is still held on disc.

- collection of data for the auditor's use. This may be data about transactions which may later be overwritten or printed out.

- addition of audit data to client's files eg of the results of stock checks or plant examination to computer files of stock or plant.

d. The use of systems software data analysis. This is somewhat similar to embedded facilities. It involves having logging facilities in the operating system or in the data base management system so that the systems operation can be monitored. This is an audit check on the general controls in the systems.

e. SCARF. This means System Control Audit Review File.

This means that special audit modules are placed within a clients application program to extract information about transactions of interest to the auditor. This information is then placed in a SCARF file on disc for review at leisure by the auditor. Information that might be gathered includes exceptional transactions, sample transactions and system errors.

Summary

27. a. Three general approaches to an audit in a computerised environment can be distinguished:

- detailed system evaluation

- substantive tests and analytical review techniques

- the use of computer assisted audit techniques.

b. The distinctions between manual and computer environments that are important to an auditor include: complexity of computer systems; user/computer department schism; non-existence of visible evidence; non-retention of files and data; existence of programmed controls; possibility of systematic errors; processing by third parties at computer bureaux.

c. Auditing differences include: need to be in at the design stage of systems; timing of audit visits; complexity and difficulty of systems reviews; differences in testing techniques; difficulties in reliance on internal control; availability of computer assisted audit techniques.

d. Loss of audit trail can be a problem but most firms have a surfeit of paper offering audit trails.

e. Planning problems for auditors include: need to be in at the design stage of systems; timing of audit visits; opportunities to record working papers on a computer; need for skilled staff.

f. Audit firm organisation may need to encompass computer audit departments.

g. Testing techniques have CAATs in addition to usual techniques. CAATs include test packs and computer audit programs.

h. Computer bureaux can cause problems for auditors as controls are difficult to verify and access to records for testing purposes is less easy.

i. In the future on-line systems, real-time systems, database systems and distributed systems will present new challenges.

j. Advanced auditing techniques in computer based systems include embedded audit facilities, systems software data analysis and SCARF.

Points to note

28. a. Most auditing examinations papers now include questions on the audit of EDP systems. In the past questions have tended to be very elementary, mostly involving losses of audit trail. However, more sophisticated questions are now being set.

b. It is essential to realise that the auditor's duty to determine for himself that the client's records form a reliable basis from which to prepare accounts does not change in any way because a computerized system is in use.

c. The modern approach to auditing, involving evaluation and testing of the system of internal control, is used on EDP systems.

d. There are, as we have seen, differences in EDP systems, but fundamentally the objectives and methods are the same for all audits.

e. The most recent problem areas in computer auditing arise in small companies with micro-computers. Particular problems include:

   i. Cheap off-the-peg software (eg sales ledger packages) which do not work well and cause progressive chaos.

   ii. Complete or partial lack of basic controls such as segregation of duties.

   iii. Insufficient training of staff.

   iv. Systems which are readily changeable so that fraud is possible and, if badly changed, chaos occurs.

   v. Because systems software is cheap, clients are unwilling to involve expensive auditors in selecting or reviewing systems before they become operational.

   This is considered in the next chapter.

f. The use of computer audit programs is growing. They can be used on:

   i. Enquiry of files.

    ii. Reperformance of processing to test such items as interest, depreciation or stock calculations.

    iii. Statistical sampling.

    iv. Analytical review calculations and comparisons.

    v. Preparation of debtors and creditor confirmation letters.

    vi. Regression calculations.

g. Problems now arise more frequently if in-house programmers have access to operational programs which in modern terminal operated distributed systems is difficult to avoid. Methods to overcome the possibility of fraudulent alteration of files include:

    i. Maintenance of separate production (operational) and development libraries. Copying of programs can be from production to development but not vice versa.

    ii. Automatic listing of program changes which can be compared with an authorised record of changes.

    iii. Automatic calculation of the space occupied by a program. Any change in space is reported to higher authority.

h. Problems which will bother the auditor of the future may include:

    i. Sabotage or holding businesses to ransom by stealing, damaging or threatening to steal or damage computer files. Hacking is now a well known phenomenon.

    ii. Establishment of database systems. This concept recognises that items of data are used in many different files and applications. For example, employee details may be required for wage roll, personnel and pension routines. The idea is to store data in one place only and then application programs become independent of files as we now know them. Instead, an application program will be supplied with data from the database by means of a database management system.

i. A more hopeful sign is that auditors will in future take their own micro's on audit and the machine will prepare all the working papers.

j. A common approach to auditing in a computerised environment is:

    – sufficient review of the systems to ensure proper accounting records exist.

    – audit evidence collection by substantive testing and analytical review techniques.

k. Many audit firms are asked to evaluate in detail new computer systems. This is a great help in subsequent audits.

l. Many companies are terrified that their systems are open to fraud, error and sabotage. Audit firms are taking audits because of their expertise in computing.

Case study for Chapter 53

Consider again the case study – Birds Nest Soups plc in Chapter 52 and your answers to it. Assume a comprehensive system of general and applications controls are in existence.

Discussion

a. What errors or frauds could exist in the purchase invoice area which could affect the true and fair view.

b. What issues could affect the auditor's approach to the audit of this area?

   c. Discuss the relative emphasis to be placed on internal control reliance, substantive testing and analytical review.

   d. What items might be included in a test pack to test the program controls in programs used to process purchase invoices?

   e. How might a computer audit program be used in this area?

Student self testing questions *Questions with answers apparent from the text*

1. a. What differences exist between manual and computer systems? (4)

   b. What detailed changes in audit approach are required? (5)

   c. How can a loss of audit trail be overcome? (8)

   d. What audit planning problems exist? (9)

   e. List detailed tests that can be applied to computer systems. (13)

   f. Where can computer audit programs be used? (17)

   g. What are the advantages and disadvantages of using computer audit programs? (17)

   h. What problems arise for an auditor when computer bureaux are used by clients? (18)

   i. What are the problems inherent in on-line and real time systems and how can they be mitigated? (22)

   j. What are the problems for users and auditors with database systems? (24)

   k. What are the problems for users and auditors in distributed systems and networks? (25)

   l. List some advanced auditing techniques used in computer based systems. (26)

Exercises

1. AHM Industrial Ltd have a system for inputting purchase and expense invoices where the operator inputs the following from each item:

Order number (a code 2345 is used for items like electricity)
Supplier name
Supplier code number
First four letters of nominal account name (entered on invoice by purchase dept manager)
Nominal account code (entered by purchase dept manager)
Date
Goods inward note number
Net amount
VAT amount
Gross amount

Required:

   a. Suggest manual operations and controls which might previously have been applied to these invoices.

   b. Suggest input controls that might be applied by the program to these items.

   c. List some audit tests that could be applied to these items indicating the purpose of the test and the relevant audit evidence gained.

2. Partco plc are a large component manufacturer. They have some 4,000 employees and 6,000 customers. Among the files used on their mainframe computer are:

- weekly payroll. All employees are paid by bank transfer. The file is printed out onto microfiche monthly and overwritten. A file is retained of employees with paye information.
- a personnel record with details of all employees. Annually left employees are divested onto microfiche.
- a file of loans to employees (these are extensive) and interest is added monthly. Loans that have been repaid are removed annually onto microfiche.
- a file of unpaid sales invoices. Statements are printed out and cash and invoices are removed monthly after extraction of the monthly statements. The company have a bad debt problem.
- a file which forms the plant register.

Required:

Suggest a number of uses of computer audit programs on the audit of the company. What audit evidence would emerge from these uses?

Examination question *(Answer begins on page 555)*

1. You are currently engaged in planning the audit of the financial statements of E Limited as at 30 June 1985. The company runs a wholesale electrical business buying directly from national and overseas suppliers and selling to both large and small retailers. This will be the first accounting period during which all transactions relating to the sales, purchases, wages and general ledger systems will be processed and recorded by computer. Your firm of Certified Accountants has experience of auditing computerised accounting systems and has decided as a matter of policy that during this year's audit of the financial statements of E Ltd it will be essential to test all the controls over the computerised accounting systems and to use computer audit programs to test the accounting records.

    Required:

    a. Outline how an audit is affected by the accounting transactions and records being processed by computer and held on computer files. (4 marks)
    b. Describe what is meant by:
        i.   Application controls
        ii. General controls (4 marks)
    c. Give two examples of specific application controls over data being processed through E Ltd's purchase system describing the purpose of each control. (4 marks)
    d. i.   Outline what you understand by the term computer assisted audit techniques (CAATs) and the benefits that may be derived from using them. (4 marks)
        ii. Give two examples of how CAATs might effectively be used in the audit of E Ltd's year-end trade debtors. (4 marks)

    (ACCA)

Examination questions without answers

2. You are assisting in the interim audit of DOOR CHEMICALS plc and are assigned the debtors and sales section by the audit senior. DOOR CHEMICALS plc maintains its accounting records on a mainframe computer system. There are about 20,000 debtors on the sales ledger which total approximately £10 million. The audit senior asks you to liaise with the computer audit department of your firm in planning and conducting the

audit of debtors. During your conversation with the computer audit manager, he uses certain terms which you are not familiar. These terms include 'computer assisted audit techniques' (CAATs), 'general controls' and 'application controls'. Further, as a result of your conversation, it seems that the computer audit department will not be able to visit the client whilst you are carrying out your work but will visit the client shortly after you have left the client. The audit senior is extremely annoyed at this and blames you for the lack of adequate planning.

Required:

a. Explain what is meant by the following terms used in connection with computer auditing.

    i.   General controls   (2 marks)

    ii. Application controls   (3 marks)

    iii. Computer assisted audit techniques (CAATs)   (4 marks)

b. Describe the essential elements of the planning process when auditing computerised systems. (6 marks)

c. List *four* ways in which CAATs may help you in the audit of sales and debtors. (4 marks)

d. Discuss whether you feel the audit senior is justified in blaming you for the lack of adequate audit planning. (3 marks)

e. List *three* disadvantages of the computer audit department visiting the client at a different time to your interim audit visit. (3 marks)

(ACCA 92)

3. You are a senior in charge of the audit of LINDELL Ltd., a company engaged in the distribution of spare parts for the motor industry. The company operates a computerised accounting system incorporating the sales, purchases, cash receipts and cheque payments day books, as well as the payroll records, stock records and the nominal ledger. The accounting system software package used by the company is a standard 'off the shelf' package and has been operating without modification for the past few years. The company employs one full-time computer operator who is responsible for all aspects of the computer system administration.

Approximately 85% of the company's overheads are represented by payroll and related costs. There are 125 full-time and 25 part-time employees.

Your audit manager has asked you to prepare a brief memorandum setting out how you intend to approach the audit of the computer system and of the payroll system.

Requirement

Draft a *brief* memorandum to your audit manager explaining clearly:

a. the general audit approach that you would adopt with regard to the company's computer system; and

b. the audit procedures that you would adopt with regard to the audit of the payroll figure.

(ICAI 95)

4. You are in charge of the audit of EDWIN DROOD ENGINEERING Ltd., which has a computer installation.

Required:

a. Explain the difference between pre-input controls and input controls.

b. What are validity checks and why are they necessary?

c. Explain why it is important to restrict the right of access to the computer.

d. Why is it essential that amendments to programs are authorised by the computer manager?

(AAT 94)

5. In the course of an audit, the external auditor uses the company's own computer to prepare an ageing analysis of the company's debts.

   i. How far is it valid for an external auditor to use the client's computer? (5 marks)

   ii. Why is this analysis useful to the external auditor? (5 marks)

   iii. State the appropriate audit method. (6 marks)

(LCC 89) (Total 16 marks)

6. 'Substantive testing of computer records is possible and necessary. Its extent depends on the degree of reliance the auditor has placed on the internal controls. The degree of that reliance will depend on the results of his review and compliance testing of the internal controls over the accounting records.'(AH Millichamp: *Auditing*.)

   Describe the two basic approaches which the auditor will use in his/her substantive testing of computer records.

(ICA 91)

7. You have just been appointed as the manager in charge of the audit of COMP Ltd., a large manufacturing company. The company is highly computerised using a mainframe computer which is supported by a computer department employing about 10 staff.

   The partner in charge of the audit is concerned that the audit approach to be used should be in accordance with Auditing Guideline L407, Auditing in a Computer Environment. He has asked you to prepare an audit plan concentrating on the computer audit aspects of the assignment.

   Requirement

   Draft a memorandum to the partner detailing the audit approach that should be adopted and the audit issues that should be considered when auditing in a computer environment such as that of COMP Ltd. (22 marks)

   NB: You are not required to detail the approach to be adopted in individual balance sheet or profit and loss account areas.

(ICAI 92)

8. In auditing the financial statements of companies which use computerised accounting systems, the auditor may find that his traditional audit trail is often obscured. Various techniques can be used in order to give the auditor greater assurance when the audit trail is lost. These methods will include 'auditing through the computer' coupled with a detailed analytical review.

   Required:

   a. Explain why there is a possible loss of audit trail when companies utilise computerised accounting systems, and why 'auditing through the computer' assists the auditor in overcoming this loss of audit trail. (6 marks)

   b. Explain how the auditor can use analytical review techniques in order to give him greater assurance when there is a loss of audit trail. (4 marks)

   c. Outline how audit software can be used by the auditor in order to assist him in carrying out his analytical review. (4 marks)

d. Explain the possible reasons and audit implications of significant changes in the following ratios when compared to the prior year's ratios:

i. The stock turnover ratio (ratio of cost of sales to average stock) has decreased from the previous year's rate.

ii. The debtors turnover ratio (ratio of credit sales to trade debtors) has decreased over the year. (6 marks)

(ACCA 91) (20 marks)

54 Audit of small businesses with computerised systems

Introduction

1. The audit of large companies who invariably have sophisticated computerised accounting records with good general and application controls has become a well established procedure. Such audits are difficult and require expert staff, but the techniques are available and usually well performed. Large volumes have been written on this subject and the last two chapters give an outline only.

2. The methodology of audit of small businesses with *manual* records is also well established.

3. In recent years computer hardware and turnkey systems have become available very cheaply to small businesses and are now commonplace. The audit of computerised systems in a small business is much more difficult. This chapter outlines some of the problem areas and the ways in which these systems can be audited.

Special characteristics

4. The special characteristics of computer systems in small businesses which distinguish them both from sophisticated computer systems in larger companies and from manual systems include:

a. Micro systems need no *special environment*. This tends to make them available with open access to all staff with attendant problems of data integrity. Larger systems usually require special environments with the possibilities of physical access controls. Sabotage by disgruntled employees is always a possibility in small systems.

b. Files are often held on *floppy discs*. These are highly portable and can be lost, stolen or damaged easily. Destruction of a complete sales ledger file by strong magnetic fields is quite possible.

c. Password protection if often non existent or easily circumvented. An employee who has access to a wage rate file could easily give himself a pay rise.

d. The client's computer is often fully understood by only *one person*. This creates opportunities for fraudulent manipulation and also for error if the person is less than competent. A system in which the only member of staff who fully understands it is able to circumvent or deactivate procedures or make alterations to programmes and files undetected, is clearly a recipe for disaster.

e. The computer can be operated by *lower grade staff*. Manual systems generally require a fair degree of intelligence and training for reasonable operation. Computer systems can be so over friendly that they can be operated by relatively less intelligent and untrained staff. The effect of this might be that obvious errors can be undetected. An out of date price file for use in producing sales invoices may be loaded in error. An intelligent and interested member of staff would spot this but it may not be picked up by a young person on a YTS scheme.

f. Chaos may build up. Errors can build up undetected in micro computer systems resulting possibly in business failure. For example, a sales ledger system which has input malfunction (eg specifying wrong record codes for input of sales or cash with items ending up on the wrong accounts) or processing malfunction (eg failing to post items entered) could end up with numerous accounts different from the purchase ledger accounts in the books of customers. The effect of this could be uncollected debts and then cash flow problems. Computer systems go on churning out faulty statements for ever.

g. Even at low levels of sophistication, *user departments* tend to lose interest in data processing through ignorance and possible fear of the computer. There is, therefore, less involvement in and hence control over data processing and output than in manual systems.

h. Commercially available systems on micro computers are usually very *sophisticated* in the way that data can be manipulated in several ways. For example, an original input of 'sale of ten widgets mark 111 (pink) to customer number 3642' can lead to: invoice creation and the updating of sales ledger, stock, sales commission, sales, sales analysis, customer analysis and other files and may activate re-order procedures. The firm becomes dependent on these procedures and could not go back to manual procedures at least in the short term. Quality and reliability in processing are essential.

i. User departments become *dependent* on the output of the system in such areas as listings of debtors, sales analysis and cash requirements for suppliers. As the computer produces these useful documents with little manpower. The ability of the few data processing staff used to produce documents manually fades away.

j. Micro systems can be operated in *real time* mode as well as in batch mode. Thus details of a sale can be input and all the associated processing carried out at any time.

k. Micro systems are very cheap. Staff savings can be achieved. Much more timely processing can be obtained and more useful information can be achieved.

These things do not happen overnight and a period of months is required for a new computer and its systems and programs to work properly. Effort is required to make the configuration work. *Control aspects* are usually ignored. It has been suggested that the original expensive computer systems were seen as worth the effort at control simply because they were expensive. A cheap micro system is not thought worthy of expensive controls, simply because it is cheap.

5. Some or all of the above characteristics can be found in most micro systems operated by small companies. They are also to be found in larger organisations where *disseminated*

systems are used. The effect of these characteristics on the approach to be adopted by an auditor can be summarised as:

a. Auditors may wish to place reliance on any internal controls.

b. Micro systems in small businesses tend to lack controls either general controls or application controls.

c. Consequently, it is rare that an auditor can place reliance on internal controls.

d. The auditor must, therefore, draw his evidence largely from substantive testing.

Internal control in small computer based systems

6. The following general points can be made about small business computer systems and internal control:

a. Effective control is necessary if the full potential of computer systems is to be realised. The full potential of computer systems is rarely realised.

b. Users may lack familiarity with computers. This is less of a problem now that computers are becoming so common.

c. Small numbers of people are usually involved. This makes the business very reliant on key people and makes segregation of duties difficult.

d. Small companies do not realise the utility of controls and find them irksome and often find ways of circumventing any that do exist.

e. The risks attached to not having controls are not realised. Poor systems can lead to incorrect invoicing, omitted transactions, failure to chase debtors, failure to keep records that conform to Companies Act requirements, VAT regulations, the Data Protection Act etc., and opportunities for fraud.

f. Small businesses tend to have few staff with little computer experience or training and the owners of the business are closely involved. Staff are usually unfamiliar with control procedures and unwilling to bother with them. All these things can lead to poor records, disclosure of confidential information, poor decision making, lost opportunities, loss of data and files, business disruption and possibly business failure.

Control procedures

7. These include:

a. *Completeness and accuracy of data.* Possible measures include:

   – accounting controls. These may be pre-listing of input documents, establishment of numbered batches with specific numbers of records, use of control accounts, reconciliations etc.

   – authorisation procedures done manually. Such procedures must always be evidenced and acknowledged.

   – authorisation procedures by the computer. These might include the edit checks listed in the previous chapter eg format checks, check digits, master file compatibility, range checks, logical inference, sequence checks, record numbers and comparison with inputted control totals.

- use of reports produced by the computer. The computer could produce lists of amendments to standing data eg sales prices, credit ratings, wage rates or names of employees.
- standing data should be printed out at intervals and checked in detail.
- review of reports of unusual items or exception reports. These can be produced by the system.
- review of the reasonableness of the results. Management in small companies are usually deeply familiar with all aspects of the business and a review of the results of processing may reveal any gross errors. In addition the use of budgetary control is often very helpful. These types of review should be systematised and a person be made responsible for them with acknowledgement.
- the maintenance of a log. This might contain the dates and times of all processing, the names of those initiating the processing, the files used and the accounting control data incorporated with record counts. All this is part of the discipline which alone permits good data processing.

b. *File storage and backup.*

Loss of data and files is not difficult to achieve and may cause great disruption and possible failure of the firm. Measures to achieve file storage control and back up include:

- regular copying of files onto floppies or by printing out. Some firms regularly copy all files on hard disc to floppies at the end of each day.
- keeping the copies in fire proof safes and/or in a separate building.
- listing all files backed up and ensuring that all are properly labelled. A proper system of file naming is essential.
- periodic testing of back up procedures.
- carefully organised and supervised deletion of redundant, obsolete or inaccurate data at intervals.

c. *Documentation of procedures.* In practice many small firms have procedures but these are not written down or documented. This can mean they are subject to random change and not always carried out properly. Documentation is essential at the implementation of the system, for new staff, for occasional users, for temporary replacements, and for infrequently used procedures (eg year end procedures).

Documentation is especially important if the system is developed by the firm and/or is spreadsheet based. It is all part of the discipline idea in general controls.

d. *Security of computers, data and files.* Considerations are:

- physical security of the hardware. It may be better to keep the apparatus in a separate room or alternatively in a situation where it is in full view of everybody to avoid unauthorised access.
- files on hard disc that are sensitive should be removed when not in use and re-entered when required.
- using machine locks to prevent unauthorised use.
- labelling all floppy discs and keeping disc files safely under lock and key.

- proper training of all users to minimise the possibility of loss or damage to the hardware or files by accident or oversight.

- restricting use by means of passwords.

e. *Maintenance*. Computers are prone to hardware and software failure. All firms should have regular maintenance of hardware and rapid access to repair facilities. Software failure is more difficult but where software is obtained from a supplier full service facilities should be available.

f. *Insurance*. Insurance should be carried against loss of equipment and programmes, the costs of any recovery action, the reinstatement of data and the loss of profits during any recovery period.

g. *Contingency plans for alternative processing*. Small firms can become totally dependent on the computer and disruption can be expensive or even fatal. It is essential to have:

- alternative facilities (additional or spare micros or possibility of hire)

- written plans for containment of disaster

- full copies of all software and files

- possibility of manual processing if a software failure cannot be corrected quickly.

- full documentation of the system used.

Audit planning

8. Where a micro computer based system exists, the audit planning process will include a section of the computer aspects of the audit. This may include the following sections:

a. Description of computer *hardware*.

b. Description of how the computer department is organised. It is often the lack of such organisation which is the problem.

c. Description of the *applications* which are computerised with details of the number and value of items processed. This may assist the auditor with an initial division of applications which are relevant to him (eg sales ledger, wages) and those having little or no relevance (eg sales analysis – however sales analysis by product may be useful in determining slow moving items and hence the value of stock). It is also an initial determination of material and non-material areas.

d. Preliminary review of *systems of control*. It may be that there are few or no controls but some controls may exist and be effective.

e. Description of *programmed procedures* in outline. It is particularly important to know of procedures which have control significance. For example, a program may incorporate a sequence check on delivery note numbers.

f. Review of available methods of *testing programmed procedures*. These may include test packs and computer audit programs. Smaller audit firms do not generally have access to these techniques.

g. Review of possibility of *file interrogation*. Against smaller audit firms may not be capable of applying CAATs and larger firms may not find them cost effective with smaller clients.

The approach to be adopted

9. The initial review will give the auditor an insight into his problem – how to approach the audit. The solution to the problem will depend on these and some other factors including:

   a. The client need. Some clients may specifically ask for a systems based audit in order to check on the workings of the system. This would be unusual in small audits but is common in larger companies.

   b. Whether any effective controls exist either *general* controls or *applications* controls.

   c. Whether there is any difference in principle between the system and a manual system. Many micro systems are effectively mechanised versions of manual systems. However, some are remarkably complex.

   d. Audit firms resources and audit costs. The audit firm may well have no separate computer audit department to call on and those firms that have may consider them too expensive to use on small clients.

10. The approaches available include:

   a. Auditing round the computer. This means treating the computer as a 'black box' whose working cannot be understood. This may seem rather a defeatist attitude to the computer, but in many situations where few application controls exist, substantive testing of the transactions and balances is the only way to obtain the necessary audit evidence. Investigating the computer applications and programs in depth would take time and resources with little return.

   b. Fully investigating the computer system and its associated internal controls with a view to placing some reliance on those controls. This would be possible only in systems which are large and have a proper control structure. It may be possible and perhaps essential to use computer assisted audit techniques in such cases.

   c. Some combination of a. and b.

General controls

11. There is usually a very weak set of general controls in micro systems in small businesses. As a consequence:

   a. Systems are often poorly developed and implemented. Emphasis is on making them work rather than on control procedures.

   b. Turn key systems do not work perfectly because of the lack of adaptation to the client's particular needs. Where they are so adapted the adaptations may not be very effective.

   c. There is an ever present risk of the integrity of files being corrupted by program malfunction, input errors, use of incorrectly dated files, loss of data and files, or omission of transactions. Corruption may be by systematic error, operator error, accident, fraud or sabotage.

12. The problem for the auditor is clearly that in situations where no reliable general controls exist he has to be assured that files have not been corrupted to the extent that:

   a. proper accounting records have not been kept;

   b. the records do not form a reliable basis for the preparation of the accounts;

   c. accounts taken from the accounting records do not give a true and fair view.

13. The substantive tests and analytical review techniques have to be convincing enough to give the assurance that the accounts give a true and fair view within acceptable materiality limits.

Some controls are easily tested. For example physical controls such as passwords and locks and keys. General controls such as file storage, back up, documentation of procedures, security of hardware, software and files, maintenance facilities, insurance and contingency plans can be inspected or observed.

Applications controls

14. Applications programs in micro systems tend not to have programmed controls. Consequently the auditor cannot place reliance on programmed controls. However manual controls such as exist in manual systems often continue into micro systems. For example, controls over cheque payments which exist in manual systems are likely to be retained when the system is converted into a computer system. Where controls do exist in programs then the auditor may choose to place reliance on them. For example sequence checks or validity checks on input may be good evidence of completeness and validity of processing. In micro systems without good general controls it is always possible for controls in programs to be circumvented by staff perhaps to perpetrate a fraud.

Where applications controls cannot be relied on because they are non-existent, weak, ineffective or easily overridden then the auditor has to gain other evidence of the completeness and accuracy of the data coming from the system. He does this in much the same way as he would in a manual system with few internal controls. Perhaps a difference is the need to examine masses of print outs instead of hard cover books.

Use of CAATS on micro based systems

15. In preceding paragraphs I have indicated that audit firms do not in general use sophisticated computer audit techniques on small firms with computer systems. It is however perfectly possible for these techniques to be used.

a. *test packs*. All programs have some validation build in and most build up totals and undertake analyses. The correct operation of these activities can be tested by the use of auditor designed test packs. These procedures require the auditor to get to know the manual and computer controls without requiring the detail of programme operations to be researched.

b. *file interrogation techniques*. It is possible to use computer programs to assist the auditor by:

– generating reports. The program may produce totals thus confirming figures or reperform calculations or tabulate information or produce exception reports (eg of overdue debts or large stock items).

– comparing files at different dates or comparing back up files with working files.

– extracting information from files by using networked facilities or remote terminals etc. This way the auditor is able to become familiar with the operating system and its shortcomings if any.

Use of microcomputers in auditing

16. Microcomputers now come in portable form and auditors can carry their own computers with them on audit and use the machine in various ways to automate the audit process. Some of the ways that micros can be used are:

   a. Word processing can be used to maintain the indexes and texts of files and of ICQs etc. These can be changed at will and printed out as desired. Audit manuals are also now word processed allowing for easy up-dating.

   b. Word processing can also be used for standard letters eg the bank letter, debtors' circulation, representation letter etc.

   c. Information can be transferred between word processing, spreadsheets and data bases allowing working schedules to be built up and data to be transferred for one year to the next and between schedules and also to be manipulated mathematically.

   d. Spreadsheets can facilitate analytical review. Figures can be input and compared with previous years. Ratios can be calculated and trends perceived.

   e. Databases can be compiled about a client or an industry. Financial and audit history can be included.

   f. It is possible for direct communication between the auditors' computer and the client's computer allowing for transfer of schedules and other data. This can sometimes be done over telephone lines or through remote terminals. On line access is possible in some cases to a client's files. This can be very useful for audit planning and for accessing information while it is available.

   g. Micros can be used for statistical work including the selection of random numbers, the assessment of statistical data in sampling and in regression analysis.

   h. Potentially auditors may use expert systems. This idea is certainly in its infancy but has recently been described in an ICAEW publication.

Summary

17. a. Micro computer based systems present problems for the auditor which differ from the manual system and the sophisticated main frame system.

   b. Special characteristics of micro systems include: open access; losable floppy discs; no password protection; domination by one person; operation by lower grade staff; systematic errors; loss of involvement by users; complexity; dependence on ill-controlled output; lack of controls.

   c. Audit plans may include sections on: description of hardware; organisation of computing; applications computerised; control systems; programmed controls; testing procedures; file interrogation possibilities; CAATs.

   d. Approaches to the audit may include:
   - systems reviews
   - systems testing with a view to relying on internal controls
   - review and testing of manual internal controls
   - substantive tests
   - analytical review techniques.

e. Internal controls that should be incorporated into micro based systems include procedures to ensure completeness and accuracy of processing (accounting controls, authorisation procedures manual or computer, use of computer reports, use of a log, budgetary control of output, review of exception reports), file storage and back up procedures, documentation of procedures, security procedures for hardware, software and files, maintenance, insurance and contingency plans.

f. Computer Assisted Audit Techniques such as the use of test packs and computer audit programmes can be used on micro systems.

g. Micro computers can be used in auditing – word processing of files, standard letters, manuals etc; spreadsheets for analytical review etc; databases for history and facts about a client; direct communication and transfer of data from clients' files; statistical work and potentially expert systems in auditing.

Points to note

18. a. The growth of micro processor systems in small businesses means that nearly all business will have computerised records within a few years. All firms of accountants will have to become competent in computer auditing matters. The whole subject is developing rapidly.

b. What has been said about micro computers in small businesses is equally true of micro computers used in large businesses and also of the personal computers or workstations used by many executives nowadays.

c. In examining the system of accounting used by a client the auditor must never forget the Companies Act requirement for proper accounting records.

d. Even small business micros are vulnerable to the hacker and the computer virus.

e. Business software is readily available at low prices and some of it is in the public domain (= it is not copyright and can therefore be obtained free). Such software should not be used indiscriminately but controls of the kind outlines in this chapter should surround its use.

Case study for Chapter 54

XS Components Ltd is a wholesaler with 2,000 lines in stock and 800 credit customers. Total sales are £1.8 million a year. The company uses a commercial turn key micro computer. The system provides for continuous stock recording, the usual accounting records and facilities such as sales analysis, debtors ageing, stock throughput etc. The system is based on the general office and is operated by Jim who has a HND in business studies and Janet. The firm employs 20 staff and is owned by Harry the sole director and his wife.

Discussion

a. What characteristics of this system distinguish if from main frame and manual systems?

b. How would the auditor verify debtors?

Student self testing questions *Questions with answers apparent from the text*

1. a. What special characteristics distinguish micro computer systems in small businesses? (4)

b. What audit approaches are possible? (10)

c. Why is internal control often ineffective in microbased systems in small businesses? (4, 5, 6)

d. What are the risks of having poor internal control in such systems? (4, 5, 6)

e. List the control procedures desirable in such system. (7)

f. List the sections on computer audit in the working papers of a small business. (8)

g. How can general controls be tested? (13)

h. How can CAATs be used on microbased systems? (15)

i. How can micro computers be used as an aid to auditing? (16)

Examination questions without answers

1. The senior partner of your firm of auditors has heard that some of the larger firms of auditors are using micro computers in their audit work. He has asked you to prepare a memorandum which gives examples of the ways in which micro computers can be used by auditors to assist in their work in carrying out an audit, both in terms of what is currently possible and what may be possible in the future.

(ACCA 3 88) (25 marks)

2. It is now quite commonplace for auditors to use portable microcomputers to perform audit tasks. The microcomputer is even used when the clients' data is not computerised, or when the clients' software is not compatible with the auditors. However, the controls which must be exercised by the audit firm over the microcomputer must be sufficiently sophisticated to prevent the corruption of data held on the computer.

Required:

a. Describe *five* ways in which a microcomputer may be utilised by the auditor in order to assist his audit work. (Other than computer assisted audit techniques.) (10 marks)

b. Describe *two* categories of software which the auditor might use on a microcomputer in order to aid his audit work. (Other than CAATs.) (4 marks)

c. Explain the controls which must be exercised when microcomputers are used by the auditor in his work. (6 marks)

(ACCA 92) (20 marks)

Some auditing problem areas

1. The auditor has a duty to all users of the financial statements he is auditing, to see that a true and fair view is given. We now deal with two problem areas: firstly related parties and then reservation of title.

55 Related parties

Introduction

1. Many entities are quite autonomous and deal at *arms length* with all persons and entities that they have contact with. They pursue their own *self interest* at all times. However some entities are not like that all the time. Some deal with persons or entities who are connected with them and transactions between them may not then be at arms length or in the interests of the reporting entity. For example the Adam family (primarily Adam himself) own all the shares in both Cain Ltd and Abel Ltd. For reasons of his own (perhaps inheritance tax reasons) Adam decides that Cain Ltd should transfer a freehold property to Abel Ltd at a nominal price unrelated to market price. In this case, Abel Ltd has gained something and Cain Ltd has lost something, not as a result of ordinary commercial dealing but as a result of dealings with Abel Ltd under the influence of Adam. Both Adam and Cain Ltd are *related parties* of Abel Ltd.

   If a reader of the financial statements of Abel Ltd or Cain Ltd wants to get a true and fair view of the affairs of these companies, that reader must be informed about the transaction described above. What is required is disclosure of all dealings with related parties. The ASB issued FRS 8 *Related party disclosures* in October 1995 after a very long gestation period. We discuss its provisions briefly in Chapter 36. It will be very interesting to see how it works out in practice. The gist of FRS 8 is that it requires disclosure of:

   – information on transactions with related parties
   – the name of the party controlling the reporting entity and, if different, that of the ultimate controlling party.

2. In November 1995, the APB issued Statement of Auditing Standards SAS 460 *Related parties* which sets out the auditors' duties on these matters.. This chapter is mainly about SAS 460. I will assume that you are familiar with the requirements of FRS 8.

The auditor's duties re related parties

3. SAS 460 requires that the auditors should:

   a. plan and perform the audit with the objective of obtaining sufficient *audit evidence* regarding he adequacy of disclosure of related party transactions and control of the entity in the financial statements

   b. when *planning* the audit, assess the *risk* that material undisclosed related party transactions may exist

c. review for completeness, *information* provided by the directors identifying material transactions with those parties that have been related parties for any part of the financial period

d. be *alert* for evidence of material related party transactions that are not included in the information provided by the directors

e. obtain sufficient appropriate audit evidence that material identified related party transactions are *properly recorded and disclosed* in the financial statements

f. obtain sufficient appropriate audit evidence that disclosures in the financial statements relating to *control of the entity* are properly stated

g. obtain written *representations* from the directors concerning the completeness of information provided regarding the related party and control disclosures in the financial statements

h. consider the implications for their *report* if:

  – they are unable to obtain sufficient appropriate audit evidence concerning related parties and transactions with such parties; or

  – the disclosure of related party transactions or the controlling party of the entity in the financial statements is not adequate.

Risk

4. It is the directors' responsibility under FRS 8 to identify, approve and disclose related party transactions and, to that end, they should implement adequate accounting and internal control systems. The auditors can then acquire an understanding of such systems. However the directors may not implement such systems or they may wish to hide transactions with related parties. Directors have been motivated in such matters by intentions to defraud the company (for example by extracting assets from it) or shareholders (for example by window dressing the financial statements) or the tax authorities (for example by transfer pricing to put profits in low tax countries) or national governments (for example by circumventing exchange control restrictions). There is therefore a risk that auditors may fail to identify some related party transactions.

5. In the planning stage of an audit, the auditors should assess the risk that there will be undisclosed related party transactions. In many audits the risk will be small but in others it will be large. The work the auditors can be expected to do depends on the degree of risk identified. There is an *inherent risk* that all relevant related party transactions will not be identified. However SAS 460 makes clear that the auditors cannot be expected to find a needle in a haystack.

6. There are some situations where the auditors need to be especially vigilant and enquire more deeply:

a. Where obvious risks exist. For example the company is one of several owned by a resident in a tax haven and the auditors know from past experience that transactions are entered into that are not motivated by purely commercial considerations

b. where there is *control risk* that is where the control environment is weak

c. where the management style does not place a high priority on financial statement disclosure.

In general auditors can, in the absence of high risk circumstances, rely upon the representations of the directors. However the auditors must undertake all audits with a proper degree of *scepticism* and be alert at all times to the possibility of undisclosed related party transactions.

Information provided by directors

7. Directors should provide representations to the auditors and this should then be checked. There are various ways of doing this:
   a. reviewing minutes and statutory books (eg register of directors' interests)
   b. reviewing large or unusual transactions especially around year ends
   c. reviewing loans received and made, and the bank letter
   d. reviewing investment transactions
   e. reviewing prior year papers
   f. reviewing pension and other trusts
   g. reviewing affiliations of directors and senior managers with other entities
   h. reviewing returns to tax authorities, Companies House, the Stock Exchange, regulatory agencies and others
   i. reviewing correspondence with lawyers

8. In the course of the audit, staff will be constantly alert to matters which may reveal an undisclosed related party. Such instances may include unexpected prices, unexpected contract terms, transactions lacking commercial logic, and transactions where substance differs from form. Such transactions after date are especially important.

9. The auditors must obtain evidence that the recording and disclosure in financial statements is appropriate. They may need to enquire more closely into disclosed transactions, and obtain third party confirmations.

Control of the entity

10. In most instances this is not a problem. But in some cases it is and then the auditors should obtain appropriate evidence. In some cases the ultimate controlling party is unknown. This seems surprising but the use of tax havens and offshore ownership chains designed to confuse regulatory and tax authorities is not uncommon. If the ultimate controlling party is not known then that fact should be disclosed.

Qualified reports

11. In a few cases the auditors may conclude that they have insufficient evidence on this subject. This is a *limitation of scope* and may require a qualified opinion or, rather unlikely, a disclaimer of opinion. If the auditors conclude that the disclosure is not adequate then they may issue a qualified opinion or an adverse opinion. They may also consider giving, in their report, the information which should have been given in the financial statements.

Summary

12. a. A true and fair view often requires the disclosure of related party transactions and of controlling parties.
    b. FRS 8 and SAS 460 appeared in late 1995.

c. The auditors have a duty to see that the provisions of FRS 8 are carried out and to obey the prescriptions of SAS 460. However they are not required to find a needle in a haystack.

d. The auditors need to assess the risk of inadequate disclosure and act accordingly

e. The directors are primarily responsible for the disclosure of related party and ownership matters and the auditors should obtain written representations from them

Points to note

13. a. Related parties can be of many kinds – owners, directors, 'shadow' directors, key management, persons who tend to act in concert, families of the others.

b. Some persons and entities are not considered to be related parties for these purposes. For example regulatory bodies, banks, major customers or suppliers despite the fact that they may have considerable influence over the conduct of the company's affairs. Related party transactions like directors' emoluments do not come into the definition either but, of course, The Companies Act 1985 has required their disclosure for many years.

c. Pension funds and pension fund trustees are related parties. This is in the wake of the Maxwell and Daily Mirror Group affair.

d. A general requirement for the disclosure of related party transactions is new with FRS 8. However there are many specific requirements by the Stock Exchange for listed companies and in The Companies Act 1985 for all companies (see sections 231, 232, 741and schedules 4 to 7).

e. This whole area is fascinating and we shall see how it works out over the next few years.

Case study 1 for Chapter 55

Convoluted Ltd is a company dealing in rare metals internationally. It has forty employees (25 in the UK). It is owned by Joe King Ltd, a company registered in the Cayman Islands and is known to deal with several other UK and overseas companies also owned by that company. The company has four directors who all UK residents and who do not own any shares in the company.

The company has a pension scheme with employee and employer trustees and is heavily indebted to its bankers.

The auditors are Chancy & Co. who are newly appointed.

Discussion

a. List some possible related parties of this company

b. From the auditors' point of view what risks are there that all the requirements of FRS 8 may not be met?

c. Set out a section in the overall audit plan covering the requirements of SAS 460.

d. List some possible substantive tests on the subject of related party transactions and ultimate control.

Case study 2 for Chapter 55

Obtain some annual reports and accounts of public companies. Explore and report on the related party and company control matters.

Student self testing questions *Questions with answers apparent from the text*

1. a. Why are related party transactions and ultimate ownership important to the true and fair view? (1)

    b. What are the two main sources of authority in this area? (2)

    c. List the requirements of SAS 460. (3)

    d. What are the risks that auditors undertake in this area ? (4-6)

    e. How might an auditor seek confirmation of directors' representations and assess their completeness? (7)

    f. What matters might give concern to an auditor in preparing the auditor's report? (11)

Examination questions without answers

1. At the end of your audit of Bulldog plc, you discover a stock book covering 'Stocks held in number 3 warehouse.' Enquiries indicate that this is a rented warehouse, paid for privately by the directors (NOT out of company funds). The directors state that the stocks held therein are obsolete company stocks that they are storing prior to final destruction and, as the premises are rented privately by the directors themselves, they will not allow you access to the stock records or to the warehouse itself.

    i.   What rights has the auditor in this matter?   (3 marks)

    ii. As auditor, what action would you take?   (12 marks)

    (LCC) (Total 15 marks)

2. Your firm has recently been appointed auditor of Ripley Manufacturing plc. Ripley Manufacturing plc is quoted on the London Stock Exchange and the directors own less than 5% of the company's shares.

    You have been asked by the senior in charge of the audit to carry out work in relation to directors transactions with the company, which are required to be disclosed in the company's annual accounts.

    Required:

    a. List and briefly describe the work you would carry out to check if the company has made any loans or quasi-loans to a director, or entered into any guarantees in connection with a loan to a director.   (7 marks)

    b. List and briefly describe the work you would carry out to check if there are any:

        i.   directors' service agreements with the company.

        ii. options granted by the company to enable directors to purchase shares in the company at a fixed price at a future date.   (5 marks)

    c. List and briefly describe the investigations you would carry out to determine whether any director has had a material interest in a contract with the company (other than those described in part b. above).   (6 marks)

    d. List and describe the work you would carry out and the matters you would consider if your investigations revealed that Ripley Manufacturing plc had purchased all the shares in Lowdham Engineering plc for £4,000,000. One of the directors of Ripley Manufacturing plc owns 50% of the shares of Lowdham Engineering plc.   (4 marks)

e. A partner of your firm has asked your advice on another transaction, in which Ilkeston Electrical Ltd. purchased all the shares in Nuthall Distributors Ltd for £40,000. Nuthall Distributors Ltd was owned by the two directors of Ilkeston Electrical Ltd, and all the shares in Ilkeston Electrical Ltd are owned by these two directors and their families. You are required to list and describe the work you would carry out and the matters you would consider in relation to the purchase of Nuthall Distributors Ltd by Ilkeston Electrical Ltd.   (3 marks)

(ACCA 3 88) (Total 25 marks)

56 Reservation of title

Introduction

1. In 1976, the case of *Aluminium Industrie Vaassen BV* v *Romalpa Aluminium Ltd.* (the Romalpa case) made the business community aware of the idea of selling goods subject to reservation of title. It is possible to sell goods under a contract of sale whereby ownership does not pass until the goods are paid for.

2. This departure from the normal contract of sales creates recording and reporting problems for the parties involved and for their auditors.

3. This chapter considers these from the point of view of accounting, reporting and audit.

Accounting treatment

4. The treatment recommended by the accounting bodies is to record 'Romalpa' sales as if they were ordinary sales, that is, the sales are recorded as they are invoiced and the realisation convention is followed. This is an example of the accounting convention of substance over form. Other examples of this convention include hire purchase, group accounts, and some leasing transactions.

5. This treatment is appropriate for 'Romalpa' sales but not for goods sold on consignment or goods sold on sale or return where a sale will only be made on fulfilment of some agreed event such as the resale of the goods by the consignee.

Disclosure in accounts – buyers

6. The matter is only relevant if creditors include a *material* amount owed to suppliers who have sold the goods subject to reservation of title. Such creditors are in effect secured and the companies Act and the true and fair view require disclosure of secured creditors. In fact it is not entirely clear, if the Companies Act does require disclosure of creditors secured in this way. As the accounts are drawn up on the going concern convention, disclosure of matters which are relevant only in liquidation seems unnecessary.

7. However it is customary to disclose the amount of creditors which are secured in this way. This creates practical difficulties in that:

    a. Purchases and creditors subject to reservation of title are not normally distinguishable from the general run of purchases and creditors.

b. It is not always clear if a particular sale is subject to a reservation of title which will stand up in a court of law.

Disclosure in accounts – sellers

8. So far as vendors are concerned, the matter is only relevant in improving the collectability of debts. Any review of the required provision for bad and doubtful debts will need to consider this point.

Audit work – purchasers

9. The following work will need to be done on *all* audits:

a. Ascertain what steps the client takes to identify suppliers selling on terms which reserve title.

b. Ascertain what steps the client has taken to quantify such liabilities.

c. If it is apparent that there are *material* liabilities to such creditors then:

   i. if the liabilities are quantified in the accounts (usually this is just a note to the accounts) then review and test the procedures which have produced the figure.

   ii. if the directors consider that exact quantification is impracticable (this is often the case) and have estimated the amount or made a general note that such liabilities exist to a material amount, then review and test the information given.

   iii. consider generally if the information given is sufficient.

d. If it appears that there are no material liabilities of this kind, then verify that this is so by reviewing the terms of sale of major suppliers.

e. Obtain formal representations from the directors that there are no material liabilities of this sort, or if there are, that they have been adequately disclosed.

Summary

10. a. Goods can be sold subject to reservation of title.

b. Such sales are called 'Romalpa' sales.

c. The convention is to record such sales as if they were ordinary sales under the accounting convention 'substance over form'.

d. In a balance sheet, if creditors include a material amount secured by reservation of title, this fact should be disclosed and, if possible, quantified.

e. The auditor has a duty to apply procedures to ensure that adequate disclosure of such liabilities has been made.

Points to note

11. a. This subject has proved popular with examiners.

b. In practice, a supplier may have difficulty in law in establishing that the subject matter of his debt were sold subject to reservation of title. Liquidators tend to refuse to accept that any debts are secured by reservation of title.

c. Legal doubts exist over the extent to which an unpaid seller can trace or identify his interest in the goods if the goods have become indistinguishable from similar goods not secured, transformed by incorporation in a product (eg eggs made into a cake) or sold.

Case study for Chapter 56

Baloo is engaged on the audit of the accounts of Bagheera Bearing Ltd who trade in industrial bearings. The time is March 1997 and the accounts are for the year ending 31.12.96. Baloo notes that most of Bagheera's suppliers supply on reservation of title contracts.

Debtors of Bagheera include £26,000 from Akela Ltd. A receiver was appointed to Akela on 26.2.97 and no dividend is likely to be paid to unsecured creditors. Invoices to Akela have been marked 'These goods are sold on the understanding that title to them passes to the purchaser only on payment of the sum due'. Turnover of Bagheera in 1996 was £340,000.

Discussion

a. Outline the audit work to be done re reservation of title and the creditors.

b. The directors have declined to make a provision against the debt due by Akela. What should Baloo do?

Student self testing questions *Questions with answers apparent from the text*

1. a. How should reservation of title transactions be treated in financial statements? (4)

   b. What audit work should be done on creditors in connection with reservation of title? (9)

   c. What audit work should be done on debtors in connection with reservation of title clauses?

Examination question without answer

1. During a period of economic recession, when many companies are experiencing severe financial problems, it is important for an auditor to consider transactions involving goods sold subject to reservation of title. You are auditing the accounts of Park Manufacturing PLC for the year ended 31 March 1984 and you are aware that it both purchases and sells some of its products under a 'subject to reservation of title' clause.

   Required:

   a. For trade creditors appearing in the accounts at the year end:

      i. describe the audit work you would perform to find those suppliers who are claiming to supply goods to the company subject to reservation of title.

      ii. what factors would you consider in determining whether the reservation of titles clause is valid.

      iii. if the reservation of title clause is valid, and Park Manufacturing PLC is a going concern, state how these purchases should be disclosed in the published profit and loss account and balance sheet, and

      iv. if Park Manufacturing PLC has going concern problems, describe why goods purchased subject to reservation of title may aggravate the company's going concern problems.

   b. For trade debtors appearing in the accounts at the year end, describe what effect a reservation of title clause will have on your consideration of the bad and doubtful provision at the year end.

   (ACCA)

Ignore Taxation.

Internal auditing

1. Auditing has been regarded, in this manual, as the activity carried on by the auditor when he verifies accounting data, determines the accuracy and reliability of accounting statements and reports, and then reports upon his efforts. It is essentially an activity carried on by an *independent person* with the aim of *reporting on the truth and fairness* of financial statements.

2. Another type of auditing – internal auditing – exists in business and this part of the manual deals with it.

3. This type of auditing is included in this manual because:

   a. Students of auditing should at least know what it is.

   b. External auditors often find their work overlaps that of the internal auditor and an understanding must be established between internal and external auditors.

   c. Examinations often include questions requiring some knowledge of internal auditing.

4. Chapter 57 deals with internal auditing. Chapter 58 deals with the reliance which an external auditor may place on the work of the internal auditor.

57 Internal auditing

Introduction

1. Very large organisations (and some small ones) has found a need for an internal audit in addition to an external audit. Internal auditors are employees of the organisation and work exclusively for the organisation. Their functions partly overlap those of the external auditors and in part are quite different.

2. The *precise* functions of external auditors are either laid down by statute or embodied in a letter of engagement. The functions (which are rarely *precisely* laid down) of internal auditors are determined by management and very greatly from organisation to organisation.

3. There is an Auditing Guideline – 'Guidance for internal auditors' issued in June 1990.

4. Internal audit can be defined as:

   'An independent appraisal function established by the management of an organisation for the review of the internal control system as a service to the organisation. It objectively examines, evaluates and reports on the adequacy of internal control as a contribution to the proper, economic, efficient and effective use of resources.'

5. Internal auditing is thus:

   a. Carried on by independent personnel. Internal auditors are employees of the firm and thus <u>independence is not always easy to achieve</u>. However it can be assisted by:

      – having the scope to arrange its own priorities and activities

- having unrestricted access to records, assets and personnel
- freedom to report to higher management and where it exists to an audit committee
- IA personnel with an objective frame of mind
- IA personnel who have no conflicts of interest or any restrictions placed upon their work by management
- IA personnel having no responsibility for line work or for new systems. A person cannot be objective about something he/she has taken responsibility for. On the other hand the IA should be consulted on new or revised systems.
- IA personnel who have no non-audit work.

Since internal auditors are employees it is difficult to ensure that they are truly independent in mind and attitude.

b. an appraisal function. The internal auditor's job is to appraise the activity of others, not to perform a specific part of data processing. For example, a person who spent his time checking employee expense claims is not performing an internal audit function. But an employee who spent some time reviewing the system for checking employee expense claims may well be performing an internal audit function.

c. as a service to the organisation.

The management requires that:

i. Its *policies* are fulfilled.

ii. The *information* it requires to manage effectively is reliable and complete. This information is *not only* that provided by the accounting system.

iii. The organisation's assets are safeguarded.

iv. The internal control system is well designed.

v. The internal control system works in practice.

The internal auditor's activities will be directed to ensuring that these requirements are met.

The internal auditor can be seen as the eye of the board within the enterprise.

d. Other duties may include:

i. Being concerned with the implementation of social responsibility policies adopted by top management. An example of this is in energy saving.

ii. Being concerned with the response of the internal control system to errors and required changes to prevent errors.

iii. Being concerned with the response of the internal control system to external stimuli. The world does not stand still and the internal control system must continually change.

iv. Acting as a training officer in internal control matters.

vi. Auditing the information given to management particularly interim accounts and management accounting reports.

vii. Taking a share of the external auditor's responsibility in relation to the figures in the annual accounts.

viii. Being concerned with compliance with external regulations such as those on the environment, money laundering, financial services, related parties etc.

Essential elements of internal audit

6. The essential elements of internal audit are:

a. Independence – see above.

b. Staffing – the internal audit unit should be adequately staffed in terms of numbers, grades and experience.

c. Training – all internal audit should be fully trained.

d. Relationships – internal auditors should foster constructive working relationships and mutual understanding with management, with external auditors, with any review agencies (eg management consultants) and where appropriate with an audit committee. Mutual understanding is the goal.

e. Due care – an internal auditor should behave much as an external auditor in terms of skill, care and judgement. He should be up to date technically and have personal standards of knowledge, honesty, probity and integrity much as an external auditor. It is desirable that an internal auditor be qualified as much because of the ethical as the technical standards implied by membership of a professional body.

f. Specifically the stages of Internal Audit Planning are:

i.   Identify the objectives of the organisation (the organisation may have a mission statement)

ii. Define the IA objectives

iii. Take account of relevant changes in legislation and other external factors (eg new legislation)

iv. Obtain a comprehensive understanding of the organisation's systems, structures and operations

v.   Identify, evaluate and rank risks to which the organisation is exposed (eg retail cash sales, potential stock losses)

vi. Take account of changes in structures or major systems in the organisation (eg a change in the computer system)

vii. Take account of known strengths and weaknesses in the Internal Control system

viii. Take account of management concerns and expectations

ix. Identify audit areas by service, functions and major systems

x.   Determine the type of audit: eg systems(eg sales or stock control), verification (eg cash balances or vehicles), or value of money (eg the internal audit department or the old peoples homes in a Local Authority)

xi. Take account of the plans of external audit and other review agencies (eg the regulatory agencies in financial services, banking or insurance)

xii. Assess staff resources required and match with resources available (there never are enough!)

g. Systems controls – the internal auditor must verify the operations of the system in much the same way as an external auditor ie by investigation, recording, identification of controls and compliance testing of the controls. However an internal auditor is also concerned with:

- the organisation's business being conducted in an orderly and *efficient* manner
- adherence to management *policies* and *directives*
- promoting the most *economic*, *efficient* and *effective* use of resources in achieving the management's policies.
- ensuring compliance with statutory requirements
- securing as far as possible the completeness and accuracy of the records
- safeguarding the assets

h. Evidence – the internal auditor has similar standards for evidence as an external auditor, he will evaluate audit evidence in terms of sufficiency, relevance and reliability.

i. Reporting – the internal auditor must produce timely, accurate and comprehensive reports to management on a regular basis. These should report on the matters outlines in g. above and with the accuracy of information given to management and give recommendations for change.

External and internal auditors compared and contrasted

7. **Common interests**

   a. An effective system of internal control.

   b. Continuous effective operation of such system.

   c. Adequate management information flow.

   d. Asset safeguarding.

   e. Adequate accounting system (for example to comply with the Companies Act 1985).

   f. Ensuring compliance with statutory and regulatory requirements.

8. **Differences**

   a. **Scope** – the extent of the work undertaken. Internal audit work is determined by management but the external auditor's work is laid down by *statute*.

   b. **Approach**. The internal auditor may have a number of aims in his work including an appraisal of the efficiency of the internal control system and the management information system. The external auditor is interested primarily in the truth and fairness of the accounts.

   c. **Responsibility**. The internal auditor is answerable only to management. The external auditor is responsible to shareholders and arguably to an even wider public. Both are of course answerable to their consciences and the ethical conceptions of their professional bodies.

9. **Areas of work overlap**. This can apply in the following areas:

   a. Examination of the system of *internal control*.

   b. *Examination of the accounting records* and supporting documents.

   c. Verification of assets and liabilities.

   d. Observation, enquiry and the making of statistical and accounting ratio measurements.

Summary

10. a. Internal auditing is a fast growing and important activity.

b. Internal auditing has a definition.

c. The essential elements of an internal audit function are: independence, staffing, training, relationships, due care, planning, controlling, recording, systems controls, evidence and reporting.

d. There are differences between internal and external audits in terms of: scope, approach, responsibility and persons to report to.

Points to note

11. a. The work of internal auditors very often includes checking documents. An example of this is that local authority internal auditors often examine the documents and authorities supporting payments. This kind of work is not included in the definition in paragraph 4. By this definition, the work of the internal auditor is directed towards the appraisal of the controls applied by other people in the organisation.

b. Internal auditing is now considered a major discipline and there are many textbooks on the subject. This manual is about external auditing and I have included internal auditing only in outline.

c. It is important that Internal Audit report to the highest level, preferably the Board or an audit committee.

d. The guideline has much to say on the objectivity, the staffing and the training of internal auditors and on planning, control and reporting. These ideas are very similar to those of guidelines for external audit.

e. The guideline gives a very good summary of the stages in a systems audit as:

  i. Identify the system parameters (eg the details of a system for identifying bad credit risks before sales)

  ii. Determine the control objectives (eg to prevent sales to bad credit risks)

  iii. Identify expected controls to meet control objectives (eg inspection of sales ledger account before granting credit to existing customer)

  iv. Review the system against expected controls (eg is inspection of the sales ledger account included in the system)

  v. Test the controls designed into the system against control objectives (eg are the sales ledger inspections and other controls adequate [or alternatively too stiff] to prevent sales to bad risks)

  vi. Test the actual controls for effectiveness against control objectives

  vii. Test the operation of controls in practice

  viii. Give an opinion based on audit objectives as to whether the system provides an adequate basis for effective control and whether it is properly operated in practice.

Note that the external auditor may have more restricted aims in examining internal controls. In our case she may only be interested in the controls because she wishes to place part reliance on the controls in assessing the adequacy of the bad debt provision.

f. The guideline is not in the list of those adopted by the Auditing Practices Board but remains a useful guide to internal audit practice.

Case study for Chapter 57

Boggle Manufacturing plc is a manufacturer of mechanical engineering products with six factories, twelve sales depots in the UK and six in Europe. They have 4,000 employees. The company have a good system of budgetary control and standard costing. The Chairman of the company is also a vice chairman of an ecological pressure group. The company have come under financial pressure to reduce costs to restore profitability.

Discussion

Draw up a job specification for the appointment of an internal auditor.

Student self testing questions *Questions with answers apparent from the text*

1. a. Define internal auditing. (4)
    b. List characteristics of independence for an Internal Auditor. (5a)
    c. Should an internal audit prepare a bank reconciliation statement? (5b)
    d. What may an organisation require from Internal audit? (5c)
    e. List some duties of an internal auditor. (5d)
    f. List the essential elements of internal audit. (6)
    g. List common interests of internal and external auditors. (7)
    h. List the differences between them. (8)
    i. List the stages in internal audit planning (6f)
    j. List the stages in a systems audit of bank reconciliations (11e)

Examination questions without answers

1. Grumbleweed plc is appointing an internal auditor.
    a. Outline the nature of internal auditing. (3 marks)
    b. What qualities would you look for when appointing an internal auditor? (3 marks)
    c. Give two examples of the work done by an internal auditor. (6 marks)
    d. To whom should an internal auditor report? (3 Marks)
    (LCCI 90) (Total 15 marks)

2. One of the roles of internal audit is the safeguarding of assets and one of the big risks to business assets is that of fraud. If the auditor is to be successful in ensuring that adequate controls exist to deter fraud and to detect it he/she should be aware of the circumstances in which fraud may be fostered.
    a. what are the main causes of, or circumstances which foster, fraud? (12 marks)
    b. What safeguards would the auditor look for to deter and detect fraud? (8 marks)
    (ICA 92) (Total 20 Marks)

3. You have just completed the interim audit of DURDLES PUBLISHING Ltd., for the year ending 31 January 1995. The company has grown rapidly in recent years and the system of accounting and internal control has been subject to an increasing number of breakdowns. Your letter of weakness highlighted many of these breakdowns. The directors wish to take steps to rectify these problems and have asked the chief accountant to effect the necessary changes to the system. The chief accountant has approached you for

advice on the advisability of appointing an internal auditor to carry out this work and to review systems on a continuous basis.

Required:

a. State the essential differences and similarities between an internal and an external auditor.

b. Describe the personal qualities required of the staff of the internal audit department.

(AAT 94)

58 Reliance on internal audit

Introduction

1. Many larger organisations have an Internal Audit department. The personnel of this department will be employees of the organisation and their work will be directed by the management or to the Audit Committee if there is one. However, they often have a degree of independence and may report to the Board directly or, at least, to top management. The work they do may include work also done by the external auditor. Consequently, it is economic good sense for the external auditor to consider whether he can reduce his own work by placing reliance on the work of an internal auditor.

2. There is a Statement of Auditing Standards SAS 500 *Considering the work of internal audit*

3. The previous chapter considers internal auditing as a separate but related discipline to external auditing.

Reasons for co-operation

4. Internal audit is an element of the Internal Control system established by management. Thus as external auditors are accustomed to place reliance on internal controls (see paragraph 5 of the Auditors Operational Standard) they will consider if reliance can be placed on this element.

5. Some of the objectives of internal audit are the same as those of the external auditor. For example, the internal auditor will perform work on the documentation and evaluation of accounting systems and internal controls and will carry out compliance and substantive tests. It makes economic sense to reduce the work of the external auditor by relying on work done by the internal auditor.

Basis of co-operation

6. The external auditor may utilize the work of the internal auditor in two ways:

a. by taking into account the work done by the internal auditor;

b. by agreeing with management that internal audit will render direct assistance to the external auditor.

Nature of internal auditing

7. The scope and objectives of internal audit are set by management and vary widely. The areas of activity may include:

a. reviewing accounting systems and internal control;

b. examining financial and operating information for management, including detailed testing of transactions and balances.

c. reviewing the economy, efficiency and effectiveness of operations and of the functioning of non financial controls;

d. review of the implementation of corporate policies, plans and procedures;

e. special investigations.

8. Some of these functions are directly relevant to the objectives of the external auditor – seeking evidence of the truth and fairness etc., of items in the Accounts. Even special investigations may be relevant. For example, an investigation into the extent of slow moving stock is relevant to the value of stock or an investigation into the viability of a branch may be evidence as to the correctness of the using of going concern values for that branch's assets.

A modern example of a relevant investigation may be into compliance with statute or regulatory body requirements. The Internal audit department may be assigned to determine the detailed controls designed to ensure compliance with some environmental requirement. This may not seem to be of interest to the external auditor but the fact may be that non-compliance may lead to the closure of a factory and consequent losses and expenses and removal of going concern values to some part of the assets. Clearly the external auditor in such a case must have assurance that compliance is assured and the internal auditor may be able to provide that assurance.

9. Some of the functions are clearly not relevant to the external auditor's objectives. For example, the cost of a control is not relevant, only its effectiveness.

10. Some internal audit work is not audit work at all but is a part of internal control. For example, internal audit in Local Authorities may scrutinize and approve expense claims. Such work is an internal control but it is not auditing.

Assessment

11. Before placing any reliance on the work of an internal auditor, the external auditor must assess the internal auditor and his work in the following areas:

a. *Independence*. The internal auditor may be an employee of the organisation, but he may be able to organise his own activities and report his findings to a high level in management. An internal auditor on whom the external auditor places reliance must be independent and be able to communicate freely with the external.

b. The *scope* and *objectives* of the internal audit function areas such as 7a. and b. are likely to be useful to the external auditor. But c., d. and e. may also. For example, an investigation into a fraud may supply evidence to the external auditor that the extent of the fraud is not material.

c. *Due professional care*. To be useful to an external auditor the internal auditor's work must be done in a professional manner. That is, it must be properly planned, controlled, supervised, recorded and reviewed. The auditor who arrives in the morning and says to himself 'what shall I do today', is not much use.

d. *Technical competence*. Membership of a professional body with its competence and ethical implications is desirable. Ongoing training in specialist areas, such as computers, is useful.

e. _Reporting standards_. A useful internal auditor will provide high standard reports which are acted upon by management.

f. _Resource available_. An internal audit department that is starved of resources will not be very useful to the external auditor.

12. The assessment should be thorough and fully documented and included in the working papers. If the conclusion is that the internal audit department is weak or unreliable, then this fact should be communicated in the external auditor's 'report to management'.

Extent of reliance

13. The extent of reliance depends on many factors including:

a. The _materiality_ of the areas or items to be tested. Petty cash expenditure may probably be left to the internal auditor.

b. The level of _audit_ risk inherent in the areas or items. The value of work in progress in a Civil Engineering company or the provision for doubtful debts in a Hire Purchase company, are high risk areas which the external auditor must see to himself.

c. The level of _judgement_ required. The level of delayed repairs in a truck leasing company requires careful judgement.

d. The sufficiency of _complementary_ audit evidence. The internal audit may be relied upon to audit debtors accounting procedures if the external auditor has evidence in the form of a debtor's circularisation.

e. _Specialist_ skills possessed by internal audit staff. In a Bank, the internal audit department will have specialist knowledge and skills in the appraisal of the Bank's computer systems.

Detailed planning

14. Having decided that he _may_ be able to place reliance on the work of the internal auditor, the external auditor should:

a. agree with the chief of internal audit the timing, test levels, sample selection procedures and the form of documentation to be used;

b. record the fact of his intended reliance, its extent and the reason for the fact and extent, in his working papers;

c. confirm with top management that he is doing so.

Controlling

15. In order to be able ultimately to place reliance on the work of the internal auditor, the external auditor should:

a. consider whether the work has been properly staffed, planned, supervised, reviewed and recorded;

b. compare the results with other evidence (eg debtors circularisation);

c. satisfy himself that any unusual or 'put upon enquiry' items have been fully resolved;

d. examined the reports made and the management's response to the reports;

e. ensure the work is to be done in time.

At the conclusion, the arrangements should be reviewed to make things even better next year.

Recording

16. The external auditor will have a high standard of recording in working papers. The internal auditor's work must be equally good if it is to be relied upon.

Evidence

17. The detailed material in this chapter is important for students, but you should not lose sight of the fact that an audit is about *audit evidence*. The work of the internal auditor is evidential material. Whether it is good evidence supplying a reasonable basis for conclusions to be reached, is a matter of judgement. It may be desirable for the external auditor to test the work of the internal auditor by supplementary procedures or by re-testing transactions or balances tested by the internal auditor.

Report to management

18. Whether or not any work of the internal auditor is relied upon, the internal auditor may uncover and report on weaknesses in internal controls. If the internal auditor reports to management and management responds, then the matter may rest there. If, however, weaknesses are material and the response by management inadequate, then it may be desirable to include the weaknesses in the external auditor's own *report to management*.

Summary

19. a. Internal and external auditors do similar work and economics dictates that they should co-operate.

b. Internal auditing has many objectives and some of these may be useful to an external auditor.

c. The external auditor must assess the internal auditor and his work.

d. The extent of reliance may depend on materiality, audit risks, level of judgement required, the level of complementary evidence and the specialist skills required.

e. The process of relying on the work of an internal auditor must be planned, controlled and recorded.

Points to note

20. a. With constant pressure on costs and fee levels, external auditors are increasingly tempted to rely on the work of the internal auditor.

b. Internal auditing is a growth field and the subject of this chapter will increase an importance.

c. In many large organisations, eg Banks, the external auditor has no choice but to rely on the work of the internal auditor.

d. Increased computerisation with its concommitant increase in potential fraud, has led to an upgrading in the importance and quality of internal audit.

e. Internal auditing can be carried out by the enterprise's own staff, a third party or the external audit firm. Whoever carries it on, it is still a part of the enterprise's activities. It can never have the necessary degree of autonomy or objectivity as is required by the external auditor when expressing an opinion on the financial statements.

Case study for Chapter 58

Shark Estate Agents Ltd is a company offering estate agency services to the public through a network of branches in the Midlands. The company has some 270 staff in all. The board consists of six people, a part time chairman, a chief executive, two other full time executives and two representatives of the owners. The company is jointly owned by an American bank and a city property group. The company have an internal audit department consisting of Legge who is a young certified accountant and Foot who is an accounting technician. They also have a secretary, Mavis. They report their activities monthly in detail to the Board and to the audit committees of the American bank and the city property group.

Discussion

a. What work would the internal audit department do?

b. In what ways may the external auditors place reliance on their work?

c. Draw up a check list which the external auditor could use to assess the internal auditors as potentially being capable of producing work on which the external auditors may rely.

Student self testing questions *Questions with answers apparent from the text*

1. a. Why might an external audit rely on the work of an internal auditor? (1)
   b. In what way may they co-operate? (6)
   c. How may the external auditor assess the internal auditor and his work? (11)
   d. What factors influence the extent of reliance in a particular area? (13)
   e. How might the co-operation be planned and controlled? (14, 15)
   f. What implications has all this for the external auditors' working papers? (16)

Examination question *(Answer begins on page 556)*

1. Your firm of Certified Accountants has been for some years auditor of Reynard PLC, a large company which has an internal audit department which is engaged in both internal control compliance and operational auditing within the company. You have a good opinion of the quality of the work of the internal auditors and you have established a good relationship with Mr. John MacDonald, the head of the Internal Audit Department and he has asked you to give a talk to the members of his department during their annual training week. He is particularly interested in your views on the different roles of external and internal auditors, the type of work that each carry out and their reporting responsibilities.

   Required:

   a. Draft the lecture notes that you will use when giving your talk, paying particular attention to the differences and similarities of the following features of external and internal auditors:

i. General role.	(2 marks)
ii. Independence.	(3 marks)
iii. The work carried out in the following areas:	
– systems of internal control, and	(3 marks)
– operational auditing.	(3 marks)
iv. Reporting responsibilities.	(3 marks)

b. Explain what evidence you would seek to satisfy yourself that the work of the internal auditors can be used in the course of your work as external auditor.

(3 marks)

c. Give three examples of internal audit work that may be used by the external auditor.

(3 marks)

(ACCA)

Examination questions without answers

2. The directors of one of your expanding client companies have decided to appoint an internal auditor.

Required:

a. Describe the essential similarities and differences between an internal and an external auditor.

(8 marks)

b. State the advantages of this appointment, both to the company and to you as external auditor.

(4 marks)

c. State the extent to which you, as external auditor, can rely on the work of the internal auditor.

(3 marks)

(AAT 92)(Total 15 marks)

3. In the course of your audit of Waymark & Willow plc, you find out that the company's internal auditor maintains and regularly updates a flow-chart covering the company's system of internal control.

What use can this be to the external auditor?

(LCCI 91) (13 marks)

4. The growing recognition by management of the benefits of good internal control, and the complexities of an adequate system of internal control have led to the development of internal auditing as a form of control over all other internal controls. The emergence of the internal auditor as a specialist in internal control is the result of an evolutionary process similar in many ways to the evolution of independent auditing.

Required:

a. Explain why the internal and independent auditors' review of internal control procedures differ in purpose.

(4 marks)

b. Explain the reasons why an internal auditor should or should not report his findings on internal control to the following selection of company officials:

i. the chief accountant,

ii. the board of directors.

(6 marks)

c. Explain whether the independent auditor can place any reliance upon the internal auditor's work when the latter's main role is to be of service and assistance to management.

(6 marks)

d. List four internal control procedures which could be performed on a regular basis by the manager of a small company which does not have an internal audit department.

(4 marks)

(ACCA 91) (20 marks)

5 As the external auditor to Wong plc, you have concluded that it is impossible for you to rely upon the work of the company's internal auditor.

What might have led you to this conclusion?

(LCC 88) (15 marks)

6. You are the external auditor of STORES plc, a large company which operates a country-wide chain of department stores selling a variety of goods including foods, clothing and household items. The company has an internal audit department which visits branches on a rotational basis.

   You are required to explain:

   a. The audit steps you consider necessary to establish to your satisfaction the completeness, accuracy and validity of the branch accounting records, and

   b. the steps you would take if your audit procedures led you to conclude that there were serious weaknesses in the application of branch procedures at several branches.

   (IComA 95)

59 Environmental auditing

Introduction

1. All enterprises in the 1990s face a climate of rapid change and escalating regulatory requirements. Among the major changes occurring are environmental obligations both legal and moral. In recent years there has been the green movement together with many pressures on business and other organisations to respond to very public issues including:

   - man-induced climatic change – the greenhouse effect
   - a need for waste management
   - a need to avoid polluting the earth, water and air
   - a need for recycling
   - a need for a safe and clean environment

   Some very public occurrences have worried the public including radiation leaks, the burial of atomic waste, Chernobyl, Three Mile Island, depletion of the ozone layer, and, in my home territory, the effects of noise, traffic flow and contaminated air of open cast mining and my readers can probably cite many others.

2. The near future is going to bring many constraints and duties on enterprises in connection with environmental factors and this brings with it new obligations and opportunities to accountants and auditors. This is an embryo area but watch out for explosive developments in the next few years. This chapter attempts a few thoughts on the area of environmental audit but is very tentative at the moment.

3. This chapter deals with the following issues:

   - a definition of environmental audit
   - BS 7750
   - European Eco Audit
   - What environment matters are relevant
   - Environmental auditors

- The impact on annual reports of accounts of environmental factors
- Publicity and annual reports
- Implications for company auditors

Definition of environmental audit

4. First let us define the environment. The environment can be seen as all of the air, water, land and air, with air including air within buildings and structures above and below ground. Aerospace industries might include outer space (which contains much orbiting rubbish) and even the moon and Mars!

5. There are many definitions of environmental audit. Among them are:

'A management tool comprising a systematic, documented, periodic and objective evaluation of how well organisations, management, and equipment are performing with the aim of contributing to safeguarding the environment by facilitating management control of environmental practices, and assessing compliance with company policies, which would include meeting regulatory requirements and standards applicable'

Some notes on this definition:

a. It is seen as a management tool but might also be used as a tool of regulatory agencies and any contact groups in assessing environmental performance.

b. It should be systematic (not haphazard), documented, periodic (not one-off), and objective (not a whitewash). My readers might compare these notions with the current annual audit of financial statements.

c. It is of performance

d. the objective is to contribute to safeguarding the environment.

e. It is a part of management system.

f. It is concerned with assessing company policies connected with regulatory requirements but also with appropriate standards as perceived by management

6. An environment audit may imply the following ideas:

- a set of planned environmental arrangements and procedures of which the enterprise and all its management and staff are aware.

- these would include legal requirements as well as management objectives and may include a response to probable future legal requirements.

- an assessment of whether the planned arrangements are effectively implemented and whether they are suitable for fulfilling the enterprise's environment policies.

- an environmental audit would include determination of the factual data necessary to evaluate performance.

BS 7750

7. Readers will already be familiar with BS 5750 (now the ISO 9000 series) which is reviewed elsewhere in this manual. There is also another British Standard BS 7750 which is concerned with environmental practices. BS 7750 envisages an overall management system for environmental matters and this would include within it an environmental audit as a major component.

8. The components of a BS 7750 system may include:

- a preparatory review. This will be detailed survey of the current environmental impact and performance.

- an environmental policy that includes a commitment to continual improvement. This policy should be made public.

- clearly defined responsibilities for personnel, including training and communication.

- up-to-date records of relevant legislation relating to the firm's activities

- a register of significant effects. This will be an examination of the direct (eg release of gases to the air) and indirect (eg waste removed by the council dustmen) environmental impacts of the company, and a record of the significant ones.

Three elements seem important – the setting of objectives, the establishment of procedures and an audit of the procedures. BS 7750 is not concerned with specific environmental standards (eg so many decibels of noise or so many units of a noxious gas up the chimney) other than legal requirements but rather that objectives are set (which will be specific), procedures planned to meet the objectives and an audit to monitor compliance with the procedures.

BS 7750 has made a significant contribution to the development of the draft international standard ISO 14001. It is also designed to be compatible with the European Union criteria for an environmental management system under the Eco Management and Audit Scheme (EMAS) – see next paragraph.

European eco audit

9. There is an EC regulation called EMAS (the EC Eco-Management and Audit Scheme) which has now been launched into the UK. This is a voluntary scheme whereby industrial companies satisfying the scheme's condition issue a public statement that includes information about a particular site's environmental performance and management systems.

An EMAS statement must be accredited by a verifier whose association with the statement will be much like that of an auditor. The verification process will be much as in an audit. Its elements may include:

- an independent view by an accredited verifier

- using the checks and balances of the systems including internal audit

- validation of the completeness and reliability of the information presented

- the formation of an opinion

- the making of a report

The verifier makes the report to the company but it will none the less be made public. It is not clear if that means that the verifier has any legal duty of skill and care to third parties and hence any potential pecuniary liability for losses engendered by negligence.

What environmental matters are relevant

10. There are many of these and my readers may well be able to add to the list. They include:

Man induced climatic change   Waste management

Recycling   Tidiness of the environment

Litigation against environment offenders   Nuclear electricity generation

Accidents   Industrial processes

Discharges to ground, water, air   Noise/vibration

Energy use   Ultimate clean-up

Storage, use and transport of hazardous materials   Resource minimisation

Landscaping and tree planting

Life cycle analysis of products   Excessive lighting

Environmental auditors

11. Audits of financial statements are carried out by suitable qualified and supervised accountants. Environmental audits are in general beyond the competence of accountants· and it is expected that environmental audits will be conducted by small teams numbering perhaps 3 or 4 persons. The teams will consist of suitable technically qualified persons from within or without the enterprise with a leader who is independent of the enterprise. It is thought that a professional person such as an accountant or lawyer may be a good leader. Qualified persons who are ready and able to conduct environmental audits are already in business and registers of accredited environmental auditors are being set up.

Accounting firms may be asked to act as verifiers for their audit clients. This makes sense in that:

- an environmental management system is part of the company's management system and the auditor is already engaged in an examination of that management system as part of the normal audit procedures.

- the actual skills required for an audit of an environmental management system are the same as those required for a financial audit. It is the management system that is being verified not the technical criteria.

However accounting firms may be precluded from acting as verifiers if they have provided consultancy services to the client within the previous two years. Nevertheless in the UK it is considered acceptable for an independent auditor of financial statements to also provide consultancy services to the same client. Perhaps in the future either the provision of consultancy services will not preclude auditors from being verifiers or, at the other extreme, the auditors of financial statements may find that they are precluded from supplying consultancy services to audit clients.

Annual reports and environmental factors

12. Already environmental factors are having an impact on annual financial statements. Some specific areas are:

a. Contingent liabilities (SSAP 18). There may be claims against an enterprise for environmental offences including, for example, nuisance or watercourse contamination or damage to health (tobacco companies can be sued).

b. Asset values may be affected. Stocks may be subject to environment concern and may need to be modified or replaced. Land may be contaminated and require clean up. Plant and Machinery may need to be replaced because it pollutes or otherwise fails to meet modern environmental standards.

c. Accounting for capital and revenue expenditure on fitting environmental safeguards and in undertaking remedial treatment following incidents of pollution.

d. Provision for future improvements in the plant required to enable the process to continue operating within stricter controls such as BATNEEC (Best Available Techniques Not Entailing Excessive Costs).

13. Financial statements are used to appraise past performance and to predict future performance and cash flows. In some companies environmental factors are likely to be significant in this appraisal. Examples are water companies, chemical companies and energy companies but there are many others. Companies may have land which is contaminated and plant which may need wholesale replacement. In some cases land may have negative value as the costs of clean-up may exceed book values. Information about these matters may need to be made available to the market or, as the Stock Exchange fears, a false market in the shares, based on incorrect values, may be established.

14. Lenders must be aware of any environmental factors affecting assets and liabilities as security may not be real (contaminated land) or cash flows may not be as expected (need to replace plant or liabilities for environment damage and offences)

15. Companies making takeover bids need to be aware of any environmental factors affecting the victim company. If the takeover is based on public knowledge including current share price and annual financial statements then the financial statements need to disclose the effect of environmental factors on assets, liabilities and future cash flows of the victim company.

16. The problems of designing a suitable FRS for environmental matters are legion and include:

  – what constitutes environmental costs and how are such costs to be distinguished from other costs? Capital expenditure on new machinery may be designed to provide enhanced efficiency but also to take into account new or expected environmental legislation.

  – should environmental costs be charged to P and L Account or be capitalised?

  – should capitalisation of environmental costs incurred subsequent to the acquisition of a capital asset be dependent on an increase in the future economic benefits expected from the asset?

  – when should future environmental expenditure be recognised as a liability and how should the liability be recognised if the amount involved is difficult or impossible to estimate?

  – how should *impairment of the value* of assets resulting from environmental concerns be recognised?

Essentially the problem is one of disclosure. Disclosure of environmental liabilities is one of trade off between relevance and reliability. Suppose Dirty PLC has a probable liability in connection with past use of its site in Tipton. The liability is future but arises out of past activities. The amount is impossible to estimate. Clearly the liability must be disclosed but should it be incorporated in the financial statements?

As the Environment Steering Group of the Financial Reporting and Auditing Group of the ICAEW put it: 'Information may be relevant although be so unreliable in nature or representation that its recognition in the financial statements may be potentially misleading'. Perhaps the problem with financial accounting is that point figures are used – for example Creditors £134,987, rather than range figures like Creditors £134,987 plus or minus £23,456 with 95% certainty!

We can expect a FRS in due course.

Publicity and annual reports

17. Environmental factors can be very important to some companies and for them any information on environmental matters may need to be made public. The reasons for this are many and various and include:

   a. to ensure investment by ethical investors. Many persons now only invest in 'ethical' companies and unit trusts and other investment vehicles exist to satisfy this demand. Companies all want a high share price and so need to court all potential investors. Hence there is a need to be or appear to be ethical in environmental and other ways. Other ways may include paying reasonable wages in developing companies or not employing child labour or even not opening on Sundays.

   b. As a part of a marketing strategy. Companies may have a marketing advantage over competitors if they are known to be environmentally clean and thus have products which appeal to green consumers.

   c. To appear to be committed to innovation and change and responsive to new factors.

18. The obvious medium for making public relevant information about a company's policies, systems and achievements in environmental affairs is the company's annual report and accounts. However other possibilities arise. These include:

   a. In advertisements and in public relations exercises

   b. By requiring all suppliers to complete a comprehensive environmental questionnaire (and ensuring this is known to the public).

   c. By stating that the company has BS 7750 on its stationery etc. Or perhaps that 'all our production sites in the EC participate in EMAS' on all its stationery and literature. Look out for this.

Implications for company auditors

19. Audit firms may well see environmental audit as a new opportunity and an extension to the services presently offered to clients and the public. However there are immediate implications for annual audits as you may have realised in reading this chapter so far. These implications include:

   a. Environmental factors may have an impact on asset values

   b. Environmental factors may have created actual or contingent liabilities

   c. Environmental factors may have implications for future capital expenditure and cash flows, that may impinge on the viability of the company as a going concern.

   d. Environmental factors may create fundamental uncertainties about the assets and liabilities of a company and its future which may lead the auditor to consider whether he can say the accounts show a true and fair view. The Statement of Auditing Standard on Auditors' Reports on Financial Statements deals with this matter but current auditing standards require qualified auditors' reports where there is material uncertainty.

e. Balance sheet items such as secured loans may not be secured if land values are affected by environmental factors

f. Insurance cover may not be adequate and hence contingent liabilities may exist which are uninsured.

g. Comprehensive legislation exists in many areas requiring environmental action. Breaches of these may not be apparent to auditors but may lead to undisclosed liabilities. Auditors may consider Section 389A of the Companies Act 1985 which makes it an offence to knowingly or recklessly make a statement to the company's auditors which conveys information to them which they require, or are entitled to require, that is misleading, false, or deceptive. The auditors could ask for a statement of environmental matters affecting the company including potential liabilities.

Summary

20. a. A major impact on companies in recent times is the environmental issue. This has come about from the green revolution and has led to large amounts of regulation.

b. Environmental audit definitions include the notions of environmental policies and objectives, systems to achieve those policies and objectives and assessments of the effectiveness of the systems and policies.

c. There is a British standard BS 7750 available to companies.

d. There is a Euro-eco scheme called EMAS.

e. Environmental matters affect companies and their assets and operations in numerous ways.

f. Environmental audit teams need to be technically qualified but may well be led by an independent professional such as an accountant.

g. Annual accounting information may need to incorporate environmental factors or assets may be overvalued, liabilities omitted and future prospects unrealistically presented.

h. Takeover bidders and lenders (and indeed all contact groups) must be wary of companies that may suffer from undisclosed environmental problems.

i. The annual report and accounts may be a good medium for dissemination of environmental information about a company but there are others.

j. Auditors of financial statements need to take account of environmental factors in their auditing procedures.

Points to note

21. a. The idea that 'The Polluter Must Pay' will have a potential major impact on many companies which currently pollute air, water or ground but expect others (national or local government or other companies for example) to pay for the clean-up.

b. The government have introduced much legislation to assist in improving or conserving the environment and many agencies and regulatory bodies now have statutory powers to require companies to take action. The government are apparently committed to the environment and readers may note the imposition of VAT on domestic fuel and power as an indication of this.

c. Environmental audits are not just an investigation into the interaction of a company with its environment and with legal requirements but rather an investigation into policies and systems and how well practices and procedures fulfil policies.

d. Some public companies include information on environmental matters in their annual reports. Examples include the water companies, British Airways, Body Shop and others. Check any accounts you see for this element.

e. Auditors need to be very alert to environmental factors in some audits but they are a factor in all audits now.

f. Some legislation imposes personal liabilities on directors and managers in the case of infringement of environmental legislation.

g. The public now expects ever rising standards in the environmental area and this subject may loom large in all areas of human activity in the near future. Auditing will be heavily affected.

h. It is important to realise that BS 7750 is not a set of environmental performance guidelines. Rather it is a standard framework for management activities in the environmental area.

i. Environmental auditing or verification as a set of procedures is not very different from the audit of financial statements.

j. This is a very fast moving area. Watch out for changes in the near future!

Case study 1 for Chapter 59

Sludgy PLC are a quoted company heavily engaged in the waste disposal industry and engage also in some open cast mining in land reclamation projects. The company sees itself as performing an unpleasant duty which the rest of the public are unwilling to do for itself. The company has inevitably acquired a reputation for being environmentally unfriendly and has noticed that the share price has fallen despite good profits and excellent prospects.

Discussion

1. Suggest factors which may have caused the company's reputation and fall in share price.
2. Suggest an action programme for improving the company's public image.

Case study 2 for Chapter 59

Wednesfield Widget Manufacturing Ltd operate from their old freehold factory on a site in a manufacturing estate in Wolverhampton which dates back to the nineteenth century. Their plant is old but is regularly maintained to a good standard. They have certification under ISO 9000 but not under BS 7750. The auditors are Wurried & Co who are aware that the company has asked for a loan from the bank to be secured on the freehold premises.

Discussion

1. Indicate some green policies the company may adopt.
2. What environmental factors may affect the audit?
3. How might Wurried & Co incorporate environmental factors in their audit?

Student self testing questions *Questions with answers apparent from the text*

1. a. Why has environmental audit become an issue? (1)
   b. Attempt a definition of environmental audit (4,5,6)
   c. List the components of system under BS 7750 (8)
   d. What will companies engaged in Euro-eco audit need to do? (9)
   e. List some relevant environmental factors (10)
   f. Who might act as environmental auditors? (11)
   g. List environmental factors which impact on annual accounts.(12)
   h. Why are environmental factors important in appraising a company's performance and prospects? (13)
   i. Why might companies seek to publicise their environmental performance? (17)
   j. How might a company publicise its environmental achievements? (18)
   k. List the implications for the annual audit of environmental factors (19)

60 Audit committees, the Greenbury code and other matters

Introduction

1. An idea whose time has definitely come is that of audit committees. These are committees of Boards of Directors of mainly listed companies and usually consist of three or more non-executive directors. Since 1978, the New York Stock Exchange has required all listed companies to have audit committees. In the UK most publicly listed companies and financial institutions now have audit committees compared with 17% in 1987. Audit committees are a requirement of the Code of Best Practice which is part of the Cadbury Report on the Financial Aspects of Corporate Governance. And the Report includes an appendix with specimen terms of reference for an Audit Committee.

2. An audit committee is usually composed of 3 to 5 non-executive directors. The boards of many public companies consist of executive directors who work full time in the business and non-executive directors who attend board meetings and bring the benefit of other experience and knowledge to the board. Such non-executive directors are often directors of other companies or retired civil servants or diplomats.

3. There is an audit brief on audit committees.

Work done by audit committees

4. The work done by an audit committee would include:

   a. Review the half year and annual financial statements before submission to the Board focusing particularly on:
      - any changes in accounting policies
      - major judgmental areas
      - significant adjustments arising from the audit

- the going concern assumption
- compliance with accounting standards
- compliance with stock exchange and legal requirements

This would enable the financial statements to receive independent critical appraisal and for contentious issues to be seriously probed and discussed.

b. Consider the appointment, remuneration and any questions of resignation or dismissal of the external auditor. The appointment of the external auditor would be, to some extent, insulated from the influence of dominant directors.

c. Discuss with the external auditor, before the audit, the nature and scope of the audit and ensure co-ordination where more than one audit firm is involved. The Committee may be able to alert the auditor to problems areas.

d. Discuss problems and reservations arising from the interim and final audits and any matters the auditors may wish to raise. This may be in the absence of executive directors if necessary. Matters that arise may involve actions of the executive directors.

e. Review the external auditors' management letter and managements' response. Without this discussion, management have tended to ignore the management letter.

f. Review the Company's statement on internal control systems prior to endorsement by the Board. This statement is not yet a legal requirement but is a recommendation of the Code.

g. Where an internal audit function exists, review the internal audit programme, ensure co-ordination between internal and external auditors and ensure that the internal audit function is adequately resourced and has appropriate standing with the company.

h. Review major findings of internal investigations and management's response.

i. Consider other topics as defined by the Board

The need for all these duties lies in the present reality of listed companies having self-perpetuating Boards of directors, often dominated by one strong man, whose priorities do not often encompass objective auditing and reporting arrangements. it is, of course, essential that the Board includes non-executive directors of adequate power, influence and independence. The Code deals with their appointments and functions.

Relations with the external auditors

5. The existence of an audit committee need not affect the work of the external auditors in any way. However, common sense indicates that the committee could be beneficial to the external auditor. Precise relations depend on the circumstances but the committee would probably discuss:

a. the contents of the *management* letter

b. any intended *qualification* in the audit report

c. any problems re the most suitable accounting treatment of contentious items and the manner and degree of *disclosure* of any items.

d. any matters where the auditor and the board disagree

e. any matters to be included in the letter of representation

f. matters pertaining to the auditors' appointment and remuneration.

Overall, the external auditor should have free access to the committee and be invited to attend its meetings if that would be helpful. Relations between auditor and board are often difficult where there are delicate and sensitive issues of a practical or technical nature. The audit committee can be a useful channel of communication between auditor and board.

Advantages of audit committee

6. These include:

   a. Assistance is provided to directors in carrying out their legal responsibilities, notably in the areas of accounting systems, internal control and reporting.

   b. Strengthening the role of non-executive directors. At present such directors have no precise role. It is contended that membership of an audit committee would increase their knowledge of the company and hence their effectiveness.

   c. Strengthening the objectivity and credibility of financial reporting. In some well publicized cases, companies have suddenly collapsed. In fact such collapses are a culmination of hidden but gradual processes followed by, perhaps, small events which precipitate disaster. It is contended that audit committees might perceive the possibility of collapse earlier than now.

   d. Strengthening the independence of the audit function. In practice an auditor reports on financial statements produced by directors who in reality appoint him and fix his remuneration. Clearly a review of the appointment, terms of engagement and remuneration by a quasi-independent committee must be a good thing.

   e. Improving the quality of the accounting and auditing functions. It is contended that a regular review of accounting systems, internal control and reporting functions will improve and strengthen these. Similarly the external (and internal) auditor will have to explain and justify his work to the committee.

   f. Improved communication between directors, auditors and management. Here perhaps lies the crux of the matter.

Drawbacks to audit committees

7. The audit brief discusses several, and generally manages to argue them away.

   a. Audit committees would split the board. As boards are individuals, splitting into factions is inevitable and, in any case, healthy.

   b. Audit committees would create conflicts within companies. Rather they would provide a forum for resolving conflicts. Knowledge and understanding usually reveals that conflicts are more apparent than real.

   c. Audit committees would encroach on management's responsibilities. There is a delicate grey area between supervision and management. This problem can be overcome with well designed terms of reference.

   d. Audit committees would be powerless if they could not enforce recommendations or report to shareholders. This is true but any airing of a problem will lead to consideration and solution.

   e. Audit committees are not practicable in the UK because there are not enough non-executive directors to serve on them. In fact, the number of non-executive directors is growing rapidly.

f. Audit committees would take up too much time and cost too much. In fact, the cost in money and time is unlikely to be material and the benefits could be substantial.

g. Audit committees will be least effective in the companies which need them most. The sort of company that most needs an audit committee is one dominated by a strong personality (the history of company failures is full of such characters). This is possibly true and is maybe an argument for compulsory establishment of audit committees.

h. Audit committees pre-empt the question of two tier boards. This is rather a large issue. In continental law, the idea of a supervisory board supervising an executive board is well established. In the UK, this may be a future development but I think it unlikely that the audit committee will pre-empt the idea as an audit committee will have a much more limited and specific role.

i. In theory, non-executive directors and audit committees are a good thing. However executive directors expect their non-executive directors to be on 'their side', that is wholly committed to the company and its welfare. Needless to say, total confidentiality is required. As a result of this, the executive directors prefer people who are known to them and perhaps personal friends or business acquaintances of long standing. You will see that this approach diminishes the idea of an independent role for the non-executives.

Greenbury report

8. In July 1995 the Greenbury committee on directors' remuneration reported amid a blaze of publicity. The committee had been formed in the wake of media disquiet at very high remuneration for company directors especially in the privatised utility industries. High remuneration included salaries, share options and compensation for loss of office. The latter, often running into millions, was a consequence of three year rolling contracts and was often paid to remove a director who had manifestly failed in his job.

The committee produced a Code of Best Practice which recommended the setting up in each listed company of a remuneration committee. This committee would be composed of non-executive directors and would fix the remuneration of the Board. They should also report annually to shareholders in the Annual Report and Accounts and set out full details of remuneration policy, actual remuneration and how it is calculated. The full report would be quite lengthy and full of detail. Try and find one to study.

9. The following points may be relevant to the auditor of a listed company:

a. The Code recommends that the amounts received by, and commitments made to, each directors should be subject to audit.

b. So far the guidance on how directors' remuneration should be calculated includes UITF Abstract 10 *Disclosure of directors' share options*.

c. The remuneration committee report is audit evidence in the auditors' consideration of the directors' remuneration part of the financial statements. Remember that the Companies Act 1985 has much to say on this subject and that S 237(4) requires the auditor to give information on directors' remuneration if it is not given in the accounts.

d. The remuneration committee report is another document which the auditor must consider in relation to whether there is a conflict of view between the financial statements and other information in documents containing audited financial statements. See SAS 160 and Chapter 48.

e. Directors' remuneration including bonuses, pension entitlements and compensation for loss of office is likely to remain a very high profile part of every Annual Report and Accounts.

f. Auditors have, at the time of writing, no specific statutory or SAS duties arising specifically out of the Greenbury Code of Best Practice. However auditors should check the application of the Code and pay particular attention to this whole area.

Board and other committees

10. The Cadbury code requires listed companies to establish a remuneration committee composed wholly or largely of non-executive directors. The terms of reference of these committees may include the remuneration of senior employees not on the Board. Some companies have a nomination committee (not part of the Code's requirements) which is concerned with the recruitment of suitable Board members Some companies combine these committees.

The audit significance of these committees has not yet been digested. However their proceedings are clearly audit evidence of remuneration both in terms of amounts paid and payable and in terms of the contracts of employment of directors and in some cases of senior staff.

Some companies have established Board Social Responsibilities Committees. Some have Environmental Advisory Panels. The explosion of interest in corporate governance will no doubt spawn other committees. The proceedings of any Board committees or of advisory panels will provide audit evidence in many areas.

Summary

11. a. Audit committees are a new but growing idea in the UK.

b. They would consist of 3 to 5 non-executive directors.

c. Their role would be to:

   i. Acquire a good understanding of the entire audit function both external and internal.

   ii. Review the whole systems of accounting, internal control and reporting.

   iii. Review the annual financial statements before submission to the board for approval.

   iv. Consider the appointment, terms of reference, remuneration and findings of the auditors.

d. The Greenbury committee's report setting out a Code of Best Practice on directors' remuneration has considerable audit implications.

e. Many companies now have remuneration, nomination and other committees.

Points to note

9. a. Audit committees would be concerned to uncover facts, ideas, problems and difficulties, not to take executive decisions or actions. The key phrase is 'open government'. Sadly, the whole emphasis in the UK has been toward secrecy in central and local government as well as in board rooms and committees.

b. The whole question of power equilibrium between the competing claims of management, employees, consumers and government and the role of an auditor is fascinating.

c. Non-executive directors and audit committees are a main platform in the reform of the financial aspects of corporate governance recommended by the Cadbury Committee. The next chapter review the whole issue and the auditing implications.

Case study 1 for Chapter 60

THE FIGWORT GROUP PLC is a quoted company in the Midlands with interests mainly in construction. However the group, which has grown rapidly by acquisition, has interests in building supplies and in Do-It-Yourself materials. The turnover is £50 million and the annual profit about £6 million. the company is dominated by Knapweed, who is a very thrusting character. He is chairman and chief executive and holds some 15% of the share capital. There are 4 other full-time executive directors who have come up through the company management structure. There are 3 non-executive directors – the solicitor who assisted in the flotation five years ago, a director of the merchant bank who advises the company and a retired regional general manager of a clearing bank.

The company are exploring the possibility of having an audit committee.

Discussion

a. Who could be members of the audit committee?

b. What benefits might the group gain?

c. Would it work?

d. Draw up a sample agenda for a meeting of the committee.

Case study 2 for Chapter 60

Jim Fixit has built up his garage business until it has become one of the UK's largest listed companies with subsidiaries in manufacture and trading in the Far East and Eastern Europe. He has been very active in the takeover market. He is the Chairman and Chief Executive of the company and the main Board has six other directors including two of his sons. All are group executives. Recently the group has been criticised for its accounting policies by the FRRP and for its takeover activities by the Takeover Panel. The company have recently made a successful hostile bid for another group requiring an increase in its gearing to very high levels.

The auditors are Supine and Thrusting who won the audit from Puce, Watermelon on a tender bid after being called in as advisers on an accounting policy which Puce, Watermelon were unhappy on.

Fixit has done very well for his shareholders and has a large and adoring following.

Discussion

Discuss the desirability of having an audit committee in this type of situation.

Student self testing questions *Questions with answers apparent from the text*

1. a. Who might compose an audit committee? (2)

    b. What work might an audit committee do? (4)

c. List the items concerning the external auditor that an audit committee might discuss. (5)

d. What are the advantages of an audit committee? (6)

e. List possible drawbacks to having an audit committee. (7)

f. Outline the recommendations of the Greenbury committee (8)

g. What audit evidence may be available from Board committees? (10)

Examination question without answers

1. After the collapse of the BCCI Bank in July 1991, a spokesman on internal audit matters issued a Press Release in which it was asserted that the internal auditors of the bank knew of the irregularities that had taken place but no notice was taken of their recommendations. They lacked, the statement said, someone of an independent mind to whom to report.

   You are required to explain:

   a. how the existence of an audit committee might have provided the independent mind to whom to report; and (10 marks)

   b. the action that should be taken by internal auditors when their reports and recommendations to management are not heeded. (10 Marks)

   (ICA 91) (Total 20 Marks)

61 The future of auditing

Introduction

1. The legal framework of auditing is subject to periodic change as new Companies Acts are promulgated. The theory and practice of auditing is being steadily developed by the professional bodies and now the Auditing Practices Board. New developments occur because of new situations and ever rising expectations and the need for higher standards.

2. Most developments in auditing have been evolutionary but currently more rapid change, which might be called revolutionary, is about to happen. This has primarily come about because of public attention on the whole way in which companies are run and governed. This is partly, but not wholly, due to scandals like the collapse of BCCI (Bank of Commerce and Credit International) and the Maxwell affair. There have been many listed companies which have collapsed suddenly and many of these have been run in a dictatorial manner by one strong character.

3. As a response to these problems in the governance of companies, the Cadbury Committee was set up and reported in late 1992 in 'The report of the Committee on the Financial Aspects of Corporate Governance'. This report recommended many changes in the Board rooms, reporting practices and auditing including a Code of Best Practice. The Report is reviewed in this chapter. The ramifications of the Cadbury Code on Corporate Governance are still being worked out and they have a substantial impact on the future of auditing in the short term.

4. The Auditing Practices Board issued a paper on 'The Future Development of Auditing' in November 1992. The purpose of this paper is to promote debate on the future of auditing in the UK and Ireland. This paper is also reviewed in this chapter. The Auditing Practices Committee produced a further document *The Audit Agenda* in December 1994 and we will review it also.

What is wrong with corporate governance?

5. Public attention has been focused on Corporate Governance (the action, manner or system of governing) and especially the financial aspects for several reasons including:

    a. the collapse of several large companies without warning and the BCCI, Barings and Maxwell affairs.

    b. concern about standards of financial reporting (the Financial Reporting Review Panel have reported several 'profits' which had to be modified)

    c. lack of accountability by companies run by dominant characters

    d. raids on company pension schemes by companies in financial difficulties

    e. apparently excessive directors pay, the rates of which seem to be fixed by the recipients themselves. Excessive severance pay for directors. The Greenbury committee reported on this in 1995.

    f. some notable frauds and incidents of insider trading

    g. a feeling that auditors cannot stand up to demanding Boards

    h. a feeling that auditors are too close to their clients as a result of carrying out much non-audit work

    i. looseness of accounting standards

    j. the practice of opinion shopping where companies seek auditors who will agree with them

    k. the expectations gap where the investing public does not understand the rather limited role of the auditor and imagines he/she is doing much more especially in the area of fraud.

6. Already there had been improvements including the Companies Acts of 1985 and 1989 with the whole panoply of regulation of auditors and the setting up of the Financial Reporting Council with the Accounting Standards Board, the Urgent Issues Task Force and the Financial Reporting Review Panel. There is also the Auditing Practices Board which is improving auditing practice.

Recommendations of the Cadbury committee

7. The Cadbury committee's report on the financial aspects of corporate governance makes many recommendations. Some of these (on Chairpersons of Boards of Directors, the role of the company secretary, non-executive directors, the roles of shareholders and especially institutional shareholders) are beyond the scope of a book about auditing but even these may have some relevance to auditing in practical situations.

8. The main recommendations are:

    a. the adoption by listed companies of a Code of Practice – see next paragraph

    b. Listed companies should include in their report and accounts a statement about their compliance with the Code of Practice with reasons for any areas of non-compliance.

c. The statements of compliance should be reviewed by the auditors before publication. Only areas which can be objectively verified should be covered. We will discuss this later in this chapter.

d. Directors' service contracts should not exceed three years without shareholders' approval. It may be that supine shareholders will allow the necessary permissions to go through at an AGM by default.

e. Interim reports should be extended to providing Balance Sheet information and perhaps cash flow information. Interim reports should not be subject to a full audit but should be reviewed by the auditors. See Chapter 48.

f. Fees paid to audit firms should be fully disclosed with the intention of disclosing the relative significance of audit work as against non-audit work. This will require some amendment to the 1991 regulations under the Companies Act 1985.

g. The accountancy profession should draw up guidelines on the rotation of audit partners. The Committee did not feel that rotation of audit firms was a good idea as it would add to costs as an audit firm's expertise and knowledge of a client built up over a period of years would be lost. In any event the number of audit firms doing listed company audits seems to steadily diminish due to mergers.

h. Directors should report on the effectiveness of their system of internal control and the auditors should report on their statement. We will review internal control reports later in this chapter.

i. The directors should state in their report and accounts that their business is a going concern with supporting assumptions as necessary and the auditors should report on this statement. Going concern is discussed in Chapter 34.

j. The government should consider introducing legislation to extend to all companies the statutory protection already available to auditors in the regulated sector (financial service companies) so that they can report reasonable suspicion of fraud freely to the appropriate investigatory authorities. Auditors who report reasonable suspicion of fraud currently direct, say to the police, lay themselves open to legal action for defamation.

k. The accountancy and legal professions should consider further the question of illegal acts other than fraud. Illegal acts are now easy to commit inadvertently as well as with moral turpitude in many fields including technical acts in such fields as employment, health and safety and in the environment. This subject is taken up in the chapter on environmental auditing. See also SAS 110 and SAS 120.

As you will see some of these recommendations will mean more work and responsibility for auditors and for the accountancy profession, the APB and the FRC.

The code of best practice

9. The contents of the Code of Best Practice include:

a. the board should meet regularly and retain full and effective control over the company and monitor the executive management.

b. there should be clear division of responsibilities (eg an independent chairperson) so that no one individual has unfettered powers of decision.

c. the Board should include non-executive directors of sufficient calibre and number (at least three).

d. the Board should have a formal schedule of matters specifically reserved to it to ensure it has full direction and control of the company.

e. there should be an agreed procedure whereby directors can take independent professional advice at the company's expense.

f. all directors should have access to the services and advice of the company secretary who should be removable only with the approval of the Board as a whole.

g. non-executive directors should:

   i. bring independent judgement

   ii. be free of any business or other relationship with the company (except as directors)

   iii. be appointed for specified periods without automatic renewal

   iv. be selected by a formal process.

h. directors service contracts should not exceed three years.

i. full and clear disclosure of directors total remuneration distinguishing between salary and performance related elements and the basis of calculation of the performance related part.

j. executive directors' pay should be subject to the recommendations of a remuneration committee made up wholly or mainly of non-executive directors.

k. the Board should establish an audit committee of at least three non-executive directors with written terms of reference.

l. the directors should explain their responsibility for preparing the accounts next to a statement by the auditors about their reporting responsibilities.

m. the directors should report on the effectiveness of the company's system of internal control.

n. the directors should report that the business is a going concern with supporting assumptions or qualifications as necessary.

o. (as a footnote) the company's statement of compliance should be reviewed by the auditors re paragraphs d, e, g (iii & iv), h, i, j, k, l, m and n.

Audit committees are reviewed in Chapter 60.

10. Most of these ideas seem fairly innocuous but a casual glance at the city pages of any newspaper will reveal abuse of power by dominant chief executives, unexpected company failures, changes of auditor, disputes over accounting policies, excessive remuneration and redundancy pay, companies desperate to sell off companies they purchased only a short time before, excessive borrowings etc.

Compliance with the code of practice on corporate governance

11. The London Stock Exchange now has a rule that a listed company incorporated in the UK must state in its annual report and accounts whether or not it has complied with the Code of Best Practice. If it has complied with only part of the code it must specify the paragraphs with which it has not complied and give reasons. The statement must be reviewed by the auditors before publication insofar as it relates to certain specified paragraphs of the Code. You will now find such a statement in all listed company annual reports. Look at some.

The APB issued Bulletin 1993/2 *Disclosures relating to corporate governance* in December 1993 and a revised version 1995/1 in 1995. It states that disclosures required by the Code which can be objectively verified include:

- schedule of matters reserved for Board decision
- process of appointment of non-executive directors
- directors' service contracts do not exceed three years without shareholder approval
- clear disclosure of directors' emoluments
- executive directors' pay is recommended by a remuneration Committee
- an audit Committee is established
- a statement of directors' responsibility for preparing accounts
- a statement of effectiveness of internal control
- going concern basis with supporting assumptions

Internal control matters are reviewed later in this chapter. Going concern in Chapter 34.

Auditors should:

- include the review in their letter of engagement
- apply such procedures as are necessary to conclude whether they are satisfied that the statement appropriately reflects the company's compliance with the relevant paragraphs of the Code
- determine if there are any areas of non-compliance which have not been disclosed
- determine if the statement is factually correct.
- report

They are not expected to review the effectiveness of the company's procedures or the appropriateness of the reasons given for non-compliance

Reporting can be done in several ways:

- a separate report in the annual report and accounts
- a separate section in the auditors' report on the financial statements
- a report to the directors with a paragraph in the directors statement of compliance confirming that the auditors have sent a report to the Board.

Internal control and financial reporting

12. The Cadbury Code requires that listed company's directors should report on the effectiveness of the company's system of internal control. Guidance on how to do this was issued by the Cadbury Committee early in 1995. The guidance defines internal control as:

'The whole system of controls, financial and otherwise, established in order to provide reasonable assurance of:

a. effective and efficient operations
b. internal financial control; and
c. compliance with laws and regulations.'

Further, as financial aspects are the focus of the Cadbury Code, *internal financial controls* are defined as:

'The internal controls established in order to provide reasonable assurance of:

a. The safeguarding of assets against unauthorised use or disposition; and

b. the maintenance of proper accounting records and the reliability of financial infor-
    mation used within the business or for publication.'

You will notice that the definition of *internal financial control* excludes efficiency, value for
money, and legal and regulatory compliance.

Directors should include a statement in the Annual Report and Accounts (most likely in
the corporate governance section):

a. acknowledgement that the directors are responsible for the company's system of
    internal financial control

b. Explanation that such a system can provide only reasonable and not absolute assur-
    ance against material misstatements or loss

c. description of the key procedures that the directors have established and which are
    designed to provide effective internal financial control; and

d. confirmation that the directors (or a Board committee) have reviewed the effective-
    ness of the system of internal financial control.

Guidance is given on the idea of key procedures. These are:

a. steps taken to ensure an appropriate control environment

b. the process used to identify major business risks

c. the major information systems that are in place

d. the main control procedures which address the financial implications of the major
    business risks

e. the monitoring system the Board uses to check the that the system is operating
    effectively.

The auditors' duties on the directors' statement comprise assessing whether it may be
misleading. This means that they must assess whether it is consistent with the
information of which they have become aware in the course of the audit of the financial
statements.

There are additional procedures when the directors have complied with the requirements of the Guidance for Directors on Internal Financial Control.

APB and the paper on the future development of auditing

13. Firstly we should consider the state of auditing as it is at present. Auditing is defined in
    the explanatory foreword to the Auditing Standards and Guidelines as:

    'the independent examination of, and expression of an opinion on, the financial state-
    ments of an enterprise.'

    This is a very narrow definition. Many business people and investors are under the
    impression that an audit has a much wider scope and this has caused the expectation
    gap which is much talked about. Auditing can have a wider scope and the APB paper
    suggests a number of additions to the scope of auditing. You will remember that in the
    audit of public bodies, by or under the supervision of the Audit Commission and the
    National Audit Office, the scope has already been widened by the emphasis on 'Value

for Money' and also in improving management and giving an assurance that money has been spent as intended or within legal restrictions.

14. The APB suggests that the reasons for change are changes in the environment in which auditing is carried on and the expectation gap but also an awareness by the public that:

- audits are concerned with the past
- auditors have sometimes yielded to pressure by directors and have been inadequately robust in standing up to them on matters of significance
- a wider circle of persons than just shareholders are interested in the results of the audit. There is a general public interest
- there are gaps in the audit in, for example, directors' stewardship, future prospects and risks, fraud, internal controls and interim reporting. These gaps are now being filled in
- auditors lack independence from their clients
- auditors' reports are uninformative and disclose very little especially about issues and concerns which arise from the audit
- competition among audit firms may have caused fee competition and hence a loss of quality and rigour in the audit
- fear of litigation has acted against proactivity and change
- accounting standards are too flexible and this makes auditing more difficult
- sudden collapse of major listed companies should somehow have been foreseen by the auditors
- the regulatory framework for auditing lacks independence, objectivity and impact – there are several regulatory bodies and they are not independent of the firms they regulate and, in any case, real regulation has only just arrived
- the audit does not encompass the way in which a company's affairs are conducted

15. The suggestions for the future of the APB paper include:

a. a new definition of an audit as:

'to provide an independent opinion to those with an interest in a company that they have received from those responsible for its direction and management an adequate account of:

(a) the proper conduct of the company's affairs

(b) the company's financial performance and position

(c) future risks attaching to the company.'

(a) and (c) are new and (b) is the traditional role of the auditor.

Under (b) it is also pointed out that the financial statements audited now comprise only a small part of the totality of information given to shareholders.

b. requiring the auditor to report on whether the company has financial and other relevant risk management controls

c. extending the audit into aspects of propriety and efficiency (as in Local and national government and the NHS). This might mean fraud beyond the present requirement to conduct their work so as to have a reasonable expectation of detecting fraud whose financial dimension is material to the view shown by the financial statements.

d. extending the audit into the area of illegal acts. Already auditors of financial service companies are empowered to report direct to regulatory agencies and this might be extended to all companies. There is a growing demand for monitoring legal (and also basic ethical) standards of corporate behaviour. Illegal acts can be in any area but notably arise in relation to health, safety, employees and the environment.

e. extending the association of the auditor to all areas of information contained in public documents including the whole annual report, interim statements and preliminary announcements. See SAS 160 on this.

f. requiring directors to provide, and auditors to report on, a summary of the principal assumptions and judgements made by the directors in preparing the financial statements.

g. directors giving an unbiased commentary on future prospects and auditors taking on some role in warning shareholders and other stakeholders (customers, suppliers, lenders, employees etc) of substantial future risks. The APB see future risks in a company being unable to sustain its core operations profitably or at all and in a style of management which might facilitate imprudence or fraud.

h. more informative reporting by auditors. This is already included in SAS 600 but may include, in the future, a comment on the directors' commentary mentioned in (g) above and a more discursive style of report including a commentary on the substantive issues concerning the company's financial position.

i. auditors might become a catalyst for best management going well beyond the management letter.

j. widening the role of the auditor to be a check and balance on the proper conduct of the enterprise in the public interest. The auditor can be seen as having a duty to stakeholders such as actual and potential customers, suppliers, employees, lenders, government departments and the public generally. Before this suggestion is considered in detail, the problem of litigation in tort against auditors needs to be addressed and some changes made.

k. increasing the independence of the auditor from the directors. This might be achieved in several ways:

  i. more involvement by shareholders in appointing auditors (to reflect the legal position rather than the practical realities) and other matters of corporate governance

  ii. audit committees – see Chapter 60

  iii. possibly giving auditors a fixed term of tenure of more than one year

  iv. rotation of audit firms or individual partners

  v. involving shareholders in commissioning auditors to provide services other than auditing. The paper does not think it right to disallow auditors from providing other services if such provision is in the best interest of shareholders

  vi. possibly reducing the proportion of fees which a firm can earn from any one client (less work for smaller firms and more for the big ones?)

  vii. trying to change auditing attitudes by more regulation, supervision and monitoring

l. involving shareholders in the audit process and other matters of corporate governance in some way. Possibilities might include:

    i. establishing a standing 'audit panel' to represent the shareholders of all listed companies.

    ii. establishing a small representative group of shareholders of each company to meet annually with the auditors.

    iii. appointing a 'trustee' for the shareholders on the analogy of trustees for debentureholders.

m. Resolving the issue of litigation against auditors. Several solutions have been proposed:

    i. use of directors and officers insurance (so that the auditor is not the only defendant with money)

    ii. more recognition of negligence by a plaintiff

    iii. limiting liabilities by agreement

    iv. proportional responsibility by the persons to blame.

    See Chapter 49 on this matter.

n. establishing a clear statement of the long term purpose of auditing as a foundation for the development of matters to be included in the scope of auditing and the persons to whom auditors should be accountable.

My readers will realise that many of these ideas will reach fruition in the not to distant future but many are more tentative.

The audit agenda

16. In December 1994 the APB issued a paper 'The Audit Agenda'. This is a long document and contains much valuable information to students of auditing. Its main proposals are:

a. that the scope of audit for listed companies and major economic entities is differentiated from that for unlisted, owner-managed businesses. The Companies Act 1985 has already done much in this area – see Chapter 38. Many new audit requirements are for entities that are listed or are in the regulated sector. The Cadbury Code and the Greenbury Code are for listed companies.

b. that the scope of listed company audits is extended to:

    – assurance to shareholders on the consistency of all textual information accompanying the financial statements with the view portrayed by the financial statements. See Chapter 48.

    – the provision of reports to the Board and audit committees on governance issues. See earlier in this chapter.

    – the provision of reports to shareholders on governance statements made by the directors. This was also covered earlier in this chapter.

c. that the APB will develop guidance on the application of auditing standards to the audit of owner-managed businesses.

d. that the ASB should develop financial reporting standards for the quantum and quality of reporting on risks and sensitivities by directors to support their statements on going concern. This will advance from SAS 130.

e. In relation to fraud:

  – that auditors of listed companies should include in their report to Boards and Audit Committees observations as to the appropriateness and adequacy of systems intended to minimise the risk of fraud

  – that the accountancy bodies should review the education and training process to develop auditor's understanding of behavioural and forensic (used in or connected with a court of law) issues and undertake seminars discussing experience and means of detecting fraud

  – that Boards should commission periodic forensic audits. A forensic audit is described as an in-depth assessment of the company's arrangements and procedures to minimise fraud and investigations into any apparent areas of weakness.

  – that the statutory framework relating to penalties for directors and staff deceiving auditors should be reviewed.

f. that the APB will undertake research jointly with the ASB into developing a framework for reporting and giving assurance to secondary (lenders, employees etc) and tertiary stakeholders (potential investors, brokers etc) – see Chapter 49.

g. that auditors' opinion should be signed by the responsible partner identifying his/her name as well as that of the firm

h. that the APB will develop standards and guidance on the qualities required of a partner responsible for an audit

i. that the partner responsible for the audit of a listed company should not have overall responsibility for the marketing of non-audit services to that company. This is a small concession to the movement in favour of auditors not supplying other services to their audit clients.

j. that audit Committees of listed companies should have specific responsibilities, as a proxy for shareholders, for the appointment and remuneration of auditors and the approval of non-audit services by the audit firm. This may already happen and is rather less than the idea of shareholder representative committees having this function.

k. that the Chairman of the audit committee should report to primary stakeholders (shareholders) on matters relating to the appointment and remuneration of auditors

l. that the that the APB will develop guidance for non-executive directors who act as members of an audit committee

m. that the APB will continue its dialogue with others on the need for a further institutional framework to support the objectivity of the total governance process

n. that the APB will seek to encourage that the extended scope of the audit in relation to listed companies and private reporting to directors on governance issues (Cadbury) can be contracted with restriction of liability (see Chapter 49)

o. that the APB will commission a review of total quality management techniques to ensure quality of the audit process at effective cost. The Audit Agenda makes the excellent point that quality control is more about improved education and training, total quality management and customer satisfaction and service than it is about rule books, checks on checks, review on review and external monitoring. The education profession has always known this but big business is just learning it. Sadly education is going down the road of rule books and procedures.

You will see that there is plenty of ideas for developing auditing as a discipline in the near future. Watch the accounting press for details as they emerge.

Summary

17. a. There is general disquiet about the governance of companies and of other entities with a public profile.

b. There is an expectation gap on the role of the auditor.

c. The Cadbury Code of Best Practice is in many ways revolutionary and its ramifications will take years to work through.

d. Compliance with the Code is reported in a statement by the directors in the annual report and the auditor now has duties in connection with that statement. Bulletin 95/1 *Disclosures relating to corporate governance (revised)* deals with this.

e. There is still some doubt on the auditors' procedures in relation to internal financial control.

f. The APB issued a paper on the future development of auditing in 1992. Some of the suggestions have now been taken up.

g. The APB issued a document *The Audit Agenda* in December 1994. This made some far reaching proposals.

h. Problems with audits and auditors are identified as: past orientation; pressure on the independence of auditors; other stakeholders are interested in the results of an audit; gaps in the audit on propriety, future prospects, risks, fraud, internal control and interim and other reports; uninformative auditors' reports; competition between auditors lowering standards and integrity; fear of litigation; flexible accounting standards; sudden collapses of listed companies; lack of impartial regulation.

i. Recommendations include: a new definition enlarging the scope of audits to proper conduct and future risks; enlarging reporting responsibilities to all published statements, financial controls, propriety, efficiency, fraud, illegality; assumptions and judgements underlying the accounts; more informative reporting by auditors; more duties to other stakeholders; improving the independence of auditors; involving shareholders with the auditors; resolving the problem of litigation. Some of these have been acted upon already.

Points to note

18. a. The Stock Exchange requires all listed companies, as a continuing obligation of listing, to state whether they are complying with the Code.

b. Any new regulation or legislation must recognise the need for companies to be entrepreneurial. It must be remembered that a camel is a horse designed by a committee!

c. Many of these suggestions require companies to be more open but there is also some need to retain commercial secrets.

d. There is now a clear view that there is a difference in the public accountability and corporate governance matters between the owner-managed business and listed companies and other entities which have responsibilities to the public.

e. There is an opinion that the independence of auditors of listed companies cannot be seen to exist when those auditors also undertake a wide range of other work for the audit client. The APB and the new auditing faculty of the ICAEW are clearly committed to continuance of the supply of other services to audit clients.

f. The scandals which may have precipitated much of the crisis in corporate governance have been partly a consequence of the recession or at least the recession causing the collapse of companies run by ruthless characters These people may be sufferers from Lord Acton's aphorism that power corrupts and absolute power corrupts absolutely.

g. There is clear distinction between the role of auditors to public sector entities which is very much concerned with value for money and the role of auditors to the private sector which is still concerned only with true and fair. However the Cadbury Code reporting is a move into the minefield of how well a company is managed.

h. Corporate governance in the past has tended to be oriented towards a duty to shareholders. Now directors need to have a duty to all stakeholders, the public at large and the environment.

i. Auditors talk of their clients. This tends to narrow their thinking down to the company when their duties and responsibilities are now wider. Perhaps the company should be called the patient or the subject or some other word. Do you have any suggestions?

j. The auditor will soon be reporting on the directors' report on compliance with the Cadbury Code's requirements on internal financial controls. At first sight this should be simple for auditors who are presumed to review internal control as part of the audit. However auditors may seek evidence form many sources and in particular areas internal control reliance may not be one of them. There are many other problems in this area and I commend to you the APB discussion paper on Internal Financial Control Effectiveness issue in April 1995.

k. There is a strong movement towards making the APB independent of the accountancy bodies.

Case study 1 for Chapter 61

Megacongom PLC is a giant group in the media and property industries. There are seven directors, all paid executives, and the Chairman and Chief Executive is Napoleon Caesar, a man of boundless ambition and fame. The Group has expanded rapidly in recent years by takeovers and there have been many rationalisations. The Group have many manufacturing subsidiaries in the Third World and Eastern Europe. Gearing is very high and the auditors, Compromise and Co, have acquiesced in some doubtful accounting policies which are probably within the accounting standards. The company engage in much switching of resources round the subsidiaries and recently the company has borrowed a large sum from its pension scheme.

Discussion

In what ways are the various sets of proposals summarised in this chapter relevant to this company?

Case study 2 for Chapter 61

Carter of Wolverhampton is owed £25,000 for goods supplied to Hippo. Hippo is a national charity registered by guarantee under the Companies Act and operates rest homes for retired carthorses and other beasts of burden.

It has suddenly been announced that receivers have been called in as the company has been the victim over a period of two years of a large fraud and several million pounds are missing. The managing director, John Devius, of the charity is missing also and is believed to be in South America. Creditors are unlikely to be paid as the company's properties are mortgaged.

Carter complains to his own auditors that the most recent accounts show a healthy position and he cannot think what the auditors were doing. He proposes to sue Rigor & Co if he is not paid.

Carter's auditor knows Bloggs of Rigor & Co (a local firm in Wolverhampton) the audit partner in charge of Hippo's audit and knows that he has done the audit of Hippo for many years and played golf with Devius.

Discussion

What lessons are there here for the future of auditing and auditors?

Student self testing questions *Questions with answers apparent from the text*

1. a. Summarise the problems of corporate governance and auditing today (5)
   b. Summarise the recommendations of the Cadbury committee (8)
   c. Summarise the Code of Best Practice (9)
   d. Define the audit as practice at present (13)
   e. Summarise the reasons for changing auditing (14)
   f. Summarise the suggestions of the APB paper (15)
   g. Summarise the proposals in the Audit Agenda (16)

Examination questions without answers

1. a. A member of the Institute, Mr. Finch, who is a partner in a small to medium sized practice, is engaged in providing a variety of financial services to his firm's clients. As part of his activities, he receives clients' funds which he uses to make payments on their behalf. To help keep a separate record of such client transactions, Mr. Finch operates a bank current account designated 'Mr. Finch – Office No 3 Account'.
   Requirement:
   i. State briefly in what way Mr. Finch is breaching professional conduct.
   ii. State briefly the manner of reporting required in the above circumstances.
   b. The audit expectation gap is the subject of much debate at present with a wide range of proposals on offer to help narrow the gap.
   Requirement
   i. Set out your understanding of what is meant by the 'audit expectation gap'.
   ii. What are the main reasons which lie behind the concern on the part of the profession about the audit expectation gap.
   iii. What action do you recommend the profession should take to close the gap.

   (ICAI 93)

2. The following statement has been made about the 'audit expectation gap' and the means of solving the problem.

'Following the Caparo decision, auditors of large companies have no responsibility to ensure that the accounts they audit are accurate, and they are not required to detect and report on error and fraud.'

Recent failures of companies and major frauds in financial institutions and pension funds indicate serious weaknesses in the quality of audits. What is required is that auditors should have responsibility:

a. to a larger range of parties than those decided in the Caparo case (8 marks)

b. for detecting and reporting all error and fraud, and (7 marks)

c. for institutions holding and investing client's money, and pension funds, auditors should be present at all times to ensure that no loss arises from investing these funds and that fraud is prevented. (10 marks)

If necessary, there should be changes in legislation to implement these proposals.

You are required to discuss this statement, particularly the matters noted in parts (a) to (c). Your answer should consider the practicality of implementing these proposals, and, if you believe they are impractical, you should make proposals which should be acceptable to both the general public and auditors. (25 marks)

(ACCA 93)

62 Auditing theory

Introduction

1. Auditing is a practical subject. It is something that people do. How it is done today is a result of a long history of marginal changes and responses to new commercial and legal developments over the centuries with the most rapid progress in the last few years. There is no real body of theory in the way that there is, for example, in accounting. In accounting there are a few recognised conventions (going concern, accruals etc) which underlie all accounting and enable applications to be made to new situations in a coherent and consistent manner. Many attempts have been made to develop theories of auditing with a small range of underlying principles but, currently, we are still managing with the large range of discrete prescriptions provided by the Auditing Practices Board.

2. This final chapter reviews some thoughts on auditing theories and principles including the auditing postulates of Mautz and Sharaf.

Enduring principles of auditing

3. The APB in the Audit Agenda identified eight enduring principles of auditing. These are:

   a. **Integrity.** If auditors did not behave with integrity (honesty, adherence to moral principles) and be seen to behave that way, then their reports would not be believed and the whole audit process would have no value. Clearly, in the UK, auditors do behave with integrity although at the margin, there may be some accommodation to client wishes when lucrative work other than audit work is performed and when there is a fear of loss of the audit fee. Partly, conforming to integrity requirements is because of the innate morality of accountants but also because of strict regulation and fear of litigation.

b. **Independence.** If auditors are not independent of the entity being audited or are not seen to be so, then their reports will not be believed and again the whole audit process will have no value. Essentially, auditors must be objective, give their opinions without fear or favour and be unaffected by conflicts of interest or pressures from any source. UK auditors tend to carry on work additional to the audit and their independence is by no means total. Your author believes that attempts to distance the auditors from the directors by such means as their relations with the company being mediated through an audit committee of non-executive directors are not much more than cosmetic. Ultimately auditors will need to be truly independent of commercial clients in the same way as they are with local authorities.

c. **Competence.** If auditors are not competent, then the whole audit process is of no value. In general UK auditors are seen as competent but a number of recent events including company failures, criminal trials and civil litigation have given rise to some doubts in the minds of the business community. The government have legislated for competence (Companies Act 1989 Sections 24 et al), the professional bodies have encouraged it (difficult exams, approved training, post qualifying education, practising certificates with inspections, etc) and the Auditing Practices Board have issued numerous prescriptions. An interesting idea is that competence is constantly being improved but at the same time economics have dictated that the time spent on auditing is constantly being reduced even though modern laws, accounting systems and structures are steadily becoming more complex.

d. **Rigour.** This word implies that auditors should apply strictness in conducting their work and in forming their opinions. Auditors should apply a degree of professional scepticism to their work, should assess the risks involved and should obtain sufficient reliable evidence on all matters from a range of sources. The evidence from negligence cases is that auditors do not always apply sufficient rigour especially in complex cases, where clients are dominated by single individuals and in the valuation of subsidiary companies.

e. **Accountability.** Auditors should act in the best interests of shareholders whilst having regard to the wider public interest. The Audit Agenda suggests that where these responsibilities conflict, auditors should generally place the interests of the shareholders first except where this could materially damage the interests of the public. It is difficult to think of specific instances of such conflicts of interest but your author tends to the view that auditors would be more highly regarded if the public interest always prevailed.

f. **Judgement.** Auditors should apply sound professional judgement. Specific areas where judgement is required include assessment of reasonable assurance, material, misstatement and risk.

g. **Communication.** There are two strands to this. Firstly auditors should openly disclose all matters necessary to a full understanding of their opinion and secondly they should make disclosure to the proper authorities of matters they should disclose in the public interest. The former is met by the long standard form of audit report which I imagine is read by nobody. The latter is a new departure and is too new to assess as yet. Auditors tend to be constrained by fears of suits for defamation and by a natural tendency to confidentiality.

h. **Providing value.** Clearly auditing should be conducted with a minimum of resource input and with a maximum of utility to the business community. There is a trade off here and some auditors would assert that despite massive improvements in auditing techniques (eg risk and materiality assessments, use of analytical review) audits are often conducted too cheaply. The Audit Agenda suggests that value can be achieved in providing greater benefits to the shareholders, in innovating new services as well as in more economical auditing. This seems to conflict with the principle of independence.

Postulates of auditing

4. These are matters which are assumed to be true and are taken for granted. It is often considered that it is useful to examine a discipline and to see what, if any, are its postulates. This was done by Mautz and Sharaf in their 1961 book 'The philosophy of auditing' and I commend this book to you. Their eight postulates are:

a. **Financial statements and financial data are verifiable.** This is an unspoken assumption by all auditors who otherwise would not attempt to verify the assertions in the accounts they are auditing. Sometimes facts are not strictly verifiable (for example the outcome of contentious litigation) and auditors content themselves with statements of the circumstances which can be verified.

b. **There is no necessary conflict of interest between the auditor and the management of the entity.** If this was not so, auditors would not believe the answers given to their questions and, given the complexity of modern businesses, would find conducting an audit impossible. It is this basic assumption which leads auditors to consider whether they should accept a new client where the integrity of the client is suspect.

c. **The financial statements are free from collusive and other unusual irregularities.** Auditors are expected to uncover material misstatements in financial statements caused by fraud or other irregularities but collusive fraud is often impossible to discover by auditing procedures. Consequently readers of financial statements are entitled to assume that the auditors have uncovered any material misstatements except those caused by collusive fraud. If there were a requirement to uncover such frauds the audit would become impossible or, at the least, require many more detailed and expensive procedures than are currently performed.

d. **The existence of a satisfactory system of internal control eliminates the probability of irregularities.** Auditors are entitled to rely on satisfactory internal controls as evidence of many assertions (eg on the completeness of sales or the accuracy of stock taking). If this postulate was not a fundamental principle of auditing they would not do so. It is interesting that SAS 300.8 requires that regardless of the assessed levels of inherent and control risk, auditors should perform some substantive procedures for financial statements assertions of material account balances and transaction classes.

e. **Consistent application of Generally Accepted Accounting Principles results in fair presentation of the results and position.** Auditors need some criterion for their assessment of the fairness of the view given by financial statements and the GAAPs supply it. If they did not then there would be no standard by which fairness could be judged.

f. **In the absence of clear evidence to the contrary, what has held true in the past for the entity will hold true in the future.** If this were not so the auditor would be unable to accept the value of debts, the value of fixed assets, the saleability of stock, the effectiveness of internal controls, the integrity of management and many other matters.

g. **When examining financial data, the auditor acts exclusively in the capacity of auditor.** This is tied up with notions like independence, useful economic function and social responsibility to the public. In the past, many auditors assumed that activities like preparing financial statements, extracting balances and preparing schedules was the same as auditing. This postulate is fundamental and yet the necessary independence of mind is still a difficult problem for many auditors.

h. **The professional status of the independent auditor imposes commensurate professional obligations.** This means that members of the professions have higher duties than economic self interest. However it is not always clear to whom professional duties are owed. Are they to the public at large, to the client company or to the shareholders? However it is certain that the professional accounting bodies impose very onerous duties on their members.

Fundamental auditing principles

5. You will appreciate that there is no agreed list of fundamental auditing principles. Here nonetheless is my list:

a. **Professional status:** independence, integrity, rigour in approach, competence, observance of ethical code, observance of the prescriptions of the law and of the Auditing Standards.

b. **Judgement:** of inherent risk, control risk, detection risk, of what constitutes material misstatement, of what constitutes reasonable assurance.

c. **Evidence:** evidence is made available to auditors, auditors have unrestricted access to required evidence, direct evidence is preferred, evidence for any assertion is collected from several sources, auditors are not biased in assessing evidence, evidence is assessed with an appropriate degree of scepticism, anomalies are probed with tenacity, auditors see for themselves.

d. **Communication:** auditors report their audit opinion without fear or favour, they also report matters which they are required to, to the proper authorities, they report in language which is clear, unequivocal and which can be understood by its recipients.

Summary

6. a. Auditing as a discipline lacks any agreed set of fundamental principles or propositions.

    b. The Audit Agenda contains a list of enduring principles of auditing.

    c. Mautz and Sharaf suggested a list of postulates of auditing.

Points to note

7. a. It is desirable that all auditors follow at all times the various principles I have enumerated in this chapter. In practice auditors are constrained from doing so by a range of influences:

    – the desire for lucrative work in addition to the audit

    – the desire to keep the audit

    – a natural desire to please immediate contact groups especially the directors

    – a desire for a peaceful life

    – a desire to produce the audit as economically as possible so as to make a profit and to avoid losing the audit to competitors

    – the accounting standards are not as rigid a set of criteria for fair view as might be desired and so acceptance of some bending of the rules is inevitable.

    b. On the other hand auditors are now pushed to conform to the principles by:

    – fear of litigation

    – practice regulation and inspection

    – more specific rules (eg the Auditing Standards) which have to be followed

Case study for Chapter 62

Sheinton Military Vehicles PLC have new auditors Thrusting & Co., who won the audit by submitting the lowest tender. They have agreed to assist the company with a range of taxation and consultancy services in IT and management. On the first audit Francis, the clerk in charge of the audit, finds a number of doubtful matters:

a. The company have illegally exported a number of vehicles to a country which is subject to trade sanctions. The chief executive explains that the law has not been broken as the export has actually been to a neighbouring country which is not embargoed.

b. The tax department of Thrusting have advised that the transfer pricing policies of the company broke the tax rules in several countries and that there was a possibility of investigations by those countries with large potential liabilities. The chief executive assures Francis that the tax authorities concerned will not pursue these matters as he has friends in high places.

c. The company have exported vehicles to a particular country where, so a junior manager in the client told Francis, they are used in a particularly brutal oppression of minorities. The chief executive told Francis that the use of the vehicles was nothing to do with them. Think, he said, of the jobs of Sheinton's employees. Francis remembers that a questioner at the last AGM was assured that the company's vehicles were not used in this way.

d. The shares in Sheinton rose in April last year as a result of buying by an unknown institution in a tax haven. This was just before Sheinton bought another company in another tax haven with an exchange of shares. Later the share price fell again as a result of selling by the unknown institution. Francis has been told that this matter should not be investigated as it is not relevant to the audit objectives.

e. Material sums have been paid to a subsidiary in a tax haven by the main operating company. These are described as management services and the accounts of the subsidiary show a small profit and have been audited by a small firm in the tax haven. The chief executive says that Francis should have no problem as he can net off the turnover in the consolidation. The major expense in the subsidiary's accounts is simply cost of sales.

Discussion

Relate this affair to the material in this chapter.

Student self testing questions *Questions with answers apparent from the text*

1. a. List the enduring principles of auditing. (3)
   b. List the postulates of auditing. (4)

Appendix 1

Introduction

This appendix contains notes on:

a. Using the questions and answers provided in the manual.
b. Effective study.
c. Examination technique.

1.1 Using the questions and answers

Types of question

1. Three types of question are provided in the manual:
   a. Those having no answers given but the answers are apparent from the text.
   b. Those examination questions having answers provided in Appendix 3.
   c. Those not having answers in the text but full answers are available to teachers from the publishers – these questions are for class/tutorial use where the book is used as a course text.

Sources of questions

2. Questions are from examinations of:
   a. The Institute of Chartered Accountants in England and Wales (ICAEW).
   b. The Chartered Association of Certified Accountants (ACCA).
   c. The Association of Accounting Technicians (AAT).
   d. The London Chamber of Commerce (LCC).
   e. The Institute of Chartered Accountants in Ireland (ICAI).
   f. The Institute of Company Accountants (ICA).
   g. The Institute of Chartered Accountants of Scotland (ICAS).

Using the questions

3. a. Those with answers apparent from the text. These do not require much thought but do require *knowledge*. Jot down the answer fully before comparing your answer with the paragraph in the book.
   b. **Examination questions** with answers. Write out a complete answer making sure your answer includes as many *points* as you can think of with each point being labelled numerically or alphabetically if that seems to be required. If the question requires you to develop an argument, then use plenty of paragraphs. A continuous narrative is difficult to read and the examiner will find it difficult to follow your reasoning or see that you have all the points.

      Having written out an answer, compare it with the outline answers to see how many points you got or whether you have hit upon the right argument.

There are three possibilities:

i. You have got the answer right and in full. Well done!

ii. You have not got all the points. Do not worry, no candidate will get all the points!

iii. You have apparently got it all wrong. Do not worry, there may be more than one possible answer. Both yours and mine may be right. However it is more likely that you have not yet fully learned or understood the material concerned.

c. **Examination questions without answers**. There are no answers provided for these given in the manual. They are designed for class discussion or as exercises to be marked by your tutors.

4. Remember that success in examinations comes from:

a. knowledge

b. imagination

c. care and attention to detail

d. endless practice in examination questions

1.2 Effective study

Introduction

1. These note are intended for those who are new to studying for examination subjects, although those who are not may also benefit. They have been written in relation to study involving the reading of text books, and they apply to all subjects. It is often extremely difficult to pick out the important principles from such books. As the AUDITING MANUAL is an INSTRUCTIONAL manual your auditing studies should be made much easier. Nevertheless careful reading of these notes will be of benefit even in studying the manual.

General

2. Study means more than just reading a piece of literature. It means close concentrated reading with a notebook at your side. Unless you're one of a few people don't kid yourself you can absorb material by just one general read through it, you cannot!

3. Read a small area, making notes as you go along. Then ask yourself – what have I just learnt? Write down what you think it was all about. Then look again and you may be surprised to find you've missed a key point or points – they must be down in your notebook and eventually in your head.

Compilation of notebook

4. A well compiled NOTEBOOK is a must. Use block capitals or different colour inks to headline the main areas and subdivisions of those areas. Notes made during lectures or private study should not go straight into your NOTEBOOK. Take them down on 'rough' paper and write them in your NOTEBOOK as soon as possible after the lecture or study period, thinking about what you are writing. This does not apply to studying the auditing manual which itself can be used as your notebook.

Memory aids

5. Mnemonics are very useful – if the sequence of points in the text book isn't significant, change it if it makes for a better mnemonic.

6. Association of the points with familiar objects which will serve to recall them is also useful.

7. Some people memorise things by saying them over and over out loud, others have to write them down time after time.

8. Many students have small blank cards and using one side of each card for each study area, put down the main points. They carry the cards everywhere with them and use every opportunity to study them. As they are small they are easily carried. It is surprising how much of your day can be utilised in this way.

Programme

9. Map out a programme for yourself; set targets and achieve them. One thing is certain, studying is not easy but it is not too difficult if you go about it in an orderly purposeful way. Many students fail their examinations through bad preparation. Tackle your studies as you would a project at work, systematically. Allocate a number of hours each week to each subject. Try fixing specific times for each subject, then keep to them by refusing to let anything keep you from your planned task.

Revision

10. Revise periodically. The nearer the examination gets, the more you should concentrate on the major headlines in your notebook and less with the supporting detail.

1.3 Examination technique

First impressions

1. However well prepared you may be, you are still likely to look at the paper on the day and say to yourself, after a quick look at the questions, 'There's not much there I can do'.

2. The atmosphere of the exam room has something to do with this. Try to blot everything from your mind other than the job in hand. Concentrate hard. If you feel a bit panicky (most people do – despite the apparent looks of serenity around you) grip the table, take a deep breath, and get on with it. Remember things are never as bad as they seem!

Time allocation

3. Allocate each question time appropriate to the number of marks. At the end of the allotted time for a question go on to the next – remember, the first 5 or 10 marks on the new question are more readily picked up that the last 1 or 2 on the previous question.

4. The temptation will be to say 'I'll write just one more sentence', but before you know where you are, you'll have written several more and probably just managed to scrape another mark, whereas the same time spent on the next question could have earned 5 or 6 marks. TIME ALLOCATION IS IMPORTANT.

5. If you are running out of time write down the main headings first, leaving a few lines between each – at least the examiner will see that you had the overall picture. Then go back putting in as much supporting detail as you can.

General approach

6. Read the instructions at the top of the paper.

7. Read the question paper once through. Make your choice of questions quickly. Pick the easiest (if one appears so) and get on with it.

Individual questions

8. a. **Read the question.**
   b. **Read it again.**
   c. Underline important words in the question.
   d. Make sure you know *exactly* what the examiner requires you to do.
   e. Do a. to d. over again.
   f. Jot down the points you want to make, add to these points others as you think of them even while writing the answer out.
   g. Stop and think for a moment.
   h. Draft *an outline plan* of your answer.
   i. Write your answer, referring back continuously to the *requirements of the question*. Take plenty of room, use short sentences and paragraphs. Number your points if you think it appropriate.
   j. Go on to next question.

Common faults in auditing answers

9. a. **Not obeying the questioners requirements.** If it says set out; tabulate; list; to what extent; examine the truth of; state; state concisely; what are the principal matters; discuss; comment on; describe; write a short essay then:
   Do what it says!
   Not doing what is says is a more common fault with auditing examinees than lack of knowledge.
   b. **Not reading the question carefully.**
   Many students on being asked to audit a partnership will ask for the memorandum and articles!
   c. **Not making enough points.**
   This is very hard to overcome but one good technique is to try to break the question down into sections. A tree approach – roots, trunk, branches, twigs, leaves – is often successful.
   d. **Not being specific.**
   'Vouch the cash book' will not often do, 'vouch the entries in the cash book with available supporting documents such as ...' might do.
   e. **Being irrelevant.**
   Tied up with not obeying instructions and not reading the question carefully.
   f. **Lack of planning, coherence and logic.**
   Planning an answer should cure this.
   g. **Lack of balance.**
   If the examiner asks for five points he does not want four pages on point one and one line each on the others.
   h. **Handwriting, grammar, spelling, punctuation.**
   Do not waste your time and opportunities by presenting your work badly or with avoidable errors.
   i. **Confusing the role of auditor with that of accountant, tax consultant, etc.**
   If asked what the auditor should do in certain circumstances, never say 'alter the accounts' because producing accounts is not the auditor's function. Neither should you

advice an action which would save your client tax, you must say what you would do as an *auditor*.

Layout and wording of answer

10. a. **Use the wording of the question** wherever you can.

    b. Answer the question in the *sequence* requested.

    c. **Obey instructions** on lay out eg tabulate.

    d. State any assumptions you make in answering the question.

However do not make assumptions which change the question to suit your knowledge.

End of exam procedure

11. Have a quick look at each answer, checking for grammatical errors and badly formed letters.

12. Ensure each answer sheet has your number on it and don't leave any lying on the table.

Conclusions

13. Good technique plays a large part in examination success; this is a fact. Refuse to be panicked, keep your head, and with reasonable preparation you should make it.

14. Remember – you don't have to score 100% to pass.

15. A final point; once you're in the examination room stay there and make use of every minute at your disposal.

16. Practise your techniques when answering the questions set in the manual.

1.4 Why do students fail auditing exams

1. There are four main reasons:

    a. Inadequate knowledge

    b. Failure to answer the questions set

    c. Failure to see the implications of the questions

    d. Failure to make enough points

Appendix 2

Answers to questions at the ends of chapters

Chapter 3

1. a. ensure accounts show a true and fair view, separation of ownership and control, need for stewards (directors) to account to owners, and also to other parties (eg bank, inland revenue, creditors etc)

    b. See para 3 or Companies Act 1985 Ss.385–387.

    c. Access, information and explanations, attendance at meetings, receipt of notices, speaking at meetings, written representations if proposed to remove him/her, right to information from subsidiary companies and their auditors (see chapter on groups), right to resign and give statement of circumstances and perhaps right to requisition a meeting, where private company election is in force to dispense with laying accounts the auditor has the right to require a meeting to be held to lay the accounts (S.253(2)), right to make his report on the accounts.

    d. Proper accounting records and lay and deliver annual accounts. By implication also to safeguard assets and prevent errors and fraud and to institute controls and systems to achieve these.

Chapter 8

1. a. Points to make are:

    The supply of services additional to the audit is customary and should be covered in the letter of engagement.

    It makes economic sense as two firms would be wasteful and it is desirable to use audit firm expertise to improve performance of businesses.

    Executive functions should not be taken on and it may be that some systems work (eg design and implementation) is an executive function.

    Accountancy services can be supplied to all companies but writing up books should not be done for plcs.

    The client must take responsibility for all accountancy work done (in writing).

    It is possible to use a Chinese Wall approach whereby different members of the firm carry on the audit and the other activities. This again seems uneconomic and is rarely found in practice.

    The letter of weakness is established practice.

    The provision of advice is acceptable and desirable but design and implementation of systems goes too far.

    The auditors must be independent and objective. They must also be seen to be so. That seems to be the problem here.

    The EC would like auditors to provide no other services to their clients. English law does not require this.

    b. Points to make:

    An ethical problem. Guide suggests greater than 15% of fees from one client may impair independence. 20% in this case. Auditors may feel that their income needs may compromise their objectivity. 20% may be reduced by giving up some other work or actively seeking additional clients (advertising is now acceptable).

Should not do accounting records work for quoted clients.

Need to be seen as independent is more important for quoted companies.

May be that Smith and Jones may not have the resources or standing to audit a quoted company.

   c. See Chapter 3 paragraph 9.

   d. See Chapter 3 paragraph 9.

   e. See Chapter 3 paragraphs 6 and 7.

Chapter 9

1. a. See paragraph 3 of Chapter 9.

    b. i. Notes on Companies Act Ss.235, 237, Definition from Chapter 1 paragraph 15d.

       ii. Not object of audit, audit tests may reveal, relevant if it affects true and fair view, will reveal to management if found, directors responsibilities for internal control, accounting records and accounts.

      iii. All are directors' responsibilities. Auditors will do if asked, PAYE, VAT, usually done by client but auditor will do if required, CT usually done by auditor. Can prepare accounts, can offer other services. Cannot do accounting records for a public company.

      iv. Time spent, grade of staff, separate billings for audit and other services, payments on account, standing orders?

Chapter 12

1. a. i. – Companies Act requirements

          – Contact groups need confidence in Annual Accounts

          – Stock Exchange requirements (not yet for Q Ltd., but later?)

       ii. – Skills, responsibilities borne and time necessarily spent.

    b. Interim, Year End, Final – for more detail see Chapter 11 paragraphs 4 to 9.

    c. Benefits: needs of non–involved members of the family; negotiating loans, selling business etc., requires credible accounts; directors have confidence in the report on their activities which is the annual accounts; auditor can also provide other services; unlikely that accounts unscrutinised by auditors would give a true and fair view or conform to legal requirements.

      Uses: Dividend decision; tax computations; loan negotiation; sale of business; flotation of company; wage negotiation.

      Note: In b. answer must relate to Q Ltd., and in c. distinguish benefits of the audit and uses of audited accounts.

Chapter 14

1. a. See paragraph 4 of Chapter 14.

    b. Any four types from paragraph 4 could be used. Remember to relate the illustration to what little you are told about Southern. Possible answers are:

      Segregation of duties. Separate persons to determine requirements for materials and to requisition them from the persons who order goods, receive them into custody, store them and account for them both as stock control and for financial accounting. Possible consequences include payment for goods not received.

Physical control. Need for physical security of stocks to guard against theft and deterioration. Possible consequences are theft of valuable parts and also breakages and deterioration.

Arithmetical and counting. Possibly continuous inventory could be maintained and regular comparisons made between physical and book stocks. Possible consequences are losses due to theft or failing to charge customers with parts.

Authorisation and approval. All requisitions and orders should be authorised and approved by duly authorised senior personnel. Possible consequences are that goods not wanted could be ordered.

c. Points to make:
- Common problem with small companies for auditor to qualify report.
- Need for auditor to rely on assurances given by management in nearly all companies of this size.
- Positive act to change from proprietorial supervision to sophisticated system of internal control. Companies rarely do it until forced.
- Unlikely to have enough staff for adequate segregation of duties.
- Rate of change inhibits development of stable systems.
- Staff will not easily change to and become familiar with more elaborate systems.
- High cost of internal control will not be perceived as justifiable.
- Management time will be taken up with operational problems not establishment of internal controls.
- Management will consider that close involvement in day to day operations will be sufficient control but will increasingly not have the time to involve themselves when the company becomes larger.
- Management will lack technical expertise to install complex systems.

Chapter 16
1. a. GP ratio – static in 49, 50 and 51. Unlikely rise in 52 and again in 53. Needs close investigation. Possible reasons – fraud or error, changes in products or markets or pricing policy. Stock turnover – rapid rise in stock (as proportion of throughput in 52 and 53) – understated in 49–51 or overstated in 52 and 53, physical or valuation problems. GP ratio change may be connected to stock magnitude.
   b. Close investigation of sales, purchases, stocks, pricing policies, cut-off. Ask directors for explanation and check it out. Seek for frauds and errors. Circumstances (eg hope to sell business or avert takeover) may have induced directors to present false accounts.

Chapter 17
1. a. Flowchart of Andrew plc Raw Material System follows.

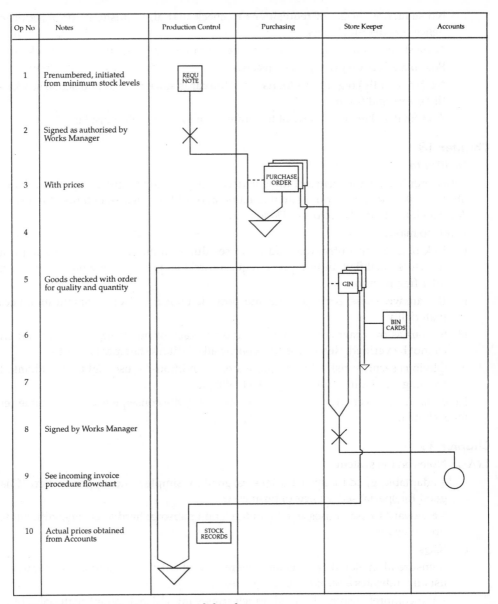

Op No	Notes	Production Control	Purchasing	Store Keeper	Accounts
1	Prenumbered, initiated from minimum stock levels	REQU NOTE			
2	Signed as authorised by Works Manager				
3	With prices		PURCHASE ORDER		
4					
5	Goods checked with order for quality and quantity			GIN	
6					BIN CARDS
7					
8	Signed by Works Manager				
9	See incoming invoice procedure flowchart				
10	Actual prices obtained from Accounts	STOCK RECORDS			

b.   – Establishment of minimum stock levels.
     – Use of bin cards to alert stockkeeper to low stocks.
     – Separately maintained stock records enable errors and unauthorised losses to be identified.
     – Authorising of requisitions by works manager.
     – Segregation of duties between departments.
     – Verification of quantities and qualities and agreement with order of incoming goods.
     – Approval of GIN and hence of goods.
     – Accounts department cannot pay invoices unsupported by a GIN and thus cannot pay for goods not received.

c.   No sequence checks of requisitions to check that all requisitions produce orders and hence possible stock outs.

No system to follow up orders to ensure prompt supply, again possible stock outs.

Possible errors on pricing stock records.

No (apparently) regular comparisons of bin cards stock records and actual stocks to identify errors and frauds.

And finally, there is no copy of the order form to send to the supplier!

Chapter 18

1.   Dodds Ltd.

Letter should be in the form including material suggested in Chapter 18 paragraphs 9 and 10. Students should decide on a suitable name and address before entering the exam room. Address letter to the Directors of Dodds Ltd.

Points to make:

i.   lack of internal control can lead to: losses due to fraud and error, including frauds by directors; qualified audit reports; request directors to review the matter now five years after first mention.

ii.   Restate weakness, consequences and possible remedies. Not in qualification because of materiality.

iii. Serious as overpayments may occur and accuracy of purchases, expenses and creditors cannot be verified. Remedy is to reconcile all creditors statements monthly.

iv.   Obvious security risk – breach of insurers' conditions? – use night safe at bank. Risk of teeming and lading. Bank daily intact takings.

Note that the answer should detail the weaknesses, the consequence and possible remedies for each item.

Chapter 19

1.(A)a. Notes on the system

+ adaptable; good for small businesses; good for simple systems; good where IC is weak; good for specialised aspects of businesses.

– awkward to use; impossible to understand or absorb; hard to change; difficult to interpret or evaluate.

b.   ICQs

+ ensure all major IC points are covered; excellent for evaluation as negative answer usually indicates a weakness; easy to use.

– too comprehensive; cluttered; much irrelevant and redundant material; not good in specialised situations.

c.   Flow charts (of documents)

+ matters cannot be missed; easy to understand; easy to interpret and evaluate and plan tests.

– require time and effort; may omit essential items (eg physical flows, supervisory controls).

In practice a combination of all these methods will be used with emphasis on one or the other depending on the situation and the extent of risk.

(B) a.   Storeman ...

– require two persons to do the checking (OK providing no collusion and this would be a temptation to the other employee)

- maintenance of independent stock records
- regular reconciliation of such records with actual and investigation of differences
- rotation of duties
- spot checks of newly arrived materials by management or internal audit.

Purchasing Officer ...

This is very hard to prevent or detect.

- ensure requisitioner is given a copy of the order, thus making sure he/she is aware of the name of the supplier
- adopt a system of tendering (this assumes that the buyer is using more expensive suppliers)
- rotate duties
- inform all staff of company rules with warnings about breaches
- monitor staff lifestyles for evidence of living beyond salary (can this really be done?)

  b. Sample as:

- purchase requisitions for authorisation and appropriateness
- sequence checks on purchase orders and test also to suppliers standards terms and conditions
- goods received notes to orders, suppliers despatch notes and invoices for quantity, quality conditions etc.
- GRNs to stock records
- purchase invoices to purchase orders etc. (note direction of enquiry)
- codings
- approval of invoice for calculation, additions etc., by signature etc.

  c. Points to make: not at present a general responsibility; note in letter of engagement; responsibility of directors; auditors plan their work to detect material mis-statements in financial statements; this work cannot be relied upon to disclose all fraud and irregularities; where fraud is discovered auditor will inform client who is then responsible for further investigations; will also report to management weaknesses in IC which may lead to frauds. Possibility of reports direct to third parties.

Chapter 20

1. Thames Engineers PLC

  a. An audit programme will encompass all the verification points on paragraph 9 except vi, x, and xvi. Special investigations will need to be done on whether plant is still in use and on the accuracy of estimates of useful lives. Also repairs will need to be examined to see no capital expenditure is included.

  b. Points to make are in SSAP 12:

Depreciation should be allocated as fairly as possible to the periods expected to benefit from their use.

Where there is a change from one method to another the unamortised cost should be written off over the remaining useful life on the new basis. The effect should be disclosed in the year of change.

Where assets are revalued the provision for depreciation should be based on the revalued amount and current estimate of remaining useful life, with disclosure in the year of change.

Note Higher assets – revaluation but lower profits in short term (reducing balance) and long term (depreciation on revalued assets).

  c. Companies Act 1985 Sch 4 50(3):

Contracts placed but not provided for.

Contracts authorised but not placed.

Verify by: enquiry, post balance sheet events, directors' minutes, representation letter, inspection of placed contracts.

  d. Companies Act Sch 4 (44):

Amount ascribable to freehold land and to leasehold land.

Leasehold land division into long and short leases.

See also Sch 4 (42)1a, 1b, 2a, 3.

Note also Sch 7 para 1. (Directors' Report)

Auditor should ensure true and fair view is given and that Companies Act requirements are met. Sch 7 is not his responsibility but consistency between accounts and Directors' Report is.

Chapter 21

1. a. The objectives of circularisation of debtors are:

   i. To obtain confirmatory evidence that the system of recording and documenting sales and debtors and the controls thereon can be relied upon to produce an accurate figure for debtors. Normally the tests which are designed to obtain evidence of the reliability of the system are called compliance tests.

   ii. To obtain evidence that the figure in the Accounts £5,866,095 is a true and fair one. This sort of evidence is called substantive because it helps to substantiate the correctness of the figure.

   iii. To obtain evidence of the correctness of cut off. Cut-off is the technical term used to ensure that in computing profit, sales are accurately compared with the costs of the goods sold. Cut-off tests can be substantive (eg examining last numbers of documents) or compliance (if controls exist, the application of which can be tested).

Thus, in this case, debtors circularisation can be viewed as both substantive and compliance testing.

  b. **Zero balances:**

   i. – to confirm that the balances are truly zero

    – to confirm completeness of the debtors figure

    – to confirm system of control over sales, debtors and cut off.

  Credit balances:

    – credit balances are prima facie 'put upon enquiry'

    – 4% of debtors ie it is material

    – to confirm system (as above)

   ii. **£1 – £1,000**

    – balances form a homogeneous population

    – statistical sampling can be used

    – select sample size using tables after determining relevant factors (eg materiality factor, risk factor, confidence level, precision interval).

    – select sample randomly

    over £20,000

    – material (46% of debtors)

    – small in number (30)

- 100% sample is possible and desirable.
iii. Audit steps – debts in hands of agencies:
  - item is material therefore worth some audit effort
  - review reports from agencies
  - circularise collection agencies for current position
  - review post balance sheet events (eg collection)
  - review credit control procedures to determine, for example, if company are relaxing credit control to obtain work.
c. Alternative auditing procedures on refusal by debtors to reply to circularisation:
  - detailed vouching of all entries in the debtors account
  - examining post balance sheet events eg settlement
  - examining of the possibility of unusual items or mis–statement
  - review of correspondence with debtor, if any
d. Additional substantive tests on debtors:
  - review of application of internal controls in the intervening period – discuss with management
  - some compliance tests of the system in the period
  - review of the data, sales, credit notes, journal entries etc. in the intervening period to seek evidence of unusual events or transactions
  - a small circularisation
  - analytical review eg debtors/sales ratio
  - post balance sheet review eg settlements, credit notes after date
  - review of age analysis of debtors
  - special attention to the largest debtors.

Chapter 22

1. a. i. Two possible reasons:
     - Incomplete processing of entry data. For example the data on some goods received notes and despatch notes may not be entered.
     - Inaccurate processing. For example the sale of a 24×20 type may be posted to the card for 23×20 tyres.
   ii. To overcome incomplete processing:
     - batching items to be processed and pre-adding numbers of items to be posted, the forming of hash totals of items to be posted, subsequent measurement of actual postings by the computer to compare with totals found in advance, input of all input document numbers with the computer assessing whether they are consecutive.

     To overcome errors in input:
     - program edit checks, use of redundant data, eg inputting size of tyre and a code for that size for computer comparison.
   b. Stocktaking instructions. Inadequate, vague or poorly communicated instructions would inevitably lead to errors.

   Use of teams of two. One person should be familiar with the stock and one should be independent. Clearly the use of two people will lead to a more accurate count and it is essential to have a knowledgeable person but also an independent person.

Cut off procedures. In practice more accounting errors occur in this area than in any other.

Stock sheets. Stock sheets should be prenumbered, issue controlled and a check made that all are collected. Clearly without this stock sheets could be completed but not processed in the final summaries.

Identification of items requiring valuation at net realisable value. Failure to do this will cause stock to be over valued.

  c. Matters on valuation:

X27 Verification of the correctness of the figure 19.

Y91 Stock levels are high in comparison to turnover (3 years supply!) and happily none are on order. Probable need to value at NRV.

Z32 Replacement cost is below cost of items in stock. However the difference is small and the tyres evidently sell well so cost will still be the correct valuation method.

Chapter 23

1. Audit program heads (with purposes in brackets).

  a. Trade creditors:

- obtain schedule (this is the sum to be audited)
- examine previous year schedule (for analytical review)
- carry out analytical review (compare with monthly purchases and previous years' ratio for reasonableness, to identify situations requiring further study)
- determine, record, evaluate and test internal control system (always necessary if any reliance is to be placed on internal controls, for example for completeness evaluation)
- cut off testing (the major source of error, to be carried out in conjunction with other areas eg stocks and sales)
- control account agreement (clearly if this does not balance then the creditors may not be correct)
- examination of individual balances (also to verify accuracy of processing)
- examine suppliers statements (to check balances with external evidence)
- possibly circularise creditors (to obtain true independent third party evidence)
- examine post balance sheet events (to determine if all creditors are included).

  b. Sundry accruals:

- obtain schedule (this is to be audited)
- obtain schedule of previous year (for comparison)
- analytical review (to see if last years items have this year items also and also to see if expected items are present)
- substantiate each item (to ensure correct amount is included)
- examine post balance sheet events (to ensure all items are included).

  c. Provisions:

- examine all provisions (are they needed?, is the amount too large merely to reduce profits?, are they too little to avoid reducing profit?)
- examine directors minutes, post balance sheet events, correspondence with lawyers etc. for evidence of the need for provisions (essential to ensure all necessary provisions are included)
- consider SSAP 18 requirements (to ensure true and fair view is given)

- legal action: examine correspondence with lawyers, read directors minutes, discuss with management, consider probabilities of payment with requirements of SSAP 18, perhaps obtain letter from the lawyer.
- factory repairs: review initial needs and the evidence of disrepair then presented and evaluated, verify and inspect the repairs costing £58,000, examine estimates and quotations and reports from builders, architects, surveyors etc., examine directors minutes and discuss with management.
- review with any evidence available (minutes, correspondence, registers, registration documents with government agencies etc) possibility of liabilities arising out of pollution or health or and safety legislation.

Chapter 24

1. a. Kinds is not a precise word. Could mean sources (see Chapter 24 paragraph 14) or techniques (see paragraphs 9 and 10).

   b. Client permission, from client (debtors circularisation etc), or direct (bank letter etc), reply to the auditor direct, follow guideline if any (eg bank letters) or other advice (debtors circs or lawyers), consider replies, relate to other evidence, consider status of third party (related?, expert?, ordinary course of business, integrity), follow up if necessary.

   c. Relevant – see paragraph 16.

   Reliable – if b, supra followed, if no suspicious circumstances, if debtor is not a related party, if debtor is known to exist (McKesson and Robbins).

   Sufficient – probably on the specific debt but problem of cut off, collectibility, after date C.N.s, not sufficient for debtors generally if this is part of a sampling operation.

   Other work – see Chapter 21 paragraph 3.

Chapter 26

1. a. See Chapter 26 paragraphs 11, 12 and 13.

   b. See Chapter 26 paragraph 17.

   c. See Chapter 26 paragraph 15 for advantages.

   For disadvantages see paragraph 11 where judgement sampling seems superior.

Chapter 28

1. a. SSAP 9 requires that the chosen method of stock valuation must provide the fairest practicable approximation to actual cost. Where standard costs are used they need to be reviewed frequently to ensure that they bear a reasonable relationship to actual costs obtaining during the period.

   b. Two matters should be included in the notion 'does not make sense':
   - The costs must (see a.) bear a reasonable relationship to the actual costs obtaining in the period.
   - Some stocks may need to be valued at net realisable value.

   In this case:

   Component A – Standard cost does seem to bear a reasonable relationship to the actual costs in the year. However the amount of stock is almost half the annual sales. The company has only three major customers and questions must be asked of the saleability of this component.

   Component B – Actual costs of the component are substantially above standard cost (£140,000 against £100,000) for the year. It may be that costs earlier in the year were higher than latterly but clearly the matter must be clarified. Actual stock is about two months throughput so it will mostly have been manufactured in the final quarter. Possibly costs were then more stable as the standard has not been materially changed in January 1985. A possible explanation of the high actual costs may be abnormal costs earlier in the year.

Component C – Here standard costs are higher than actual costs so there is a risk of the component being overvalued. This is confirmed by a downward change (£1.85 to £1.55) in the standard from 1.1.85.

c. Two critical matters in considering standard labour costs are:
- The rate of pay which should be of the grade of labour involved and include other standard labour costs including social security for the production of the component.

Two audit tests that may be performed may be:

On rates: testing the wages system to see standard rates approximate to actual wage rates paid: Examining the allocation of other wage costs (including national insurance).

On time: examine component design and production schedules which should specify times taken and grades of labour used: enquiry of production staff, examination of production records and actual observation to determine reasonableness of times included.

Chapter 32

1. a. See para 7.

   b. This is a matter of uncertainty in that the auditor cannot obtain all the evidence he needs because of absence of records. In the circumstances the amount may not be material or if it is, then the difference revealed if the records were available is likely to be less than £10,000. I would include the matter in the letter of representation, gather whatever other evidence is available in the area, make a full description in the working papers and leave it at that. The government grant has been wrongly treated in accordance with SSAP 4 and I would ask the directors to change the accounts to accord with SSAP 4. If this is not done then the matter is one of disagreement and a qualification is required if the matter is material.

   c. 'As explained in note x an amount of £25,000 has been credited to Profit and Loss Account and included in exceptional items. SSAP 4 requires that such items should be recognised and credited to Profit and Loss Account over the expected useful economic lives of the related plant and machinery. The effect of the change would be to make operating profit £y instead of £z with a corresponding change in shareholders funds.'

   d. The directors are solely responsible for the directors' report and the auditors have no general responsibility for it. However they are required to consider whether the information in the Directors' report is consistent with the accounts. If they are of the opinion that the valuation particulars are inconsistent with any information given in the accounts then they must say so in their report. This is unlikely but any information at all in the Directors' report which seems to the auditor dubious would put the auditor on enquiry.

Chapter 33

1. a. Points to make:
   - SSAP 17 deals with events which occur between the date of the balance sheet and the date the accounts are drawn up. These events may need to be incorporated in the accounts.

- those that do are called adjusting events and the others are called non adjusting events.
- adjusting events are those that provide additional information on the conditions existing at the balance sheet date.
- some post balance sheet events are customarily incorporated (eg tax and dividends)
- going concern evidence is always incorporated
- even non adjusting events should be disclosed by way of note if the matters are very relevant to an understanding of the position of the enterprise.
- truth and fairness is all and counts above a cut off of information at the balance sheet date.

b. See Chapter 33 paragraph 9.

c. i. Check facts ie original cost, examine correspondence with planning authority, review estimates of NRV by reference to external valuers certificates etc.

Decline in value occurred only on refusal of planning permission. Worth at least cost till then and hence non adjusting.

Alternatively, original value (cost) incorporated information that planning permission would be obtained. PBSEs cast new light on that assumption and are thus adjusting. Correct view is adjusting!

ii. Check all facts eg costs to accounting date and to completion, work certified to accounting date and to completion, cash paid. Consider retentions and possible guarantee work. Examine contract and all papers connected with the contract including the costings. Check calculations for accounting treatment. This is clearly an adjusting event as it given evidence on conditions subsisting at the balance sheet date.

iii. Verify facts and opinions by examining share certificate, share quotation, correspondence and accounts from liquidator.

It is clear that the asset had a value at balance sheet date as it was quoted. However it seems that at that time the real value of the company was nil and as such it should be valued at nil.

Chapter 36

1. a. See Chapter 36 paragraph 10 b.

b. Examine each fixed asset purchase and determine if it is eligible for grant, if it is then verify correct amount has been received, examine documentation and correspondence, verify correct accounting treatment according to SSAP 4.

c. Request change policy to SSAP 4 requirements, if they refuse and matter is material then qualify report for disagreement.

Chapter 37

1. a. See Chapter 3 paragraph 9, statement of circumstances or statement that there are no ....

b. S 392 (3).

c. By the directors (S 388).

d. See letter in Chapter 37 paragraph 3 at end.

e. Reply stating there are no reasons known to LEE why nominees should not accept appointment, perhaps state actual reasons, give whatever information new people ask for. NB it is not usual for old auditors to hand over all their files. See Chapter 37 paragraph 3 middle

f.   Lee have a right to retain any books of account, files and papers which their clients have delivered to them and also any documents which have come into their possession in the course of their ordinary professional work, until any outstanding fees have been paid.

Item i. belongs to Lee but items ii. and iii. belong to the client. As such (subject to lien) Lee are obliged to hand over ii. and iii.

Chapter 39

1. a.   Audit evidence of ownership of fixed asset, make, type, first registered, registration number, in name of client, is genuine, see it agrees with fixed asset schedule or register.

b.   Suppliers statement, evidence of a liability and indirectly of internal control over creditors, supplier name, date, amount due in terms of total and detail, see if apparently genuine, agreement with bought ledger account, if part of IC is a checking of statements then see evidence that the checking has been performed.

c.   Evidence of existence and ownership of an asset, amount, date, building society name, interest credited, dates, see if genuine (it should come direct to the auditor) agree with data in the accounting records.

d.   HP agreement, evidence of a liability and support of several payments, HP company name, goods price, deposit, interest, instalments, APR if relevant, dates. Verify detail agrees with entries in the accounting records.

e.   Policy, evidence for insurance payment, indirect evidence re property and its value, schedule of property included and its value, premium and renewal date, verify agreement with property register and with premium payment. Enquire into any uninsured property or risks.

Chapter 49

1. a.   Liable to: any person/institution with whom the accountant has contractual relations, clients (individuals, partnerships, companies etc), persons who may rely on the work of the accountant (providing the audit knew or ought to have known that the person would rely on the work). Precise extent of parties to whom auditor may be liable is unclear. Note the House of Lords on CAPARO.

b.   If the auditor was negligent, if the negligence led to a monetary loss by the complainant party, if the auditor had a duty of care to the complainant party (see a.).

c.   Possible defences: standard of care adopted was satisfactory, auditing standards and guidelines were followed meticulously, claim does not come from a person who the auditor owes a duty of care (eg a shareholder), complainant did not lose money as a result of the negligence, any losses are recoverable (eg from inland revenue for tax overpaid), other persons should be sued and losses are recoverable from them (eg the director).

Chapter 50

1. a.   Prima facie, the MD may be guilty of:
    –   S 389A false statements to auditors
    –   S 450 falsifying company documents
    –   S458 intent to defraud creditors
    –   Theft Act ss 15–18 Misuse of company property

    All these may lead to fines and/or imprisonment. He may also be sued for recovery of the monies taken by the liquidator.

b. Auditors have completed one year only. Auditor may not have been negligent if fraud was undiscoverable and auditor did all a reasonable auditor would have done and followed the standards and guidelines. Company did suffer loss after auditor failed to find fraud so may be liable for that part of loss (cf London Oil Storage) General liability should be discussed in terms of Caparo etc. Note that liquidator can sue as company had contractual relationship with auditors but shareholders did not and Caparo etc is all about whether non-contracted stakeholders can sue.

c. Similar with previous auditors. Main thing would be for plaintiff to show auditors had been negligent.

Chapter 53

1. a. Points to make include:
   - Audit must still be conducted in accordance with the Auditing Standards.
   - Auditor needs additional skills.
   - Auditor must adapt to change in nature of internal control in a computer environment.
   - Loss of audit trail.
   - Timing problems. Must be present when files exist and programs to be tested are still being used.
   - General controls are most important especially those over setting up programs and systems and maintaining integrity of programs and files.

   b. i. Applications controls are those which are applied to specific applications eg to invoice production or gross wage calculation. They are designed to ensure completeness, accuracy and validity of entries in the accounting records. They may be manual or programmed.

   ii. General controls are controls which are concerned with the environment in which data processing is carried on. The objectives are to ensure the integrity of applications development and of programs and files and of computer operations.

   c. Many controls are possible. Some are:
   - Establishing control totals of batches of incoming invoices for subsequent checking with the computer generated total. Several totals may be required including hash totals.
   - Sequence checking of prenumbered purchase orders. This could be a program control.
   - Automatic matching of files eg of orders with invoices or stock movements.

   The purpose of these controls would be to ensure that all the batch was processed (for example an invoice could not be omitted or a fraudulent invoice to be put in by a computer operator).

   d. i. CAATs are audit techniques performed through the computer or using an independent computer. The two main kinds are:

   Audit software which can be used to search or examine the contents of a computer file and/or perform logical or mathematical operations on the data in the file.

   Test packs which are real or dummy transactions which the auditor inputs to an operational program to determine if the program performs as it is supposed to.

   The benefits that can be derived are:
   - They enable the auditor to search files and do tests and other operations (eg take out statistical samples or check calculations).

– They enable the audit to be conducted more rapidly and economically (and more impressively!).

ii. CAATs may be used in the audit of the year-end trade debtors by:

– Stratifying the debtors so that for example all large debtors, all overseas debtors, all debtors overdue can be printed out.

– Selecting a sample of debtors for detailed analysis using perhaps monetary unit sampling.

Chapter 58

1. a. i. Both report, both are concerned with systems and with information, both operate on same basic data and use same basic techniques, but in reporting EA report outside on true and fair view and IA report inside on very specific matters.

ii. External – subject to statutory and professional requirements, IA – desirable in general approach and in position in company hierarchy.

iii. IC – IA specific tasks, EA means to an end and may ignore if other forms of evidence are sufficient. Operational auditing – investigation into validity of operational objectives, information reliability, efficiency and effectiveness of activities and is also an agent for change by analysing and suggesting solutions to managerial problems. All this is not a EA matter.

b. See paragraphs 11, 13, 15, Chapter 59.

c. Visits to branches, IC compliance tests in general (eg in a bank), stock counts.

Appendix 3

Auditing case study 1

Objectives

The objectives of this case study is to explore the issues of professional independence, and of ethical matters generally. A subsidiary aim is to give students practice in drafting letters and audit documentation.

All Change Ltd

Brown And Co. is a small firm of Chartered Accountants in Brickhampton. There are two partners, George Smith and Charles Jones, both in their forties. They have been partners for twelve years. The original principals of the firm have been dead for many years. The firm specialises in small clients of the incomplete records type with a few small manufacturing companies. They have some 300 clients and gross fees are about £190,000. They have five audit staff, all unqualified and two typists.They occupy modern offices in the centre of Brickhampton. Both partners are anxious to expand the practice and to this end are members of several clubs and societies. George is a member of the Brickhampton Golf Club and regularly plays golf with William Robinson who has recently been appointed managing director of Robinson Widgets Ltd, in succession to his uncle who has recently died.

Robinson Widgets Ltd, was established in 1930 to make Widgets for the engineering industry. Some facts about the company are:

Turnover £10 million, including exports via overseas depots of £6 million, profit before tax £220,000, net assets £1.6 million, number of employees 156, location – a factory at Brickhampton and twelve depots in the UK and abroad.

The company keep their records on a new mini-computer. Directors are William Robinson who is chairman and Managing Director, Philip Robinson and Daniel Robinson who are his cousins and three others who are employees with many years service but who have no shares in the company. Share holders are William Robinson with 15%, Philip Robinson 10%, Daniel Robinson 10%, ten other members of the Robinson family, none of whom are close to the directors 52%, former employees or their heirs 4%, John Wilkes who is senior partner in Wilkes & Son, Certified Accountants the company's auditors 9%. John Wilkes acquired his shares in the 1960's when the company went through a difficult period.

One morning in March George Smith received a letter from the company signed by William Robinson asking Brown & Co, to accept nomination as auditors of the company in place of Wilkes & Son, at the AGM to be held on May 5th. George then contacted William to obtain more information.

He discovered:

1. William dislikes John Wilkes and wishes to have as auditor an accountant that he likes.
2. Wilkes and Son do not wish to lose their client and propose to exercise their statutory rights.
3. Total remuneration to Wilkes & Son was about £25,000 in the last year.
4. William would like Brown & Co. to prepare half yearly and annual accounts as well as acting as auditors. They will also be required to advise the directors on tax matters and to agree the company's corporation tax assessments. William would also like George to give financial advice when required and to attend the directors' meeting when the annual dividend is considered.

Classwork

1. The partners of Brown & Co. feel it is necessary to draw up a checklist of matters that they should consider before accepting a new client. Draw up such a checklist with four sections: legal, ethical, practical, other matters.
2. Use the checklist to decide whether or not Brown & Co. should accept the audit.
3. Wilkes & Son wish to exercise their statutory rights to persuade the shareholders not to replace them. Draft representations from them to the shareholders designed to persuade the shareholders.
4. Draft the letters which the firms of accountants would exchange under the professional etiquette rules.
5. Draft the statement of circumstances that Wilkes & Co. should make.
6. Brown & Co. are finally appointed auditors to Robinson Widgets Ltd. Draft the letter of engagement which they will agree with the company.
7. Debate the proposition that an effective auditor must:
    a. be totally independent of his client and
    b. perform no work other than an audit for his client.

Auditing case study 2

Objectives

This case study is designed to give students practice in the audit of systems, including the drafting of flowcharts.

Allan Castings Limited

Allan Castings Limited is an old established company manufacturing castings for the heavy engineering industry. The company is owned and run by two brothers, Aaron and Robin Allan, both of whom have been with the company since they left school. Statistics about the company include:

Turnover £4 million, profit before directors fees and taxation £180,000, net assets £600,000.

Hourly paid workers 105, salaried workers 20.

The factory is old but is owned by the company and is in good repair.

Most records are maintained on a micro computer but wages records are still manual and are processed by a small staff including Miss Jones who has been with the company for many years and is in sole charge of the wages computation and administration.

The auditors were changed at the last AGM from a small firm to a medium size firm, Swan and Gander, who, in addition to the audit have been engaged to prepared the accounts from a trial balance and to deal with tax matters.

In the interim stage of their first audit, Swan and Gander elucidated the following description of the manual wages system from a questioning of Miss Jones, the gatekeeper and other employees:

All manual employees are paid at an hourly rate agreed with the Union. Hours in excess of eight per day and all hours on Saturdays are paid at time and one half. All employees clock on and off at the gate using a modern time clock. Supervision of the time clock is by Charlie the gatekeeper who is present from 8.00 a.m. to 5.00 p.m. His duties also include supervision and recording of goods and visitors entering and leaving the factory. Employees have access to the factory before and after Charlie's duty hours if a foreman or director is present. Discharging and taking on new workers is the responsibility of the directors who send appropriate memos to Miss Jones. At the beginning of each week, Miss Jones collects the time cards for the previous week and computes the wages due and does a coin analysis.

On Friday mornings, she passes a note to the bookkeeper of the amount of the cash requires for manual wages. A cheque is then made out by the bookkeeper and signed by the two directors. The cash is collected from the bank by Securicor. On arrival of the cash Miss Jones puts the cash in wage envelopes together with a carbon copy of the details of each workers pay and deductions. On Friday afternoon the four shop foremen collect the wage packets for the men in their departments and give them out to the men. If any men are absent, the foremen return the absent workers' packets to Miss Jones and these workers collect the packets from her on their return to work. The bookkeeper deals with the payment of PAYE and NHI by extracting the details from Miss Jones' wages sheets once a month.

The company have no costing system, prices being changed periodically after an ad hoc cost investigation. The company have no personnel department or officer.

Classwork

1. Flowchart this system.
2. Identify and list the good features of internal control found in this system.
3. Identify and list the weaknesses in this system that constitute opportunities for error or fraud to occur. Explain how these errors and fraud could occur.
4. Suggest possible improvements to the system. Assume that no new staff can be engaged but that some time is available from other officers of the company.
5. Draft a letter of weakness to be sent to the directors. Assume that there are no weaknesses in other parts of the company's systems.
6. List the walkthrough tests, tests of control and substantive tests that Swan and Gander could apply to manual wages.
7. Suggest a computerised system with modern methods of payment.
8. Debate the auditor's duty on the discovery of fraud and error by client staff.

Auditing case study 3

Objectives

This case study is designed to give practice in basic auditing techniques, dealing with audit problem areas and drafting qualified audit reports.

Thark Social and Sports Club

This is an old established club, registered as a company limited by guarantee. You are the auditor and are conducting the audit for the year ending 31 December 19-5. The club is run by an elected committee of twelve. The committee include the Chairman who is now ageing and somewhat vague, the Secretary who is very sharp and receives an honorarium of £1,000 a year and the Honorary Treasurer who is a retired optician. The bar is managed by the full time steward who controls three part time staff.

During the audit of the year ending 31 December 19-5 the following matters arose:

a. Subscriptions are £60 a year and are payable annually or monthly. This year the treasurer has been ill and subscriptions are £7,200 in arrear. The full amount of these arrears has been included as a debtor. There are 900 members.

b. The club received a legacy during the year of £100,000 from a former member. The whole sum has been invested on the stock exchange in a 29 separate quoted securities. In due course the investments will be realised and new sports facilities are proposed.

c. Bar profits are down and the auditor considers that the internal control system is inadequate.

d. During the year two members gave gifts to the club. One was a piece of land adjacent to the club which has now been turned into a croquet lawn. The other was a set of an antique table and chairs with a silver service for use by the committee. Nothing appears in the accounts in respect of these gifts.

e. During the year a fraud was committed by a former secretary of the bowls section and the club lost £2,000. The matter was hushed up and the loss is included in the accounts in a global figure of miscellaneous expenses.

f. During the year the roof of the main building was repaired with a contract price of £16,000. £10,000 of this has been paid and the remainder remains unpaid as the club insist the work was poorly carried out. The builder rejects this and the matter is going to court in due course. There is a note to the accounts but no provision.

g. In the accounts for the year ending 31 December 19-4 there was a figure for stock of sporting goods which was unfortunately not counted. You qualified your report in respect of this matter. The 19-5 stock was correctly counted and valued.

Required:

i. Outline a programme for the audit of the subscriptions.

ii. Design an audit programme for the audit of the investments. How should the investments be accounted for in the accounts?

iii. Design an internal control system for the bar.

iv. How should the two gifts be accounted for?

v. What should the auditor do about the fraud?

vi. What audit work should be done on the roof provision?

vii. Write out your audit report on the assumption that you are dissatisfied with:
  - the collectibility of the outstanding subscriptions
  - the completeness of recording of bar takings
  - the roof provision

You should invent suitable figures.

Auditing case study 4

Objectives

The objectives of this case study are to give the student practice in the auditing of computer systems.

Martian Sales and Marketing Limited

Martian Sales and Marketing Limited are wholesalers of fast moving consumer goods with a turnover of £3 million. The company is a wholly owned subsidiary of an American group but is wholly independent except for capital expenditure decisions. The auditors, a multi-national firm, are engaged on the interim audit of the company two months before the financial year end. After the year end the audited accounts have to be in America within one month of the year end.

An investigation of the computerised disc-based sales system revealed the following:

Orders

Orders are received over the telephone or through the post and come directly from customers or through the company's four representatives. Orders are processed in real-time mode by being entered through terminals. The effect of each entry is:

a. Each order is assigned a number by the system.

b. The order is priced from data on the master stock file and trade discounts are applied according to data held on the customer master file. Special price terms can be applied by the operator.

c. The customer's name is compared with data on the customer master file. If not found there or if the customer is marked 'deleted' the order is rejected. The total value of each order is added as a 'memo' to the customer master file.

d. Stock codes are compared with stock master file. If not found, the order is rejected. The order is added to 'allocated' stock and deducted from 'free' stock on the stock master file.

e. Selection list/despatch note is printed on a printer in the warehouse.

Despatch

During the day, goods are selected, packed and despatched to customers together with the despatch note. The selection list is batched and used at the end of each day to update files. Entries are made through a terminal in the warehouse. Only quantities on the selection list/despatch note can be altered by the warehouse staff.

The effect of each entry is:

a. Invoice details are assembled on an invoice file from the selection list, customer descriptive information on the customer master file and stock descriptive information on the stock master file.

b. The customer master file balances are updated and the 'memo' downdated.

c. The stock master file record is amended by a reduction of 'allocated' stock.

d. A despatch confirmation report is printed.

Invoices

After the despatch information has been processed the invoices are printed using the data in the invoice file.

Sales Ledger

Category A – Data on the invoice file is posted onto a Transit file and the invoice file deleted.

Category B – Manual invoices (which are very few), credit notes (which are produced manually) and journal entries are entered in batch mode daily through a terminal. The effect of these entries is:

a. The data is compared with the customer master file and data is rejected is no customer is found or the customer file is marked 'deleted'.

b. The data is added to the Transit file.

c. The customer master file is updated.

d. A batch listing is printed with control totals.

Category C – Cash. Details of cash received are batched and entered through a terminal. The effect of each entry is:

a. Cash is matched where possible against open items in the transit file. Each item so matched is marked accordingly.

b. Customer master file is updated.

Invoices and credit notes are further posted to a daybook file.

Daybook

The daybook file is printed out as a daily listing and the file zeroised.

Debtors' Aging Report

This program prints monthly:

a. individual open items and an age summary of the balance for each customer

b. an aged summary of the total outstanding.

Statements

This program uses the transit file and the customer master file:

a. to cancel matched open items

b. to print statements for all accounts.

Master-file Maintenance

Amendment forms to update the customer master file are input via a terminal from forms made out by the credit control department. Updating is in real time mode with access to the customer master and transit files.

For amendments:

a. Additional customers are accepted if the customer code does not exist on the file.

b. Amendments to customer records are accepted only if the customer code exists. Value fields cannot be amended.

c. Deletions of customer records can only be accepted if the customer code exists, the balance is zero and there are no open items in the transit file.

Classwork

1. Prepare a systems flowchart (run chart) of this system.

2. Suggest additions to the system to improve control. (Hint: areas for improvement include credit control, more printouts, terminal access controls, user pre-lists).

3. Draw a program flowchart for the master file maintenance program.

4. Assuming the amendments suggested by you have been adopted, list the compliance tests that you would apply to this system.

5. Draw up lists of:

   a. Controls that are essential for auditor satisfaction.

   b. Controls that are desirable for management but not essential from an audit point of view.

6. Debate the idea that auditors need to gain detailed understanding of computer programs.

Auditing case study 5

This case study brings together a number of matters of difficulty for auditors. These include the analytical review, the problem of secondary auditors, accounting policies, letters of representation, materiality and qualified audit reports.

Compton Widgets (Holdings) plc

Compton Widgets (Holdings) plc is a multi-national group with a stock exchange listing. Group turnover in 19-6 is £600 million, profits before tax £15 million, the group employs 12,000 people worldwide and operates in 16 countries. Capital employed is £205 million. The principal activities are the manufacture and marketing of widget making machines and of machine tools generally. Subsidiary activities included airline operations in Africa, publishing and a hotel. The shareholding is among 10,000 individual members with 70% of the shares in institutional hands. The directors are all former employees who have been promoted except the part-time Chairman who is a merchant banker and the chief executive who was appointed from a rival group. The auditors are Watermelon and Company, an international firm. Accounts in previous years have been unqualified.

During the audit of the group accounts for 19-6, the following matters have arisen:

a. The group's subsidiary in San Antonio, a Central American Republic, has net assets included in the group 19-6 balance sheet of £4 million and net profit after tax of £2,400,000. Civil war has now broken out and although it is known that the subsidiary is still trading, no audit has been possible.

b. A subsidiary, Compton Factories Limited, has won a contract of £25 million to build a complete widget factory in a Middle Eastern oil producing country. The construction work is expected to extend over five years and at the end of 19-6, the work is about half complete. Difficulties have arisen with subcontractors and with the government concerned and litigation is taking place in several countries. Estimates have been given to the directors that the possible outcomes of the contract range from a loss of £10 million to a profit of £5 million.

c. Compton Widgets (Australia) Limited, a subsidiary in Sydney, is audited by an Australian firm unconnected with Watermelon and Company. The net assets of this subsidiary are £4.6 million and the profit before tax £900,000. The audit report of the Australian firm includes a qualification to the effect that the physical assessment of stock and work in progress had been badly organised and that confusion occurred on the day. The value of stock and work in progress in the accounts was £2.7 million.

d. The airline subsidiary's statement of accounting policies includes the following:

    'A new scheduled cross continent route was commenced during the year. Expenditure on training of flight and ground personnel, the costs of training flights, and the cost of extensive advertising and publicity have been capitalised and are being amortised over five years.'

    The amount capitalised is £2.3 million. The auditors, a local partnership of Watermelon and Company report that the advertising £950,000, included £425,000 which was actually payments to ministers and civil servants to induce them to grant licences.

e. A newly acquired American subsidiary has stock valued on a L.I.F.O. basis at £3 million at the end of 19-5 and £3.6 million at the end of 19-6.

f. The publishing subsidiaries, Widget Books Limited, suffered a major set back during the year when they lost a libel action and had to pay £800,000 in costs and damages. The directors propose to treat the payment as an extraordinary item.

g. A comparison of the stock levels and annual usage of the different raw materials by Compton Widget Manufacturing Limited disclosed that as major component in the widget making machines had been overbought in 19-6 and that the stock of the component at the end of 19-6 was valued at cost at £3.7 million and represented two years usage.

h. During the year, the Hotel subsidiary had been formed and had converted at a cost of £3.2 million, a derelict Victorian mansion costing £450,000 into a magnificent and now flourishing hotel. The directors have not depreciated the hotel in the accounts on the grounds that as the fabric would be regularly maintained to a high standard, the hotel would retain its value in real terms.

i. In February, 19-7, the group received notification that the principal customer of the products of Widget Manufacturing Limited's Glasgow plant had switched its purchasing to a competing Hong Kong company. The board had made a rapid decision to close the factory and this was in process with an estimated overall reduction in net assets of £900,000. The change in assets and liabilities involved had been incorporated in the 19-6 accounts.

Classwork

1. Draft a programme for a final review of the financial statements.
2. With regard to item c., the Australian company, draft a questionnaire to be sent to the Australian firm to determine if:
   a. the Australian firm had audited the subsidiary to an adequate standard
   b. matters relating to the group had received proper attention.
3. With regard to £425,000 mentioned in d, discuss the auditor's duties towards this item.
4. Draft paragraphs for inclusion in the letter of representation for items g. and h.
5. Discuss each of the items in relation to the accounting concept of materiality in the context of the group accounts.
6. Many of these items may lead to Watermelon issuing a qualified audit report. Draft a comprehensive check list of possible reasons for qualification which could be used for all audits by the Reporting Partner. Use your check list to consider the items in the Case Study.
7. Assuming that Watermelon and Company decide to issue a qualified audit report in respect of all the items mentioned, draft the audit report in full.

Index

References are to chapter and paragraph

Index